An Index of Gregorian Chant, Volume I

An Index of Gregorian Chant

Volume I: Alphabetical Index

Compiled by John R. Bryden and
David G. Hughes

Harvard University Press, Cambridge, Massachusetts, 1969

Distributed in Great Britain by Oxford University Press, London
Library of Congress Catalog Card Number 71–91626
SBN 674–44875–8
Printed in the United States of America

PREFACE

The present form of the <u>Index of Gregorian Chant</u> is the result of an unusual combination of circumstances. Some years ago both of the compilers were at work on indexes of Gregorian melodies, each without knowledge of the other's work. Both chanced, by good fortune, to write to Professor Willi Apel within a period of a few months. Professor Apel, seeing the similarity of the two projects, kindly put us into communication with each other. Of course, the thought of publishing two competing indexes was ridiculous; and, although Professor Bryden's work was the further advanced, he generously consented to become a partner in the production of an index more comprehensive than either of us could have accomplished alone. By extraordinary good fortune, we had used methods of recording our data that, while dissimilar, were easily convertible from one system to another. As a result, there was little wasted labor, and our several thousand filing cards could be freely intermingled.

Once the decision to collaborate had been reached, in 1963, the remaining work was divided on the only basis possible to collaborators working far from each other: Professor Bryden undertook the completion of the Gradual, and I that of the Antiphonal. Despite abundant correspondence and a few personal meetings during the years that followed, and despite careful checking of the final cards, certain inconsistencies between the handling of the Mass chants and those of the Office may have crept in. For these, and for the inevitable errors that no caution can entirely eliminate from a work such as this, we ask the user's indulgence.

Among the many persons who have aided us in the production of the <u>Index</u>, we must mention with special gratitude Professor Gustave Reese, who made suggestions of great value; Professor Apel, for his part in putting the compilers in touch with each other; Miss Mary Lou Little of the Eda Kuhn Loeb Music Library, Harvard University, whose assistance was unfailing; and the graduate students who have worked on the <u>Index</u>--Mrs. Carol Marsh Rowan, Mr. Dennis Dufalla, and particularly Miss Kathryn Reichardt. A special debt is owing to Mrs. Doris Carlin, who performed with astonishing accuracy the arduous task of converting our often illegible cards to a typescript. For financial support that paid for the occasional assistance of graduate students and for the production of the final typescript, we acknowledge the generosity of the Harvard Graduate Society and Transylvania College. The staff of the Harvard University Press has given encouragement and assistance over the years. Finally, the compilers owe an incalculable debt to their wives, who not only suffered patiently the seemingly endless blizzard of file cards, but also contributed actively to the work of checking.

For the compilers,

David G. Hughes

INTRODUCTION

The index presented here has one purpose only: to save time and trouble for students and
scholars whose work involves them in one way or another with plainsong. It is intended, therefore,
to be a practical work, with the limitations and (we hope) the advantages that the word implies.
The following paragraphs will give the user an idea of the nature of the Index, and of how to use
it to best advantage.

Scope

The Index deals only with what is usually referred to as Gregorian chant. Ambrosian chant
and the local Roman dialect of Gregorian chant (the "Old-Roman" or "City-Roman" repertory) are not
included. Also omitted are all of the various mediaeval accretions to the liturgy: tropes, proses
or sequences, versus and conductus, prosulae, and the like, whether occurring in manuscript or printed
sources. The only post-Gregorian categories included in the Index are the melodies for hymns and for
the Ordinary of the Mass. Their inclusion might be questioned on logical grounds, but practical con-
siderations seemed more important: chants of this type were used very frequently in polyphonic settings of later periods, and their omission would have deprived the Index of much of its value.

The Index attempts to cover that portion of the chant that was in general use for a considerable period of time. There can be no question of "complete" coverage: any such attempt would be the
work of several lifetimes, and the modest advantages to be gained would hardly be commensurate with
the labor involved. But even the determination of a body of chant "in general use" is not without
its difficulties. The scientific procedure would involve the consultation of a large number of manuscripts, widely scattered in place and time, and the use of only those chants common to a large number
of them. Again, the practical rewards of such a laborious procedure are rather slight. The simpler
method of choosing relatively few representative sources and indexing their entire contents includes
virtually all that the more scientific approach would, and differs only in admitting also a certain
number of rare or peculiar items.

Sources[1]

The Index draws its material from the modern printed chant books, from five selected manuscripts,
and from certain special studies dealing with specific categories of chant. The use of the modern
printed books of chant produced by the monks of Solesmes hardly needs justification. These volumes
are convenient in size, low in price, and available to everyone. Among them they contain a considerable body of chant, mostly in versions very similar to those of the mediaeval manuscripts. To be sure,
their use introduces into the Index a certain number of chants adapted or even composed at Solesmes,
but these are easily detected and create no problem. (In fact, some new feasts have resurrected authentic chants otherwise missing from the modern repertory.)

It is true that excessive reliance on these publications in scholarly work is to be deplored.
It is foolish to make a detailed comparison between the cantus firmus of a Josquin motet and a chant
of the same title found in the Liber usualis; but it is just as foolish to use a twelfth-century manuscript for the purpose. What is needed in such a case is a source that Josquin himself might have
consulted. Nevertheless, the Liber usualis can and does perform a valuable function in the initial
stages of one's work: from it one can at least learn whether Josquin was using a melody roughly the
same as the one traditionally associated with the text. From there, one must go back to the appropriate sources for detailed work--and the proper sources for Josquin are not necessarily those proper
for Dufay or for Leoninus.

---

[1]Complete bibliographical information is given below, pp. xii-xiv.

The modern books, however, cannot contribute the entire substance of the Index; too much is missing from them. Many feasts once widely observed are no longer celebrated, and their Propers are not a part of the modern liturgy. Moreover, the relative neglect of matins has resulted in the loss of the majority of the great responsories, and of a large number of antiphons. Clearly, some recourse to manuscripts is also necessary.

Only manuscripts fulfilling two conditions could be considered: they must be in diastematic notation (since otherwise melodic incipits derived from them would be at least in part conjectures of the compilers); and they must be available to the musicological public (since there is not much use giving a reference to a source that is not likely to be available to the user). These conditions immediately suggest sources like those reproduced in the Paléographie musicale. After careful consideration, five such manuscripts were selected for indexing: the Antiphonals of Lucca and Worcester, and the Graduals of Benevento, St. Yrieix, and Sarum--all except the last from the Paléographie musicale. It would have been desirable to supplement these with a French antiphonal, but no suitable manuscript is available in facsimile. The inclusion of the Sarum Antiphonal could be argued, but one English manuscript for the Office seemed sufficient.

Two major areas of weakness, however, remain: neither hymns nor chants of the Ordinary are adequately represented. Fortunately, several recent publications were available to fill these gaps: for the hymns, Bruno Stäblein's collection of melodies; and for the Kyrie, Gloria, Sanctus, and Agnus, specialized studies with catalogues giving melodic incipits. In addition, Ott's Offertoriale provides a considerable number of offertory verses. With these additions, all major areas of chant are well represented.

Naturally, the presence of a given chant in one of the five manuscripts, or in Stäblein's hymn collection (based largely on early sources), is sufficient guarantee that the piece is not a modern one. But the opposite conclusion should not be so easily drawn. A number of authentic chants found in the modern Gradual and Antiphonal do not happen to occur in any of the manuscripts used for the Index; and the special studies of Ordinary chants use a number of post-mediaeval sources as well as early ones. Proving a given chant to be modern involves more than mere consultation of this Index.

Method

The general plan of the Index is simple: the same information is given in both volumes, but in Volume I the entries are arranged in the alphabetical order of the textual incipits, while in Volume II they are arranged in the numerical order of the melodic incipits.

All chants having verses (e.g., graduals, responsories, even some antiphons) are indexed for the verse as well as for the main chant. Thus the user will find the gradual Sederunt principes in its proper place, and, among the A's, he will also find the verse Adjuva me Domine, with the appropriate cross reference to Sederunt. Anyone who has attempted to find the responsory to which an isolated verse belongs will appreciate the utility of this feature. Only the verses of the short responsories, which are extremely short and of little importance, have been omitted. Page references for verses invariably refer to the page on which the entire piece begins--not that where the verse appears.

Secondly, the melodies, as well as the texts, are indexed. In Volume II of the Index, the order is based on the melodic incipit in a manner explained below (p. ix). Certain texts, however, have no need for the inclusion of a melodic incipit--namely, those sung to some sort of standard tone. In this class belong the psalm verses of the introits and communions, the short responsories, most of the verses of the great responsories, and certain less common forms. All these are given normal entries, lacking only the melodic incipit, in Volume I; and are omitted from Volume II. Lections, psalms, prayers, versicles, doxologies, and the like are omitted altogether.

Melodic variants among the sources used are, in almost all cases ignored: in principle, each melody for a given text is given only one entry. When, however, a variant occurs in one source that would result in a melodic incipit different from that given in the entry, the reference to that source is preceded by an asterisk. The absence of an asterisk shows that the source involved has an incipit identical to that given in the entry, but does not preclude the occurrence of variants later in the melody. Incipits that are identical except for the presence or absence of a flat are regarded as the same, and no asterisk is used in such cases.

The Melodic Code

The system of coding melodies used here is that described by N. Bridgman ("L'Etablissement d'un catalogue par incipit musicaux," _Musica disciplina_ IV [1950], 65). In it, the starting tone of the melody is reckoned as 0, a semitone above it as 1, a whole tone above as 2, a minor third as 3, and so on. Tones below the starting tone are reckoned in the same way, but as negative numbers. Thus a minor third below the starting tone would be -3, a perfect fifth below, -7. This system is particularly congenial to the repertoire involved, since it accommodates modal melodies (as some systems do not) and brings together transposed versions of the same tune.

Each melodic incipit consists of eight numbers divided into two groups of four by a space. These represent the first eight pitches of the melody after the first note (which is by definition 0, and is not represented numerically, but by its letter name). If a note is directly repeated, the appropriate number still appears only once. Thus the familiar introit of the first Christmas Mass is coded D 3 5 3 0 3 0 3 -2, the direct repetitions of the F being ignored. Liquescent notes, quilismas, and other ornamental signs are represented as if they were ordinary notes. In a few cases, a melody is so short, or repeats the same tone so often, that it does not contain eight different pitches. In this event the pitches occurring are given, and the remaining places are filled with bracketed zeros. This is the sole case where a number will be found directly repeated. Whenever entries are arranged in numerical order (throughout Volume II, and in many places in Volume I), the algebraic signs are taken into account. Thus -7 comes before -6, which comes before -5, and so on. This algebraic filing (a deviation from the Bridgman system) is necessary here. One of the purposes of the _Index_ is to group together pieces having the same melodic beginning. If the minus signs were disregarded in filing, members of different groups would be interspersed (e.g., melodies beginning 5 2 0 2, 5 2 0 -2, and -5 -2 0 -2 would all be mixed together.)

Proceeding the melodic incipit, each entry gives a pitch letter, using the usual designations (GG for low G, capitals for A-G above, and small letters from the next octave). This is merely for the information of the user, and has no effect on the numerical filing of the incipit. Thus C 3 5 7 5 will precede A 3 5 7 8.

The Entries

The entries in Volume I give the following information: (The order described here is that of Volume I. For the order of Volume II, see the Introduction to Volume II.)

1. _Mode_. The number at the extreme left of the entry indicates the mode of the piece, as given by the sources. Occasionally these disagree, one giving the authentic, the other the plagal, form of the mode. In such cases, the mode is given as "1 2". The tonus peregrinus is indicated by "tp"; irregular tones by "ir". Mode is not given for verses or subdivisions of a piece, nor for pieces (such as short responsories) that do not have melodic incipits and that may be given settings in various modes. In general, the modes given by the modern printed books have been taken over without question, except in the case of obvious errors. For the manuscripts, the indices of the _Paléographie musicale_ reproductions have served as primary source, with consultation of the psalm- or verse-tones when appropriate. For the St. Yrieix and Beneventan Graduals, the indices of which do not list mode, the choice has been based on the notation, which normally shows the intended mode clearly. In the case of Stäblein's hymn collection (see below, p.xii), which generally does not give modes, we have applied modal designations on our own initiative.

2. _Textual incipit_. This is the basis for the alphabetical ordering of the entries. The alphabetization is of the separate-word type, so that, for example, all texts beginning with the

word "A" are listed before the first "Ab" appears. The spelling used is that of modern liturgical
Latin, and the orthography of sources not conforming to this has been altered where necessary. Thus,
the user will find no entries beginning "Ihesus" ("Jesus" is used instead), or "celi" ("caeli" is
used). For those unfamiliar with the vagaries of mediaeval spelling, a little experimentation may
be necessary.

Every effort has been made to distinguish texts with identical beginnings and different
continuation, by the usual device of three periods followed by the first word different in the
two texts. When two versions of the same text exist of which the longer includes all of the
shorter plus further material, the longer has the incipit of the shorter plus three periods and
the first word of the continuation. This method is not always followed, however, when the texts
are those of pieces that would naturally differ considerably in length. Thus, for example, an
antiphon and a responsory may be listed with identical incipits: the reader may assume that the
responsory text would include all of the antiphon, plus a continuation.

It often happens that a text may occur with somewhat different beginnings. Doubtless many
of these cases have not been detected, with the result that each form has its own entry in the
Index. When the identity has been observed, however, the variant version has been given an entry
in its proper place, containing only the text incipit followed by "see [the fully indexed form]".
In some instances, an entry for a text is followed by "see also [a variant form of the same text]".
This merely warns the user that a similar text is present in the Index and may be useful. Further
cases of this type may be found in Volume II, where melodic identity has brought together two different forms of the same text.

In addition, a few more general "see also" references have been provided: "Cum: see also Dum,"
for example, is a general warning that texts beginning with one of these words should also be looked for
under the other, since there are frequent variations. The Index does not, however, pretend to either
completeness or consistency in the matter of cross references.

In general, minor variations of text not affecting the alphabetization of the incipit have been
wholly ignored. These occur frequently but are of small importance. Only in cases where the liturgical
destination of the text is thereby altered (as in the case of the Gaudeamus introits, for example), has
it been felt necessary to record them.

Whenever the textual incipits of two or more entries are identical, the following principles of
arrangement have been observed: (1) those entries lacking a melodic incipit are placed before those
having one. Entries without melodic incipit are arranged alphabetically by the category of chant to
which they belong. This places the verses (which constitute the majority of such entries) at the end
of the group without melodic incipit, and places, for example, verses of communions before verses of
introits and verses of responsories. Among several verses of the same type (introit verses, for example),
the arrangement is by alphabetical order of the chants to which the verses belong. (2) Entries having
melodic incipits are arranged in the numerical order of the incipits. In the few cases where these also
are identical, the arrangement is first by category, then by source, then by page number within a single
source. The presence of two entries identical in tune, text, and category suggests that the melodies
have been examined and found difficult (on the slightly different principle used in dealing with hymn
melodies, see below, p. xii.

The liturgical use of a chant is not given in the Index. This omission was dictated by the
nature of the chants. A fair number of them are regularly and predictably associated with a given
feast: for these, it suffices to turn to the first source at hand to discover their liturgical desti-
nations. Many others, however, were not so regularly employed. Particularly noteworthy in this re-
spect are the great responsories, which vary to the extent that only rarely do two dioceses have the
same list for a given feast. For chants such as these, the listing of one or two liturgical possi-
bilities (as much as would have been possible in the Index) would be of very little use. They must
be studied individually, within the context of the time and place involved.

3. Category to which the chant belongs. This is indicated by a two- to four-letter lower-
case abbreviation (see the list at the end of the Introduction, p.xvii. When the abbreviation ends
with "v", the item indexed is the verse of the chant indicated by the remainder of the abbreviation
(except that "inv" stands for invitatory). The textual incipit of the "parent" chant is, in such
cases, given below the incipit of the verse, indented, thus:

                        A Domino factum est   rev
                        Vere felicem

This should be read: "A Domino factum est in the verse of the responsory Vere felicem." The
incipits of the parent chants are shortened as much as clarity permits. The indentation used here
is deeper than that employed when the text incipit is so long that it runs over into a second line.

4. Sources. Each source is represented by an abbreviation in capitals (see the list at the
end of the Introduction, p. xvii), followed by the page number (or numbers) where the piece in question
may be found. For all the sources indexed, every complete appearance of the piece in all the sources
indexed is given. (When a source gives only the incipit of a piece, this is not indexed except in such
cases--notably introit verses--when both text and melody can be reconstructed with certainty.) The
presence of an asterisk before the source-abbreviation or page number signifies (as was mentioned above)
that the melodic incipit in that source or on that page is not identical to that given in the Index,
although the melody is fundamentally the same in all the sources cited. (Naturally, when two different
melodies are used for the same text, they receive separate entries.)

In most cases the page references create no problems, although the user should note that
manuscript references are to the page numbers of the Paléographie musicale reproductions, and not
to the original foliation. However, certain of the modern chant books--the Antiphonale, the Graduale,
and, especially, the Liber usualis--have been issued in a large number of editions in which the pagination is not always exactly the same (for details see below pp. xii-xiv). There is no solution for
this difficulty: listing the paging for each edition is clearly out of the question; using only the
Vatican edition would eliminate the problem, but the Vatican books are far less commonly used than
the Tournai publications, and the majority of users would be seriously inconvenienced by such a step.
The compilers therefore elected to give page numbers for the editions actually used (these are speci-
fied in the list at the end of the Introduction, pp. xii-xiv). This will, fortunately, give correct
results in the vast majority of cases, since the Solesmes editors have tried to avoid page changes as
much as possible. In those cases where the user does not find the piece he wants on the page speci-
fied, he will merely have to consult the index of the edition he is using. This will not, we believe,
happen very often, except in the Holy Week section of the Liber usualis, where liturgical changes have
caused fairly extensive re-numbering of pages.

5. First note of the chant. As has been mentioned above, this information is given for the
user's convenience. It is not in any way an integral part of the melodic incipit following, and does
not affect the algebraic filing of the latter. When a chant appears in different sources on two different pitches (F and c, for example), only the pitch of the first source cited is given. Difference
in pitch is not signaled by an asterisk.

6. Melodic incipit. The coding system has been described above under "The Melodic Code."
Here we need only observe that, in addition to pieces lacking a melodic incipit because they are sung
to a standard formula, a few other pieces do not have this information. Where the incipit of a melody
is illegible, or where music is not given, this is indicated by "inc illeg" or "nm".

7. Final. This is not given for verses, or for entries lacking a melodic incipit.

Functions

It is to be hoped that the Index will prove to be useful in a variety of ways. Some of the
functions it is best adapted to perform may be mentioned here.

Its most obvious utility is in the finding of sources for a known liturgical text. Without the Index this can be a laborious procedure, since it involves searching through a large number of different indexes (each one generally having separate alphabets for different categories of chant). With the Index the user will be assisted by the entries for verses (not indexed at all in any publication known to us), and by the single overall alphabet, which will show him directly what texts have different settings in different liturgical forms (for example, hundreds of texts exist as responsories, as verses of responsories, and also as antiphons). The user will also be able to find sources for differing settings of the same text in the same category. These will be most useful, perhaps, in the case of hymns, which were often sung to a large number of tunes; other categories normally have no more than three or four settings of a single text.

For all of this work, of course, Volume I of the Index will be used; and, in fact, it may be said that the purpose of the first volume is not to enable things of a new kind to be done, but merely to facilitate the doing of familiar tasks. With Volume II the situation is somewhat different, since published indexes of this kind do not, to our knowledge, exist (except for small fractions of the repertoire). For the student of plainsong, the principal advantage of Volume II is that it brings together in one place melodies having the same incipit. It will be easy to find the answer to the question: "With what texts was a given Alleluia or responsory melody sung?"

Perhaps of more general interest is the facility offered by the Index of identifying a melody that has been transmitted without text, or with a text clearly not the original one. (The most obvious type of case is that in which the cantus firmus of a polyphonic composition is not identified by the composer.) In principle, one has only to code the incipit of the cantus firmus and turn to Volume II of the Index: a melody that matches the code of the unknown tune should be what is required. In practice, however, the matter is not that simple. The user may find no matching melody at all, or he may find one or even many that match but are clearly inappropriate.

In the first case it may be that the desired melody is simply not in the Index. It is, however, just as likely that the particular version used in the polyphonic piece contains a variant somewhere near the beginning. This, of course, would alter the melodic coding and cause the desired piece to appear some distance away from the place suggested by the cantus firmus code (for example, the mere filling-in of an initial third -- F-G-a for F-a -- will cause a displacement of many hundreds of entries). The user must be prepared, in this sort of work, to experiment by introducing likely variants into his unknown melody, in the hope that he will finally hit upon the one leading to the correct result. Although this is tedious work, it is still a good deal more expeditious than the traditional page-by-page search through a liturgical book or manuscript.

The second case -- finding entries that appear to solve the problem, but in reality do not -- is merely a variant of the first. Just as melodic variations can move an entry in the Index away from the place where it is looked for, so also can they move "foreign" entries to the correct place. If all the matching entries can, in fact, be eliminated as possible solutions, one is reduced to experimenting with artificial variations, as was just described.

We have discussed this matter in some detail in order to emphasize that the Index cannot, by its nature, provide an automatic solution to problems of identifying a cantus firmus. It will offer considerable help and save considerable time, but success will still ultimately depend on the user. Above all, one should not conclude, after a single search, that the melody sought is not represented in the Index, or use the Index as "proof" that a given melody is not pre-existent. Either conclusion may, in any given case, be true, but neither can be established without considerable labor.

The Sources

1. Printed

Graduale sacrosanctae Romanae ecclesiae . . . (Paris, Tournai, Rome; Desclée No. 696; 1952)
[GR]. Pagination differs slightly in different editions. Pages 1-658, proprium; [1]-[149]; commune
sanctorum; 1*-159*, ordinarium missae; 1**-142**, "missae aliquibus in locis celebrandae." The edition used here has a supplement, pp. (1)-(43), containing Masses for the Benedictine Order. A few
insertions have been accommodated by means of superscript numbers added to the normal pagination.

Antiphonale sacrosanctae Romanae ecclesiae . . . (Paris, Tournai, Rome; Desclée No. 820; 1949)
[AR]. Arranged like the Graduale: pp. 1-931, ordinarium and proprium; [1]-[192], commune; 1*-218*,
toni communes, and various chants. Different editions have various short supplements, each with its
own pagination. In the Index, these are indicated as "4 (sup 1)," but without any confidence that
other copies will have the same supplements in the same order.

Antiphonale monasticum pro diurnis horis . . . (Paris, Tournai, Rome; Desclée No. 818; c.1934)
[AM]. Pagination is continuous, with a few superscripts. The copy used here has an 8-page supplement,
dated 1960.

The Liber usualis with introduction and rubrics in English (Tournai, New York; Desclée No. 801;
1961) [LU]. Difference in pagination between different editions is at its greatest here, since the basic
pagination is continuous. The publishers have made every effort to minimize the problem by liberal use
of superscripts (p. 776 goes up to 776^{KK}), but in several sections, notably in Holy Week, the numbers
given in the Index will not be correct for earlier editions. The edition dated 1963 is, however, substantially the same as the one used here, and it is unlikely that there will be further changes.

Officium hebdomadae sanctae et octavae Paschae . . . (Rome, Tournai, Paris, New York; Desclée
No. 914: 1962) [OHS]. Continuously paginated 1-852, with a section of toni communes, pp. 1*-18*.

Liber responsorialis pro festis I. classis . . . (Solesmes, 1895) [LR]. Subsequently reprinted
without change. See note below at Variae preces.

Processionale monasticum ad usum congregationis Gallicae . . . (Solesmes, 1893) [PM]. Subsequently reprinted without change. See note below at Variae preces.

Variae preces ex liturgia tum hodierna tum antiqua collectae aut usu receptae (Solesmes; 5th
ed., 1901) [VP]. Subsequently reprinted without change. The Variae preces contains a large number
of proses, monophonic conductus, and the like. In keeping with the general policy observed throughout
the Index, these have not been indexed.

These last three sources often give versions different from those of later publications. In
general, the later versions have been preferred as base readings for the Index.

Carolus Ott, ed., Offertoriale sive versus offertoriorum cantus Gregoriani (Paris, Tournai, Rome,
Desclée; 1935) [OTT]. This important source for offertory verses is unfortunately marred by editorial
emendations (see Ruth Steiner, "Some questions about the Gregorian offertories and their verses,"
Journal of the American Musicological Society, XIX [1966], 162 ff.).

Bruno Stäblein, ed., Hymen (I): Die mittelalterlichen Hymnenmelodien des Abendlandes (Monumenta
monodica medii aevi, I; Kassel and Basel, 1956) [ST]. The matter of variants is treated somewhat dif-
ferently for this volume, since it is useful to have available several versions of a tune, especially
when dealing with polyphonic settings. Hence, all versions showing a difference in the first eight pitches
are given separately, even when the continuations show that the melodies are substantially the same.

Moreover, all combinations of melodies and texts are indexed, even when Stäblein does not print them in full, but gives brief references such as "Somno refectis artubus . . . Mel. 142$_3$" (p. 213). The user is warned, however, that a number of these references are incorrect, usually by only a single digit (e.g., Mel. 1$_4$ for Mel. 1$_5$). The correct melody can usually but not always be determined by consulting Stäblein's indices. In the Index such errors have been corrected without comment whenever the corrections were reasonably certain. References posing insoluble problems have been omitted.

Margareta Melnicki, Das einstimmige Kyrie des Lateinischen Mittelalters (Forschungsbeiträge zur Musikwissenschaft, I; Regensburg [1954]) [MEL]. Like the three items that follow, this is a source of a different kind. It contains, not the melodies themselves, but a catalogue of melodic incipits, together with references to manuscript sources (about 400 manuscripts were used in preparing the catalogue). The user of the Index will therefore have to go beyond MEL to a manuscript if he wishes to find a complete melody; but the information collected in MEL and the three sources following is so useful that their inclusion in the Index was a matter of course.

All references to MEL are to melody numbers, not page numbers.

Detlev Bosse, Untersuchung einstimmiger mittelalterlicher Melodien zum "Gloria in excelsis Deo," (Forschungsbeiträge zur Musikwissenschaft, II; Regensburg, n.d. [1954?]) [BOS]. The remarks made above concerning MEL apply equally to BOS. Again, references in the Index are to melody numbers, not pages.

Peter Josef Thannabaur, Das einstimmige Sanctus der römischen Messe in der handschriftlichen Überlieferung des 11. bis 16. Jahrhunderts (Erlanger Arbeiten zur Musikwissenschaft, I; Munich, 1962) [THAN]. The remarks made concerning MEL apply here also. In both BOS and THAN, some incipits are described as mere variants of numbered melodies. These variants, especially numerous in THAN, are not indexed here, in accordance with the general policy of the Index. References are to melody numbers, not pages.

Martin Schildbach, Das einstimmige Agnus Dei und seine handschriftliche Überlieferung vom 10. bis zum 16. Jahrhundert (Dissertation Erlangen-Nürnberg, 1967) [SCH]. The remarks concerning MEL apply here also. References are to melody numbers, not page numbers. SCH was received too late for its entries to be incorporated into the main body of Volume I: they are given as an Appendix, pp. 445-456. In Volume II, they are integrated into the numerical series with the rest of the entries.

2. Manuscript

Le Codex 903 de la Bibliothèque Nationale de Paris (XIe siècle); Graduel de Saint-Yrieix (Paléographie musicale, XIII; Tournai, 1925) [SYG]. The manuscript is written in Aquitanian notation and is, for the most part, easily legible. In a few cases, however, an unequivocal determination of the starting tone could not be made. In such cases the pieces are given in the alphabetical part of the Index without melodic incipit, and are of course omitted from Volume II. Some of the entries that do give a melodic incipit are uncertain, in that a different choice of starting tone would yield a different result.

Tropes, prosulae, and their like are not indexed, nor are chants of the Ordinary.

SYG references are to page numbers, which run consecutively through the facsimile. Pages 1*-8*, consisting of plates chosen to illustrate the Introduction, are not indexed.

Le Codex VI. 34 de la Bibliothèque Capitulaire de Bénévent (XIe-XIIe siècle): Graduel de Bénévent avec prosaire et tropaire (Paléographie musicale, XV; Tournai, 1937) [GB]. The Beneventan notation used in this source is generally free from ambiguities. Tropes, prosulae, and Ordinary chants are not indexed.

References are to folio (not page) numbers. Verso pages are indicated by a superscript "v" following the number.

Walter Howard Frere, ed., Graduale Sarisburiense; a Reproduction in Facsimile of a Manuscript of the Thirteenth Century . . . (London, 1894; and a reprint, 1966) [GS]. Square notation.
References are to page numbers, as follows: A-M, a-z, after which an Ordinarium (not indexed) follows, paginated by numbers followed by a mark like a double sharp. Then follows the main body of
the manuscript, paginated 1-236. In the reprint, the numbered pages came first.

Antiphonaire monastique; XIIe siècle: Codex 601 de la Bibliothèque Capitulaire de Lucques
(Paléographie musicale, IX; Tournai, 1906) [LA]. Italian notation, free from ambiguities. Indexed
in its entirety, except for the versiculi. References are to page numbers.

Antiphonaire monastique; XIIIe siècle: Codex F. 160 de la bibliothèque de la cathedrale de
Worcester (Paléographie musicale, XII; Tournai, 1922) [WA]. Square notation. Rubbing, however, has
made a few areas illegible. Indexed complete, except for versiculi and a few miscellaneous items, and
except for the hymnary, which is given in ST. References are to page numbers. In the copy used,
pp. 335 and 336 are wrongly numbered 345 and 346, and the reverse. The Index gives the correct page
numbers.

Notes on the Various Categories of Chant

Alleluias.[2] As used here, this title refers only to the Alleluia of the Mass, other items with
this text being assigned to their own categories. Each Alleluia has two entries. The first is given
as "Alleluia: Excita Domine," and refers to the beginning of the piece. The second, "Excita Domine,"
refers to the verse. In a few cases there is a second verse. Thus, in SYG, Alleluia: laetatus sum
has the second verse Stantes erant, which is indexed:

          Stantes erant   alv   SYG 3
            Laetatus sum

Naturally the first verse, like all single verses, does not need the mention of Laetatus sum on the
second line.

The manuscripts often give only the first few notes of the jubilus, assuming that the singer
will know it, or at least know where to find it (certain melodies, such as the Alleluia: dies sanctifi-
catus, were employed with a large number of verses). In all such cases, the melodic incipit was com-
pleted from another occurrence of the same melody in the same source, and the final tone similarly
supplied. It was not thought necessary to indicate this by the use of brackets.

Antiphons. Those alleluiatic antiphons that exist also with regular text have been treated
as follows: when the source explicitly indicates the non-Paschal text at the beginning of the alleluiatic version (a frequent occurrence), no separate listing is made under "Alleluia," and the page numbers
for both alleluiatic and non-alleluiatic versions are given under the normal text. There are often
melodic variations between the two versions, and an entry like

          Cito euntes   an   WA 129 *136

indicates this as usual by an asterisk preceding the variant appearance. There is, of course, nothing
in the entry to show that the second appearance has the text "Alleluia" instead of "Cito euntes," but
those experienced in liturgy would be able to make a shrewd guess--and, in any case, a glance at WA 136
would settle the matter.

When, on the other hand, the source does not indicate the texted version, the antiphon is merely
listed under "Alleluia": such melodic identities are evident in the Volume II of the Index.

---

[2]The number of Alleluias listed could perhaps have been increased by the indexing of Karl-Heinz
Schlager, Thematischer Katalog der ältesten Alleluia-melodien . . . (Erlanger Arbeiten zur Musikwissenschaft, II; Munich, 1965), but this publication appeared too late to be considered.

Verses of antiphons are generally sung to standard tones, or to formulae so simple that melodic indexing would serve no purpose. In a few cases, more elaborate melodies are used, and these are given melodic incipits in the normal way.

Communions. The communions themselves present no difficulties. Their verses were sung to the same tones as the introit verses, and hence are not indexed melodically. Manuscript sources frequently indicate them only by a very brief textual incipit. When this is so short as to permit ambiguity (e.g. "Cantate," which might refer to one of several texts), the verse is not indexed.

Graduals. In general, these do not require special comment. The gradual Haec dies, with its numerous verses for use on various days after Easter, has been given entries in this manner:

        Dextera Domini fecit   grv   GR 250(241)
            Haec dies

These entries constitute an exception to the general rule that page numbers in verse entries refer to the beginning of the whole piece. The first page number is that of the verse Dextera Domini. The page number in parentheses (note that it follows the first number without space) refers to the page on which the gradual itself may be found--since neither printed nor manuscript sources write it out each time.

Hymns. The special principles governing the indexing of variant hymn melodies are given in the description of the sources, at "Stäblein, Hymnen." No special indication is made for processional hymns.

Since ST--the major source for hymns--does not indicate mode for the most part, the modal designations are often those of the compilers. The assignment to an authentic or plagal form is frequently subject to question, and it may happen that the same tune (with different texts) has been called authentic in one instance, plagal in another. Such conflicts are eliminated in the thematic part of the Index.

Ordinary chants. The identifying numbers used in the modern books are retained, as they are often used in the literature. The first entry for each Ordinary chant is given at some length, and succeeding entries are abbreviated: "Gloria in excelsis Deo; Gloria."

Trope titles have been retained for the Kyrie, to aid in identification, but the order of the melodies is solely numerical. "(etc)" after a trope title indicates that other tropes were also used for the same tune.

Tropes are not given for Gloria melodies, as the combination of trope and tune is a very complex matter. But entries are given for "Et in terra," as well as the actual beginning, to assist in identifying polyphonic settings. For the Credo, Sanctus, and Agnus Dei the indexing follows the usual procedures.

Since the specialized sources MEL, BOS, and THANN contain only incipits, the Index can give only such modal information as appears in those studies. In BOS the final tone is given, and is said (p. 83) to indicate the mode. Hence entries in the Index give the maneria (in Roman numerals). In MEL the final tone is given, but without indication that this is a modal determinant (i.e. that transpositions have been noted). Hence no mode has been given except where it could be supplied from another source. THAN gives the ambitus as well as the final, and mode has been derived from this information. SCH indicates mode, often in conflict with the final (e.g. D-4). Its modal designations have been retained.

Responsories. Verses are not given melodic incipits except when idiomelic. In a few cases, when an incipit is given, it is identical with the beginning of one of the tones. This shows that while the beginning of the verse follows the standard tone, the continuation is free.

Occasionally a responsory verse will appear with only the incipit of the respond. Such cases are treated like the gradual Haec dies (above): the page number of the verse is given; then, in parentheses and without space, the page where the whole respond may be found.

Doxologies are not indexed, except in the few cases where they have special text.

Short responsories. These are sometimes so short that the first words of the verse had to be included in the textual incipit to show which form of a text was being used. The verses themselves are not otherwise indexed. Melodic incipit is not given for short responsories, since the tunes are all more or less standard.

Tracts. The recent Roman usage of reverting to the term "canticle" for the Holy Saturday tracts has not been followed here, as the pieces are tracts from a musical point of view.

Sigla Used for the Sources
(for full titles, see pp. xiii-xv)

AM	Antiphonale monasticum
AR	Antiphonale Romanum (or Liber antiphonarius)
BOS	Bosse, Untersuchung . . . Gloria
GB	Graduel de Bénévent (Pal. mus. XV)
GR	Graduale Romanum (or Liber gradualis)
GS	Graduale Sarisburiense
LA	Antiphonaire monastique . . . de Lucques (Pal. mus. IX)
LR	Liber responsorialis
LU	Liber usualis
MEL	Melnicki, Das einstimmige Kyrie
OHS	Officium hebdomadae sanctae
OTT	Ott, Offertoriale
PM	Processionale monasticum
SCH	Schildbach, Das einstimmige Agnus Dei
ST	Stäblein, Die Hymnen
SYG	Graduel de Saint-Yrieix (Pal. mus. XIII)
THAN	Thannabaur, Das einstimmige Sanctus
VP	Variae preces
WA	Antiphonaire . . . de Worcester (Pal. mus. XII)

Abbreviations for Categories of Chant

al	Alleluia
alv	Alleluia verse
an	antiphon
anv	antiphon verse
co	Communion
cov	Communion verse
gr	Gradual
grv	Gradual verse
hy	hymn
int	Introit
intv	Introit verse
inv	invitatory
of	Offertory
ofv	Offertory verse
re	great responsory
rev	verse of great responsory
sr	short responsory
tr	Tract
trv	verse of Tract

Other Abbreviations

inc illeg	incipit (either textual or musical) illegible
ir	tonus irregularis
nm	no music
sup	supplement
tp	tonus peregrinus
var	variant

<u>A N I N D E X O F G R E G O R I A N C H A N T</u>

ALPHABETICAL INDEX

No.	Title		Sources										
2	A bimatu et infra	an	AR 284 LU 427 AM 260 *WA 46	D	2	3	5	2	3	2	0	3	D
7	A Christo de caelo vocatus	re	WA 263 (inc illeg)										G
	A Christo de caelo vocatus / Magnus sanctus Paulus	rev	PM 129 LA 430 WA 265										
6	A Christo de caelo vocatus	gr	SYG 44	D	3	7	5	7	5	3	5	3	F
8	A Christo de caelo vocatus	an	WA 264 LA 345	G	5	2	0	2	0	-2	0	2	G
7	A Christo suscepta	an	WA 336	G	5	4	5	7	9	7	5	7	G
8	A dextris est mihi Dominus	re	LA 81 *WA 60	G	2	4	5	2	5	4	2	4	G
	A Domino factum est / Vere felicem	rev	WA 289										
	A Domino factum est / Benedictus qui venit	grv	GR 31 LU 404 GS E GB 15^V SYG 15	F	4	7	9	7	4	7	9	11	
	A Domino sanctum est / Pro te Jesu	rev	WA 249	c	2	5	4	5	4	2	4	2	
2	A facie furoris tui	re	LA 305 WA 186	A	3	5	7	5	3	7	5	7	D
1	A finibus terrae laudes	an	LA 23	D	-2	3	5	3	7	9	7	5	D
	A fructu frumenti / Redemit Dominus	rev	LA 305 WA 184										
2	A fructu frumenti	an	LR 121 LU 923	C	5	4	2	0	5	7	4	2	D
	A judiciis tuis non declinavi / Ab omni via mala	rev	LA 134 WA 89										
8	A patre unigenite	hy	ST 366	G	-5	-2	0	2	0	-2	0	5	G
8	A patre unigenite	hy	ST 221	G	-3	-2	-5	-2	2	0	-2	0	G
8	A patre unigenite	hy	ST 81	G	-2	-3	-5	-2	2	0	-2	0	G
	A periculis cunctis libera nos	sr	AR 7 8 sup										
2	A planta pedis	an	AR 843 LU 1639 AM 1048	F	-1	-5	-1	0	-3	-1	-5	-3	D
2	A porta inferi erue Domine	an	AR 441 [179] OHS 622 LU 776^A 1802 AM 447 448 1164 *WA 127 *LA 206 559	D	-2	0	3	2	0	2	0	-2	D
4	A saeculo non est auditum	an	WA 105	G	2	5	7	5	7	9	7	5	a
	A sagitta volante / Qui habitat	trv	GR 95 LU 533 *GS 35 *GB 65 *SYG 73	D	3	2	3	5	7	5	7	5	
	A solis ortu et occasu / Obsecro Domine	rev	LA 5										
4	A solis ortu usque ad occasum	an	AR 299 LU 452 *AM 277	F	-3	0	-1	-3	-1	0	-3	-1	E
3	A solis ortus cardine	hy	ST 143	E	-2	3	5	8	7	5	3	5	E
8	A solis ortus cardine	hy	ST 410	G	2	-2	0	2	5	4	2	0	G
3	A solis ortus cardine	hy	ST 31 219 275 366 AM 242	D	2	3	5	7	0	2	3	5	E
3	A solis ortus cardine	hy	ST 81 178 AR 266 LU 400	D	2	3	5	7	0	2	5	3	E

5 A solis ortus cardine	hy	ST 337	F	4	0	2	0	-1	-3	0	4	F
3 A somno pigros excita	hy	ST 338	D	5	7	9	10	9	7	5	7	E
A summo caelo egressio Omnis pulchritudo	rev	PM 85 LR 97 LA 245 WA 147										
4 A summo caelo egressio	an	LR 95 *WA 147 *LA 244	a	-2	0	3	5	3	5	7	5	a
7 A summo caelo egressio	alv	GR 85**	F	2	4	2	7	6	4	2	9	
A summo caelo egressio In sole posuit tabernaculum	gr	GR 14 LU 344 GS 8 *SYG 10 GB 8^{v}	a	3	5	7	5	3	2	3	0	
2 A summo caelo egressio	gr	GR 13 LU 343 *SYG 10 *GS 8 *GB 8	E	3	5	8	5	7	8	5	3	a
2 A timore inimici	an	AR 192 *AM 52 53 *WA 67 LA 95	F	-1	-3	0	-1	-3	-5	-3	0	D
4 A viro iniquo	an	AM 150 *WA 68 *LA 99	E	3	5	7	5	3	1	3	5	E
3 Ab adolescentia pugnando	an	WA 289	E	-2	3	5	3	5	8	7	8	E
Ab altitudine Miserere mihi ... conculcavit	intv	GS 73										
8 Ab hominibus iniquis libera me	an	AR 436$_{D}$OHS 627 LU 776^{D} AM 431 432 WA 121 *LA 194	G	2	0	-2	2	5	4	5	2	G
1 Ab insurgentibus in me	an	OHS 500 LU 706 WA 123 LA 198	D	-2	3	5	3	5	7	8	7	D
1 Ab ipso pueritiae suae	an	LR 318 WA 296 LA 366	D	-2	3	5	3	5	7	5	3	D
2 Ab occultis meis munda me Domine	gr	GR 130 *SYG 81 *GS 57 *GB 84^{v}	E	3	5	8	5	7	8	5	3	a
4 Ab occultis meis munda me Domine	co	GR 142 SYG 103 GB 91^{v} GS 65	G	4	7	5	4	0	2	0	2	
Ab omni via mala prohibui Deus docuisti	trv	GR 72**	G	2	4	5	4	0	2	0	2	
8 Ab omni via mala prohibui	re	LA 134 WA 89	F	4	7	9	7	6	9	11	7	G
3 Ab Oriente adducam semen	gr	GR (4)	F	-5	-3	0	-1	0	2	4	2	E
Ab Oriente venerunt Videntes stellam	rev	LA 72 WA 55										
8 Ab Oriente venerunt	an	AR 331 AM 297 *WA 56 LA 75	a	-4	-2	0	-2	-4	0	3	0	G
8 Ab ortu solis usque ad occasum	tr	GR [97] LU 1282	D	3	5	2	3	5	0	-2	0	G
1 Abiit Jesus foras	an	WA 89	D	7	9	7	5	3	5	7	5	D
1 Abiit Jesus trans mare	an	WA 103	D	-2	0	2	3	2	0	-2	3	D
8 Abraham et semen ejus	an	WA 69	F	2	4	7	6	4	2	4	2	G
2 Abraham pater vester	an	AR 415 LU 577 *AM 393 *LA 172	C	2	4	5	7	9	5	4	2	D
2 Abraham pater vester	an	WA 108	C	2	5	7	5	4	2	5	2	D

	Incipit		Sources										
	Abraham stabat coram Deo Clamor inquit	rev	WA 81										
6	Abscondi tamquam aurum	re	LA 85 WA 61	a	3	5	3	5	7	5	7	5	c
8	Abscondite eleemosynam in sinu	re	LA 129 *WA 86	D	3	5	7	5	7	5	7	5	G
4	Absolve Domine animas eorum	co	SYG 237	F	-1	-3	-1	2	0	-1	-3	-1	E
7	Absolve Domine animas eorum	re	LA 558 *WA 438	G	2	5	7	5	4	5	7	9	G
8	Absolve Domine animas omnium	tr	GR 95* LU 1809	G	2	4	2	0	2	0	5	7	G
4	Absque tuo imperio non movebit	an	AR 5 (sup)	G	2	5	7	9	7	5	7	9	a
8	Absterget Deus omnem lacrimam	re	LR 178 LA 514 *WA 420	G	2	4	5	4	2	5	2	4	G
7	Absterget Deus omnem lacrimam	an	AM 652 *AR [47] *LU 1156 LA 392	G	5	4	5	7	5	4	2	4	G
	Abyssus vallavit me Fluctus tui	rev	LA 305 WA 186										
3	Accedens Petrus ad Jesum	an	WA 100	E	-2	3	5	3	5	8	7	5	E
2	Accedentes carnifices	an	WA 234	C	2	5	2	4	2	0	2	5	D
1	Accedentes discipuli	re	LA 453 *WA 363	C	2	4	2	9	11	9	7	9	D
	Accedentes principes sacerdotum Sepulto Domino	rev	OHS 618 LU 773 LA 202										
2	Accedite ad Dominum et illuminamini	of	GR 106**	A	3	5	7	5	7	8	10	7	D
	Accedite ad eum et illuminamini Immittet angelus	ofv	OTT 102 GB 71 *SYG 79	d	-5	-3	-2	0	2	0	3	0	
	Accedite ad eum et illuminamini Venite filii	grv	GR 336 (39) LU 1010 GS 67 148 168 GB 93 SYG 105	F	4	7	6	4	7	6	2	4	
1	Accepite autem omnes	an	WA 190 *LA 165	D	3	0	2	0	-2	3	5	3	D
	Accepit ergo centuplum Ecce jam cari	rev	WA 300	c	2	5	4	5	4	2	4	2	
1	Accepit ergo Jesus panes benedixit	an	WA 104	D	3	0	2	0	-2	3	5	3	D
1	Accepit ergo Jesus panes et cum	an	AR 398 LU 559 AM 374	D	3	0	-2	3	5	3	7	5	D
1	Accepit ergo Jesus panes et cum	an	WA 104	D	3	0	2	0	-2	3	5	3	D
6	Accepit Jesus calicem	re	LR 128 LU 932	F	2	0	2	4	0	-3	-1	0	F
6	Accepit Joseph puerum	an	LR 304	F	2	4	0	-1	-3	-1	-5	-3	F
	Accepit regnum decoris Induit eum	trv	GR 13**	G	-5	0	2	5	4	5	2	0	
4	Acceptabis sacrificium justitiae	co	GR 347 SYG 67 GB 63^v GS 33 152 LU 1023	D	7	3	5	7	8	5	7	2	E
1	Accepto pane Judas	an	LA 188	D	-2	3	5	3	5	7	5	3	D
3	Accessistis ad Sion montem	an	AR 763 LU 1528 *AM 948B	G	5	2	0	2	0	2	5	4	E
1	Accessit Jesus et tetigit	an	WA 190	D	3	0	2	0	-2	3	5	7	D
	Accingimini filii potentes Dixit Judas Simoni	rev	LA 297										

	Text	Type	Sources										
8	Accingimini filii potentes	an	WA 180 LA 300	G	-2	-5	-2	0	2	0	2	0	G
	Accingite vos sacerdotes / Plange quasi virgo	rev	OHS 603 LU 761 LA 202										
8	Accinxit fortitudine	an	PM 238 LR 220 *LA 540 *WA 433	G	-5	-2	0	2	0	2	0	-2	G
2	Accinxit fortitudine	re	LR 228	A	3	5	7	5	3	5	8	7	D
8	Accipe me ab hominibus	an	LA 500	G	5	4	0	2	5	2	0	2	G
	Accipiens Simeon puerum / Adorna thalamum	rev	LA 348 WA 268										
	Accipiens Simeon puerum / Senex puerum	rev	LA 348 WA 270										
3	Accipiens Simeon puerum	an	AR 620 LU 1366 AM 802 WA 272 *LA 355	G	4	5	2	5	4	0	2	4	E
4	Accipite jucunditatem gloriae	int	GR 298 LU 890 *SYG 185 GB 191^v GS 138	G	-5	-2	0	2	0	-5	-2	0	E
7	Accipite spiritum sanctum	an	AR 507 LU 877 AM 523 IA 262	G	5	4	5	7	2	4	5	4	G
	Acuerunt linguas suas / Eripe me	trv	GR 208 OHS 534 LU 725 *GS 99 *GB 116^v *SYG 137	D	3	2	3	5	7	5	7	5	
	Ad annuntiandum mane	sr	LA 102 WA 70										
	Ad annuntiandum mane / Bonum est confiteri	rev	LA 240 WA 144										
	Ad annuntiandum mane / Justus ut palma	ofv	OTT 150 *GB 25^v *SYG 24	F	-3	2	0	-1	0	-1	0	2	
	Ad annuntiandum mane / Bonum est confiteri	trv	GR 497	C	2	5	7	5	7	5	2	5	
	Ad annuntiandum mane / Justus ut palma	grv	GR [42]LU 1201 GS 202 GB 23 SYG 195	a	3	5	7	5	3	2	3	0	
	Ad annuntiandum mane / Bonum est confiteri	grv	GR 360 LU 1041 *GS 53 158 *GB 81 *SYG 92	F	4	0	4	7	9	11	7	9	
4	Ad coenam agni providi	hy	ST 190	a	-2	0	-2	-4	-2	-4	-5	-4	E
8	Ad coenam agni providi	hy	ST 387	a	-2	0	2	3	0	2	0	-2	G
4	Ad coenam agni providi	hy	ST 113	F	-1	-3	-5	-1	-3	2	0	-3	E
4	Ad coenam agni providi	hy	ST 35	F	-1	-3	-1	2	4	0	-1	2	E
1	Ad coenam agni providi	hy	ST 53	D	2	0	2	0	7	9	7	5	D
8	Ad coenam agni providi	hy	ST 419	G	2	0	2	4	5	2	4	2	G
1	Ad coenam agni providi	hy	ST 290 (var)	D	2	3	2	0	-2	3	5	7	D
6	Ad coenam agni providi	hy	ST 290	F	2	4	5	2	0	4	2	0	F
8	Ad coenam agni providi	hy	ST 189	G	2	4	5	4	2	0	2	-2	G
1	Ad coenam agni providi	hy	ST 92	C	2	4	7	4	2	5	4	2	D
7	Ad coenam agni providi	hy	ST 190	G	2	5	4	5	7	9	7	5	G

	Text	Type	Source										
1	Ad coenam agni providi	hy	ST 91	a	3	0	-2	-4	-2	0	-5	-7	D
8	Ad coenam agni providi	hy	ST 91 AM 459 467	a	3	0	-2	3	2	3	5	3	G
1	Ad coenam agni providi	hy	ST 290	D	3	0	-2	3	5	7	5	10	D
1	Ad coenam agni providi	hy	ST 229	D	3	2	0	-2	3	5	7	5	D
2	Ad Christi laudem virginis	hy	ST 435	G	-3	-2	0	-2	-3	-5	0	-2	D
	Ad dandam scientiam Tu puer propheta	cov	SYG 199										
	Ad dandam scientiam Tu puer	rev	LR 358										
8	Ad dandam scientiam	an	WA 67	G	5	2	0	-2	0	2	0	5	G
	Ad Dominum dum tribularer	alv	GB 263^v	G	2	-2	0	2	0	2	0	-2	
5	Ad Dominum dum tribularer	gr	GR 321 LU 961 *SYG 91 *GB 80 GS 53 142	D	3	5	3	0	3	5	2	3	F
8	Ad hanc vocem Christi ... Dionysius	an	WA 387	G	-2	0	2	0	-2	0	2	0	G
1	Ad hanc vocem Christi ... Sebastiani	an	LA 330	D	-2	3	5	3	5	7	5	3	D
	Ad hoc tantum sub clamide Christo cotidie	rev	LA 328										
1	Ad hoc tantum sub clamide	an	LA 324	D	3	0	-2	3	5	3	5	7	D
5	Ad honorem regis summi	hy	ST 111	c	-3	-2	-3	-5	-2	0	-3	-7	F
3	Ad hujus quoque spectat	an	WA 291	E	-2	3	5	3	5	8	7	3	E
1	Ad Jesum autem cum venissent	an	AR 538^{13} LU 979 AM 570	D	3	0	-2	3	5	3	7	10	D
2	Ad laudem sanctae Mariae	hy	ST 456	a	-2	2	0	-2	-5	-4	-2	-4	D
2	Ad laudem sanctae Mariae	hy	ST 432	D	2	0	-2	0	3	2	3	5	D
1	Ad manus autem illum	an	LA 342 WA 262 (inc illeg)	G	-7	-5	2	4	2	0	2	4	D
	Ad montem quoque Qui persequebantur	rev	LA 158										
1	Ad monumentum Lazari	an	WA 105	D	3	2	3	5	0	3	5	3	D
3	Ad nutum Domini nostrum	re	AR 130* *PM 187 *WA 365	G	2	0	2	4	2	4	5	7	E
1	Ad occasum vergens	re	WA 251	D	-2	0	2	3	0	2	-2	0	D
8	Ad omnia quae mittam te	an	LR 346 WA 320 *LA 400	G	-2	-5	-3	-2	0	2	0	2	G
1	Ad perennis vitae fontem	hy	ST 463	e	-2	-4	-2	-4	-5	-7	-9	-4	a
3	Ad quantum vero messem	an	WA 238	G	2	0	-3	-5	0	2	5	4	E
4	Ad regias agni dapes	hy	AR 454 LU 814	F	-1	-3	-5	-1	-3	2	0	-1	E
8	Ad regias agni dapes	hy	AR 453 LU 812	G	2	5	4	2	0	5	4	5	G
2	Ad sacros virgo	hy	AM 1132	A	5	3	5	8	7	5	7	8	D
	Ad te clamant omnes rei O praeclara stella	rev	VP 187	a	-4	-2	-4	-2	0	3	5	3	

	Title	Type	References	Mode									End
	Ad te clamaverunt et salvi Deus Deus meus	trv	GR 180 OHS 109 LU 594 GS 86 GB 109 SYG 122	F	2	0	2	0	-3	0	-1	0	
	Ad te Clamaverunt patres nostri Media vita	rev	AR 152* PM 45 VP 106	D	7	5	7	8	7	5	7	8	
7	Ad te de luce	an	AR 354 GR 297 AM 327 WA 79 *LA 124	G	4	5	7	9	7	5	4	5	G
3	Ad te Deus de luce	an	WA 251	G	2	0	-2	-3	-5	-3	-5	0	E
	Ad te Domine clamabo		see also Ad te Domine clamavi										
	Ad te Domine clamabo Dominus fortitudo	intv	GR 334 LU 1006 GS 146 GB 249 SYG 242										
	Ad te Domine clamavi In Deo speravit	grv	GR 348 LU 1025 *GS 60 152 *GB 87^v SYG 98	F	4	7	9	7	9	11	7	9	
	Ad te Domine clamavi Salvum fac populum	grv	GR 119 *GS 43 50 171 GB 78 SYG 88	G	5	7	9	10	12	10	7	5	
	Ad te Domine levavi animam ... Deus De necessitatibus	intv	GR 104 GS 41 GS 72 SYG 80										
	Ad te Domine levavi animam ... Deus Dirige me Domine	intv	GB 74^v										
	Ad te Domine levavi animam ... Deus Oculi mei	intv	GR 123 LU 552 GS 54 GB 82 SYG 92										
	Ad te Domine levavi animam ... Deus Reminiscere	intv GS	GS 39 47 GB 69 SYG 77										
	Ad te Domine levavi animam ... Deus Respice in me	intv	GR 327 LU 981 GS 143 GB 248 SYG 240										
2	Ad te Domine levavi animam ... Deus	re	LA 84 *WA 61	C	2	4	5	4	0	2	5	4	D
	Ad te Domine levavi animam ... Deus ... neque De necessitatibus	trv	GR 102 LU 841^A GS 39 *GB 69^v SYG 78	C	2	5	7	5	7	9	7	5	
2	Ad te Domine levavi animam ... Deus ... neque	of	GR 3 LU 321 OTT 5 SYG 2 GB 1^v GS 2 33 51 152	A	3	5	3	5	3	5	8	7	D
4	Ad te Domine levavi animam ... veni	an	AR 242 AM 217 *WA 20 *LA 27	a	3	5	3	5	7	3	5	7	a
8	Ad te levavi animam ... Deus ... neque	int	GR 1 LU 318 SYG 1 GS A	G	-5	-2	0	2	0	5	2	0	G
	Ad te levavi oculos ... qui Sicut oculi	intv	GR 99 GS 37 GB 67 SYG 75										
8	Ad te levavi oculos ... qui	tr	GR 124 LU 554 *SYG 93 *GB 82^v GS 55	D	3	5	2	3	5	0	-2	0	G
3	Ad thronum majestatis	an	WA 358	E	-2	3	5	8	7	5	3	5	E
4	Ad tua solemnia	hy	ST 355	E	1	3	1	0	1	0	-2	0	E

#	Incipit	Genre	Sources										
	Ad unius jussionis Mox ut vocem	rev	LA 498										
8	Adam vetus quod polluit	hy	ST 367	G	2	0	2	0	-2	0	2	5	G
	Adaperiat Dominus cor Exaudiat Dominus	rev	WA 180										
6	Adaperiat Dominus cor ... Dominus	an	LA 299	F	2	4	2	4	2	0	2	4	F
3	Adaperiat Dominus cor ... in diebus	re	LR 425 LA 295 WA 180	G	2	5	4	5	2	0	2	0	E
8	Adaperiat Dominus cor ... in diebus	an	AR 550 LU 993 AM 587	G	5	2	0	-2	0	2	0	-2	G
8	Adducam eos in montem	of	GR 446 LU 1387	D	3	5	7	5	7	5	3	5	G
	Adducentur in laetitia Afferentur regi ... post eam	ofv	OTT 163 *SYG 5 *GB 4^V	D	-2	0	3	5	3	0	3	-2	
	Adducentur in laetitia Audi filia	trv	GR [62] LU 1227	C	2	5	7	2	0	2	5	7	
	Adducentur in laetitia Omnis gloria	trv	GR 104**	C	2	5	7	2	0	2	5	7	
	Adducentur in laetitia Diffusa est gratia	trv	SYG 49	C	2	5	7	5	4	2	4	5	
	Adducentur regi virgines	sr	WA 394										
8	Adducentur regi virgines	tr	GB 45	G	-5	-2	0	2	0	2	0	-2	G
3	Adducentur regi virgines	alv	GR [61] LU 1217 *GS 231 GB 29^V	C	2	4	5	7	5	7	10	7	
	Adducentur regi virgines Audi filia	trv	GR [62] LU 1227	D	3	2	3	5	7	5	7	5	
	Adducentur regi virgines Omnis gloria	trv	GR 104**	D	3	2	3	5	7	5	7	5	
8	Adducunt beato Mauro caecum	re	LR 278	G	2	0	2	0	-2	2	5	7	G
	Adduxerunt autem eum Jesum tradidit	rev	OHS 507 LU 711 *LA 199	f	-1	0	2	0	-1	0	-1	-3	
	Adduxi vos per desertum Popule meus	rev	WA 103										
7	Adduxi vos per desertum	re	LA 160 *WA 103	G	2	-2	0	2	0	2	0	2	G
7	Adduxisti sanctos tuos	re	LA 551	G	2	0	2	4	5	4	2	4	G
	Ade vero non inveniebatur Dixit Dominus Deus non est	rev	LA 110 WA 73										
5	Adeamus cum fiducia	int	GR 587^1 43** LU 1612^1	F	4	7	9	7	9	7	4	2	F
4	Adeptus est sedem	an	WA 41 *LA 54	F	-1	-3	-1	0	2	0	-1	-3	E
1	Adest dies praeclara	an	WA 358	D	3	0	-2	0	3	2	0	2	D
6	Adest frater curiosus	an	WA 292	c	2	4	0	2	0	-3	-1	0	c
1	Adest multitudo monachorum	an	WA 404 (inc illeg)										
1	Adest namque beati Dionysii	an	WA 389	C	2	9	11	9	7	9	11	9	D
8	Adest namque beati Dionysii	re	WA 387	D	3	5	7	5	7	5	7	9	G

1 Adest praeclara festivitas	an	WA 335	C	2	4	2	0	2	5	4	5	D
3 Adeste sancti plurimo	hy	AM 906	E	1	3	1	0	-2	0	-2	-4	E
8 Adeste sancti plurimo	hy	LR 451	C	5	4	5	7	9	7	5	7	G
1 Adesto Deus unus	an	WA 158	D	3	5	7	5	7	5	3	5	D
6 Adesto dolori meo Deus	re	LA 286	D	3	5	3	7	3	7	10	5	F
8 Adesto dolori meo Deus	re	WA 174	D	3	5	7	5	3	7	5	7	G
1 Adesto sancta trinitas	hy	AR 180*	D	-2	3	2	0	7	5	3	2	D
3 Adesto sancta trinitas	hy	ST 114	E	-2	3	5	8	7	5	3	5	E
8 Adesto sancta trinitas	hy	ST 392	G	2	0	-3	-2	-3	-5	-3	0	G
4 Adesto summa suavitas	hy	ST 233	E	1	-2	1	-2	-4	-2	0	-2	E
3 Adhaereat lingua mea	an	AR 160 LU 297	G	5	2	0	2	5	4	5	7	E
8 Adhaesit anima mea	an	AR 388	a	-4	-2	-4	0	3	2	-2	2	G
8 Adhaesit anima mea ... cremata	an	AR 814 LU 1597 AM 1006	G	4	5	2	0	4	5	2	5	G
8 Adhaesit anima mea ... cremata	an	WA 350 LA 440	G	5	2	0	5	2	5	4	7	G
8 Adhaesit anima mea ... lapidata	an	AR 274 LU 418 1583A AM 250 *LA 47 *WA 37	G	4	5	2	0	4	5	2	5	G
3 Adhuc eo loquente	an	AR 806 LU 1589	G	2	0	2	5	4	2	4	2	E
6 Adhuc eo loquente	an	AM 999	F	2	4	0	-1	-3	-5	-3	0	F
Adhuc esca erat in ore Manducaverunt	cov	GB 61										
1 Adhuc loquente Petro	an	WA 327	C	2	5	7	5	4	2	4	2	D
Adhuc me loquente et orante Oravi Deum	ofv	OTT 107 *GB 256V *SYG 250	a	3	5	3	2	3	2	-2	0	
5 Adhuc multa habeo	an	AR 482 AM 497 *LA 242	F	4	7	9	7	6	9	11	7	F
Adimplebis me laetitia eum Notas mihi fecisti	cov	GS 59										
2 Adjuro vos filiae	an	WA 353	D	-2	0	3	2	0	-2	0	3	D
7 Adjutor et protector noster	int	GR 485 LU 1277A	G	5	4	5	7	9	7	9	5	G
4 Adjutor et susceptor meus	re	LR 414 *LA 168 WA 108	F	-1	0	-3	0	-1	0	2	4	E
3 Adjutor in opportunitatibus	gr	GR 74 LU 498 *GB 56 GS 24 *SYG 58	G	5	0	2	5	2	0	2	5	E
1 Adjutor in tribulationibus	an	OHS 297 (nm) WA 65 *LA 90	a	-2	-5	-4	-2	-4	-5	-7	[0]	D
Adjutor meus esto	sr	LA 114 WA 75										
8 Adjutor meus et liberator	an	AR 164 LU 300	G	-2	2	5	4	0	-2	0	2	G
2 Adjutor meus et liberator	gr	GR 115 SYG 87 GB 76V GS 48	A	3	5	7	0	3	5	7	8	D

#	Title	Type	Sources		1	2	3	4	5	6	7	8	
5	Adjutor meus tibi psallam	re	LA 94 *WA 66	a	-4	0	3	0	3	2	3	5	F
	Adjutorium nostrum in nomine	sr	AM 277 LA 90 WA 64										
1	Adjutorium nostrum in nomine	an	AR 120 OHS 287 LU 285 *LA 99	F	2	4	2	0	2	0	-1	0	D
	Adjuva me Domine Deus Confitebor Domino	ofv	OTT 74 *GB 162 *SYG 178	a	3	5	3	5	3	5	3	5	
	Adjuva me Domine Deus Sederunt principes	grv	GR 36 LU 416 *SYG 22 GB 21 GS 15	F	4	5	7	9	7	4	7	9	
8	Adjuva me et salvus ero	an	AM 94 96 WA 64 *LA 89	G	5	4	0	4	5	2	4	2	G
	Adjuva nos Deus salutaris noster Emendemus in melius	rev	PM 47 GR 86 LU 524 WA 85										
2	Adjuva nos Deus salutaris noster	tr	GR [131]	D	-2	0	-2	-5	-2	0	-2	0	D
	Adjuva nos Deus salutaris noster Domine non secundum	trv	GR 89 LU 527 OHS 209 *GS 31 *SYG 66	F	2	4	5	4	2	4	0	-3	
	Adjuva nos Deus salutaris noster Propitius esto	grv	GR 107 LU 999 GS 42 51 145 170 GB 78^v *SYG 81	F	4	5	7	9	7	2	7	9	
6	Adjuva sancte tuos precibus	gr	SYG 230	F	2	0	2	0	4	2	4	2	F
	Adjuvabit eam Deus vultu suo	sr	AR [94] LU 1257 AM 676 1178 1179 WA 434										
	Adjuvabit eam Deus vultu suo Accinxit fortitudine	rev	LR 228										
7	Adjuvabit eam Deus vultu suo	an	LR 214 247 375 *LA 541 *WA 432	d	-3	0	2	0	-3	-2	-3	-7	G
5	Adjuvabit eam Deus vultu suo	gr	GR [56] LU 1221 *SYG 50 *GB 50 GS 181	F	4	7	4	7	6	7	6	4	F
	Adjuvent nos eorum merita Concede nobis	rev	PM 202 *WA 393	a	-2	0	-2	-4	-2	0	-2	0	
5	Adjuvit eam Deus mane	an	LR 261	a	-4	0	3	5	3	2	3	0	F
8	Admirabile est ... in universa terra	an	LR 260	G	2	0	-5	-2	-3	-2	-5	-3	G
1	Admirabile est ... quia gloria	an	LR 382 *WA 395 *LA 475	C	2	9	10	9	7	5	7	9	D
5	Admirabile nomen Jesu	inv	LR 430	F	4	7	9	7	11	9	7	4	F
	Admirandus cunctis O beatum praesulem	rev	WA 295	D	7	5	7	3	5	3	2	5	
1	Admoniti Magi in somnis	an	AR 334 LU 483 *AM 300 *LA 69 *WA 57	D	-2	3	5	3	7	5	8	7	D
8	Admonitus in somnis Joseph	an	LR 308	G	-5	-3	-2	0	2	0	2	5	G
4	Adnue Christe saeculorum Domine	hy	ST 100	F	-1	-3	-5	-3	0	-3	-1	0	E
4	Adnue Christe saeculorum Domine	hy	ST 195	F	-1	-3	-5	-3	0	-3	0	-1	E

1	Adnue Christe saeculorum Domine	hy	ST 130	D	3	2	0	-2	0	7	5	3	D
1	Adolescens tibi dico	an	WA 190	C	2	9	11	9	7	9	11	9	D
3	Adonai Domine Deus	re	LR 424 LA 290 *WA 178	E	-2	3	5	8	5	7	8	7	E
3	Adonai Domine Deus	an	AR 549 LU 993	E	1	3	1	0	-2	3	5	8	E
8	Adonai Domine Deus	an	AM 586 *WA 176	G	2	0	-2	0	-2	-5	-2	-3	G
8	Adonai Domine Deus	an	LA 294	G	5	2	0	2	0	-2	0	2	G
	Adorabo ad templum sanctum	alv	GR [73] LU 1251 GS 175 k GB 174^v SYG 48 236	G	5	7	5	7	2	0	2	-2	
	Adorabo ad templum sanctum Si ambulavero	ofv	OTT 118 GB 86^v *SYG 97	G	5	7	5	7	5	7	9	7	
	Adorabunt eum omnes reges	sr	AR 894^{12} LU 1715										
	Adoramus te Christe	sr	AR 703 LU 1458 AM 896 1038 WA 309 370										
	Adoramus te Christe Tuam crucem adoramus	rev	WA 369										
4	Adoramus te Christe et benedicimus	re	WA 369	F	-3	0	-1	0	2	0	-1	0	E
2	Adoramus te Christe et benedicimus	tr	GR [104]	D	-2	0	-2	-5	-2	0	-2	0	D
1	Adoramus te Christe et benedicimus	an	OHS 584 SYG 141 LU 746 WA 370	C	2	9	10	9	7	9	10	9	D
1	Adoramus te Christe et hymnum	an	GB 115^v	C	2	9	11	9	7	9	11	9	D
6	Adorate Deum alleluia	an	LR 74	F	-1	2	4	-1	0	-3	-5	0	F
7	Adorate Deum omnes Angeli	int	GR 70 LU 488 *SYG 42 GB 39 GS 23	G	5	7	5	7	5	9	7	9	G
	Adorate Dominum alleluia	sr	AR 317 LU 463										
6	Adorate Dominum alleluia in aula	an	LR 74 *LA 69 *WA 54	F	-1	2	4	-1	0	-3	-5	0	F
6	Adorate Dominum alleluia omnes	an	WA 54 LA 69	F	-1	2	4	0	-1	-3	-5	0	F
8	Adorate Dominum in aula	an	LR 233 *LA 82 *WA 61	G	-2	2	5	7	5	4	2	5	G
7	Adorate eum omnes angeli	an	LR 338	G	2	5	9	7	5	7	10	9	G
7	Adoraverunt viventem	re	LA 58 *WA 46	a	-4	0	3	5	3	0	3	5	G
2	Adoremus Christum regem confessorum	inv	WA 287	C	2	4	5	4	2	4	2	4	D
2	Adoremus conditorem cunctorum	inv	WA 335	C	2	4	5	4	2	4	2	5	D
	Adoremus crucis signaculum O crux gloriosa	rev	VP 151	c	-3	-5	-1	0	2	0	-1	-3	
4	Adoremus crucis signaculum	an	WA 371 *LA 464	E	-2	-4	-2	0	-2	0	1	3	E
7	Adoremus crucis signaculum	an	SYG 139	G	2	5	4	2	4	5	7	9	G
4	Adoremus Deum qui in sanctis	inv	WA 43	D	3	2	0	3	2	3	5	3	E

4	Adoremus Dominum qui fecit	inv	LA 80 *WA 60 165	C	4	7	5	2	5	4	5	2	E
6	Adoremus Dominum qui vos	inv	WA 109	F	2	0	2	4	0	2	4	2	F
6	Adoremus Dominum quoniam	inv	LA 96 WA 67	c	2	0	2	4	0	2	4	2	c
5	Adoremus in aeternum sanctissimum		AR 92* LU 1853	a	-2	0	-2	-4	3	5	3	2	F
4	Adoremus regem apostolorum	inv	LA 48 *WA 38	C	2	4	5	7	5	4	2	0	E
4	Adoremus regem saeculorum	inv	WA 238	F	-1	-3	0	-1	0	2	0	-1	E
7	Adoremus victoriosissimum	inv	WA 232	G	5	4	5	7	5	7	9	7	G
6	Adorna thalamum ... amplectere	an	GR 430 PM 134 LU 1359 GS i 180 *SYG 46 *GB 46^v	F	4	7	9	7	9	7	6	4	c
8	Adorna thalamum ... quem	re	LA 348 *WA 268	F	4	7	9	7	9	7	6	7	G
5	Adoro te devote latens Deitas	hy	AR 100* LU 1855 VP 13	F	4	7	9	7	5	4	2	0	F
	Adspice	see Aspice											
2	Adstemus mente vigili	hy	ST 376	d	-2	-3	-5	-2	0	-2	-5	-7	d
	Adstiterunt	see Astiterunt											
	Adstitit	see Astitit											
8	Advenerunt nobis dies	an	AR 87 *AM 97 112 *PM 48 WA 89	G	2	0	2	0	2	4	0	-2	G
5	Adveniente Petro	an	WA 326	a	-2	-4	0	3	2	0	-2	3	F
	Advenit ignis divinus Spiritus sanctus procedens	rev	PM 87 LR 111 LA 261 WA 154										
8	Advenit ignis divinus	re	WA 153	G	-2	2	4	2	0	5	4	2	G
7	Advenit ignis divinus	re	LR 116 *LA 259	G	2	4	5	4	2	4	2	0	G
6	Adversio parvulorum	re	WA 171	a	-2	3	5	8	7	5	3	5	c
5	Adversum me exercebantur	co	GR 189 LU 614 OHS 279 SYG 126 GB 113^v GS 91	a	-4	0	3	5	3	0	1	0	F
	Adversum me exercebantur Improperium exspectavit	ofv	OTT 49 GB 110^v SYG 123	D	3	5	3	5	7	5	0	5	
	Adversus me	see Adversum me											
6	Aedificabuntur in te deserta	of	GR (5)	D	3	5	3	0	3	5	3	-2	F
	Aedificata est ut civitas Iste est Ode	rev	PM 210										
	Aedificato altari Igitur Abraham	rev	WA 82										
	Aedificavit ex lapidibus Dom iret Jacob	rev	LR 406										
	Aedificavit ibi Jacob Dom iret Jacob	rev	WA 91										
6	Aedificavit Moyses altare	an	LR 233 WA 318 LA 549	F	2	4	2	0	2	4	2	0	F

3 Aedificavit Noe altare	re	LA 117 *WA 78	C	2	5	2	5	7	5	4	2	E
4 Aedomans corpus iuvenis	an	WA 292	F	-3	-1	0	2	0	2	4	2	E
4 Aegypte noli flere	re	LA 14 *WA 14	a	-2	0	-4	-7	-4	-5	-7	-4	E
1 Aemula prosequitur	re	WA 284	D	3	2	0	-2	0	3	5	7	D
Aemulor enim vos Dei	alv	GS 227	a	-2	0	-4	-7	-9	-7	-5	-4	
4 Aestimatus sum cum descendentibus	re	OHS 617 LU 772 *LA 205 *WA 126	F	-3	-1	0	-1	2	0	-3	-1	E
Aestimatus sum cum descendentibus Repleta est malis	grv	GR 9**	C	2	5	7	9	7	5	7	5	
4 Aeterna caeli gloria	hy	AR 168 AM 72	E	-4	-2	1	0	1	3	1	0	E
1 Aeterna caeli gloria	hy	AM 72	a	2	0	-2	-4	-2	0	-2	-4	D
3 Aeterna caeli gloria	hy	ST 214	D	2	3	5	3	5	3	2	3	E
8 Aeterna caeli gloria	hy	ST 363	D	2	3	5	7	3	5	0	2	G
8 Aeterna Christi munera	hy	ST 16	G	-2	-3	-2	0	2	0	2	5	G
5 Aeterna Christi munera	hy	ST 100 103	F	2	4	2	0	2	4	6	4	F
3 Aeterna Christi munera apostolorum	hy	ST 195	E	-2	3	5	8	7	5	7	8	E
3 Aeterna Christi munera apostolorum	hy	LR 134	E	1	0	-2	3	5	8	7	5	E
6 Aeterna Christi munera apostolorum	hy	ST 402	c	2	4	2	0	2	4	5	4	c
1 Aeterna Christi munera apostolorum	hy	LR 429	C	2	4	7	5	4	2	4	5	D
3 Aeterna Christi munera et apostolorum	hy	ST 60	E	-2	3	5	8	7	5	8	7	E
2 Aeterna Christi munera et martyrum	hy	ST 44	D	-2	-3	-2	0	-2	0	2	5	D
3 Aeterna Christi munera et martyrum	hy	LR 175	E	1	0	-2	3	5	8	7	5	E
3 Aeterna Christi munera et martyrum	hy	LR 164	E	1	3	1	0	-2	0	1	-2	E
8 Aeterna Christi munera et martyrum	hy	ST 140	G	2	0	-2	-3	-2	0	2	0	G
6 Aeterna Christi munera et martyrum	hy	ST 403	c	2	4	2	0	2	4	5	4	c
3 Aeterna sapientia	hy	ST 233	E	1	3	1	0	-2	0	1	-2	E
5 Aeterna sapientia	hy	ST 127	F	2	4	2	0	2	4	7	5	F
8 Aeterne patris unice	hy	AM 976	G	2	4	5	4	2	0	2	-2	G
5 Aeterne rector siderum	hy	AR 867	F	4	7	9	6	7	9	11	7	F
2 Aeterne rerum conditor	hy	ST 2	D	-5	-3	-2	0	2	0	-2	0	D
8 Aeterne rerum conditor	hy	ST 211	G	-5	-2	2	-2	0	5	2	5	G
2 Aeterne rerum conditor	hy	ST 26	D	-5	-2	2	0	-2	0	5	2	D
1 Aeterne rerum conditor	hy	ST 251	E	1	3	7	5	3	5	3	8	D
6 Aeterne rerum conditor	hy	ST 358	c	2	4	2	5	4	2	0	2	c
1 Aeterne rerum conditor	hy	AR 6 AM 34 ST 84 181	F	2	4	5	4	2	4	2	7	D

#	Title	Cat	Source	M									End
1	Aeterne rerum conditor	hy	ST 262	F	2	5	4	2	4	5	2	7	D
1	Aeterne rerum conditor	hy	ST 262	F	2	5	4	2	5	4	5	2	D
3	Aeterne rerum conditor	hy	ST 323	E	3	5	8	3	5	8	7	5	E
8	Aeterne rex altissime	hy	ST 93 390	G	2	4	2	0	-2	2	0	2	G
8	Aeterne rex altissime	hy	ST 37	G	2	5	2	0	-2	2	0	2	G
8	Aeterne rex altissime	hy	GR 156* PM 96 LR 94 LU 957 ST 470	G	2	5	4	2	0	-2	2	0	G
1	Aeterni patris filium	hy	ST 306	a	1	0	-2	-4	-5	-2	0	-4	D
8	Aeterni regis immensam ... Annae	an	WA 339	C	2	5	2	0	2	7	9	7	G
1	Aeterni regis immensam ... Magdalenae	an	WA 335	C	2	5	2	0	2	7	9	7	D
	Afferens autem urceum Dixit Romanus	anv	LA 433 WA 347										
	Afferentur		see also Offerentur										
2	Afferentur in laetitia	an	LR 335	D	5	3	2	3	0	-2	0	3	D
1	Afferentur regi virgines post	of	GR 437 LU 1370 OTT 163 *SYG 5 GS 229 GB 4^v	C	2	5	2	4	2	5	7	5	D
	Afferentur regi virgines post Diffusa est gratia	trv	SYG 49	C	2	5	7	9	5	4	7	5	
1	Afferentur regi virgines post	re	LR 223	C	2	5	7	9	7	4	5	2	D
4	Afferentur regi virgines proximae	of	GR [54] LU 1219 OTT 155 *SYG 29 *GB 30 GS 229	D	3	0	3	2	3	5	7	2	E
	Afferte Domino familiae	sr	AR 894^11 LU 1714 AM 1089										
	Afferte Domino filii Dei Psallite Domino	rev	WA 396										
7	Afferte Domino filii Dei	an	LR 69 *LA 66 *WA 53	G	4	5	7	9	7	9	5	2	G
	Afferte Domino gloriam	sr	AR 305 LU 450										
5	Afferte Domino patriae gentium	of	GR [129] LU 1296	c	-3	0	-3	0	4	2	0	-1	F
	Affirmans quia hic Saulus autem multo	anv	WA 264										
8	Afflicti pro peccatis nostris	re	VP 262 LA 84 *WA 62	D	3	5	7	5	7	9	7	5	G
	Afflige opprimentes nos Aperi caelos	rev	WA 182										
	Affluens ergo misericordiae Servus Dei Nicholaus	rev	WA 241	F	2	4	2	0	2	4	7	4	
	Agatha		see also Agathes										
7	Agatha ingressa carcerem	an	LA 360	G	4	5	7	5	7	9	7	5	G
7	Agatha laetissime et glorianter	an	PM 138 LA 356	d	-2	-3	-2	0	2	0	-2	-3	G
8	Agatha laetissime et glorianter	re	LA 357	F	2	4	2	4	2	4	2	4	G

2 Agatha laetissime et glorianter	re	WA 273		C	2	4	2	5	4	2	4	5	D
8 Agatha sancta dixit	an	LA 357		a	2	3	0	-2	-4	-2	0	-2	G
8 Agathae sacrae virginis	hy	ST 41		G	-2	0	2	5	4	5	7	5	G
Agathes		see also Agatha											
8 Agathes ingressa carcerem	an	WA 274		F	2	4	2	0	4	2	7	9	G
8 Agathes sancta dixit	an	WA 273		G	5	2	0	-2	0	2	0	4	G
Age nunc virgo Christi Gaudens perenniter	trv	SYG 238		F	2	4	2	4	2	4	5	4	
1 Agmina sacra angelorum	re	WA 391		C	2	5	0	4	2	5	2	4	D
4 Agnes beatae virginis	hy	ST 39		a	-2	-5	-7	-2	0	3	0	-2	E
8 Agnes beatae virginis	hy	ST 15		G	-2	0	2	4	5	4	5	7	G
3 Agnes beatae virginis	hy	ST 329		E	3	5	7	8	7	5	3	1	E
8 Agnetis festum martyris	hy	ST 425		G	-2	-5	-3	-2	0	2	0	-2	G
2 Agnetis festum martyris	hy	ST 373		D	2	0	-2	3	5	7	2	0	D
1 Agnoscat omne saeculum	hy	ST 218		D	2	-2	2	5	7	5	2	3	D
1 Agnoscat omne saeculum	hy	ST 255		G	2	-2	2	5	7	5	3	2	G
8 Agnoscat omne saeculum	hy	ST 367		G	2	0	2	0	-2	0	2	5	G
3 Agnosce o Vincenti	an	WA 261		G	5	2	4	2	0	2	5	4	E
1 Agnosce o Vincenti	re	WA 259		D	7	5	7	10	7	9	7	5	D
4 Agnum sponsum virginum	inv	WA 430		E	-4	-2	0	1	0	1	3	1	E
2 Agnus Dei Christus	re	WA 126		C	2	4	2	5	4	5	7	5	D
5 Agnus Dei qui tollis peccata XVII*		GR 57* OHS 145 LU 61		c	-3	-7	-5	-7	-3	0	2	0	F
4 Agnus Dei X		GR 38* LU 45		E	-2	-4	-2	0	3	5	3	1	E
4 Agnus Dei I		GR 7* OHS 715 LU 18		b	-2	0	-2	-4	0	3	5	3	b
8 Agnus Dei VII		GR 27* LU 36		a	-2	3	5	3	5	0	-4	0	G
6 Agnus Dei ad lib. II		GR 93* LU 88		b^b	-1	-3	-1	-5	-6	-5	-3	-5	F
4 Agnus Dei III		GR 14* LU 25		F	-1	-3	-1	0	-1	-3	-5	-3	E
1 Agnus Dei II		GR 10* OHS 851 LU 21		D	2	-2	2	3	2	0	2	0	D
8 Agnus Dei XIV		GR 50* LU 56		G	2	0	-2	-3	-5	-2	0	2	G
8 Agnus Dei VI		GR 24* LU 33		G	2	0	-2	0	2	0	2	5	G
1 Agnus Dei XIII		GR 47* LU 53		D	2	0	-2	3	2	0	2	5	D
8 Agnus Dei XVIII		GR 58* OHS 213 LU 63		G	2	0	2	-2	0	2	0	2	G
8 Agnus Dei VIII		GR 31* LU 39		F	2	0	2	4	0	2	0	-3	F
1 Agnus Dei XI		GR 41* LU 48		D	2	3	0	-2	0	2	5	7	D
6 Agnus Dei IV		GR 17* OHS 421 LU 27		F	2	4	2	0	-1	0	2	4	F

*Over two hundred additional Agnus Dei listings are given in the Addenda, pp. 449 ff.

#	Title	Type	Sources										
4	Agnus Dei V		GR 20* LU 30	C	2	4	5	4	2	0	2	4	E
1	Agnus Dei XV		GR 53* LU 58	D	3	0	-2	2	0	5	7	5	D
1	Agnus Dei XVI		GR 54* LU 60	E	3	1	0	-4	-2	0	-2	0	D
2	Agnus Dei XII		GR 44* LU 50	A	3	5	8	7	8	7	5	7	D
8	Agnus Dei ad lib I		GR 92* LU 87	G	4	5	2	0	4	2	0	-3	G
5	Agnus Dei IX		GR 34* OHS 462 LU 42	F	4	7	4	2	7	9	7	9	F
8	Agnus Dei ... requiem		GR 101*	G	2	0	2	-2	0	2	0	2	G
8	Ait autem Abraham	re	WA 81	D	3	5	7	5	7	5	7	9	G
1	Ait autem angelus ne timeas	an	AR 661 LU 1408	D	-2	3	5	3	5	7	10	7	D
3	Ait Dominus Deus ad serpentem	an	AR 587 LU 1315 *AM 765	G	5	2	0	2	5	4	5	4	E
1	Ait dominus villico	an	AR 559 AM 598	D	2	3	5	2	5	7	3	2	D
	Ait illi Jesus / Dixit Dominus mulieri	trv	SYG 85 *GS 47	F	-1	0	2	4	2	4	2	4	
	Ait illis Pilatus / Egressus Jesus	rev	WA 123	e	1	0	-2	3	5	3	0	1	
1	Ait latro ad latronem	an	AR 438 OHS 511 LU 715 AM 439 440 *WA 124 LA 200	D	3	0	-2	3	5	3	7	10	D
2	Ait Petrus principibus	an	WA 326	C	2	0	2	4	5	2	0	2	D
	Ait puella matri suae / Puellae saltanti	rev	LA 452										
3	Alabastrum unguenti	an	WA 335	G	2	0	2	5	4	2	4	2	E
4	Ales diei nuntius	hy	AR 109 AM 51	E	-4	-2	1	0	1	3	1	0	E
1	Ales diei nuntius	hy	AM 51	a	2	0	-2	-4	-2	0	-2	-4	D
3	Ales diei nuntius	hy	ST 213	D	2	3	5	3	5	3	2	3	E
8	Ales diei nuntius	hy	ST 363	D	2	3	5	7	3	5	0	2	G
8	Alias oves habeo	an	AR 472 *AM 486	G	-2	-5	-3	-2	0	2	0	-2	G
	Alieni insurrexerunt in me / Tradiderunt me	rev	OHS 505 LU 710 LA 197										
4	Alieni insurrexerunt in me	an	OHS 494 LU 701 WA 122 *LA 197	G	2	5	7	5	7	9	7	5	a
8	Alieni non transibunt	re	WA 10 LA 4	D	3	5	7	5	7	5	7	9	G
8	Alleluia	an	PM 238	G	-5	-2	0	2	0	-2	0	2	G
8	Alleluia	an	PM 231	G	-5	-2	2	0	2	5	4	5	G
8	Alleluia	an	AR 119 LU 285 288	a	-4	-2	-4	0	3	0	2	3	G
8	Alleluia	an	AM 118	a	-4	-2	0	2	3	0	2	3	G
6	Alleluia	an	AM 29	F	-3	-1	0	-1	-3	-5	0	2	F
6	Alleluia	an	WA 65	F	-3	0	-1	-3	-5	0	2	4	F
1	Alleluia	an	AR 158 LU 295 298	a	-2	-5	-4	-5	-4	-2	-5	-4	D

1 Alleluia	an	AM 43	a	-2	-4	-5	-4	-2	-5	-4	-5	D
8 Alleluia	an	AR 31 LU 239 AM 32 87	a	-2	-4	-2	0	-2	0	3	0	G
1 Alleluia	an	WA 64	a	-2	0	-2	-5	-4	-2	-4	-5	D
6 Alleluia	an	AR 165	a	-2	0	-2	-4	-2	0	-2	-4	F
8 Alleluia	an	AR 145	a	-2	0	-2	-4	-2	0	2	3	G
4 Alleluia	an	WA 69	E	-2	0	-2	-4	-2	1	-2	1	E
1 Alleluia	an	WA 66	a	-2	0	-2	-4	-2	3	0	-2	D
ir Alleluia	an	AM 113	a	-2	0	-2	0	-2	-4	-2	0	a
2 Alleluia	an	PM 218	D	-2	0	3	5	3	2	0	2	D
8 Alleluia	an	WA 131	G	-2	2	5	4	0	[0	0	0]	G
8 Alleluia	an	WA 127	G	-2	2	5	4	0	4	5	4	G
1 Alleluia	an	AM 68	F	-1	-3	-5	0	2	0	4	2	D
2 Alleluia	an	AM 56	F	-1	-3	0	-1	-3	-5	-3	-1	D
7 Alleluia	an	AM 84	c	-1	-3	0	2	4	0	-3	-1	G
8 Alleluia	an	AM 138 141	c	-1	0	-3	-5	-7	-5	-3	-1	G
8 Alleluia	an	AM 154 157	c	-1	0	-3	-5	-1	-3	-1	0	G
8 Alleluia	an	AM 103	c	-1	0	-3	0	-5	-3	-5	-7	G
4 Alleluia	an	AM 79	E	1	-2	0	1	3	1	0	-2	E
7 Alleluia	an	AR 48 463 741 LU 256 812 AM 127 476	b	1	3	5	3	1	-2	1	0	G
4 Alleluia	an	AM 47	E	1	3	5	3	5	3	1	-2	E
8 Alleluia	an	AR 447 OHS LU 784	G	2	-2	2	5	7	5	4	5	G
2 Alleluia	an	AR 43 LU 246 249	F	2	0	-3	-1	0	-1	-5	0	D
8 Alleluia	an	AR 56 58 209 LU 266 285 289 294 300 307 316	G	2	0	-2	2	5	4	5	2	G
4 Alleluia	an	AM 73 75	F	2	0	-1	-3	-1	0	2	4	E
8 Alleluia	an	WA 71	c	2	0	-1	-3	2	0	-1	-3	G
8 Alleluia	an	AR 187	c	2	0	-1	0	-3	-7	-5	-3	G
8 Alleluia	an	AR 37 LU 244	c	2	0	-1	0	2	0	-3	0	G
7 Alleluia	an	AM 162 473	c	2	0	2	0	-1	-3	0	-1	G
6 Alleluia	inv	WA 136 137	F	2	0	2	0	2	4	0	2	F
8 Alleluia	an	AM 61	F	2	0	4	7	6	4	6	7	G
5 Alleluia	an	AM 50	F	2	0	4	7	9	7	6	4	F
6 Alleluia	an	AM 90	F	2	4	0	2	0	-3	-1	0	F
6 Alleluia	an	AR 205 452 LU 312 AM 39 41	F	2	4	0	2	0	-1	-3	0	F

6 Alleluia	an	GR 237 QHS 688 LU 776 KK AM 450	F	2	4	0	2	4	2	0	-3	F
6 Alleluia	an	WA 68	F	2	4	2	0	2	0	-1	-3	F
3 Alleluia	an	AM 92	G	2	4	2	0	4	5	2	0	E
4 Alleluia	an	AR 172* VP 153	C	2	4	2	0	4	7	9	7	E
6 Alleluia	an	LA 206	F	2	4	2	4	0	2	4	2	F
1 Alleluia	an	AR 99 LU 280 283 AM 132 136	F	2	4	2	4	2	-1	0	2	D
6 Alleluia	an	AM 64	F	2	4	2	4	2	0	-3	0	F
6 Alleluia	an	AR 5 458 AM 32 475	F	2	4	2	4	2	0	2	4	F
3 Alleluia	an	AR 180 LU 301 304	G	2	5	4	2	0	2	-3	-2	E
3 Alleluia	an	AR 125 AM 143 147 149 152	G	2	5	4	2	0	2	0	-2	E
2 Alleluia	an	WA 136	C	2	5	4	5	4	2	4	2	D
4 Alleluia	an	AM 93	G	2	5	7	5	7	9	5	7	a
6 Alleluia	an	WA 130	D	3	2	0	-2	0	3	5	3	F
1 Alleluia	an	AM 71	D	3	2	0	-2	3	5	7	5	D
2 Alleluia	an	AM 123 LU 290 292	D	3	2	0	2	-2	0	-2	0	D
2 Alleluia	an	AR 139	D	3	2	0	2	3	2	0	-2	D
2 Alleluia	an	AR 106	D	3	2	3	0	3	2	0	-2	D
7 Alleluia	an	AM 54	G	4	5	7	5	2	5	4	2	G
7 Alleluia	an	AR 70	G	4	5	7	9	7	5	4	2	G
7 Alleluia	an	PM 232	G	4	5	7	9	7	9	7	5	G
5 Alleluia	an	PM 228	F	4	7	6	4	2	7	9	7	F
8 Alleluia	an	AM 29 474	G	5	2	0	-2	0	2	0	4	G
8 Alleluia	an	AM 6 87	G	5	2	0	2	0	-2	0	2	G
2 Alleluia	an	WA 71	C	5	2	4	5	2	5	7	5	D
8 Alleluia	an	WA 70	D	5	3	2	3	5	7	5	3	G
8 Alleluia	an	AM 98	G	5	4	0	4	5	2	0	2	G
3 Alleluia	an	AR 19 LU 225 229	G	5	4	2	0	2	-2	0	-2	E
7 Alleluia	an	PM 236	G	5	4	2	4	0	4	5	7	G
8 Alleluia	an	WA 127	G	5	4	5	2	0	-2	0	2	G
7 Alleluia	an	AR 18 LU 224	G	5	4	7	9	7	9	5	4	G
7 Alleluia	an	AM 84	G	7	5	4	5	7	9	7	5	G
7 Alleluia	an	PM 225	G	7	5	4	5	9	7	9	5	G
1 Alleluia	an	AM 108	D	7	9	7	5	3	5	7	3	D

1 Alleluia	an	AM 90	D	7	10	7	5	7	5	7	5	D
7 Alleluia a summo caelo egressio ejus	al	GR 85**	G	2	0	-2	0	2	0	5	4	G
8 Alleluia ad Dominum dum tribularer	al	GB 263^v	G	2	-2	0	2	-2	0	-2	2	G
3 Alleluia adducentur regi virgines	al	GR [61] LU 1217 *GS 231 GB 29	E	1	-2	3	7	3	5	7	8	E
7 Alleluia adorabo ad templum sanctum	al	GR [73] LU 1251 GS 175 k SYG 48 263 *GB 174^v	G	2	-2	0	5	2	5	7	9	G
1 Alleluia aemulor enim	al	GS 227	C	2	4	5	4	2	4	5	7	D
4 Alleluia amavit eum Dominus	al	GR [39] LU 1191 *GS 222 *GB 271^v *SYG 214	C	2	5	2	4	5	7	4	5	E
1 Alleluia angelus Domini apparuit	al	GR 5**	C	2	0	4	2	5	9	7	5	D
8 Alleluia angelus Domini descendit	al	GR 245 OHS 775 LU 786 *GS 125 *GB 131 *SYG 159	G	-2	-5	-3	-2	0	2	0	-2	G
7 Alleluia angelus Domini descendit cum splendore	al	SYG 162	G	2	0	-2	2	5	0	2	0	G
2 Alleluia apparuerunt apostolis	al	SYG 186	C	2	5	0	4	2	0	2	4	D
2 Alleluia architectus Deus fundavit	al	GB 174	D	-2	-3	-2	0	-2	2	5	7	D
3 Alleluia ardens est cor meum	al	SYG 167	E	3	0	3	5	3	5	7	5	E
1 Alleluia ascendens Christus in altum	al	GS 135	D	-2	2	5	2	-2	0	2	5	D
5 Alleluia ascendens Christus in altum	inv	WA 146	F	4	7	5	7	9	7	11	9	F
4 Alleluia ascendit Deus in jubilatione	al	GR 286 LU 848 GS 135 SYG 180 *GB 177	F	-3	-1	0	2	4	2	4	5	E
7 Alleluia ascendo ad patrem	al	SYG 180	G	7	9	7	4	7	5	4	2	
4 Alleluia assumpta est Maria ... angeli	al	GS 195 *SYG 216	C	2	5	4	5	4	2	4	5	E
5 Alleluia assumpta est Maria ... exercitus	al	GR 584 LU 1603	C	2	4	5	7	9	7	11	12	C
6 Alleluia attendite popule meus	al	GB 253 *SYG 243 *GS 149	a	2	3	2	0	-2	3	5	7	c
6 Alleluia audi filia ... quia concupivit	al	GB 272^v	D	3	5	3	8	7	5	7	3	F
1 Alleluia auditui meo dabis	al	GR [142]	F	2	4	2	0	4	2	7	6	G
8 Alleluia audivi quasi vocem	an	WA 142	F	2	4	2	0	4	2	7	6	G
1 Alleluia audivimus eam in Ephrata	re	LA 238 WA 144	F	2	4	2	4	2	4	2	0	D
2 Alleluia ave Maria gratia plena	al	GR [77] LU 1265 GS 184	C	2	5	2	4	5	4	0	2	D
1 Alleluia ave Maria gratia plena	al	GB 11^v	C	2	5	4	5	7	4	2	5	D
1 Alleluia ave rex noster tu solus	al	GR [108]	C	2	5	4	5	7	5	4	5	D
3 Alleluia beata Agathes ingressa	al	SYG 51	E	-2	0	3	0	1	0	-2	0	E

3	Alleluia beata es virgo Maria	al	LU 1476[c]	E	3	1	0	1	0	-2	0	-2	E
3	Alleluia beatam me dicent omnes	al	GR 587[5]	E	1	-2	3	7	3	5	7	8	E
8	Alleluia beati estis ... qui cotidie	al	SYG 222	G	2	0	2	5	4	0	2	5	G
1	Alleluia beati estis ... qui meruistis	al	SYG 222	D	-2	2	5	3	2	-2	0	2	D
3	Alleluia beati qui habitant in domo	al	GR 2**	F	-3	2	4	0	-1	0	-3	2	E
2	Alleluia beati qui persecutionem	al	GB 267[V]	C	2	0	2	4	5	7	5	7	D
1	Alleluia beati quorum remissae sunt	al	SYG 241	C	2	4	2	4	5	7	4	2	D
1	Alleluia beatus es Simon	al	GB 204[V]	D	2	3	0	2	0	2	0	2	D
1	Alleluia beatus homo qui audit me	al	GR 62	C	2	9	10	9	7	4	5	7	D
1	Alleluia beatus Laurentius dum in craticula	al	SYG 217	D	2	0	-2	0	2	3	2	0	D
8	Alleluia beatus Laurentius oravit	al	GB 217[V]	F	4	6	7	6	4	2	4	2	G
1	Alleluia beatus Petrus dum penderet	al	SYG 203	D	2	0	2	0	-2	2	3	5	D
3	Alleluia beatus quem elegisti	al	GR 519 LU 1479	C	4	2	7	9	7	9	7	12	E
1	Alleluia beatus qui lingua sua	al	GR 29**	D	2	0	-2	2	5	7	5	3	D
1	Alleluia beatus vir qui suffert	al	GR [43] LU 1202 *GS 207 *SYG 218	D	3	2	5	7	3	5	3	2	D
5	Alleluia beatus vir qui timet Dominum	al	GR [46] LU 1205 GS 208 SYG 44 GB 270	F	4	7	4	7	9	7	9	7	F
5 7	Alleluia beatus vir sanctus Martinus	al	GR 652 LU 1747 *GB 242[V]	C	4	5	7	9	7	9	11	12	C
5 7	Alleluia bene fundata est domus Domini	al	GR [73] LU 1252 *GB 174	C	2	4	5	7	9	7	11	12	C
4	Alleluia benedic anima mea Dominum	al	GR 636	F	-3	-1	0	2	4	2	4	5	E
1	Alleluia benedicamus patrem	al	GR [85] LU 1274	D	2	3	2	0	-2	3	5	7	D
1	Alleluia benedicamus patrem ... in saecula	al	SYG 261	D	3	0	-2	3	5	7	9	10	D
1	Alleluia benedicamus patrem ... laudemus	al	SYG 261	C	2	5	7	5	4	2	5	4	D
4	Alleluia benedicat vobis Dominus	al	GR [124] LU 1290	E	1	-2	3	5	1	0	1	-2	E
4	Alleluia benedicite Domino omnes virtutes	al	GR 612 LU 1664	F	-3	-1	0	2	4	2	4	5	E
7	Alleluia benedicta tu inter mulieres	al	SYG 217	F	2	4	7	6	4	6	2	4	G
8	Alleluia benedicta tu inter mulieres	al	SYG 216	a	-2	0	2	0	-2	-4	-5	-4	G
1	Alleluia benedictio Dei in mercedem	al	GR 452	D	2	3	5	7	2	3	5	3	D
3	Alleluia benedictus Dominus Deus meus	al	GR 465	E	1	-2	3	7	3	5	7	8	E
6	Alleluia benedictus es Dei filius	al	GB 148	c	2	4	0	2	0	2	0	2	[c]
8	Alleluia benedictus es Domine Deus patrum ... saecula	al	GR 306 309 LU 904 911 *GS c *SYG 260 *GB 213	G	2	4	0	2	0	2	5	4	G

1 Alleluia benedictus es Domine Deus patrum ... superexaltatus	al	SYG 261	D	-2	0	2	3	5	3	2	0	D
1 Alleluia benedictus es Domine super sceptrum	al	SYG 261	D	2	3	5	2	3	5	2	0	D
8 Alleluia benedictus sit Dei filius	al	SYG 261	G	2	4	0	2	5	4	2	0	G
8 Alleluia biduo vivens pendebat	al	SYG 231	G	-2	-5	-3	-2	0	2	0	-2	G
1 Alleluia bonum certamen certavi	al	SYG 205	C	2	4	2	4	5	7	5	4	[D]
3 Alleluia caeli enarrant gloriam Dei	al	GB 267	E	3	0	-2	3	5	3	5	7	E
7 Alleluia caeli enarrant gloriam Dei	al	SYG 239	G	5	4	5	7	5	7	4	7	G
7 Alleluia candor est lucis aeternae	al	GR 572 LU 1586	F	2	4	0	2	4	2	0	4	G
1 Alleluia cantabant sancti	al	SYG 26	D	7	9	10	9	7	5	7	5	D
1 Alleluia cantantibus organis	al	SYG 228	D	7	5	3	0	-2	5	3	5	D
6 Alleluia cantate Domino canticum novum	al	GB 150	D	3	0	-2	0	3	5	3	7	F
1 Alleluia cantate Domino canticum novum	al	GR 364 LU 1045 SYG 247	D	3	5	3	7	5	7	10	7	D
1 Alleluia cantate Domino canticum novum	al	SYG 248	D	7	5	3	2	0	-2	0	-2	D
Alleluia caritas Dei diffusa est	al	SYG 187	D	3	5	8	5	3	7	3	5	F
8 Alleluia caritas Dei diffusa est	al	GB 194	D	3	5	7	9	10	12	10	9	G
7 Alleluia caro mea vere est cibus	al	GR 314 [96] LU 1045	F	2	4	0	2	4	2	0	4	G
3 Alleluia casta generatio in perpetuum	al	GR 100**	E	-2	0	3	5	0	1	0	-2	E
6 Alleluia cernentibus discipulis elevatus	al	GB 178^V	D	3	0	-2	0	3	5	3	7	F
1 Alleluia Christo confixus sum cruci	al	GR 427 LU 1354^V	C	2	4	5	7	5	4	2	5	D
5 Alleluia Christum Dominum ascendentem	inv	LR 94	F	4	7	9	7	11	9	7	6	F
6 Alleluia Christus hodie	inv	WA 128	F	2	4	2	4	5	4	2	0	F
2 Alleluia Christus mortuus est propter delicta	al	GS 127	G	2	5	2	4	2	0	5	7	D
1 Alleluia Christus passus est pro nobis	al	GR 481	C	2	0	2	5	7	4	2	4	D
1 Alleluia Christus resurgens ex mortuis	al	GR 269 LU 827 *SYG 165 *GB 135^V GS 126	D	-2	0	3	5	3	2	0	3	D
8 Alleluia Christus resurgens ex mortuis	al	SYG 168	E	-2	3	5	7	5	3	5	3	G
2 Alleluia cives apostolorum et domestici	al	GB 268	C	2	4	5	2	0	4	5	7	D
3 Alleluia cognoverunt discipuli Dominum	al	GR 264 LU 817	E	3	1	0	1	0	-2	0	-2	E
1 Alleluia concaluit cor meum	al	GR 502 LU 1473	D	7	5	3	2	5	7	9	10	D
7 Alleluia concussum est mare	al	GR 609 LU 1655 GS 198	F	2	4	0	2	4	2	0	4	G
6 Alleluia condemnat autem justus	al	GR 71**	c	2	4	0	-3	-5	0	-1	0	c
2 Alleluia confessor Domini Benedicte	al	SYG 207	C	2	0	2	0	2	0	2	4	D
8 Alleluia confiteantur Domino misericordiae	al	GR 411	F	2	4	2	4	6	7	6	4	G

8	Alleluia confitebor tibi Domini in toto	al	GB 169	C	2	4	5	7	9	7	5	7	G
4	Alleluia confitebuntur caeli ... et veritatem	al	SYG 172	F	-3	-1	0	2	4	2	4	6	E
7	Alleluia confitebuntur caeli ... etenim	al	GR [16] LU 1147 1465^B SYG 171 GS 216 (n m)	G	2	0	5	4	7	9	7	5	G
6	Alleluia confitebuntur caeli ... etenim	al	GB 163^V	D	3	0	-2	0	3	5	3	7	[F]
2	Alleluia confitemini Domino et invocate nomen	al	GR 376 LU 1060 SYG 250 *GB 162 GS 157	G	2	5	2	5	7	5	7	9	a
7	Alleluia confitemini Domino in saeculum	an	AR 18 LU 228	G	5	4	7	9	7	9	5	4	G
8	Alleluia confitemini Domino quoniam bonus	al	PM 80 GR 282 GS 132 *GB 161^V	F	2	4	7	9	6	7	4	2	G
8	Alleluia confitemini Domino quoniam bonus	al	GR 236 LU 776^{II} OHS 682 SYG 152 *GB 122 *GS 115	E	3	5	7	3	5	3	5	7	G
1	Alleluia constitues eos principes	al	SYG 221	C	2	4	2	4	2	0	2	5	D
4	Alleluia constitues eos principes	al	GR [2^3]$_5$ LU 1122^5 *SYG 194	C	2	4	5	7	5	4	2	0	E
1	Alleluia corona aurea super caput	al	GR 14**	D	-2	2	5	2	-2	0	2	5	D
1	Alleluia corona tribulationis effloruit	al	GR 15**	D	7	5	3	2	0	-2	5	3	D
2	Alleluia corpora sanctorum in pace	al	GR [23] LU 1164	C	2	4	5	2	4	5	4	2	D
8	Alleluia crastina die delebitur	al	GR 25 LU 361	G	2	4	0	2	0	2	5	4	G
2	Alleluia crastina die delebitur	al	SYG 13	C	2	4	2	4	5	7	5	4	D
4	Alleluia crastina die delebitur	al	GS 13	D	3	0	3	5	8	7	8	10	E
3	Alleluia crastina erit vobis salus	al	GB 12^V	E	1	-2	3	7	3	5	7	8	E
3	Alleluia crucifixus surgens	al	SYG 164	F	-3	2	6	2	4	6	7	9	E
1	Alleluia cum esset Stephanus	al	SYG 22	D	2	0	-2	0	2	3	5	3	D
3	Alleluia cum sederit filius	al	SYG 157	G	2	4	2	4	5	7	4	0	E
4	Alleluia cum venerit paraclitus spiritus	al	SYG 181	C	2	4	2	4	5	7	4	2	E
4	Alleluia custodi innocentiam	al	GR 529	D	3	5	3	2	3	0	3	5	E
6	Alleluia data est mihi	al	SYG 160	D	2	0	-2	3	5	2	3	0	F
4	Alleluia de excelso misit ignem	al	GR 501 LU 1473	D	3	5	3	2	3	0	3	5	E
7	Alleluia de profundis clamavi ad te	al	GR 388 LU 1076 *SYG 255 *GB 264^V GS 164	G	2	0	5	4	7	9	7	5	G
1	Alleluia de quacumque tribulatione	al	GR 486 LU 1441	C	4	7	9	11	9	7	9	7	D
1	Alleluia de utero senectutis	al	GB 198^V	C	2	4	2	4	5	7	5	4	[D]
1	Alleluia declinabo super eum	al	GR 509 LU 1482	D	2	3	5	7	2	3	5	3	D

7 Alleluia dedisti hereditatem	al	SYG 218	G	5	4	5	7	9	7	9	7	G
1 Alleluia dedisti mihi protectionem	al	GR 465	C	2	5	7	4	2	5	4	5	D
8 Alleluia dedit illi Dominus scientiam	al	GB 272	G	2	0	2	5	4	2	0	2	G
2 Alleluia deduc me Domine	an	AR 29 LU 237	C	5	4	2	4	2	0	2	5	D
3 Alleluia defecit caro mea et cor meum	al	GR 506 LU 1479	G	2	4	2	0	2	4	5	4	E
3 Alleluia delectatio bona	re	WA 144	F	-1	0	-1	-3	2	4	0	-1	E
2 Alleluia Deus a Libano	al	SYG 4	C	2	4	7	9	5	4	7	5	D
2 Alleluia Deus autem rex noster	al	GR 79**	D	-2	0	-2	-5	-2	0	2	0	D
1 Alleluia Deus docuisti me a juventute	al	GR 519	C	2	0	4	2	5	9	7	5	D
8 Alleluia Deus judex justus	al	GR 328 LU 982 SYG 239 *GB 248^v *GS 142	G	-3	-5	0	2	0	-5	-3	-5	G
7 Alleluia Deus qui sedes super thronum	al	GR 331 LU 999	G	2	5	2	5	2	5	9	5	G
7 Alleluia Deus qui sedes super thronum	al	GB 36^v	G	2	5	2	5	9	5	7	5	G
2 Alleluia Deus venerunt gentes	al	SYG 222	C	5	4	2	0	2	0	2	4	D
4 Alleluia Deus virtuum convertere	al	GR [132]	F	-3	-1	0	2	4	2	4	5	E
4 Alleluia dextera Dei fecit virtutem	al	GR 269 LU 827 SYG 254 GB 234^v *GS 161	D	3	0	-2	3	5	7	9	10	E
8 Alleluia dicite in gentibus quia Dominus	al	GR 256 491 LU 801 1455 OHS 817 *SYG 173 *GS 122	G	2	5	4	2	5	7	5	0	G
2 Alleluia Dies sanctificatus illuxit nobis	al	GR 34 LU 409 GB 17^v GS G *SYG 19	C	2	5	7	5	7	4	2	5	D
8 Alleluia diffusa est gratia	al	SYG 5	F	2	4	0	2	4	2	0	4	G
8 Alleluia diffusa est gratia	al	GR 405 LU 1323 *SYG 5 *GB 4^v GS 228	F	2	4	2	4	6	7	6	4	G
1 Alleluia dignus es Domine accipere	al	GR 540	D	-2	0	3	0	2	0	-2	3	D
1 Alleluia dilectus meus mihi	al	GR (10)	C	2	4	5	7	9	7	5	4	D
8 Alleluia dilexi quoniam exaudivit	al	GB 262	G	2	0	-2	0	2	5	2	5	G
1 Alleluia dilexisti justitiam	al	SYG 229	D	2	0	2	3	5	2	0	3	D
1 Alleluia dilexit Andream Dominus	al	GR 393 LU 1305 *SYG 231 *GB 246 GS g	C	2	5	2	5	4	5	7	5	D
5 Alleluia diligam te Domine	al	GB 249 *SYG 239 *GS 143	F	4	7	6	4	7	6	4	6	F
8 Alleluia dispersit dedit pauperibus	al	GR 556 LU 1480	G	2	0	-2	0	-2	2	5	4	G
2 Alleluia disposui testamentum	al	GB 272 *SYG 34 *GS 222	D	3	5	3	5	2	0	3	5	D
3 Alleluia dixit Dominus Domino meo	al	SYG 248	E	1	0	-2	3	5	1	3	0	E

1	Alleluia Domine Deus meus in te speravi	al	GR 322 LU 962 GB 248 *GS 167 f	D	-2	2	5	3	2	-2	0	-2	D
3	Alleluia Domine Deus salutis meae	al	GR 351 LU 1029 GS 152 *SYG 245 *GB 254	E	3	1	0	1	0	-2	0	-2	E
8	Alleluia Domine dilexi decorem	al	GB 174	F	4	2	4	7	6	4	7	6	G
2	Alleluia Domine diligo habitaculum	al	LU 1623^D	C	2	5	7	5	7	4	2	5	D
7	Alleluia Domine exaudi orationem	al	GR 367 LU 1049 *GB 256^V	G	5	4	7	5	7	9	7	12	G
6	Alleluia Domine in virtute tua	al	GR 333 LU 1003 GB 249^V GS 144 *SYG 240	D	3	5	3	8	7	5	7	3	F
7	Alleluia Domine refugium factus es nobis	al	GR 355(39) LU 1034 GS 153 SYG 245 *GB 254^V	G	2	0	5	4	7	9	7	9	G
6	Alleluis Dominus dabit verbum evangelizantibus	al	GR 59**	F	2	0	2	5	4	5	2	0	F
8	Alleluia Dominus dixit ad me	al	GR 29 LU 394 SYG 15 *GB 14 GS 14	F	2	4	2	4	6	7	6	4	G
8	Alleluia Dominus in Sina in sancto	al	GR 286 LU 848 GS 136 SYG 179 *GB 178^V	F	2	4	2	4	6	7	6	4	G
6	Alleluis Dominus regnavit decorem	an	AR 2	F	-3	-1	0	-1	-3	-5	0	-1	F
2	Alleluia Dominus regnavit decorem ... fortitudinem	al	GR 31 LU 405^V SYG 16 GB 15^V *GS E	C	2	5	7	5	4	5	7	9	D
8	Alleluia Dominus regnavit exsultet terra	al	GR 72 LU 490 GS 23 SYG 42	F	2	4	2	4	6	7	6	4	G
8	Alleluia Dominus salvavit manum tuam	al	GR 464	F	2	4	2	4	6	7	6	4	G
2	Alleluia dulce carmen	hy	ST 378	C	2	5	4	2	0	5	7	9	D
8	Alleluia dulce lignum dulces clavos	al	GR 491 LU 1456 GS 185 235 SYG 174 *GB 165	E	3	5	3	8	7	5	3	8	G
1	Alleluia dum complerentur dies	al	GR 305 LU 903 *GB 187 *SYG 183	C	2	5	2	5	4	5	7	5	D
5	Alleluia ecce adest dies	al	SYG 216	F	4	7	4	7	9	7	9	7	F
1	Alleluia ecce concipiet et pariet	al	GR 3**	C	2	5	7	4	2	5	4	5	D
8	Alleluia ecce jam venit plenitudo temporis	al	GB 31	C	2	4	5	7	9	7	12	11	G
1	Alleluia ecce miles Christi	al	SYG 214	C	2	4	5	7	4	2	5	4	D
8	Alleluia ecce mitto vos	al	GB 268	F	2	4	2	0	4	7	6	4	G
8	Alleluia ecce quam bonum et quam	al	GR 568	G	-3	-2	0	2	4	2	0	-2	G
8	Alleluia ecce quam bonum et quam	al	GB 201^V	G	2	0	2	5	7	5	7	5	G
8	Alleluia ecce quam bonum et quam	al	GB 201^V	F	2	4	2	4	2	0	4	7	G

1	Alleluia ecce sacerdos magnus qui ... et inventus	al	SYG 215	D	-2	2	5	3	2	0	2	3	D
8	Alleluia ecce vir Dei Benedictus reliquit	al	GB 55	F	2	4	2	4	2	0	4	6	G
2	Alleluia ecce virgo concipiet	al	SYG 2	A	3	5	3	5	3	5	3	5	D
1	Alleluia eduxit Dominus populum	al	SYG 161	C	2	4	5	7	5	4	2	5	D
2	Alleluia ego autem cantabo	al	GR 469	G	2	5	2	5	7	5	7	9	a
8	Alleluia ego dilecto meo et ad me	al	GR 626 LU 1691	G	2	4	0	4	7	5	4	2	G
1	Alleluia ego dilecto meo et dilectus	al	GR 52**	D	3	2	3	5	2	0	3	0	D
2	Alleluia ego Dominus dabo eis	al	GR 105**	C	2	5	7	5	7	4	2	5	D
1	Alleluia ego Dominus inebriabo animam	al	GR 91**	C	2	0	4	2	5	9	7	5	D
1	Alleluia ego rogabo patrem	al	SYG 185	D	3	5	3	7	5	7	3	7	D
4	Alleluia ego sum pastor bonus et cognosco	al	SYG 164	E	1	3	1	3	1	5	3	1	E
1	Alleluia ego sum pastor bonus et cognosco	al	GR 47 264 LU 818	D	2	3	2	0	-2	3	5	7	D
8	Alleluia ego sum pastor bonus et cognosco	al	GS 127	F	2	4	5	4	2	5	7	9	G
1	Alleluia ego sum pastor bonus qui pasco	al	SYG 165	D	2	3	2	0	-2	3	5	7	D
2	Alleluia ego sum vitis vera	al	SYG 171	C	2	0	2	5	2	4	5	7	D
1	Alleluia ego sum vitis vera ... estis	an	LA 389 392	C	2	9	11	9	7	9	7	4	D
1	Alleluia ego sum vitis vera ... veri	an	WA 306	C	2	9	11	9	7	5	7	5	D
1	Alleluia ego veritatem dico	al	SYG 167	D	3	5	3	7	5	7	3	7	D
1	Alleluia ego vos elegi de mundo	al	GR 630 LU 1487	D	3	2	3	5	2	0	3	0	D
2	Alleluia elegit te Dominus sibi	al	GB 28^V *GS 223	D	3	5	3	5	2	0	3	5	D
4	Alleluia emitte spiritum tuum	al	GR 293 LU 879 SYG 183 *GB 187^V GS M 137	F	-3	-1	0	2	4	2	4	5	E
1	Alleluia erat lucerna ardens	al	SYG 197	C	2	5	7	5	4	2	0	2	D
2	Alleluia eripe me de inimicis	al	GR 343 LU 1018 *SYG 242 *GB 251 GS 147	C	2	5	2	4	5	4	0	2	D
1	Alleluia erit autem sanguis vobis	al	GR 540	C	2	5	2	0	4	2	4	5	D
7	Alleluia euntes in mundum	al	SYG 181	G	2	5	2	7	5	7	5	7	[G]
3	Alleluia evangelizare pauperibus	al	GR 67**	C	2	4	5	4	2	7	5	4	E
5	Alleluia exaltabo te Deus	al	GR 54	F	4	7	6	7	6	4	2	7	F
7	Alleluia exaudi Deus orationem	al	GB 246^V *SYG 243	G	2	0	2	0	-2	2	4	5	G
7	Alleluia exaudi orationem meam	al	GR 21**	G	7	9	5	4	5	7	5	7	G
4	Alleluia excita Domine potentiam	al	GR 8 LU 336 GS 4 SYG 7 GB 5^V	F	-3	-1	0	2	4	2	4	5	E

7	Alleluia exivi a patre et veni	al	GR 272 LU 831	d	-5	0	-2	0	2	3	5	3	G
1	Alleluia expansis manibus beata	al	GB 244	C	2	0	2	4	5	7	5	7	D
7	Alleluia exsultabo et laetabor	al	GR [148] *LU 841^B	G	2	0	5	4	7	9	7	5	G
7	Alleluia exsultabunt sancti in gloria	al	SYG 169 GS 216 (n.m.)	G	4	2	5	7	5	4	7	5	G
7	Alleluia exsultate Deo adjutori	al	GR 348 LU 1026 GS 150 SYG 244 GB 253	G	5	4	5	7	5	7	4	7	G
3	Alleluia exsultent justi Dei in conspectu	al	GB 269^V	E	1	-2	3	7	3	5	7	8	[E]
8	Alleluia fac nos innocuam Joseph	al	GR 486 LU 1441	E	1	3	5	3	0	3	1	0	G
5	Alleluia faciem tuam Domine	an	AR 41 LU 247	a	-4	0	3	2	3	5	3	7	F
1	Alleluia factus est repente	al	SYG 183 *GS 140	C	2	4	2	4	5	7	5	4	D
4	Alleluia fecisti viriliter et confortatum	al	GR 39**	F	-3	-1	0	2	4	2	4	5	E
8	Alleluia felix es sacra virgo Maria	al	GR 542 LU 1539	G	2	0	-2	0	2	5	2	5	G
3	Alleluia felix namque es nimium beate Stephane	al	SYG 211	E	3	0	-2	3	5	3	7	8	E
7	Alleluia filii tui de longe venient	al	GR 46**	G	5	4	5	7	2	5	4	5	G
1	Alleluia flores apparuerunt in terra nostra	al	GR 442	C	2	4	5	2	4	2	0	5	D
1	Alleluia Franciscus pauper et humilis	al	GR 602 LU 1643	C	2	5	7	4	2	5	4	5	D
1	Alleluia fulgebunt justi et tamquam	al	GR 575 *SYG 193 GB 268^V GS 225	C	2	4	5	4	2	7	4	5	D
7	Alleluia fundamenta ejus	al	SYG 263	G	2	0	2	5	2	7	5	7	G
1	Alleluia fundata est domus ... super	al	SYG 264	D	7	5	3	2	0	3	5	2	D
7	Alleluia fundata est domus ... supra	al	SYG 264	G	2	0	2	5	4	5	7	5	G
4	Alleluia gaudete justi in Domino	al	GR 406 LU 1327 SYG 169	D	3	2	3	5	7	5	3	5	E
2	Alleluia gavisi sunt discipuli	al	SYG 163	C	2	4	5	7	5	4	2	0	D
2	Alleluia gloria et honore coronasti ... Domine et constituisti	al	GS 208	C	2	5	7	5	7	4	2	5	D
7	Alleluia gloria et honore coronasti ... Domine et constituisti	al	GB 23 *SYG 201	G	5	4	5	7	2	5	4	5	G
1	Alleluia gloriosae virginis Mariae	al	GB 231^V	C	2	4	2	4	5	7	5	4	D
2	Alleluia gressus meos dirige	al	GR [143]	G	2	5	2	5	7	5	7	9	a
2	Alleluia gustate et videte quoniam	al	GR 616	C	2	5	7	5	7	4	2	5	D
1	Alleluia habet in vestimento	al	GR 641 LU 1712	D	-2	2	5	2	-2	0	2	5	D
8	Alleluia haec dies quam fecit	al	GR 259 LU 805 OHS 827 GS 123 SYG 161 *GB 142^V	F	2	4	2	4	6	7	6	4	G
7	Alleluia haec est generatio quaerentium	al	GR 114**	G	5	4	5	7	2	5	4	5	G

8 Alleluia haec est vera fraternitas	al	GR 495 LU 1492^A 1508 *GB 231^V	G	2	0	5	4	5	7	5	4	G
4 Alleluia haec est virgo sapiens et una	al	GR [57] LU 1222	C	2	4	2	4	2	0	5	7	E
2 Alleluia haec est virgo sapiens quam	al	GS 228	D	2	3	0	-2	3	5	7	5	D
2 Alleluia hic est discipulus ille	al	GR 39 LU 422 GS 17 *GB 24^V *SYG 24	C	2	5	7	5	7	4	2	5	D
2 Alleluia hic est sacerdos quem coronavit	al	GR [8] [34] LU 1184	C	2	5	7	5	7	4	2	5	D
2 Alleluia hic est vere martyr quem coronavit	al	SYG 226	D	3	5	3	5	2	0	3	5	[D]
1 Alleluia hic est vere martyr qui pro Christo	al	SYG 229	D	2	3	2	0	-2	3	5	7	D
2 Alleluia hic Martinus pauper	al	SYG 227 GS 200	C	2	5	7	4	2	5	4	5	D
1 Alleluia hic martyr Domini	al	SYG 223	D	3	0	-2	3	5	7	9	10	D
7 Alleluia hoc est praeceptum	al	SYG 194	c	-3	-1	-3	-5	-7	-3	-1	-3	G
1 Alleluia hoc jam tertio	al	SYG 160	C	2	0	7	4	5	4	2	4	D
8 Alleluia hodie Maria virgo caelos ascendit	al	SYG 216 GS 195	E	1	3	5	3	0	3	1	0	G
7 Alleluia hodie omnes apostoli	an	PM 88 *LA 264 SYG 182	G	5	4	5	7	5	4	5	7	G
1 Alleluia hortus conclusus est	al	GB 232	D	2	0	-2	2	3	5	7	5	D
8 Alleluia hosanna filio David	al	SYG 2	E	-2	3	5	7	5	3	5	8	G
4 Alleluia imperatrix reginarum	al	VP 51	D	3	2	3	5	3	5	7	5	E
4 Alleluia in conspectu angelorum ... adorabo	al	GR 635 LU 1700	C	2	5	2	4	0	2	7	4	E
4 Alleluia in conspectu angelorum ... Domine	al	GR [87] LU 1276 GS 197	C	2	5	2	4	0	2	7	4	E
1 Alleluia in Deo salutare meum	al	GR 622^4	D	-2	0	3	5	7	5	7	5	D
1 Alleluia in Deo speravit cor meum	al	GR [146]	D	2	3	2	0	-2	0	-2	3	D
7 Alleluia in die resurrectionis	al	GR 262 LU 809 GS 121 SYG 169 GB 140	G	2	-2	2	5	4	2	5	7	G
2 Alleluia in exitu Israel ex Aegypto	al	GR 381 LU 1068 *GB 261	C	2	4	5	7	4	5	2	0	D
2 Alleluia in exitu Israel ex Aegypto	al	SYG 248	D	3	5	3	5	2	3	2	0	D
8 Alleluia in multitudine presbyterorum	al	GR 528 LU 1513	G	-5	0	2	4	5	2	0	2	G
1 Alleluia in omnem terram exivit sonus apostolorum	al	SYG 209	a	-2	0	-2	-4	-5	-4	-5	-7	D
1 Alleluia in omnem terram exivit sonus eorum	al	GB 267	C	2	4	2	9	11	9	7	9	D
6 Alleluia in omnem terram exivit sonus eorum	al	GS x	D	3	5	3	8	7	5	7	3	F
8 Alleluia in omnem terram exivit sonus eorum	al	GB 267	F	4	2	4	7	6	4	7	6	[G]

6	Alleluia in resurrectione tua Christe	al	GB 146^V	C	2	4	0	2	0	2	0	5	c
3	Alleluia in te Domine speravi	al	GR 335 LU 1008 *GS 146 *GB 250 *SYG 241	F	2	4	2	4	6	4	2	7	E
	Alleluia in tua patientia	al	SYG 5										
8	Alleluia inebriabuntur ab ubertate	al	GR 425	F	2	4	2	4	6	7	6	4	G
3	Alleluia ingressa Agnes turpitudinis	al	GB 45	E	1	-2	3	7	3	5	7	8	E
1	Alleluia ingressus Zacharias templum	al	SYG 198	a	-2	0	-2	-4	-5	-4	-5	-7	D
2	Alleluia initio cognovi de testimoniis	al	GR 82**	D	2	0	-2	0	2	0	2	3	D
2	Alleluia initium sapientiae timor	al	GR 112**	A	3	5	3	5	3	5	8	7	D
7	Alleluia inter natos mulierum	al	SYG 196	G	2	4	5	7	9	7	10	12	G
4	Alleluia inter natos mulierum	al	GS m	C	2	5	2	4	0	2	7	4	E
1	Alleluia interrogabat magos Herodes	al	GB 33^V *SYG 31	C	2	4	7	4	5	2	0	4	D
2	Alleluia inveni David servum meum	al	GR 514 LU 1489 GS 222 SYG 38	C	2	5	7	5	7	4	2	5	D
1	Alleluia ipse est directus divinitus	al	GR 566 LU 1581	D	-2	2	0	2	5	2	0	2	D
1	Alleluia iste cognovit justitiam	al	SYG 189	C	2	4	5	4	2	4	7	4	D
8	Alleluia iste est qui ante Deum	al	SYG 211	E	1	3	5	3	0	1	-2	-4	G
1	Alleluia iste est qui pro lege Dei	al	SYG 210	D	3	2	3	5	2	0	3	0	D
8	Alleluia iste sanctus digne in memoriam	al	SYG 226 GS 207	G	2	0	-3	-2	-5	-3	-2	0	G
1	Alleluia isti sunt duae olivae	al	SYG 199 *GS n	D	-2	2	0	3	5	3	2	3	D
1	Alleluia isti sunt duo viri	al	SYG 208	D	2	-2	0	2	3	5	3	2	D
8	Alleluia isti sunt qui venerunt	al	SYG 194	C	2	4	5	7	9	7	5	7	G
8	Alleluia ite nuntiate fratribus	al	SYG 163	a	-2	0	2	0	-2	-4	-5	-4	G
3	Alleluia iterum autem videbo vos	al	GS 129 *SYG 166	F	2	4	0	2	4	2	0	4	E
1	Alleluia iterum videbo vos	al	SYG 166	D	2	3	2	0	-2	3	5	7	D
7	Alleluia Jesus autem eo quod maneat	al	GR [101] LU 1283^B	G	5	4	5	7	5	7	4	7	G
2	Alleluia Joannes est nomen ejus	al	GB 198^V	C	5	4	5	7	0	2	4	2	D
1	Alleluia jubilate Deo omnis terra	al	GB 148	D	-2	2	5	3	2	3	2	0	D
3	Alleluia jubilate Deo omnis terra	al	GR 65 LU 479 *SYG 32 GB 256 *GS 20	E	1	-2	3	7	5	7	8	7	E
7	Alleluia jubilate Deo omnis terra	al	GR [127] LU 1294	G	5	4	5	7	2	5	4	5	G
2	Alleluia jubilemus Christo	inv	WA 311	C	2	4	5	4	2	0	2	4	D
3	Alleluia judica judicium	re	WA 144	F	-1	0	-1	-3	2	6	2	4	E
1	Alleluia judicabunt sancti nationes	al	SYG 188 GS 199	D	-2	2	5	2	-2	0	2	5	D
8	Alleluia juravi et statui custodire	al	GR 73**	G	-2	-3	-2	-5	-3	-2	0	2	G

	Incipit		Sources										
1	Alleluia juravit Dominus et non paenitebit	al	GR [37] LU 1187 SYG 189 *GB 41^v	C	2	4	7	4	5	4	2	4	D
4	Alleluia justi confitebuntur nomini	al	GR 96**	F	-3	-1	0	2	4	2	4	5	E
1	Alleluia justi confitebuntur nomini	al	SYG 190	C	2	4	2	5	4	2	9	7	D
1	Alleluia justi epulentur et exsultent ... delectentur	al	GR [27] LU 1168 SYG 190 *GB 269^v GS 216	D	3	2	3	5	2	0	3	0	D
1	Alleluia justi epulentur et exsultent ... parasti	al	GR 56**	D	3	2	3	5	2	0	3	0	D
6	Alleluia justi fulgebunt sicut sol	al	GB 268^v	c	2	4	0	2	0	2	0	2	c
8	Alleluia justi quasi virens folium	al	GR (21)	G	5	4	5	7	2	4	5	4	G
1	Alleluia justorum animae in manu Dei	al	GR 561 GB 268	D	3	0	-2	3	5	7	9	10	D
8	Alleluia justum deduxit ... gloriam	al	SYG 229	G	2	0	-2	0	2	0	-2	2	G
8	Alleluia justum deduxit ... regnum	al	GB 271	G	2	0	2	4	5	4	5	2	G
7	Alleluia justum deduxit ... regnum	al	SYG 214	G	2	0	5	4	7	9	7	9	G
2	Alleluia justum deduxit ... regnum	al	GB 271	D	3	5	3	5	2	0	3	5	D
1	Alleluia justus germinabit sicut lilium	al	GR [40] (42) LU 1192 *SYG 207 *GB 270^v GS 222	D	3	5	3	5	7	5	7	3	D
2	Alleluia justus non conturbabitur	al	GR 573 GS 208 *SYG 34 *GB 270	C	2	5	7	5	7	4	2	5	D
1	Alleluia justus ut palma florebit	al	GR [49] (41) LU 1207 GS 207 *SYG 198 *GB 230	C	2	5	2	5	4	5	7	5	D
8	Alleluia laetabitur justus in Domino	al	SYG 209 GS 207	F	2	4	0	2	4	2	0	4	G
4	Alleluia laetamini cum Jerusalem	al	GR 510 LU 1483	D	3	5	3	2	3	0	3	5	E
8	Alleluia laetamini in Domino et exsultate	al	GB 269 GS 217 (nm)	F	2	4	0	2	4	7	6	7	G
1	Alleluia laetatus sum in his	al	GR 5 LU 329 *SYG 3 *GB 3 GS 162	D	-2	3	5	3	8	7	8	10	D
2	Alleluia lapidem quem reprobaverunt	al	SYG 161	D	3	5	3	5	2	0	3	5	D
5	Alleluia lapis revolutus est	an	PM 67 *WA 138	c	2	4	2	0	2	-3	-5	-3	F
8	Alleluia lauda anima mea	al	SYG 256 GS 166	F	2	4	2	4	6	7	6	4	[G]
4	Alleluia lauda Jerusalem Dominum	al	GR [136] LU 1285 SYG 259	F	-3	-1	0	2	4	2	4	5	E
8	Alleluia laudanda tremenda	al	GB 213^v	G	4	5	4	2	0	2	4	2	G
4	Alleluia laudate Deum omnes angeli	al	GR 68 LU 486 GS 22 SYG 35 GB 168^v	F	-3	-1	0	2	4	2	4	5	E
1	Alleluia laudate Dominum de caelis	an	AR 5	C	2	9	10	9	7	9	7	4	D
3	Alleluia laudate Dominum Deum nostrum	al	GR 41**	E	-2	3	5	8	7	5	8	7	E
4	Alleluia laudate Dominum in sanctis ejus	al	SYG 224	F	-3	-1	0	2	4	2	4	5	E
2	Alleluia laudate Dominum omnes gentes	al	SYG 256 GS b *GB 263^v	A	3	5	3	5	3	5	3	5	D

4 Alleluia laudate pueri Dominum	al	GR 42 260 OHS 827 LU 428 805 GS p 123 216 SYG 161 *GB 142^v	D	3	2	3	5	7	5	3	5	E
1 Alleluia laudem Domini loquetur	al	GR 52 LU 448	D	-2	2	5	3	2	-2	0	-2	D
8 Alleluia Laurentius bonum opus	al	GB 218	F	2	4	0	2	4	7	6	7	G
1 Alleluia leva in circuitu oculos tuos	al	GR 45**	C	2	4	2	9	10	9	7	9	D
7 Alleluia levita Laurentius bonum opus	al	SYG 213	G	2	-2	2	5	4	2	5	7	G
7 Alleluia levita Laurentius bonum opus	al	GR 579 LU 1595 GS 194	F	2	4	0	2	4	2	0	4	G
7 Alleluia lingua pravorum peribit	al	GR 29**	G	2	4	5	4	0	2	0	5	G
1 Alleluia loquebantur variis linguis	al	GR 297 LU 888 GS 139 *GB 193 *SYG 184	D	-2	0	3	2	3	0	2	0	D
2 Alleluia loquebar de testimoniis	al	GS 228	G	2	5	2	4	5	4	0	2	a
2 Alleluia loquebar Domine de testimoniis	al	GR 437 LU 1369	D	-2	-5	-2	0	-2	3	2	0	D
1 Alleluia loquebar Domine de testimoniis	al	SYG 39 *GB 244	D	-2	3	5	7	9	10	7	9	D
8 Alleluia lux perpetua lucebit	al	GB 163^v	E	1	3	5	7	8	10	8	7	G
6 Alleluia magnificat anima mea Dominum	al	GR 587^3 49** LU 1612^2	D	3	5	3	8	7	5	7	3	F
1 Alleluia magnus Dominus ... in civitate	al	SYG 242	D	2	0	-2	2	5	3	2	5	D
7 Alleluia magnus Dominus ... in civitate	al	GR 340 LU 1014	G	7	5	7	5	2	5	7	5	G
1 Alleluia magnus sanctus Paulus	al	GB 208	C	2	4	5	7	4	2	5	4	D
2 Alleluia magnus sanctus Paulus	al	GR 419 LU 1346 GS 178 189	C	2	5	7	5	7	4	2	5	D
1 Alleluia magnus sanctus Paulus	al	GS 178 189	D	3	2	3	5	2	0	3	0	D
1 Alleluia mane nobiscum Domine	al	GS 126	C	2	5	2	0	2	4	5	7	D
7 Alleluia mane nobiscum Domine	al	SYG 156	G	2	5	7	9	7	5	7	9	G
1 Alleluia manum suam aperuit inopi	al	GR 632 LU 1695	C	2	4	5	7	9	7	5	4	D
2 Alleluia Martialis magnus	al	SYG 208	D	3	5	3	5	2	0	3	5	[D]
8 Alleluia Martinus Abrahae sinu	al	SYG 226	G	2	0	-2	2	5	4	2	0	G
1 Alleluia Martinus hic pauper	al	SYG 227	C	2	4	2	4	5	7	5	4	D
1 Alleluia Martinus signi potens	al	SYG 227	a	-2	-4	0	-2	-4	-5	-7	-5	D
7 Alleluia memento Domine David	al	SYG 181	b	3	0	1	-2	-4	-2	0	-2	G
7 Alleluia minuisti eum Domine paulo	al	GR 451	F	2	4	0	2	4	2	0	4	G
1 Alleluia mirabantur omnes de his	al	SYG 42	C	2	4	5	4	5	2	0	5	D
1 Alleluia mirabilis Dominus noster	al	GR 414 GS 216 SYG 176 GB 268^v	D	2	3	2	0	-2	3	5	7	D
7 Alleluia miserere mei Deus	al	SYG 234	G	2	0	-2	2	5	0	2	0	G

1 Alleluia misericordias Domini	al	SYG 245	C	2	4	7	5	4	5	2	4	D
1 Alleluia misso Herodes spiculatore	al	GS 196	C	2	5	2	5	4	5	7	5	D
3 Alleluia missus est angelus Domini	al	GR 637	a	3	2	0	3	2	0	2	-2	E
8 Alleluia mittat tibi Dominus	al	SYG 232	F	2	4	2	4	6	7	6	4	[G]
8 Alleluia mittat vobis Dominus	al	GR [123] LU 1289	F	2	4	2	4	6	7	6	4	G
8 Alleluia modicum et non videbitis	al	SYG 166 GS 128 *GB 273^v	E	1	3	5	3	0	3	1	0	G
8 Alleluia multae tribulationes	al	SYG 200	F	2	4	2	4	6	4	2	6	G
7 Alleluia multifarie olim Deus loquens	al	GR 49 LU 441 GS H SYG 19 GB 31^v	G	2	0	-2	2	5	0	2	0	G
8 Alleluia nativitas gloriosae virginis	al	GS u	F	2	4	0	2	4	2	0	4	G
2 Alleluia nativitas tua Dei genitrix	al	GB 232	A	3	5	3	5	3	5	3	5	D
4 Alleluia ne timeas Zacharia ... deprecatio	al	SYG 198	C	2	5	4	2	4	7	5	2	E
7 Alleluia ne timeas Zacharia ... oratio	al	GB 196^v *SYG 196	G	2	5	7	5	7	10	12	9	G
7 Alleluia nihil iniquinatum in eam	al	GR 51**	G	5	4	5	7	5	7	4	7	G
8 Alleluia nimis honorati sunt	al	SYG 207 *GS y	G	-2	-3	-2	0	2	0	2	4	G
8 Alleluia nimis honorati sunt	al	GR 644 LU 1720 *GB 267^v	F	2	4	2	4	6	7	6	4	G
5 Alleluia noli flere Maria	an	PM 67 *WA 138 LA 222	c	2	4	2	0	2	-3	-5	-3	F
5 Alleluia non derelinquet Dominus sanctos	al	GR 446	C	2	4	5	7	9	7	11	12	C
1 Alleluia non dilexerunt animas suas	al	GR 109**	D	-2	2	5	2	-2	0	2	5	D
7 Alleluia non nobis Domine non nobis	al	GB 261^v	G	5	4	5	7	9	5	7	2	G
1 Alleluia non vos me elegistis	al	SYG 172 GS y	C	2	5	2	4	5	2	4	0	D
7 Alleluia non vos relinquam orphanos dicit	al	GB 182^v	G	2	-2	2	5	4	2	5	7	G
1 Alleluia non vos relinquam orphanos vado	al	GR 289 LU 856 GS K SYG 187	D	2	3	2	0	-2	0	-2	3	D
2 Alleluia nonne cor nostrum ... loqueretur	al	GB 131	E	-2	1	-2	0	-2	-4	-2	0	D
1 Alleluia nonne cor nostrum ... loqueretur	al	GS 118 SYG 155	D	2	3	2	0	-2	0	-2	3	D
8 Alleluia nonne cor nostrum ... nobiscum loqueretur	al	SYG 164	E	3	0	-2	3	5	7	5	7	G
1 Alleluia nos autem gloriari	al	GB 165 *GS v	D	2	5	7	9	7	5	7	5	D
2 Alleluia nunc cum eo regnas	al	LU 1476^D	C	2	5	7	5	7	4	2	5	D
4 Alleluia nunc ergo ora pro nobis	al	GR 39**	D	3	2	3	5	7	5	3	5	E
1 Alleluia nuptiae factae sunt	al	SYG 35	D	-2	0	-2	0	2	3	0	2	D

7	Alleluia O adoranda trinitas	al	SYG 261	G	2	0	-2	2	5	0	2	0	G
1	Alleluia O Joachim sancte conjux	al	GR 585 LU 1609	C	2	4	5	4	0	4	5	7	D
7	Alleluia O quam beata es virgo	al	GB 223	G	2	0	2	5	7	5	4	2	G
7	Alleluia O quam beatus est Dei apostolus	al	GB 227	G	2	0	2	5	7	5	4	2	G
1	Alleluia O quam bonus et suavis est	al	GR 303 LU 898	C	2	5	2	5	4	5	7	5	D
7	Alleluia O quam gloriosum est	al	SYG 222	G	2	5	7	9	7	9	10	12	G
7	Alleluia O quam pretiosum est regnum	al	GB 239^v	G	5	7	9	7	9	10	12	10	G
4	Alleluia O quam pulchra	al	GR [58] LU 1223 GB 223^v	C	2	4	2	0	5	7	9	10	E
1	Alleluia O quam pulchra ... immortalis	al	GR 104**	C	2	4	5	4	0	4	5	7	D
2	Alleluia O vos omnes qui transitis	al	GR 597 LU 1634^v	F	4	2	4	0	-1	-3	0	2	D
3	Alleluia obtulerunt discipuli	al	SYG 156	G	2	4	2	0	2	4	5	4	E
2	Alleluia obtulerunt discipuli	al	GB 133^v	D	3	5	3	5	2	0	2	3	D
8	Alleluia oculis ac manibus in caelum	al	SYG 225	G	2	4	0	2	5	4	2	0	G
2	Alleluia oculis ac manibus in caelum	al	GB 242^v	D	3	5	3	5	2	0	3	5	D
2	Alleluia oculus Dei respexit illum	al	GR 604 LU 1646	A	3	5	3	5	3	5	8	7	D
1	Alleluia omnes gentes plaudite manibus	al	GR 337 LU 1011 SYG 241 *GS 133 GB 177	D	3	5	3	7	5	7	10	7	D
7	Alleluia omnibus omnia factus sum	al	GR 68**	G	5	4	5	7	5	7	4	7	G
4	Allcluia omnis terra adoret te	al	GB 37^v SYG 35	C	2	4	2	4	5	7	4	5	E
4	Alleluia oportebat pati Christum	al	GR 267 LU 822 GS 126 SYG 155 GB 133^v	E	-2	0	-2	-4	-2	-4	-2	-4	E
8	Alleluia optimam partem elegit	al	GS p 191	F	2	4	0	2	4	2	0	4	G
2	Alleluia ora pro nobis beate Clemens	al	GB 245	D	3	5	3	5	2	0	3	5	[D]
7	Alleluia os justi meditabitur	al	GB 40^v	G	2	4	5	7	4	2	5	2	G
1	Alleluia os justi meditabitur	al	SYG 199	C	2	4	5	7	9	7	5	4	D
3	Alleluia ostende mihi faciem tuam	al	GR 440 LU 1377	F	2	4	2	4	7	4	2	7	E
8	Alleluia ostende nobis Domine	al	GR 2 LU 320 GS 1 SYG 2 *GB 1	F	2	4	2	4	6	7	6	4	G
1	Alleluia paraclitus spiritus sanctus	al	GS 138	D	3	2	3	5	2	0	3	0	D
8	Alleluia paras mihi mensam	al	LU 1623^c	F	2	4	2	4	6	7	6	4	G
3	Alleluia paratum cor meum Deus	al	GR 378 LU 1064 GB 259^v *GS 158 SYG 253	E	1	-2	3	7	3	5	7	8	E
7	Alleluia pascha nostrum immolatus est Christus	al	GR 242 LU 779 OHS 710 GS 117 *SYG 153 *GB 125^v	G	2	5	2	7	4	7	4	7	G
8	Alleluia pater cum essem	al	SYG 178	E	1	3	1	5	8	5	3	1	G

	Text		Source										
4	Alleluia pauper et inops laudabunt	al	GR 424 LU 1352^v	D	3	2	3	5	7	5	3	5	E
4	Alleluia per manus autem apostolorum	al	GS y	C	2	5	4	5	4	2	4	5	E
1	Alleluia per signum sanctae crucis	al	SYG 174	D	2	3	2	0	-2	3	5	7	D
1	Alleluia per te Dei genitrix nobis est	al	GR 552 LU 1557 GS u	D	2	3	5	2	3	5	2	0	D
1	Alleluia plantatus in domo	al	SYG 189	D	3	2	3	5	2	0	3	0	D
1	Alleluia positis autem genibus	al	SYG 22	D	-2	0	3	5	0	3	2	0	D
1	Alleluia positis genibus	al	SYG 22	D	7	5	3	5	7	10	7	9	D
7	Alleluia post dies octo ... stetit	al	GR 262 LU 810 *GS 124 SYG 163 GB 144^v	G	2	0	2	0	-2	2	5	7	G
1	Alleluia post dies octo ... stetit	al	SYG 163	D	3	2	3	5	2	0	3	0	D
1	Alleluia post excessum beatissimi Martini	al	SYG 227	D	2	3	2	0	-2	3	5	7	D
4	Alleluia post partum virgo inviolata	al	GR [77] LU 1265 GS r *SYG 48 *GB 220^v	C	2	5	4	5	4	2	4	5	E
8	Alleluia posui adjutorium super potentem	al	GS 224	G	2	-2	0	5	2	5	7	5	G
2	Alleluia posui adjutorium super potentem	al	GB 272	D	3	5	3	5	2	0	3	5	D
1	Alleluia posui vos ut eatis	al	GR 568	C	2	4	5	7	4	5	2	0	D
1	Alleluia posuisti Domine super caput	al	GR [17] LU 1148 GS 206 GB 270	C	2	5	7	4	2	5	4	5	D
6	Alleluia posuisti Domine super caput	al	SYG 217	D	3	0	-2	3	5	3	5	7	F
2	Alleluia potens in terra erit semen	al	GR 585	G	2	5	7	5	7	4	2	5	a
1	Alleluia potestas ejus potestas aeterna	al	GR 639 LU 1711	D	-2	0	3	5	3	2	0	3	D
4	Alleluia pretiosa in conspectu Domini	al	GR [19] LU 1151 SYG 218	E	1	-2	3	5	1	0	1	-2	E
8	Alleluia Pretiosa in conspectu Domini	al	GB 164	F	2	4	7	2	4	2	0	2	G
5	Alleluia primus ad Sion dicet	al	SYG 170 GS v 204	F	4	7	4	7	9	7	9	7	F
4	Alleluia pro omnibus mortuus	al	GR 480 LU 1434	G	2	0	-3	-2	-3	-5	-3	-5	E
1	Alleluia propitius esto Domine peccatis	al	GR [148] LU 841 *SYG 234	C	2	4	5	2	0	4	2	5	D
2	Alleluia propter veritatem ... deducet	al	GR [67] LU 1237	C	2	5	7	5	4	5	7	9	D
4	Alleluia propter veritatem ... exaltabit	al	SYG 232	D	2	-2	3	0	2	0	-2	0	E
	Alleluia psallite Domino	sr	WA 150										
2	Alleluia psallite Domino	al	GB 182	D	-2	0	2	3	2	0	-2	0	D
7	Alleluia psallite Domino	al	SYG 180	G	2	5	2	7	5	7	5	7	[G]
1	Alleluia puer meus dicit Dominus	al	SYG 213	C	2	5	7	4	2	5	4	5	D
8	Alleluia pulchra facie	al	SYG 42	E	-2	3	5	7	5	3	5	8	G

1	Alleluia quae est ista quae progreditur	al	GR 75**	D	-2	2	5	2	-2	0	2	5	D
	Alleluia qualis pater talis filius	al	SYG 261										
1	Alleluia quam magna multitudo	al	GR 628	C	2	4	5	4	2	4	5	7	D
6	Alleluia quasi cedrus exaltata es	al	GB 224	c	2	4	2	4	5	4	2	0	c
1	Alleluia quasi modo geniti infantes	al	GB 144^v	C	2	5	2	4	2	0	2	5	D
7	Alleluia quasi palma exaltata	al	GR 34**	G	4	7	5	4	5	7	5	4	G
7	Alleluia quasi rosa plantata	al	GR 614 LU 1669	G	4	7	5	4	5	7	5	4	G
5	Alleluia quem quaeris mulier	an	PM 67 LA 221 *WA 138	c	2	4	2	0	2	-3	-5	-3	F
7	Alleluia qui ad justitiam erudiunt	al	GR 497 LU 1467	G	4	7	5	4	5	7	5	4	G
1	Alleluia qui confidunt in Domino	al	SYG 255 *GS 163	a	-2	0	-2	-4	-5	-4	-5	-7	D
1	Alleluia qui confidunt in Domino	al	GB 266^v	D	2	3	0	2	0	-2	0	2	D
1	Alleluia qui docti fuerint fulgebunt	al	GR 496 LU 1466	C	2	4	5	7	9	7	5	4	D
4	Alleluia qui facit angelos suos	al	GR 461 GB 168^v	C	2	4	2	9	10	9	7	4	E
1	Alleluia qui me invenerit inveniet vitam	al	GR 26**	D	-2	0	3	5	0	3	2	0	D
4	Alleluia qui posuit fines tuos	al	GR [137] LU 1286 GS f ·	F	-3	-1	0	2	4	2	4	5	E
3	Alleluia qui sanat contritos corde	al	SYG 258 *GS d	E	1	-2	3	5	1	0	1	-2	E
2	Alleluia qui sequitur me non ambulat	al	GR [13] LU 1139	D	2	0	-2	2	3	5	3	2	D
1	Alleluia qui timent Dominum sperent	al	GR 385 LU 1072 *GS 160 SYG 249	D	3	5	3	7	5	7	10	7	D
3	Alleluia qui timent te videbunt me	al	GR 73**	E	3	1	0	1	0	-2	0	-2	E
2	Alleluia quia factus es susceptor	al	GR 470	D	2	0	2	3	5	3	2	3	D
3	Alleluia quid bonum ejus est	al	GR 55**	E	1	-2	3	7	3	5	7	8	E
	Alleluia quid quaeris	see	Alleluia quem quaeris										
7	Alleluia quinque prudentes virgines	al	GS 231	a	-2	0	3	5	0	3	2	0	G
7	Alleluia quinque prudentes virgines	al	GR 416 LU 1339 *SYG 45 GB 273^v	G	2	0	-2	2	5	4	2	5	G
3	Alleluia quis sicut Dominus Deus	al	GR 19**	E	3	1	0	1	0	-2	0	-2	E
3	Alleluia quis vestrum habebit	al	SYG 177	a	3	0	3	0	2	-2	0	3	E
3	Alleluia quoniam confirmata est	al	SYG 250	E	1	-2	3	7	3	5	7	8	E
7	Alleluia quoniam Deus magnus	al	GR 361 LU 1042 GS 156 SYG 246 GB 255^v	G	2	5	7	9	7	5	7	9	G
2	Alleluia reddet Deus mercedem	al	GS 216	D	-2	0	3	5	0	3	2	0	D
1	Alleluia reddet Deus mercedem	al	SYG 191	D	-2	0	3	5	3	2	0	-2	D
2	Alleluia redemptionem misit Dominus	al	GR 266 LU 822 *SYG 248	C	2	5	7	5	7	4	2	5	D

5 Alleluia regem martyrum	inv	LA 386	F	4	7	4	7	9	7	11	9	F
1 Alleluis regi autem saeculorum	al	SYG 262	D	-2	0	2	3	2	0	2	0	D
7 Alleluia regnabit Deus super gentes	al	SYG 180	G	2	-2	2	5	4	2	5	7	G
1 Alleluia regnavit Dominus super omnes	al	GR 288 LU 855 *GB 179^v *GS K	D	2	0	-2	2	5	7	5	3	D
1 Alleluia repleti fructu justitiae	al	GR 545 LU 1545	C	2	5	7	4	2	5	4	5	D
1 Alleluia repleti sunt apostoli	al	GB 192	C	2	4	2	4	5	7	5	4	[D]
2 Alleluia repleti sunt omnes	al	SYG 186	D	2	0	-2	0	2	0	2	3	D
1 Alleluia repletus sum consolatione	al	GR 547	D	-2	0	3	5	3	5	7	5	D
Alleluia resurrexit Dominus	sr	WA 142										
5 Alleluia resurrexit Dominus	an	WA 138	c	2	4	2	0	2	0	-1	-3	F
2 Alleluia resurrexit tamquam dormiens	al	GB 126	D	2	-2	0	3	2	0	-2	0	D
1 Alleluia rogavi pro te Petre	al	GR 543 LU 1543	C	2	4	7	4	5	4	2	4	D
4 Alleluia rosa vernens caritatis	al	VP 52	E	1	-2	3	5	0	3	5	3	E
8 Alleluia sacerdos Dei Martine	al	SYG 226	C	2	4	5	7	9	7	5	7	G
2 Alleluia sacerdos sit sanctus sicut	al	GR [119]	D	2	0	2	3	5	3	2	3	D
3 Alleluia sacerdotes tui Domine Deus	al	GR 89**	G	2	4	2	0	2	4	5	4	E
6 Alleluia sacerdotes tui Domine induantur	al	GB 272 *SYG 211	c	2	4	2	0	2	4	5	7	c
1 Alleluia salva nos Christe	al	SYG 173	C	2	5	2	4	2	0	5	7	D
1 Alleluia salvabo populum meum Israel	al	GR [140]	D	-2	0	3	5	7	5	7	5	D
5 Alleluia salve mater misericordiae	al	GR 44**	C	2	4	5	7	9	7	11	12	C
8 Alleluia salve regina misericordiae	al	LU 1476^E	F	2	4	2	4	6	7	6	4	G
7 8 Alleluia salve virga florens	al	VP 53	G	5	7	5	10	9	7	0	3	G
3 Alleluia salvum me fac Deus	al	GR [139]	E	-2	3	5	8	7	5	8	5	E
1 Alleluia Sancte Benedicte qui in caelis	al	SYG 207	C	2	5	2	4	5	2	4	0	D
8 Alleluia Sancte Michael archangele	al	GR 609 LU 1655	D	5	3	7	5	2	3	0	3	G
8 Alleluia Sancte Paule apostole intercede	al	GB 208^v	F	2	4	6	7	2	4	2	0	G
8 Alleluia Sancte Paule apostole praedicator	al	GR 535 LU 1526	D	5	3	7	5	2	3	0	3	G
8 Alleluia Sancte Vincenti levita	al	GB 46	G	4	5	4	2	0	2	4	0	G
7 Alleluia sancti et justi in Domino gaudete	al	GS 215	G	2	0	-2	2	5	0	2	0	G
7 Alleluia sancti et justi in Domino gaudete	al	SYG 222	G	2	0	2	0	-2	2	5	7	G
2 Alleluia sancti tui Domine benedicent	al	GR 415 LU 1336 GS 215 *GB 269^v *SYG 40	C	2	5	7	5	7	4	2	5	D

8	Alleluia sancti tui Domine florebunt	al	SYG 222	G	2	0	2	4	5	7	5	2	G
8	Alleluia sancti tui Domine florebunt	al	GR [19] LU 1150 GS 215 GB 239	F	2	4	2	4	2	0	4	2	G
7	Alleluia sanctorum sicut aquilae	al	SYG 210	G	2	0	-2	2	4	5	2	0	G
1	Alleluia sapientia hujus mundi stultitia	al	GR 473 LU 1428	C	2	4	2	4	2	0	4	5	D
1	Alleluia sapientiam ipsorum narrent	al	GR 445 LU 1386	C	2	4	2	9	10	9	7	9	D
1	Alleluia Saturninus pontifex magnus	al	SYG 230	D	3	5	3	5	2	0	3	5	D
8	Alleluia scitote quoniam Dominus ipse est	al	GR [129] LU 1296	E	3	5	7	5	1	3	8	3	G
1	Alleluia senex puerum portabat puer autem	al	GR 434 LU 1363 GB 47^v	C	2	5	2	5	4	5	7	5	D
4	Alleluia si enim non abiero	al	SYG 168	E	1	-2	3	7	5	7	8	10	E
3	Alleluia si filii et heredes	al	GR 480 LU 1434	E	-2	3	5	8	7	5	7	8	E
3	Alleluia si testimonium hominum accipimus	al	GR 538 LU 1534	E	3	1	0	1	0	-2	0	-2	E
2	Alleluia sicut cinnamomum	al	GR 34**	A	3	5	3	5	3	5	8	7	D
7	Alleluia sicut oliva fructifera	al	GR 622^4	G	5	7	5	4	7	5	2	0	G
7	Alleluia solemnitas gloriosae virginis	al	GR 620 LU 1676^A	F	2	4	0	2	4	2	0	4	G
1	Alleluia solve jubente Deo terrarum	al	GR 563 LU 1576 GS 192 *SYG 203	C	2	4	2	0	4	2	5	7	D
2	Alleluia specie tua et pulchritudine	al	SYG 41	D	-2	0	2	3	5	3	2	0	D
8	Alleluia specie tua et pulchritudine	al	GR [70] LU 1218 GS 227 SYG 29 *GB 273	F	2	4	2	4	6	7	6	4	G
1	Alleluia speciosum fecit rex angelorum	al	SYG 219	C	2	5	2	0	4	5	7	4	D
3	Alleluia sperent in te qui noverunt	al	GR 94**	F	-3	2	4	0	-1	0	-3	2	E
8	Alleluia spiritus Dei ornavit caelos	al	SYG 185	F	2	4	7	2	4	2	0	2	G
4	Alleluia spiritus Domini replevit orbem	al	GS a 140	G	2	5	0	2	5	2	0	5	E
3	Alleluia spiritus Domini replevit orbem	al	SYG 183	E	3	5	7	5	7	8	7	5	E
5	Alleluia spiritus Domini replevit orbem	inv	LR 107 LU 863 *LA 255 *WA 152	F	4	7	9	7	11	9	7	6	F
1	Alleluia spiritus Domini super me	al	GR [102] LU 1283^C	C	2	4	7	4	5	4	2	4	D
8	Alleluia spiritus ejus ornavit caelos	al	GR 305 LU 902	F	2	4	7	2	4	2	0	4	G
8	Alleluia spiritus est Deus	al	SYG 187	F	2	4	2	4	6	7	6	4	G
8	Alleluia spiritus est qui vivificat	al	GR 304 LU 901	G	2	5	4	2	5	7	5	0	G
8	Alleluia spiritus omnia scrutatur	al	SYG 186	F	2	0	2	4	2	7	4	7	G
2	Alleluia spiritus paraclitus docebit vos	al	GB 192	D	2	5	7	4	2	5	4	5	D
2	Alleluia spiritus qui a Patre	al	GB 191^v	C	2	0	2	5	4	2	5	4	D
1	Alleluia spiritus qui a Patre	al	SYG 185	C	4	5	7	4	5	4	2	0	D

8	Alleluia spiritus sancti gratia	al	SYG 24	G	-2	-5	-3	-2	0	2	0	-2	G
8	Alleluia spiritus sanctus docebit vos	al	GR 299 LU 891 GB 191	F	2	4	2	7	9	11	9	7	G
1	Alleluia spiritus sanctus in te	al	SYG 2	D	-2	0	2	3	2	0	-2	0	D
2	Alleluia spiritus sanctus procedens	al	GS M 137	C	2	0	2	0	2	5	4	2	D
3	Alleluia spiritus ubi vult spirat	al	SYG 186	E	3	5	7	5	7	8	7	5	[E]
2	Alleluia stabat sancta Maria	al	GR 596 LU 1633[V]	D	3	2	0	-2	3	2	0	5	D
2	Alleluia stabunt justi in magna constantia	al	SYG 172	D	2	0	-2	0	2	3	2	0	D
2	Alleluia stabunt justi in magna constantia	al	GS 185	D	3	2	0	-2	3	2	0	5	D
7	Alleluia stetit Jesus in medio	al	SYG 162	a	-2	2	0	-2	0	2	3	5	G
1	Alleluia surgens Dominus Jesus	al	SYG 156	D	3	2	3	5	2	0	3	2	D
1	Alleluia surgens Jesus Dominus ... stans	al	SYG 163	D	-2	2	5	3	2	-2	0	-2	D
2	Alleluia surgens Jesus Dominus ... stetit	al	GS 119	C	2	5	2	4	5	4	0	2	D
7	Alleluia surrexit altissimus de sepulcro	al	SYG 158 GS 127	G	2	0	5	4	7	9	7	9	G
1	Alleluia surrexit altissimus de sepulcro	al	SYG 168	D	7	8	7	5	7	5	7	5	D
7	Alleluia surrexit altissimus Dominus	al	GB 146	G	2	0	2	5	4	5	7	9	G
1	Alleluia surrexit Christus et illuxit	al	GR 271 LU 831 *GS 127 SYG 165	C	2	4	5	4	2	7	4	5	D
6	Alleluia surrexit Christus jam	al	GS 131	F	2	0	2	5	4	5	2	0	F
2	Alleluia surrexit Christus qui creavit	al	GR 254 OHS 808 LU 798 SYG 159 GB 150 GS 129	A	3	5	3	5	3	5	3	5	D
	Alleluia surrexit Dominus de sepulcro	sr	WA 143										
1	Alleluia surrexit Dominus de sepulcro	al	GR 248 LU 790 OHS 785 *GB 137[V]	C	2	4	2	9	10	9	7	9	D
1	Alleluia surrexit Dominus et occurrens	al	SYG 163 *GS 120	C	2	4	2	0	2	4	5	7	D
8	Alleluia surrexit Dominus vere	al	GR 251 OHS 797 LU 794 GS 130 *SYG 155 GB 135[V]	F	2	4	7	2	4	2	0	4	G
8	Alleluia surrexit pastor bonus ... grege	al	GS 128	G	-2	-3	-2	-5	-3	-2	0	2	G
1	Alleluia surrexit pastor bonus ... ovibus	al	SYG 164	C	2	5	2	4	5	2	0	2	D
8	Alleluia surrexit quasi ignis	al	GR 66**	C	4	7	4	2	4	5	4	2	G
4	Alleluia suscitans a terra inopem	al	GR 20**	D	3	2	3	5	7	5	3	5	E
1	Alleluia suxerunt mel de petra	al	GB 151[V]	D	-2	2	3	5	3	2	3	2	D
8	Alleluia tamquam filiis dico dilatamini	al	GR 547	G	2	0	4	5	7	5	4	0	G

8 Alleluia tamquam prodigium factus sum	al	GR 622² LU 1681³	G	2	0	4	7	5	4	2	5	G
8 Alleluia tanto tempore vobiscum sum	al	GR 489 LU 1465^C	G	2	4	0	2	0	2	5	4	G
7 Alleluia te decet hymnus Deus	al	GR 346 LU 1022 GS 148 *SYG 242 *GB 252	G	4	7	5	4	5	7	5	4	G
5 Alleluia te gloriosus apostolorum chorus	al	GR 588 LU 1613	C	2	4	5	7	9	7	11	12	C
5 Alleluia te martyrum candidatus laudat	al	GR [30] LU 1171 GS 18 217 SYG 192 GB 268^V	C	2	4	5	7	9	7	11	12	C
7 Alleluia tibi gloria hosanna	al	GR [109]	G	2	4	2	0	4	5	7	9	G
4 Alleluia timebunt gentes nomen tuum	al	SYG 249	C	2	4	2	4	5	4	2	4	E
1 Alleluia timebunt gentes nomen tuum	al	GR 373 LU 1056 GB 39^V *GS 167	D	3	0	-2	3	5	3	5	7	D
1 Alleluia timete Dominum omnes sancti	al	SYG 192	C	2	4	5	7	5	4	2	4	D
1 Alleluia timete Dominum omnes sancti	al	SYG 212	D	3	5	3	7	5	7	10	7	D
7 Alleluia tolle puerum	al	SYG 30	G	7	9	7	4	7	5	4	2	G
3 Alleluia tollite jugum meum	al	GR 325 [112] LU 972	C	2	4	5	4	2	7	5	4	E
1 Alleluia tota pulchra es Maria	al	GR 402 LU 1318	D	3	5	3	2	0	3	5	7	D
1 Alleluia tristitia implebit cor vestrum	al	SYG 168	F	2	-1	-3	0	-3	0	4	6	D
7 Alleluia tu Domine pater noster	al	GB 151^V	G	2	4	5	7	9	7	10	12	G
1 Alleluia tu es altissimus super omnem	al	GB 178^V	C	7	9	7	2	4	2	4	5	D
2 Alleluia tu es Petrus et super hanc petram	al	GR 409 534 LU 1122³ 1520 *SYG 203 *GB 202^V	C	2	5	7	5	7	4	2	5	D
8 Alleluia tu es sacerdos in aeternum	al	GR [4][33] LU 1183 1495^B *SYG 38 *GB 272^V	D	5	3	5	7	10	7	3	5	G
1 Alleluia tu es Simon Bar Jona	al	SYG 203 *GS 189	D	2	0	-2	0	2	3	5	2	D
6 Alleluia tu es vas electionis	al	SYG 205	D	3	5	7	5	3	5	7	5	F
7 Alleluia tu gloria Jerusalem tu laetitia	al	GR 403	G	7	9	7	4	7	5	4	2	G
2 Alleluia tu puer propheta altissimi	al	GR 524 LU 1501 GS 1 188 *SYG 196 *GB 197^V	C	2	5	7	5	7	4	2	5	D
1 Alleluia tuam crucem adoramus	al	SYG 173	C	2	4	2	4	5	7	5	4	D
8 Alleluia tuus sum ego	an	AR 35 LU 241 243	G	5	2	0	2	0	-2	0	2	G
8 Alleluia universae angelorum virtutes	al	GB 169	F	2	4	7	2	4	2	0	2	G
4 Alleluia usque modo non petistis	al	SYG 168 *GS 130	C	2	4	5	4	2	4	5	7	E
1 Alleluia vado ad eum qui misit me	al	SYG 167 *GS 130	D	7	5	3	5	7	10	7	9	D
1 Alleluia valde honorandus	al	SYG 24	C	2	4	2	4	2	0	4	7	D

Mode	Text	Type	Source	Start	1	2	3	4	5	6	7	8	End
8	Alleluia venerunt de tribulatione	al	GR 108**	G	-2	-5	-3	-2	0	2	0	-2	G
3	Alleluia veni Domine et noli tardare	al	GR 22 LU 354 SYG 7 GB 11 *GS 12	E	1	-2	3	7	3	5	7	8	E
1	Alleluia veni Domine visitare	al	SYG 13	D	7	5	3	2	0	-2	0	2	D
1	Alleluia veni electa mea	al	GS 227	C	2	4	2	9	10	9	7	9	D
2	Alleluia veni sancte spiritus	al	GR 293 [92] LU 880 GB 187 GS 138 234	C	2	4	5	4	2	0	2	7	D
3	Alleluia veni sponsa Christi accipe coronam	al	SYG 208	D	2	5	7	3	2	5	3	2	E
8	Alleluia veni sponsa Christi accipe coronam	al	GB 273^V	F	4	2	4	7	6	4	7	6	[G]
7	Alleluia veni sponsa Christi accipe coronam	al	GB 272^V	G	5	2	0	2	4	2	0	5	G
1	Alleluia veni sponsa Christi accipe palmam	al	SYG 208	C	2	5	2	0	2	4	5	4	D
8	Alleluia venite ad me omnes qui laboratis	al	GR 648 [114] LU 973 1726 *SYG 218	G	-2	2	0	2	0	5	7	5	G
8	Alleluia venite ad me sancti mei	al	SYG 207	a	-2	0	-2	-4	-2	0	-2	0	G
8	Alleluia venite benedicti Patris	al	GB 267^V	G	2	4	0	2	4	5	4	2	G
1	Alleluia venite comedite panem meum	al	GR 627	C	2	5	2	0	4	2	4	5	D
7	Alleluia venite exsultemus Domino	al	GR 358 LU 1038 *GS 154 GB 255 *SYG 245	G	5	4	7	9	7	5	2	5	G
7	Alleluia venite filii audite	al	GB 250^V	G	5	4	5	7	9	7	5	2	G
7	Alleluia venite justi ad prandium	al	SYG 44	d	-2	0	2	0	5	3	2	0	G
2	Alleluia verba mea auribus percipe	al	GR 312 *GS 141 *SYG 239 *GB 247^V	C	2	0	2	4	2	4	5	7	D
8	Alleluia verbo Domini caeli firmati	al	GR 300 LU 893	G	-2	-5	-3	-2	0	2	0	-2	G
2	Alleluia verbo Domini caeli firmati	al	SYG 240	C	2	5	2	4	5	2	0	2	D
8	Alleluia vere tu es rex absconditus	al	GR 61 LU 472	G	2	-2	-3	-5	-3	-2	0	-2	G
1	Alleluia verumtamen existimo omnia	al	GR 474 LU 1428	C	2	4	2	5	7	5	4	2	D
7	Alleluia vicerunt draconem	al	GR 99**	G	2	0	-2	2	5	4	2	5	G
8	Alleluia videbitis et gaudebit cor	al	GR 510 LU 1483	G	2	0	2	0	4	2	0	4	G
2	Alleluia video caelos apertos	al	GR 37 LU 416 GS 15 *GB 21^V *SYG 22	C	2	5	7	5	7	4	2	5	D
1	Alleluia vidi speciosam	al	SYG 177	C	2	4	5	4	2	0	5	7	D
2	Alleluia vidimus stellam ejus	al	GR 58 LU 460 GS 19 *GB 33^V *SYG 31	C	2	5	7	5	7	4	2	5	D
4	Alleluia vindica Domine sanguinem	al	SYG 175 191	E	1	3	1	0	1	-2	1	3	E
1	Alleluia vindica Domine sanguinem	al	SYG 210	C	2	5	2	4	2	5	4	2	D

4	Alleluia vindica Domine sanguinem	al	GB 269	C	4	7	5	4	5	2	5	7	E
6	Alleluia vir Dei Benedictus	al	GR (25)	D	3	5	3	8	7	5	7	3	F
1	Alleluia vir Domini Benedictus	al	SYG 207	D	3	5	3	7	5	7	3	7	D
7	Alleluia vir obediens loquetur	al	GR (5)	G	2	0	5	7	4	0	2	5	G
8	Alleluia virga Jesse floruit	al	GR [79] LU 1267	E	3	5	3	8	7	5	7	3	G
1	Alleluia virgo Dei genitrix	al	GR 623 LU 1684	C	2	4	2	9	10	9	7	9	D
8	Alleluia viriliter agite	al	GR (36)	G	2	0	-3	-5	-3	-2	-5	-3	G
8	Alleluia virtutes caeli movebuntur	al	GS 3 SYG 4	G	-2	2	0	5	2	4	2	0	G
1	Alleluia vita nostra est abscondita	al	GR 63	D	3	0	-2	2	5	7	5	10	D
7	Alleluia vos estis lux	al	GB 235[V] *SYG 218	G	2	0	2	4	5	7	5	4	G
8	Alleluia vos estis qui permansistis	al	GR 548 LU 1548	G	2	-2	0	-2	2	5	4	2	G
8	Alleluia vos qui secuti estis me	al	GB 267[V]	G	-3	-5	0	2	0	-5	-7	-5	[G]
7	Alleluia vota mea Domino reddam	al	GR 36**	G	2	5	7	9	7	9	10	12	G
8	Alleluia vox exsultationis et salutis	al	GB 269 *SYG 176 *GS 215	D	5	7	9	7	5	7	9	7	G
4	Alleluia vox turturis audita est	al	GR 442 LU 1379[1]	G	2	0	-3	-2	-3	-5	-3	-5	E
	Allide virtutem eorum Domine Deus qui conteris	rev	LA 292 WA 178										
1	Alliga Domine in vinculis	an	AM 411 WA 117 LA 188	F	4	5	4	2	4	2	0	2	D
4	Alma Christi quando fides	hy	ST 301	F	-1	0	-3	-5	-3	0	-3	0	E
8	Alma Dei genitrix succurre	co	GS s	G	-5	-2	0	2	0	-2	-3	-2	G
3	Alma Dei porta David	hy	ST 315	b	1	0	-2	-4	-2	-4	-6	-7	E
5	Alma redemptoris mater	an	AR 69 LR 46 LU 277 AM 178	C	4	5	7	9	7	9	11	12	C
5	Alma redemptoris mater	an	AR 65 LU 273 *AM 173 *WA 303	F	4	5	7	9	12	11	9	7	F
1	Alma Scholastica	re	LR 290	D	7	5	7	10	12	10	7	10	D
1	Alme confessor Domini	an	WA 428	C	2	0	2	5	2	4	2	0	D
8	Alme dictatis resonante gratis	hy	ST 67	G	-2	-3	-5	0	2	0	2	4	G
3	Alme pater Augustine doctor	hy	ST 235	D	2	3	5	3	2	0	2	0	E
	Alme pater Augustine ora	sr	WA 316										
5	Alme pater clericorum	hy	ST 458	F	2	0	-1	0	5	4	2	4	F
	Alme pater Wulstane	sr	WA 252										
8	Almi beati martyris	hy	ST 392	G	-5	-2	0	2	0	-2	0	5	G
2	Almi prophetae progenies pia	hy	ST 53	D	-2	2	5	7	5	3	0	2	D
8	Almi prophetae progenies pia	hy	ST 296	G	2	0	5	0	2	5	7	5	G
8	Almi prophetae progenies pia	hy	ST 433	F	2	4	2	7	6	2	4	7	G
8	Almi prophetae progenies pia	hy	ST 12	G	2	4	5	4	2	4	5	7	G

	Title	Type	Source									
8	Almi prophetae progenies pia	hy	ST 430	G	5	2	4	2	0	2	4	2	G
7	Almi prophetae progenies pia	hy	ST 393	G	5	2	5	7	5	7	5	7	G
1	Almi prophetae progenies pia	hy	ST 42	D	7	8	7	5	7	9	10	7	D
	Altaria tua Domine / Adduxisti sanctos	rev	LA 551										
	Altaria tua Domine / Postquam sexaginta	rev	LR 286										
	Altaria tua Domine / Cor meum	trv	GR 626	G	2	4	5	4	5	7	5	0	
1	Alto ex Olympi vertice	hy	AR [108] LU 1242	C	2	5	2	0	5	7	10	7	D
7	Amande praesul inclite	hy	ST 165	G	7	9	12	10	9	7	10	9	G
1	Amator tuus semper	an	WA 233	D	3	0	-2	3	5	7	9	7	D
	Amavit eum Dominus et ornavit	sr	AR [62][63][83] LU 117 AM 659 672 853 966 WA 427										
	Amavit eum Dominus et ornavit	alv	GR [39] LU 1191 GS 222 *GB 271[V] *SYG 214	C	2	5	2	4	5	4	2	4	
1	Amavit cum Dominus et ornavit	an	AR 577[16][4] [65] LU 262[4] 1181 AM 663 740 WA 428 *LA 537	C	2	5	4	2	0	2	5	4	D
2	Amavit eum Dominus et ornavit	re	PM 223 LR 201 LA 532 *WA 427	A	3	7	5	8	7	8	5	7	D
1	Ambiens speciosus ejus	an	WA 40	D	2	0	3	5	3	2	0	-2	D
8	Ambulabant martyres Christi	an	WA 378	G	-5	-2	0	2	0	-2	2	5	G
2	Ambulabunt mecum in albis	re	LA 57 WA 45	D	2	-2	0	3	0	2	0	-2	D
4	Ambulabunt mecum in albis	an	LA 56	D	2	3	5	2	5	2	0	3	E
1	Ambulans Jesus juxta mare	an	WA 232 *LA 497	D	2	0	3	5	2	3	0	-2	D
6	Ambulate in dilectione sicut / et Christus	of	GR 483 LU 1435	C	2	5	7	5	7	9	7	5	F
1	Amen amen dico vobis antequam	an	WA 109	C	2	9	11	9	7	9	11	9	D
1	Amen amen dico vobis iterum videbo	an	AR 477 *AM 391	D	3	0	-2	3	5	3	7	5	D
1	Amen amen dico vobis qui credit	an	WA 157	D	3	2	0	3	2	3	5	3	D
8	Amen amen dico vobis qui non	an	WA 156	G	2	5	2	4	2	4	0	2	G
8	Amen amen dico vobis quia plorabitis	an	AR 474 LU 825 *AM 489	G	2	0	-2	2	4	0	2	0	G
1	Amen amen dico vobis quia plorabitis	an	LA 236	D	3	0	-2	3	5	3	5	7	D
1	Amen amen dico vobis si quis sermonem	an	AR 414 LU 574	D	3	0	-2	3	5	3	7	10	D
	Amen dico tibi hodie / Velum templi	rev	WA 123										
1	Amen dico vobis mundus plorabit	an	LA 236	D	-2	3	5	3	7	5	7	9	D
8	Amen dico vobis nisi abundaverit	an	WA 188	G	-2	0	-7	-5	-2	0	2	0	G

	Incipit	Type	Sources										
1	Amen dico vobis quia nemo propheta	an	AR 391 LU 1089 AM 366 *WA 99 *LA 154	D	-2	3	5	3	7	5	3	5	D
1	Amen dico vobis quia non praeteribit	an	AR 576 LU 1080 AM 618	D	-2	3	5	3	7	5	3	5	D
1	Amen dico vobis quidquid orantes	co	GR 389 LU 1077 SYG 259 GB 265 GS f 167	C	2	9	10	9	7	12	11	12	D
1	Amen dico vobis quod uni	an	AM 829 974	D	-2	3	5	3	7	5	3	5	D
4	Amen dico vobis quod uni	co	GR 101 GS 219 *GB 68 *SYG 193	D	2	3	2	3	5	3	2	5	E
1	Amen dico vobis quod vos	co	GR [47] LU 1206 *GS 179 SYG 45 55 *GB 209^v	D	2	3	2	3	5	3	2	5	D
1	Amice non facio tibi	an	LA 116	C	2	9	10	9	7	9	7	5	D
	Amici mei et proximi Fratres mei	rev	WA 110										
6	Amicus Dei Nicholaus	an	WA 242	c	2	4	2	5	4	2	0	2	c
8	Amicus meus osculi me	re	OHS 388 LU 643 LA 191	G	-2	-5	-3	-2	-3	-5	-7	-5	G
4	Amo Christum in cujus thalamum	re	LA 333	a	3	0	3	5	3	0	2	0	b
7	Amo Christum in cujus thalamum	re	WA 254	G	3	2	0	3	2	3	5	3	G
4	Amor Jesu dulcissime	hy	AM 1000	a	-2	-5	-7	-2	0	2	0	-2	E
2	Amore Christi nobilis	hy	ST 9	D	-2	-5	-7	-2	0	2	3	2	D
2	Amore Christi nobilis	hy	ST 39	a	-2	-5	-7	-2	0	3	2	0	a
8	Amorem sensus erige	hy	ST 384	G	2	4	2	0	-2	2	0	2	G
4	Amorem sensus erige	hy	ST 224	D	7	5	3	2	0	2	3	5	E
	Amove Domine a me	an	OHS 239 (n.m.)										
	Amplius lava me ab injustitia Ne recorderis	rev	WA 437										
	Amplius lava me Domine Domine secundum actum	rev	AR [172] LU 1798 LA 555										
8	Amplius lava me Domine	an	WA 67 *LA 95	G	-2	2	5	4	0	4	5	2	G
7	Amplius lava me Domine	an	AR 130 AM 52	G	4	5	7	5	2	5	4	5	G
2	Ancilla Christi sum	an	WA 273 LA 357	D	3	2	3	5	2	3	0	3	D
1	Ancilla dixit Petro	an	AR 432 OHS 358 AM 411 *LA 187	D	-2	0	3	2	0	-2	3	5	D
1	Ancilla fidelis et sponsa	an	AM 1132	D	-2	3	5	3	7	8	7	5	D
4	Andrea pie	hy	ST 240	F	-1	-3	-5	-3	0	-3	-1	0	E
6	Andreas apostolus	an	WA 232	c	2	4	2	5	4	2	0	2	c
	Andreas Christi famulus Mox ut vocem	rev	WA 233										
8	Andreas Christi famulus	an	AR 580 LU 1308 AM 755 WA 234 LA 504	G	5	2	0	-2	0	2	0	4	G

2 Angeli archangeli ... Cherubim	co	GR [89] LU 1277	F	-3	-5	0	4	2	-1	-3	0	D
7 Angeli archangeli ... laudate	an	AR 857 LU 1660 AM 1059 WA 384 LA 472	d	-2	-3	-2	0	2	0	-2	0	G
2 Angeli archangeli ... patriarchae	an	AR 897 LU 1721 AM 1101 LA 479	C	2	0	2	4	5	2	4	2	D
1 Angeli Dei qui nobis	re	VP 225	D	-2	0	3	2	-2	2	0	2	D
tp 4 Angeli Domini Dominum	an	AR 857 LU 1660 AM 1059 *LA 472	D	-2	0	3	5	7	5	7	5	G
8 Angeli eorum ... patris	an	AR 284 AM 260 LU 431 *LA 61	G	2	0	-2	0	2	5	4	2	G
1 Angeli eorum ... qui est	an	AR 866, LU 1665	D	-2	0	3	5	7	5	3	5	D
Angelis suis Deus mandavit	see also	Angelis suis mandavit										
2 Angelis suis Deus mandavit	tr	GR [144]	D	-2	0	-2	-5	-2	0	-2	0	D
8 Angelis suis Deus mandavit	an	AR 865 LU 1665 *AM 1067	G	5	2	0	-2	0	2	0	-2	G
1 Angelis suis Deus mandavit	re	PM 193 *LA 130 WA 87	D	7	10	12	10	7	3	7	3	D
Angelis suis mandavit	see also	Angelis suis Deus mandavit										
2 Angelis suis mandavit	gr	GR 94 LU 533 *GS 34 *SYG 72 *GB 65	G	4	2	5	2	4	5	2	0	a
2 Angelorum esca nutrivisti populum	an	AR 530 LU 940 *AM 550	D	-2	-5	-2	0	2	3	0	2	D
7 Angelorum regi Deo	inv	WA 379	G	7	9	7	5	4	2	5	4	G
7 Angelus ad pastores ait	re	LR 63 LA 32	G	2	0	2	5	4	5	7	5	G
7 Angelus ad pastores ait	an	AR 264 LU 397 AM 241 *WA 32 LA 37	G	7	5	7	9	10	9	7	9	G
7 Angelus archangelus Michael	an	WA 380 LA 472	d	-2	-3	-2	0	2	0	-2	0	G
8 Angelus autem Domini descendit	an	AR 443 OHS 723 765 LU 782 *AM 453 WA 129 *136 LA 214 229	G	5	2	0	-2	0	2	0	-2	G
7 Angelus Domini apparuit in somnis Joseph	an	AR 320 LU 467	d	-2	-3	-2	0	2	0	-2	-5	G
2 Angelus Domini apparuit in somnis Joseph	tr	GR 6**	D	-2	0	-2	-5	-2	0	-2	0	D
Angelus Domini apparuit in somnis Joseph	alv	GR 5**	C	2	5	2	0	2	0	2	4	
3 Angelus Domini apparuit in somnis Joseph	int	GR 4**	G	5	4	5	2	0	2	5	4	E
5 Angelus Domini apparuit Joseph	an	AR 649 LU 1401	a	-4	0	3	5	3	5	3	2	F
2 Angelus Domini apparuit Joseph	re	LR 310	A	3	5	7	3	0	5	3	5	D
Angelus Domini astitit Surge Petre	rev	PM 172 LR 363 LA 416 WA 327										

#	Incipit	Cat.	Sources										
4	Angelus Domini astitit	an	LA 415	F	-1	-3	-1	2	4	2	0	2	E
4	Angelus Domini astitit	an	WA 328	C	2	5	4	2	7	5	7	5	E
4	Angelus Domini descendebat de caelo	an	AR 377 LU 1084 AM 350 *WA 90 LA 135	a	-2	0	3	5	3	5	7	5	a
	Angelus Domini descendit ... cum splendore	alv	SYG 162	G	2	0	-2	2	5	0	2	0	
3	Angelus Domini descendit ... et accedens	re	LR 83 OHS 695 (nm) *LA 208 *WA 128	G	2	-2	-3	-2	2	0	4	2	E
	Angelus Domini descendit ... et accedens	alv	GR 245 OHS 775 LU 786 GS 125 GB 131 SYG 159	C	2	4	5	7	5	4	5	7	
3	Angelus Domini descendit ... et accedens ... et dixit	an	SYG 147	E	-2	3	5	7	3	5	8	7	E
8	Angelus Domini descendit ... et dixit	of	GR 246 OHS 776 OTT 57 LU 787 GS 118 SYG 155 GB 132	F	2	4	7	4	2	0	2	4	G
	Angelus Domini descendit ... et lumen Caeciliam intra	rev	LA 491 WA 407										
	Angelus Domini locutus est / Angelus Domini descendit	rev	LA 208 WA 128										
5	Angelus Domini locutus est	re	LA 208 WA 128	a	-4	0	3	5	3	0	3	5	F
	Angelus Domini nuntiavit	sr	AM 859 860 863										
1	Angelus Domini nuntiavit	an	AR 219 AM 191 *LR 251 LA 7 380 WA 8	D	-2	2	3	5	3	0	-2	3	D
5	Angelus Domini Raphael apprehendit	gr	GR 634 LU 1699	F	2	0	2	4	2	4	2	0	F
2	Angelus Domini vocavit	re	LA 121 WA 82	A	3	5	7	3	0	5	3	5	D
7	Angelus Gabriel apparuit Danieli	an	AR 660 LU 1410	G	4	5	7	9	7	5	4	5	G
4	Anglorum jam apostolus	hy	LR 434 AM 831	F	-1	-3	-1	2	4	0	-1	2	E
1	Angularis fundamentum	hy	ST 107	D	7	5	3	5	7	0	3	7	D
8	Angustiae mihi undique	re	LA 304 *WA 185	D	3	5	7	5	7	5	7	9	G
7	Anima mea liquefacta est	an	PM 275 *WA 361	G	4	5	7	9	10	7	9	10	G
	Anima mea turbata est valde / Hei mihi Domine	rev	AR [165] LU 1791 LA 555 WA 436										
5	Anima nostra sicut passer	gr	GR 41 [26] LU 1167 GS 17 *SYG 25 *GB 26	F	2	0	-3	0	2	-1	0	2	F
6	Anima nostra sicut passer	co	GB 210^v SYG 206 GS 219	F	2	0	4	2	0	2	0	2	F
2	Anima nostra sicut passer	of	GR 43 OTT 145 LU 430 SYG 26 GB 27^v GS 18	A	3	5	8	5	8	12	10	8	D
5	Anima nostra sustinet Dominum	gr	GR 111**	F	2	0	-3	0	2	-1	0	2	F

	Incipit		Sources										
5	Anima Scholasticae ex arca	re	LR 300	F	4	7	6	7	6	4	7	9	F
	Animae enim viventis Intempestae noctis	rev	WA 334										
	Animae eorum bonis		see Animae eorum in bonis										
	Animae eorum in bonis Domine Jesu Christe	ofv	OTT 189 SYG 235	D	-2	0	2	3	2	0	2	0	
	Animae eorum in bonis Requiem aeternam	grv	GB 265^V *GS 232	D	3	5	7	5	3	2	0	-2	
	Animae fidelium quas assumpsisti Domine Jesu Christe	ofv	OTT 189 SYG 235	D	-2	-5	-2	0	2	3	2	0	
8	Animae impiorum fremebant	an	WA 109 *LA 166	F	2	4	7	6	2	4	2	4	G
7	Animam de corpore quam assumpsisti	an	LA 560	d	-2	-3	-2	0	2	0	-2	-3	G
6 8	Animam meam dilectam	re	OHS 499 LU 704 LA 197	F	2	4	2	0	2	4	2	0	G
	Animas fidelium		see Animae fidelium										
7	Annulis septem subarrhavit	an	AM 1131	d	-3	0	2	0	-2	0	2	0	G
7	Annulo suo subarrhavit me	an	AR 603 LU 1340 AM 786 *WA 253 LA 338	d	-3	0	2	0	-2	0	2	0	G
	Annuntiabitur Domino Deus Deus meus	trv	GR 180 OHS 109 LU 594 *GS 86 *GB 109 *SYG 122	E	-4	-2	1	3	-2	1	3	1	
2	Annuntiate de die in diem	an	LR 337	D	-2	0	3	2	3	5	2	3	D
	Annuntiate et auditum facite Audite verbum	rev	LA 4 WA 4										
	Annuntiate et auditum facite Canite tuba	rev	LR 396 LA 18										
	Annuntiate in finibus terrae Canite tuba	rev	WA 22										
8	Annuntiate inter gentes gloriam	tr	GR [128] LU 1295	D	3	5	3	5	3	0	2	-2	G
4	Annuntiate populis et dicite	an	AR 241 AM 216 *WA 18 *LA 24	a	-2	0	3	5	3	5	7	5	a
3	Annuntiaverunt inter gentes	an	LR 140	E	-2	3	5	3	5	8	7	8	E
8	Annuntiaverunt opera Dei	an	LR 136 WA 411 LA 506	G	-2	2	5	4	0	4	5	2	G
5	Annuntiavi justitiam in coetu	gr	LU 1623^B	D	3	5	3	5	7	5	7	5	F
8	Annuntiavi justitiam tuam	tr	GR [2^2] LU 1122^4	F	2	4	2	4	2	0	2	4	G
	Ante cujus conspectum Recessit pastor ... nam	rev	WA 125										
1	Ante diem festum Paschae ... cum	an	AR 429 OHS 193 AM 408 LA 186	C	2	9	10	9	7	9	10	9	D
4	Ante diem festum Paschae ... ut	an	WA 213 *GS 97	G	2	-3	-2	-3	-5	0	2	0	E
3	Ante diem festum Paschae ... ut	an	SYG 134	E	3	1	0	1	0	-2	0	-2	E
2	Ante luciferum genitus ... mundo	an	AR 312 LU 463 AM 290 *WA 56 *LA 73	D	2	-2	0	5	7	3	2	-2	D

2 Ante luciferum genitus ... nasci	an	WA 29 *LA 37	E	-2	-4	-2	3	5	1	0	-2	D
1 Ante me non est formatus	an	AR 230 LU 334 *AM 203 *WA 13 *LA 12	D	3	5	3	5	3	5	7	5	D
8 Ante sex dies passionis	an	GS 81	D	3	5	7	3	2	0	3	0	G
8 Ante sex dies solemnis Paschae	an	PM 57 GR 174 *WA 207 *SYG 119 *GB 106^v	D	3	5	7	5	3	2	3	2	G
Ante sex dies solemnitatis	see also	Ante sex dies solemnis										
8 Ante sex dies solemnitatis	an	GS 80	G	-2	-5	-2	0	0	2	0	-2	G
4 Ante torum hujus virginis	an	LR 213 246 *WA 353 *LA 541	G	2	5	7	5	4	5	7	5	a
7 Antequam comedam suspiro	re	LA 282 *WA 172	G	2	0	2	0	-2	2	5	7	G
1 Antequam convenirent	an	AM 191 *AR 220 *WA 8 LA 6	D	-2	3	5	3	7	5	8	7	D
Antequam exires de vulva Ecce constitui	rev	LA 406 WA 322										
2 Antequam te ascenderet	an	WA 233	D	-2	0	3	5	3	2	0	2	D
3 Antiochena polis divini	an	WA 277 (inc illeg)										
2 Antra deserti teneris sub annis	hy	ST 95	D	-2	0	3	2	0	2	0	-2	D
2 Antra deserti teneris sub annis	hy	AM 928A *LR 345	C	2	5	2	4	2	0	2	4	D
4 Anxiatus est in me spiritus meus	an	AR 438 OHS 510 LU 714 AM 438 439 *WA 124 *LA 200	F	-3	-1	0	2	0	-1	0	-3	E
2 Aperi caelos tuos	re	WA 182	C	2	4	2	5	4	5	4	2	D
Aperi mihi soror mea Hortus conclusus	rev	LR 270										
7 Aperi mihi soror mea	an	WA 163	G	7	5	7	10	9	7	9	7	G
7 Aperi nobis festinanter	re	WA 345	F	2	4	2	0	2	4	2	0	G
Aperi nobis velocius Vade Luciane	rev	WA 342										
Aperi os tuum Sancte Martine Christi	rev	LA 485										
Aperiam in parabolis Attendite popule	rev	LA 159 WA 102										
Aperiam in parabolis Portas caeli	ofv	OTT 60 *GB 136^v *SYG 158	a	-2	0	3	5	3	5	3	5	
8 Aperiens Petrus os suum	an	WA 326	F	2	4	2	4	2	0	4	2	G
8 Aperiens Tobias os suum	re	WA 177	G	2	0	2	0	-2	2	5	4	G
Aperiet os suum Ecce homo sine querela	rev	WA 426										
Aperis tu manum tuam Oculi omnium	grv	GR 314 [96] LU 944 GS 59 164 GB 86^v SYG 97	d	2	0	-3	-2	0	-2	-3	0	
3 Aperite illi portas	an	WA 439	G	2	5	2	5	4	2	0	2	E

	Incipit	Type	Sources										
3	Aperite mihi portas justitiae	int	GR 33**	E	-2	3	5	8	7	8	5	8	E
	Aperti sunt oculi caecorum Sanctissimus monachorum	rev	PM 168 LR 371	D	7	5	7	5	3	2	0	3	
1	Apertis thesauris suis	an	AR 313 LU 463 AM 291 WA 56 LA 74	F	4	2	4	2	0	2	-3	4	D
	Apertum est os Zachariae Innuebant patri	rev	LR 354 LA 406 WA 322										
8	Apertum est os Zachariae	an	AR 739 LU 1499 AM 926 *WA 323 LA 408	a	-4	-2	0	2	3	2	0	-2	G
4	Apollinaris martyris	hy	ST 15	C	2	4	5	7	5	4	2	4	E
1	Apostolorum mystica	hy	ST 451	D	7	5	7	9	10	9	7	5	D
8	Apostolorum passio	hy	ST 12	G	-2	-3	-2	0	-2	-5	-7	-8	G
2	Apostolorum passio	hy	ST 42	a	-2	3	2	0	7	5	3	2	a
6	Apostolorum passio	hy	ST 431	F	2	4	2	0	2	4	5	4	F
4	Apostolorum splendido	hy	ST 292	F	-1	-3	-5	-3	0	-1	-3	0	E
8	Apostolorum supparem	hy	ST 13	G	-2	0	2	4	5	4	5	7	G
8	Apostolorum supparem	hy	ST 42	G	-2	0	2	5	4	5	7	5	G
4	Apostolus Petrus respondit	an	WA 327	F	-1	-3	-1	2	4	6	4	2	E
	Apparebit in finem Ecce apparebit	rev	LR 393 LA 13 WA 13										
7	Apparuerunt apostolis dispertitae	re	LR 112 *LA 260 *WA 156	G	2	0	5	4	5	7	4	5	G
	Apparuerunt apostolis dispertitae	alv	SYG 186	C	2	4	5	2	4	2	0	2	
4	Apparuerunt caelestes spiritus	an	AM 1136	G	-2	-5	-3	-2	-3	-2	0	-2	E
2	Apparuit caro suo	re	WA 41	D	-2	0	2	3	0	2	0	-2	D
7	Apparuit caro suo	an	WA 39 *LA 51	G	4	5	7	9	7	9	7	5	G
1	Apparuit Dominus Jesus	re	PM 175	D	-2	0	3	0	-2	0	3	5	D
3	Apparuit iterum sanctus Gamaliel	an	WA 346	G	2	5	4	2	4	2	0	-5	E
	Apparuit nubes obumbrans In splendenti nube	rev	PM 173										
4	Appenderunt mercedem meam	an	AR 426 OHS 189 215 AM 405 WA 114 LA 184	D	2	3	5	2	5	7	3	2	E
	Apprehende arma et scutum Ne derelinquas ... pater	rev	LA 279 WA 169										
	Apprehende arma et scutum Numquid Dominus	rev	LA 285 WA 173										
	Appropiaverunt persequentes		see Appropinquaverunt persequentes										
1	Appropinquabat autem dies	an	AR 419 LU 1100 *AM 397 *WA 110 *LA 174	F	-5	-3	4	5	4	2	4	2	D
3	Appropinquante Jesu	an	SYG 120	E	3	1	5	3	1	0	-2	0	E
	Appropinquaverunt persequentes me Benedictus ... et non tradas	ofv	OTT 48 *GB 104 SYG 116 GS 77	a	-2	0	3	5	7	5	7	5	

2 Apud Dominum gressus hominis	tr	GR 528	D	-2	0	-2	-5	-2	0	-2	0	D
4 Apud Dominum misericordia	an	AR 271 LU 412 AM 246 WA 33 *LA 39	G	2	5	7	5	7	9	7	5	a
4 Apud Dominum propitiatio	an	AR 538³ LU 966 AM 561	G	2	5	7	5	7	9	7	5	a
7 Aqua comburit peccatum	an	WA 59 LA 77 VP 96	G	7	5	4	7	9	5	7	5	G
Aqua cubitis quindecim / Arca ferebatur	rev	WA 77										
Aqua quam ego dedero	see	Aquam quam ego dedero										
7 Aqua sapientiae potavit eos	int	GR 247 OHS 783 LU 789 *GS 119 *SYG 156 GB 133	G	7	9	7	5	7	2	5	9	G
Aquae multae non potuerunt / Prolapso in lacum	rev	LR 276										
5 Aquae multae non potuerunt	gr	GR 625 (10) LU 1690	F	2	0	-3	0	2	-1	0	2	F
5 Aquae multae non potuerunt	an	LR 215	c	2	0	-1	0	-3	0	-1	-5	F
8 Aquam quam ego dedero	an	AR 394 LA 155 WA 100	c	-1	-3	-5	-3	-1	-3	-5	-3	G
4 Aras nefandi numinis	hy	ST 40	a	-2	-5	-7	-2	0	3	0	-2	E
1 Arbor decora fulgida	an	SYG 143	D	3	0	-2	3	5	7	9	10	D
1 Arca ferebatur super aquas	re	WA 77	D	3	0	-2	3	5	7	10	7	D
Archangele Christi per gratiam / Hic est Michael	rev	WA 382										
8 Archangele Christi per gratiam	an	PM 154 WA 383 LA 470	G	-2	-5	-3	-2	0	2	0	-2	G
8 Archangele Michael constitui te	an	AR 856 LU 1660 AM 1059 *WA 383 *LA 472	G	-2	2	5	7	5	4	2	5	G
8 Archangeli Michaelis interventione	re	LA 470 *WA 383	G	-2	0	-7	-5	-2	0	2	4	G
1 Archangeli Michaelis interventione	an	WA 381 LA 473	D	3	0	-2	3	5	3	5	7	D
1 Archangelus Gabriel ait ad Mariam	an	AR 666 LU 1413	C	2	5	4	2	4	2	0	2	D
Archangelus Michael praepositus / paradisi / Hic est Michael	rev	PM 153										
Architectus Deus fundavit	alv	GB 174	D	2	0	2	5	4	5	7	5	
8 Ardens est cor meum	an	AR 466 AM 479 *WA 139	F	2	4	2	0	4	6	7	9	G
Ardens est cor meum	alv	SYG 167	E	3	0	3	5	3	5	7	5	
4 Ardua spes mundi	hy	ST 490	C	2	5	4	2	0	2	4	5	E
7 Argentum et aurum	an	AM 934 *AR 751 *LU 1515 LA 412 WA 328	G	7	4	7	9	7	9	7	5	G
Arguebat Herodem Joannes / Misit Herodes	rev	PM 183 LA 450										

	Incipit		Sources										
1	Arguebat Herodem Joannes	an	AR 829 LU 1620 AM 1027 *WA 361 *LA 450	C	2	5	2	4	5	4	0	5	D
3	Arridebat parvulus occisori	an	WA 43	G	2	0	2	5	4	2	0	2	E
7	Artem fabri fideliter	an	LU 1446	G	4	5	7	5	9	7	5	9	G
2	Ascendant nostrae protinus	hy	ST 42	a	-2	-5	-7	-2	0	3	2	0	a
	Ascendens Christus in altum		see also Ascendens in altum alleluia										
	Ascendens Christus in altum	sr	AR 494 LU 850 AM 505 506 LA 251 WA 150										
	Ascendens Christus in altum Ascendit Deus	rev	LR 103 LA 247 WA 148										
4	Ascendens Christus in altum	re	LR 102	F	-1	0	-3	-1	0	2	4	2	E
	Ascendens Christus in altum	alv	GS 135	C	2	5	2	0	4	5	7	4	
6	Ascendens Christus in altum	inv	LA 252 *WA 150	a	3	5	3	5	3	5	7	5	c
2	Ascendens ergo Deus	re	WA 81	C	2	5	2	0	4	5	7	5	D
	Ascendens in altum alleluia		see also Ascendens Christus in altum										
4	Ascendens in altum alleluia	re	WA 148 *LA 247	F	-1	0	-1	0	2	4	2	-1	E
1	Ascendens Jesus in navim	an	AR 555 LU 1103 *AM 593 *WA 187 *LA 311	D	-2	0	2	3	0	-2	0	2	D
	Ascendens Moyses in montem Moyses famulus	rev	LA 158										
3	Ascendente Jesu in naviculam	an	WA 71	E	-2	3	5	3	5	8	10	8	E
6	Ascendente Jesu in naviculam	an	AR 338 LU 1108 *AM 308 LA 107	c	2	0	2	4	5	4	2	0	c
6	Ascendit autem Joseph a Galilaea	an	AR 688	F	2	4	0	2	0	-1	-3	2	F
6	Ascendit Christus super caelos	an	PM 179 *WA 358	F	2	4	0	2	4	0	2	4	F
	Ascendit Deus in jubilatione	sr	AR 494 LU 846 AM 510 LA 251 WA 149										
	Ascendit Deus in jubilatione Ascendens Christus	rev	LR 102										
	Ascendit Deus in jubilatione Ascendens in altum	rev	WA 148 LA 247										
3 4	Ascendit Deus in jubilatione	re	LR 103 LA 247 *WA 148	F	-3	2	4	0	-1	0	-1	0	E
	Ascendit Deus in jubilatione	alv	GR 286 LU 848 GS 135 *SYG 180 *GB 177	a	-2	0	-2	-5	-4	-2	-4	-2	
1	Ascendit Deus in jubilatione	of	GR 287 LU 849 OTT 75 *GS 136 *SYG 179 GB 177	D	-2	0	2	3	5	7	9	10	D
4	Ascendit Deus in jubilatione	an	AR 875 LR 99 LU 1675 AM 1075 *WA 147 *LA 247	a	-2	0	3	5	3	5	7	5	a

	Incipit		Sources										
	Ascendit fumus aromatum	sr	AR 860 LU 1658 AM 1055 1056 1065										
4	Ascendit fumus aromatum	an	WA 379 *LA 465	b	-4	-2	1	3	1	3	5	3	a
5	Ascendit haec virga Jessea	an	WA 359	a	-2	-4	0	3	5	3	5	3	F
1	Ascendit Joseph a Galilaea	an	LR 302	D	2	3	5	2	5	7	3	2	D
2	Ascendit Joseph a Galilaea	re	LR 311	A	3	5	7	5	8	10	8	7	D
	Ascendit Moyses in montem Moyses famulus	rev	WA 101										
	Ascendo ad patrem meum	sr	AR 495 LU 850										
	Ascendo ad patrem meum	alv	SYG 180	G	4	5	7	9	7	5	7	9	
7	Ascendo ad patrem meum	an	AR 492 LU 845 AM 510 WA 150 LA 251	G	4	5	7	9	12	7	9	7	G
	Aspectus earum et opus Cum aspicerem	rev	WA 374										
4	Asperges me Domine hyssopo	an	GR 4* LU 13	F	-1	-3	-1	2	4	5	4	2	E
7	Asperges me Domine hyssopo	an	GR 1* PM 9 LU 11 *WA 7	G	2	5	4	2	4	5	7	9	G
7	Asperges me Domine hyssopo	an	GR 3* LU 13	G	2	5	4	5	7	9	10	9	G
1	Aspice Domine de sede	re	LA 301 WA 183	D	-2	3	5	7	5	7	5	7	D
1	Aspice Domine quia facta	an	AR.552 LU 996 AM 590 LA 308	D	-2	0	2	3	0	2	0	-2	D
1	Aspice Domine quia facta	re	LA 302 *WA 183	F	-1	-3	-1	0	-1	0	-3	-1	D
8	Aspice in me Domine	an	WA 64 *LA 89	c	2	0	-1	-3	0	-1	-3	-7	G
8	Aspice in me Domine ... et miserere	an	AM 101	c	-1	0	-3	0	-5	-3	-5	-7	G
	Aspice in me et miserere ... secundum Participem me fac	rev	LA 132 WA 88										
	Aspice in oriente et vide Dum esset gens	intv	SYG 173										
6	Aspiciebam in visu noctis	re	LA 3	c	2	0	-1	0	2	0	-1	0	c
7	Aspiciens a longe ecce video	re	PM 18 *LA 2	d	-2	0	-2	0	2	0	-2	0	G
8	Aspiciens in caelum	an	LA 41	G	-2	-5	-3	-2	0	2	0	-2	G
	Aspicientes in auctorem fidei Christo igitur	trv	GR 482	D	-2	0	3	5	7	3	2	5	
7	Assertor aequi non ope regia	hy	ST 399	G	5	2	5	7	5	7	5	7	G
1	Assertor aequi non ope regia	hy	ST 42	D	7	8	7	5	7	9	10	7	D
	Assis nobis pater Ad occasum	rev	WA 251	D	7	10	9	5	7	5	3	5	
	Assiste mater gloriosa Sancta Maria succurre	rev	WA 353										
2	Assumpsit Jesus discipulos	an	AR 380 LU 1085 AM 353 *WA 90 *LA 136	G	4	2	5	4	2	-2	2	4	a

	Title	Type	Sources									
1	Assumpsit Jesus Petrum	an	AR 805 LU 1588	F	-5	-3	4	5	4	2	4	2	D
1	Assumpsit Jesus Petrum	an	AM 998	C	2	9	11	9	7	9	11	9	D
	Assumpta est Maria ... angeli	sr	AR 823 LU 1605 AM 1012 1012^A										
	Assumpta est Maria ... angeli	alv	SYG 216	C	4	5	4	2	0	2	4	0	
	Assumpta est Maria ... angeli	alv	GS 195	F	-1	0	-3	-1	-3	-5	-3	-1	
8	Assumpta est Maria ... angeli	of	GR (32) OTT 167 GB 226	F	2	4	7	4	2	0	2	4	G
7	Assumpta est Maria ... angeli	an	AR 820 875 AM 1013 1076 LU 1605 LA 448 *WA 358	G	4	5	7	9	5	7	4	5	G
	Assumpta est Maria ... angeli Hodie Maria	rev	LR 379	D	7	5	3	2	0	3	7	5	
	Assumpta est Maria ... gaudent	alv	GS 195	F	-1	0	-3	-1	-3	-5	-3	-1	
	Assumpta est Maria ... gaudet	alv	GR 584 (32) LU 1603	C	2	5	4	5	7	5	4	2	
8	Assumpta est virgo Maria	re	LA 446	G	2	0	-3	-2	0	2	0	-3	G
1	Assumptus ex eculeo	an	WA 261	D	-2	0	3	0	2	0	-2	0	D
7	Assumptus ex eculeo	re	WA 258	G	2	0	-2	0	2	0	2	0	G
1	Assunt festa jubilaea	hy	ST 140	a	-2	-4	-5	-4	-2	-7	-5	-4	D
	Astantes cives clamore Stans in aede	rev	WA 251	a	-4	0	3	5	3	7	8	10	
8	Astiterunt justi ante Dominum	an	WA 324	F	2	4	2	0	4	7	9	7	G
1	Astiterunt justi ante Dominum	an	AR 742 LU 1506 AM 929 LA 411	C	2	9	10	9	7	9	10	9	D
	Astiterunt reges terrae Tradiderunt me	rev	WA 123	c	2	5	4	5	4	2	4	2	
8	Astiterunt reges terrae	an	OHS 478 LU 688 *WA 121 *LA 195	G	3	0	-2	0	2	0	-2	0	G
8	Astiterunt reges terrae	re	OHS 616 LU 771 *LA 205	D	3	5	7	5	7	9	7	5	G
	Astitit regina a dextris Ornatam monilibus	rev	PM 259 VP 220 LR 253 LA 445 WA 356										
	Astitit regina a dextris Quam pulchra	rev	LR 224										
2	Astra polorum super ascendit	hy	ST 350	D	-2	0	-2	3	2	0	-2	3	D
	At illa dixit etiam Dixit dominus mulieri	trv	SYG 85 GS 47	D	-2	0	3	5	7	3	2	5	
	At illa intincta tunica Extrahentes Joseph	rev	LA 147										
1	At Jesus conversus	an	AR 574 LU 1077 AM 615 LA 320	D	2	3	5	3	2	0	-2	3	D
8	Athleta Christi Antoninus martyr	hy	ST 55	G	2	0	-3	-2	-5	-3	-5	-7	G
8	Athleta Christi Vincenti	an	WA 261	G	-5	-2	2	-2	0	2	5	7	G

8	Attende caelum et loquar	tr	GR 231 LU 776^U OHS 656 GS 112 *SYG 151 GB 119^v	G	2	4	2	0	2	0	5	7	G
7	Attende Domine ad me	re	OHS 63 (nm) LA 176 *WA 110	a	-4	0	3	2	3	2	0	3	G
	Attende Domine de caelo Obsecro Domine	rev	WA 5										
5	Attende Domine et miserere		AR 158* LU 1871	C	4	7	12	11	7	9	7	12	C
	Attende fili mi sapientiam Praebe fili cor	rev	LA 280 WA 170										
8	Attendite a falsis prophetis	an	AR 558 LU 1104 AM 596	a	-4	-2	0	2	3	2	0	-2	G
1	Attendite a falsis prophetis	an	WA 188 LA 313	C	2	9	11	9	12	9	7	9	D
	Attendite popule meus in legem meam Portas caeli	ofv	OTT 60 GB 136^v SYG 158	G	2	0	2	-2	0	2	0	2	
	Attendite popule meus in legem vestram	alv	GB 253 SYG 243 GS 149	a	3	0	-2	3	5	3	7	5	
	Attendite popule meus legem Accipite jucunditatem	intv	GR 298 LU 890 GS 138 SYG 185 GB 191^v										
	Attendite popule meus legem Dum sanctificatus	intv	GB 93										
	Attendite popule meus legem Eduxit eos	intv	GR 255 LU 800 OHS 816 GS 122 GB 140 SYG 160										
	Attendite popule meus legem Lex veritatis	intv	GR 526 LU 1511										
	Attendite popule meus legem Salus populi ego sum	intv	GR 375 LU 1059 GS 59 163 GB 86 SYG 97										
	Attendite popule meus legem Sitientes venite	intv	GR 149 LU 565 GS 70 GB 96 SYG 108										
	Attendite popule meus legem Spiritus Domini super me	intv	GR 564 LU 1579										
8	Attendite popule meus legem	re	LA 159 WA 102	D	3	5	7	5	7	5	7	9	G
	Attendite universi populi O vos omnes	rev	OHS 610 LU 767 LA 204 WA 125										
7	Attendite universi populi	an	AR 440 OHS 621 LU 776 *AM 446 447 *WA 127 *LA 206	b	3	0	3	5	3	0	3	5	G
	Attollens autem Joseph Iste est frater	rev	LA 150 WA 97										
1	Auctor beate saeculi	hy	AM 1255	D	7	5	7	5	3	2	5	7	D
1	Auctor donorum spiritus	an	WA 292	D	2	0	-2	3	5	3	5	7	D
2	Auctor salutis unicus	hy	ST 386	D	-2	0	2	3	0	3	0	-2	D
2	Audi benigne conditor	hy	ST 381	D	-2	0	2	3	0	3	0	-2	D
2	Audi benigne conditor	hy	ST 283	D	-2	0	3	0	3	0	-2	0	D
2	Audi benigne conditor	hy	ST 32 88 AR 362 LU 539 AM 337	D	-2	0	3	2	3	0	2	0	D

2 Audi benigne conditor	hy	ST 225		D	-2	0	3	2	3	0	3	0	D
4 Audi benigne conditor	hy	ST 185		D	2	3	5	3	2	3	0	2	E
2 Audi benigne conditor	hy	ST 185		C	2	5	4	5	2	4	2	0	D
2 Audi benigne conditor	hy	ST 416		D	3	0	2	0	-2	0	3	5	D
2 Audi benigne creator	hy	ST 18		D	-2	0	3	5	-2	0	-2	0	D
1 Audi Domine hymnum	re	LA 272 WA 167		F	2	4	2	4	2	0	2	4	D
Audi fili mi 　　Fili noli deficere	rev	WA 170											
7 Audi fili mi	re	WA 171		G	2	0	2	0	-2	0	2	5	G
Audi filia 　　Concupivit rex	grv	GR [65] LU 1230		D	7	10	7	5	3	2	5	7	
7 Audi filia ... et concupiscet	gr	GR 583 LU 1602		G	5	4	5	7	5	7	5	4	G
Audi filia ... et obliviscere 　　Propter veritatem	rev	WA 431											
4 Audi filia ... et obliviscere	an	PM 270		G	-2	0	-5	0	-2	0	-2	-3	E
1 Audi filia ... et obliviscere	re	VP 250 WA 433		D	-2	0	3	0	2	0	-2	0	D
Audi filia ... et obliviscere 　　Diffusa est gratia	trv	SYG 49		F	2	4	2	0	2	4	2	4	
Audi filia ... et obliviscere 　　Diffusa est gratia	trv	GS 228		F	2	4	2	4	2	5	2	0	
2 Audi filia ... quia concupivit	tr	GR [62] LU 1227		D	-2	0	-2	-5	-2	0	-2	0	D
Audi filia ... quia concupivit	alv	GB 272^V		F	2	0	5	4	2	4	0	2	
Audi filia ... quia concupivit 　　Propter veritatem	grv	GR 620 (31) LU 1676 GS s GB 222^V SYG 215		F	4	7	9	7	9	7	9	4	
Audi filia ... quia concupivit 　　Specie tua	grv	GB 42^V		F	4	7	9	7	9	7	9	4	
7 Audi filia ... quia concupivit	gr	GR 655 LU 1755 GS 195 t SYG 228 GB 243^V		G	5	4	5	7	5	7	5	4	G
2 Audi Israel praecepta Domini	re	LA 160 WA 102		F	-1	0	-3	-5	-3	0	-3	-5	D
Audi popule meus et loquar 　　In die sollemnitatis	ofv	OTT 61 GB 139^V SYG 159		F	-3	-5	-3	0	-3	0	-3	0	
7 Audiam Domine vocem laudis	re	LA 84 WA 61		G	2	5	4	5	4	2	5	7	G
1 Audiebam sonum alarum	re	WA 375		D	-2	0	3	0	2	-2	0	3	D
4 Audiens Christi confessor	re	WA 240		E	1	-2	1	0	1	-2	1	3	E
5 Audiens ergo Lucianus	an	WA 346		a	-4	0	3	2	0	-2	3	5	F
5 Audiens Joseph quod Archelaus	an	LR 308		a	-4	0	3	2	0	-2	3	5	F
8 Audistis quia dictum est	an	AR 556 LU 1103 AM 594 *LA 311		G	5	2	0	2	0	-2	0	2	G
1 Audit tyrannus anxius	hy	LR 430		C	2	4	7	5	4	2	4	5	D
Auditam fac mihi mane	sr	LA 105											
Audite audientes 　　Sitientes venite	intv	GS 70											

	Audite disciplinam et estote sapientes trv Nunc ergo filii		GR 587³	G	2	4	5	4	5	4	0	2	
8	Audite et intelligite	an	AR 393 LU 1090 AM 367 WA 100 LA 155	G	5	4	0	4	5	2	0	2	G
	Audite haec omnes gentes Postquam surrexit Dominus	anv	GS 97										
	Audite insulae et attendite De ventre matris	inv	SYG 196										
	Audite itaque domus David Confortamini et iam	ofv	OTT 9 *GB 7 SYG 8	F	-1	0	-1	0	2	4	2	4	
	Audite preces Cives apostolorum	rev	WA 414										
3	Audite verbum Domini gentes	re	LA 4 WA 4	E	-2	3	5	7	8	5	3	1	E
8	Audite vocem hymni	hy	ST 498	F	2	0	2	4	6	7	9	11	G
	Auditor Dei Nicodemus Cum scirem ego	rev	WA 343										
3	Auditor legis non surdus	re	WA 282	G	2	5	0	5	2	0	2	5	E
1	Auditu auris andivi	an	LA 287	D	-2	0	3	2	0	2	0	-2	D
8	Auditu auris audivi	re	WA 175	D	3	5	7	5	7	3	0	3	G
	Auditui meo dabis gaudium	alv	GR [142]	C	2	4	5	7	9	7	5	4	
2	Audivi vocem de caelo dicentem	an	WA 435	D	3	2	3	5	0	3	2	3	D
1	Audivi vocem de caelo venientem	re	PM 236 *WA 394	D	-2	0	3	5	3	0	2	3	D
	Audivi vocem dicentem Oravi Deum	ofv	OTT 107 *GB 256ᵛ SYG 250	D	7	10	9	5	7	5	3	0	
	Audivi vocem in caelo angelorum		see Audivi voces ...										
7 8	Audivi vocem in caelo tamquam	re	LA 225 *WA 140	G	2	-2	0	2	0	2	4	5	G
1	Audivi voces in caelo angelorum	re	LA 226 *WA 140	G	2	-2	0	2	0	2	4	5	D
1	Audivi voces occisorum	an	WA 44	C	2	5	7	5	2	5	2	4	D
	Audivit autem vocem Et subito circumfulsit	anv	LA 340										
7	Audivit Dominus et misertus	int	GR 91 GS 33 SYG 68 GB 63ᵛ	G	5	4	5	9	7	5	7	10	G
2	Aufer a me opprobrium	co	GR 370 GS 170 SYG 252 *GB 258	F	2	4	2	0	2	4	2	4	D
	Aufer a plebe tua opprobrium Benedictus es ... in labiis	ofv	GB 60	E	1	0	-2	0	-5	-4	-2	0	
	Auferte deos alienos Praeparate corda	rev	LA 268 WA 166										
1	Auférte ista hinc	an	WA 104	D	-2	0	3	2	0	-2	3	5	D
3	Auferte ista hinc	an	AR 400 LU 1093 *AM 376 LA 163	G	5	2	0	2	5	2	5	4	E
6	Aula Maria Dei casta	an	WA 367	c	2	5	4	2	0	2	0	2	c
4	Aurea luce et decore roseo	hy	ST 394	F	-3	-5	-3	0	-3	-5	0	2	E

4 Aurea luce et decore roseo	hy	ST 95		F	-1	-3	-5	-3	0	-3	-1	0	E
4 Aurea luce et decore roseo	hy	ST 233		F	-1	-3	-5	-3	0	-3	-1	0	E
4 Aurea luce et decore roseo	hy	ST 432		F	-1	-3	-5	-3	0	-3	-1	0	E
4 Aurea luce et decore roseo	hy	ST 191		F	-1	-3	-5	-3	0	-3	0	-1	E
4 Aurea luce et decore roseo	hy	ST 296		F	-1	-3	-5	-3	0	-1	0	-3	E
4 Aurea luce et decore roseo	hy	ST 296 (var)		E	1	0	-2	-4	-2	1	0	1	E
1 Aurea luce et decore roseo	hy	ST 191 *AM 932		D	7	9	5	7	9	10	9	7	D
7 Aures ad nostras deitatis preces	hy	ST 383		c	-1	-3	-1	0	-5	-3	-5	-7	G
8 Aures ad nostras deitatis preces	hy	ST 414		c	-1	-3	-1	0	-1	-3	-5	-7	G
2 Auribus percipe Domine	re	LA 91 *WA 65		D	-2	0	-2	-5	-2	0	-2	0	D
Auribus percipe Domine Salvum fac servum	grv	GR 105 *GS 41 GB 72 SYG 80		D	7	5	7	3	7	8	7	5	
Auribus percipe vester Deus in nomine tuo	intv	GB 91											
8 Auribus percipite	an	WA 65		c	-1	0	-3	-5	-1	-3	-1	0	G
4 Auro virginum	an	WA 239		F	-3	-1	0	-3	-1	-3	-5	-3	E
8 Aurora caelum purpurat	hy	AR 458		G	2	0	2	4	5	2	4	5	G
3 Aurora caelum purpurat	hy	AR 459		E	3	5	3	5	7	8	7	5	E
4 Aurora jam spargit polum	hy	AR 190 AM 80		E	-4	-2	1	0	1	3	1	0	E
1 Aurora jam spargit polum	hy	AM 80		a	2	0	-2	-4	-2	0	-2	-4	D
3 Aurora jam spargit polum	hy	ST 214		D	2	3	5	3	5	3	2	3	E
8 Aurora jam spargit polum	hy	ST 363		D	2	3	5	7	3	5	0	2	G
2 Aurora lucis rutilat	hy	ST 419		G	-2	0	2	0	-2	0	3	2	G
6 Aurora lucis rutilat	hy	ST 229		D	-2	0	2	0	-2	2	-2	0	C
8 Aurora lucis rutilat	hy	ST 387		a	-2	0	2	3	0	2	0	-2	G
8 Aurora lucis rutilat	hy	ST 92		a	-2	0	3	2	0	-2	3	-2	G
2 Aurora lucis rutilat	hy	ST 118		D	-2	3	2	0	-2	0	3	5	D
4 Aurora lucis rutilat	hy	ST 449		G	2	0	-5	-3	-2	0	2	0	E
7 Aurora lucis rutilat	hy	ST 288		G	2	0	-2	2	5	4	2	0	G
8 Aurora lucis rutilat	hy	AM 455 470		G	2	0	2	4	5	2	4	5	G
8 Aurora lucis rutilat	hy	ST 287		G	2	0	5	4	5	7	9	7	G
6 Aurora lucis rutilat	hy	ST 230		F	2	4	5	2	0	4	2	0	F
6 Aurora lucis rutilat	hy	ST 316		C	2	5	7	5	2	4	5	4	C
8 Aurora lucis rutilat	hy	ST 287		G	4	5	7	9	7	4	5	7	G
4 Aurora lucis rutilat	hy	ST 452		E	5	3	1	0	1	3	5	3	E
3 Aurora rubens fugat noctis stellas	hy	ST 332		C	2	4	5	4	2	7	5	7	E
2 Aurora soli praevia	hy	AR 632 VP 69		a	-2	-5	-7	-2	0	3	2	0	a
2 Aurora solis nuntia	hy	LU 1438		a	-2	-5	-7	-2	0	3	2	0	a

8	Aurora surgit aurea	hy	AM 966	G	-5	0	2	0	-3	-2	0	2	G
8	Aurora velut fulgida	hy	ST 398	G	2	0	-2	0	2	4	0	-2	G
5	Austriae decus princeps et patrone	hy	ST 331	F	4	6	7	4	7	9	7	4	F
1	Auxilium meum a Domino	an	AR 100 OHS 224 LU 282 h	D	-2	3	5	7	5	3	5	3	D
4	Ave caeli janua	hy	ST 56	D	2	5	7	5	9	5	7	2	E
	Ave gratia plena Dei genitrix Beata es Maria quae	rev	WA 270										
1	Ave gratia plena Dei genitrix	an	VP 103 SYG 46 *GB 46^v GS 180	F	-1	2	0	-1	-3	-1	0	-3	D
1	Ave gratia plena Dominus tecum	of	GR 443 LU 1379	D	3	5	3	0	-2	3	7	5	D
4	Ave Katherina martyr et regina	hy	ST 297	E	1	0	-2	-4	-2	1	0	3	E
7	Ave Katherina martyr et regina	hy	ST 238	G	7	9	5	9	10	12	10	9	G
8	Ave Maria Dei genitrix intacta	an	PM 247	F	2	4	2	4	2	-3	0	2	G
	Ave Maria gratia plena Beata es Maria quae	rev	WA 357 (270) LA 353										
	Ave Maria gratia plena Beata es virgo ... quae	rev	AR 126* LR 249 PM 260										
	Ave Maria gratia plena O magnum mysterium	rev	LR 61 LU 382										
5	Ave Maria gratia plena	inv	WA 7	F	2	0	2	4	2	0	2	4	F
	Ave Maria gratia plena Beata es virgo ... Dei	rev	LR 258 VP 200 LA 445	F	2	5	4	5	4	2	4	2	
7	Ave Maria gratia plena	inv	LR 435 WA *238 301 LA 376	G	5	4	5	7	5	7	9	7	G
1	Ave Maria gratia plena ... benedicta	an	AR 252 668 872 [139] LU 1416 1679 *AM 228 862 1073 *WA 301 *LA 6 376	F	-5	-3	4	5	4	2	0	2	D
8	Ave Maria gratia plena ... benedicta	tr	GB 55^v	G	-5	-2	0	2	0	2	0	-2	G
8	Ave Maria gratia plena ... benedicta	of	GR 23 [79] OTT 13 LU 355 1268 GS 6 GB 12	F	2	4	2	4	0	4	0	2	G
	Ave Maria gratia plena ... benedicta	alv	GR [77] LU 1265 GS 184	C	2	4	5	2	4	0	2	4	
8	Ave Maria gratia plena ... benedicta	of	GR 404 LU 1318	F	2	4	7	4	2	5	4	2	G
	Ave Maria gratia plena ... et benedictus	sr	AM 703 704 708 1030 1181 1182 LA 355										
2	Ave Maria gratia plena ... et benedictus	tr	GR 459 LU 1412 GS 183 SYG 57	D	-2	0	-2	-5	-2	0	-2	0	D
	Ave Maria gratia plena ... et benedictus	alv	GB 11^v	F	-1	2	0	-1	0	-3	5	7	
1	Ave Maria gratia plena ... sancta Maria	an	AR 123* LU 1861	F	-5	-3	4	5	4	2	0	2	D
7	Ave Maria gratia plena ... spiritus	re	PM 244 LA 3 378	G	2	0	2	0	-2	2	5	7	G

4 Ave maris stella Dei mater alma	hy	ST 175	F	-3	-5	-3	-1	2	4	7	6	E
4 Ave maris stella Dei mater alma	hy	ST 375	F	-3	-5	-3	0	-3	-1	2	7	E
1 Ave maris stella Dei mater alma	hy	ST 133	a	-2	0	-2	-4	-5	-7	-2	0	D
4 Ave maris stella Dei mater alma	hy	ST 91	F	-1	-3	-5	-3	-1	2	4	6	E
4 Ave maris stella Dei mater alma	hy	ST 429 AR [118] LU 1261 AM 704	F	-1	-3	-5	-3	0	-3	-1	2	E
4 Ave maris stella Dei mater alma	hy	ST 281	F	-1	-3	-5	-3	0	-1	2	4	E
4 Ave maris stella Dei mater alma	hy	ST 281	E	1	0	-2	-4	-2	1	0	3	E
7 Ave maris stella Dei mater alma	hy	ST 500	d	2	-2	0	-3	0	-2	-3	-5	G
7 Ave maris stella Dei mater alma	hy	AR [119] LU 1262	G	2	0	-2	-3	-2	0	-2	0	G
7 Ave maris stella Dei mater alma	hy	ST 222	G	2	0	-2	-3	-2	0	2	5	G
7 Ave maris stella Dei mater alma	hy	ST 124 AR [127]	G	2	4	0	2	4	5	4	2	G
5 Ave maris stella Dei mater alma	hy	ST 115	E	3	5	3	8	7	3	5	1	C
4 Ave maris stella Dei mater alma	hy	ST 428	E	5	3	5	8	5	3	1	0	E
1 Ave maris stella Dei mater alma	hy	ST 40	D	7	5	7	9	12	10	9	7	D
1 Ave maris stella Dei mater alma	hy	AR [126] AM 712	D	7	8	7	5	7	5	7	5	D
1 Ave maris stella Dei mater alma	hy	ST 193	D	7	9	5	7	9	10	12	10	D
1 Ave maris stella Dei mater alma	hy	AR [117] PM 288 LU 1259 AM 704	D	7	9	5	7	9	12	10	9	D
6 Ave o theotocos virgo	an	WA 366	c	2	5	4	2	0	2	4	2	c
1 Ave pater Wulstane	an	WA 248	D	2	-2	3	0	3	5	7	3	D
8 Ave praesul alme	hy	ST 401	G	2	0	-2*	0	2	5	2	0	G
8 Ave praesul gloriose	an	WA 424	G	-2	-5	-2	0	2	0	-2	0	G
6 Ave regina caelorum ave	an	AR 66 OHS 174 LU 274 AM 175 *WA 360	c	-2	-3	-2	-5	-3	0	2	4	c
6 Ave regina caelorum ave	an	AR 69[1] OHS 175 LR 47 LU 278 AM 179	F	-1	-3	-5	-3	0	2	0	4	F
1 Ave regina caelorum mater regis	an	PM 270 LU 1864	D	3	0	-2	3	5	7	8	7	D
2 Ave rex gentis Anglorum	an	WA 405	D	3	0	-2	3	5	7	8	7	D
1 Ave rex noster fili David	an	OHS 102 *WA 209 *SYG 118 *GS 85	F	-3	-1	-5	-1	0	2	4	-1	D
Ave rex noster tu solus	**alv**	GR 108	F	-3	-1	-5	-3	-1	0	2	4	
2 Ave sancte rex Edwarde	an	WA 199	D	-2	0	3	5	3	2	0	-2	D
4 Ave senior Stephane	an	WA 37 (inc illeg)										
7 Ave stella matutina peccatorum medicina	an	PM 277	G	4	5	7	9	10	12	10	9	G
7 Ave superne	an	WA 42 (inc illeg)										
6 Ave verum corpus natum		AR 100* LU 1856	F	2	4	0	2	0	5	4	2	F
8 Ave virgo ...	an	WA 360 (inc illeg)	G	2	0	-2	0	-5	-2	0	2	G

Avertantur retrorsum et erubescant Deus in adjutorium	intv	GR 350 LU 1027 GS 51 154 GB 78^v SYG 89										
8 Avertantur retrorsum et erubescant	an	OHS 370 LU 628 *WA 118 *LA 189	c	2	0	2	0	-1	-3	-1	0	G
Avertantur retrorsum et erubescant Domine in auxilium	ofv	OTT 106 GB 80^v SYG 91	F	4	2	0	4	2	0	4	7	
Avertatur obsecro furor Civitatem istam	rev	LA 307 WA 186										
2 Averte Domine faciem	an	WA 82	F	-3	-5	-3	0	-1	-3	-1	-3	D
Averte mala Deus in nomine	intv	GS 64										
Averte oculos meos Deduc me in semitam	rev	LA 240 WA 145										
8 Avertet Dominus captivitatem	an	WA 65 LA 92	G	-2	2	5	4	0	4	5	2	G
8 Avete solitudinis	hy	AM 1119	G	2	0	-2	2	5	4	0	2	G
7 Baptista contremuit	an	VP 96 WA 59 *LA 78	G	7	5	4	7	9	7	5	7	G
8 Baptizat miles regem	an	PM 44 WA 58 *LA 76	G	-2	-5	-2	-3	-5	-7	-5	-2	G
7 Baptizatur Christus	an	WA 59 *LA 77	G	4	5	7	5	9	7	4	7	G
2 Barrabas latro dimittitur	re	WA 122	A	3	5	7	5	7	5	8	7	D
4 Bartholomaee	hy	ST 402	F	-3	-5	-3	0	-3	-5	0	2	E
4 Bartholomaee	hy	ST 241	F	-1	-3	-5	-3	0	-3	-1	0	E
1 Beata Agatha ingressa carcerem	re	PM 137 LA 362 *WA 275	D	2	0	2	0	2	0	2	-2	D
Beata Agathes ingressa carcere	alv	SYG 51	E	-2	0	3	0	1	0	-2	0	
8 Beata Agnes in medio flammarum	an	AM 785 *AR 602 *LU 1338 LA 338 WA 252	G	5	2	0	-2	0	2	0	2	G
7 Beata Caecilia dixit ad Tiburtium	an	WA 407 *LA 489	G	4	5	7	9	7	9	7	5	G
8 Beata Caecilia dixit Tiburtio	re	LA 492 *WA 407	D	3	5	7	5	7	5	7	9	G
Beata civitas Jerusalem O quam gloriosum	rev	VP 84										
7 Beata Dei genitrix Maria cujus	re	LR 62 LU 383 *LA 34 *WA 29	G	2	5	2	4	2	0	2	5	G

8 Beata Dei genitrix Maria virgo	an	AR 923 LU 1754 *AM 714	G	-2	-3	-5	-3	-2	2	0	-2	G
8 Beata Dei genitrix Maria virgo ... alleluia	an	AM 1138	G	-3	-2	-3	-5	-2	0	2	0	G
8 Beata Dei genitris Maria virgo ... ora pro populo	an	AR [130] *WA 361 *LA 449	G	-2	-3	-5	-3	-2	2	0	-2	G
7 Beata Dei genitrix nitor	hy	ST 398	G	2	4	5	4	2	0	5	7	G
1 Beata Dei genitrix virgo	an	AM 36 130 165 749	D	-2	3	5	3	5	7	8	7	D
2 Beata Dei genitrix virgo	an	AR 52 577[23] LU 260	C	2	5	4	2	4	2	0	2	D
Beata es Maria	see also	Beata es virgo										
1 Beata es Maria mater Domini	an	PM 277	C	2	5	2	0	2	4	2	0	D
8 Beata es Maria quae credidisti	an	AR 233 769 [123] LU 339 1538[v] AM 207 709 953 *WA 12 *LA 379	G	5	2	0	2	-2	0	2	0	G
1 Beata es Maria quae Dominum	re	LA 353 *WA 270	D	3	0	-2	3	5	7	5	3	D
7 Beata es N. quae propter Deum	re	LR 230	G	2	0	2	0	-2	0	2	0	G
Beata es quae credidisti Gaude Maria	rev	VP 130	c	2	0	2	5	4	2	7	9	
Beata es virgo	see also	Beata es Maria										
Beata es virgo gloriosa O beata Caecilia	rev	LA 489										
1 Beata es virgo Maria Dei genitrix	an	AR 874 LU 1674 AM 1074	D	-2	0	3	2	-2	2	3	0	D
6 Beata es virgo Maria Dei genitrix	re	LR 258 VP 200 LA 445 WA 357	D	3	5	3	5	3	5	7	5	F
1 Beata es virgo Maria quae Dominum	an	PM 252	D	3	0	-2	0	3	5	3	2	D
1 Beata es virgo Maria quae Dominum	re	AR 126* *LR 249 *PM 260	D	3	0	-2	3	5	7	5	7	D
8 Beata es virgo Maria quae omnium	an	AM 1081 *AR 882[2] *LU 1686	a	-4	-2	0	-2	-4	-2	0	-4	G
8 Beata es virgo Maria quae omnium	of	GR [83] LU 1272 GB 220[v]	F	2	4	7	4	2	0	2	4	G
Beata es virgo Maria quae sub cruce	alv	LU 1476[c]	E	1	0	-2	3	5	8	7	5	
Beata et venerabilis	see also	Benedicta et venerabilis										
Beata et venerabilis Felix namque	ofv	OTT 188	F	2	4	7	4	2	0	2	4	
2 Beata et venerabilis virgo	re	LA 35 *WA 48	D	3	0	-2	0	-2	0	3	2	D
Beata gens cujus est Laudabilis populus	rev	LA 304 WA 184										
1 Beata gens cujus est	gr	GR 366 [91] LU 1048 *SYG 105 *GB 93 GS 67 160 234	D	3	5	3	2	3	7	5	3	D
7 Beata Lucia dixit	an	WA 244	G	7	5	4	5	7	9	7	5	G

2	Beata mater et innupta virgo	an	WA 302 LA 215 449	D	3	0	-2	0	-2	0	3	2	D
2	Beata mater et intacta virgo ... intercede	an	AR [129] AM 713 PM 243	D	3	0	-2	0	-2	0	3	2	D
2	Beata mater et intacta virgo Maria ... intercede	an	LU 1476[H]	D	3	0	-2	0	2	0	-2	0	D
8	Beata mater et intacta virgo ... sentiant	an	AR 881 LU 1681 *AM 1080	G	5	2	0	2	0	7	5	4	G
8	Beatam nimium et Deo	an	WA 389	G	5	2	0	2	0	2	0	2	G
4	Beata nobis gaudia	hy	ST 354	E	-2	0	-4	-2	0	1	0	-2	E
4	Beata nobis gaudia	hy	ST 449	F	-1	-3	-1	-3	-5	-3	-1	2	E
4	Beata nobis gaudia	hy	ST 232	E	1	-2	1	-2	-4	-2	0	-2	E
7	Beata nobis gaudia	hy	ST 122	G	2	0	2	4	5	4	2	0	G
8	Beata nobis gaudia	hy	ST 294	G	2	0	2	5	4	2	4	2	G
3	Beata nobis gaudia	hy	ST 146	D	2	3	5	7	0	3	5	3	E
7	Beata nobis gaudia	hy	ST 258	F	2	4	2	7	6	4	7	4	G
8	Beata nobis gaudia	hy	ST 294	F	2	4	2	7	6	4	7	4	G
1	Beata nobis gaudia	hy	AR 505 LU 876 AM 522 ST 38 94	C	2	9	10	9	7	9	7	5	D
1	Beata nobis gaudia	hy	ST 421	D	3	0	-2	3	5	7	5	10	D
1	Beata nobis gaudia	hy	ST 339	a	3	2	0	-2	0	-2	-4	-2	D
7	Beata nobis gaudia anni	hy	ST 391	G	2	4	5	4	2	0	5	7	G
7	Beata progenies unde Christus	re	PM 262 LR 249 *LA 459 *WA 367	G	2	0	2	0	-2	2	5	7	G
8	Beata quae credidisti	an	LU 1476[A]	G	5	2	0	-2	0	2	0	4	G
	Beata quae credidit quoniam Beata Dei genitrix	rev	LR 62 LU 383 LA 34										
1	Beata vere mater ecclesiae	re	LR 388	D	3	0	-2	0	2	-2	0	2	D
	Beata viscera Mariae Nesciens mater	rev	WA 48										
1	Beata viscera Mariae	co	GR [80] LU 1268 *GB 220[v] GS 195	D	3	2	3	5	2	3	2	0	D
7	Beata viscera Mariae	re	LU 389 *LR 65 LA 33 *WA 29	G	2	4	5	7	5	4	5	7	G
	Beatae de proelio Feliciter virgines	rev	WA 394	D	-2	0	3	2	3	5	3	2	
7	Beatae Gertrudis verba	an	AM 1135	G	4	5	7	5	4	5	7	9	G
	Beatam Aredii animam	gr	SYG 219	a	-5	0	2	0	-2	2	0	-2	[c]
	Beatam me dicent ... quia ancillam Congratulamini mihi	rev	PM 248 LR 248 WA 49										
	Beatam me dicent ... quia ancillam	alv	GR 587[5] LU 1612[4]	C	2	4	5	7	5	7	9	10	
8	Beatam me dicent ... quia ancillam	an	AR 246 773 [125] AM 221 711 957 LU 1263 1542 WA 16 LA 17 *383	G	5	2	0	2	0	-2	0	2	G

	Text		Sources										
6	Beatam me dicent ... quia fecit	co	GR 584 LU 1604	D	3	5	3	7	5	3	5	3	F
8	Beatam me dicent ... quia fecit	re	PM 258 LR 257 LA 444 *WA 356	D	3	5	7	5	7	9	7	5	G
8	Beatam me dicent ... quia fecit	an	AR 585 LU 1313 AM 763	G	5	2	0	2	0	-2	0	2	G
4	Beate pastor Petre	hy	AR 599 752 LU 1516	F	-1	-3	-5	-3	0	-3	-1	0	E
4	Beate Simon	hy	ST 403	F	-3	-5	-3	0	-3	-5	0	2	E
4	Beate Simon	hy	ST 241	F	-1	-3	-5	-3	0	-3	-1	0	E
1	Beati eritis cum vos	an	AM 1121 WA 415 *LA 478	C	2	5	4	2	4	2	0	5	D
7	Beati estis cum maladixerint	re	LR 142	G	2	0	-2	0	2	0	2	0	G
	Beati estis sancti ... meruistis	alv	SYG 222	D	-2	2	5	3	2	-2	0	2	
1	Beati estis sancti ... meruistis	an	AM 877	D	-2	3	2	0	-2	0	3	5	D
1	Beati estis sancti ... meruistis ... ideoque	an	WA 394	D	-2	3	2	0	-2	0	3	5	D
7	Beati estis sancti ... meruistis ... ideoque	re	LR 389 *WA 396	G	2	0	2	0	2	5	4	2	G
	Beati estis sancti ... qui cotidie	alv	SYG 222	G	2	0	2	4	2	4	5	4	
	Beati immaculati in via Ecce lignum crucis	anv	SYG 139										
	Beati immaculati in via Mandatum novum do vobis	anv	SYG 130 GS 96										
	Beati immaculati in via Maria ergo	anv	GS 96										
	Beati immaculati in via Confundantur superbi	cov	SYG 228										
	Beati immaculati in via Feci judicium	cov	SYG 40										
	Beati immaculati in via In salutari tuo	cov	SYG 258										
	Beati immaculati in via Tu mandasti mandata	cov	SYG 98										
	Beati immaculati in via Beatus Martinus obitum	intv	GB 242										
	Beati immaculati in via Cognovi Domine	intv	GR [68] LU 1239 GS t 226 GB 229^V										
	Beati immaculati in via Custodivit anima mea	intv	GR 70**										
	Beati immaculati in via Etenim sederunt principes	intv	GR 36 LU 414 GS 15 GB 21 SYG 21										
	Beati immaculati in via In voluntate tua	intv	GR 380 LU 1066 GS 165 GB 261^V SYG 256										
	Beati immaculati in via Justus es Domine	intv	GR 365 LU 1047 GS 160 GB 256 SYG 250										

	Chant	Type	References	Mode									End
	Beati immaculati in via Loquebar de testimoniis	intv	GR [51]LU 1215 GS 225 GB 42^v SYG 39										
	Beati immaculati in via Me exspectaverunt	intv	GR [55] LU 1220 GS 226 GB 44^v SYG 1										
	Beati immaculati in via Narraverunt mihi	intv	GR 473 LU 1427										
	Beati immaculati in via Omnia quae fecisti	intv	GR 377 LU 1063										
	Beati immaculati in via Prope es tu	intv	GR 11 GS 6 GB 8 SYG 9										
	Beati immaculati in via Confitebor tibi	ofv	OTT 44 *GB 98 SYG 110	D	-2	3	5	7	5	7	5	8	
	Beati immaculati in via Benedictus ... in labiis	ofv	OTT 28 *GB 60 *SYG 62	c	-1	0	2	0	2	0	-3	-1	
4	Beati martyres Christi	re	LA 410 *WA 324	F	-3	0	-1	0	2	0	-1	0	E
8	Beati martyres Christi	an	WA 377 LA 409	G	-2	0	-7	-5	-2	0	2	0	G
1	Beati mundo corde quoniam ipsi	an	WA 414	a	-2	-4	-2	0	3	2	0	-2	D
1	Beati mundo corde quoniam ipsi	co	GR 650 LU 1727	a	-2	0	3	2	0	2	0	-2	D
1	Beati mundo corde quoniam ipsi	co	SYG 223	D	3	0	-2	3	5	7	5	3	D
	Beati omnes qui diligunt te Aperiens Tobias	rev	WA 177										
	Beati omnes qui timent Ecce sic benedicetur	cov	SYG 234										
	Beati omnes qui timent Deus Israel conjungat	intv	GR [121] LU 1288										
	Beati omnes qui timent Gaudeamus ... Joachim et Annae	intv	GR (28)										
2	Beati omnes qui timent	an	AR 139 OHS 354 LU 290 *AM 121 *LA 102	D	3	2	0	2	3	2	0	-2	D
6	Beati omnes qui timent	gr	SYG 234	D	3	5	7	9	7	5	7	5	F
	Beati pacifici beati mundo O quam gloriosum ... gaudent	rev	WA 396										
1	Beati pacifici beati mundo	an	AR [4] LU 1112 AM 623 *WA 412 *LA 511	D	-2	3	5	3	5	7	5	8	D
1	Beati pauperes spiritu quoniam ipsorum	co	GR 24**	D	3	2	3	5	7	5	7	8	D
8	Beati qui audiunt	an	WA 99	a	-4	-2	0	-2	0	-2	0	-2	G
6	Beati qui custodiunt judicium	of	GR 91**	F	2	0	2	4	0	2	0	4	F
	Beati qui custodiunt judicium Confitemini Domino	trv	GR 113 LU 547 GB 75	F	2	4	2	4	2	0	2	0	
	Beati qui custodiunt judicium Confitemini Domino	trv	SYG 86	C	2	4	5	7	5	2	5	7	

	Incipit		Source										
8	Beati qui habitant in domo	an	AR 177 LU 279[Q]	G	5	2	0	2	0	-2	0	2	G
	Beati qui habitant in domo ... in saecula Benedic Domine	rev	LA 548										
	Beati qui habitant in domo ... in saecula	alv	GR 2**	F	-3	2	4	0	-1	0	-3	2	
	Beati qui habitant in domo ... in saecula Unam petii a Domino	grv	GR 60 LU 471	F	4	7	9	11	7	9	7	6	
8	Beati qui habitant in domo ... in saecula	an	LR 236 *WA 429	G	5	2	0	-2	0	2	0	4	G
8	Beati qui lavant stolas	an	AR 764 LU 1529 *AM 949	a	-4	-2	0	-4	-5	-7	-5	-4	G
1	Beati qui persecutionem	an	LR 186 *WA 412	a	-4	-2	0	-2	3	0	2	-2	G
	Beati qui persecutionem	alv	GB 267[V]	D	3	5	3	5	0	-2	3	5	
	Beati quorum remissae sunt Laetamini in Domino	ofv	OTT 140 GB 44 SYG 41	D	-2	3	5	7	5	7	5	8	
	Beati quorum remissae sunt	alv	SYG 241	D	3	2	0	3	0	-2	3	5	
8	Beati quos elegisti	an	WA 412	a	-4	-2	0	1	0	-2	0	-4	G
8	Beati quos elegisti ... clamabunt	an	LA 476	G	5	2	0	-2	0	2	4	2	G
8	Beati quos elegisti ... etenim	an	WA 395	G	5	2	0	-2	0	2	4	2	G
1	Beati servi illi quos cum venerit	co	GR 97**	a	-2	0	3	2	0	2	0	-2	D
6	Beati Stephani aperientes	an	WA 344	c	-1	0	-3	-1	-5	0	2	4	F
	Beati vero Hippolyti Jussit Valerianus	rev	WA 351										
	Beati viri corpus O quantus erat luctus	rev	LA 486 WA 401										
	Beatissimae virginis Mariae Cum jucunditate celebremus	rev	LA 460										
	Beatissimae virginis Mariae Gloriosae virginis	rev	WA 365										
	Beatissimae virginis Mariae Hodie nata est	rev	LA 456										
4	Beatissimae virginis Mariae	re	LA 457 *WA 365	F	-3	0	2	0	-1	-3	-1	-3	E
2	Beatissimae virginis Mariae	an	WA 364	D	-2	0	3	2	0	3	5	3	D
8	Beatissimus Christi martyr	re	WA 351	D	3	5	7	5	7	3	0	3	G
4	Beatissimus Dionysius Christi	re	WA 386	F	-3	0	-1	0	2	0	-1	0	E
3	Beatissimus Stephanus projectus	an	WA 343	G	5	2	0	2	5	2	5	4	E
	Beatorum animae sanctorum Beatus Dionysius Rusticus	rev	WA 388										
1	Beatorum martyrum veneranda	an	WA 379	D	-2	0	3	5	3	2	0	-2	D
1	Beatum canimus Dei apostolum	co	GB 229	D	3	2	3	5	2	3	2	3	D
	Beatus Aigulfus Obviam sacratissimis	rev	LR 370										

	Incipit	Genre	Sources										
8	Beatus Andreas de cruce	re	WA 235	D	3	5	7	5	7	5	7	9	G
2	Beatus Andreas de cruce	re	LA 502	A	3	5	7	5	8	7	8	10	D
8	Beatus Andreas orabat	an	AR 579 LU 1307 AM 755 *LA 504 WA 237	G	5	2	0	2	0	-2	0	2	G
3	Beatus Anselmus saeculi	an	AM 872	E	1	0	-2	3	5	3	5	3	E
1	Beatus Dei athleta	re	WA 259	C	2	0	2	5	7	5	2	5	D
8	Beatus Dionysius caelestis	an	PM 198	G	5	2	0	-2	0	2	0	-2	G
	Beatus Dionysius Rusticus Tres viri isti	rev	WA 389										
1	Beatus Dionysius Rusticus	re	WA 388	D	3	2	0	-2	0	-2	3	5	D
6	Beatus Dunstanus exilio	re	WA 313	c	-1	0	-3	-1	-3	-5	-3	0	c
1	Beatus es care Dei	re	WA 315	D	-2	0	3	2	0	3	5	3	D
	Beatus es Christi martyr Zoe uxor	rev	LA 327										
	Beatus es Christi martyr ... et Beatus es tu et bene	rev	LA 328										
	Beatus es egregie Dei doctor Beatus es vas	rev	LA 345 *WA 265										
	Beatus es et bene tibi Elegit Dominus virum	rev	LA 329										
8	Beatus es et bene tibi	an	PM 128 LA 331	c	-1	0	2	0	-1	-3	-1	0	G
	Beatus es Simon Bar-Jona Quem dicunt	rev	LR 366 LA 419 WA 279										
	Beatus es Simon Bar-Jona	alv	GB 204^V	D	3	5	3	2	0	2	3	2	
6	Beatus es Simon Bar-Jona	re	LR 367 *LA 418 WA 328	D	3	5	3	5	3	5	7	5	F
	Beatus es Simon Petre Tu es Petrus	ofv	OTT 187 SYG 53	C	2	4	7	4	2	0	2	4	
	Beatus es Simon Petre Tu es Petrus	alv	SYG 203	D	3	5	7	5	7	5	7	5	
4	Beatus es tu et bene tibi	re	LA 328	F	-3	0	-1	0	2	0	-1	0	E
4	Beatus es vas electionis	re	LA 345 *WA 265	D	-2	-5	-2	0	-2	2	5	3	E
1	Beatus Gamaliel doctoris	re	WA 342	a	-2	0	-2	-5	-2	0	-2	0	D
1	Beatus Gregorius a diebus	an	WA 289	D	-2	3	5	3	5	7	3	5	D
1	Beatus Gregorius in cathedra	an	AM 832	D	-2	3	5	3	5	7	5	7	D
	Beatus homo qui audit me Nunc ergo filii	trv	GR 587^3 LU 1612^3	G	2	5	4	2	5	2	0	2	
	Beatus homo qui audit me	alv	GR 62	C	2	9	10	9	7	9	5	4	
	Beatus homo qui audit me Ego sapientia	grv	GR 25**	F	4	7	9	11	7	9	7	6	
3	Beatus Hugo piscator Dei	re	PM 149	E	1	0	-2	3	5	3	5	8	E
7 8	Beatus ille servus quem cum venerit	an	AR [74] LU 1196 AM 671 *WA 427 *LA 540	G	2	4	2	0	2	0	7	5	G

No.	Incipit	Type	Sources											
1	Beatus iste sanctus qui confisus	an	LR 191 WA 424 LA 529	C	2	9	10	9	7	9	7	9	D
4	Beatus Laurentius Christi martyr	inv	LR 446 *WA 347	C	2	4	5	4	2	0	2	4	E
2	Beatus Laurentius clamavit	re	LA 438 *WA 349	A	3	5	7	5	8	7	8	5	D
	Beatus Laurentius dixit Gratias ago	anv	WA 349										
	Beatus Laurentius dixit Quo progrederis	anv	WA 347 LA 433										
8	Beatus Laurentius dixit Domine	an	WA 347	G	5	2	0	2	0	-2	2	0	G
7	Beatus Laurentius dixit ego	re	LA 438	d	-3	-2	0	2	0	-3	-2	0	G
2	Beatus Laurentius dixit ego	re	WA 349	D	-2	0	-2	-5	-2	0	3	0	D
8	Beatus Laurentius dixit mea	an	WA 347 *LA 434	G	5	2	0	2	0	-2	2	0	G
	Beatus Laurentius dum in craticula	alv	SYG 217	C	2	4	2	4	5	4	2	4	
8	Beatus Laurentius dum in craticula	an	AR 816 LU 1598 AM 1009 *WA 347 LA 441	G	5	2	0	-2	0	2	0	-2	G
8	Beatus Laurentius orabat ... Domine	an	LA 432	G	5	2	0	2	0	2	0	-2	G
8	Beatus Laurentius orabat ... gratias	an	AR 814 LU 1597 AM 1006 WA 350 LA 437	G	5	2	0	2	0	2	0	-2	G
4	Beatus Laurentius oravit et dixit	re	WA 350	F	-3	0	-1	0	-1	0	2	0	E
2	Beatus Laurentius oravit et dixit	re	LA 440	A	3	5	7	5	8	7	8	5	D
	Beatus Laurentius oravit et dixit	alv	GB 217^{V}	F	4	6	7	9	7	6	4	2	
7	Beatus Martinus dixit Juliano	an	WA 399	d	-3	0	2	0	-3	-2	0	-5	G
8	Beatus Martinus dixit Juliano	an	LA 483	G	5	2	0	-2	0	2	0	4	G
	Beatus Martinus obitum O beatum virum Martinum	rev	WA 400										
3	Beatus Martinus obitum	re	LA 484 *WA 399	F	-3	2	4	2	4	7	6	7	E
7	Beatus Martinus obitum	int	GB 242	G	2	-2	2	0	2	5	7	9	G
1	Beatus Maurus a teneris	an	AM 779	E	-4	-2	5	7	5	3	1	3	D
3	Beatus Maurus patricio	an	AM 778	E	-2	3	5	7	8	7	8	10	E
1	Beatus Nicholaus adhuc	an	WA 242	D	2	0	-2	0	3	2	0	2	D
6	Beatus Nicholaus jam triumpho	re	WA 241	G	5	7	10	9	5	7	5	7	c
8	Beatus Petrus apostolus	an	WA 332 *LA 421	G	5	2	0	-2	0	2	0	5	G
	Beatus Petrus dum penderet	alv	SYG 203	D	2	0	2	0	-2	2	3	5	
8	Beatus populus cujus Dominus	an	AR 203 OHS 42 LU 309	c	-1	-3	-5	-3	-5	-7	-3	0	G
8	Beatus quem elegisti	an	LR 154 *WA 417 *LA 524	a	-4	-2	0	2	3	0	-2	-4	G
	Beatus quem elegisti	alv	GR 519 LU 1479	C	7	5	4	2	4	5	4	2	
2	Beatus qui audit me	co	GR3**	F	-3	-1	0	-1	-5	0	2	0	D
	Beatus qui audit verba Exemplo vitae	rev	LR 291										

No.	Incipit	Type	Source										
	Beatus qui intelligit super egenum Christo confixus sum	intv	GR 479 LU 1433										
	Beatus qui intelligit super egenum Majorem hac dilectionem	intv	GR 553 LU 1559										
	Beatus qui intelligit super egenum Ego dixi Domine miserere mei	grv	GR 311 GS 141 GB 247 SYG 239	F	4	7	9	11	7	6	9	11	
	Beatus qui lingua sua	alv	GR 29**	D	-2	2	0	3	5	2	0	3	
5	Beatus quicumque times	gr	LU 1442	D	3	5	7	5	2	3	5	3	F
3	Beatus servus quem cum venerit	co	GR [45] LU 1203 GS 223 SYG 28 GB 29	a	1	-2	3	5	3	5	7	8	a
	Beatus Sixtus dixit Non ego te desero	anv	LA 433 WA 347										
4	Beatus Stephanus Christi martyr	inv	WA 33	C	2	5	4	5	4	2	0	2	E
1	Beatus Stephanus jugi legis	an	WA 33	D	-2	0	3	2	0	2	0	-2	D
1	Beatus Stephanus levita	an	WA 38 LA 47	D	-2	0	3	2	3	5	3	2	D
	Beatus venter qui Mariam O felix Anna	rev	PM 171										
8	Beatus venter qui te	an	WA 47 *LA 33	c	-1	-3	-5	-7	-5	-3	0	-1	G
3	Beatus Vincentius applicatus	an	WA 258	E	-2	3	5	7	5	3	5	8	E
7	Beatus Vincentius cujus jam	an	WA 258	G	5	4	5	7	9	7	9	12	G
1	Beatus vir Benedictus	an	AM 851 WA 301 (inc illeg) *LA 374	D	2	-2	0	2	3	5	3	2	D
8	Beatus vir cujus est auxilium	tr	GR 450 LU 1394	G	2	4	2	0	2	0	2	0	G
5	Beatus vir cujus est nomen	gr	GR 20**	D	3	5	2	3	0	5	2	3	F
	Beatus vir qui in lege	an	OHS 56 (n m)										
3	Beatus vir qui in lege ... voluntas	an	LR 191 WA 424 *LA 529	E	-2	3	5	8	7	8	10	8	E
1	Beatus vir qui inventus est	re	PM 229 LR 209	D	3	0	-2	3	5	7	5	3	D
	Beatus vir qui metuit Fulgebat in venerando	rev	WA 287										
8	Beatus vir qui metuit	re	LR 165 LA 384 WA 304	D	3	5	7	5	7	3	0	3	G
	Beatus vir qui non abiit Qui meditabitur	cov	SYG 67										
	Beatus vir qui non abiit Miseratio hominis	intv	GR 631 LU 1693										
1	Beatus vir qui suffert tentationem	an	LA 528	D	-2	0	3	2	0	2	0	-2	D
7	Beatus vir qui suffert tentationem	re	LR 160 *WA 418	G	2	0	2	5	4	5	7	5	G
	Beatus vir qui suffert tentationem	alv	GR [43] LU 1202 *GS 207 SYG 218	C	4	7	9	7	4	5	4	2	
	Beatus vir qui timet Dicit Dominus sermones mei	intv	GR 656 LU 1758										

	Incipit		Sources										
	Beatus vir qui timet Dispersit dedit	intv	GR 576 LU 1607 GS 193 GB 216 SYG 212										
	Beatus vir qui timet Vir Dei Benedictus	intv	GB 54										
8	Beatus vir qui timet	tr	GR [8] LU 1442 GS 203 SYG 55 *GB 52^v	G	2	4	2	0	2	0	5	7	G
5	Beatus vir qui timet	gr	GR [11] LU 1136 *GS 206 SYG 51 GB 51	D	3	5	2	3	0	5	2	3	F
4	Beatus vir qui timet	an	WA 63	E	3	5	3	1	3	1	-2	1	E
	Beatus vir qui timet	alv	GR [46] LU 1205 *GS 208 *SYG 44 GB 270	F	4	6	7	9	7	2	5	4	
	Beatus vir sanctus Martinus	alv	GR 652 LU 1747 *GB 242^v	C	4	5	7	9	7	9	11	12	
2	Beatus Wulstanus Domini	re	WA 250	D	-2	0	3	2	3	0	2	-2	D
1	Bellator armis inclitus	hy	ST 43	C	2	4	7	5	4	2	5	4	D
8	Bellator armis inclitus	hy	ST 6	D	3	5	3	7	5	0	3	5	G
8	Bene fac Domine bonis	an	LA 102	c	-1	0	-3	-5	-1	-3	-1	0	G
8	Bene fundata est domus Domini	an	AR [107] LU 1247 AM 698 WA 319 LA 552	c	-1	-3	-5	-3	-1	-3	-5	-8	G
	Bene fundata est domus Domini	alv	GR [73] LU 1252 *GB 174	C	2	5	4	5	7	5	4	2	
5	Bene omnia fecit	an	AR 563 LU 1027 AM 602 WA 189 LA 315	F	4	7	6	4	2	7	9	7	F
	Benedic anima Domino Faciam te in gentem	intv	GR (24)										
5	Benedic anima mea Domino et noli	of	GR 105 OTT 110 *GS 42 169 SYG 80 *GB 72	F	4	7	9	7	9	4	2	4	F
	Benedic anima mea Domino et omnia Benedicite Dominum omnes angeli	intv	GR 607 LU 1653 GS v GB 168										
	Benedic anima mea Domino et omnia Caritas Dei	intv	GR 304 501 LU 900 1472										
8	Benedic anima mea Dominum	an	WA 70 LA 103	c	-1	0	-3	-5	-7	-5	-3	-1	G
	Benedic anima mea Dominum Domine Emitte spiritum	ofv	OTT 77 *GB 184 *SYG 182	F	2	-1	0	-1	-5	-3	0	2	
	Benedic anima mea Dominum et omnia	alv	GR 636	a	-2	1	0	-2	0	-4	-5	-4	
	Benedic anima mea Dominum et omnia Benedicite Dominum	grv	GR 608 LU 1654 GS 197 GB 168	E	3	0	3	5	3	1	-2	0	
8	Benedic Domine domum istam	re	LR 235 LA 548	D	3	5	7	5	7	5	7	9	G
	Benedic domum istam Benedictus es in templo	rev	LR 243										
	Benedicam Dominum in omni tempore	sr	AR 91 AM 136 141 147 152 157 LA 87 WA 163										

	Text	Abbr	Sources										
	Benedicam Dominum in omni tempore Venite, venite	anv	GS 94										
	Benedicam Dominum in omni tempore Gustate et videte	cov	SYG 244										
	Benedicam Dominum in omni tempore Clamaverunt justi	intv	GR 455 GS 210 GB 167^v SYG 172										
	Benedicam Dominum in omni tempore Dum sanctificatus	intv	GR 145 (38) LU 859 GS 66 SYG 104										
	Benedicam Dominum in omni tempore Exclamaverunt ad te	intv	SYG 172										
	Benedicam Dominum in omni tempore Multae tribulationes	intv	GR 515 LU 1507 GS m 212 GB 201 SYG 199										
	Benedicam Dominum in omni tempore Timete Dominum	intv	GR 574 GS 211 GB 215^v SYG 192										
	Benedicam Dominum in omni tempore Venite filii	intv	GR 589 LU 1615										
7	Benedicam Dominum in omni tempore	gr	GR 350 LU 1028 SYG 246 GB 253^v *GS 154	G	2	0	2	5	2	0	2	0	G
	Benedicam Dominum in omni tempore Immittet angelus	ofv	OTT 102 *GB 71 *SYG 79	F	2	7	9	7	9	6	7	4	
5	Benedicam Dominum in omni tempore	re	LA 88 WA 63	F	4	7	4	7	9	7	9	5	F
2	Benedicam Dominum qui mihi tribuit	an	WA 70	D	-2	0	3	2	0	-2	0	3	D
1	Benedicam Dominum qui mihi tribuit	of	GR 116 511 LU 1004 1484 OTT 88 *SYG 87 *GB 76^v GS 49 146	C	2	9	10	9	7	9	12	9	D
4	Benedicam te in vita mea	an	AR 3 (sup 1)	G	2	5	7	5	7	9	7	5	a
7	Benedicam te in vita mea	an	AR 3	G	5	4	5	7	5	4	2	4	G
2	Benedicamus Domino Ia		AR 59* LU 124	D	-5	-2	0	-2	0	3	0	-2	D
	Benedicamus Domino		PM 83	a	-4	0	-2	0	-2	-4	-5	-7	E
	Benedicamus Domino		GR 55* 59* AR 62*	a	-4	0	-2	0	-2	-4	-5	[0]	E
5	Benedicamus Domino IIb		AR 60* LU 125	c	-3	-5	-3	-2	-3	-5	-7	-5	F
8	Benedicamus Domino VIb		AR 62*	G	-2	-3	-2	-5	-2	2	0	-2	G
1	Benedicamus Domino VIa		AR 62*	a	-2	0	-2	-7	-4	-5	-7	-9	D
2	Benedicamus Domino IIIb		AR 61* LU 126	a	-2	0	-2	-4	-5	-7	-2	0	a
2	Benedicamus Domino IIa		AR 60* LU 125	D	-2	0	3	2	3	5	3	0	D
5	Benedicamus Domino Ib		AR 59* LR 44 LU 124	c	-1	-5	-3	-5	-8	-7	-5	10	C
1	Benedicamus Domino V		AR 61* LU 126	a	1	0	-2	0	-7	-4	-2	0	D
8	Benedicamus Domino IIc		AR 60* LU 126	G	2	0	-2	2	5	4	2	0	G
6	Benedicamus Domino VIII		AR 62* LU 127	F	2	0	-1	-3	-5	0	2	4	F
6	Benedicamus Domino XVIIb		GR 57*	F	2	0	2	4	7	5	4	2	F

5 Benedicamus Domino Id		AR 59* LU 125	G	2	0	5	7	5	4	0	2	C
6 Benedicamus Domino Ic		AR 59* LU 125	F	2	4	2	5	4	0	2	0	F
1 Benedicamus Domino IIIa		AR 61*	F	2	4	5	4	2	4	0	-1	D
1 Benedicamus Domino XVIIa		GR 57*	C	2	5	4	2	0	2	5	2	D
1 Benedicamus Domino IV		AR 61* LR 44 LU 126	D	3	5	7	5	3	2	0	3	D
7 Benedicamus Domino		LU 127	G	4	5	7	5	7	9	7	4	G
Benedicamus Domino alleluia		AR 447	G	-3	-2	-3	-5	-7	0	2	0	C
Benedicamus patrem et filium cum	sr	AR 521 LU 909 AM 532 WA 162										
Benedicamus patrem et filium cum Benedicta sit	anv	GR 203										
Benedicamus patrem et filium cum Benedicta sit	intv	GS b SYG 260										
Benedicamus patrem et filium cum	alv	GR [85] LU 1274	a	-2	-4	-5	-9	-5	-2	-4	-5	
8 Benedicamus patrem et filium cum	tr	GB 214^{V}	G	2	4	2	0	2	0	5	7	G
Benedicamus patrem et filium cum ... in	alv	SYG 261	a	-2	0	-2	-5	-2	-4	-2	0	
Benedicamus patrem et filium cum ... laudemus Benedictus sit	ofv	OTT 81 *GB 215 *SYG 262	F	-5	-3	-1	0	-1	2	0	-1	
8 Benedicamus patrem et filium cum ... laudemus	re	LA 477 *WA 160	G	-2	0	-5	-2	0	2	0	-2	G
Benedicamus patrem et filium cum ... laudemus	alv	SYG 261	C	2	5	7	5	4	2	5	4	
6 Benedicamus patrem et filium in	an	WA 82	c	2	4	2	5	4	2	0	2	c
4 Benedicat Dominus corda	an	SYG 134	C	2	4	5	4	5	4	5	4	E
Benedicat Israel Domino Benedictus es in firmamento	trv	GS 44	G	5	4	0	5	7	9	5	2	
2 Benedicat nos Deus	an	WA 103 *LA 162	F	-1	-3	0	-1	0	2	-5	-3	D
1 Benedicat nos Deus ... et metuant	re	WA 158	D	3	5	3	0	3	2	0	-2	D
Benedicat nos Deus ... et metuant Confiteantur tibi	grv	GR [126] LU 1294	F	4	2	7	9	7	9	7	11	
2 Benedicat nos Deus ... filius	tr	SYG 263	D	-2	0	-2	-5	-2	0	-2	0	D
Benedicat nos sancta majestas Benedicat nos Deus	trv	SYG 263	C	2	5	7	5	2	4	5	4	
Benedicat nos sancta trinitas Benedicat nos Deus	trv	SYG 263	F	2	4	2	4	2	0	2	4	
1 Benedicat te hodie Deus	int	SYG 233	D	7	10	9	10	7	5	3	7	D
Benedicat terra Domino Benedictus es in firmamento	trv	GS 44	G	5	4	0	5	7	9	5	4	
Benedicat tibi Dominus ex Sion Ecce sic benedicetur	trv	GR [123] LU 1290	D	3	0	3	7	3	5	3	5	
Benedicat vobis Dominus ex Sion	alv	GR [124] LU 1290	E	1	-4	-2	3	8	5	3	5	

	Benedicens benedicam tibi Dixit angelus ad Jacob	rev	WA 93										
	Benedicens benedicam tibi Locutus est Dominus ad Abram	rev	LR 402 LA 120 WA 80										
6	Benedicens ergo Deus	re	WA 78	c	-2	-3	-2	0	2	0	2	4	c
	Benedicimus Deum caeli	see also	Benedicite Deum caeli										
4	Benedicimus Deum caeli	co	GR 310 LU 912 *SYG 262 *GB 215^v GS c	a	-2	-4	-2	0	-2	-5	-2	-5	E
	Benedicite Anania Azaria Benedictus es in firmamento	trv	GS 44	G	4	5	7	5	9	7	9	5	
	Benedicite aquae quae super Benedictus es in firmamento	trv	GS 44	G	4	5	7	5	9	7	9	7	
	Benedicite Deum caeli	see also	Benedicimus Deum caeli										
	Benedicite Deum caeli Tempus est	rev	WA 177										
5	Benedicite Deum caeli	an	AR 891 LU 1701	a	-2	1	0	-2	0	-4	0	3	F
1	Benedicite Deum caeli	re	PM 113 LA 289 WA 177	G	2	5	4	5	2	0	2	0	D
	Benedicite Deum caeli Benedictus es Dominus qui	grv	SYG 260 GS c *GB 213	F	4	7	6	4	7	6	2	4	
	Benedicite Domino	see also	Benedicite Dominum										
8	Benedicite Domino in opere	an	LR 269	G	5	2	0	-2	0	2	0	2	G
	Benedicite Domino omnes virtutes ejus	alv	GR 612 LU 1664	a	-2	1	0	-2	0	-4	-5	-4	
	Benedicite Domino omnes virtutes ejus Benedicite Dominum	trv	GR [87] LU 1276	C	2	5	7	2	5	7	5	4	
	Benedicite Domino omnia opera ejus Benedicite Dominum	trv	GR [87] LU 1276	C	2	5	7	5	7	5	2	4	
	Benedicite Dominum	see also	Benedicite Domino										
3	Benedicite Dominum omnes angeli	gr	GR 608 LU 1654 *GB 168 *GS 197	F	-5	-3	-1	0	-1	0	-3	0	E
2	Benedicite Dominum omnes angeli	tr	GR [87] LU 1276	D	-2	0	-2	-5	-2	0	-2	0	D
3	Benedicite Dominum omnes angeli	an	LA 476	G	2	5	2	5	0	2	4	5	E
3	Benedicite Dominum omnes angeli	int	GR 607 LU 1653 *GS v *GB 168	G	2	5	4	5	2	7	5	7	E
1	Benedicite Dominum omnes angeli	of	GR 612 LU 1664	C	2	9	10	9	12	9	7	9	D
8	Benedicite Dominum omnes angeli	an	WA 396	G	5	2	0	2	0	2	4	2	G
8	Benedicite Dominum omnes electi	an	AR 899 LU 1729 AM 1103 *WA 397	G	5	2	0	-2	0	2	0	-2	G
7	Benedicite Dominum omnes electi	an	LU 1831	G	5	4	5	7	9	7	9	12	G
	Benedicite Dominum omnes virtutes Laudate Dominum	trv	GR 636	G	2	4	5	4	5	4	0	2	
3	Benedicite Dominum omnis	in	GB 168	G	4	5	2	7	5	7	5	4	E
	Benedicite frigus Benedictus es in firmamento	trv	GS 44	G	5	2	4	0	2	4	0	2	

6 Benedicite gentes Deum	an	WA 66 *LA 93	G	2	0	-2	0	-2	-5	-2	0	F
2 Benedicite gentes Dominum	of	GR 272 OTT 71 LU 832 GS 67 131 SYG 105 GB 93^{v}	A	3	5	7	3	0	3	0	3	D
Benedicite ignis et aestus Benedictus es in firmamento	trv	GS 44	G	5	2	4	0	2	4	0	2	
Benedicite maria et flumina Benedictus es in firmamento	trv	GS 44	G	5	2	4	0	2	4	0	2	
Benedicite nomini ejus Cantate Deo	rev	LA 240 WA 143										
3 Benedicite omnes angeli Domini	co	GR 611 LU 1657 *GB 171 GS 198	E	1	-2	0	3	5	3	1	-2	E
Benedicite omnia opera Sacerdotes Dei	intv	GR [7] LU 1132 GS 220 GB 52 SYG 55										
Benedicite omnia opera Benedictus es in firmamento	trv	GS 44	G	5	2	4	0	2	4	0	2	
Benedicite spiritus et animae Benedictus es in firmamento	trv	GS 44	G	5	2	0	4	0	2	5	4	
Benedicite stellae caeli Benedictus es in firmamento	trv	GS 44	G	5	2	4	0	2	4	0	2	
Benedicite volucres caeli Benedictus es in firmamento	trv	GS 44	G	5	2	4	0	2	4	0	2	
8 Benedico te pater Domini ... quia per apostolum	an	AR 625 LU 1371 AM 808 *WA 276 *LA 363	G	-5	-2	0	2	5	4	2	4	G
8 Benedico te pater Domini ... quia per filium	an	AR 592 604 925 LU 1324 1341 1757 AM 770 786 1141 *WA 255 408 *LA 322 338 494	G	-5	-2	0	2	5	4	2	4	G
Benedicta a filio	see also	Benedicta filia tu										
7 Benedicta a filio tuo	an	WA 358 *LA 448	G	5	4	5	7	5	7	9	7	G
5 Benedicta es tu virgo Maria	gr	GR 401 LU 1317	D	3	7	5	7	5	3	7	8	F
7 Benedicta es tu virgo Maria	an	AR 587 631 LU 1321 1381 AM 764	G	5	4	5	7	9	7	5	9	G
Benedicta es virgo	see also	Benedicta et venerabilis										
4 Benedicta es virgo Maria	gr	GS q	F	-1	0	2	0	-3	-1	-3	0	E
Benedicta et venerabilis	see also Beata et venerabilis and Benedicta es virgo											
Benedicta et venerabilis ... cujus viscera Beata es virgo	rev	WA 357										
5 Benedicta et venerabilis ... cujus viscera	re	PM 261 LR 257	F	2	4	2	4	5	4	2	0	F
4 Benedicta et venerabilis ... cujus viscera	re	LA 447 *WA 271	D	3	0	3	5	3	0	2	0	E
5 Benedicta et venerabilis ... quae sine tactu	co	GR 77**	c	-3	0	2	0	2	0	2	4	F

4	Benedicta et venerabilis ... quae sine tactu	gr	GR [76] LU 1264 GB 220	F	-1	0	2	0	-3	-1	-3	0	E
2	Benedicta et venerabilis ... quae sine tactu	re	PM 249	D	2	3	2	0	-2	0	-2	0	D
6	Benedicta et venerabilis sancta	an	WA 364	a	3	0	2	3	2	0	-2	5	c
	Benedicta filia	see also	Benedicta a filio										
7	Benedicta filia tu a Domino	an	AR 821 882³ LU 1606 1686 AM 1014 1082 LA 448 *WA 358	c	-1	0	2	0	2	4	2	4	G
7	Benedicta gloria Domini	an	LR 238 LA 549 *WA 318	G	2	5	7	5	7	9	10	12	G
6	Benedicta sit creatrix	an	AR 520 LU 908 *AM 538 *WA 162	c	2	0	2	4	5	4	2	4	c
	Benedicta sit sancta trinitas Benedicamus patrem	trv	GB 214ᵛ	G	2	4	5	4	5	4	5	0	
2	Benedicta sit sancta trinitas	an	GR 203	C	2	5	2	0	2	5	4	2	D
8	Benedicta sit sancta trinitas	int	GR 308 *SYG 260 *GB 212ᵛ *GS b	G	5	4	5	2	0	-2	0	2	G
	Benedicta tu in mulieribus Salve sancta parens	intv	GS q										
	Benedicta tu in mulieribus Benedicta et venerabilis	rev	PM 261 LR 257 LA 447 WA 271										
	Benedicta tu in mulieribus Ingressus angelus	rev	WA 301										
	Benedicta tu in mulieribus Sancta et immaculata	rev	AR 130* PM 38 LR 62 247 VP 39 LU 384 AM 1184 LA 34 WA 29										
	Benedicta tu in mulieribus Ave Maria	trv	GR 459 LU 1412 *GS 183 *SYG 57	C	2	5	7	2	7	5	4	5	
4	Benedicta tu in mulieribus	an	AR 221 AM 193 LR 246 375 WA 9 268 *LA 7 444	G	2	5	7	5	7	9	7	5	a
	Benedicta tu inter mulieres Ave Maria	trv	GB 55ᵛ	G	2	4	5	4	2	5	2	0	
	Benedicta tu inter mulieres	alv	SYG 217	F	2	4	7	6	2	4	0	2	
7	Benedicta tu inter mulieres	an	AR 772 LU 1541	G	4	5	7	4	5	7	9	7	G
	Benedicta tu inter mulieres	alv	SYG 216	E	5	7	5	3	5	3	0	1	
	Benedictae tam efficaces Cumque perfusis	rev	LR 295										
	Benedictio Dei in mercedem	alv	GR 452	C	2	9	7	2	4	7	9	4	
8	Benedictio et claritas	an	WA 162	G	-2	-5	-2	0	2	0	2	0	G
1	Benedictio et claritas	re	WA 160	D	3	2	0	-2	0	3	2	3	D
6	Benedictio perituri super me	of	GR 60**	C	2	5	9	7	9	5	2	5	F
	Benedictionem omnium gentium Ecce sacerdos magnus	inv	SYG 226										

	Benedictionem omnium gentium Ecce sacerdos magnus	rev	AR 82* PM 308 LR 194 LU 1841 LA 530 WA 425										
6	Benedictionem omnium gentium	co	GR (26)	D	3	2	3	7	5	7	8	7	F
7	Benedictionem omnium gentium	an	AR 2 (sup 1) AM 979	G	4	5	7	9	7	5	2	4	G
7	Benedictiones patris tui	re	LR 307	G	5	4	5	7	5	7	5	4	G
5	Benedictionis tuae Domine	an	WA 33	a	-4	0	3	2	0	3	5	3	F
tp	Benedictum nomen gloriae	an	AR 302	C	2	5	7	9	10	9	7	5	G
3	Benedictum propheticis condecoremus	an	LR 329	E	-2	3	5	8	7	10	8	7	E
	Benedictus Abraham Deo Revertenti Abraham	rev	WA 80	a	3	2	-2	0	3	2	0	3	
8	Benedictus Dei famulus	an	WA 300	G	4	5	2	0	-2	0	2	0	G
6	Benedictus Deus Israel	an	AM 45 LA 89	F	2	4	0	2	0	2	0	-3	F
8	Benedictus Deus patrum	an	SYG 136	F	-1	0	2	0	2	4	2	7	G
5	Benedictus Deus qui misit	an	AR 866 LU 1665 AM 1068	F	4	7	4	2	7	9	7	9	F
4	Benedictus Dominus Deus Israel	an	AR 75	G	-2	-3	-2	-5	-2	-3	-2	0	E
2	Benedictus Dominus Deus Israel	re	LR 337 *WA 159	D	-2	0	-2	-5	-2	0	3	0	D
7	Benedictus Dominus Deus Israel	gr	GR 64 LU 478 SYG 32 GB 36 GS 20	G	2	4	2	0	2	0	5	7	G
6	Benedictus Dominus Deus meus	an	AM 155 156 *WA 70 *LA 102	F	2	4	0	2	0	-1	-3	0	F
	Benedictus Dominus Deus meus	alv	GR 465	C	2	4	5	7	9	7	5	7	
3	Benedictus Dominus die cotidie	in	SYG 238	G	5	2	0	4	5	4	2	5	E
6	Benedictus Dominus in aeternum	an	WA 69 *LA 100	F	2	4	2	0	2	0	-1	-3	F
	Benedictus Dominus qui creavit Benedixit te Dominus	rev	LA 291 WA 178										
4	Benedictus Dominus quia visitavit	an	WA 64	F	-1	-3	-1	0	2	0	-1	-3	E
	Benedictus Dominus quoniam mirificavit Quoniam respexisti	grv	GR (35)	F	4	2	7	9	7	4	7	9	
6	Benedictus Dominus susceptor	an	AR 203 OHS 41 LU 308	F	2	4	0	2	0	-1	-3	-1	F
	Benedictus es Dei filius	alv	GB 148	C	4	5	4	2	0	2	4	2	
	Benedictus es Domine		see also Benedictus es tu Domine										
	Benedictus es Domine Deus	alv	GB 213	c	4	5	4	2	0	2	4	2	
7	Benedictus es Domine Deus ... gloriosus	hy	GR 16 *SYG 11 *GB 120ᵛ 183 GS 9	G	5	4	5	7	5	7	4	2	G
	Benedictus es Domine Deus ... in saecula	alv	GR 306 309 LU 904 911 *GS c *SYG 260 *GB 213	G	5	4	2	0	2	4	2	0	
	Benedictus es Domine Deus ... superexaltatus	alv	SYG 261	D	-2	0	2	3	5	3	2	0	

8 Benedictus es Domine doce me ... et non tradas	of	GR 165 OTT 48 *SYG 116 GB 104 *GS 77	G	4	7	5	2	4	5	4	7	G
3 Benedictus es Domine doce me ... in labiis	of	GR 83 OTT 28 LU 514 *SYG 62 GB 60 *GS 29	G	4	7	5	2	4	5	4	7	E
Benedictus es Domine in firmamento	sr	AR 522										
Benedictus es Domine in firmamento Benedictio et claritas	rev	WA 160	a	3	2	-2	-4	-2	0	-2	0	
Benedictus es Domine in firmamento Benedictus ... qui intueris	grv	GR 308 LU 910 GB 213 SYG 260	F	4	7	6	4	7	6	2	4	
Benedictus es Domine in firmamento Benedicamus patrem	rev	LA 477 *WA 160	G	5	4	0	2	4	2	4	5	
5 Benedictus es Domine qui intueris	gr	GR 308 LU 910 SYG 260 GB 213 *GS c	D	3	7	5	7	5	3	7	8	F
Benedictus es Domine qui non derelinquis Adonai Domine	rev	LR 424 LA 290 WA 178										
Benedictus es Domine super sceptrum	alv	SYG 261	D	2	3	5	?	3	5	2	0	
3 Benedictus es in firmamento ... gloriosus	hy	SYG 82 GB 9^V 73 193^V 258^V	G	4	7	5	2	0	5	4	7	E
8 Benedictus es in firmamento ... gloriosus	tr	GS 44	G	4	7	5	2	0	5	4	7	G
1 Benedictus es in firmamento ... in saecula	an	AR 342 AM 312 *WA 74 LA 114	F	-1	0	-1	-3	-5	0	2	4	D
1 Benedictus es in templo sancto	re	LR 243	C	2	4	2	9	10	9	7	5	D
Benedictus es qui intueris abyssos Benedictus sit	ofv	OTT 81 GB 215 *SYG 262	G	5	2	0	5	4	5	2	4	
Benedictus es tu Domine	see also Benedictus es Domine											
Benedictus es tu Domine In toto corde	rev	LA 239										
3 Benedictus in dies	an	LR 323	G	2	0	2	5	4	5	2	4	E
Benedictus qui venit in nomine	sr	WA 51										
8 Benedictus qui venit in nomine	of	GR 260 LU 806 OHS 828 OTT 64 GS 124 SYG 161 GB 144	F	2	0	-1	-5	-3	0	2	4	G
Benedictus qui venit in nomine Haec dies	grv	GR 256(241) OHS 817(709) LU 801(778) GS 122(117) SYG 160(152) GB 140(125)	a	3	5	7	5	3	2	3	0	
5 Benedictus qui venit in nomine	gr	GR 31 SYG 15 *GB 15^V GS E	F	4	7	4	7	6	7	9	7	F
5 Benedictus qui venit in nomine	re	LA 37 WA 48	F	4	7	4	7	6	7	9	7	F
Benedictus sit Dei filius	alv	SYG 261	G	4	5	4	2	0	2	4	2	

3	Benedictus sit Deus Pater	of	GR 309 LU 911 OTT 81 GS c SYG 262 *GB 215	D	5	7	10	9	10	12	10	9	E
1	Benedictus sit Dominus	an	WA 251	D	3	2	0	2	0	-2	3	5	D
	Benedictus venit in nomine Hic est dies	rev	LR 370	D	7	5	7	5	3	2	5	7	
8	Benedixerunt eam omnes una voce	of	GR 41**	G	2	0	-2	0	5	2	4	2	G
8	Benediximus vobis in nomine	an	WA 64 LA 90	c	-1	-5	-3	-1	-3	-1	0	-3	G
	Benedixisti Domine terram tuam Dominus dabit benignitatem	cov	SYG 3										
	Benedixisti Domine terram tuam Dicit Dominus ego cogito	intv	GR 386 LU 1074 GS e GB 264 SYG 258										
	Benedixisti Domine terram tuam Gaudete in Domino	intv	GR 6 LU 334 GB 5 SYG 6										
	Benedixisti Domine terram tuam Loquetur Dominus pacem	intv	LU 1492 GR 516 GB 196 GS 212										
	Benedixisti Domine terram tuam Rorate caeli	intv	GR [81] LU 1269										
6	Benedixisti Domine terram tuam	an	WA 68 *LA 98	F	2	4	2	0	2	0	-1	-3	F
	Benedixisti Domine terram tuam Deus tu convertens	ofv	OTT 6 GB 3 SYG 4	G	2	5	7	5	4	7	9	7	
4	Benedixisti Domine terram tuam	of	GR 8 LU 337 OTT 8 GS 5 *SYG 7 *GB 6	E	3	0	3	5	3	1	-2	1	E
	Benedixisti Domine terram tuam Ostende nobis Domine	grv	GR 11 GS 7 GB 8 SYG 9	a	3	5	7	5	3	2	3	0	
7	Benedixisti Domine terram tuam	an	AR 166	G	4	5	7	5	7	5	4	2	G
1	Benedixit te Dominus in virtute	re	LA 291 WA 178	C	2	4	2	9	11	9	7	5	D
7	Benedixit te Dominus in virtute	an	AR 872 LU 1679	G	5	4	5	7	9	7	4	5	G
	Benedixit te Dominus in virtute Tota formosa	grv	GR 60**	D	7	10	7	5	3	2	5	7	
4	Benigne fac Domine	an	AR 191	F	2	0	-1	0	-1	-3	0	-1	E
4	Benigne fac Domine	an	LA 104	D	3	0	2	3	5	2	3	5	E
4	Benigne fac in bona	an	AM 73	F	2	0	-1	-3	0	-1	-3	-1	E
8	Benignitatem fecit Dominus	an	LR 126	G	-2	2	5	4	0	4	5	2	G
	Benjamin et Manasse Qui regis	trv	SYG 11	G	4	2	4	5	7	5	4	0	
5	Bernardus doctor inclitus	hy	ST 45	F	2	4	2	4	5	4	2	0	F
1	Bernardus doctor mellifluus	an	AM 1022	C	2	5	4	2	4	2	0	5	D
7	Bernardus inclitis ortus natalibus	hy	ST 46	G	7	9	7	5	4	5	7	4	G
7	Bethlehem civitas Dei	re	LA 13 *WA 14	G	5	7	9	10	7	5	7	5	G
4	Bethlehem non est minima	an	WA 9	C	2	5	4	2	7	5	7	5	E
	Biduanis ac triduanis Cantantibus organis	rev	LA 489 WA 406										
2	Biduanis ac triduanis	an	WA 406	D	-2	0	3	5	3	2	0	3	D

	Chant	Type	Sources										
	Biduo vivens pendebat Dilexit Andream	rev	LA 503										
1	Biduo vivens pendebat	an	WA 237 *LA 500	F	-1	-3	-5	-3	-1	-3	0	2	D
	Biduo vivens pendebat	alv	SYG 231	a	3	2	0	2	-2	0	-2	-4	
4	Biennio ante mortem siluit	re	LR 284	F	-3	0	-1	2	0	-3	-1	-3	E
	Biennium est enim Dixit Joseph undecim	rev	LA 151 WA 98										
	Biennium est quod	see	Biennium est enim										
4	Bina caelestis	hy	ST 402	F	-3	-5	-3	0	-3	-5	0	2	E
4	Bina caelestis	hy	ST 240	F	-1	-3	-5	-3	0	-3	-1	0	E
	Bonas facite vias Disrumpam vincula	rev	WA 182										
5	Bonitas Domini Dei	of	LU 1444	F	2	0	2	0	2	4	7	4	F
3	Bonorum meorum non indiges	an	AM 21	G	4	5	2	5	4	0	2	0	E
	Bonum certamen certasti O beata Caecilia	rev	WA 408										
	Bonum certamen certavi Reposita est mihi corona	rev	LA 427										
1	Bonum certamen certavi	an	WA 331 LA 422	D	-2	0	2	3	5	3	0	-2	D
2	Bonum certamen certavi	re	LA 427 WA 330	C	2	5	2	0	2	5	7	5	D
	Bonum certamen certavi	alv	SYG 205	F	4	2	-1	0	2	0	2	-3	
	Bonum certamen certavit Maxima pars	rev	LR 285										
6	Bonum doctrinae gratia nomine	hy	ST 311	F	-3	-5	-3	0	2	4	2	4	F
5	Bonum doctrinae gratia nomine	hy	ST 311	F	2	4	2	4	5	4	2	0	F
	Bonum ei fuerat	see	Bonum erat ei										
	Bonum erat ei si natus Amicus meus	rev	OHS 388 LU 643 LA 191										
5	Bonum est confidere in Domino	gr	GR 358 LU 1037 SYG 107 GB 95 *GS 69 157	F	2	0	-1	0	2	4	5	2	F
	Bonum est confiteri Domino Exiit sermo	cov	SYG 25										
	Bonum est confiteri Domino De ventre matris	intv	GR 523 LU 1499 GS 1 GB 198										
	Bonum est confiteri Domino In medio ecclesiae	intv	GR [38] LU 1190 GB 24 SYG 24										
	Bonum est confiteri Domino Justus ut palma	intv	GR [45] LU 1204 GB 197 SYG 195 GS 205										
	Bonum est confiteri Domino Loquebar de testimoniis	intv	GR 591 LU 1618										
2	Bonum est confiteri Domino	tr	GR 497	D	-2	0	-2	-5	-2	0	-2	0	D
8	Bonum est confiteri Domino	an	AM 67 68 *WA 69 *LA 101	c	-1	-3	-5	-3	-5	-3	-7	-5	G

#	Title		Sources										
5	Bonum est confiteri Domino	gr	GR 360 LU 1041 *SYG 92 *GB 81 GS 53 *158	F	2	0	-3	0	2	-1	0	2	F
8	Bonum est confiteri Domino	off	GR 76 LU 501 OTT 26 *SYG 59 *GB 57 *GS 25	F	4	2	-3	2	4	7	4	2	G
	Bonum est confiteri Domino / Justus ut palma	ofv	OTT 150 GB 25^v	F	4	5	4	2	4	5	4	0	
7	Bonum est confiteri Domino alleluia	re	LA 240 *WA 144	a	3	5	3	5	3	2	5	8	G
4	Bonum est Domine tibi confiteri	an	WA 283	C	2	5	4	2	4	5	7	5	E
8	Bonum est sperare in Domino	an	AR 396 AM 372 WA 103 *LA 161	F	2	4	2	-1	0	2	4	0	G
	Bonum est sperare in Domino / Bonum est confidere	grv	GR 358 LU 1037 GS 69 157 GB 95 SYG 107	F	4	7	9	7	9	7	9	4	
2	Bonum mihi Domine	re	LA 142 WA 93	D	-2	0	-2	-5	-2	0	-2	0	D
	Bonus est Dominus omnibus / Desiderium cordis	rev	LR 296	F	2	5	4	5	4	2	4	2	
	Bracchia peccatorum conterentur	an	OHS 236 (n m)										
8	Brachia peccatorum conterentur	co	GR 467 LU 1421	F	2	4	?	4	7	6	4	7	G
	Butirum et mel comedet / Ecce virgo concipiet	cov	SYG 9										
	Cadent a latere tuo mille / Qui habitat	trv	GR 95 LU 533 GS 35 GB 65 SYG 73	F	2	4	2	4	2	0	2	0	
1	Caecilia famula tua	an	WA 407	D	-2	3	5	7	8	7	5	3	D
3	Caecilia famula tua	an	AR 925 LU 1757 *AM 1140 LA 494	E	-2	3	5	8	7	5	3	5	E
3	Caecilia me misit	an	LA 491	E	-2	3	5	8	5	8	7	3	E
3	Caecilia me misit	re	LA 491 WA 406	E	-2	3	5	8	7	5	3	5	E
7	Caecilia me misit	an	WA 406	G	4	5	7	5	7	9	7	4	G
	Caecilia valedicens fratribus / Dum aurora finem	rev	LA 493 WA 408										
8	Caecilia virgo almachum	an	WA 405 *LA 488	G	-2	-5	-3	-2	0	2	0	-2	G
3	Caeciliam intra cubiculum	re	LA 491 *WA 407	G	5	2	0	5	7	5	4	2	E
	Caeco illuminato / Beatissimus Christi	rev	WA 351										

#	Incipit	Type	Sources		1	2	3	4	5	6	7	8	
1	Caecus magis ac magis	an	AR 357 LU 516 AM 330 WA 83 *LA 125	D	2	3	5	2	3	2	0	3	D
8	Caecus sedebat secus	re	LR 401 *LA 123 *WA 83	G	2	0	-2	2	5	4	5	7	G
7	Caecus sedebat secus	an	WA 81 *LA 125	G	4	5	7	5	9	7	9	7	G
1	Caeleste beneficium introivit	an	WA 366	D	-2	3	5	3	5	7	3	5	D
1	Caeleste beneficium introivit	an	PM 171	D	3	0	-2	3	5	3	5	7	D
1	Caeleste beneficium introivit	re	WA 366	D	3	0	-2	3	5	7	5	3	D
8	Caelestis agni nuptias	hy	AR 729 LU 1491	G	2	4	5	4	2	0	2	-2	G
2	Caelestis aulae nuntius	hy	AR 873 LU 1672 AM 1074	a	-2	-5	-7	-2	0	3	2	0	a
1	Caelestis urbs Jerusalem	hy	AR [104] LU 1248	C	2	5	2	0	5	7	10	7	D
7	Caelestium contemplator	re	WA 313	G	2	0	2	0	-2	0	-2	0	G
8	Caelestium minister donorum	re	WA 294	F	2	4	2	4	2	0	4	7	G
	Caeli aperti sunt Hodie in Jordane	rev	WA 53										
	Caeli aperti sunt In columbae specie	rev	PM 43 LR 71 LA 68 WA 68										
5	Caeli aperti sunt	an	WA 54 LA 76	c	-1	-3	0	-1	-3	-5	0	2	F
2	Caeli caelorum laudate	an	AM 56 WA 65 *LA 95	F	-1	-3	0	-1	-3	-5	-3	-1	D
5	Caeli cives applaudite	hy	ST 351	a	-2	0	3	0	-2	0	-2	-5	C
6	Caeli cives applaudite	hy	ST 325	F	2	4	0	5	4	2	4	0	F
1	Caeli Deus sanctissime	hy	ST 363 AM 148	F	2	4	0	2	0	-1	2	0	D
1	Caeli Deus sanctissime	hy	AR 142	F	2	4	2	0	-1	2	-1	0	D
8	Caeli Deus sanctissime	hy	AM 148	D	3	5	3	7	5	0	3	5	G
2	Caeli Deus sanctissime	hy	ST 214	D	3	5	7	3	5	3	5	2	D
	Caeli enarrant gloriam Dei Ab occultis meis	cov	SYG 103										
	Caeli enarrant gloriam Dei Dicit Dominus Petro	intv	GR 530 GS o GB 202 SYG 201										
	Caeli enarrant gloriam Dei Dominus secus mare Galilaeae	intv	GR 390 GS g GB 245 SYG 231										
	Caeli enarrant gloriam Dei Lex Domini	intv	GR 122 GS 53 GB 81 SYG 91										
	Caeli enarrant gloriam Dei Meditatio cordis	intv	GR 148 GS 69 GB 95 SYG 107										
	Caeli enarrant gloriam Dei Rorate caeli	intv	GR 21 LU 353 GS 183 GB 6^v SYG 8										
	Caeli enarrant gloriam Dei	alv	GB 267	E	3	0	-2	3	5	7	5	3	
	Caeli enarrant gloriam Dei A summo caelo	grv	GR 13 LU 343 GS 8 SYG 10 *GB 8^v	a	3	5	7	5	3	2	3	0	

	Incipit		Sources										
	Caeli enarrant gloriam Dei In omnem terram	grv	GR 629 LU 1486 GS x GB 202^v	a	3	5	7	5	3	2	3	0	
	Caeli enarrant gloriam Dei In omnem terram	ofv	OTT 130 SYG 54 GB 236	E	3	7	5	7	5	3	5	3	
	Caeli enarrant gloriam Dei	alv	SYG 239	G	5	4	5	7	9	5	4	5	
1	Caeli enarrant gloriam Dei annuntiant	an	LR 289	D	7	8	7	5	7	5	3	2	D
1	Caeli enarrant gloriam Dei ... quia	re	WA 410	D	-2	0	-2	0	2	3	5	3	D
8	Caeli laetentur sidera	hy	ST 401	G	2	0	-2	0	2	5	7	5	G
	Caelicus ordo sacram reveretur Virginitas caelum	rev	AR 132* VP 203	D	7	10	9	5	3	2	5	7	D
1	Caelitum Joseph decus	hy	AR 690 LU 1879 AM 888 *LR 302	a	-2	0	-2	-4	-7	-9	-2	-4	D
2	Caelorum regi psallite	hy	ST 15	D	-2	0	3	5	0	-2	0	-2	D
4	Caelum terra pontus aethra	hy	ST 465	G	2	4	0	-3	-2	-3	-5	-7	E
1	Caesar dixit ad Hippolytum	an	WA 352	a	-2	0	-2	-4	0	3	0	-2	D
2	Caeteri tantum cecinere vatum	hy	ST 393	D	-2	0	2	3	0	3	0	-2	D
	Calciatus caligis Beatus Gamaliel	rev	WA 342										
2	Calicem salutaris ... et nomen	an	AR 436 OHS 477 (nm) *AM 429 430 *WA 121 LA 194	D	2	3	0	-2	0	3	2	-2	D
3	Calicem salutaris ... et sacrificabo	an	AR 526 LU 956 *AM 544	E	-2	3	5	8	7	8	10	8	E
5	Caligaverunt oculi mei	re	OHS 508 LU 712 *LA 203 *WA 123	a	-4	0	3	5	3	2	3	0	F
1	Calix benedictionis	re	LR 132	D	2	0	-2	3	2	0	2	0	D
4	Calix benedictionis	of	GR 541 LU 1535	D	3	5	3	0	-2	0	-2	3	E
	Calix tuus inebrians Calix benedictionis	rev	LR 132										
1	Candida virginitas paradisi	re	PM 264 VP 40	D	-2	0	3	5	3	2	0	2	D
1	Candidato martyrum choro	an	PM 196	D	-2	0	3	5	3	5	7	5	D
2	Candidi facti sunt Nazaraei	re	PM 220 LR 172 *LA 387 WA 306	C	2	5	2	0	2	5	4	5	D
	Candidiores nive Candidi facti	rev	PM 220 LR 172										
	Candidiores nive Qui sunt isti qui ut nubes	rev	WA 414	D	7	5	7	5	3	5	7	9	D
4	Candor est lucis aeternae et	an	AR 630 LU 1380	E	3	1	0	-2	-4	-2	-4	-2	E
	Candor est lucis aeternae speculum	alv	GR 572 LU 1586	G	5	4	2	4	0	2	0	-2	
1	Canite tuba in Sion quia prope	an	AR 250 LU 356 *AM 226 *WA 24 *LA 21	F	-5	-3	4	5	4	2	0	2	D
1	Canite tuba in Sion vocate	re	LR 396 *LA 18 WA 22	F	-5	-3	4	5	4	2	0	2	D

Mode	Incipit	Genre	Sources										
	Cantabant sancti canticum	alv	SYG 26	a	-2	0	2	-2	0	-2	-4	-2	
1	Cantabant sancti canticum	re	LA 58 WA 45	C	2	9	11	9	7	5	7	9	D
8	Cantabant sancti canticum	an	WA 46 *LA 61	G	5	2	-2	0	4	5	7	5	G
	Cantabimus et psallemus Exaltare Domine	rev	LA 246 WA 147										
2	Cantabo Domino qui bona tribuit	co	GR 323 LU 963 GS 143 *SYG 240 *GB 248	F	2	5	2	5	4	5	7	5	a
2	Cantabo Domino qui bona tribuit	an	AM 18 *LA 99	D	3	2	3	2	0	3	2	0	D
8	Cantabo Domino qui bona tribuit	an	WA 68	G	5	4	0	2	4	5	4	2	G
1	Cantantibus organis Caecilia Domino	an	AR 924 LU 1756 AM 1140 *WA 408 LA 493	D	3	2	3	5	3	2	0	2	D
	Cantantibus organis Caecilia virgo	alv	SYG 228	C	2	4	2	4	2	0	2	0	
8	Cantantibus organis Caecilia virgo	re	LA 489 WA 406	D	3	5	7	5	7	5	3	5	G
2	Cantate Deo alleluia	re	LA 240 *WA 143	D	3	2	3	5	3	7	5	7	D
2	Cantate Domino alleluia	co	GR 273 LU 833 SYG 169 GB 152^v GS 131	a	3	2	3	5	3	2	3	2	a
	Cantate Domino benedicite nomen Confessio et pulchritudo	ofv	OTT 166	D	5	7	9	7	5	10	7	3	
	Cantate Domino benedicite nomen Laetentur caeli	ofv	OTT 15 GB 15 SYG 15	D	5	7	9	7	5	10	7	3	
6	Cantate Domino canticum	an	WA 67	F	2	4	2	0	2	0	-3	0	F
6	Cantate Domino canticum ... alleluia	int	GR 268 LU 826 *SYG 167 *GB 149^v GS 129	D	3	2	3	5	3	5	3	7	F
	Cantate Domino canticum ... cantate Confessio et pulchritudo	intv	GR 578 LU 1593 GS 40 194 GB 70^v SYG 79										
	Cantate Domino canticum ... cantate In sermonibus	intv	GR 622^1 LU 1681^1										
	Cantate Domino canticum ... cantate Venite benedicti	intv	GR 250 OHS 795 LU 792 GS 120 GB 135 SYG 157										
	Cantate Domino canticum ... cantate In ecclesiis	rev	WA 143										
	Cantate Domino canticum ... cantate Exsultabunt sancti	ofv	OTT 143 GB 195 SYG 191	D	5	7	5	7	10	7	5	3	
	Cantate Domino canticum ... cantate Confessio et pulchritudo	ofv	OTT 166	D	5	7	9	7	5	10	7	3	
	Cantate Domino canticum ... cantate Laetentur caeli	ofv	OTT 15 GB 15 SYG 15	D	5	7	9	7	5	10	7	3	
	Cantate Domino canticum ... laus Exsultabunt sancti	grv	GR 646 GS 214 GB 210 SYG 205	a	3	5	7	5	3	2	3	0	
7	Cantate Domino canticum ... laus	an	AR 230 AM 202 WA 13 *LA 5	G	4	5	7	9	7	9	5	2	G

	Text		Sources									
	Cantate Domino canticum ... quia Cantemus Domino	intv	GR 38**									
	Cantate Domino canticum ... quia Ecce virgo concipiet	intv	GR 622^6 LU 1683									
	Cantate Domino canticum ... quia Puer natus	intv	GR 33 LU 408 GS G SYG 18									
	Cantate Domino canticum ... quia Sciens Jesus	intv	GR 53**									
	Cantate Domino canticum ... quia Signum magnum	intv	GR 582 LU 1601									
	Cantate Domino canticum ... quia Victricem manum	intv	GR 252 LU 796 OHS 805 GS 121 GB 137									
	Cantate Domino canticum ... quia	alv	GR 364 LU 1045 *SYG 247	C	2	9	7	10	9	10	7	5	
	Cantate Domino canticum ... quia	alv	GB 150	D	3	0	-2	0	3	5	3	7	
7	Cantate Domino canticum ... quia	an	LR 294	G	4	5	7	9	7	9	5	2	G
	Cantate Domine canticum ... quia	alv	SYG 248	D	7	5	3	5	3	2	0	-2	F
2	Cantate Domino et benedicite	an	AR 106 *WA 69 *LA 101	D	3	2	3	2	0	3	2	3	D
	Cantate Domino psalmum dicite Confirma hoc	ofv	OTT 79 *GB 189^V SYG 183	D	3	5	3	2	3	-2	0	3	
	Cantate ei canticum novum Gaudete justi	rev	LR 174										
	Cantate ei canticum novum Sacerdotes Dei	rev	WA 429										
	Cantate ei canticum novum Sumite psalterium	rev	PM 192										
ir	Cantemus Domino gloriose	an	AM 61 63	F	4	5	2	0	2	4	[0	0]	a
8	Cantemus Domino gloriose enim honorificatus	re	LA 157 *WA 101	G	2	-2	0	2	0	2	0	2	G
8	Cantemus Domino gloriose enim honorificatus	tr	GR 229 LU 776^R OHS 652 SYG 150 GB 119 GS 111	G	2	4	2	0	2	0	5	7	G
5	Cantemus Domino gloriose enim magnificatus	int	GR 38**	F	4	2	4	0	4	7	4	7	F
8	Capillus de capite vestro	of	GR (22)	D	3	5	7	5	7	5	3	5	G
8	Captabunt in animam justi	an	OHS 503 LU 708 WA 123 *LA 199	G	5	4	0	4	5	2	0	2	G
	Caput circuitus eorum Eripe me	trv	GR 208 LU 725 OHS 534 GS 99 GB 116^V SYG 137	F	2	4	2	4	2	0	2	0	
7	Caput draconis salvator	an	WA 59 *LA 78 *VP 96	G	7	5	4	7	9	5	7	0	G
6	Caput tuum ut Carmelus	an	AM 971 *AR 787	F	2	0	2	4	5	2	0	2	**F**
	Caritas benigna est Sanctus Benedictus dilectum	rev	LR 277										

No.	Incipit	Type	Sources		1	2	3	4	5	6	7	8	
1	Caritas Dei diffusa ... inhabitantem	an	AR 515 AM 531 *PM 90	D	-2	3	5	3	5	7	5	2	D
	Caritas Dei diffusa ... inhabitantem	alv	SYG 187	F	2	5	2	0	4	0	2	5	
3	Caritas Dei diffusa ... inhabitantem	int	GR 304 501 LU 900 1472 *SYG 187 *GS a *GB 193	G	5	2	4	2	0	2	4	2	E
7	Caritas Dei diffusa ... spiritum	an	LA 267	d	-3	0	2	0	-2	0	-3	-2	G
	Caritas Dei diffusa ... spiritum	alv	GB 194	G	2	4	5	4	2	0	2	0	
7	Caritas est summum bonum	an	SYG 132	G	2	4	5	4	2	4	7	5	G
7	Caritas pater est	an	WA 159	G	5	4	5	7	9	5	4	5	G
	Caritatis gratia repletus Ecce jam coram te	rev	PM 31 VP 79	a	-2	-4	-2	0	-4	-5	-7	-4	D
6	Carminibus hymnidicis	hy	ST 149	F	2	4	5	4	2	4	2	0	F
2	Carnales viriliter edomuit	an	WA 289	D	-2	0	-2	0	3	2	0	3	D
	Carnifices vero urgentes Strinxerunt corporis	alv	LA 436 WA 348										
	Carnifices vero urgentes Strinxerunt corporis	rev	LA 437 WA 348										
	Caro et sanguis non revelavit Ego pro te	rev	LR 365										
4	Caro et sanguis non revelavit	an	WA 281	b	-4	-2	1	3	1	3	5	3	a
7	Caro mea requiescit	an	OHS 593 LU 753 *WA 125 LA 201	d	-3	0	2	3	0	-3	-2	-5	G
7	Caro mea vere est cibus	an	AR 4 (sup 2)	d	-3	0	2	3	0	-3	-2	-5	G
4	Caro mea vere est cibus ... qui	co	LU 1623^E	D	2	3	-2	2	0	3	5	7	E
	Caro mea vere est cibus ... qui	alv	GR 314 [96] LU 944	G	5	4	2	4	0	2	0	-2	G
7	Caro mea vere est cibus ... qui	an	LR 130	G	7	5	4	5	7	9	7	5	G
8	Casta Columba nidificans	an	AM 1135	a	-4	-2	0	-2	0	-2	-4	-2	G
	Casta generatio in perpetuum	alv	GR 100**	C	2	4	2	4	7	9	4	5	
	Caste viventes apostolus Quid cruciaris	rev	WA 246										
	Castra verterunt exterorum Sancti per fidem	rev	LR 180										
	Catervatim ruunt populi Ex ejus tumba	rev	PM 118 VP 61 *WA 241										
	Causa salutis erant spinae Naufragantis carnis	rev	WA 249										
1	Celebremus ... apostoli quia	an	WA 267 (inc illeg)	C	2	5	4	2	0	2	5	4	D
8	Celebremus conversionem beati Pauli	an	LA 346	G	-5	-2	0	2	0	-2	2	5	G
1	Celebremus conversionem beati Pauli	re	LA 345 *WA 266	C	2	5	7	9	7	5	2	5	D
1	Celebremus diem istum	re	WA 248	C	2	4	5	4	2	0	5	4	D
1	Celebremus solemniter	re	WA 282	C	2	4	5	2	4	0	2	0	D

	Celsa omnipotentis In columbae specie	trv	GB 54[v]	G	5	7	9	5	0	5	7	9	
1	Centum quadraginta	re	LA 60 WA 45	D	-2	0	3	5	3	5	0	2	D
	Cernentibus discipulis elevatus	alv	GB 178[v]	D	3	0	-2	0	3	5	3	7	
	Cernere divinum lumen gaudete Solem justitiae	rev	AR 128* PM 185 VP 211 WA 366	D	7	5	3	2	0	3	7	5	
8	Certamen magnum habuerunt	re	LR 185 *LA 518	G	2	5	4	2	0	2	0	2	G
	Cherubim quoque et Seraphim Te sanctum Dominum	rev	AR 196* PM 109 VP 216 WA 382	D	7	5	7	5	3	2	0	5	
8	Chorus angelorum	an	WA 8	G	5	2	0	-2	0	2	0	4	G
4	Chorus novae Jerusalem	hy	ST 36	E	1	3	1	0	-2	0	-2	-4	E
3	Chorus novae Jerusalem	hy	ST 230	E	1	3	1	0	-2	0	1	-2	E
4	Chorus novae Jerusalem	hy	ST 289	E	1	3	1	0	-2	1	0	-2	E
2	Christe caelorum habitator alme	hy	ST 423	F	2	0	2	4	2	0	2	4	D
3	Christe caelorum habitator alme	hy	ST 406	G	2	4	2	0	5	0	2	4	E
3	Christe caelorum habitator alme	hy	ST 277	C	2	5	7	5	4	2	0	4	E
1	Christe cunctorum dominator alme	hy	ST 14	c	-5	-3	0	2	0	2	0	4	a
8	Christe cunctorum dominator alme	hy	ST 45	a	-4	-2	0	-2	-4	0	3	0	G
2	Christe cunctorum dominator alme	hy	ST 107	D	-2	0	3	2	0	2	0	-2	D
4	Christe cunctorum dominator alme	hy	ST 44	E	-2	0	3	5	3	5	3	1	E
6	Christe cunctorum dominator alme	hy	ST 423	c	2	0	-1	0	-3	-5	0	2	c
4	Christe cunctorum dominator alme	hy	ST 406	D	2	3	5	7	5	3	2	0	E
1	Christe cunctorum dominator alme	hy	ST 159	D	3	0	-2	3	5	7	8	7	D
1 2	Christe Deus misericordiarum	an	VP 117	D	-2	-5	-2	0	2	0	-2	0	D
3	Christe Deus plebem tuam	int	SYG 230	F	-3	0	-1	0	2	4	0	-5	E
	Christe fili Dei vivi	sr	AR 19 20 21 LU 229 230										
1	Christe pater misericordiarum	an	SYG 69	D	-2	-5	-2	0	2	0	-2	0	D
8	Christe patris altissimi	hy	ST 373	G	-5	-2	0	2	0	-2	0	5	G
2	Christe qui lux es et dies	hy	ST 5	E	-2	-4	-2	0	1	0	-2	1	D
2	Christe qui lux es et dies	hy	ST 176	D	2	0	-2	0	2	3	0	3	D
2	Christe qui lux es et dies	hy	ST 382	D	2	0	-2	0	2	3	2	0	D
2	Christe qui lux es et dies	hy	VP 29	D	3	0	-2	0	2	3	0	-2	D
2	Christe qui lux es et dies	hy	ST 29 89	D	3	0	-2	0	2	3	0	3	D
2	Christe qui lux es et dies	hy	ST 210 254 270	D	3	0	-2	0	2	3	2	0	D
4	Christe qui virtus sator et vocaris	hy	ST 369	G	2	4	2	0	5	0	2	4	E
8	Christe redemptor omnium conserva	hy	LR 380 AM 1100	G	2	0	-2	2	5	4	0	2	G
7	Christe redemptor omnium conserva	hy	ST 400	F	2	4	6	7	6	4	2	4	G
1	Christe redemptor omnium conserva	hy	ST 237	C	2	4	7	5	4	5	2	0	D

8	Christe redemptor omnium conserva	hy	ST 98	G	2	5	2	0	-2	-3	-5	-2	G
8	Christe redemptor omnium ex patre	hy	ST 81	G	-2	-3	-5	-2	2	0	-2	0	G
3	Christe redemptor omnium ex patre	hy	ST 177	G	-2	2	5	4	2	0	2	4	E
3	Christe redemptor omnium ex patre	hy	ST 117	E	-2	3	5	8	7	5	3	5	E
8	Christe redemptor omnium ex patre	hy	ST 410	G	2	0	-2	0	2	4	0	-2	G
6	Christe redemptor omnium ex patre	hy	ST 366	c	2	4	5	4	2	4	5	7	c
1	Christe redemptor omnium ex patre	hy	AM 238	C	2	4	7	4	2	5	4	2	D
7	Christe redemptor omnium ex patre	hy	ST 274	F	2	4	7	5	2	5	4	2	G
1	Christe redemptor omnium ex patre	hy	LR 54	C	2	4	7	5	4	2	4	5	D
1	Christe redemptor omnium ex patre	hy	ST 218	C	2	4	7	5	4	5	2	0	D
8	Christe redemptor omnium ex patre	hy	ST 81	G	2	5	2	0	-2	-3	-5	-2	G
2	Christe redemptor omnium ex patre	hy	ST 318	C	2	5	4	2	4	5	4	2	D
8	Christe redemptor omnium ex patre	hy	ST 177	G	4	2	5	4	2	5	4	2	G
4	Christe salvator pietatis auctor	hy	ST 239	E	-2	0	3	5	3	1	0	-2	E
2	Christe sanctorum decus angelorum	hy	ST 119	D	-2	-3	-2	0	2	0	-2	-3	D
1	Christe sanctorum decus angelorum	hy	AR 659 857 889 LU 1409 1702	a	-2	0	-2	-4	-5	-4	-2	-5	D
1	Christe sanctorum decus angelorum	hy	AM 1061	a	-2	0	-2	-4	-5	-2	-5	-4	D
7	Christe sanctorum decus angelorum	hy	ST 57	a	-2	0	3	2	0	-2	3	5	G
2	Christe sanctorum decus angelorum	hy	ST 97	D	-2	0	3	2	0	2	0	-2	D
4	Christe sanctorum decus angelorum	hy	ST 454	F	-1	-3	-5	-3	-1	-3	-1	0	E
4	Christe sanctorum decus angelorum	hy	ST 316	E	1	0	-2	-4	-2	0	1	0	E
8	Christe sanctorum decus angelorum	hy	ST 237	G	2	0	-3	-2	0	2	0	-2	G
6	Christe sanctorum decus angelorum	hy	ST 429	c	2	0	-1	0	-3	-5	0	2	c
4	Christe sanctorum decus angelorum	hy	ST 399	G	2	4	2	0	5	0	2	4	E
2	Christe sanctorum decus angelorum	hy	ST 160	C	2	4	2	5	0	2	0	2	D
8	Christe sanctorum decus atque virtus	hy	ST 427	G	2	0	-2	2	5	4	2	4	G
3	Christe sanctorum decus atque virtus	hy	ST 369	G	2	4	2	0	5	0	2	4	E
1	Christe sanctorum decus atque virtus	hy	ST 395	a	5	7	5	3	5	7	3	5	a
4	Christe supreme dominator alme	hy	ST 300	C	2	5	7	5	4	2	0	4	E
1	Christi factus sum ego	of	GR 622[5] LU 1681[3]	D	-2	0	2	3	5	8	5	3	D
2	Christi fortis hic athleta	an	WA 295	C	2	4	2	0	2	4	5	4	D
2	Christi mater dilectissima	re	VP 268 WA 303	D	-2	0	-2	-5	-2	0	-2	0	D
2	Christi miles pretiosus	hy	ST 84	a	-2	-4	-2	0	-7	-4	-2	-5	D
1	Christi miles pretiosus	re	WA 259	D	-2	0	3	2	0	-2	3	5	D
	Christi virgo dilectissima		see Christi mater dilectissima										
1	Christi virgo nec terrore	an	WA 254 *LA 86 331	F	2	-1	0	-3	0	-1	-3	-5	D

	Incipit		Source										
2	Christianissimus Francorum rex	re	LR 283	D	-2	0	2	3	5	2	3	0	D
4	Christo caelorum agmina	hy	ST 301	D	2	3	5	7	5	3	2	0	E
2	Christo caelorum agmina	hy	ST 151	D	3	2	0	-2	0	3	2	3	D
4	Christo confixus sum cruci	int	GR 479 LU 1433	F	-3	0	-1	0	-1	0	2	4	E
	Christo confixus sum cruci	alv	GR 427 LU 1354^V	C	2	4	5	7	5	4	2	5	
	Christo cotidie sedulum In isto loco	rev	LA 330										
4	Christo cotidie sedulum	re	LA 328	F	-3	0	-1	0	2	0	-1	0	E
7	Christo cotidie sedulum	an	LA 324	G	5	4	5	7	9	7	9	7	G
8	Christo datus est principatus	an	PM 45 OHS 831 WA 57 *LA 77	G	-2	-5	-2	0	2	0	2	0	G
2	Christo igitur passo in carne	tr	GR 482	D	-2	0	-2	-5	-2	0	-2	0	D
	Christo stella coruscans O regem caeli	rev	WA 30										
7	Christum Dei filium qui putari	inv	LR 301	G	5	4	5	7	5	7	9	7	G
4	Christum Dei filium qui suo nos	inv	LR 441	C	2	4	2	5	4	2	0	2	E
4	Christum in cujus pace	inv	LR 451	C	2	4	5	4	2	5	4	2	E
4	Christum natum qui beatum	inv	LR 428 *LA 40	D	3	0	3	2	3	5	3	0	E
4	Christum pro nobis passum	inv	LR 333	C	2	4	5	4	2	5	4	2	E
4	Christum regem adoremus	inv	AR 102* LR 119 LU 918 VP 6	C	2	4	2	5	4	2	0	2	E
4	Christum regem crucifixum	inv	LR 437	C	2	4	5	4	2	5	4	2	E
6	Christum regem crucifixum	inv	LR 437	D	3	5	3	5	7	5	3	5	F
7	Christum rogemus et patrem	hy	ST 42	G	-2	2	0	2	4	5	4	2	G
6	Christus apparuit nobis	inv	WA 57	F	2	0	2	4	0	2	4	2	F
4	Christus apparuit nobis	inv	LR 68 WA 53	D	2	3	5	7	5	7	5	7	E
7	Christus circumdedit me	an	WA 253 LA 334	d	-3	0	2	0	-2	0	-3	-2	G
1	Christus Dei filius	an	LU 1446	D	2	3	5	2	3	5	3	2	D
	Christus Deus noster In patre manet	rev	WA 50										
	Christus dilexit nos et lavit	sr	AR 768 LU 1536 AM 950										
7	Christus Dominus fabri	an	LU 1437	b	1	3	5	3	5	3	1	3	G
8	Christus est vita veniens in orbem	hy	ST 411	F	2	4	6	4	2	0	4	2	G
	Christus factus est pro nobis Agnus Dei	rev	WA 126										
5	Christus factus est pro nobis	an	AR 434 OHS 410 LU 659 AM 420	F	2	0	2	0	2	4	0	-1	F
5	Christus factus est pro nobis	gr	GR 196 OHS 444 LU 669 GS v 94 235 SYG 129 GB 115	F	2	0	2	0	2	4	0	-1	F
2	Christus infans non despexit	an	WA 43	D	3	2	0	-2	0	-2	0	3	D

4	Christus Jesus splendor Patris	an	AR 804 LU 1584 *AM 997	C	2	0	2	5	2	4	5	7	E
4	Christus lux indeficiens	hy	ST 47	F	-1	-3	-1	2	-1	-3	0	-1	E
8	Christus me misit	an	WA 235 *LA 498	G	5	2	0	-2	0	2	0	4	G
	Christus mortuus est propter delicta	alv	GS 127	D	3	2	3	0	-2	0	-2	3	
4	Christus natus est nobis	inv	LU 368 LR 54 LA 31 WA 27	D	2	3	5	7	5	7	5	7	E
	Christus passus est pro nobis	alv	GR 481	D	2	0	-2	2	3	5	3	2	
4	Christus pro nobis humiliavit	int	SYG 128	D	3	2	3	5	3	0	3	2	E
	Christus resurgens a mortuis		see Christus resurgens ex mortuis										
	Christus resurgens ex mortuis	alv	GR 269 LU 827 *SYG 165 *GB 135^V GS 126	D	-2	0	3	5	3	2	0	3	
4	Christus resurgens ex mortuis	re	OHS 822	E	1	-2	1	3	0	1	3	5	E
	Christus resurgens ex mortuis	alv	SYG 168	G	2	0	5	4	2	4	2	4	
2	Christus resurgens ex mortuis	re	AR 164* PM 66 VP 141 *WA 223	C	2	4	2	5	4	2	5	9	D
1 2	Christus resurgens ex mortuis	an	WA 133 *SYG 147	C	2	4	2	5	4	2	9	7	D
8	Christus resurgens ex mortuis	co	GR 252 OHS 799 LU 795 *SYG 158 *GS 121 *GB 137	G	5	4	5	2	5	7	4	2	G
8	Christus semel oblatus est	co	GR 541 LU 1535	F	4	2	4	-1	0	2	6	4	G
3	Christus unam pro peccatis	of	GR [103] LU 1283^D	G	2	5	4	5	4	7	5	4	E
2	Cibavit eos ex adipe frumenti	int	GR [95] SYG 184 LU 1282 GB 191	A	3	5	3	5	8	5	3	5	D
2	Cibavit eos ex adipe frumenti ... alleluia	int	GR 297 313 LU 887 943 GS 138	A	3	5	3	5	8	5	3	5	D
	Cibavit illos ex adipe frumenti	sr	AR 534 LU 955 AM 546										
	Cibavit illum Dominus pane Stola jucunditatis	rev	LR 156 LA 524 WA 417										
1	Cibavit illum Dominus pane	co	GR 83**	D	3	2	3	7	5	3	5	3	D
	Cibavit illum Dominus pane Misit me vivens	rev	AR 116* LR 131 LU 938	G	5	4	2	5	7	5	2	0	
7	Cibavit illum Dominus pane	re	LA 54	G	5	7	9	10	5	7	4	5	G
	Cibavit illum pane		see also Cibavit illum Dominus pane										
2	Cibavit illum pane vitae	re	WA 41 426	A	3	5	8	7	8	10	8	7	D
8	Cibavit nos Dominus	an	LR 125 LU 935	G	-2	-5	-2	-3	-2	2	0	-2	G
	Cilicio Caecilia membra Virgo gloriosa	rev	LA 490 WA 406										
8	Cilicio Caecilia membra	re	LA 491 WA 406	D	3	5	7	5	7	5	7	5	G
8	Cilicio Caecilia membra	an	WA 406 *LA 488	G	5	2	0	2	0	-2	0	2	G
1	Cinctus ergo fide	an	WA 385	D	-2	3	5	3	5	7	5	3	D

	Incipit	Type	Sources										
6	Circuibo et immolabo	co	GR 336 LU 1009 *SYG 243 GB 250^v *GS 147	c	-5	-2	2	0	4	0	2	0	c
1 2	Circumdantes circumdederunt me	an	AR 422 OHS 66 AM 400 *WA 113 LA 181	F	-1	-3	-1	0	2	4	2	-1	D
7	Circumdate Scholasticam	an	LR 290	b	1	3	1	0	1	5	3	1	G
5	Circumdederunt me gemitus mortis	int	GR 73 LU 497 SYG 58 *GB 56 *GS 24	F	4	2	4	0	4	7	4	7	F
2	Circumdederunt me viri mendaces	re	PM 52 OHS 63 (nm) 303 (nm) LA 183 WA 113	D	-2	0	-2	-5	-2	0	5	7	D
7	Circumduxit eam et docuit	co	GR 618 LU 1671	G	2	0	5	4	5	7	5	2	G
	Circumfulsit eum lux Saule Saule	anv	WA 262										
	Cito euntes dicite Maria Magdalene	rev	LA 209										
7	Cito euntes dicite	an	WA 129 *137 *LA 216	G	4	5	7	9	7	5	2	7	G
	Cives apostolorum et domestici	alv	GB 268	C	2	4	5	2	0	4	5	7	
7	Cives apostolorum et domestici	re	WA 414	G	2	5	4	2	4	0	2	0	G
1	Cives caelestis patriae	hy	ST 65	F	2	0	2	5	4	5	4	2	D
	Civitas Jerusalem noli flere Confortate manus	rev	LA 4										
1	Civitas Jerusalem noli flere	re	PM 24 *LA 8 WA 10	a	3	-2	0	-2	-4	-2	0	3	D
2	Civitatem istam tu circumda	re	LA 307 *WA 186	A	3	5	7	8	7	8	10	5	D
6	Clama in fortitudine	re	LR 394 LA 23 *WA 17	F	5	2	4	2	0	-3	0	2	F
1	Clama ne cesses	an	LA 126	a	-2	-4	-2	-7	-4	-5	-7	-9	D
1	Clamabat autem mulier	an	WA 94 *LA 142	C	2	0	2	5	4	2	4	2	D
8	Clamabat Eliseus ad Eliam	an	LA 275	G	5	2	0	2	0	2	0	-2	G
2	Clamant clamant clamant	an	PM 36 VP 85	F	-1	-3	0	-1	-3	-5	-3	-1	D
2	Clamant clamant clamant	an	WA 44	C	2	4	0	2	4	5	4	2	D
	Clamantes et dicentes advenisti Libera me Domine de viis	rev	AR [173]LU 1798 PM 317 *LA 556 WA 438	a	-2	0	-2	-4	-5	-2	0	1	
	Clamaverunt justi et Dominus Inseparabilis fides	anv	LA 427										
7	Clamaverunt justi et Dominus	gr	GR [29] LU 1170 *GS 213 SYG 188 *GB 194	G	-2	0	-2	0	2	0	2	4	G
2	Clamaverunt justi et Dominus	int	GR 455 SYG 172 GB 167^v *GS 210	D	-2	2	0	3	5	7	3	0	D
7	Clamaverunt justi et Dominus	an	LR 135 *WA 411 LA 505	c	-1	0	2	0	2	4	2	0	G
7	Clamavi et Dominus	an	AR 100 OHS 223 LU 281	b	3	0	3	5	3	1	3	1	G

2	Clamavi et exaudivit	an	LA 93	a	-2	-5	-4	-2	-4	-5	-7	-9	D
ir	Clamavi et exaudivit	an	AM 111	a	-2	-4	-2	0	1	-2	1	0	a
	Clamavi in toto corde meo	sr	AR 42 LU 247										
8	Clamavit populus ad regem	an	PM 143	G	5	2	0	2	0	-2	0	2	G
	Clamor filiorum Israel Locutus est Dominus ad Moysen	rev	LR 411										
1	Clamor inquit Dominus	re	WA 81	D	3	5	2	3	0	-2	0	3	D
1	Clamor meus ad te	an	WA 70 LA 103	a	-2	0	-2	-5	-4	-2	-5	-4	D
8	Clamor meus Domine	an	AR 198 LU 279^S	c	-3	2	0	2	0	-1	-5	-3	G
	Clamor meus in conspectu ejus Populum humilem	ofv	OTT 93 GB 95^V SYG 107	c	-3	0	-3	-5	0	4	2	0	
2	Clara diei gaudia modulizet ecclesia	hy	ST 108	D	2	-2	0	3	5	3	0	-2	D
	Clara quippe voce Qui cum audissent	rev	WA 240	c	2	0	-1	-3	-1	-3	0	2	
1	Clarifica me pater	an	AR 420 427 OHS 192 LU 1101 AM 398 406 *WA 110 *LA 175	D	-2	3	5	3	7	8	7	5	D
3	Claris conjubila Gallia laudibus	hy	PM 338 LR 427	D	2	3	5	7	5	7	10	12	E
4	Claris psallendo vocibus	hy	ST 304	E	-2	-4	-2	1	3	1	0	-2	E
8	Clarissimis cotidie viris	an	LA 324	G	5	2	0	2	0	2	0	-2	G
8	Clarissimis viris Marcelliano	re	LA 327	G	-2	0	-7	-5	-2	0	-2	0	G
3	Claro paschali gaudio	hy	AM 634	E	1	3	1	0	-2	0	-2	-4	E
7	Clarum decus jejunii	hy	ST 187	G	2	4	0	2	5	4	2	4	G
2	Clarum decus jejunii	hy	ST 226 278	C	2	4	5	7	5	4	2	0	D
2	Clarum decus jejunii	hy	ST 380	C	2	5	7	5	4	2	0	2	D
3	Claudus quidam cum vidisset	an	LA 412	G	2	0	2	4	5	4	2	0	E
8	Claudus quidam cum vidisset	an	WA 340	G	2	5	4	2	0	4	2	0	G
4	Claves pater possedisti	an	WA 313	c	2	5	4	2	4	7	9	7	E
2	Clementissime Christi confessor	an	LA 537	D	-5	-2	0	2	0	-2	0	-2	D
3	Clementissime Domine qui pro nostra	an	LA 559	G	2	5	4	2	0	2	4	5	E
	Coarctabatur enim Substrato cilicio	rev	LR 287										
1	Coena facta dixit	an	WA 121	F	-1	-3	-1	-3	-1	-3	-1	-3	D
2	Coena facta sciens Dominus	an	SYG 133	F	2	0	-1	-5	-3	0	2	0	D
1	Coenantibus autem accepit Jesus	an	AR 437 *AM 434 *LA 195	D	-2	3	5	3	5	7	5	7	D
	Coenantibus autem illis accepit Jesus	an	OHS 477 (nm)										
5	Coenantibus illis accepit Jesus	re	AR 115* LR 127 LU 931	F	4	2	7	9	7	6	4	2	F
1	Coeperunt omnes turbae	an	OHS 98 LU 585 *LA 184 *SYG 118 GB 106^V	C	2	5	2	0	2	0	2	5	D

7	Coepit Hippolytus tristis	re	WA 352	G	2	0	2	0	2	0	2	5	G
5	Cogitationes cordis ejus	int	GR 324 [111] LU 970	F	4	7	9	7	9	7	6	2	F
8	Cogitaverunt autem principes	re	WA 112 GS 83	G	2	0	-2	2	5	7	5	7	G
8	Cogitaverunt impii et locuti sunt	an	AHS 384 LU 639 *WA 118 *LA 190	c	-1	2	0	2	-3	-7	-5	-3	G
3	Cognoscetur Dominus ab Aegypto	of	GR 7**	G	4	7	5	2	4	5	4	7	E
	Cognoscetur Dominus judicia / Sperent in te	ofv	OTT 85 *GB 100 *SYG 112	G	2	0	4	5	4	5	4	7	
	Cognoverunt discipuli Dominum	alv	GR 264 LU 817	E	1	0	-2	3	5	8	7	5	
	Cognoverunt Dominum alleluia	sr	WA 146										
6	Cognoverunt Dominum alleluia	an	AR 478 *AM 492	F	-1	2	4	-1	0	-3	-5	0	F
1	Cognoverunt omnes a Dan	an	AR 538^{14} LU 980 AM 571 WA 164 *LA 273	D	2	3	5	3	2	0	3	5	D
3	Cognovi Domine quia aequitas	int	GR [68] LU 1239 GB 229^V GS 226	E	1	-2	3	0	3	5	10	8	E
	Cognovi Domine quia aequitas / Gressus meos	ofv	OTT 39 *GB 88^V *SYG 99	D	5	0	5	7	5	3	5	0	
3	Cognovimus Domine quia peccavimus	an	SYG 65	G	5	2	4	2	0	2	4	5	E
3	Cognovit autem pater quia illa hora	an	AR 571 LU 1066 *AM 612 WA 191 LA 319	G	5	2	0	2	5	2	4	5	E
8	Cognovit eum Dominus	an	LR 197	G	2	0	-2	0	2	0	2	0	G
3	Collaudabunt multi ... ejus	an	WA 428 *LA 539	G	5	2	0	2	5	2	5	4	E
8	Collaudabunt multi ... sanctorum	an	WA 373	G	2	5	4	2	4	2	0	2	G
8	Collaudate regem	an	WA 149	F	2	0	4	7	9	7	4	6	G
	Collegerunt pontifices / Seniores populi	rev	OHS 398 LU 651 IA 193										
2	Collegerunt pontifices	re	GR 166 *GB 105^V *GS 84	D	-5	-7	-5	-3	-2	0	-2	0	D
2	Collegerunt pontifices	an	WA 210 *SYG 117	F	-5	-3	0	2	0	2	5	7	G
1	Colligite primum zizania	an	AR 339 LU 494 AM 309 LA 107	C	2	9	10	9	12	9	7	9	D
	Collocavit ante paradisum / Ecce Adam	rev	WA 74										
	Collocet eos Dominus	see	Collocet eum Dominus										
8	Collocet eum Dominus	an	AR [10] LU 1114 AM 626 WA 415 LA 421 512	c	-1	-3	-5	-3	-1	-3	-5	-3	G
1	Columna es immobilis	an	AR 593 AM 771 *WA 247 *LA 322	D	2	3	0	2	3	0	3	7	D
2	Comedetis carnes et saturabimini	re	LR 123 LU 927	D	-2	0	2	3	2	0	2	3	D
8	Comedi favum cum melle	an	WA 355 *LA 458	G	5	4	2	0	2	0	-2	-3	G
	Comedi favum meum	see	Comedi favum cum ...										

	Incipit		Sources										
8	Comedite pinguia et bibite	co	GR 370 *SYG 251 GB 258 GS 169	D	3	7	5	7	5	7	5	3	G
4	Commendemus nosmetipsos	an	AR 92 AM 100 102 115 117 WA 89	G	2	5	7	9	7	5	7	9	a
	Commissa mea pavesco / Domine quando veneris	rev	PM 319 AR [160] LU 1787 LA 554 WA 437										
	Commoverunt itaque plebem / Surrexerunt quidem	rev	LA 42										
8	Commovisti Domine terram	tr	GR 78 LU 507 SYG 60 GB 58 *GS 27	E	3	5	8	5	7	8	10	8	G
1	Communicantes Christi passionibus	co	GR 484 LU 1436	D	3	2	3	5	3	2	3	0	D
5	Communicantes Christi passionibus	gr	GR 508 LU 1482	F	4	7	6	9	7	9	7	4	F
3	Communione calicis quo Deus	an	LR 121 LU 924	E	-2	3	5	8	7	5	3	5	E
1	Compassus nutrici suae	an	WA 298 LA 369	C	2	9	11	9	12	9	7	9	D
	Compatiens nobis pietatis / O diligens	rev	WA 337										
8	Complaceat tibi Domine ... festina	an	LA 556	G	5	2	0	-2	0	2	0	-2	G
2	Complaceat tibi Domine ... respice	an	AR [167] LU 1793	D	2	3	0	2	0	-2	0	3	D
2	Complaceat tibi Domine ... respice	an	WA 437	a	3	0	-2	0	-2	0	-2	-4	a
	Complacuit per eum reconciliare / Vos qui aliquando	rev	VP 186	a	-4	0	3	2	0	-2	3	5	
8	Completa oratione	an	AM 964	a	-4	-2	0	-2	0	-2	-4	0	G
8	Completi sunt dies Mariae	an	AR 260 LU 364 *WA 27 *LA 31	a	-4	-2	0	3	-2	0	-2	3	G
	Concaluit cor meum intra me	alv	GR 502 LU 1473	D	-2	0	3	2	0	5	3	2	
	Concaluit cor meum intra me / Eructavit cor meum	grv	GR 65**	F	4	7	9	7	4	7	0	4	
1	Concede nobis Domine quaesumus	re	PM 202 WA 393	D	-2	0	3	0		-2	3	5	D
7	Concede nobis hominem	an	AR 581 *AM 757 WA 236 LA 504	G	2	5	4	5	7	9	7	5	G
6	Conclusit vias meas	re	LA 176 *WA 115	E	-2	-4	-2	0	1	0	-2	0	C
6	Concordi laetitia propulsa		AR 136*	F	2	4	0	2	-1	0	7	9	F
	Conculcaverunt me inimici mei / Miserere mihi	intv	GR 156 GS 73 GB 99 SYG 111										
1	Concupivit rex decorem tuum	gr	GR [65] LU 1230	D	7	8	7	5	7	5	3	7	D
8	Concussum est mare	an	WA 381 LA 467	G	5	2	0	-2	0	2	0	4	G
	Concussum est mare	alv	GR 609 LU 1655 *GS 198	G	5	4	2	4	0	2	0	-2	
	Condemnat autem justus	alv	GR 71**	c	2	0	5	4	2	0	2	4	
3	Condescende nobis pietatis	an	WA 336	G	2	5	4	2	0	2	0	2	E

4 Conditor alme siderum	hy	AM 182 ST 30	b	-4	0	3	5	1	3	5	1		b
4 Conditor alme siderum	hy	ST 271	F	-3	-5	-1	2	4	2	0	2		E
4 Conditor alme siderum	hy	ST 364	F	-3	-1	-3	-5	-3	-1	2	4		E
4 Conditor alme siderum	hy	ST 215 255	E	-2	-4	0	3	5	3	1	3		E
4 Conditor alme siderum	hy	ST 170	E	-2	-4	1	3	5	3	1	3		E
4 Conditor alme siderum	hy	ST 70	F	-1	-3	-1	-3	-5	-3	-1	2		E
1 Conditor alme siderum	hy	ST 70	D	3	0	-2	3	5	7	5	10		D
3 Confessio et pulchritudo	int	GR 578 LU 1593 *SYG 79 *GB 70^v *GS 40 194	E	-2	3	3	5	8	5	8	5	3	E
4 Confessio et pulchritudo	of	GR 580 LU 1595 OTT 166 *GB 219 *GS 194 g SYG 213	F	2	4	5	4	2	0	4	7		E
3 Confessio et pulchritudo	an	LR 293	G	2	5	2	5	4	0	2	4		E
Confessionem et decorem induisti / Ponis nubem	rev	PM 84 LR 105 AM 1186											
Confessionem et decorem induisti / Emitte spiritum	ofv	OTT 77 GB 184 *SYG 182	G	2	5	4	5	7	5	4	7		
1 Confessor Dei Nicholaus	re	WA 239	D	3	5	3	0	-2	0	2	0		D
1 Confessor Domini Benedicte	an	WA 334	D	-2	0	3	2	0	2	0	-2		D
Confessor Domini Benedicte	alv	SYG 207	A	3	5	8	10	5	7	5	3		
2 Confessor Domini Maure	hy	ST 424	D	-2	0	2	3	5	3	2	0		D
2 Confessorum regem adoremus	inv	LA 366 WA 296	C	2	4	5	2	4	2	0	4		D
1 Confide filia quia fides	an	WA 191	D	-2	0	3	0	2	0	-2	0		D
8 Confido in Domino	an	WA 399 LA 480	G	5	2	0	-2	0	2	0	-2		G
Confirma hoc Deus / Spiritus Domini	intv	SYG 183											
8 Confirma hoc Deus	an	AR 86* PM 328 LR 112 LU 869 1844 *WA 152 LA 257	c	2	0	-1	0	-3	0	-1	-3		G
4 Confirma hoc Deus	of	GR 295 [94] LU 882 OTT 79 *GS 137 234 *GB 189^v *SYG 183	D	2	3	2	3	5	7	3	8		E
1 Confirmatum est cor virginis	re	PM 166 *WA 49	C	2	4	2	9	10	9	12	9		D
3 Confiteantur Domino misericordiae	gr	GR 631 LU 1694	F	-5	-3	0	-1	0	2	4	2		E
Confiteantur Domino misericordiae	alv	GR 411	c	-1	2	0	-1	0	2	0	-3		
Confiteantur Domino misericordiae / Exaltent eum	grv	GB 244^v SYG 53	D	3	5	7	5	3	2	3	0		
Confiteantur Domino misericordiae / Exaltent eum	grv	GR 408 [2^1] LU 1122^2 GS 182	F	4	7	4	7	4	7	4	7		
Confiteantur Domino misericordiae / Misit Dominus verbum suum	grv	GR 68 LU 485 GS 21 GB 37^v SYG 35	F	4	7	4	7	4	7	4	7		
7 Confiteantur Domino misericordiae	co	GR 80**	G	5	4	5	7	9	10	9	7		G

3	Confiteantur tibi Domine	int	GR 92**	F	-1	0	-3	2	-1	2	4	9	E
	Confiteantur tibi populi Deus Deus misereatur	intv	GR [126] LU 1292										
5	Confiteantur tibi populi Deus	gr	GR [126] LU 1294	D	3	2	3	5	7	5	3	5	F
6	Confitebor Domino nimis in ore	of	GR 283 LU 842 OTT 74 *SYG 178 GB 162 *GS 132	C	2	9	10	9	10	9	12	9	F
8	Confitebor Domino nimis in ore	an	WA 70	D	5	3	2	3	5	7	5	3	G
7	Confitebor Domino nimis in ore	an	LA 104	G	7	5	4	5	7	9	7	5	G
	Confitebor nomini tuo alleluia	sr	AR 692 LU 1443 AM 888										
5	Confitebor nomini tuo Domine	an	AR 160 LU 298	a	-2	-4	3	2	3	5	3	2	F
1	Confitebor tibi Domine Deus	of	GR 54 LU 448 OTT 44	C	2	9	10	9	12	9	7	9	D
4	Confitebor tibi Domine Deus	re	LA 100 *WA 69	D	3	0	2	3	2	3	2	3	E
	Confitebor tibi Domine in toto corde Narrabo omnia mirabilia	cov	SYG 88										
	Confitebor tibi Domine in toto corde Sermo meus	intv	GR 544 LU 1543										
	Confitebor tibi Domine in toto corde	alv	GB 169	C	2	4	5	7	9	7	11	12	
1	Confitebor tibi Domine in toto corde	of	GR 155 LU 573 OTT 44 SYG 110 GB 98 GS 72	C	2	9	10	9	12	9	10	12	D
	Confitebor tibi Domine in toto corde Domine Deus meus in te	ofv	OTT 173	D	3	2	3	0	-2	3	5	7	
8	Confitebor tibi Domine quoniam	an	AR 342 AM 312 *WA 74 *LA 113	F	2	0	4	7	9	7	6	4	G
	Confitebuntur caeli mirabilia ... et	alv	SYG 172	E	-4	-2	5	7	5	3	5	3	
3	Confitebuntur caeli mirabilia ... et	gr	GR 512	F	-3	0	-1	0	2	0	-1	-3	E
	Confitebuntur caeli mirabilia ... et	alv	GB 163^V	D	3	0	-2	3	5	3	7	3	
7	Confitebuntur caeli mirabilia ... et	of	GR [17] LU 1148 OTT 138 SYG 170 *GB 153 GS 209	G	4	7	5	7	5	7	9	7	G
	Confitebuntur caeli mirabilia ... etenim	alv	GR [16] LU 1147 1465^B SYG 171 GS 216 (nm)	G	2	0	5	4	5	7	9	10	
8	Confitebuntur caeli mirabilia ... etenim	gr	SYG 190	F	4	2	4	2	4	0	2	4	G
	Confitebuntur tibi populi	an	OHS 297 (nm)										
	Confitemini Domino et invocate Aqua sapientiae	intv	GR 247 LU 789 OHS 783 GS 119 SYG 156										
	Confitemini Domino et invocate Benedicta sit	intv	GB 212^V										
	Confitemini Domino et invocate Eduxit Dominus	intv	GR 258 LU 804 OHS 825 GS 123 GB 142^V SYG 161										

	Text	Type	Sources										
	Confitemini Domino et invocate Erit quasi signum	intv	GR 84**										
	Confitemini Domino et invocate Introduxit vos Dominus	intv	GR 244 OHS 773 LU 785 SYG 154										
	Confitemini Domino et invocate Laetetur cor	intv	GR 146 GS 68 169 GB 94^v SYG 106										
	Confitemini Domino et invocate Victricem manum tuam	inv	SYG 158										
	Confitemini Domino et invocate	alv	GR 376 LU 1060 *SYG 250 GB 162 GS 157	a	3	5	3	7	5	3	0	2	
5	Confitemini Domino filii	an	WA 228	F	4	7	9	7	9	7	9	7	c
3	Confitemini Domino quia	an	AR 159 LU 296	G	2	5	4	5	7	5	4	0	E
	Confitemini Domino quoniam bonus Vidi aquam	anv	GR 2* LU 12 PM 10 GS 116										
	Confitemini Domino quoniam bonus Aperite mihi portas	intv	GR 33**										
	Confitemini Domino quoniam bonus Aqua sapientiae	intv	GB 133										
	Confitemini Domino quoniam bonus Eduxit Dominus populum	intv	GS 123										
	Confitemini Domino quoniam bonus Introduxit vos Dominus	intv	GB 129										
	Confitemini Domino quoniam bonus Memento nostri Domine	intv	GB 11										
	Confitemini Domino quoniam bonus Salvos nos fac	intv	GR [133]										
	Confitemini Domino quoniam bonus Venite benedicte	intv	GS 120										
	Confitemini Domino quoniam bonus Victricem manum	intv	GS 121										
2	Confitemini Domino quoniam bonus	tr	GR 113 LU 547 SYG 86 GB 75	D	-2	0	-2	-5	-2	0	-2	0	D
	Confitemini Domino quoniam bonus Haec dies	grv	GR 241 LU 778 OHS 709 GS 117 *GB 125 *SYG 152	a	3	5	3	5	7	8	7	3	
	Confitemini Domino quoniam bonus	alv	GR 236-282 LU 776^{II} OHS 682 *PM 80 *SYG 152 *GB 122 161^v GS *115 132	G	5	2	0	4	0	2	5	4	
	Confitemini Domino quoniam bonus	alv	SYG 177	G	5	4	5	2	0	4	0	2	
3	Confitemini Domino quoniam in aeternum	an	AR 158 LU 295	G	2	5	4	2	0	4	2	0	E
	Confitemini ei coram omnibus Tempus est ut ... vos	rev	LA 290										
	Confitemini illi quoniam bonus Laudate Dominum Deum	rev	WA 178										
5	Confiteor tibi pater	gr	GR 613 LU 1668	D	3	5	3	5	3	5	7	5	F

	Incipit	Gen.	Sources		1	2	3	4	5	6	7	8	
	Conforta me rex sanctorum	an	LA 294 (nm)										
2	Conforta me rex sanctorum	re	WA 179	A	3	5	7	5	8	7	8	10	D
4	Confortamini et jam nolite	of	GR 10 OTT 9 *SYG 8 *GB 7 GS 12	C	2	5	4	5	7	5	4	5	E
1	Confortate manus fatigatas	re	LA 4	C	2	4	2	9	11	9	7	5	D
7	Confortatus est principatus	an	AR [11] LU 1115 AM 627 WA 415 LA 421 512	c	-1	0	2	0	2	4	2	4	G
	Confringam illos nec poterunt / Persequar inimicos	trv	GR 463 LU 1420	C	2	5	7	5	2	5	7	9	
4	Confundantur et revereantur	an	OHS 492 LU 699 WA 122 *LA 197	G	2	5	7	5	7	9	7	5	a
	Confundantur et revereantur / Adjutor meus	grv	GR 115 GS 48 GB 76^v SYG 87	C	2	5	7	9	7	5	7	5	
	Confundantur omnes inimici / Noli esse mihi	rev	LA 177 WA 111										
8	Confundantur omnes qui	an	AR 139 OHS 355 LU 290	G	2	0	4	2	5	4	2	4	G
4	Confundantur qui me persequuntur	an	AR 422 OHS 70 AM 400 WA 113 *LA 182	G	2	5	7	5	7	9	7	5	a
1	Confundantur superbi quia injuste	co	GR [54] LU 1220 SYG 228 GB 244^v GS 231	F	-1	0	2	4	0	-1	-3	-5	D
8	Congaudete mecum et congratulamini	an	AR 604 LU 1341 AM 787 WA 255 LA 338	G	-2	-5	-3	-2	0	2	0	4	G
7	Congratulamini mihi omnes ... quia / cum essem	re	PM 248 LR 248 WA 49	G	5	4	5	7	5	4	7	9	G
3	Congratulamini mihi omnes ... quia / quem quaerebam	rc	OHS 803 *LR 91 *WA 132	E	-2	3	5	3	5	7	8	7	E
7	Congratulamini mihi quia inveni	an	WA 187	G	5	4	5	7	5	2	5	4	G
8	Congregatae sunt gentes	re	LA 298 WA 181	D	3	5	7	5	7	5	5		G
4	Congregate illi sanctos ejus	int	GR 63**	F	-3	-1	0	2	4	2	4	5	E
	Congregate illi sanctos ejus / Ex Sion species	grv	GR 4 LU 328 GB 2^v SYG 3 GS 3	F	4	7	4	7	4	7	4	7	
1	Congregati sunt Deus	re	AR 197*	D	-2	0	3	2	5	2	3	0	D
1	Congregati sunt inimici	re	LA 297 WA 181	C	2	4	2	9	11	9	7	9	D
	Congregaverunt iniquitatem / Seniores populi	rev	WA 119										
1	Congregavit Christus	an	WA 214 SYG 132	C	2	5	4	2	0	4	5	2	D
	Congregavit nos Christus		see Congregavit Christus										
	Congregavit nos in unum / Ubi caritas	anv	GR 204 OHS 451	F	2	4	2	4	5	4	2	4	
1	Congregavit nos in unum	an	SYG 132	F	4	2	5	4	2	4	0	-1	D
8	Conscendat usque sidera	hy	ST 396	G	-2	0	2	5	4	5	7	5	G

	Incipit		Sources										
4	Conscendat usque sidera	hy	ST 234	E	1	-2	1	-2	-4	-2	0	-2	E
	Conscriptus numero eorum Exsultemus ... in Domino	rev	WA 314										
6	Consecrandus ad altare	re	WA 250	c	-2	-3	-5	0	2	4	2	0	c
	Conserva me Domine Notas mihi fecisti	cov	SYG 97										
	Conserva me Domine A dextris est mihi	rev	LA 81 WA 60										
2	Conserva me Domine	an	LA 102	E	-2	-4	-2	0	1	3	1	0	D
	Conserva me Domine Benedicam Dominum	ofv	OTT 88 GB 76^v SYG 87	C	2	9	10	9	10	9	7	9	
2	Considera oves tuas	an	WA 279	D	-5	-2	0	2	0	2	3	0	D
7	Considerabam ad dexteram	an	AR 437 OHS 630 LU 776^F AM 433 *WA 121 *LA 194	G	4	7	5	2	4	5	7	4	G
1	Consilium fecerunt inimici	an	WA 115 LA 186	D	-2	3	5	7	8	7	5	8	D
2	Consolamini consolamini popule	an	AM 231 *AR 254 LA 17 *WA 18	F	-1	-3	-5	-3	0	-5	-3	0	D
4	Consors paterni luminis	hy	ST 363	G	-3	0	-2	-3	-2	-5	-3	-2	E
4	Consors paterni luminis	hy	ST 213 253	D	2	3	5	3	5	3	2	3	E
8	Conspicit in caelis	an	WA 376	G	2	5	2	0	2	0	-2	-3	G
8	Constantes estote videbitis	re	LA 29 WA 25	D	3	5	7	5	7	5	7	9	G
2	Constantes estote videbitis	an	AR 242 *AM 217 *WA 20 *LA 26	D	5	3	2	-2	0	3	2	-2	D
	Constantes estote videbitis Judaea et Jerusalem	rev	AM 1183 *PM 26 *WA 27	D	7	5	3	2	0	2	3	5	
	Constitues eos principes	sr	AR [9] LU 1113 1521 AM 620 931 1170 WA 414										
4	Constitues eos principes	re	LA 510	F	-3	0	-1	-5	-3	2	0	-1	E
	Constitues eos principes	alv	GR [2^3]_5 LU 1122^5 SYG 194	C	2	4	7	4	5	2	0	2	
2	Constitues eos principes	re	LR 143 *WA 413	A	3	5	7	5	8	7	8	5	D
5	Constitues eos principes	gr	GR 393 533 LU 1519 SYG 202 GB 204 *GS x	D	3	7	5	7	5	3	7	8	F
7	Constitues eos principes	an	LR 135 LA 505 *WA 411	G	4	7	5	2	5	4	5	7	G
3	Constitues eos principes	of	GR 534 LU 1520 OTT 131 SYG 203 *GB 206^v GS z 203	D	5	7	10	9	10	12	10	9	E
	Constitues eos principes	alv	SYG 221	D	7	5	7	5	3	5	7	9	
	Constituit eum Dominum domus	sr	AR 656 691 LU 1403 1439 AM 843 884										
2	Constitutus a Deo	an	WA 33	C	2	4	2	0	2	4	2	0	D

4 Consul aeterni trabeate regni	hy	ST 468	E	-2	0	-2	-4	-2	0	1	0	E
1 Consummatus in brevi	int	GR 81**	C	2	5	2	4	0	5	7	9	D
1 Consummatus in brevi	gr	GR 70**	C	2	9	10	9	7	5	9	7	D
2 Consummatus in gloria	an	WA 313	D	3	2	-2	0	-2	0	-2	0	D
Consumpta vero omni carne / Deletis cunctis	rev	WA 77										
2 Consurge consurge induere	an	AR 254 AM 230 / WA 18 *LA 17	D	5	3	2	-2	0	2	0	3	D
4 Consurgens Joseph accepit	an	LR 304	F	-1	-3	-1	2	-1	0	-1	-3	E
4 Contemplativae vitae magna	an	WA 335	F	-3	-1	0	-1	2	4	2	0	E
8 Continet in gremio	re	WA 50	F	2	4	2	4	2	4	7	2	G
3 Continge ergo sepulchrum	an	WA 243	G	2	0	2	5	4	2	0	2	E
Continuerunt aures suas / Impii super justum	rev	LA 45 WA 35										
2 Contra spem in spem	co	GR 426 LU 1353^v	D	-2	2	3	2	0	2	0	3	D
Contristatus est Petrus / Simon Joannis	cov	SYG 204										
8 Contristatus est rex	re	WA 362	D	3	5	7	5	7	5	7	9	G
Contristatus sum in exercitatione / Exaudi Deus	intv	GR 143 GS 65 / GB 91^v SYG 103										
2 Contristatus sum in exercitatione	tr	GR 622^3	D	-2	0	-2	-5	-2	0	-2	0	D
8 Contritum est cor meum	an	AR 433 OHS 402 / LU 654 AM 416 / WA 120 LA 193	a	-4	-2	0	-2	0	-2	-4	-2	G
8 Contumelias et terrores ... et Dominus	an	AR 430 OHS 306 316 / AM 410 WA 117 LA 187	c	-1	-5	-3	0	2	0	-1	0	G
7 Contumelias et terrores ... qui erant	re	OHS 241 (nm) / LA 178 *WA 116	c	-1	0	2	0	2	-1	0	-1	G
Conturbata sunt omnia ossa / Miserere mihi	grv	GR 133 GS 58 / GB 85^v SYG 96	G	7	10	7	5	2	0	2	-2	
Conturbatus sum a voce inimici / Exaudi Deus	ofv	OTT 36 *GB 84 / *SYG 95	G	5	7	5	0	5	7	5	4	
Convenerunt autem ibi / Dominus Jesus	rev	WA 112 GS 83										
8 Conventione autem facta	an	WA 75	G	-5	-2	0	2	0	2	0	2	G
1 Conventione autem facta	an	AR 343 LU 496 / AM 314 *LA 114	D	-2	3	5	3	7	5	3	5	D
8 Conversus est furor	an	AR 76 AM 41 / WA 64 *LA 89	a	-4	-2	0	3	2	3	0	3	G
Converte nos Deus salutaris / A facie furoris	rev	LA 305 WA 186										
2 Convertere animam meam	gr	GB 265^v	A	3	5	8	5	8	5	3	7	
5 Convertere Domine aliquantulum / et deprecare	gr	GR 108 LU 1007 / SYG 81 GB 250 / GS 43 147 169	D	3	5	7	8	5	3	5	3	F

8	Convertere Domine aliquantulum et ne	an	AR 241 AM 216 *WA 19 LA 25	G	5	2	0	-2	0	2	0	-2	G
1	Convertere Domine et **deprecabilis**	an	AR 150	D	2	3	5	2	3	2	0	3	D
8	Convertere Domine et eripe animam	an	AR [156] LU 1783 *WA 436 LA 553	G	-2	-5	**-3**	-2	0	2	0	2	G
8	Convertimini ad Dominum	an	WA 84	G	5	2	0	-2	0	2	0	-2	G
	Convertimini ad eum Praeparate corda	rev	PM 110 LR 420										
1	Convertimini ad me	an	WA 84	C	2	5	4	2	0	2	0	2	D
8	Convertimini omnes simul	an	SYG 65	G	2	4	5	4	5	4	2	4	G
4	Convocatis Jesus duodecim ... dedit	an	AR 513 *AM 529 WA 157	F	-3	0	-1	-3	-1	0	2	0	E
1	Convocatis Jesus duodecim ... misit ... egressi	an	WA 371	E	-2	-4	-2	1	0	-2	0	-2	D
8	Convocatis Jesus duodecim ... misit ... et sanare	an	LA 266	G	5	2	0	2	0	2	0	-2	G
	Coöperante gratia spiritus Reposita est	anv	LA 426 WA 331										
3	Copiosae caritatis	an	WA 242	E	-2	3	5	8	7	5	3	5	E
3	Cor arca legem continens	hy	AR 538[8] VP 21*	E	-2	3	5	8	7	5	3	5	E
6	Cor arca legem continens	hy	VP 169	F	2	-1	0	2	4	5	4	2	F
1	Cor arca legem continens	hy	AM 567	D	7	5	7	5	3	2	5	7	D
6	Cor contritum et humiliatum	an	AR 170	F	-5	-3	0	-1	0	2	4	0	F
4	Cor dulce Jesu quis tuum	hy	AR 1 (sup 2)	F	-1	0	2	4	2	0	-3	0	E
1	Cor Jesu sacratissimum miserere		AR 92* LU 1853	a	-2	1	0	-2	-4	-2	0	-2	D
5	Cor meum conturbatum est	int	GR 8**	F	4	2	0	2	0	4	7	4	F
1	Cor meum et caro mea	co	GR 503 LU 1474	F	2	0	-3	-1	-5	-3	0	2	D
8	Cor meum et caro mea	tr	GR 626	G	2	4	2	0	2	0	-2	0	G
1	Cor mundum crea in me	an	AR 365 AM 341 *WA 88 206 211 LA 132	C	2	9	10	9	7	9	5	7	D
	Corde et animo Christo Regali ex progenie	rev	LA 458										
8	Corde et animo Christo	an	AR 835 LU 1626 AM 1033 WA 368 *LA 461	G	-2	-5	-3	-2	0	2	0	2	G
4	Corde et animo Christo	re	WA 367	G	2	0	2	5	2	0	4	0	E
1	Corde et animo Christo	re	LA 459	D	2	3	2	0	-2	3	5	7	D
4	Corde et voce simul	inv	WA 364	G	2	5	4	2	4	2	0	-3	b
3	Corde natus ex parentis	hy	ST 367	E	-2	3	5	3	5	8	5	3	E
3	Corde natus ex parentis	hy	ST 341	c	-1	-5	-3	-7	-8	-5	-8	-12	E
3	Corde natus ex parentis	hy	ST 274	E	1	0	-2	3	5	3	5	8	E

	Title		References										
1	Cornelius centurio vir religiosus	re	PM 125 *WA 279	D	-2	0	-2	-5	-2	0	3	2	D
7	Cornelius centurio vir religiosus	an	WA 326	G	2	5	4	5	7	9	7	5	G
	Corona aurea super caput In diademate	rev	PM 225 LA 385 WA 141										
3	Corona aurea super caput	re	LR 158 *LA 524 *WA 417	c	-5	-3	0	-1	0	2	0	-1	E
	Corona aurea super caput	alv	GR 14**	C	2	5	2	0	4	5	7	4	
3	Corona aurea super caput	gr	GR 12**	G	2	5	4	5	2	4	5	7	E
	Corona tribulationis effloruit Induit eum	trv	GR 13**	G	2	5	4	2	5	2	0	2	
	Corona tribulationis effloruit	alv	GR 15**	C	2	9	7	5	7	5	4	2	
	Coronam auream super caput		see Corona aurea ...										
	Corpora ipsorum in pace Electi mei	grv	GR 444 LU 1386	c	2	-1	0	-3	-5	-3	-1	0	
1	Corpora sanctorum in pace	an	AR [41] LU 1153 AM 648 *WA 423 *LA 520	D	-2	3	5	3	7	5	7	3	D
	Corpora sanctorum in pace	alv	GR [23] LU 1164	C	2	4	5	2	4	5	4	5	
1	Corpora sanctorum in pace	re	PM 200 LR 188 *LA 519	D	3	5	3	0	3	5	3	5	D
	Corpore mente habitu In sanctis crescens	rev	WA 293										
	Corpore tantum cum coenantibus O Juda qui	rev	WA 120										
	Corpus in cibum Transiturus	rev	LR 132	F	2	4	2	5	4	2	0	4	
	Corripe me Domine in misericordia Non abscondas me	rev	PM 112										
8	Corripies me Domine	an	AR 112	G	2	0	-2	2	5	4	5	2	G
8	Cosmas et Damianus	an	WA 377	G	5	2	0	-2	0	2	0	4	G
2	Cotidie apud vos eram	an	WA 62 117 *LA 188	D	-5	-2	0	2	3	0	-2	0	D
	Crastina die delebitur	sr	AR 258 LU 363 WA 26										
	Crastina die delebitur	alv	GS 13	a	-2	0	-2	-5	-2	-4	-2	0	
4	Crastina die delebitur	an	AR 256 LU 363 AM 232 *WA 26 *LA 30	a	-2	0	3	5	7	5	3	5	a
	Crastina die delebitur	alv	SYG 13	C	2	4	2	4	5	7	5	4	
	Crastina die delebitur	alv	GR 25 LU 361	G	5	4	2	0	2	4	2	0	
	Crastina erit vobis salus	sr	AR 258 LU 364										
8	Crastina erit vobis salus	an	AR 256 LU 363 *WA 26 LA 30	c	-3	0	-1	-3	-5	-3	-7	-3	G
	Crastina erit vobis salus	alv	GB 12^V	C	2	4	5	7	5	7	12	7	

	Incipit	Type	Sources										
4	Creator alme siderum	hy	AR 210 LU 324	E	-4	0	3	5	1	3	5	1	E
	Creator omnium Deus / Tua est potentia	rev	AM 1203 VP 262 / LA 295 WA 180										
	Creator omnium rerum / Libera me de morte	rev	WA 439 (438)										
2	Crede mater Agathen	an	WA 243	D	-2	-5	-2	0	2	0	-2	0	D
8	Credidi propter quod locutus	an	AM 134 135 / *WA 64	c	-1	-3	-5	-3	-5	-3	-7	-5	G
	Credidit Abraham Deo / Eduxit Dominus	rev	WA 80										
2	Credimus Christum filium	an	WA 407 *LA 490	F	-1	-3	-5	-3	-1	-3	-1	0	D
5	Credo III		GR 64* LU 68	c	-3	-7	-2	-3	-5	-7	-3	-2	F
1	Credo IV		GR 67* LU 71	G	-3	-2	-5	-3	0	2	-5	2	D
4	Credo II		GR 62* LU 66	G	-3	-2	-5	-3	0	2	0	-2	E
4	Credo I		GR 59* LU 64 / OHS 139	G	-3	-2	-5	-3	0	2	3	2	E
4	Credo V		GR 69* LU 90	G	-3	-2	-5	-3	0	2	3	2	E
4	Credo VI		GR 72* LU 92	G	-3	-2	-5	-3	0	2	3	2	E
4	Credo V		GR 69* LU 90	G	-2	-3	-2	0	-2	-3	-5	-3	E
4	Credo VI		GR 72* LU 92	G	-2	-3	-2	0	-2	-3	-5	2	E
8	Credo quod redemptor meus	re	PM 320 AR [158] / LU 1785 LA 554 / WA 436	G	5	2	5	4	5	7	5	4	G
4	Credo videre bona Domini	an	AR [163] OHS 605 / LU 763 1789 / *WA 125 437 / *LA 203 555	E	1	-2	0	-4	-2	0	1	3	E
	Crescebat quotidie fames / Esuriente terra	rev	LR 306										
2	Crucem sanctam subiit	an	AR 704 LU 1461 / AM 131 166 468 750 / 903 *WA 132 *LA 399	C	2	4	5	4	2	4	7	4	D
4	Crucem tuam adoramus	an	GR 217 OHS 577 / LU 741 *VP 273 / *LA 463 *GS 102 / SYG 141	E	3	5	3	5	7	8	5	0	E
	Crucifixum in carne / Sedit angelus ad	anv	WA 222 *SYG 146	G	2	4	2	4	2	7	5	4	
	Crucifixus surgens a mortuis	alv	SYG 164	D	2	3	5	7	5	7	10	7	
6	Crucifixus surrexit a mortuis	an	AR 54 577[24] / LU 261 *AM 37 167 / 471 750 WA*136 138 / LA 216	F	2	4	2	4	0	2	4	2	F
8	Crucifixus surrexit tertia die	an	LA 399	G	-2	-5	-3	-2	2	0	-2	2	G
3	Crudelis Herodes Deum regem	hy	AR 308 LU 464	D	2	3	5	7	0	2	5	3	E
8	Crudelis Herodes Deum regem	hy	AR 309 LU 465	F	2	4	7	2	4	0	2	7	G
7	Crux alma fulget	an	PM 153 *SYG 142	G	2	4	5	7	9	7	5	7	G

8	Crux benedicta nitet	an	WA 370	G	-2	2	5	4	2	5	7	5	G
8	Crux benedicta nitet	hy	ST 483	G	2	0	-2	-5	-2	-5	-2	2	G
6	Crux fidelis inter omnes ... dulcia	an	WA 370	c	2	4	0	2	5	4	2	0	c
3	Crux fidelis inter omnes ... sustinens	hy	ST 33	E	1	-2	3	5	8	10	8	5	E
2	Crux fidelis inter omnes ... sustinens	hy	ST 228	a	-2	-4	-2	0	-7	-4	-2	-5	D
1	Crux fidelis inter omnes ... sustinens	hy	ST 481 WA 216 GS 102	C	4	7	9	7	9	12	11	9	D
8	Crux fidelis inter omnes ... sustinet	an	WA 370 SYG 143	G	-5	-2	0	2	0	2	0	2	G
1	Crux fidelis inter omnes ... sustinet	hy	GR 218 222 VP 269 22*	D	2	5	7	5	7	10	9	7	D
7	Crux fidelis inter omnes ... sustinuit	re	PM 152 WA 369	G	2	0	2	5	4	5	7	5	G
2	Crux Jesu Christi adaperiat	co	SYG 130	D	-2	0	3	2	3	0	2	0	D
	Cui cum Nicostratus / Sanctus Sebastianus	rev	LA 329										
	Cui pro veritate / Beatus Dunstanus	rev	WA 313										
	Cui sacerdos respondit / Igitur dissimulata	rev	WA 342										
2	Cui sol luna	an	WA 379	C	2	0	2	4	5	2	0	2	D
	Cui vivere Christus fuit / O beati viri	rev	LR 210 WA 297										
	Cujus caput datum / Contristatus est rex	rev	WA 362										
	Cujus caput datum / Misso Herodes	rev	WA 363										
	Cujus intercessio nobis / Vir inclitus	rev	WA 387										
	Cujus partus / Rosa vernans	alv	VP 52	E	1	-2	3	5	0	3	5	3	
	Cujus pulchritudinem sol / Mel et lac	rev	WA 254										
2	Cujus pulchritudinem sol	an	WA 254 LA 334	D	-2	0	3	2	0	-2	0	3	D
	Cujus vita gloriosa / Caeleste beneficium	rev	WA 366										
8	Cultor Dei memento	hy	ST 113	c	-1	-3	-1	0	-3	0	-1	-5	G
	Cum	see also Cumque											
	Cum	see also Dum											
1	Cum accepisset acetum	an	AR 440 OHS 477 (nm) AM 444 LA 188	D	-2	3	5	3	5	7	8	7	D
1	Cum ambularent animalia	re	WA 374	E	-2	-4	0	3	5	7	5	3	a
	Cum ambularent animalia / Audiebam sonum	rev	WA 375	D	7	5	3	2	5	7	5	7	
7	Cum angelis et pueris	an	AR 422 GR 175 PM 58 OHS 69 98 LU 585 *AM 400 *WA 113 209 *LA 181	b	1	3	1	0	1	5	3	1	G

	Incipit	Type	Sources										
7	Cum appropinquaret Dominus Jerosolymam	an	GR 171 *PM 54 WA 208 *GS 79 *SYG 118 GB 105	G	2	4	0	-2	0	2	5	4	G
1	Cum appropinquaret Dominus Jerosolymam	an	AR 560 LU 1104 AM 599 *WA 188 *LA 314	D	3	-2	0	7	8	7	5	3	D
2	Cum ascendisset Petrus	an	WA 327	D	-2	0	3	2	3	0	2	0	D
7	Cum aspicerem animalia	re	WA 374	G	2	0	-2	2	5	4	2	7	G
1	Cum audisset Jacob quod Esau	re	LA 141	D	3	0	-2	3	5	7	5	3	D
1	Cum audisset Job nuntiorum	an	AR 546 LU 991 *AM 582 *WA 171 *LA 286	D	-2	3	5	8	7	8	10	8	D
5	Cum audisset populus quia Jesus	an	GR 172 PM 56 GS 80 *SYG 117	C	2	0	5	7	5	7	9	7	C
8	Cum audisset populus quia Jesus	an	GB 107	G	2	4	0	-2	0	2	5	4	G
5	Cum audisset populus quia Jesus	an	WA 208	c	4	7	9	7	9	7	2	4	c
8	Cum audisset salutationem Mariae	an	AR 772 AM 955	G	-5	-2	0	2	0	2	0	-2	G
1	Cum audisset turba quia venit	re	WA 112	D	-2	0	3	2	3	5	3	0	D
	Cum aurora	see Dum aurora											
7	Cum autem complacuit	an	WA 262 LA 346	G	5	4	5	7	9	7	9	10	G
8	Cum autem descendisset Jesus	an	AR 337 LU 1108 AM 307 WA 71 LA 106	G	2	0	-2	0	2	5	4	0	G
8	Cum autem ducerentur	an	WA 378	G	2	0	-3	-2	0	-2	2	5	G
	Cum autem esset Stephanus Intuens in caelum	rev	LA 43										
8	Cum autem sero	an	WA 75	G	5	4	5	7	5	2	5	4	G
8	Cum autem venerit	an	WA 145 *LA 242	G	5	4	5	7	5	4	2	5	G
1	Cum coetu virgineo adveniens	an	PM 215	D	2	0	-2	0	3	2	3	5	D
3	Cum complerentur dies Pentecostes	re	LR 109 LU 873 LA 255 *WA 152	F	-1	-3	2	4	2	4	6	7	E
	Cum elevarentur animalia Cum ambularent	rev	WA 374										
	Cum ergo accepisset acetum Tenebrae factae	rev	LA 200 WA 123										
	Cum ergo cognovisset Responsum acceperat	rev	WA 269										
	Cum ergo fleret Tulerunt Dominum	rev	OHS 802 LR 90 LA 211 WA 131										
1	Cum essem parvula placui	an	AR 882³ LU 1686 AM 1082	D	-2	3	5	3	5	7	8	7	D
	Cum essent in unum	see Dum ergo essent in unum											
8	Cum esset desponsata ... antequam ... quod	an	WA 26 LA 31	G	-2	-5	-3	-2	0	2	0	-2	G
3	Cum esset desponsata ... ejus	of	GR 624 LU 1685	G	2	5	2	0	4	7	5	2	E

No.	Incipit	Genre	Source	Mode									Final
3	Cum esset desponsata ... Jesu	an	AR 649 687 LU 1437 *AM 837 885	E	-2	3	5	8	5	3	5	8	E
4	Cum esset plenus spiritu	re	LA 42	F	-3	0	-1	0	2	0	-1	0	E
	Cum esset rex	see Dum esset rex											
1	Cum esset sero die illa	an	AR 456 LU 807 AM 475 *LA 223	C	2	5	2	0	2	0	2	5	D
4	Cum esset sero die illa	an	WA 136	D	2	5	3	2	0	2	-2	3	E
	Cum esset Stephanus	alv	SYG 22	C	2	4	7	4	5	4	2	0	
1	Cum esset summus pontifex	an	WA 426	D	-2	3	5	3	5	7	9	7	D
7	Cum evigilasset Jacob	an	WA 318 *LA 547	G	4	5	7	9	5	7	5	4	G
	Cum exarserit in brevi Servite Domino	rev	LA 83										
1	Cum facis eleemosynam	an	AR 361 AM 334 WA 84 LA 126	D	-2	3	5	3	5	7	8	7	D
7	Cum factus esset Jesus	an	LA 106	G	2	5	4	5	7	9	7	5	G
	Cum fortis armatus	see Dum fortis armatus											
8	Cum his qui oderunt pacem	an	AR 436 OHS 626 LU 776D AM 430 431 WA 121 *LA 194	G	5	2	0	-2	0	2	0	4	G
	Cum igitur saxorum crepitantium Stephanus servus Dei	rev	PM 30 LA 44 WA 51(36)										
1	Cum immundus spiritus exierit	an	AR 390 LU 557 AM 364 *WA 99 *LA 153	D	-2	3	5	3	5	7	5	8	D
3	Cum in die magni sabbati	an	AM 875	G	2	4	5	4	5	7	5	4	E
	Cum inducerent puerum Hodie Maria virgo puerum	rev	LA 353										
	Cum inducerent puerum Suscipiens Jesum	rev	VP 102 LA 350										
1	Cum inducerent puerum	an	AM 803 *AR 621 LA 347 WA 268	D	-2	3	5	7	8	7	5	3	D
	Cum inducerent puerum Responsum accepit	anv	PM 135	C	2	5	2	4	2	0	2	4	
6	Cum inducerent puerum	re	LR 312	C	2	5	7	5	7	5	7	9	F
1	Cum inducerent puerum ... dicens	re	LA 352	D	2	3	5	3	2	3	5	7	D
1	Cum inducerent puerum ... dixit	re	WA 270	D	3	5	3	0	3	5	3	5	D
7	Cum intraret Jesus in domum	an	AR 567 AM 607 *LA 316	G	4	5	7	9	4	5	7	5	G
2	Cum invocarem te exaudisti	co	GR 102 SYG 77 *GB 69 *GS 38	D	2	3	0	3	5	7	5	7	D
1	Cum iratus fueris	an	AR 172	D	-2	3	5	3	5	7	5	7	D
1	Cum iter maris cepisset	an	AR 928 AM 1146 LA 496	D	3	0	-2	3	5	3	7	10	D
7	Cum jejunatis nolite fieri	an	AR 359 AM 332 *WA 84 *LA 126	G	4	5	7	9	7	5	7	5	G

#	Incipit	Type	Sources	Mode									Final
8	Cum jucunditate celebremus	re	LA 460 *WA 367	C	5	4	5	7	5	7	5	7	G
7	Cum jucunditate maternitatem	an	AR 882² LU 1683 AM 1081	G	5	4	5	7	9	7	5	9	G
	Cum jucunditate nativitatem Beatissimae virginis	rev	LA 457 WA 365										
7	Cum jucunditate nativitatem	an	AR 835 LU 1626 AM 1033 WA 368 LA 461	d	-3	0	2	0	2	0	-3	-2	G
	Cum multa turba	see Cum turba multa											
	Cum natus esset Jesus Magi veniunt	rev	LA 68 WA 53										
4	Cum non posset levare	re	WA 283	F	-1	-3	-5	-3	0	-3	-1	0	E
5	Cum omnibus se fratribus	an	LR 274	a	-4	0	3	5	3	5	7	5	F
	Cum orasset Cornelius Cornelius centurio	rev	PM 125 *WA 279	D	7	5	7	5	3	5	8	7	
7	Cum orasset Judas	an	WA 309 *LA 398	G	4	5	7	5	9	7	4	7	G
8	Cum ortus fuerit sol	an	AR 262 LU 367 AM 239 WA 27	G	-5	-2	0	2	0	2	0	2	G
8	Cum palma ad regna	an	AR [41] LU 1153 AM 648 WA 423 LA 519	a	-4	-2	0	3	2	3	0	3	G
	Cum pastoribus ovium Cuthbertus	rev	WA 292										
1	Cum pervenisset beatus Andreas ... exclamavit	an	AR 582 LU 1308 AM 758 WA 237 LA 504	D	-2	0	3	2	0	2	0	-2	D
3	Cum pervenisset beatus Andreas ... videns	an	WA 232	E	-2	3	5	8	7	8	7	8	E
7	Cum Placidus ex aqua	an	AM 965	G	5	4	5	7	9	5	4	5	G
7	Cum plebe clerus monachi	hy	ST 153	G	2	4	2	5	4	2	0	-2	G
2	Cum redirent remansit puer	an	AR 652 LU 1406 AM 841	D	-5	-2	0	-2	3	5	2	0	D
6	Cum respexisset Petrus crucem	an	PM 161	F	-3	-5	0	2	0	2	4	0	F
8	Cum rex gloriae Christus	an	SYG 148	D	2	5	3	5	7	5	7	5	G
3	Cum rex gloriae Christus	an	WA 225	D	3	5	7	5	3	5	7	5	E
5	Cum sancto sancte	re	WA 283	F	4	7	5	4	2	7	9	7	F
7	Cum sanctus Benedictus in cella	re	LR 327 *LA 370 *WA 299	G	2	0	5	4	5	7	5	7	G
7	Cum sanctus Benedictus post triduum	an	AM 816	G	5	4	5	7	5	7	9	7	G
5	Cum scirem ego Gamaliel	re	WA 343	F	4	2	7	9	7	6	7	6	F
	Cum sederit filius ... coeperit Vos amici mei qui secuti	anv	WA 331										
	Cum sederit filius ... coeperit Hoc signum crucis	rev	LA 396 WA 308										
1	Cum sederit filius ... coeperit	an	SYG 70 *WA 206	D	-2	0	3	2	3	0	2	0	D

	Incipit		Source										
	Cum sederit filius ... tunc	alv	SYG 157	E	-2	3	5	7	5	7	8	10	
1	Cum sol autem occidisset	an	LA 155	D	3	0	-2	3	5	3	7	3	D
1	Cum sublevasset oculos	an	AR 398 LU 1093 *AM 373 WA 191 *LA 162	D	-2	0	3	0	2	0	-2	0	D
	Cum transieris per aquam Ab oriente	grv	GR (4)	E	-2	3	5	7	8	10	5	3	
	Cum transiret Dominus	see	Dum transiret Dominus										
4	Cum transisset sabbatum	re	OHS 696 (nm) LR 84 LA 213 WA 129	C	2	5	7	5	2	5	7	5	E
8	Cum turba multa esset	an	AR 557 LU 1103 AM 595 *LA 312	G	-5	-2	0	2	0	-3	-2	-3	G
1	Cum turba plurima convenirent	re	LR 400	D	-2	0	3	0	2	0	-2	0	D
8	Cum turba plurima convenirent	an	AR 349 AM 321 WA 79 LA 119	G	5	2	0	2	0	2	4	2	G
1	Cum venerimus ante	an	WA 205 SYG 70	D	2	0	-2	2	5	7	9	7	D
8	Cum venerit filius	an	AR 238 *WA 17	c	-1	0	2	0	-1	-3	-1	0	G
8	Cum venerit paraclitus quem ego	an	AR 496 LU 854 AM 513 WA 151 *LA 254	C	2	5	4	5	7	5	9	7	G
	Cum venerit paraclitus spiritus	alv	SYG 181	E	3	1	0	3	0	-2	3	5	
8	Cum venerit paraclitus spiritus	an	AR 481 AM 496	G	5	2	0	2	0	-2	0	2	G
2	Cum venit paraclitus spiritus	an	WA 145	D	3	2	0	2	0	-2	0	3	D
	Cum videris nudum Frange esurienti	rev	LA 131										
8	Cum videris nudum	an	LA 126	G	5	2	0	2	0	-2	0	2	G
1	Cum videritis abominationem	an	AR 575 LU 1110 AM 617	C	2	5	4	2	4	2	0	2	D
8	Cum vidissent turbae	an	LA 163	G	5	2	0	2	0	-2	0	-2	G
1	Cum vidisset beatus Andreas	re	LA 498	C	2	9	11	9	12	9	7	9	D
8	Cum vidisset Jesus matrem	an	AR 677 LU 1425 *AM 868	G	-5	-2	0	2	0	2	3	2	G
8	Cum vidisset turba	an	WA 191	G	5	2	0	4	2	0	2	0	G
7	Cum vocatus fueris	an	AR 568 LU 1047 AM 608 *WA 190 *LA 317	G	4	5	7	4	5	7	9	7	G
	Cum vos oderint homines Beati estis	rev	LR 142										
	Cumque	see also	Cum										
	Cumque abisset Ruben Dixit Judas	rev	WA 96										
5	Cumque ad mensam sederent	re	LR 292	a	-4	0	3	2	3	0	3	5	F
2	Cumque ascendisset	an	WA 309 *LA 398	C	2	4	5	4	2	0	4	5	D
	Cumque aspiceret beatus Intuens in caelum	rev	WA 34										

Cumque audisset Jacob Nuntiaverunt Jacob	rev	LR 410 LA 152 WA 98										
Cumque audisset populus	<u>see also</u> Cum audisset populus											
Cumque audisset populus quod Jesus Ingrediente Domino	rev	PM 60 OHS 104 GR 177 LU 590 LA 181 WA 112 GS 85										
4 Cumque carnifices apostolum	an	WA 232	F	-1	-3	0	-1	0	2	4	6	E
Cumque carnifices ducerent Homo Dei ducebatur	rev	LA 500 WA 233										
Cumque complesset apostolus Apparuit caro	rev	WA 17	a	-2	-4	-2	0	2	0	-2	0	
Cumque ducerent eum Homo Dei ducebatur	rev	PM 117										
Cumque duo pergerent Factum est dum	rev	LA 272 WA 167										
Cumque duo simul	<u>see</u> Cumque duo pergerent											
Cumque evigilasset Jacob Mane surgens	rev	LR 240 LA 552										
Cumque evigilasset Jacob Vere Dominus	rev	WA 91										
Cumque evigilasset Jacob Terribilis est	rev	WA 317	D	7	5	3	2	0	3	2	3	
Cumque exitum suum Transiens ex hoc mundo	rev	WA 314	a	3	2	-2	0	2	0	3	5	
Cumque extendisset manum Angelus Domini vocavit	rev	LA 121 WA 82										
Cumque illi omnia Igitur Lucianus	rev	WA 345	c	-1	-5	-3	-1	-3	0	2	0	
Cumque in sopore Veniens vir splendidissimus	ofv	SYG 174	F	2	4	0	2	4	6	4	2	
8 Cumque in specu	an	WA 300	F	2	4	6	4	2	4	2	0	G
Cumque injecissent manus Tamquam ad latronem	rev	OHS 496 LU 702 LA 196										
Cumque intraveritis terram Vos qui transituri	rev	LR 412 *LA 161 *WA 102	F	4	7	4	2	7	9	7	12	
Cumque intuerentur in caelum Viri Galilaei	intv	SYG 179 GS 135										
Cumque intuerentur in caelum Viri Galilaei	ofv	OTT 172 *SYG 180 *GB 180^v	C	2	4	5	7	5	7	9	7	
8 Cumque intuerentur in caelum	an	AR 491 LU 851 *AM 509 *WA 149 LA 250	F	2	4	6	2	4	2	0	4	G
Cumque intuerentur in caelum Viri Galilaei	rev	LR 105 *LA 250 *WA 149	G	5	7	9	7	5	7	9	10	
Cumque mature surrexisset Dixit angelus ad Jacob	rev	LA 140										
Cumque obdormisset vidit Surgens ergo mane	rev	LA 550										

	Text	Type	Sources										
	Cumque obduxero in nubibus / Ponam arcum meum	rev	LA 118 WA 78										
	Cumque orationem complesset / Orante sancto Clemente	rev	LA 495										
	Cumque per singulos dies / Sexto die	rev	LR 331 LA 373										
8	Cumque perfusis lacrimis	re	LR 295	F	2	4	2	0	2	-5	-3	0	G
	Cumque pro signo acceperitis / Caecilia me misit	rev	LA 491 WA 406										
	Cumque sanctus Benedictus		see Cum sanctus Benedictus										
7	Cumque sibi conspicerent	an	LA 370	G	7	5	4	7	9	5	7	2	G
	Cumque stetisset Abraham / Dum staret	rev	WA 81										
	Cumque venatu aliquid / Tolle arma	rev	LR 405 LA 136 WA 91										
	Cumque vidissent Joseph / Videntes Joseph	rev	LR 408 LA 146 WA 96										
	Cumque vidisset ventum / Domine si tu es	rev	LR 362 LA 414 WA 327	G	5	4	0	2	4	2	5	7	
ir	Cunctis diebus vitae	an	AM 47 48	C	2	4	5	2	5	4	2	0	a
4	Cunctis diebus vitae	an	WA 65 *LA 92	C	2	4	5	2	5	4	2	0	E
1	Currebant duo simul	an	AR 452 OHS 825 AM 465 *WA 136 *LA 222	D	-2	3	5	3	7	10	7	5	D
	Currus Pharaonis et exercitum / Cantemus Domino gloriose	rev	LA 157 WA 101										
3	Custodes hominum psallimus angelos	hy	AR 863 LR 449 LU 1666	D	2	3	5	7	5	7	10	12	E
7	Custodes hominum psallimus angelos	hy	AM 1065	G	4	5	7	9	7	5	7	0	G
	Custodi innocentiam et vide	alv	GR 529	a	-2	1	0	1	-2	-4	-2	-4	
	Custodi innocentiam et vide / Propter fratres	grv	GR 527 LU 1512	F	4	2	7	9	7	9	7	11	
7	Custodi me a laqueo	an	AR 437 OHS 629 LU 776^E AM 432 *WA 121 LA 194	G	4	7	5	7	5	4	2	5	G
1	Custodi me Domine de manu	of	GR 189 LU 614 OHS 278 OTT 52 *SYG 126 GB 113 *GS 91	D	-2	0	3	5	3	0	3	-2	D
	Custodi me Domine de manu / Eripe me	trv	GR 208 LU 725 OHS 534 GS 99 GB 116^V SYG 137	F	2	4	2	0	2	0	-3	-1	
	Custodi me Domine ut pupillam / Perfice gressus	ofv	OTT 90 *GB 58^V *SYG 61	F	-3	2	4	7	6	7	4	9	
1	Custodi me Domine ut pupillam	gr	GR 345 LU 1021 *SYG 79 *GB 70^V GS 41 151	D	-2	0	3	2	5	3	2	3	D
4	Custodiebant testimonia	an	LR 140 *WA 412 LA 508	a	-2	0	3	5	3	5	7	5	a

4 Custodiebant testimonia ... quae dedit	an	WA 412	b	-4	-2	1	3	1	3	5	3	a
Custodit Dominus omnia ossa Pretiosa	rev	LR 166										
8 Custodivit anima mea testimonia	int	GR 70**	G	2	4	5	4	5	2	0	2	G
Custodivit eum ab inimicis Justum deduxit	rev	LR 200										
Custodivit eum Dominus Cibavit illum	rev	WA 426										
1 Cuthbertus puer bone	re	WA 292	D	-2	0	3	5	3	5	0	2	D
Cutis mea denigrata Versa est in luctum	rev	LA 286 WA 174										
1 Da fabricator noctis et diei	hy	ST 332	D	7	10	7	5	7	5	3	2	D
Da gaudiorum praemia Gloria patri	rev	WA 160	F	4	2	7	6	4	2	7	9	
4 Da mercedem Domine	an	AR 239 AM 214 WA 17 *LA 23	G	2	5	7	9	7	5	7	9	a
Da mihi Domine sedium Emitte Domine	rev	LA 276 WA 169										
1 Da mihi Domine sedium	re	LA 277 WA 169	a	-2	0	-4	0	-2	-4	-2	-4	D
4 Da mihi in disco caput	an	AR 830 LU 1621 AM 1027 *WA 363 LA 454	a	-2	0	3	7	5	3	5	7	a
8 Da mihi in disco caput	re	LA 453	F	2	4	2	4	2	4	6	4	G
Da mihi intellectum ut discam Domine vivifica	ofv	OTT 31 GB 64 *SYG 68	c	2	4	2	4	2	4	0	-1	
7 Da nobis Deus auxilium	int	GR 106**	G	2	-2	2	0	2	5	9	7	G
5 Da nobis Deus auxilium	gr	GR 107**	D	3	5	3	5	7	5	7	5	F
2 Da nobis Domine auxilium	an	WA 66 LA 93	D	3	2	0	3	2	0	-2	0	D
Da nobis Domine locum Conforta me rex	rev	WA 179										
Da nobis Domine virtutum Haec tua sunt	rev	WA 316	a	-2	-4	-2	0	-2	0	-2	-4	
2 Da pacem Domine in diebus nostris	an	AR 144* LU 1867 VP 17 13* LA 300	D	-2	0	3	5	3	2	3	5	D
8 Da pacem Domine in diebus nostris	an	WA 180	C	2	5	4	5	7	9	7	9	G
1 Da pacem Domine sustinentibus te	int	GR 372 [135] LU 1056 SYG 253 GB 259^v GS 161	D	7	8	7	8	7	10	7	8	D

Dabit ei Dominus Deus sedem   rev   LA 15 380
    Ecce radix Jesse

Dabit ei Dominus Deus sedem   rev   PM 23 LA 3 377
    Missus est Gabriel

1 Dabit ei Dominus sedem   an   AR 669 [140]   D -2   3   5   3   5   7   8   7   D
                                              LU 1417 AM 862
                                              WA 19 LA 24 379

1 Dabit illi Dominus Deus sedem   an   AR 894^5 LU 1704   D   2   3   0   2   0 -2   3   5   D
                                              AM 1091

4 Dabit illi Dominus Deus sedem   re   WA 302   C   2   5   4   5   4   5   2   0   E

Dabo in Sion salutem   rev   LA 8 WA 10
    Sicut mater

8 Dabo in Sion salutem   an   AR 231 LU 338   G -2 -5 -2 -3   -2   0   2   0   G
                                              *AM 204 WA 16
                                              *LA 16

8 Dabo sanctis meis locum   an   LR 177 AM 981   G   2   0 -2   0   2   5   4   2   G
                                              WA 420 *LA 513

2 Daemonis saeva perit hic rapina   hy   ST 107   D -2   0   3   2   0   2   0 -2   D

7 Damasci praepositus gentis   re   WA 265   G   2   0   2   5   7   5   4   5   G

8 Damasci praepositus gentis   re   LA 424   F   2   4   2   4   6   4   2   4   G

8 Damasci praepositus gentis   an   AR 610 757   G   5   2   0 -2   0   2   0   4   G
                                              LU 1349 *AM 793 942
                                              WA 266 *LA 431

8 Dansque illi sancta   an   WA 386   G   5   2   0 -2   0   2   0   4   G

Dantur ergo laudes Deo   rev   WA 259
    Beatus Dei athleta

8 Dantur ergo laudes Deo   an   WA 261   G -2 -5 -2 -3   -2   0   2   0   G

Data est mihi omnis potestas   sr   AR 894^{11}
                                              LU 1709 AM 1093

8 Data est mihi omnis potestas   an   AR 452 OHS 820   G -2   2   5   4   0   4   5   2   G
                                              LU 803 AM 465
                                              *WA 135 LA 222

1 Data est mihi omnis potestas   co   GR 258 OHS 819   F -1 -3   0   2   0   2   4   0   D
                                              LU 803 *SYG 161
                                              *GB 142 *GS 123

Data est mihi omnis potestas   alv   SYG 160   F   2   0   2   4   6   7   6   7

Data est potestas   rev   WA 383
    Hic est praepositus

Data est potestas   rev   WA 381
    Venit Michael

8 Data sunt ei incensa   an   WA 381 *LA 467   c -1   0 -3 -5   -3 -5 -7 -5   G

Date ei de fructu manuum   rev   LR 222
    Fallax gratia

7 Date ei de fructu manuum   an   AR 577^{22}[101]   c -1 -3   0   2   0   4   5   4   G
                                              LU 1236 AM 688 747

Date eleemosynam et ecce   rev   LA 129 WA 86
    Abscondite eleemosynam

3	Date et dabitur vobis mensuram	co	GR 634 LU 1696	E	1	-2	0	3	5	3	0	1	E
	Date magnificentiam		see Date magnitudinem										
6	Date magnitudinem Deo	an	AM 75 78	F	2	4	0	2	0	-1	-3	0	F
	Date magnitudinem Deo / Attende caelum	trv	GR 231 OHS 656 LU 776^U *GS 112 *GB 119^V *SYG 151	G	2	4	5	4	5	7	5	0	
4	Date nobis de oleo	an	WA 431	F	-1	-3	0	-1	0	-1	0	2	E
	Datiano frustra cogitante / Pretiosus martyr	rev	WA 260	a	-2	0	3	1	-2	0	-2	-4	
7	Datum est opus	an	WA 376	G	7	5	2	5	9	7	9	5	G
	De bono thesauro cordis sui	sr	AR 7 (sup 2)										
7	De caelo veniet dominator	an	AR 227 LU 1082 *AM 199 *WA 12 *LA 11 381	G	4	5	7	9	7	5	7	5	G
	De caetero reposita / Bonum certamen	anv	WA 331										
	De excelso misit ignem	alv	GR 501 LU 1473	a	-2	1	0	1	-2	-4	-2	-4	
6	De fructu operum tuorum	co	GR 353 LU 1031 SYG 247 *GB 254 *GS 155	F	2	4	2	4	2	0	2	0	F
8	De fructu ventris tui	an	AR 272 LU 412 AM 247 *WA 272 *LA 39	G	5	4	0	4	5	2	0	2	G
8	De illa occulta habitatione	re	WA 25	G	5	4	5	2	4	2	5	4	G
	De illustratione sancte Paule / Laetemur omnes	intv	GS h 177										
	De Jacob exiet / Orietur stella	rev	WA 5										
3	De luce sanctus praesul	an	WA 285	E	-2	3	5	7	8	7	8	10	E
8	De manu filiorum	an	WA 110 LA 201	G	2	0	-2	0	2	5	4	2	G
1	De manu omnium	an	AR 129 AM 58	F	4	2	4	0	2	-3	0	-1	D
	De medio autem ejus / In visione Dei	rev	WA 372	a	-2	-4	-5	-2	0	3	5	3	
	De mundi hujus / Occasum tanti	rev	WA 285	c	-1	2	0	-3	0	-1	-3	-5	
5	De necessitatibus meis eripe	an	WA 70	a	-4	0	3	2	0	3	0	-2	F
2	De necessitatibus meis eripe	tr	GR 102 LU 841^A SYG 78 GB 69^V GS 39	D	-2	0	-2	-5	-2	0	-2	0	D
4	De necessitatibus meis eripe	int	GR 104 *SYG 80 *GB 72 GS 41	D	3	2	3	0	3	2	3	2	E
8	De necessitatibus meis libera	an	LA 104	c	-1	-5	-3	-1	-3	0	-3	-5	G
	De ore leonis libera me	sr	AR 37 LU 244 AM 382 383										
	De ore leonis libera me / Erue a framea	rev	LA 171 WA 108										

	Text	Type	Sources										
2	De ore leonis libera me	re	LA 172	A	3	5	7	5	8	7	8	10	D
7 8	De ore prudentis procedit mel	re	OHS 780 *PM 230 *LR 88 *LA 384 *WA 306	a	3	5	3	5	2	3	2	-2	G
2	De patre verbum prodiens	hy	ST 369	G	-3	-2	0	2	0	-2	-3	-5	D
3	De patre verbum prodiens	hy	ST 220	E	-2	3	5	8	7	5	8	7	E
	De profundis clamavi ad te Requiem aeternam	intv	GB 265^v										
	De profundis clamavi ad te Si iniquitates	intv	GR 383 LU 1070 GS d GB 263^v SYG 259										
	De profundis clamavi ad te Domine exaudi orationem	rev	LA 103										
	De profundis clamavi ad te Memento mei Deus	rev	AR [164] LU 1791										
8	De profundis clamavi ad te	an	AR 140 OHS 356 LU 291 AM 138 139 WA 66 LA 93	c	-1	0	-3	-5	-7	-5	-3	-1	G
	De profundis clamavi ad te Rogamus te Domine	rev	LA 557	c	-1	0	2	0	-1	0	-1	-3	
	De profundis clamavi ad te	alv	GR 388 LU 1076 *SYG 255 *GB 264^v *GS 164	G	2	0	5	4	7	9	7	9	
8	De profundis clamavi ad te	tr	GR 75 LU 499 SYG 59 GB 56^v GS 25	G	2	4	2	0	2	0	-2	0	G
2	De profundis clamavi ad te	of	GR 388 LU 1076 OTT 126 SYG 258 *GB 265 *GS f 167	A	3	5	8	5	8	5	3	5	D
	De quacumque tribulatione	alv	GR 486 LU 1441	a	-2	-5	-2	0	-2	-5	-4	-5	
1	De quinque panibus	an	AR 399 LU 559 AM 374 WA 102 LA 162	D	-2	3	5	3	5	7	8	7	D
	De reliquo reposita Scio cui	anv	WA 330										
1	De sacro tabernaculo	hy	ST 351	D	7	5	3	2	0	3	5	3	D
	De sensibus enim Numquam inquinatum	rev	WA 245										
	De Sion exibit lex Erumpant montes	rev	LA 10										
2	De Sion exibit lex	an	AR 221 AM 192 *WA 9 61 LA 7	D	5	3	2	-2	0	3	2	-2	D
1	De Sion veniet Dominus	an	AR 241 AM 216 *WA 19 LA 25	F	2	4	2	4	-1	0	2	0	D
1	De Sion veniet qui regnaturus	an	AR 241 AM 216 *WA 19 LA 25	F	2	4	2	4	2	-1	0	2	D
7	De sub cujus pede fons	an	AR 928 LU 1760 AM 1145 *LA 496	d	-3	0	2	0	-3	-2	-3	-7	G
1	De sub cujus pede fons	an	WA 410	D	-2	3	5	3	5	7	9	7	D

2	De sublime praeceps	an	WA 249	A	3	5	8	10	8	7	5	12	D
7	De terra plasmasti	an	WA 439	c	-1	-3	-1	0	2	4	0	2	G
	De utero senectutis	alv	GB 198ᵛ	F	2	4	2	-1	0	2	0	2	
7	De ventre matris meae	re	LR 350	G	2	5	4	2	4	2	0	5	G
1	De ventre matris meae	int	GR 523 LU 1499 SYG 196 GB 198 GS 1	D	3	0	2	-2	3	5	7	5	D
	De vultu tuo judicium / Custodi me	grv	GR 345 LU 1021 GS 41 151 GB 70ᵛ SYG 79	C	2	9	10	9	7	9	7	9	
8	Debitas laudes Domino canentes	hy	ST 438	G	-2	-5	-3	-2	-3	-5	-3	-2	G
6	Decantabat populus in Israel	re	LA 226 WA 141	F	4	7	9	7	9	7	9	7	c
4	Decantande speciosis	an	WA 241	F	-1	-3	-5	-3	-1	-3	0	-1	E
1	Decantaverunt Domine nomen	co	GR 471	D	2	-2	0	3	5	7	3	5	D
6	Decantemus Domino canticum	an	WA 250	F	2	4	2	0	2	-3	-5	-3	F
	Decimo enim mense / Requievit arca	rev	WA 77										
6	Decius dixit ad beatum	an	WA 352	c	-1	0	-3	-5	0	2	0	2	c
	Declara super nos Deus	sr	LA 153 WA 99										
	Declaratio sermonum tuorum / Gressus meos	ofv	OTT 39 *GB 88ᵛ SYG 99	F	2	7	4	7	6	4	7	9	
	Declinabo super eum	alv	GR 509 LU 1482	D	2	-2	0	7	5	0	2	5	
4	Decora lux aeternitatis auream	hy	AR 747 LU 1522	F	-1	-3	-5	-3	0	-3	-1	0	E
1	Decora lux aeternitatis auream	hy	AR 749 LU 1523	D	7	9	5	7	9	10	9	7	D
	Decursis omnibus poenis / Gloriosus Dei	rev	VP 199	D	7	5	7	5	3	2	5	7	
2	Decus morum dux minorum	hy	ST 444	C	2	5	4	2	0	4	5	4	D
1	Decus praesulum Dunstanus	an	WA 315	D	-2	0	3	5	3	2	0	2	D
1	Dederunt hostiam pro Domino	an	WA 269	D	2	3	5	2	5	7	3	2	D
8	Dederunt in celebratione	an	WA 375	G	-5	-2	0	2	0	2	0	-2	G
	Dederunt in escam meam fel / Improperium	grv	GR [107]	C	2	5	7	9	7	5	7	5	
	Dedi spiritum meum / Ecce puer meus	rev	WA 39										
	Dedisti Domine habitaculum / Invenerunt in modum	rev	WA 409										
1	Dedisti Domine habitaculum	an	AR 929 LU 1761 AM 1148 *PM 213 WA 410 LA 496	D	-2	3	5	3	5	7	10	7	D
8	Dedisti Domine habitaculum	re	LA 495 WA 409	D	3	5	7	5	7	5	7	5	G
8	Dedisti haereditatem timentibus	an	LR 136 WA 411 LA 506	G	5	4	0	4	5	2	0	2	G
	Dedisti haereditatem timentibus	alv	SYG 218	G	7	5	7	9	7	5	7	5	
	Dedisti mihi protectionem	alv	GR 465	C	2	5	7	4	2	5	4	5	

#	Incipit		Source										
	Dedit autem Jeremias Hic est fratrum	rev	WA 182										
1	Dedit ei Dominus potestatem	an	AR 894⁶ LU 1705 AM 1092	D	-2	3	5	3	5	7	10	7	D
3	Dedit illi Deus sapientiam	int	GR 422 LU 1352	E	1	-2	3	8	5	3	8	5	E
	Dedit illi Dominus scientiam	alv	GB 272	G	2	4	2	0	2	4	2	0	
	Dedit Mariae Dominus Elegit Mariam	rev	LR 264										
1	Dedit mihi Dominus linguam	int	GR 28**	D	7	8	7	5	7	5	3	5	D
7	Dedit mihi Dominus pennas	an	AM 819	G	5	4	5	7	9	7	5	7	G
7	Dedit pater penitenti	an	WA 95	d	-2	-3	0	2	-2	0	-2	-3	G
8	Dedit se ut liberaret	an	AR 304 *AM 281	G	5	2	0	2	0	2	0	-2	G
6	Deduc me in justitia	an	AR 75	F	2	4	2	4	2	0	2	0	F
1	Deduc me in semitam	re	LA 240 *WA 145	C	2	9	11	9	7	9	11	9	D
	Deduc quasi torrentem Jerusalem luge	rev	LA 202 WA 125										
	Deduc quasi torrentem Jerusalem surge	rev	OHS 598 LU 757										
	Deduxisti sicut oves Magna enim sunt	rev	WA 170										
	Defecerunt prae lacrimis	sr	AR 846 LU 1638 AM 1048										
	Defecit caro mea et cor	alv	GR 506 LU 1479	G	2	4	2	0	2	4	5	4	
	Defecit caro mea et cor Aquae multae	grv	GR 625 LU 1690	F	4	2	7	9	7	4	7	0	
	Defende nos Domine Per signum crucis	trv	SYG 129	F	2	4	2	4	2	4	5	2	
	Deferens autem signum Volens scire	rev	WA 77	a	3	2	-2	0	2	0	-2	0	
1	Deficiente vino jussit	an	AR 336 LU 488 AM 306 *WA 63 *LA 106	D	-2	3	5	3	7	10	7	5	D
8	Defuncto Herode angelus	an	LR 304	G	5	2	0	2	0	4	5	7	G
2	Dei fide qua vivimus	hy	ST 187	a	-2	-4	-5	-4	-2	-4	-5	-7	D
4	Dei fide qua vivimus	hy	ST 284	a	2	0	-2	-4	-2	0	-2	-4	E
2	Dei fide qua vivimus	hy	ST 416	a	2	0	-2	-4	-2	0	-2	-4	D
8	Dei fide qua vivimus	hy	ST 381	c	2	0	-1	-3	0	-3	0	-1	G
4	Dei fide qua vivimus	hy	ST 157	D	3	2	[0	0	0	0	0	0]	E
	Dei genitrix intercede pro nobis Gaude Maria	trv	GR [78] LU 1266	C	2	5	2	0	2	0	2	0	
	Dei gratia doctor Cum sancto sancte	rev	WA 283										
4	Dele Domine iniquitatem	an	AM 45	E	1	3	5	3	5	3	1	-2	E
4	Dele iniquitatem meam	an	AR 111	F	-1	-3	-5	-3	0	-1	0	2	E

5	Delectare in Domino et dabit	re	LA 88 WA 64	F	4	7	6	4	7	9	7	6	F
	Delectare in Domino et dabit Spera in Domino	grv	GR 423 LU 1352[V]	D	7	5	7	3	7	8	7	5	
2	Deletis cunctis substantiis	re	WA 77	D	-2	0	-2	-5	-2	0	3	2	D
8	Delicta juventutis meae	an	AR [161] LU 1788 *WA 437 LA 555	a	-4	-2	0	-2	0	-2	-4	-2	G
	Delicta juventutis meae Congregati sunt	rev	AR 197*	a	-2	-4	0	3	0	-2	0	2	
2	Denariorum numero	hy	ST 33	E	-2	0	-2	-4	-2	0	3	5	D
8	Deo nostro jucunda	an	AR 147 AM 161 WA 60 *LA 105	c	-1	0	-3	-5	-7	-5	-3	-1	G
	Deponet omnes iniquitates Qui venturus	rev	LA 13 WA 14										
1	Deposuit Dominus potentes	an	AR 184	D	-2	3	5	3	5	7	5	7	D
1	Deposuit potentes sanctos	an	WA 67 *LA 103	D	-2	3	5	3	5	7	5	8	D
1	Deprecamur te Domine	an	WA 227	C	2	9	10	9	7	9	12	11	a
2	Deprecamur te Domine	an	GB 157	A	3	5	7	5	7	8	7	8	D
1	Deprecatus enim sum	re	WA 345	C	2	9	11	9	7	5	7	9	D
	Deprecatus sum vultum tuum Confitebor tibi	ofv	SYG 110 GB 98	C	2	9	11	9	7	9	12	9	
	Derelinquat impius viam Scindite corda	rev	LA 129										
8	Derelinquat impius viam	re	LA 131	G	2	0	2	0	-2	0	2	5	G
	Derelinquerunt me proximi Fratres mei	rev	LA 176										
	Dereliquo reposita est Bonum certamen	alv	LA 423										
	Dereliquo reposita est Scio cui credidi	anv	LA 422										
	Dereliquo reposita est Scio cui credidi	intv	SYG 204										
2	Deriventur fontes tui	gr	GR 555 LU 1562	F	2	4	0	2	4	7	4	7	a
1	Descendentibus illis	an	WA 90 (inc illeg)										D
4	Descendet Dominus sicut pluvia	re	LA 14 380 *WA 15	F	-3	0	-1	0	2	0	-1	0	E
7	Descendi in hortum nucum ... alleluia	an	LR 252	G	4	5	7	9	12	7	9	7	G
7	Descendi in hortum nucum ... revertere	an	PM 243 WA 356 LA 458	G	4	5	7	9	12	7	9	7	G
7	Descendit angelus Domini	re	LR 352 *LA 402 *WA 321	G	2	5	4	2	4	2	0	7	G
8	Descendit angelus Domini	an	LR 355	G	5	2	0	-2	0	2	0	-2	G
7	Descendit angelus Domini	an	WA 325	G	5	4	5	7	5	2	5	4	G
1	Descendit de caelis Deus	re	LR 59 LA 32	D	3	0	-2	3	5	7	5	3	D
1	Descendit de caelis missus	re	PM 27 WA 31	D	3	0	-2	3	5	7	5	3	D

8 Descendit hic justificatus	an	AR 562 LU 1023 AM 601	G	5	2	0	2	0	-2	0	2	G
8 Descendit Jesus cum eis	re	LR 316	G	-2	-5	-3	-2	-3	-5	-7	-5	G
8 Descendit Jesus cum eis	an	AR 325 654 LU 474 1407 AM 842	G	-2	-5	-3	-2	0	2	0	-2	G
1 Descendit Jesus cum eis	co	GR 63 LU 473	F	2	0	-3	-1	-5	-3	0	2	D
8 Descendit Jesus cum Maria	an	LU 1439	G	5	2	0	-2	0	2	0	4	G
Descendit Moyses de monte Splendida facta est	rev	LA 159 WA 101										
Descendit spiritus sanctus Hodie in Jordane	rev	LR 71 LA 67 WA 58(53)										
6 Descendit spiritus sanctus	an	LA 75	c	-1	-3	-5	-3	0	2	0	2	c
Descenditque cum illo Honestum fecit	rev	LR 154 LA 526										
4 Desiderio desideravi hoc Pascha	an	AR 419 LU 1100 AM 396 WA 110 *LA 174	G	2	5	7	5	7	9	7	5	a
Desiderium animae ejus Posuisti	rev	LR 156 LA 526										
8 Desiderium animae ejus	re	LA 525	G	-5	0	2	4	2	0	2	4	G
8 Desiderium animae ejus	tr	GR [5] LU 1131 SYG 52 *GB 51^v GS 208	F	2	4	2	4	2	0	2	4	G
Desiderium animae ejus Posuisti Domine	ofv	OTT 136 *GB 233^v	F	2	5	2	0	-3	-5	-3	0	
Desiderium animae ejus Posuisti Domine	grv	GR (6) GB 45^v SYG 43 GS 206	C	2	9	12	9	7	9	7	4	
4 Desiderium animae ejus	re	LR 155 207 *WA 416	D	3	0	3	2	5	3	0	2	E
6 Desiderium animae ejus ... Domine	of	GR [50] OTT 153 LU 1208 SYG 215 GB 53^v GS 224	C	2	5	9	7	9	5	2	5	F
6 Desiderium cordis ejus	re	LR 296	a	-4	-2	-4	-5	-4	-2	-4	-2	F
1 Desiderium cordis ejus	gr	GR 82**	C	2	9	10	9	7	5	7	9	D
5 Desiderium meum omnipotens	re	WA 175	F	4	7	9	7	6	4	7	9	F
2 Desiderium pauperum exaudivit	of	GR 589 LU 1616	A	3	5	7	3	0	3	2	3	D
Despecta namque praesentis O veneranda martyrum	rev	VP 255 *WA 423										
Destruxit quidem claustra Recessit pastor ... nam	rev	OHS 608 LU 766 LA 203										
Destruxit quidem claustra Recessit pastor ... portas	rev	LR 341										
7 Det tibi Deus de rore	re	LA 137 WA 91	G	5	4	5	7	5	7	9	7	G
Det vobis cor omnibus Exaudiat Dominus	rev	LA 299										
2 Det vobis Deus idipsum	of	GR [133]	E	3	5	7	5	3	5	7	5	a

Incipit		type	sources										
	Det vobis Dominus suam Dominus Deus Israel	intv	SYG 233										
2	Deum time et mandata	re	WA 88	D	-2	0	3	5	3	2	0	-2	D
4	Deum verum unum in trinitate	inv	LR 440 WA 158	C	2	4	5	4	2	5	4	2	E
4	Deum vivum in quem cor	inv	LR 451	C	2	4	5	4	2	5	4	2	E
1	Deus a Libano veniet	an	AR 243 AM 218 WA 19 LA 26	D	-2	0	2	3	5	3	2	0	D
	Deus a Libano veniet Domine audivi	trv	GR 206 OHS 529 LU 721 *GS 98 GB 116 SYG 136	F	2	4	2	4	2	4	5	2	
	Deus a Libano veniet	alv	SYG 4	C	2	4	7	9	5	4	7	5	
8	Deus adjuvat me	an	OHS 612 AR 135 LU 521 768 *WA 126 LA 204	G	2	0	-2	0	2	0	-2	0	G
	Deus auribus nostris Exsurge Domine	anv	PM 133										
	Deus auribus nostris Exsultabo in Jerusalem	intv	GR 507 LU 1481										
	Deus auribus nostris Exsurge quare obdormis	intv	GR 77 LU 504 GS 26 GB 57^V SYG 60										
	Deus auribus nostris Exsurge Domine	grv	GR 143 *GS 65 *GB 91^V SYG 103	a	3	2	3	5	3	2	3	2	
tp	Deus autem noster in caelo	an	OHS 159 AR 48 LU 256	C	2	5	4	5	7	9	5	4	G
	Deus autem rex noster	alv	GR 79**	D	-2	0	-2	-5	-2	-3	-2	0	
8	Deus canticum novum	re	LA 239 WA 145	D	3	5	7	5	7	5	7	9	G
8	Deus caritas est	an	SYG 131	F	2	4	6	7	6	4	2	0	G
4	Deus creator omnium	hy	ST 254	a	-2	-4	-5	-7	-2	0	3	0	E
4	Deus creator omnium	hy	ST 144	F	-1	2	4	2	0	2	4	2	E
8	Deus creator omnium	hy	ST 214	D	2	3	5	3	5	7	5	3	G
1	Deus creator omnium	hy	VP 28	C	2	4	0	2	5	4	2	4	D
7	Deus creator omnium	hy	ST 364	G	2	4	5	4	2	0	5	7	G
2	Deus creator omnium	hy	ST 5	D	3	2	5	3	2	5	0	2	D
8	Deus creator omnium	hy	ST 28	G	4	2	5	4	2	5	0	2	G
	Deus cui adstat angelorum Locus iste	grv	GR [72] LU 1251 GS 175 GB 173^V *SYG 263	F	4	7	9	11	7	9	7	2	
4	Deus cujus sedes est caelum	an	PM 241	F	-1	-3	2	0	-3	4	2	0	E
1	Deus de caelis qui es pius	an	GB 157^V	D	-2	0	3	2	0	2	0	-2	D
4	Deus deorum Domine	hy	ST 247	a	-2	-4	-5	-7	-2	0	-2	0	E
	Deus deorum Dominus Congregate illi sanctos	intv	GR 63**										
8	Deus deorum Dominus	an	OHS 299 (nm) WA 65 LA 90	c	-1	-3	-5	-3	-5	-7	-5	-3	G

	Incipit		Sources										
2	Deus Deus meus ad te	of	GR 265 OTT 66 LU 818 *SYG 165 *GB 147^V *GS 128	C	2	5	2	0	2	4	5	4	D
1	Deus Deus meus ad te	an	AR 342 AM 312 *WA 74 LA 113	D	3	2	0	-2	3	5	7	8	D
	Deus Deus meus respice Domine ne longe facias	intv	GR 178 OHS 106 LU 592 GS 86 GB 108^V SYG 121										
	Deus Deus meus respice Deus meus es tu	rev	WA 106										
2	Deus Deus meus respice	tr	GR 180 OHS 109 LU 594 SYG 122 GB 109 GS 86	D	-2	0	-2	-5	-2	0	-2	0	D
	Deus docuisti me	alv	GR 519	C	2	0	2	5	2	0	2	0	
8	Deus docuisti me	tr	GR 72**	G	2	4	2	0	2	0	2	0	G
8	Deus Domini mei Abraham	re	LA 122 *WA 83	G	2	0	2	0	-2	2	5	4	G
3	Deus dum egredereris	int	GR 300 LU 892 SYG 186 GB 191^V GS 139	G	-5	-3	-2	0	2	0	2	0	E
	Deus enim creavit me Ego ex ore	rev	LR 266										
8	Deus enim firmavit	of	GR 32 LU 406 OTT 16 *GB 16 *GS F H *SYG 16	a	-4	0	-2	0	-2	0	3	0	G
	Deus et pater Domini Damasci praepositus	anv	WA 266 LA 431										
	Deus et pater Domini Damasci praepositus	rev	LA 424 WA 265										
8	Deus exaudi orationem meam	gr	GR 156 SYG 111 GB 99 GS 73	F	4	2	4	2	4	0	2	4	G
	Deus fidelis in quo Attende caelum	trv	GR 231 LU 776^U OHS 656 *GB 119^V GS 112 *SYG 151	G	2	4	5	4	5	7	5	0	
7	Deus in adjutorium meum	int	GR 350 LU 1027 SYG 89 GB 78^V GS 51 154	c	5	2	0	2	-2	0	2	5	G
	Deus in cujus conspectu Oravit Jacob	rev	LA 140 WA 92										
5	Deus in loco sancto suo	int	GR 347 LU 1024 SYG 245 GB 253 GS 152	c	2	0	2	0	-3	-5	-3	-1	F
	Deus in nomine tuo salvum	sr	LA 90 WA 164										
	Deus in nomine tuo salvum Ecce Deus adjuvat	intv	GR 342 LU 1016 GS 150 GB 252										
	Deus in nomine tuo salvum Peccantem me quotidie	rev	AR [171] LU 1797 *LA 556 *WA 437	a	-2	0	-2	-5	-2	0	2	3	
4	Deus in nomine tuo salvum	int	GR 141 *SYG 103 *GS 64 *GB 91	E	3	1	-2	3	5	3	5	6	E
	Deus in nomine tuo salvum Deus exaudi	grv	GR 156 *GS 73 *SYG 111 GB 99	G	5	7	5	4	5	7	9	7	

	Incipit		Source										
	Deus in te speravi Repleatur os meum	intv	GB 192^v										
3	Deus in te speravi	re	LA 97	G	2	5	2	4	5	4	5	7	E
	Deus in te speravi Esto mihi in Deum	grv	GR 339 LU 1013 GS 64 149 GB 91 SYG 103	F	4	7	9	7	9	11	7	9	
	Deus iniqui insurrexerunt Misericordia tua	rev	LA 100										
	Deus injusti insurrexerunt Misericordia tua	rev	WA 69										
3	Deus Israel conjungat vos	int	GR [121] LU 1288	G	5	2	4	5	7	5	4	0	E
8	Deus Israel propter te	re	OHS 241 (nm) WA 114	c	2	0	2	0	-5	-3	-5	-7	G
	Deus judex justus	alv	GR 328 LU 982 *SYG 239 GB 248^v GS 142	G	2	0	-5	-3	-5	-3	-7	0	
8	Deus judex justus	an	AM 14	G	2	4	2	0	2	0	-2	0	G
	Deus judicium tuum Dignus est angus	intv	GR 638 LU 1709										
	Deus judicium tuum Ecce advenit	intv	GR 57 LU 459 GS J GB 32 SYG 30										
	Deus judicium tuum Reges Tharsis	ofv	OTT 21 GB 34 *SYG 31	c	-3	2	0	-1	-3	0	-1	-3	
	Deus laudem meam Domine fac mecum	ofv	OTT 37 GB 85^v SYG 96	b	1	0	1	0	1	0	1	0	
7	Deus magnus Dominus	inv	LA 80	d	-2	2	0	-2	-3	-2	0	-2	G
4	Deus majestatis intonuit	an	AR 71	F	-3	-1	0	2	-1	0	2	4	E
1	Deus manens primordium	hy	ST 161	D	7	8	7	5	7	9	12	10	D
	Deus meus clamabo per diem Deus Deus meus	trv	GR 180 OHS 109 LU 594 GS 86 *GB 109 *SYG 122	D	3	2	3	5	7	5	7	5	
8	Deus meus eripe me	an	OHS 371 LU 629 *WA 118 *LA 189	c	-1	-3	-1	0	-1	-5	-3	-5	G
8	Deus meus eripe me	re	LR 413 *LA 168 *WA 107	c	2	-1	0	2	0	-3	-1	0	G
	Deus meus es tu et confitebor Deus canticum	rev	LA 239										
	Deus meus es tu et confitebor In conspectu angelorum	rev	LA 466										
8	Deus meus es tu et confitebor	an	AR 354 *WA 79 *LA 123	c	2	0	-1	0	2	0	-1	-3	G
8	Deus meus es tu me discedas	re	LA 167 *WA 106	G	5	4	5	2	0	4	0	2	G
4	Deus meus impolluta via	int	GR 97**	D	3	5	7	5	7	5	2	3	E
8	Deus meus in te confido	an	AR 114 LU 279^E	c	-1	-5	-1	-3	0	-3	-5	-7	G
3	Deus meus misericordia	an	AR 139 LU 279^M	c	-1	-3	-5	-10	-8	-7	-5	-7	E
	Deus meus ne elongeris a me Deus meus eripe	rev	LR 413 LA 168 WA 107										

	Incipit	Genre	Sources										
	Deus meus pone illos ut rotam Sciant gentes	grv	GR 78 LU 506 GS 26 GB 58 *SYG 60	a	-2	0	3	0	3	-2	-4	0	
8	Deus misereatur et benedicat	an	WA 98 *LA 152	F	2	4	7	6	7	4	2	0	G
	Deus misereatur nostri ... nobis Nos autem gloriari	intv	GR 195 490 LU 667 1454 OHS 257 439 GS 90 235 SYG 125 GB 112^v										
3	Deus misereatur nostri ... nobis	int	GR [126] LU 1292	G	-5	-3	-2	0	2	0	2	0	E
8	Deus misereatur nostri ... nos	an	AR 111	F	2	4	7	6	7	4	7	6	G
	Deus misereatur nostri ... nos Deus Benedicat nos	rev	WA 158	a	-2	0	-2	-4	-5	-2	0	-2	
	Deus ne elongeris	see	Deus meus ne elongeris										
	Deus omnipotens praecinxit	sr	AR 588 LU 1316 AM 765										
1	Deus omnium exauditor	re	LA 267 *WA 165	D	2	3	0	2	0	2	3	0	D
8	Deus piorum gaudium	hy	ST 400	G	-5	-2	0	2	0	-2	0	5	G
	Deus qui in sanctis Domum istam protege	anv	SYG 135										
2	Deus qui mundum crimine jacentem	hy	ST 377	D	-2	0	2	3	5	7	5	3	D
8	Deus qui mundum crimine jacentem	hy	ST 428	G	2	0	-2	2	5	4	2	0	G
	Deus qui perduxisti Deus Domini mei	rev	WA 83										
7	Deus qui praecinxit me virtute	gr	GR 463 LU 1419	G	5	2	0	2	0	-2	0	2	G
2	Deus qui quosvis eligis	hy	ST 234	D	-2	0	3	0	-5	0	-2	0	D
	Deus qui sedes super thronum	alv	GB 36^v	G	2	5	2	5	9	5	7	2	
	Deus qui sedes super thronum ... esto	alv	GR 331 LU 999	G	2	5	2	5	2	5	9	5	
4	Deus qui sedes super thronum ... esto ... quia	re	LA 81 *WA 60	F	2	0	-3	-1	2	4	0	-1	E
1	Deus qui sedes quper thronum ... esto ... quia	an	WA 70	D	2	0	-2	0	3	5	3	2	D
8	Deus sacrati nominis	hy	ST 423	G	2	0	-2	0	2	4	0	-2	G
	Deus tentavit illos Justorum animae	rev	LR 189										
4	Deus tu conversus	an	AR 170	F	-1	-3	-1	-5	-3	-1	0	2	E
3	Deus tu convertens vivificabis	of	GR 6 OTT 6 LU 330 *SYG 4 *GS 3 7 *GB 3	G	2	5	7	5	4	5	2	4	E
4	Deus tuorum militum	hy	ST 404	a	-2	-5	-7	-2	0	3	0	-2	E
4	Deus tuorum militum	hy	ST 243	a	-2	-4	-5	-7	-2	0	-2	0	E
2	Deus tuorum militum	hy	ST 61	a	-2	-4	-2	0	-5	-2	-4	-7	D
4	Deus tuorum militum	hy	AR [25]	E	-2	-4	0	3	1	-2	-4	-2	E
8	Deus tuorum militum	hy	AM 254	G	-2	-3	-5	-2	2	0	-2	0	G

8	Deus tuorum militum	hy	ST 16	G	-2	-3	-2	0	2	0	2	5	G
3	Deus tuorum militum	hy	AR [13²] LU 1127	E	-2	3	5	8	7	5	7	8	E
3	Deus tuorum militum	hy	AR [24] AM 630	E	1	3	1	0	-2	0	-2	-4	E
3	Deus tuorum militum	hy	LR 163	E	1	3	1	0	-2	0	1	-2	E
1	Deus tuorum militum	hy	AR 277 LR 428 LU 419	C	2	4	7	5	4	2	4	5	D
2	Deus tuorum militum	hy	ST 457	C	2	5	4	0	2	4	5	4	D
1	Deus tuorum militum	hy	ST 196	D	3	0	-2	3	5	7	5	10	D
7	Deus tuorum militum	hy	ST 44	G	4	5	7	9	7	5	4	5	G
8	Deus tuorum militum	hy	ST 197	G	5	2	0	5	4	5	7	5	G
8	Deus tuorum militum	hy	ST 388 400	G	5	2	0	5	7	5	4	2	G
8	Deus tuorum militum	hy	AR [13¹] LR 148 LU 1126 AM 639	C	5	4	5	7	9	7	5	7	G
8	Deus tuorum militum corona	hy	ST 100	a	3	0	-2	3	2	3	5	3	G
	Deus ultionum Dominus Expandi manus	rev	LA 502 WA 236										
	Deus ultionum Dominus Factus est mihi	rev	LA 101 WA 69										
	Deus venerunt gentes Intret in conspectu	intv	GR [21] LU 1162 GS 210 GB 43ᵛ SYG 40										
	Deus venerunt gentes	alv	SYG 222	C	5	4	2	0	2	4	2	7	
	Deus virtuum convertere	alv	GR [132]	D	7	8	7	5	7	5	2	3	
	Deus vitam meam annuntiavi	sr	AR 679										
8	Deus vitam meam nuntiavi	gr	GR 128 SYG 94 GB 83ᵛ GS 56	F	4	2	4	2	4	0	2	4	G
2	Devota mente socii	hy	ST 396	G	-3	-2	0	2	0	-2	-3	-5	D
8	Devota mente socii	hy	ST 432	G	2	0	-2	0	2	4	0	-2	G
	Devotae plebi subveni Sanctissime confessor	rev	PM 145 LR 330 AM 1194 LA 372 WA 299										
	Dextera Dei fecit virtutem	alv	GR 269 LU 827 SYG 254 GB 234ᵛ GS 161	a	-2	0	-2	-5	-2	-4	-2	0	
8	Dextera Domini fecit virtutem	an	AR 379 AM 352 WA 93 LA 141	c	-1	-3	-5	-3	-1	-3	-5	-3	G
	Dextera Domini fecit virtutem Haec dies	grv	GR 250(241) OHS 796(709)LU 793(778) GS 120(117) SYG 157(152) GB 135ᵛ(125)	a	3	5	7	5	3	2	3	0	
2	Dextera Domini fecit virtutem	of	GR 72 196 492 OHS 455 LU 677 1457 OTT 25 *SYG 43 GB 39ᵛ GS 23 57 95	E	3	5	7	5	3	5	7	5	a
8	Dextera Domini salvavit eos	an	LR 140	c	-1	0	-3	-5	-3	-5	-3	-5	G

Mode	Incipit		Sources	Fin	1	2	3	4	5	6	7	8	Fin
	Dextera tua Domine glorificata est Gloriosus Deus	grv	GR [22] LU 1163 *GS 212 GB 43^V SYG 40	D	7	5	7	3	7	8	7	5	D
	Dexteram meam et collum Ipsi sum desponsata	rev	LA 335 WA 255										
7	Dexteram meam et collum	an	WA 253 *LA 332	d	-3	0	2	0	-3	-2	0	-2	G
5	Dexteram meam et collum	re	LA 333 WA 253	F	4	7	9	7	9	7	6	4	F
	Dic mihi fili mi Vae nobis quia peccavimus	anv	SYG 139	C	4	5	7	5	4	2	4	5	
	Dicant nunc Judaei Christus resurgens	rev	AR 164* PM 66 VP 141 WA 223	F	2	-1	-3	0	-1	-5	-3	-1	
	Dicant nunc Judaei Christus resurgens	anv	WA 133 SYG 147	F	2	0	-1	-3	0	-1	-5	-3	
7	Dicant nunc qui redempti	re	LR 418 LA 241	a	3	5	3	5	3	2	5	8	G
	Dicant nunc qui redempti Haec dies	grv	GR 247(241) OHS 784(709) LU 790(778) *GS 119(117) SYG 156(152) *GB 133(125)	a	3	5	3	5	7	8	7	3	
	Dicat nunc Israel Haec dies	grv	GR 245(241) OHS 774(709) LU 786(778) *GS 118(117) *SYG 155(152) *GB 131(125)	a	3	5	3	5	7	8	7	3	
	Dicat nunc Israel Saepe expugnaverunt	trv	GR 153 LU 571 GS 72 GB 97^V SYG 110	D	3	0	3	7	3	5	3	5	
1 2	Dicebat enim intra se	an	AR 573 LU 1108 AM 615 WA 191 LA 320	D	-2	0	2	3	5	3	2	0	D
	Dicebat enim regi Joannes Interrogatus Joannes	rev	LA 451										
3	Dicebat Jesus turbis ... propterea	an	AR 412 LU 1097 *AM 390	G	5	2	0	2	5	2	4	5	E
7	Dicebat Jesus turbis ... responderunt	an	LA 173	G	5	2	0	2	5	2	4	5	G
	Dicet Domino susceptor meus es Scapulis suis	ofv	OTT 32 GB 66^V SYG 74	c	2	-3	-7	-3	-5	-3	-5	-7	
	Dicet Domino susceptor meus es Qui habitat	trv	GR 95 LU 533 GS 35 GB 65 SYG 73	F	2	-3	0	2	0	-1	0	-1	
8	Dicit Andreas Simoni	co	GR 392 *SYG 231 *GB 245^V *GS g	c	2	0	-1	0	-1	-5	-1	0	G
	Dicit Dominus Domino meo		<u>see</u> Dixit Dominus ...										
6	Dicit Dominus ego cogito	int	GR 386 LU 1074 *SYG 258 GB 264 GS e	D	-4	-2	0	-2	3	5	3	7	F
6	Dicit Dominus implete hydrias aqua	co	GR 70 LU 487 SYG 37 GB 39 GS 22	F	4	5	4	2	4	2	0	2	F

8	Dicit Dominus paenitentiam	an	AR 253 AM 229 *WA 16 LA 17	G	-2	-5	-2	-5	-3	-2	0	2	G
4	Dicit Dominus Petro	int	GR 530 *SYG 201 *GB 202 GS o	E	3	1	0	1	3	5	3	5	E
1	Dicit Dominus sermones	int	GR 656 LU 1758 SYG 228 GB 244^{v} GS 200	D	7	8	7	5	7	5	3	5	D
3	Dicit mater Jesu	re	LR 315	F	-1	-3	2	4	7	6	9	7	E
	Dicite Deo quam terribilia Jubilate Deo	intv	GR 265 LU 821 GS 128 GB 148 SYG 165										
	Dicite Domino quam terribilia Fili quid fecisti	cov	SYG 33										
	Dicite in gentibus quia Dominus	alv	GR 256 491 LU 801 1455 OHS 817 SYG 173 *GS 122	G	4	5	4	0	2	4	2	0	
8	Dicite invitatis ecce prandium	an	AR 570 AM 610 *WA 190 *LA 318	F	2	0	2	4	2	4	2	4	G
7	Dicite pusillanimes confortamini	co	GR 9 LU 337 *SYG 7 *GB 6^{v} *GS 5	G	2	-2	2	0	2	5	4	5	G
1	Dicite pusillanimes confortamini	an	AR 229 AM 202 WA 13 *LA 12	F	2	4	2	4	2	-1	0	2	D
	Dicite quidnam vidistis Quem vidistis	rev	LU 377 LR 58 LA 36 WA 49(30)										
8	Dico autem vobis amicis meis	co	GR [28] LU 1169 SYG 214 GB 219^{v} GS q	G	2	0	-2	0	2	4	5	0	G
5	Dico vobis gaudium	co	GR 330 LU 984 *SYG 260 *GB 248^{v} *GS e	c	-3	0	2	4	2	0	-1	2	F
4	Dico vobis gaudium	an	WA 187 *LA 85	F	2	0	-1	0	2	4	-1	-3	E
8	Diem festum sacratissimae	re	LA 332 WA 253	D	3	5	7	5	7	5	2	3	G
6	Diem festum virginis	of	GB 50^{v}	D	-2	0	2	3	2	0	3	-2	F
8	Diem sacrati nominis	hy	ST 401	G	2	4	5	4	2	0	5	7	G
3	Dies absoluti praetereunt	hy	ST 224	E	1	-2	3	5	8	5	3	1	E
4	Dies absoluti praetereunt	hy	ST 283	E	1	0	-2	3	5	8	5	3	E
4	Dies absoluti praetereunt	hy	ST 283	E	1	3	5	8	5	3	1	0	E
1	Dies absoluti praetereunt	hy	ST 333	D	3	5	7	12	10	9	7	10	D
	Dies diei eructat In omnem terram	ofv	SYG 54	E	3	5	-2	0	3	5	8	7	
	Dies diei eructat In omnem terram	ofv	GB 236	A	3	7	5	7	5	3	5	3	
1	Dies Domini sicut fur	an	WA 25 LA 17	C	2	9	11	9	7	9	7	4	D
	Dies illa dies irae calamitatis Libera me de morte	rev	PM 321 AR [174] GR 102* LU 1767 LA 557 *WA 438	F	-1	0	-3	-1	-3	-5	-3	-1	

	Incipit		Sources										
	Dies mei sicut umbra Induta est caro	rev	WA 172										
	Dies mei sicut umbra Velociter exaudi	rev	LA 104										
	Dies mei sicut umbra Rogamus te Domine	rev	LA 557	c	-1	0	2	0	-1	0	-1	-3	
2	Dies mei sicut umbra	gr	GB 104^v	G	4	2	5	2	5	2	0	4	a
	Dies mei velocius transierunt Induta est caro	rev	LA 283										
	Dies sanctificatus illuxit nobis	sr	WA 56										
	Dies sanctificatus illuxit nobis Beata viscera	rev	LR 65 LU 389 LA 33 WA 29										
	Dies sanctificatus illuxit nobis Hic est dies	rev	LR 81 LA 68 WA 55										
	Dies sanctificatus illuxit nobis	alv	GR 34 LU 409 GB 17^v *GS G SYG 19	D	-2	0	2	3	5	7	5	3	
8	Dies sanctificatus illuxit nobis	re	LR 73 LA 70 WA 55	G	5	2	0	-5	0	2	0	2	G
3	Diffusa est gratia in conceptione	an	LR 261	G	4	5	2	0	4	2	5	4	E
	Diffusa est gratia in labiis Specie tua	rev	LR 217 LA 542										
4	Diffusa est gratia in labiis	re	LR 216 254 *LA 542 *WA 431	F	-3	0	-1	0	-1	0	-1	2	E
2	Diffusa est gratia in labiis	tr	SYG 49 GS 228	F	-2	0	-2	-5	-2	0	-2	0	D
	Diffusa est gratia in labiis Afferentur regi	ofv	OTT 155 *GB 30 *SYG 29	E	-2	3	5	8	5	8	5	8	
	Diffusa est gratia in labiis	alv	GR 405 LU 1323 SYG 5 GB 4^v GS 228	c	-1	2	0	-1	0	2	0	-3	
	Diffusa est gratia in labiis	alv	SYG 5	a	3	2	0	2	-2	0	-2	-4	
8	Diffusa est gratia in labiis	of	GR [58] OTT 156 LU 1223 *SYG 46 *GB 49 *GS 181	D	3	2	3	5	7	5	7	5	G
6	Diffusa est gratia in labiis	co	GR 559 LU 1572 *SYG 6 GB 5 GS 230	D	3	5	3	5	7	5	7	5	F
5	Diffusa est gratia in labiis	gr	GR [69] LU 1240 SYG 28 *GB 29^v *GS 227	D	3	5	7	5	7	3	5	3	F
1	Diffusa est gratia in labiis	an	LR 56 LU 373 *WA 49 *LA 31	F	4	2	4	-1	0	2	-1	2	D
1	Digna Deo Cilinia	hy	ST 143	C	2	5	4	2	0	2	4	2	D
4	Dignare me laudare te	an	LR 251 *WA 268 LA 348	a	-2	0	3	7	5	3	5	7	a
8	Dignas promamus Domino	of	GB 228^v	F	2	4	2	4	0	4	0	2	G
	Dignis ergo veneremur Praesul Christi	rev	WA 250	c	-2	-3	-5	0	2	0	2	4	

	Dignissime namque devotis Celebremus solemniter	rev	WA 282	a	-2	0	-2	-4	-5	-2	0	-2	
5	Dignum canentes angeli	hy	ST 19	C	4	5	7	9	7	9	11	12	C
5	Dignum namque est	an	WA 364	a	-2	-4	0	3	5	3	1	3	F
5	Dignum namque est	an	PM 253	c	-1	0	-1	-3	-5	-7	-3	0	F
8	Dignum sibi Dominus computavit	an	LA 497	d	-3	0	2	0	-2	0	-3	-2	G
6	Dignus a dignis	an	WA 43	F	-1	0	-3	-5	0	2	4	5	F
	Dignus es Domine accipere	alv	GR 540	D	-2	0	3	0	2	0	-2	3	
7	Dignus es Domine accipere	re	LR 416 AM 1199 *LA 224 WA 139	G	5	4	5	7	5	7	5	4	G
1	Dignus es Domine Deus	an	WA 139	D	-2	2	3	5	3	0	-2	3	D
4	Dignus es Domine Deus	an	GS 82	C	4	2	0	2	5	4	5	7	E
	Dignus est agnus Ecce vicit	rev	PM 68 OHS 789 LR 89										
3	Dignus est agnus	int	GR 638 LU 1709	E	1	0	-2	3	5	3	5	8	E
	Digreditur namque vir Patriarchae nostri	rev	WA 293										
6	Dilectae animam e carcere	an	AM 1136	F	2	4	0	2	0	-1	0	-3	F
8	Dilecti Deo et hominibus	an	WA 375	F	2	4	2	0	2	4	7	6	G
8	Dilectio Dei honorabilis	int	GR 603 LU 1645	G	5	4	5	2	-2	0	2	0	G
	Dilectio et benignitas Mecum est maxima	rev	WA 387										
	Dilectio illius custodia Initium sapientiae	rev	LA 278										
1	Dilectus Deo et angelis	an	WA 316	C	2	5	2	0	2	0	2	0	D
2	Dilectus meus candidus	an	AR 674 LU 1423	D	-2	-5	-2	0	3	2	0	2	D
	Dilectus meus mihi	alv	GR (10)	C	2	9	10	9	7	9	5	4	
	Dilectus meus mihi Sicut lilium	grv	GR 75**	F	4	2	7	9	7	4	7	4	
	Dilexi quoniam exaudivit	alv	GB 262	G	2	0	-2	0	2	5	2	5	
	Dilexisti justitiam et odisti Beata es N.	rev	LR 230										
	Dilexisti justitiam et odisti Diffusa est	rev	WA 431										
	Dilexisti justitiam et odisti Veni sponsa	trv	GR [52] LU 1217	G	-5	0	2	5	7	5	0	2	
6	Dilexisti justitiam et odisti	co	GB 226^v	c	-3	0	-1	0	-3	-5	-7	-5	F
8	Dilexisti justitiam et odisti	an	LR 289	G	-2	-5	-3	-2	0	2	0	2	G
3	Dilexisti justitiam et odisti	re	LR 221 *LA 543 *WA 431	G	2	0	2	5	0	2	0	2	E
8	Dilexisti justitiam et odisti	gr	GR [52]LU 1216 *SYG 5 *GB 4 *GS 226	C	2	0	7	5	2	0	7	4	G

Num	Incipit	Type	Sources										
8	Dilexisti justitiam et odisti	int	GR [60] LU 1225 *SYG 5 *GB 4 *GS 225	G	2	5	0	-2	0	2	4	5	G
	Dilexisti justitiam et odisti	alv	SYG 229	C	2	5	4	2	5	2	0	5	
	Dilexisti justitiam et odisti / Diffusa est gratia	trv	SYG 49	C	2	5	7	9	5	4	7	5	
4	Dilexisti justitiam et odisti	co	GR [71] LU 1241 SYG 217 *GB 219^V	G	4	7	5	4	0	2	0	-2	b
	Dilexit Andream Dominus	sr	WA 237										
4	Dilexit Andream Dominus	re	LA 503 *WA 236	F	-3	-1	0	2	6	2	4	6	E
	Dilexit Andream Dominus	alv	GR 393 LU 1305 SYG 231 GB 246 GS g	a	-2	-5	-4	-2	-4	-2	-7	-9	
8	Dilexit Andream Dominus	an	LA 497	G	5	2	0	2	0	-2	0	2	G
	Dilexit justitiam et odisti / Fuit sacra	rev	WA 433	d	-2	-4	-5	-2	0	-2	0	2	
	Diligam te Domine fortitudo / Dominus firmamentum	cov	SYG 241										
	Diligam te Domine fortitudo / Circumdederunt me	intv	GR 73 LU 497 GS 24 GB 56 SYG 58										
	Diligam te Domine fortitudo / Deus meus impolluta	intv	GR 97**										
	Diligam te Domine fortitudo / Exaudivit de templo	intv	GR 282 LU 840 GS 132 GB 161^V SYG 177										
	Diligam te Domine fortitudo / Factus est Dominus	intv	GR 320 LU 961 GS 142 GB 247^V SYG 239										
	Diligam te Domine fortitudo / Liberator meus	intv	GR 159 GS 74 GB 100^V SYG 113										
	Diligam te Domine virtus mea	an	OHS 179 (nm)										
4	Diligam te Domine virtus mea	re	LR 342 *LA 82 *WA 61	F	-3	-1	0	2	-1	0	2	4	E
	Diligam te Domine virtus mea / Intonuit de caelo	ofv	OTT 58 *GB 134^V *SYG 156	D	3	5	3	2	-2	0	3	0	
	Diligam te Domine virtus mea	alv	SYG 239 GB 249 *GS 143	F	4	7	9	7	9	7	9	7	
5	Diligamus in invicem	an	WA 214 *SYG 131 *GS 96	F	7	5	4	5	7	9	7	5	F
	Diligamus nos invicem	see	Diligamus in invicem										
4	Diligebat autem eum Jesus	an	LA 48	C	2	0	2	4	5	4	2	0	E
3	Diligebat autem eum Jesus	re	LA 55 *WA 40	G	2	0	2	4	5	4	2	0	E
8	Diligis justitiam et odisti	of	OHS 418 LU 663	D	3	2	3	5	7	5	7	5	G
2	Diligite Dominum omnes sancti	an	LR 385 WA 395 LA 475	D	-2	0	3	2	0	3	5	3	D
1	Diligite Dominum omnes sancti	gr	GR 93**	D	-2	0	3	2	3	5	3	2	D

2 Dimitte Domine peccata	an	VP 263 *WA 229	D	-5	-2	2	0	-2	0	3	5	D
Dinumerabo eos et super arenam Nimis honorati	grv	GR 391 LU 1326 GS w GB 235 SYG 54	a	3	5	7	5	3	2	3	0	
7 Dirigatur oratio mea	gr	GR 109 LU 1060 SYG 76 GB 68v GS 38 163 171	G	7	4	5	7	2	0	5	4	G
Dirige Domine Deus meus Ne recorderis	rev	AR [166] LU 1792 LA 555										
7 Dirige Domine Deus meus	an	AR [154] LU 1782 *WA 436 *LA 553	d	-3	0	2	0	2	0	-2	-5	G
Dirige in conspectu tuo Intende voci	ofv	OTT 83 GB 87v SYG 98	c	2	0	-5	0	2	0	-7	-3	
2 Dirige me Domine in veritate	int	GB 74v	C	2	-1	2	0	2	5	7	9	D
Dirige me in veritate tua Ad te Domine	ofv	OTT 5 *SYG 2 *GB 1v	D	7	10	7	5	7	5	7	10	
Diriget mansuetos in judicio Dulcis et rectus	grv	GR 324 [112] LU 971	D	7	5	7	10	7	5	3	2	
7 Dirupisti Domine vincula mea	an	AR [10] LU 1114 AM 626 *WA 419 *LA 527	G	2	5	7	9	7	5	2	5	G
Dirupisti vincula mea Dominus mihi adjutor	grv	GR 35**	C	2	9	12	9	7	9	4	5	
8 Discede a me pabulum	an	WA 252 *LA 332	G	5	2	-2	0	5	4	2	5	G
8 Discerne causam meam Deus	an	AR 111	c	-1	-3	-5	-3	-7	-5	-3	0	G
7 Discerne causam meam Domine	an	AR 428 OHS 244 254 *AM 407 *WA 115 *LA 186	b	3	0	3	5	3	5	6	5	G
5 Discerne causam meam Domine	gr	GR 158 SYG 112 GB 100 GS 74	D	3	5	3	5	7	3	5	3	F
Disciplina pacis nostrae Vere languores	trv	GR [108]	C	2	5	7	2	5	7	9	7	
8 Disciplinam et sapientiam	re	LR 114 *LA 257 *WA 154	D	3	5	7	5	7	5	7	10	G
Disperge illos in virtute Congregati sunt inimici	rev	LA 297 WA 181										
Dispersit dedit pauperibus Levita Laurentius	anv	LA 437										
Dispersit dedit pauperibus Initium sapientiae	rev	WA 170										
Dispersit dedit pauperibus Levita Laurentius	rev	PM 174 LA 434 WA 347										
Dispersit dedit pauperibus	alv	GR 556 LU 1480	G	2	0	-2	0	-2	2	5	2	
2 Dispersit dedit pauperibus	gr	GR 576 LU 1608 SYG 212 GB 216v *GS 193	E	3	5	8	5	7	8	5	3	a
8 Dispersit dedit pauperibus	an	AR 851 LU 1649	G	5	2	0	2	0	-2	0	2	G
3 Dispersit dedit pauperibus	int	GR 576 LU 1607 *SYG 212 *GB 216 GS 193	G	5	2	0	5	2	0	2	5	E

	Disposui testamentum	alv	SYG 34 GS 222 *GB 272	F	2	4	2	0	2	0	-3	-1			
	Disputabat enim cum Graecis Mirabantur omnes qui	anv	LA 343												
	Disputabat enim cum Graecis Ingressus Paulus	ofv	SYG 45	C	7	9	11	9	7	12	9	7			
8	Disrumpam vincula populi	re	WA 182	D	3	5	7	5	7	5	7	5	G		
	Divertit ab oneribus Joseph cum intraret	rev	LA 148												
7	Dives ille guttam aquae	an	AR 385 LU 1087 AM 359	b	1	3	5	3	5	6	5	3	G		
	Dividunt sibi indumenta mea	an	OHS 471 (nm)												
	Divina namque praeventus Sanctus Benedictus plus	rev	PM 144 LR 321 LA 368 WA 297												
6	Divine ductor Raphael	hy	VP 233	F	4	7	9	7	6	7	9	11	F		
6	Divinis donis Aurea	hy	ST 470	F	2	4	0	2	4	5	4	2	F		
	Divinis gradibus Praeditus hinc	rev	WA 284												
	Divinum munus votum praevenit Unam quam petiit	rev	PM 266	a	-2	-4	0	3	5	3	0	1			
8	Diviserunt sibi vestimenta mea	an	OHS 479 LU 688 *WA 122 LA 195	G	2	0	4	2	5	4	2	5	G		
	Divites eguerunt et esurierunt Gustate et videte	trv	GR 95**	G	-5	0	2	4	2	5	7	5			
	Dixerunt discipuli ad beatum Martinum Beatus Martinus obitum	rev	WA 399												
6	Dixerunt discipuli ad beatum Martinum	gr	GB 242	D	3	5	3	5	7	5	7	5	F		
2	Dixerunt discipuli ad beatum Martinum	re	LA 484 *WA 399	E	3	5	7	5	8	7	8	5	a		
7	Dixerunt discipuli ad beatum Martinum	an	AR 917 LU 1748 AM 1115 WA 402 *LA 486	G	4	5	7	9	7	5	4	2	G		
1	Dixerunt impii apud se	re	OHS 302 (nm) LA 179 *WA 116	a	-2	0	2	3	5	3	2	0	D		
8	Dixerunt impii opprimamus virum	an	AR 429 OHS 247 284 *AM 408 *WA 115 LA 186	G	-2	-3	-5	-7	-2	0	2	0	G		
	Dixerunt viri tabernaculi mei Coenantibus illis	rev	AR 115* LR 127 LU 931												
	Dixi custodiam vias Dedit mihi Dominus	intv	GR 28**												
	Dixi custodiam vias Auribus percipe	rev	LA 91 WA 65												
	Dixi Domino Deus meus Eripe me	trv	GR 208 OHS 534 LU 725 GS 99 GB 116v SYG 137	F	2	-3	0	2	0	-1	0	-1			
	Dixi Domino Deus meus Custodi me	ofv	OTT 52 *SYG 126	G	2	4	5	7	5	4	5	7			
	Dixi Domino Deus meus Custodi me	ofv	GB 113	C	5	7	5	2	5	7	9	5			

7	Dixi iniquis nolite loqui	an	OHS 391 LU 646 WA 119 LA 192	d	-3	-2	0	2	0	-2	-5	-2	G
	Dixi sapientiae soror mea Super salutem ... dilexi	rev	LA 279 WA 169										
4	Dixi vobis jam	an	WA 104	c	-1	-3	-5	-3	-8	-7	-5	-3	E
7	Dixit angelus ad Jacob	re	LA 140 *WA 93	G	2	0	2	0	2	4	0	2	G
1	Dixit angelus ad Mariam	re	WA 302	F	-3	0	-3	-5	0	2	4	2	D
8	Dixit angelus ad Petrum	an	AR 751 799 LU 1515 1577 AM 935 989 *WA 328 *LA 415	c	-1	-3	-1	0	-1	-5	-1	0	G
8	Dixit autem discipulis	an	LA 220	G	2	4	5	2	0	2	0	-2	G
5	Dixit autem Dominus ad Abraham	re	WA 80	c	2	4	0	2	0	-3	-5	0	c
7	Dixit autem dominus ad cultorem	an	LA 317	G	5	4	5	7	9	7	9	7	G
	Dixit autem Dominus in visu Vade Anania et quaere	anv	WA 263										
7	Dixit autem dominus servo	an	WA 191	G	4	5	7	9	7	5	2	4	G
8	Dixit autem dominus servo	an	AR 572 LU 1107 *AM 612 *LA 319	G	5	2	0	-2	0	2	4	2	G
1	Dixit autem Jesus ad mulierem	an	SYG 132	G	5	2	0	4	5	4	5	7	[D]
1	Dixit autem Maria ad angelum ... ecce	re	WA 302	F	-3	0	-3	-5	0	2	4	2	D
3	Dixit autem Maria ad angelum ... quomodo	an	AR 662 LU 1409	G	5	2	0	4	5	4	5	2	E
8	Dixit autem pater ad servos	an	AR 386 LU 551 *AM 361 WA 95 (inc illeg) *LA 146	G	5	2	0	2	0	-2	0	2	G
8	Dixit autem paterfamilias	an	AR 346 *AM 317 WA 75 *LA 115	G	5	2	0	2	0	-2	0	2	G
8	Dixit Caesar ad Hippolytum	an	WA 352	F	2	4	2	0	4	7	6	2	G
7	Dixit Dominus ad Adam	re	WA 73	G	2	0	2	0	2	5	7	5	G
8	Dixit Dominus ad Adam	an	AR 341 LU 496 AM 311 LA 1	D	3	5	7	5	3	2	3	5	G
	Dixit Dominus ad Moysen Precatus est Moyses	ofv	OTT 97 *GB 79 *SYG 89	a	3	5	3	0	-2	3	5	2	
8	Dixit Dominus ad Noe	an	AR 347 LU 503 AM 319 *LA 1	G	2	0	-2	2	4	5	2	0	G
6	Dixit Dominus ad Noe	re	LR 399 *LA 116 *WA 76	F	2	5	2	5	7	5	4	0	F
5	Dixit Dominus Deus non est	re	LA 110 *WA 73	F	2	0	4	6	7	2	0	2	F
	Dixit Dominus Domino meo In splendoribus sanctorum	cov	SYG 15										
	Dixit Dominus Domino meo Juravit Dominus	intv	GR [100] LU 1283										
	Dixit Dominus Domino meo Juravit Dominus	rev	LR 195 LA 531 WA 425										

	Dixit Dominus Domino meo Juravit Dominus	grv	GS 221 SYG 33 GB 40v	E	1	-2	3	5	3	5	7	8	
7	Dixit Dominus Domino meo	an	OHS 156 AR 45 LU 252 AM 125 *LA 86	b	1	3	5	3	1	-2	1	0	G
	Dixit Dominus Domino meo	alv	SYG 248	G	2	0	2	4	5	7	5	9	
	Dixit Dominus Domino meo Tecum principium	grv	GR 28 LU 393 GS 13 GB 13v SYG 14	a	3	5	7	5	3	2	3	0	
1	Dixit Dominus Jesus quid est	an	LA 266	D	2	3	5	3	2	0	3	0	D
4	Dixit Dominus Mariae	re	WA 336	F	2	0	-1	-3	-5	0	2	4	E
2	Dixit Dominus mulieri	tr	SYG 85 GS 47	D	-2	0	-2	-5	-2	0	-2	0	D
8	Dixit Dominus mulieri	an	WA 94 *LA 143	D	3	5	3	5	7	5	-2	0	G
1	Dixit Dominus paralytico	an	AR 569 AM 609 WA 190 LA 318	D	2	3	5	2	5	7	3	2	D
2	Dixit Dominus Simoni	an	WA 338	D	-2	0	2	3	5	3	2	0	D
1	Dixit Dominus villico	an	WA 188 LA 313	D	2	3	5	2	5	7	3	2	D
1	Dixit Jesus ad legisperitos	an	WA 190	D	3	2	0	2	0	-2	3	5	D
	Dixit Jesus discipulis suis In hoc cognoscent	anv	GR 202 OHS 450										
	Dixit Jesus discipulis suis Si quis mihi ministraverit	anv	LA 437										
8	Dixit Jesus discipulis suis afferte	an	AR 450 OHS 800 *AM 463 LA 220	G	5	2	0	2	0	-2	0	2	G
8	Dixit Jesus discipulis suis ego mittam	an	WA 151	G	2	4	2	-2	0	4	5	7	G
1	Dixit Jesus discipulis suis venite	an	LA 220	D	7	10	7	5	7	8	7	5	D
6	Dixit Jesus discipulo ecce mater	of	GR 86**	F	4	7	4	6	7	2	4	2	F
8	Dixit Jesus matri suae mulier	co	GR 587^6 LU 1612^4	G	2	0	-2	2	4	0	2	4	G
1	Dixit Jesus ut sciatis	an	AR 514 AM 530	C	2	5	7	5	4	0	2	5	D
7	Dixit Joseph undecim fratribus	re	LA 151 *WA 98	G	2	0	2	0	2	0	2	4	G
7	Dixit Judas fratribus	re	LA 147 *WA 96	c	-1	0	2	0	2	4	2	4	G
7	Dixit Judas Simoni	re	LA 297 *WA 182	c	-1	0	2	0	2	4	2	4	G
4	Dixit mater ejus ad illum	an	AR 653 LU 1406 AM 842	F	-1	0	-3	-5	-3	0	-1	-3	E
4	Dixit mater Jesu	an	AR 324 LU 474	F	-1	0	-3	-5	-3	0	-1	-3	E
	Dixit Moyses ad populum Erit vobis	ofv	OTT 63 *GB 141v SYG 160	F	2	4	2	0	2	0	-3	-1	
	Dixit Moyses et Aaron Precatus est Moyses	ofv	OTT 97 GB 79 *SYG 89	G	2	0	2	-2	0	-2	-3	-2	
7	Dixit paterfamilias operariis	an	AR 345 LU 503 AM 315 *LA 115	G	5	4	5	7	9	7	5	2	G
7	Dixit Romanus ad beatum	an	WA 347 *LA 433	G	4	5	7	5	9	7	4	7	G

	Dixit Ruben fratribus suis Merito haec patimur	rev	LA 151 WA 97										
8	Dixit Ruben fratribus suis	re	LA 150 *WA 97	G	2	0	2	0	-2	0	2	-2	G
8	Dixit sanctus Vincentius	an	WA 259	G	-2	-5	-3	-2	0	-2	0	2	G
8	Dixit Simon Petrus Domine	an	LA 365	G	2	4	5	2	0	2	4	7	G
	Dixitque Dominus Abraham Dum staret Abraham	rev	LA 121										
8	Doceam iniquos vias	re	WA 106	F	2	4	2	4	2	4	2	4	G
2	Docebit nos Dominus vias	re	LA 15 *WA 10	A	3	5	7	5	8	7	8	5	D
7	Docebo te quae ventura	re	LA 307 *WA 185	G	2	-2	0	2	0	2	0	5	G
3	Docete filios vestros	re	LA 387 *WA 142	G	5	2	5	4	5	2	0	2	E
3	Doctor bonus et amicus	re	LA 499 *WA 234	D	3	2	3	5	3	0	2	0	E
4	Doctor egregie Paule	hy	LR 433	F	-3	-5	-3	0	-3	-1	0	-3	E
4	Doctor egregie Paule	hy	ST 234	F	-1	-3	-5	-3	0	-3	-1	0	E
4	Doctor egregie Paule	hy	AM 790 936	E	1	0	-2	-4	-2	1	-2	0	E
4	Doctrinam quasi antelucanum	of	GR 530 LU 1513	D	3	0	2	3	0	5	3	0	E
	Dolens ego pro meis Libera me de morte	rev	WA 438	D	-2	0	3	2	3	5	2	3	
1	Doleo super te	an	WA 165 LA 274	D	-2	0	3	2	0	3	0	-2	D
4	Dolorosa et lacrimabilis	gr	GR 595 LU 1633^V	F	-1	0	2	0	-3	-1	-3	0	E
1	Domare cordis impetus	hy	AR 781	D	-2	0	3	0	3	2	3	5	D
5	Dominabitur a mari	gr	GR 639 LU 1710	F	2	4	2	4	7	9	6	7	F
2	Dominator Domine caelorum	re	PM 113 LA 292 *WA 178	A	3	5	8	7	8	5	7	5	D
	Domine abstraxisti ab inferis Exaltabo te	ofv	OTT 96 *GB 62^V SYG 66	c	-1	0	-3	0	-3	0	-3	-5	
8	Domine abstraxisti ab inferis	an	OHS 606 LU 764 WA 125 *LA 203	G	2	0	-2	0	2	5	4	2	G
6	Domine ad adjuvandum me	of	GR 147 OTT 42 SYG 106 GS 68	F	4	5	4	2	4	2	0	4	F
2	Domine ad adjuvandum me	of	GB 104^V	D	5	7	5	3	5	3	0	3	D
	Domine audivi auditum tuum Beata et venerabilis	rev	LA 35										
	Domine audivi auditum tuum Benedicta et venerabilis	rev	PM 249										
	Domine audivi auditum tuum O magnum mysterium	rev	LA 35 WA 28										
4	Domine audivi auditum tuum	an	AM 68 69 WA 69 LA 102	F	-3	-1	0	2	-1	0	2	4	E
2	Domine audivi auditum tuum	tr	OHS 529 GR 206 LU 721 SYG 136 GB 116 GS 98	D	-2	0	-2	-5	-2	0	-2	0	D
1	Domine bonum est	an	AR 380 LU 545 AM 354 *WA 90 (inc illeg) *LA 136	F	2	4	2	-1	0	2	0	-1	D

Incipit		Src	Sources										
8 Domine clamavi ad te		an	AR 182 LU 303 AM 151 152 *WA 68 *LA 99	c	-1	0	-3	-5	-1	0	-3	-5	G
6 Domine convertere et eripe		of	GR 322 OTT 84 LU 963 GS 73 142 SYG 111 GB 99^v	F	2	0	-3	0	2	0	2	4	F
1 Domine descende ut sanes		an	WA 191	F	2	4	0	2	0	2	-1	2	D
Domine Deus caeli Spem in alio		rev	WA 179										
Domine Deus Domini mei Deus Domini mei		rev	LA 122										
2 Domine Deus in adjutorium		an	WA 66 LA 95	F	-1	-3	0	-1	-3	-5	-3	-1	D
6 Domine Deus in simplicitate cordis		of	GR [74] OTT 159 LU 1252 SYG 264 GB 175^v GS 175	F	2	0	2	4	2	0	2	0	F
Domine Deus Israel Afflicti pro peccatis		rev	VP 262 LA 84 WA 62										
Domine Deus meus clamavi Exaltabo te		grv	GR 160 *GS 75 GB 101 SYG 113	E	-2	3	5	7	8	5	8	5	
8 Domine Deus meus exaltasti		an	WA 435	G	-2	-5	-3	-2	0	2	0	-2	G
8 Domine Deus meus in te speravi		an	LA 92	F	2	4	2	0	4	6	7	6	G
1 Domine Deus meus in te speravi		an	WA 66	F	4	2	4	2	0	2	0	-1	D
2 Domine Deus meus in te speravi libera		co	GR 111 LU 544 SYG 84 *GB 74^v *GS 47	F	-3	0	-1	-5	-3	-1	0	-5	D
Domine Deus meus in te speravi salvum		alv	GR 322 LU 962 GB 248 *GS 167 f	a	-2	0	-2	-4	-5	-9	-5	-2	
1 Domine Deus meus in te speravi salvum		of	OTT 173	D	3	0	3	2	0	-2	3	5	D
8 Domine Deus meus magnificatus		an	AR 200 LU 279^T	G	-2	-3	-5	-2	0	2	0	2	G
Domine Deus meus si feci istud Domine Deus meus in te		ofv	OTT 173	D	3	0	3	2	0	-2	3	5	
Domine Deus meus speravi		see Domine Deus meus in te speravi											
2 Domine Deus noster qui cum patribus		an	PM 46 VP 107	D	-2	0	3	2	0	3	0	-2	D
8 Domine Deus noster qui cum patribus		an	WA 227	G	2	0	-2	0	2	0	2	0	G
2 Domine Deus qui conteris		re	LA 292 *WA 178	C	2	4	2	5	4	5	7	2	D
Domine Deus salutis meae Caritas Dei diffusa est		intv	GB 193 GS a										
Domine Deus salutis meae Intret oratio		intv	GR 106 LU 541 GS 42 GB 73 SYG 81										
Domine Deus salutis meae		alv	GR 351 LU 1029 GS 152 *SYG 245 *GB 254	E	1	0	-2	3	5	8	7	5	
8 Domine Deus salutis meae		of	GR 110 307 LU 544 905 OTT 112 SYG 84 *GB 74 *GS b 46 173	D	2	3	5	3	5	7	10	7	G

	Title	Type	Sources	Mode									
	Domine Deus tu cognovisti Exspectans exspectavi	ofv	OTT 104 GB 92 SYG 104	c	2	0	-3	-5	-1	-3	-5	-7	
6	Domine Deus virtutum beati	an	LR 386 WA 396 LA 476	F	-1	-3	-5	-3	-5	-3	0	2	F
	Domine Deus virtutum converte Non discedimus	rev	WA 24										
8	Domine Deus virtutum converte	tr	GR 53	G	-2	-5	-3	-7	-5	-2	0	2	G
2	Domine Deus virtutum converte	gr	GR 15 LU 345 *SYG 10 *GS 8 *GB 9	G	4	2	5	2	4	5	2	0	a
	Domine Deus virtutum exaudi Protector noster	grv	GR 108 LU 1003 GS 37 43 144 171 GB 67^V SYG 75	F	4	2	7	9	7	4	7	9	
6	Domine Deus virtutum non discedimus	int	GR 111**	F	2	0	2	4	0	2	0	2	F
	Domine dilexi decorem Audiam Domine	rev	LA 84 WA 61										
4	Domine dilexi decorem	re	LA 548	F	-1	-3	0	-1	0	2	4	2	E
	Domine dilexi decorem	alv	GB 174	c	-1	2	0	-1	0	2	0	-3	
8	Domine dilexi decorem	int	SYG 85	D	3	5	7	5	-2	0	3	5	G
	Domine diligo habitaculum	alv	LU 1623^D	D	-2	0	2	3	5	7	5	3	
2	Domine dimitte eam	an	WA 93 *LA 143	D	2	0	-2	0	3	5	3	2	D
	Domine Domine virtus salutis Eripe me	trv	GR 208 OHS 534 LU 725 GS 99 *GB 116^V SYG 137	D	-2	0	3	5	3	2	3	2	
	Domine Dominus noster Benedicta sit	intv	GR 308										
	Domine Dominus noster Caritas Dei	intv	SYG 187										
	Domine Dominus noster Christe Deus	intv	SYG 230										
	Domine Dominus noster Ex ore infantium	intv	GR 40 LU 427 GS 17 SYG 25										
	Domine Dominus noster Gloria et honore	intv	GB 233^V SYG 200 GS 204										
	Domine Dominus noster In nomine Jesu	intv	GR 50 LU 446										
	Domine Dominus noster Justi decantaverunt	intv	GR 444 LU 1384										
2	Domine Dominus noster	co	GR 117 SYG 87 *GB 77 GS 49	D	-2	2	3	2	0	2	0	3	D
5	Domine Dominus noster	gr	GR 342 LU 1017 *SYG 244 GB 252 GS 150	F	2	0	2	4	2	4	2	0	F
	Domine Dominus noster Gloria et honore	ofv	OTT 133 *GB 23^V *SYG 34	D	7	8	5	10	9	7	5	8	
1	Domine Dominus noster	an	LR 192 *WA 420 424 LA 530	D	7	8	7	10	7	5	7	8	D

#	Incipit		Sources										
	Domine exaudi orationem meam Potum meum cum fletu	cov	SYG 128										
	Domine exaudi orationem meam Dicit Dominus sermones	intv	GB 244^v SYG 228 GS 200										
	Domine exaudi orationem meam In nomine Domini	intv	GR 190 LU 616 OHS 320 GS 91 GB 113^v SYG 126										
7	Domine exaudi orationem meam ... perveniat	int	GB 104^v	G	2	-2	2	0	2	5	7	9	G
8	Domine exaudi orationem meam ... perveniat	re	LA 103	F	2	4	2	4	6	4	2	4	G
3	Domine exaudi orationem meam ... perveniat	of	GR [142] OHS 345 OTT 53 LU 623 SYG 128 *GS 93 GB 114^v	D	2	3	5	3	5	7	5	7	E
3	Domine exaudi orationem meam ... perveniat ... ne	of	GR 194	D	2	3	5	3	5	7	5	7	E
2	Domine exaudi orationem meam ... veniat	tr	GR 191 OHS 324 LU 619 SYG 127 GB 114 GS 92	D	-2	0	-2	-5	-2	0	-2	0	D
	Domine exaudi orationem meam ... veniat	alv	GR 367 LU 1049 *GB 256^v	G	5	4	7	5	7	9	10	12	
4	Domine fac mecum misericordiam	of	GR 133 OTT 37 *SYG 96 *GB 85^v *GS 58	c	-3	-1	0	2	0	-3	-5	-1	b
6	Domine in auxilium meum respice	of	GR 364 OTT 106 LU 1046 SYG 91 GB 80^v GS 53 160	F	-5	-3	-5	-3	0	2	0	2	F
	Domine in caelo misericordia	sr	LA 89 WA 64										
8	Domine in caelo misericordia	an	AR 146 AM 40 *WA 64 *LA 89	c	-1	0	-3	-5	-1	-3	-1	0	G
	Domine in lumine vultus Laetentur omnes	rev	PM 122 VP 97	g	2	0	2	0	-3	-2	-3	-5	
5	Domine in lumine vultus	of	GR 101**	F	4	7	9	7	9	4	2	4	F
5	Domine in tua misericordia	int	GR 310 *SYG 238 GB 247 GS 141	F	4	2	0	2	0	-3	0	2	F
	Domine in virtute tua In virtute tua Domine	intv	GB 51										
	Domine in virtute tua Ne timeas Zacharia	intv	GR 521 GS 188 GB 196 SYG 195										
	Domine in virtute tua	alv	GR 333 LU 1003 GB 249^v GS 144 *SYG 240	F	2	0	5	4	2	4	0	2	
8	Domine in virtute tua	an	OHS 182 (nm) WA 60 *LA 80	F	2	4	2	0	4	7	6	4	G
6	Domine inminuti sumus	an	WA 228	F	2	4	2	4	2	4	2	0	F
8	Domine iste sanctus habitabit	an	LR 196 *WA 425	F	2	4	2	4	2	4	2	4	G
4	Domine jam satis est	an	WA 404 (inc illeg)										
	Domine Jesu Christe judex O pie Deus	ofv	OTT 178 *SYG 237	D	-2	-5	-2	0	2	0	-2	0	

2 Domine Jesu Christe magister	an	WA 237	C	5	4	5	2	5	7	5	4	D		
8 Domine Jesu Christe pastor	re	LA 492 *WA 407	F	2	4	2	4	2	-1	2	0	G		
2 Domine Jesu Christe rex gloriae	of	GR 100* LU 1813 *SYG 235 *GB 266 *GS 232	D	-2	0	-2	0	3	0	-2	3	D		
8 Domine Jesu Christe seminator	an	PM 212 336 *WA 407 LA 488	F	2	4	2	4	2	0	-1	0	G		
Domine labia mea aperies Doceam iniquos	rev	WA 106												
7 Domine labia mea aperies	an	AR 378 AM 352 WA 93 LA 141	d	-2	-3	0	-2	-3	0	2	-2	G		
Domine libera animam meam Ad Dominum dum tribularer	grv	GR 321 LU 961 GS 53 142 GB 80 SYG 91	c	2	0	-1	-3	2	-1	0	2			
3 Domine libera animam meam	an	WA 66	G	2	5	4	2	0	-2	0	-2	E		
4 Domine magnus es tu	an	AR 127 *AM 55 56	c	2	4	2	0	2	-3	2	0	a		
8 Domine memorabor justitiae tuae	co	GR 365 LU 1046 SYG 107 GB 95 GS 69 160	F	2	4	2	0	2	0	2	-3	G		
3 Domine mi rex da mihi	an	AR 829 LU 1620 *AM 1026 *WA 363 LA 454	c	-3	-1	0	-1	-5	0	-1	-3	E		
2 Domine mi rex omnipotens	re	LR 425 *LA 293 *WA 179	C	2	5	2	4	2	5	4	5	D		
Domine ne in furore Ne derelinquas me	intv	GR 118 GS 50 GB 78 SYG 88												
Domine ne in furore Qui cognoscis Domine	intv	SYG 234												
Domine ne in ira tua Ego dixi Domine	rev	LA 91												
1 Domine ne in ira tua	re	LR 398 *LA 81 *WA 60	D	2	3	2	0	2	3	2	0	D		
Domine ne in ira tua Domine convertere	ofv	OTT 84 GB 99ᵛ *SYG 111	F	4	0	2	4	2	-1	0	2			
8 Domine ne longe facias	int	GR 178 OHS 106 LU 592 SYG 121 GB 108ᵛ *GS 86	D	3	5	7	5	-2	0	3	5	G		
Domine ne memineris Domine non secundum	trv	GR 89 OHS 209 LU 527 *SYG 66 GS 31	D	3	2	3	5	7	5	3	5			
Domine nomen tuum Laudate Dominum	ofv	OTT 40 *GB 90 *SYG 102	c	2	0	-3	-5	-3	-5	-3	-1			
2 Domine non aspicias peccata	tr	SYG 56	D	-2	0	-2	-5	-2	0	-2	0	D		
2 Domine non aspicias peccata	re	LR 322 *LA 369 *WA 298	C	2	5	2	5	4	5	2	4	D		
2 Domine non est alius	an	WA 228	A	3	5	8	7	8	10	8	5	D		
1 Domine non est exaltatum	an	AR 140 OHS 356 LU 291	F	2	4	2	4	2	0	-1	0	D		
7 Domine non habeo	an	WA 90 (inc illeg) LA 135	c	-1	0	2	4	2	0	2	0	G		

	Title	Type	References	Mode	1	2	3	4	5	6	7	8	End
2	Domine non secundum peccata	tr	GR 89 OHS 209 LU 527 SYG 66 GS 31	D	-2	0	-2	-5	-2	0	-2	0	D
	Domine non sum dignus / Domine puer meus	rev	LR 402 WA 84										
1	Domine non sum dignus	an	AR 360 *AM 334 *WA 84	F	2	4	2	4	2	4	2	-1	D
1	Domine nonne bonum semen	an	AR 339 LU 1109 AM 309 *LA 107	D	7	8	7	3	5	7	5	7	D
	Domine ostende nobis patrem / Tanto tempore vobiscum	rev	PM 151 WA 307										
7	Domine ostende nobis patrem	an	AR 694 LU 1465^E AM 893 *WA 307 LA 393	c	-1	0	2	-1	2	4	2	0	G
5	Domine pater et Deus	re	LA 276 WA 169	c	-3	0	2	0	-1	0	2	0	F
4	Domine praevenisti eum	gr	GR [48] LU 1207 *SYG 224 *GB 53 GS 222	F	-1	0	2	0	-3	-1	-3	0	E
8	Domine praevenisti eum	re	PM 219 LR 159 205 LA 523 *WA 416	F	2	4	2	4	6	4	2	4	G
1	Domine praevenisti Saturninum	int^t	SYG 229	D	-2	0	3	0	2	0	-2	3	D
	Domine probasti me / Mihi autem nimis	intv	GR 392 LU 1304 GS w GB 235 SYG 54										
	Domine probasti me / Nunc scio vere	intv	GR 532 LU 1518 GB 204 SYG 202										
	Domine probasti me / Resurrexi	intv	GR 240 OHS 708 LU 777 GS K GB 123 SYG 152										
	Domine probasti me / Scio cui credidi	intv	GR 417 LU 1344 GS 189 GB 207^v										
	Domine probasti me / Mihi autem	ofv	OTT 128 GB 203 SYG 201	E	1	3	5	3	0	1	3	5	
3	Domine probasti me	an	AR 179 LU 301 *AM 149 150 WA 68 *LA 99	G	2	5	4	2	0	2	0	-3	E
3	Domine puer meus jacet	re	WA 84 (inc illeg)										
1	Domine puer meus jacet	re	LR 402	F	-1	0	-3	-5	0	2	4	7	D
1	Domine puer meus jacet	an	AR 360 *AM 333 *WA 84 *LA 107	F	2	4	2	4	2	4	2	-1	D
8	Domine quando veneris judicare	re	PM 319 AR [160] LU 1787 LA 554 *WA 437	G	-2	-3	-2	0	-2	0	2	0	G
	Domine qui custodis pactum / Exaudisti Domine	rev	LA 271 WA 166										
	Domine qui dixisti mihi / Cum audisset Jacob	rev	LA 141										
	Domine qui me creasti / Beata Agatha	rev	PM 137 LA 362 WA 275										
6	Domine qui operati sunt	an	LR 382 WA 395 *LA 475	F	-1	0	-3	-5	0	2	0	2	F

	Text		Sources										
	Domine quinque talenta Euge serve	rev	LR 193 LA 530 WA 425										
7	Domine quinque talenta	co	GR 396 LU 1311 *SYG 38 *GB 42 *GS 223	b	1	-2	0	1	-4	0	1	-2	G
1	Domine quinque talenta	an	AR [74] LU 1195 AM 670 *WA 425 LA 532	F	2	4	5	4	2	5	2	4	D
6	Domine quis habitabit	co	GR 131 SYG 96 GS 58 GB 85	F	-1	0	-3	-1	-3	-5	0	2	F
	Domine quis habitabit Qui ambulat fraudulenter	grv	GR 30**	a	3	5	7	5	3	2	3	0	
	Domine refugium factus es	sr	LA 99 WA 68										
	Domine refugium factus es Immutemur habitu	anv	GB 61^v										
	Domine refugium factus es Convertere Domine	grv	GR 108 LU 1007 GS 43 147 169 GB 250 SYG 81	c	2	0	-1	-3	0	-1	-5	-3	
	Domine refugium factus es	alv	GR 355 (39) LU 1034 GS 153 SYG 245 GB 254^v	G	2	4	5	4	5	4	2	0	
2	Domine refugium factus es	gr	GR 381 LU 1067 SYG 256 *GS 34 165 *GB 262	G	4	2	5	2	4	5	2	0	a
5	Domine refugium factus es	int	GR 101 SYG 76 *GB 68 *GS 38	F	4	7	9	7	9	7	6	2	F
	Domine refugium factus es	ofv	OTT 175 GB 163 SYG 171	D	7	8	7	10	9	7	5	8	
6	Domine refugium factus est	an	AR 145 *AM 60 61 *WA 68 LA 98	F	2	4	0	2	0	-3	0	2	F
2	Domine rex Deus	an	WA 231	D	-5	-2	0	-2	0	2	0	3	D
	Domine rex omnipotens		see also Domine mi rex										
6	Domine rex omnipotens creator	an	GB 160^v	C	2	4	2	5	4	5	2	4	F
1 2	Domine rex omnipotens in ditione	an	AR 549 LU 993 AM 587 *WA 176 *LA 294	C	2	5	7	5	4	2	0	2	D
1	Domine salva nos	an	AR 338 LU 492 AM 308	F	2	4	0	2	4	2	0	2	D
8	Domine secundum actum meum	re	AR [172] LU 1798 *LA 555 *WA 437	G	2	0	2	0	-3	-2	0	2	G
	Domine si adhuc in praesenti Domine si adhuc populo	rev	WA 400										
	Domine si adhuc populo ... laborem O beatum virum Martinum	rev	LA 482										
7	Domine si adhuc populo ... laborem	an	AR 917 LU 1749 *AM 1115 WA 402 LA 486	d	-3	0	2	0	2	0	-3	-2	G
2	Domine si adhuc populo ... subire	re	LA 481 WA 400	C	2	4	2	0	2	5	7	5	D
	Domine si conversus fuerit Benedic Domine	rev	LR 235										

8	Domine si conversus fuerit	re	LA 271 WA 167	F	2	4	2	0	2	4	2	4	G
1	Domine si hic fuisses	an	AR 404 LU 1096 AM 380 WA 105 (inc illeg) *LA 165	F	2	4	2	5	2	4	2	4	D
1	Domine si iratus fueris	an	SYG 64	F	-3	0	-1	-5	-3	-5	0	2	D
8	Domine si tu es jube me	re	LR 362 *LA 414 *WA 327	G	2	0	2	-3	0	-2	-3	-5	G
1	Domine si tu vis	an	AR 337 LU 491 AM 307	F	2	4	2	5	2	4	2	-1	D
	Domine spes mea Confiteor tibi	grv	GR 613 LU 1668	c	2	0	-3	0	2	4	0	2	
5	Domine spes mea	gr	GR 518 LU 1494	F	2	0	2	4	2	4	2	0	F
3	Domine spes sanctorum	an	LR 386 *WA 395 *LA 475	G	2	5	2	5	4	5	7	9	E
4	Domine suscipe me	an	WA 40 *LA 51	C	2	5	4	2	5	4	5	7	E
5	Domine tu mihi lavas pedes	an	GR 201 OHS 448 LU 673 SYG 130	c	-1	-3	-5	0	2	4	2	0	F
3	Domine ut video propheta	an	AR 395 LU 1092	G	2	4	5	2	5	4	5	7	E
1	Domine ut video propheta	an	AM 370 WA 100 (inc illeg)	F	2	4	6	4	2	4	0	2	D
3	Domine vim patior responde	an	AR 429 OHS 246 *AM 408 *WA 115 *LA 186	G	2	4	5	2	5	4	5	7	E
8	Domine virtus et laetitia	an	WA 35	c	-1	-3	-5	-3	-5	-3	-5	-7	G
3	Domine vivifica me	of	GR 92 OTT 31 *SYG 68 *GB 64 *GS 34	c	-3	-1	0	2	0	-3	-5	-1	E
	Domini est terra Hodie scietis	intv	GR 24 LU 359 GS 12 GB 12ᵛ SYG 13										
	Domini est terra Tollite portas	ofv	OTT 14 *GB 13 *SYG 14	c	-1	0	2	-1	0	2	-3	-5	
8	Domini est terra	re	LA 83 *WA 61	F	2	4	2	4	6	4	2	4	G
4	Domino sanctorum praesulum	inv	WA 292 (inc lacking)										E
6	Dominum Deum nostrum	inv	LA 103 WA 70	F	2	0	2	4	0	2	4	2	F
8	Dominum Deum tuum	an	AR 371 LU 538 AM 344 WA 88 LA 134	F	2	4	2	4	2	0	2	4	G
4	Dominum qui fecit mare	inv	WA 80	C	2	4	5	4	2	4	5	7	E
6	Dominum qui fecit nos	inv	LA 100 WA 69	c	2	0	2	4	0	2	4	2	c
5	Dominum qui fecit nos	inv	LA 80 *WA 95	F	4	7	9	4	7	9	7	9	F
	Dominum tuum illum constitui Quis igitur ille	rev	LA 138										
8	Dominus ab utero	an	LR 347 WA 320 *LA 401	G	-2	-5	-3	-2	0	2	0	2	G
5	Dominus aedificet nobis	an	AR 121 OHS 290 LU 287	a	-2	0	-4	0	3	5	3	5	F

	Incipit	Type	Sources	Mode									
	Dominus conterens bella Cantemus Domino	trv	GR 229 OHS 652 *GB 119 *SYG 150 *GS 111	G	2	4	5	7	5	0	2	0	
2	Dominus custodit te ab omni	an	LA 560	F	-1	0	-3	0	-1	-3	-1	-3	D
8	Dominus custodit te ab omni	an	AR [144] LU 1773 AM 1152 *WA 435	F	2	4	2	4	2	0	4	7	G
1	Dominus dabit benignitatem	co	GR 3 LU 322 SYG 3 GB 2 GS 2	F	4	2	4	0	-1	0	-1	-3	D
	Dominus dabit verbum	alv	GR 59**	F	2	0	-3	0	2	5	4	5	
1	Dominus dabit virtutem	an	AR 76	D	-2	0	3	2	0	2	0	-2	D
	Dominus de caelo prospexit	an	OHS 177 (nm)										
7	Dominus de summo caelo	an	WA 288	d	-3	0	2	0	-3	-2	0	-2	G
1	Dominus dedit Dominus abstulit	an	LA 287	D	7	9	10	7	5	7	9	7	D
1	Dominus defensor vitae	an	WA 61	F	2	4	2	4	2	0	-1	0	D
2	Dominus Deus auxiliator	an	AR 421 OHS 65 AM 399 *WA 113 LA 181	D	2	3	0	2	0	-2	0	3	D
	Dominus Deus Hebraeorum Stetit Moyses	rev	LA 156 WA 101										
3	Dominus Deus Israel	int	SYG 233	G	5	2	0	4	5	2	4	5	E
8	Dominus dixit ad me	an	LR 55 LU 371 *WA 27 *LA 31	c	-1	0	-3	-5	-1	0	-3	0	G
	Dominus dixit ad me	alv	GR 29 LU 394 SYG 15 GB 14 *GS 14	c	-1	2	0	-1	0	2	0	-3	
2	Dominus dixit ad me	int	GR 27 LU 392 SYG 14 GB 13^V GS 13	D	3	5	3	0	3	0	3	-2	D
	Dominus erigit elisos Lauda anima	ofv	OTT 67 *GB 149 *SYG 166	G	2	5	2	0	2	5	7	5	
2	Dominus firmamentum meum	co	GR 332 LU 1001 *SYG 241 GB 249 *GS 145	F	-1	0	-3	0	-5	0	-1	0	D
2	Dominus fortitudo plebis suae	int	GR 334 LU 1006 SYG 242 GB 249^V GS 146	A	3	5	7	5	3	5	3	8	D
	Dominus illuminatio mea Exaudi Domine vocem ... adjutor	intv	GR 332 LU 1002 GS 145 GB 249 SYG 241										
	Dominus illuminatio mea Exaudi Domine vocem ... tibi	intv	GR 287 LU 854 GS 136 SYG 181 GB 182										
	Dominus illuminatio mea Exspecta Dominum	intv	GR 158 GS 73 GB 99^V SYG 112										
	Dominus illuminatio mea Tibi dixit	intv	GR 117 GS 49 GB 77 SYG 88										
2	Dominus illuminatio mea	int	GR 330 LU 998 *SYG 241 GB 248^V GS 144	A	3	5	7	5	3	5	8	5	D

6	Dominus in caelo alleluia	an	LR 100 *WA 148 *LA 247	F	-1	2	4	-1	0	-3	-5	0	F
	Dominus in nomine tuo Ecce Deus	intv	SYG 244										
	Dominus in Sina in sancto	alv	GR 286 LU 848 GS 136 SYG 179 GB 178ᵛ	c	-1	2	0	-1	0	2	0	-3	
6	Dominus in Sion alleluia	an	LR 100 *WA 148 *LA 247	F	-1	2	4	-1	0	-3	-5	0	F
3	Dominus in Sion magnus	an	LR 127	G	5	2	0	2	0	2	5	4	E
8	Dominus in templo sancto	an	LR 95 WA 147 LA 244	c	-1	-5	-1	0	-3	-5	-3	-5	G
8	Dominus in templo sancto ... sedes	an	LR 232	c	-1	-5	-1	0	-3	-5	-3	-5	G
2	Dominus Jesus ante sex dies	re	WA 112 GS 83	D	-5	-2	0	2	0	-2	0	2	D
8	Dominus Jesus Christus	an	WA 400 *LA 482	G	5	2	0	-2	0	2	0	4	G
2	Dominus Jesus postquam coenavit	an	GR 201 OHS 448 LU 672 *WA 213	F	-1	-3	-1	0	-5	-3	0	-5	D
2	Dominus Jesus postquam coenavit	co	GR 197 OHS 463 LU 679 SYG 129 GB 115ᵛ *GS 95	F	-1	-3	-1	0	-5	-3	0	-5	D
1	Dominus Jesus postquam locutus	an	WA 150	F	4	2	0	2	0	4	2	4	D
3	Dominus judex noster	an	AR 894² LU 1716	G	2	4	5	2	5	4	0	2	E
1	Dominus judicabit fines	an	AM 54 55 *WA 67 LA 95	F	2	4	2	4	2	-1	0	2	D
3	Dominus legifer noster	an	AR 242 *AM 217	G	2	4	5	2	5	4	0	2	E
1	Dominus legifer noster	an	WA 19	F	2	4	5	4	2	5	4	0	D
6	Dominus legifer noster	an	LA 25 *WA 19	G	2	5	2	5	4	0	2	4	F
7 8	Dominus mecum est tamquam	re	LA 178 *WA 111	c	2	0	2	4	2	0	-1	0	G
8	Dominus mihi adjutor est	an	AR 387 AM 362 WA 98 *LA 152	F	2	4	2	-1	0	2	4	0	G
1	Dominus mihi adjutor non timebo	gr	GR 35**	D	7	8	7	5	3	7	5	7	D
8	Dominus possedit me	an	WA 167 *LA 281	a	3	2	0	-2	0	3	2	0	G
	Dominus quasi vir pugnator Fortitudo mea	trv	GR 468	G	2	4	5	4	0	2	0	2	
	Dominus qui eripuit me Deus omnium	rev	LA 267 WA 165										
8	Dominus qui eripuit me	re	LA 268 WA 165	F	2	4	2	0	2	4	2	4	G
1	Dominus quidem Jesus	an	LA 253	F	4	2	4	2	0	2	0	4	D
4	Dominus regit me	an	WA 60 *LA 80	b	-4	-2	1	3	1	3	5	3	a
2	Dominus regit me	co	GR 151 LU 567 SYG 109 *GB 97 *GS 71	F	-1	0	-3	-1	0	-1	-5	0	D
	Dominus regnavit decorem induit Deus enim firmavit	ofv	OTT 16 *GB 16 *SYG 16	D	3	5	3	0	5	10	7	3	

	Dominus regnavit decorem induit	alv	GR 31 LU 405 SYG 16 *GB 15^V GS E	D	5	7	5	3	0	5	3	5	
	Dominus regnavit decorem indutus Dum medium silentium	intv	GR 44 LU 433 GS 18 GB 30^V SYG 29										
	Dominus regnavit decorem indutus Lux fulgebit	intv	GR 30 LU 403 GS E GB 15 SYG 15										
	Dominus regnavit exsultet terra Adorate Deum	intv	GR 70 LU 488 GS 23 GB 39 SYG 42										
	Dominus regnavit exsultet terra Terribilis est	intv	GB 172^V GS 174										
	Dominus regnavit exsultet terra	alv	GR 72 LU 490 GS 23 SYG 42	a	-1	2	0	-1	0	2	0	-3	
3	Dominus regnavit exsultet terra	an	AR 125	G	2	5	4	2	0	2	0	-2	E
	Dominus robur est In Deo confisum	grv	OHS 416 LU 662	F	4	7	9	7	9	7	9	4	
	Dominus salvavit manum tuam	alv	GR 464	c	-1	2	0	-1	0	2	0	-3	
7	Dominus Scholasticae dedit	an	LR 293	d	-3	0	2	0	2	3	2	0	G
5	Dominus Scholasticam	an	LR 298	a	-4	0	3	5	3	5	7	5	F
1	Dominus secus mare Galilaeae	int	GR 390 SYG 231 GB 245 GS g	F	-1	0	-3	-5	0	2	4	2	D
2	Dominus tamquam ovis ad victimam	an	AR 433 OHS 400 LU 653 *AM 414 415 *WA 120 LA 193	D	2	3	0	2	0	-2	0	3	D
1	Dominus veniet occurrite	an	AR 251 256 LU 357 AM 227 233 *WA 19 24 *LA 21	D	-2	3	5	3	5	7	10	7	D
	Dominus vias suas docebit	sr	AR 328 LU 473										
3	Dominus virtutum ipse est rex	co	GR 157 *SYG 112 *GB 99^V *GS 73	c	4	2	4	0	-1	-3	-5	-3	E
7	Domum Dei decet sanctitudo	inv	LR 231 *LA 547	G	5	4	5	7	5	7	9	7	G
	Domum istam protege Domine	sr	WA 319										
3	Domum istam protege Domine	an	LA 550 *SYG 135	G	2	0	2	4	5	4	2	0	E
	Domum tuam Domine decet	sr	AR [111] LU 1244 1245 AM 698 699 LA 553 WA 319										
7	Domum tuam Domine decet	an	AR [106] LU 1246 AM 697 WA 319 *LA 552	G	2	5	7	9	7	4	7	5	G
8	Domus Jacob de populo	an	WA 64	c	-1	-3	-5	-3	-5	-7	-5	-3	G
	Domus mea domus orationis	tr	SYG 264 (nm)										
5	Domus mea domus orationis	co	GR [74] LU 1253 *SYG 265 GB 176^V GS 175	G	-2	0	2	4	2	0	2	0	F

1	Domus mea domus orationis	an	AR [107] LU 1247 AM 697 *WA 89 317 LA 134 552	C	2	5	7	9	7	5	7	9	D
1	Domus mea domus orationis	re	LR 241	D	7	8	7	5	3	5	7	5	D
	Domus pudici pectoris Confirmatum est	rev	PM 166 WA 49										
	Domus pudici pectoris Nesciens mater	rev	PM 250 LA 35										
4	Donet eis Dominus requiem	co	GB 266^v	F	-3	-1	0	2	4	2	0	-1	E
	Donetur nobis eorum Hodie martyrum	rev	WA 46	D	7	5	7	5	3	2	0	5	
1	Dormiunt in terrae pulvere	co	GR (22)	D	3	2	3	5	2	0	3	2	D
1	Dormivit Abraham cum patribus	re	WA 82	C	2	5	2	4	2	0	4	2	D
	Duae pennae singulorum Similitudo vultus	rev	WA 372										
7	Ductus est Jesus in desertum ... accedens	re	LA 131 WA 87	G	2	0	2	0	2	5	4	5	G
1	Ductus est Jesus in desertum ... cum	an	AM 342 *AR 369 WA 88 LA 133	C	2	5	2	0	2	0	2	4	D
	Dulce lignum dulces clavos O crux gloriosa	rev	WA 369										
1	Dulce lignum dulces clavos	an	WA 308 *LA 395 462	a	-2	0	3	5	0	-4	-2	0	D
	Dulce lignum dulces clavos	alv	GR 491 LU 1456 GS 185 235 SYG 174 *GB 165	E	3	5	3	8	7	5	3	5	
8	Dulce lignum dulces clavos	re	LA 396 WA 308	D	5	3	5	7	5	7	5	7	G
1	Dulcis et rectus Dominus	gr	GR 324 [112] LU 971	D	7	8	7	5	3	7	5	7	D
	Dum		see also Cum										
	Dum adhuc longe esset Surgam et ibo	rev	VP 117	e	1	3	1	0	1	0	-2	-4	
2	Dum adhuc paene vigilaret	an	WA 342	D	-2	-5	-2	0	2	0	-2	0	D
	Dum anxiaretur cor Exaudi Deus	rev	WA 66										
8	Dum aurora finem ... dixit	an	WA 408	G	-2	0	2	0	2	0	-2	-3	G
7	Dum aurora finem ... dixit	re	LA 493	c	-1	0	2	0	2	4	2	4	G
8	Dum aurora finem ... dixit	re	WA 408	D	3	5	7	5	7	5	7	9	G
1	Dum aurora finem ... exclamavit	an	AR 925 AM 1142	C	2	9	10	9	7	5	7	9	D
1	Dum aurora finem ... exclamavit	an	LA 494	D	3	0	-2	3	5	3	5	7	D
6	Dum autem irent emere	an	WA 431	c	2	5	4	2	0	2	4	2	c
1	Dum beatus vir	re	WA 333 (inc illeg)	C									D
8	Dum caeli sphaera volvitur	hy	ST 469	G	2	0	-3	-2	0	2	0	-2	G

3 Dum clamarem ad Dominum	int	GR 344 LU 1020 SYG 67 GB 63 GS 32 151	E	1	-2	3	0	3	5	3	5	E
Dum clamarem ad Dominum Jacta cogitatum	grv	GR 328 LU 982 GS 32 49 143 *GB 63^V *SYG 67	G	5	7	5	7	4	5	7	2	
1 Dum commiterent bellum	an	WA 383 *LA 471	C	2	0	5	7	9	7	9	11	D
Dum complerentur dies		see also Cum complerentur										
Dum complerentur dies	alv	GR 305 LU 903 *SYG 183 *GB 187	a	-2	-5	-4	-2	-4	-2	-7	-9	
3 Dum complerentur dies	an	AR 503 LU 884 *AM 520 *WA 153 LA 261 264	E	-2	3	5	8	10	8	5	7	E
1 Dum conturbata fuerit anima	an	AR 439 OHS 513 LU 716 AM 441 442 WA 124 LA 201	D	-2	3	5	3	5	7	8	7	D
4 Dum deambularet Dominus	re	LA 111 *WA 73	F	2	0	-3	-1	-3	0	-3	0	E
5 Dum duceretur Petrus apostolus	an	AR 194* VP 183 *GB 207	C	4	7	4	7	9	7	4	7	C
Dum enim in corpore Translate ad caelestia	rev	WA 315	D	7	5	7	5	3	5	7	5	
Dum ergo essent in unum Cum complerentur	rev	LR 109 LA 255										
Dum ergo essent in unum Spiritus sanctus replevit	rev	LR 116 WA 156 LA 258										
Dum ergo fleret		see Cum ergo fleret										
6 Dum ergo sint apud Deum	an	WA 342	F	2	4	2	4	2	0	-1	0	F
2 Dum esset gens congregata	int	SYG 173	C	2	5	4	2	0	2	5	4	D
3 Dum esset rex in accubitu suo	an	AR [97] [114] LU 1232 1258 *AM 686 706 *WA 434 *LA 543	G	5	2	0	2	5	2	5	4	E
1 Dum esset summus pontifex	an	AR 577^{16} [66] LU 262^4 1181 *AM 663 741 826 *LA 532	D	-2	3	5	3	5	7	5	8	D
1 Dum exiret Jacob de terra	re	LA 138 WA 91	F	2	4	2	4	2	0	2	4	D
8 Dum fabricam sacri Cluniacensis	an	PM 211	G	-5	-2	0	2	-2	0	-2	0	G
2 Dum fabricator mundi	an	WA 215 SYG 140 GS 103	D	-5	0	-2	0	3	2	3	0	D
7 Dum flerem ad monumentum	an	WA 139	G	4	5	7	9	5	7	5	7	G
3 Dum fortis armatus custodit	an	AR 388 LU 1089 *AM 363 *LA 153 *WA 99	G	5	2	0	2	5	2	4	5	E
1 Dum in hac terra	an	LR 319 WA 296 LA 367	D	-2	3	5	3	5	7	5	3	D
7 Dum ingrederetur beata Agatha	re	LA 358 WA 273	G	5	4	5	7	5	7	5	4	G
1 Dum ingrederetur Jesus	an	WA 189	C	2	4	2	5	4	2	0	5	D

	Incipit	Type	Sources										
1	Dum intraret Jesus	an	AR 564 LU 1106 *AM 604	D	-2	0	3	0	-2	0	3	0	D
6	Dum inventum esset	an	WA 346	c	-1	-3	-1	-3	-5	-3	0	2	c
1	Dum iret Jacob	re	LR 406	C	2	5	2	4	5	2	4	2	D
7	Dum iret Jacob	re	WA 91	G	2	5	2	4	5	2	5	2	G
3	Dum jactantur puppes	an	WA 292	G	2	0	2	5	4	2	4	2	E
	Dum lucem habetis / Ecce ego mitto	rev	LR 136 LA 506 WA 411										
8	Dum medium silentium ... iter	int	GR 44 LU 433 SYG 29 GB 30^v GS 18	C	2	7	5	7	9	7	10	9	G
8	Dum medium silentium ... perageret	an	AR 288 LU 433 AM 265 WA 48 LA 62	G	-5	-2	0	2	0	2	0	-3	G
3	Dum nocte pulsa lucifer	hy	AR 712	E	1	3	1	0	-2	0	-2	-4	E
4	Dum oraret in obscuro	re	WA 288	F	-3	0	-1	0	-3	0	2	0	E
3	Dum oraret sanctus	an	WA 249	E	-2	3	5	7	3	5	8	7	E
	Dum ortus fuerit	see	Cum ortus fuerit										
7	Dum paginae sacrae	an	AM 832	G	5	4	5	7	9	7	5	4	G
	Dum perambularet Dominus / Venite post me	rev	WA 233										
4	Dum perambularet Dominus	re	LA 498 *WA 233	F	-3	0	-1	0	2	4	2	6	E
7	Dum praeliaretur Michael	an	AR 856 LU 1659 AM 1058 WA 383 *LA 471	G	4	5	7	5	7	9	7	5	G
	Dum sacramenta offerret / Oculis ac manibus	rev	LA 483										
4	Dum sacramenta offerret	re	LA 483 WA 399	F	-3	0	-1	0	-1	0	2	0	E
4	Dum sacramenta offerret	an	LA 483	E	-2	0	3	7	5	3	5	7	E
	Dum sacramenta offerret / Ora pro nobis beate Martine	grv	SYG 225	F	4	7	6	4	7	6	2	4	
8	Dum sacrum mysterium beatus Dionysius	an	WA 386	G	-2	-5	-3	-2	0	2	0	2	G
8	Dum sacrum mysterium cerneret	an	AR 855 LU 1652 AM 1057 WA 379 LA 464	G	-5	-2	0	2	0	2	0	2	G
5	Dum sacrum mysterium sanctus Dionysius	re	PM 197 *WA 386	a	3	0	3	0	3	-2	0	-2	F
3	Dum sanctificatus fuero	int	GR 145 (38) LU 859 *SYG 104 *GB 93 *GS 66	E	1	0	-2	3	5	3	5	8	E
1	Dum staret Abraham	re	LA 121 WA 81	D	3	0	-2	3	5	3	5	7	D
1	Dum staret Abraham	an	WA 80	D	3	5	3	2	0	-2	0	3	D
2	Dum steteritis ante reges	an	LA 505	D	-5	-2	0	2	0	3	2	0	D
3	Dum steteritis ante reges	re	LR 138 *LA 506 *WA 412	E	-2	3	5	8	7	8	7	3	E

8 Dum tolleret Dominus Eliam	an	AR 542 LU 988 AM 578 *LA 275	G	-2	-5	-3	-2	0	2	0	2	G
5 Dum transiret Dominus	an	AR 563 LU 1105 AM 602 LA 315	F	4	7	5	4	5	7	9	7	F
1 Dum transiret Jesus	an	LA 315	C	2	5	2	0	2	5	2	5	D
Dum transisset Sabbatum	see Cum transisset											
7 Dum tribularer clamavi	an	AR 429 OHS 245 280 AM 408 *WA 115 LA 186	G	4	5	7	5	7	5	4	2	G
8 Dum venerit filius	an	AM 212 LA 22	c	-1	0	2	0	-1	-3	-1	0	G
Dum venerit paraclitus	see also Cum venerit											
8 Dum venerit paraclitus spiritus	co	GR 270 LU 828 *SYG 168 *GB 151 GS 130	a	3	2	3	0	1	0	-4	0	G
8 Dum veniet filius	an	WA 17	a	3	2	3	5	3	2	0	3	G
1 Dum vero adhuc penderet	re	WA 239	D	-2	0	3	2	0	2	0	-2	D
Dum virgo Deum et hominem Gaude Maria	trv	GR [78] LU 1266	F	2	4	2	0	2	4	2	4	
6 Dum vitam in ara Golgothae	hy	ST 22	F	2	0	-3	-5	-3	0	5	4	F
7 Dunstane pater inclyte	an	WA 312	G	7	5	7	2	5	9	5	7	G
8 Dunstanus archiepiscopus	re	WA 314	D	3	5	3	5	0	3	5	7	G
Dunstanus columbae Dei Caelestium contemplator	rev	WA 313	G	7	5	7	9	10	12	10	9	
1 Dunstanus praesul inclytus	an	WA 311	C	2	4	2	4	2	4	2	0	D
4 Duo homines ascenderunt	an	LA 314	F	-1	-3	-1	0	2	0	2	4	E
1 Duo mihi Domine talenta	an	LA 532	D	-2	3	5	3	5	7	9	7	D
Duo rogavi te Verbum iniquum	rev	LA 278										
1 Duo seraphim clamabant	re	AR 179* PM 107 LR 418	D	-2	-5	-2	0	2	0	-2	0	D
Duplici doctrina fratribus praetuit N. praeesse	rev	PM 231	D	7	5	7	5	3	2	5	7	

	Incipit	Type	Sources										
4	E Corde Jesu prodiit	hy	AR 5 (sup 2)	F	-1	0	2	4	2	0	-3	0	E
	E secretis extrahitur / Veriloquus	rev	WA 294										
8	Ecce Adam quasi unus	re	LA 112 *WA 74	G	-2	-5	-3	-2	-3	-5	-7	-5	G
	Ecce adest dies	alv	SYG 216	F	4	6	7	9	7	2	6	4	
8	Ecce advenit dominator Deus	an	WA 47	c	-1	-3	-5	0	-3	-5	-7	-5	G
2	Ecce advenit dominator Dominus	int	GR 57 LU 459 SYG 30 GB 32 GS J	A	3	5	7	5	3	5	7	8	D
	Ecce agnus Dei / Rex noster	rev	WA 12										
7	Ecce agnus Dei	re	LR 64 *LA 36	G	2	5	4	2	4	2	0	5	G
8	Ecce ancilla Domini	an	AR 247 669 [140] LU 1417 AM 223 863 LA 379	c	-1	-3	-5	-3	-1	-3	-5	-3	G
3	Ecce angelus Domini apparuit	an	LR 303	E	-2	3	5	8	7	8	7	5	E
8	Ecce annuntio vobis	re	LA 36	G	2	0	-2	0	2	0	2	0	G
7	Ecce apparebit Dominus et non mentietur	an	AR 224 LU 332 AM 196 WA 12 *LA 11	G	4	5	7	5	7	9	7	9	G
1	Ecce apparebit Dominus super nubem	re	LR 393 *LA 13 WA 13	a	-2	0	-2	-4	-2	1	0	-2	D
	Ecce appropinquabit	see	Ecce appropinquat										
	Ecce appropinquat hora / Tristis est	rev	OHS 378 LU 635 LA 189 WA 118										
4	Ecce ascendimus ... et consummabuntur	an	AR 355 AM 328 WA 82 LA 124	F	-1	-3	-1	-3	-5	-3	-1	0	E
7	Ecce ascendimus ... et consummabuntur ... prophetas	an	LA 124	a	2	3	5	7	5	3	2	0	G
7	Ecce ascendimus ... et filius	an	AR 383 LU 1086 AM 357 WA 94 *LA 144	G	4	5	7	9	7	5	4	2	G
2	Ecce carissimi dies illa	an	WA 207 *SYG 72	C	2	0	2	5	4	2	4	2	D
8	Ecce completa sunt	an	AR 255 AM 220 231 WA 27 LA 31	c	-1	-3	-5	-3	-1	-3	-5	-3	G
	Ecce concipies et paries / Dixit angelus ad Mariam	rev	WA 302										
8	Ecce concipies et paries	re	WA 302	G	-2	0	-7	-5	-2	0	2	0	G
	Ecce concipies et paries / Ave Maria	trv	GR 459 LU 1412 *SYG 57	F	2	4	2	4	2	0	2	0	
	Ecce concipiet et pariet	alv	GR 3**	a	-4	0	-4	0	-2	-4	-2	-4	
8	Ecce constitui te	re	LA 406 *WA 322	F	2	4	2	4	2	4	6	4	G
1	Ecce crucem Domini	an	AR 700 LU 1460 AM 899 1041 WA 369 *LA 463	D	2	3	5	2	3	5	3	2	D
	Ecce cum virtute / Ecce Dominus veniet ... erit	rev	WA 10										

	Ecce dabit vocem Psallite Deo	rev	WA 150										
8	Ecce de quo Joannes	an	WA 47	F	2	0	2	4	7	6	2	4	G
8	Ecce dedi te in lucem	an	AR 894[2] LU 1716 AM 1089	G	-2	-5	-2	0	-2	2	5	4	G
	Ecce dedi verba mea Priusquam te formarem	rev	LA 402 WA 322										
7	Ecce dedi verba mea	an	LR 347 WA 320 LA 401	d	-3	0	2	0	2	0	-2	0	G
3	Ecce dedi verba mea	of	GR [2[4]] LU 1122[6]	G	2	5	4	5	4	7	5	4	E
5	Ecce Deus adjuvat me	int	GR 342 LU 1016 SYG 244 GB 252 *GS 150	c	-3	0	-3	-7	-3	-2	-5	-7	F
8	Ecce Deus meus	an	AR 242 AM 217 WA 19 *LA 25	G	-5	-2	0	2	0	2	0	-2	G
8	Ecce dies veniunt	re	PM 20 *LA 10 WA 11	G	-2	0	-7	-5	-2	0	2	0	G
	Ecce dominator Dominus Ecce Dominus ... protector	rev	LR 9										
	Ecce dominator Dominus Germinaverunt campi	rev	LA 26 WA 18										
	Ecce dominator Dominus Paratus esto	rev	PM 25 LA 18										
	Ecce Dominus in fortitudine Civitas Jerusalem	rev	PM 24 LA 8 WA 10										
	Ecce Dominus in fortitudine Ecce Dominus veniet	rev	LA 19	a	-2	-4	-5	-7	-9	-7	-5	-7	
	Ecce Dominus in virtute Ecce veniet	rev	LA 8										
1	Ecce Dominus meus omnia	an	AR 1 (sup 1)	D	2	3	0	-2	3	5	3	7	D
3	Ecce Dominus noster	an	AR 225 LU 333 AM 197 *WA 12 *LA 11	G	2	4	5	2	4	2	0	2	E
5	Ecce Dominus veniet et omnes ... erit	an	AR 214 [138] LU 324 AM 187 WA 6 LA 6	c	-3	0	-1	-5	-1	-3	-5	-7	F
5	Ecce Dominus veniet et omnes ... erit	re	WA 10	c	-3	0	2	0	-2	0	-2	-3	F
6	Ecce Dominus veniet et omnes ... et erit	co	GR 12 *SYG 9 GB 8 *GS 7	c	-3	-5	-3	-7	-5	0	2	0	c
1	Ecce Dominus veniet et omnes ... tunc	re	LA 19	C	2	0	2	0	5	4	5	7	D
5	Ecce Dominus veniet protector	re	LA 9	c	-3	0	2	0	-2	0	-2	-3	F
	Ecce Dominus veniet ut salvos Sanctificamini filii	rev	LA 29										
1	Ecce ego Joannes vidi	an	WA 371	C	2	4	2	4	5	2	0	2	D
8	Ecce ego mitto angelum	an	PM 194	G	2	5	2	5	7	9	5	4	G
1	Ecce ego mitto vos	an	LA 512	D	-2	0	2	0	2	3	2	0	D

	Incipit	Type	Sources										
7	Ecce ego mitto vos	re	LR 136 LA 506 *WA 411	G	2	0	2	0	2	0	2	5	G
	Ecce ego statuam / Aedificavit Noe	rev	LA 117 WA 78										
	Ecce ego sternam / Lapides pretiosi	rev	LA 550										
6	Ecce ego vobiscum sum alleluia	an	LA 222	F	-1	2	4	0	-3	-5	0	-1	F
8	Ecce ego vobiscum sum omnibus diebus	an	AR 10 (sup 2)	F	2	0	4	7	6	7	9	7	G
3	Ecce ego vobiscum sum omnibus diebus	co	GR 58**	D	3	0	3	2	3	5	3	2	E
	Ecce elongavi fugiens / Angelus Domini apparuit	intv	GR 4**										
	Ecce enim ex hoc beatam / Magnificat	rev	LR 270										
	Ecce enim ut facta / Repleta est spiritu	rev	PM 164	a	-2	0	-2	-4	-2	0	-2	0	
6	Ecce exaltata est	an	WA 359	c	-1	0	-3	-5	-3	0	2	0	c
5	Ecce factus est sacer ille	an	PM 190 *WA 377	F	4	7	6	4	7	6	4	2	F
8	Ecce fidelis servus et prudens	an	AR 658 LU 1407 AM 846	a	-2	-4	0	3	2	3	0	-2	G
5	Ecce gens quae	an	WA 287	a	-2	0	-2	-4	0	3	2	0	F
	Ecce homo sine querela / Ecce vir prudens	rev	VP 257										
	Ecce homo sine querela / Iste est qui ante	rev	LR 208										
7	Ecce homo sine querela	re	WA 426	G	2	0	2	0	2	0	2	5	G
	Ecce homo sine querela / Iste homo ab adolescentia	rev	LA 534 *WA 426	G	5	4	0	2	4	2	5	7	
	Ecce in fortitudine		see Ecce Dominus in fortitudine										
1	Ecce in nubibus caeli Dominus	an	AR 224 LU 331 AM 195 WA 12 20 LA 11 377	D	-2	0	2	3	5	3	2	0	D
1	Ecce in nubibus caeli filius	an	WA 16	D	-2	0	2	3	5	3	2	0	D
	Ecce in pulvere sedeo / Paucitas dierum	rev	LA 284 WA 173										
	Ecce inimici tui Domine / Bonum est confiteri	ofv	OTT 26 GB 57 *SYG 59	G	5	4	5	4	5	7	2	-2	
6	Ecce jam cari noscite	re	WA 300	c	2	0	5	4	5	7	5	4	c
1	Ecce jam coram te protomartyr	re	PM 31 VP 79	C	2	5	7	4	2	5	4	5	D
4	Ecce jam in sublime	an	WA 258	F	-3	-1	2	4	2	0	-1	-3	E
4	Ecce jam in sublime	re	WA 258	F	-3	0	-3	-5	-3	0	-1	0	E
4	Ecce jam noctis tenuatur umbra lucis	hy	ST 263	F	-3	0	-1	0	-3	-5	-3	0	E
4	Ecce jam noctis tenuatur umbra lucis	hy	ST 212	E	-2	0	3	5	3	5	3	1	E
2	Ecce jam noctis tenuatur umbra lucis	hy	ST 166	D	-2	0	3	5	3	5	7	5	D
4	Ecce jam noctis tenuatur umbra lucis	hy	ST 359	c	-1	-3	-5	-1	-3	-5	-3	-1	b

	Incipit		Sources										
4	Ecce jam noctis tenuatur umbra lucis	hy	ST 85 AM 35	E	1	0	-2	0	-2	-4	-2	0	E
8	Ecce jam noctis tenuatur umbra lucis	hy	ST 264	G	2	0	-3	-2	0	2	-2	2	G
8	Ecce jam noctis tenuatur umbra lucis	hy	ST 251	G	2	0	-3	-2	0	2	0	-2	G
1	Ecce jam noctis tenuatur umbra lux	hy	AR 9	D	-2	0	3	5	3	5	7	5	D
4	Ecce jam noctis tenuatur umbra lux	hy	AR 8	F	-1	-3	-1	-3	-5	-3	-1	-5	E
4	Ecce jam tristes abiere luctus	hy	LR 453	a	-2	0	-2	-4	-5	-4	-2	-5	E
	Ecce jam veniet		see Ecce jam venit										
	Ecce jam venit plenitudo	alv	GB 31	C	2	4	5	7	9	7	12	11	
5	Ecce jam venit plenitudo	an	AR 238 AM 213 WA 17 *LA 22	F	4	7	4	7	9	7	5	4	F
5	Ecce jam venit plenitudo	re	WA 23	F	4	7	9	7	5	7	9	7	F
6	Ecce lignum crucis	an	GR 211 OHS 570 LU 735 *WA 215 GS 102	F	-3	-1	0	-1	-3	-5	0	2	F
2	Ecce Maria genuit	an	AR 295 LU 444 AM 273	E	-4	-2	1	0	-2	0	-2	-4	D
5	Ecce Maria genuit	an	WA 50 *LA 65	a	-4	0	3	2	0	-2	-4	-2	F
	Ecce Maria venit	an	SYG 47										
	Ecce mater nostra Ecce carissimi dies	anv	SYG 72	D	2	0	-2	0	-2	0	3	2	
4	Ecce merces sanctorum	an	LR 181 *LA 516	F	-3	0	-1	-3	-5	-3	2	0	E
	Ecce miles Christi	alv	SYG 214	C	2	4	5	7	4	2	5	2	
4	Ecce mitto angelum ... praecedat	re	LA 157 *WA 102	D	3	0	2	3	0	-2	0	2	E
8	Ecce mitto angelum ... praeparabit	an	AR 228 LU 1083 AM 201 WA 13 *LA 12	G	2	5	7	9	5	4	2	5	G
	Ecce mitto vos	alv	GB 268	G	2	4	5	7	4	5	4	2	
5	Ecce nomen Domini Emmanuel	an	AR 149* PM 29 VP 72	G	-2	-3	-2	0	-2	-3	-2	0	C
1	Ecce nomen Domini venit	an	AR 211 LU 317 AM 186 *LA 1	D	-2	3	5	3	5	7	9	10	D
8	Ecce nunc palam loqueris	an	WA 146 *LA 243	F	2	0	4	7	6	4	2	0	G
	Ecce nunc tempus ... commendemus In omnibus exhibeamus	rev	LA 127										
	Ecce nunc tempus ... [commendemus] Paradisi portas	rev	LA 129 WA 86										
3	Ecce nunc tempus ... commendemus	re	LR 403 LA 127 *WA 85	D	3	0	3	2	3	2	3	5	E
8	Ecce nunc tempus ... in his	an	AR 372 IU 540 AM 345 *WA 85 *LA 134	F	2	0	4	7	6	7	4	0	G
	Ecce nunc tempus ... nemini In omnibus exhibeamus	rev	WA 85										
8	Ecce nunc tempus ... operemur	an	SYG 71	G	2	-2	0	-5	-7	-5	-2	0	G

#	Incipit		Sources										
3	Ecce oculi Domini super timentes	int	GR 494 SYG 176 GB 171^V GS 212	E	1	-2	3	0	3	5	10	8	F
7	Ecce odor filii mei	re	LA 137 *WA 91	G	2	5	2	4	2	0	5	4	G
7	Ecce panis angelorum	re	AR 96*	d	-2	0	-3	-2	-5	-9	-7	-3	G
	Ecce praecedat vos Angelus Domini locutus	rev	WA 128										
1	Ecce puer meus electus	an	AR 280 LU 424 AM 256 *WA 42 *LA 56	D	-2	3	5	3	7	5	8	7	D
7	Ecce puer meus quem elegi	re	LA 54 *WA 39	G	2	4	5	4	2	4	2	0	G
	Ecce quam bonum et quam jucundum Ubi fratres in unum	anv	SYG 131										
	Ecce quam bonum et quam jucundum Haec est vera fraternitas	rev	PM 222 LR 187 LA 409 WA 422										
	Ecce quam bonum et quam jucundum Propter testamentum	rev	PM 207 LR 186 LA 517										
	Ecce quam bonum et quam jucundum Quadam die	rev	LR 295										
1	Ecce quam bonum et quam jucundum	an	AR 158 LU 295 *AM 140 141 *LA 93	a	-2	-5	-4	-2	-5	-4	-7	-5	D
	Ecce quam bonum et quam jucundum	alv	GB 201^V	F	2	4	2	0	4	6	7	6	
	Ecce quam bonum et quam jucundum	alv	GB 201^V	F	2	4	6	7	9	7	6	2	
8	Ecce quam bonum et quam jucundum	an	AR 640 AM 821	G	4	2	4	5	4	0	2	0	G
	Ecce quam bonum et quam jucundum Haec est vera fraternitas	rev	LA 517	G	5	4	2	4	2	0	-3	0	
1	Ecce quam bonum et quam jucundum	gr	GR 384 455 LU 1071 SYG 199 GB 201 GS d n 214	D	7	8	7	5	3	7	5	7	D
	Ecce quam bonum et quam jucundum ... sicut	alv	GR 568	G	2	-3	-2	0	2	4	5	2	
4	Ecce quod concupivi jam video	an	AR 604 AM 787	D	2	3	5	7	5	2	3	5	E
1	Ecce quod cupivi jam video	an	WA 255	D	2	3	5	7	5	2	3	5	D
4	Ecce quomodo moritur	re	OHS 611 LU 766 *LA 198 *WA 126	C	2	5	4	5	4	5	4	5	E
8	Ecce radix Jesse ascendet	re	LA 15 380 WA 15	G	2	0	2	0	2	5	4	5	G
4	Ecce rex veniet	an	AR 228 LU 1082 AM 200 WA 12 19 *LA 12	G	2	5	7	9	7	5	7	9	a
	Ecce rex venit	see Ecce rex veniet											
1	Ecce sacerdos magnus Martinus	int	SYG 226	D	3	0	-2	0	-2	3	5	7	D
5	Ecce sacerdos magnus qui	gr	GR [32] LU 1183 1495^A SYG 27 GB 28^V GS 220	F	2	0	2	4	0	2	0	-1	F
7	Ecce sacerdos magnus qui ... et inventus	an	AR [55] LU 1176 AM 657 WA 427 *LA 536	d	-3	0	2	0	-3	-2	-3	-7	G

	Ecce sacerdos magnus qui ... et inventus	alv	SYG 215	C	2	4	5	4	2	4	2	0	
8	Ecce sacerdos magnus qui ... ideo	re	AR 82* PM 308 LR 194 LU 1841 LA 530 *WA 425	F	2	4	2	4	6	4	2	4	G
8	Ecce sic benedicetur omnis	tr	GR [123] LU 1290	G	-2	-5	-3	-7	-5	-2	0	2	G
6	Ecce sic benedicetur omnis	co	GR [125] LU 1292 SYG 234	F	-1	0	-3	-1	-3	-5	0	2	F
	Ecce sicut oculi servorum Ad te levavi	trv	GR 124 LU 554 GS 55 GB 82v *SYG 93	G	2	4	5	4	2	5	4	2	
	Ecce sicut sol Beatus es care	rev	WA 315	D	7	5	7	5	3	2	0	5	
1	Ecce sto ad ostium et pulso	co	GR 453 LU 1396	F	-1	-3	0	2	4	2	0	-1	D
8	Ecce te rogavi	an	AM 815	G	-2	2	5	4	0	4	5	2	G
	Ecce tu Domine cognovisti Mihi autem	ofv	OTT 128 *GB 203 *SYG 201	G	5	4	5	2	0	-3	-2	0	
3	Ecce tu pulcher es	an	WA 162	E	1	3	1	0	-2	-4	3	5	E
1	Ecce tu pulchra es	an	WA 354 *LA 455	D	3	0	2	0	-2	3	5	7	D
	Ecce turba et qui vocabatur Barrabas latro	rev	WA 122										
1	Ecce veniet desideratus	an	AR 251 LU 357 AM 227 *WA 19 24 LA 21	D	-2	3	5	3	7	8	7	5	D
1	Ecce veniet Deus et homo	an	AR 222 LU 1081 AM 193 *WA 9 *LA 7	D	7	9	7	9	10	7	5	7	D
5	Ecce veniet Dominus et omnes	re	LA 8	c	-3	0	2	0	-1	0	-1	-3	F
	Ecce veniet Dominus exercituum Aegypte noli flere	rev	LA 14 WA 14										
4	Ecce veniet Dominus princeps	an	AR 237 AM 212 WA 17 *LA 22	G	2	5	7	9	7	5	7	9	a
5	Ecce veniet Dominus princeps	re	LA 15	F	4	7	4	7	9	7	9	7	F
5	Ecce veniet Dominus protector	re	WA 10	c	-3	0	2	0	-2	0	-2	-3	F
4	Ecce veniet Dominus ut sedeat	an	AR 240 AM 215 WA 18 *LA 24	G	2	5	7	9	7	5	7	9	a
4	Ecce veniet propheta	an	AR 214 LU 324 AM 188 WA 7 20 *LA 6	G	2	5	7	5	7	9	7	5	a
4	Ecce venit ad templum sanctum	inv	LR 433 LA 347 *WA 268	D	3	0	3	2	3	5	3	0	E
4	Ecce venit rex occuramus	inv	LA 1 *WA 13	C	2	4	5	4	2	4	5	4	E
	Ecce vere Israelita Ecce vir prudens	rev	LA 533 WA 390										
	Ecce vere Israelita Hodie praeclarissimus	rev	WA 289										
2	Ecce vere Israelita	re	LR 195 LA 533 *WA 390	D	-2	-5	-2	0	3	0	-2	0	D

1 Ecce vere Israelita	an	LA 540	F	-1	-3	-1	0	2	4	2	4	D
Ecce vere Israelita Consecrandos	rev	WA 250	c	2	5	4	5	4	2	4	2	
7 Ecce vicit leo	re	OHS 789 *PM 68 LR 89 LA 209 *WA 134	G	2	4	5	4	2	4	2	0	G
4 Ecce video caelos apertos	an	AR 274 LU 418 1583[B] AM 251 WA 37 *LA 47	G	2	5	7	5	7	9	7	5	a
1 Ecce vidi agnum stantem	an	WA 47	D	-2	0	3	2	3	5	3	2	D
4 Ecce vidi agnum stantem	re	LA 59	C	2	5	7	5	2	5	7	5	E
5 Ecce vidimus eum	re	OHS 381 LU 637 *LR 336 *LA 190 *WA 118	b	3	1	-2	0	-2	1	0	1	F
Ecce vir Dei Benedictus	alv	GB 55	F	2	4	2	0	4	6	7	6	
7 Ecce vir Oriens nomen ejus	an	AR 894[1] LU 1715 AM 1089	G	4	5	7	9	7	9	5	2	G
1 Ecce vir prudens	re	VP 257 LA 533 WA 390 (inc illeg)	C	2	5	2	4	5	7	5	2	D
3 Ecce virgo concipiet ... admirabilis	re	LA 5 380 *WA 5	G	2	5	4	2	0	4	5	2	E
Ecce virgo concipiet ... Emmanuel Radix Jesse	rev	LA 20 378										
3 Ecce virgo concipiet ... Emmanuel	int	GR 622[6] LU 1683	G	2	5	4	2	0	4	5	4	E
1 Ecce virgo concipiet ... Emmanuel	an	LA 17 379	C	2	9	11	9	7	9	11	9	D
1 Ecce virgo concipiet ... Emmanuel	co	GR 23 462 LU 356 *SYG 9 *GB 7[V] GS 6	D	3	2	3	5	0	-2	2	5	D
Ecce virgo concipiet ... Jesum	alv	SYG 2	A	3	5	8	5	3	7	8	10	
2 Ecce virum a virtute	re	WA 249	A	3	5	8	7	5	7	5	3	D
8 Ecclesia illisque necdum	an	WA 385	G	5	2	0	2	0	-2	0	2	G
Ecclesia illius virtute roboratur	see Ecclesia virtute											
Ecclesia virtute roboratur O beatum virum in cujus	rev	VP 243 LA 485 WA 401										
1 Ecclesia virtute roboratur	re	WA 401	D	-2	0	2	3	0	2	0	-2	D
4 Ecclesiae principatum	an	WA 311	E	-2	-4	-2	0	1	3	1	0	E
2 Ecclesiae sanctae frequentans	an	WA 242	D	-5	-2	0	3	2	0	2	0	D
8 Ecclesiae sponsum virgo	re	PM 269	G	-2	0	-7	-5	-2	0	2	0	G
2 Educ de carcere animam	re	LA 163 *WA 103	GG	2	5	7	5	7	9	10	9	D
3 Educ de custodia	an	AR 182 LU 304	G	2	5	2	5	4	0	2	4	E
Educas panem de terra	sr	AR 535 LU 955										
5 Eduxit Dominus Abram	re	WA 80	F	4	7	9	7	5	4	5	7	F
7 Eduxit Dominus populum	int	GR 258 OHS 825 LU 804 *SYG 161 *GB 142[V] GS 123	c	2	-3	0	4	2	5	4	0	G

	Chant	Type	Sources										
	Eduxit Dominus populum	alv	SYG 161	D	3	2	3	5	7	9	5	3	
4	Eduxit eos Dominus in spe	int	GR 255 OHS 816 LU 800 SYG 160 *GB 140 *GS 122	F	2	-3	0	2	0 . 4	2	0		E
	Effuderunt furorem suum — Insurrexerunt in me	rev	OHS 185 (nm) WA 115(111)										
8	Effuderunt sanguinem sanctorum	tr	GR 42 LU 429 SYG 26 *GB 26^v	F	2	4	2	4	2	0	2	4	G
4	Effuderunt sanguinem sanctorum	re	LA 58 *WA 44	G	2	5	7	5	7	9	7	9	b
	Effugarunt aciem — Martyres sancti	rev	WA 423										
	Effunde frameam et conclude — Judica Domine	intv	GR 185 LU 606 GS 89 GB 111										
	Effunde frameam et conclude — Exsurge Domine	grv	GR 185 OHS 208 LU 607 *GS 89 *GB 111^v *SYG 124	E	1	-2	3	5	8	5	8	10	
	Effundit cor meum verbum — Gaudeamus ... reginae	intv	LU 1476^B										
1	Effusum est in terra	int	GR 554 LU 1561	C	2	9	10	9	7	9	10	9	D
	Ego autem ad Deum clamavi — Exaudi Deus	ofv	OTT 36 *GB 84 SYG 95	d	2	-2	-3	-2	0	2	-2	-3	
	Ego autem ad Deum clamavi — Contristatus	trv	GR 622^3	C	2	5	7	5	2	5	7	9	
4	Ego autem ad Dominum	an	AR 243 AM 218 WA 20 *LA 26	G	2	5	7	5	7	9	7	5	a
4	Ego autem adjuvata	re	LA 361 *WA 274	D	3	0	3	2	3	5	3	2	E
	Ego autem apostolus — Medicinam carnalem	rev	LA 362										
	Ego autem cantabo fortitudinem	alv	GR 469	G	2	5	4	5	2	7	5	4	
1	Ego autem cum justitia	int	GR 121 SYG 91 GB 80 GS 52	F	2	4	7	4	2	5	4	5	D
	Ego autem cum justitia — Perfice gressus	ofv	OTT 90 *GB 58^v SYG 61	G	2	5	2	5	7	5	4	0	
2	Ego autem cum mihi molesti	of	GR 604 LU 1646	D	-2	2	0	-2	0	3	5	3	D
8	Ego autem cum mihi molesti	tr	GR 566	G	2	4	2	0	2	0	5	7	G
	Ego autem dixi in mea — Exaltabo te	ofv	OTT 96 *GB 62^v *SYG 66	F	2	4	2	4	6	4	6	4	
	Ego autem dum mihi molesti — Pacifice loquebantur	rev	LA 170 WA 107										
3	Ego autem dum mihi molesti	gr	GR 187 OHS 258 LU 610 *SYG 125 *GB 112^v *GS 90	C	2	5	4	5	4	5	4	5	E
3	Ego autem in Domino gaudebo	an	AR 299 LU 451 *AM 277	E	-2	3	5	8	7	8	10	8	E
1	Ego autem in Domino gaudebo	int	GR 467	F	2	4	7	4	2	5	4	5	D
	Ego autem in Domino sperabo		see Ego autem in Domino speravi										
1	Ego autem in Domino speravi	int	GR 132 GB 85 *GS 58 *SYG 96	F	2	4	7	4	2	5	4	5	D

No.	Incipit	Type	Sources										
	Ego autem in innocentia Proba me Domine	grv	SYG 85	E	1	-2	3	5	3	5	6	5	
	Ego autem in innocentia Lavabo	ofv	SYG 86	E	1	-2	3	5	7	8	5	3	
	Ego autem mendicus sum Beatus vir cujus est	grv	GR 20**	c	2	-1	0	-3	-5	-3	-1	0	
3	Ego autem sicut oliva	int	GR [1] *SYG 170 *GB 22^v *GS 202	E	1	-2	3	8	5	3	5	7	E
	Ego autem sum vermis Deus Deus meus	trv	GR 180 OHS 109 LU 594 GS 86 GB 109 SYG 122	C	2	5	7	5	2	5	7	9	
3	Ego clamavi quoniam exaudisti	int	GR 130 *GB 84^v GS 57 *SYG 95	F	-3	2	7	4	2	7	6	7	E
2	Ego clamavi quoniam exaudisti	co	GB 264	D	2	-2	0	-3	-2	-5	-2	0	D
8	Ego clamavi quoniam exaudisti	co	GR 386 LU 1073 SYG 240 GS 144	F	2	4	0	2	-1	0	-3	0	G
5	Ego crucis Christi	an	WA 232	F	4	7	6	4	2	7	9	7	F
8	Ego daemonium non habeo	an	AR 412 LU 568 AM 391 *WA 108 LA 172	c	-1	0	2	0	-1	-3	-1	0	G
	Ego dilecto meo et ad me	alv	GR 626 LU 1691	G	2	4	5	4	2	4	2	0	
3	Ego dilecto meo et dilectus meus	of	GR 399	c	-3	-1	0	2	0	-3	-5	-1	E
4	Ego dilecto meo et dilectus meus	co	GR 629 LU 1692	G	-2	-3	0	2	0	2	-2	0	E
8	Ego dilecto meo et dilectus meus	co	GR 74**	F	2	4	7	6	2	4	0	2	G
	Ego dilecto meo et dilectus meus	alv	GR 52**	D	3	2	5	3	2	3	0	7	
	Ego dilecto meo et dilectus meus Nihil inquinatum	grv	GR 48**	a	5	7	5	7	5	0	5	3	
	Ego diligentes me diligo Speciosa facta	rev	WA 139										
8	Ego diligentes me diligo	tr	GR 61**	G	2	4	2	0	2	0	2	0	G
	Ego diligentes me diligo Meum est consilium	trv	GR 26**	G	5	4	5	2	5	2	0	2	
	Ego dixi Domine miserere	sr	AR 538^11 LU 976 AM 562										
4	Ego dixi Domine miserere	re	LA 91 *WA 65	F	2	0	-3	-1	-3	0	-1	0	E
5	Ego dixi Domine miserere	gr	GR 311 SYG 239 GB 247 GS 141	F	2	0	-1	2	4	5	2	0	F
	Ego Dominus dabo	alv	GR 105**	D	2	0	-2	0	2	3	5	7	
	Ego Dominus inebriabo	alv	GR 91**	C	2	5	2	0	2	0	2	4	
3	Ego Dominus prope feci	an	AR 244	G	2	4	5	2	5	4	0	2	E
8	Ego dormivi et somnum	an	OHS 755 WA 128 LA 212 224	c	2	0	-1	0	-1	-3	0	-1	G
	Ego eduxi vos de terra Adduxi vos per desertum	rev	WA 103 LA 160										
1	Ego elegi vos et posui vos	co	GR (6)	D	7	8	5	3	7	5	7	8	D

	Incipit		Sources										
4	Ego enim ex Deo	an	WA 90	C	2	0	2	5	4	2	4	2	E
	Ego enim habeo mamillas Medecinam	rev	WA 275										
1	Ego enim jam delibor	an	LA 431	D	3	0	-2	3	5	3	5	7	D
	Ego enim ostendam Vade Anania	rev	LA 344 WA 264										
	Ego enim sum Dominus Deus qui Sancti Dei dedit	rev	WA 393										
	Ego enim sum Dominus Deus tuus Jerusalem cito	rev	LR 392	a	3	0	-2	0	-4	-5	-2	0	
	Ego enim sum Dominus Deus vester Octava decima	rev	WA 22										
1	Ego ex ore altissimi	re	LR 266	D	3	0	-2	0	2	0	7	8	D
8	Ego gloriam meam	an	AR 414 LU 569 AM 391	c	-1	0	2	0	-3	0	-1	-3	G
3	Ego gloriam meam	an	WA 108 *LA 169	G	2	5	4	2	5	4	2	0	E
	Ego habeo mamillas integras Dum ingrederitur beata	rev	LA 358 WA 273										
8	Ego in altissimis habitavi	an	AR 544 LU 990 AM 580 WA 168 *LA 281	c	-1	0	2	0	2	0	-1	-3	G
	Ego in altissimis habito Gyrum caeli	rev	LA 277										
	Ego in altissimis inhabitavi In principio Deus antequam	rev	WA 168										
	Ego mater pulchrae dilectionis	sr	AR 634 LU 1380										
	Ego me obtuli Gaudeo plane	rev	LA 439 WA 349										
1	Ego mittam vobis	an	WA 152	D	-2	3	5	3	5	7	9	7	D
8	Ego non ab homine	an	WA 95	G	5	2	0	-2	0	2	0	2	G
8	Ego pascam oves meas	tr	GR 66**	G	-2	-5	-3	-7	-5	-2	0	2	G
8	Ego per istos tres annos	an	WA 244	G	2	0	-2	2	5	2	5	7	G
8	Ego plantavi Apollo rigavit	an	AR 609 756 LU 1348 AM 792 941 *WA 266 *LA 430	G	5	2	0	2	0	-2	0	2	G
8	Ego principium qui et loquor	an	AR 382 LU 1085 AM 355 *WA 94 LA 144	c	-1	0	2	0	-3	-1	-3	-5	G
4	Ego pro te rogavi	re	LR 365 LA 417 *WA 278	C	2	4	2	5	7	9	7	9	E
8	Ego pro te rogavi	an	WA 280 *LA 419	G	5	2	0	-2	0	2	0	2	G
8	Ego qui loquor justitiam	an	AR 759 LU 1537 AM 945	c	-1	0	2	0	-1	-3	0	-1	G
	Ego quidem baptizavi Me oportet minui	rev	LR 18										
	Ego quidem plantavi Vinea mea	rev	WA 122										

	Ego rogabo patrem Non turbetur	rev	LR 102 LA 248 WA 147										
	Ego rogabo patrem	alv	SYG 185	a	-4	0	-2	-5	-3	-7	-4	-5	
3	Ego rogabo patrem	re	LR 104	G	2	4	5	2	4	5	4	2	E
7	Ego rogabo patrem	re	LA 248	G	2	4	5	4	2	4	0	2	G
4	Ego rogavi Dominum ... in	an	WA 247	F	-1	-3	-1	-3	-5	-3	-1	-3	E
8	Ego rogavi Dominum ... mihi	an	LA 323	G	5	2	0	2	0	-2	2	0	G
5	Ego sapientia habito	gr	GR 25**	F	2	0	2	0	2	4	5	2	F
7	Ego si patibulum crucis	an	LA 499	d	-3	0	2	0	2	0	-3	-2	G
3	Ego sicut vitis fructificavi	re	PM 256 LA 225 WA 139 305	G	2	5	4	5	2	7	5	7	E
7	Ego signo crucis	an	WA 399 LA 480	d	-3	0	2	0	2	0	-3	-2	G
	Ego statuam pactum		<u>see</u> Ecce ego statuam										
1	Ego sum alpha et omega ... ego sum	an	PM 69	C	2	0	2	5	4	2	0	5	D
1	Ego sum alpha et omega ... manus	an	WA 136 225 *SYG 147 *GS 125	D	2	0	2	5	4	2	0	5	D
	Ego sum angelus ille Docebo te	rev	WA 185										
3	Ego sum Deus patrum	an	AM 982	G	2	4	5	4	5	7	5	4	E
3	Ego sum Deus patrum	an	WA 227 *GB 153^v	G	2	5	4	5	2	5	7	5	E
6	Ego sum Gabriel angelus	an	AR 662 LU 1408	F	-3	-5	0	2	0	2	4	2	F
8	Ego sum Gamaliel	an	WA 343	F	2	0	4	7	6	4	2	4	G
8	Ego sum lux mundi	an	LA 165	G	5	2	0	-2	0	2	0	4	G
1	Ego sum lux mundi ... dicit	an	WA 105	D	2	0	-2	0	3	5	3	2	D
8	Ego sum ostium dicit Dominus	an	AR 511 AM 527 *LA 265	G	5	2	0	-2	0	2	0	-2	G
7	Ego sum panis vitae	re	LR 128	G	4	5	7	9	7	5	7	9	G
8	Ego sum panis vivus dicit Dominus	an	AR 512 LU 895 AM 528 LA 266	G	5	2	0	-2	0	2	0	4	G
	Ego sum panis vivus qui Ego sum panis	rev	LR 128	d	-2	-5	-7	-2	-3	-2	0	2	
1	Ego sum panis vivus qui	an	AM 553	D	-2	0	3	2	0	-2	3	7	D
8	Ego sum panis vivus qui	an	WA 157	F	2	0	4	2	4	0	2	4	G
1	Ego sum panis vivus qui	an	AR 533 LU 942 AM 553	D	7	5	3	5	7	8	7	5	D
1	Ego sum panis vivus qui ... et panis	an	AR 512 AM 528	D	-2	3	5	3	7	5	2	3	D
2	Ego sum pastor bonus alleluia	co	GR 265 LU 439 819 *SYG 165 GB 47^v *GS 128	E	1	-2	0	1	-4	0	1	-2	D
	Ego sum pastor bonus et cognosco	alv	GR 47 264 LU 818	a	-2	-4	-5	-9	-5	-2	-4	-5	

2 Ego sum pastor bonus et cognosco	co	GR 48 LU 438	E	1	-2	0	1	-4	0	1	-2	D
Ego sum pastor bonus et cognosco	alv	SYG 164	E	1	3	7	3	5	7	8	7	
Ego sum pastor bonus et cognosco	alv	GS 127	F	2	4	6	4	2	7	9	7	
Ego sum pastor bonus qui pasco	alv	SYG 165	a	-2	-4	-5	-9	-5	-2	-4	-5	
3 Ego sum pastor bonus qui pasco	an	AR 469 LU 820 *AM 483 *WA 142 LA 231 235	G	2	5	2	5	4	0	2	4	E
8 Ego sum pastor ovium	an	AR 467 LU 816 AM 481 WA 142 LA 235	F	2	0	4	7	6	7	4	2	G
8 Ego sum pauper et dolens	co	GR 605 LU 1647	F	2	4	0	2	-1	0	-3	0	G
1 2 Ego sum qui sum	an	OHS 753 LR 83 WA 128 LA 207 *224	F	-1	0	-3	-1	-5	-3	0	2	D
8 Ego sum qui testimonium	an	AR 407 LU 568 AM 388	G	-2	-5	-3	-2	0	2	0	2	G
8 Ego sum qui testimonium	an	WA 105	G	2	5	4	2	0	2	5	4	G
8 Ego sum radix et genus	tr	GR 45**	G	-2	-5	-3	-7	-5	-2	0	2	G
5 Ego sum Raphael angelus	an	AR 890 LU 1698	a	-2	-4	0	-2	0	1	-2	0	F
3 Ego sum Raphael angelus ... alleluia	an	AR 893	c	-1	-3	0	-1	-3	-5	-3	-8	E
2 Ego sum resurrectio et vita	co	SYG 237	D	-5	-2	0	-2	0	-2	0	2	D
2 Ego sum resurrectio et vita	an	AR [181][186] GR 111* LU 1769 1804 *AM 1166 LA 559	F	-1	0	-3	-5	-3	0	-3	-1	D
2 Ego sum resurrectio et vita	co	GB 266[V]	F	-1	0	-3	-1	-3	-5	-3	-5	D
Ego sum vestra redemptio / Ego sum alpha et omega ... manus	anv	SYG 147 *GS 125	a	-2	0	-2	-4	-2	2	-2	0	
7 Ego sum via	an	WA 62 63 307	G	2	0	-2	0	-2	0	2	5	G
7 Ego sum via ... nemo	an	AP. 695 AM 894 *LA 394	c	-1	-3	-5	2	0	2	4	2	G
8 Ego sum vitis vera	co	GR (19) *SYG 171 *GB 163 *GS 210	b	1	-2	0	1	-4	0	1	-2	G
5 8 Ego sum vitis vera	re	OHS 790 *LR 89 *WA 305	b	1	-2	0	1	-4	0	1	-2	G
Ego sum vitis vera	alv	SYG 171	D	2	0	-2	0	3	2	0	2	
6 Ego sum vitis vera alleluia	an	AR 465 *AM 479	F	-1	2	4	-1	0	-3	-5	0	F
1 Ego te tuli de domo	re	LA 270 WA 166	E	-2	0	-2	-4	-2	0	-2	0	D
Ego veniam et sanabo / Alieni non transibunt	rev	LA 4 WA 10										
Ego veritatem dico vobis	alv	SYG 167	a	-4	0	-2	-5	-4	-7	-4	-5	
3 Ego veritatem dico vobis	an	WA 145	G	2	5	4	5	7	5	2	4	E
7 Ego veritatem dico vobis	an	AR 480 *AM 496 *LA 241	G	4	5	7	5	4	2	4	0	G

	Text	Type	Source										
	Ego vero orationem meam Improperium exspectavit	ofv	OTT 49 *GB 110^v *SYG 123	c	-5	-3	0	-3	-5	0	-5	0	
8	Ego vos elegi ... quia mundus	an	WA 413	c	-1	-5	-1	0	-3	-5	-3	-5	G
1	Ego vos elegi ... ut eatis	co	GR 513 LU 1388 SYG 190 GB 195 GS 219	a	3	0	-2	2	0	2	3	0	D
	Ego vos elegi ... ut eatis	alv	GR 630 LU 1487	D	3	2	5	3	2	3	0	7	
1	Ego vox clamantis	an	LA 16	D	2	3	2	0	2	0	-2	0	D
4	Egredere Emmanuel	hy	ST 273	E	1	3	1	0	-2	1	0	1	E
7	Egredere modo frater	an	AM 815	d	-3	0	2	0	-3	-2	0	-3	G
	Egredietur Dominus de loco	sr	WA 25										
	Egredietur Dominus de loco Ite dicite Joanni	rev	LA 10										
4	Egredietur Dominus de loco	an	AR 238 AM 213 *WA 17 *LA 22	a	-2	0	3	5	7	5	3	5	a
3	Egredietur Dominus de Samaria	re	LA 9 *WA 11	E	-2	3	5	7	5	7	5	3	E
3	Egredietur Dominus et proeliabitur	re	LA 24 *WA 14	D	-2	3	5	7	5	7	5	3	E
7	Egredietur virga ... et flos	gr	GR 622^6 LU 1684	G	2	0	7	4	5	7	2	0	G
1	Egredietur virga ... et flos	re	LR 395 LA 15	D	3	0	-2	0	7	5	3	5	D
1	Egredietur virga ... et replebitur	an	AR 245 WA 17 *LA 22	D	-2	3	5	7	8	7	8	7	D
1	Egredimini et videte ... Gertrudem	an	AM 1130	D	2	9	11	9	12	9	7	9	D
2	Egredimini et videte ... regem	int	GR 11**	a	-4	-2	0	-2	3	2	0	2	a
1	Egregie Christi martyr Sebastiane	an	LA 326	D	2	3	2	0	-2	5	3	2	D
7	Egregie Christi martyr Sebastiane	re	PM 127	G	2	4	2	0	2	4	2	0	G
7	Egregie Dei antistes	an	WA 311	G	4	5	7	5	7	5	2	5	G
4	Egregie doctor Paule mores instrue	hy	AR 607 752 LU 1349	F	-1	-3	-5	-3	0	-3	-1	0	E
8	Egregio beatitudinis tuae	an	WA 287	F	2	4	2	0	2	4	6	4	G
8	Egregius Dei martyr Vincentius	an	WA 261	F	2	4	2	4	2	0	4	7	G
7	Egressi de ergastulo	an	WA 378	G	4	5	7	10	9	5	9	7	G
1	Egressi duodecim apostoli	an	WA 157	C	2	9	11	9	7	4	5	7	D
5	Egressus Jesus de praetorio	re	WA 123	c	-3	0	2	4	5	4	2	0	c
1	Egressus Jesus secessit	an	AR 376 *AM 349 *WA 93 *LA 142	C	2	5	2	0	5	7	9	7	D
	Ejecitque Dominus Deus Adam Ecce Adam quasi unus	rev	LA 112										
1	Ejicientes eum extra civitatem	an	LA 41	D	-2	0	3	2	0	-2	3	5	D
4	Ejus quoque laudabile	an	WA 291	D	2	3	5	3	0	2	3	2	E
6	Electa mea candida sicut nix	re	LR 263	F	4	2	5	4	2	4	0	2	F
5	Electi mei non laborabunt	gr	GR 444 LU 1386	D	3	5	3	5	7	5	7	5	F

7	Electi sunt in Christo	an	WA 373	G	-2	2	5	7	5	4	0	-2	G
1	Electus a Deo pontifex	an	WA 285	D	3	0	-2	0	-2	3	5	7	D
1	Electus est a Domino	an	AM 779	D	7	9	7	5	7	10	7	5	D
1	Electus et dilectus	re	WA 290	D	3	0	-2	3	5	7	5	3	D
1	Eleemosynas illius enarrabit	an	AR 851	D	2	3	5	2	3	2	0	-2	D
8	Elegerunt apostoli Stephanum	of	GR 37 LU 417 OTT 161 *SYG 23 *GB 22 GS 16	C	2	5	4	5	7	9	4	0	G
	Elegi abjectus esse Beatus vir	trv	GR 450 LU 1394	G	2	4	5	4	2	5	7	0	
3	Elegisti Domine Deus	an	WA 283	G	-3	-2	-3	-5	-3	-5	0	2	E
8	Elegit Deus beatum Hilarium	re	PM 342	D	3	5	7	5	2	3	0	2	G
7	Elegit Dominus sacerdotem	re	LA 534	G	5	4	5	7	10	9	10	9	G
3	Elegit Dominus Sion	an	AR 141 OHS 357 LU 292	G	4	2	5	4	2	0	2	0	E
8	Elegit Dominus virum de plebe	an	LA 331	G	-2	-5	-2	0	2	0	2	0	G
7	Elegit Dominus virum de plebe	re	LA 329	G	2	0	2	4	5	7	5	4	G
	Elegit eam Deus	sr	AR [95] LU 1258 WA 8 310										
6	Elegit eos ex omni	an	WA 372	c	-2	-3	-2	0	2	0	2	4	c
8	Elegit eum Dominus et excelsum	re	PM 311	D	3	5	7	5	7	5	7	10	G
	Elegit eum Dominus sacerdotem	sr	AR [63] LU 1174 1175 AM 654 1174 1175										
5	Elegit Mariam Deus	re	LR 264	F	4	7	9	7	9	11	7	4	F
7	Elegit te Dominus sacerdotem	re	LR 204 *LA 534	G	5	4	5	7	9	7	10	9	G
8	Elegit te Dominus sibi	int	SYG 232	G	2	-2	0	2	0	2	0	2	G
	Elegit te Dominus sibi	alv	GB 28^v *GS 223	D	2	0	-2	0	3	5	3	2	
5	Elevamini portae aeternales	an	LR 55 96 335 OHS 604 LU 762 *WA 27 125 *LA 63 203	c	2	0	-5	-3	-5	-3	-7	-3	F
8	Elevare elevare consurge	an	AR 246 AM 222 WA 18 *LA 17	G	-2	-5	-3	-2	0	2	0	4	G
	Elevata est magnificentia	sr	WA 150										
	Elevata est magnificentia Exaltare Domine	rev	LR 98										
4	Elevata est magnificentia	an	LR 95 WA 147 LA 244	G	2	5	7	5	7	9	7	5	a
	Elevatio manuum mearum Dirigatur oratio	grv	GR 109 LU 1060 GS 38 163 171 *GB 68^v *SYG 76	c	2	7	5	7	9	5	2	0	
4	Elevatis Jesus manibus	an	WA 149	G	2	5	7	9	7	5	7	9	a
4	Elevatis manibus benedixit eis	an	AR 492 LU 851 AM 509	G	2	5	7	9	7	5	7	9	a

4 Elevatis manibus ferebatur	an	LA 251	D	2	5	9	7	5	7	9	7	E
5 Elisabeth pacis et patriae mater	an	AR 784 LU 1553	a	-4	0	3	5	3	5	8	7	F
Elisabeth Zachariae magnum virum	sr	AR 741 LU 1503										
7 Elisabeth Zachariae magnum virum	re	PM 158 LR 348 LA 401 WA 321	a	-4	0	3	5	0	3	5	8	G
3 Elisabeth Zachariae magnum virum	an	AR 735 LU 1503 *AM 924 WA 323 LA 407	G	2	5	2	5	4	0	2	4	E
Elongatus a nutrice Puer fletum	rev	WA 299	D	7	5	3	2	5	3	2	0	
2 Emendemus in melius	re	PM 47 GR 86 LU 524 *LA 128 *WA 85	A	3	5	8	5	8	7	8	5	D
4 Emissiones tuae paradisus	an	WA 354 *LA 456	F	-1	-3	-1	0	2	4	2	4	E
Emitte agnum Domine	sr	WA 12										
Emitte agnum Domine Rorate caeli	rev	LA 26 WA 19										
4 Emitte agnum Domine	an	AR 239 AM 214 *WA 17 *LA 23	a	-2	0	3	5	7	5	3	5	a
2 Emitte agnum Domine	re	LR 395 LA 26 382 *WA 18	A	3	5	7	5	8	7	8	5	D
1 Emitte Domine sapientiam	re	LA 276 WA 169	a	-2	0	-4	0	-2	-4	-2	-4	D
Emitte Domine spiritum Venit Michael	rev	LA 468										
Emitte lucem tuam Judica me Deus	intv	GR 151 LU 569 GS 71 SYG 109										
Emitte lucem tuam Discerne causam	grv	GR 158 GS 74 GB 100 SYG 112	F	4	2	7	9	7	9	7	11	
1 Emitte spiritum sanctum	an	SYG 21	D	3	5	7	5	7	5	3	5	D
8 Emitte spiritum tuum	of	GR 290 OTT 77 LU 860 *SYG 182 GB 184 *GS L	D	-2	0	2	3	5	3	7	10	G
Emitte spiritum tuum	alv	GR 293 LU 879 SYG 183 GB 187^v *GS M 137	a	-2	1	0	-2	0	-4	-5	-4	
Emitte spiritum tuum Spiritus Domini replevit orbem	ofv	SYG 185	E	1	5	7	5	7	5	7	8	
8 Emitte spiritum tuum	an	LR 115 *WA 152 *LA 259	c	2	0	-1	0	-3	0	-1	-3	G
2 Emitte spiritum tuum	tr	GR [93] LU 1279	A	3	5	2	3	5	0	-2	0	D
2 En adest pastor vigil et superno	hy	LR 440	A	5	3	5	8	7	5	7	8	D
1 En clara vox redarguit	hy	AR 215	E	-4	0	3	5	7	5	3	5	a
En dilectus meus loquitur Moram faciente	rev	PM 139 LR 297										
4 En martyris Laurentii	hy	ST 397	D	2	3	5	3	0	-2	0	3	E
1 En rex venit mansuetus		GS 81	F	-1	-3	-1	-5	-3	0	2	4	D

	Incipit		Sources	Mode									End
3	En ut superba criminum	hy	AR 538[3] LU 978 VP 19*	E	-2	3	5	8	7	5	3	5	E
6	En ut superba criminum	hy	LR 334 VP 168	F	2	-1	0	2	4	5	4	2	F
1	En ut superba criminum	hy	AM 563	D	7	5	7	5	3	2	5	7	D
3	Enixa est puerpera	hy	ST 31	D	2	3	5	7	0	2	3	5	E
	Eodem vero anno		see also Ipso anno										
4	Eodem vero anno	re	LA 372	F	-3	0	-1	0	2	0	-1	0	E
8	Epistolam ad se	an	LR 281	G	-5	-2	0	2	0	2	0	-2	G
	Epulemur in azymis Pascha nostrum	alv	SYG 153 *GB 125[v] GS 117	d	3	0	-2	-5	-7	-2	-7	-2	
	Epulentur et exsultent In sanctis suis	rev	LA 387										
	Epulentur et exsultent Justi autem in perpetuum	rev	LA 478										
7	Eram quasi agnus	re	OHS 396 LU 649 *LA 192 *WA 119	G	2	4	5	4	2	4	2	0	G
	Erant enim piscatores Dum perambularet	rev	LA 498 WA 233										
	Erant gaudentes et alacres Ibant apostoli	rev	WA 411										
8	Erat autem aspectus ejus	an	AR 444 OHS 726 767 LU 782 *AM 454 *WA 129 137 *LA 214	c	2	0	-5	-1	2	0	2	0	G
	Erat autem visio Quatuor animalia	rev	WA 373										
3	Erat ei pro omnibus	an	WA 287	c	-1	-3	-5	-3	-8	-7	-3	-1	E
	Erat enim exercitus Refulsit sol	rev	LA 295 WA 182										
8	Erat enim in sermone	an	LA 324	c	2	0	-1	0	-3	0	-1	-5	G
	Erat enim valde compatiens Confessor Dei Nicholaus	rev	WA 239	a	-2	-4	-2	0	-2	0	3	2	
1	Erat Jesus ejiciens	an	WA 99	D	-2	0	3	2	0	2	0	-2	D
	Erat Joannes in deserto Fuit homo	rev	LR 348 WA 321										
	Erat Joannes in deserto Hic praecursor	rev	LA 404										
8	Erat Joseph et Maria	an	LA 62	F	2	4	2	4	2	4	2	4	G
	Erat lucerna ardens	alv	SYG 197	C	2	5	7	5	4	2	0	2	
	Erat namque in sermone Sebastianus Mediolanensium	rev	LA 325										
8	Erat namque in sermone	re	LA 325	D	3	5	7	5	7	5	7	9	G
1	Erat pater ejus	an	AR 321 LU 468	D	2	3	5	2	3	2	-2	0	D
1	Erat pater Jesu	an	LR 309	D	-2	3	5	3	5	7	5	7	D
1	Erat Petrus dormiens	an	WA 340 LA 415	D	-2	3	5	3	5	7	5	3	D

	Incipit	Type	Sources										
1	Erat quidam regulus	an	AR 571 LU 1107 *AM 611 LA 318	D	-2	3	5	3	5	7	5	3	D
4	Erat vir domini Benedictus	an	WA 334 *LA 374	C	2	4	5	4	2	0	2	4	E
1	Erat vultu placido	re	LA 373 *WA 333	D	2	3	0	2	3	2	0	-2	D
	Erecta namque in virtutis / Grata facta est	rev	LA 321 WA 244										
2	Erectus in culmine	re	WA 285	D	-2	-5	-2	0	-2	3	5	7	D
	Erexit Dominus nobis		see Erexit nobis Dominus										
7	Erexit Jacob lapidem	an	LR 238 *WA 318	G	4	5	7	5	2	5	4	7	G
7	Erexit nobis Dominus	an	AR 110 AM 51 LA 92	G	4	5	7	5	4	5	7	9	G
6	Erexit nobis Dominus ... sicut	an	WA 65	c	2	4	0	-3	-2	0	2	0	c
8	Ergo pater sancte	an	WA 286	G	-2	-5	-2	-3	-2	0	2	0	G
5	Erigitur itaque infantium	an	WA 43	a	-4	0	3	5	3	5	8	7	F
7	Eripe me de inimicis meis Deus	of	GR 161 OTT 46 SYG 113 GB 101^v GS 75	G	2	0	2	0	2	5	4	5	G
	Eripe me de inimicis meis Deus	alv	GR 343 LU 1018 *SYG 242 *GB 251 GS 147	C	2	4	5	2	4	0	2	4	
2	Eripe me de inimicis meis Domine	an	AR 165	D	-2	0	2	3	0	2	-2	0	D
3	Eripe me de inimicis meis Domine ... doce	of	GR 186 OHS 210 OTT 51 LU 608 SYG 125 GB 111^v GS 89	E	1	3	5	3	5	3	1	3	b
	Eripe me de inimicis meis et ab / Adjutor meus tibi	rev	LA 94 WA 66										
	Eripe me Domine ab homine malo / Ne perdas cum impiis	rev	LA 168										
2	Eripe me Domine ab homine malo	tr	GR 208 OHS 534 LU 725 SYG 137 GB 116^v GS 99	D	-2	0	-2	-5	-2	0	-2	0	D
	Eripe me Domine ab homine malo / Custodi me	ofv	OTT 52 GB 113 SYG 126	D	-2	0	3	5	7	5	7	3	
3	Eripe me Domine de inimicis	gr	GR 152 LU 570 *SYG 109 *GB 97^v GS 71	F	-5	-3	-1	0	-1	2	-1	2	E
	Eripiam eum et glorificabo / Qui habitat	trv	GR 95 LU 533 GS 35 GB 65 SYG 73	F	2	0	2	0	-3	0	-1	0	
	Eripuit Dominus animam tuam / Per unum hominem	rev	LR 262										
	Erit autem sanguis vobis	alv	GR 540	C	2	5	2	0	4	2	9	12	
	Erit enim magnus / Gabriel angelus	rev	LR 356 LA 407 WA 321										
	Erit enim magnus / Ipse praeibit	rev	LR 357 LA 404 WA 321										
7	Erit enim magnus	an	LR 352	G	2	5	7	9	5	7	9	5	G

4 Erit enim magnus	an	LA 403	D	2	5	7	9	5	9	7	5	E
1 Erit mihi Dominus in Deum	re	LA 139 WA 92	a	-2	0	-2	-4	-2	0	-2	0	D
4 Erit mihi Dominus in Deum	an	LR 233 WA 318 *LA 547	G	2	5	7	5	7	9	7	5	a
Erit nobis hic dies	<u>see</u> Erit vobis hic dies											
7 Erit quasi signum in manu	int	GR 84**	c	2	-3	0	4	2	5	4	0	G
3 Erit sanguis agni vobis	an	AR 767 LU 1531 *AM 951 *PM 164	G	2	0	2	5	2	0	2	0	E
6 Erit vobis hic dies	of	GR 257 OTT 63 LU 802 OHS 818 SYG 160 *GB 141^v GS 123	D	5	3	5	7	5	7	9	5	F
Erravi sicut ovis Septies in die	rev	LA 154 WA 99										
4 Erubescant et conturbentur	co	GR 106 SYG 81 GB 72^v GS 42	F	-1	0	2	4	5	4	2	0	E
7 Erubescant et revereantur	co	GR 187 OHS 214 LU 608 SYG 125 GB 112 GS 90	c	-1	0	2	4	5	4	2	0	G
Eructavit cor meum Diffusa est gratia	cov	SYG 6										
Eructavit cor meum Adeamus cum fiducia	intv	GR 587¹ LU 1612¹										
Eructavit cor meum Dilexisti justitiam	intv	GR [60] LU 1225 GS 225 GB 4 SYG 5										
Eructavit cor meum Gaudeamus ... Agathae	intv	GR 436 LU 1368 GB 49^v										
Eructavit cor meum Gaudeamus ... Annae	intv	GR 559 LU 1571										
Eructavit cor meum Gaudeamus ... assumptione	intv	GR (30) GS s										
Eructavit cor meum Gaudeamus ... Bartholomaei	intv	GB 226^v										
Eructavit cor meum Gaudeamus ... boni consilii	intv	GR 24**										
Eructavit cor meum Gaudeamus ... solemnitate	intv	GR 582 619 LU 1556 1675										
Eructavit cor meum Laetemur hodie	intv	SYG 227										
Eructavit cor meum Omnis gloria ejus	intv	GR 47**										
Eructavit cor meum Salve sancta parens	intv	GR [75] LU 1263 GB 220										
Eructavit cor meum Vidi civitatem	intv	GR 439 LU 1376										
Eructavit cor meum Vultum tuum	intv	GR [64] LU 1229 GS 231 GB 29 221 SYG 28										

	Eructavit cor meum Afferentur regi ... post eam	ofv	OTT 163 SYG 5 *GB 4^v	D	-2	0	3	0	-2	3	5	3	
	Eructavit cor meum Filiae regum	ofv	OTT 157 GB 43 SYG 39	a	-2	0	3	0	3	5	3	0	
	Eructavit cor meum Afferentur regi ... proximae	ofv	OTT 155 *GB 30 *SYG 29	E	1	-2	3	5	3	5	8	7	
	Eructavit cor meum Constitues eos	ofv	OTT 131 GB 206^v SYG 203	E	1	-2	3	8	10	8	10	8	
6	Eructavit cor meum	an	WA 64 *LA 88	F	2	4	2	0	2	0	-3	0	F
	Eructavit cor meum Afferentur regi ... post	ofv	GB 4^v	C	2	4	5	2	0	5	7	5	
	Eructavit cor meum Speciosus forma	grv	GR 45 LU 434 GB 31 SYG 30	G	2	4	5	4	5	4	5	7	
	Eructavit cor meum Regnum mundi	rev	LR 227 PM 234 VP 260 *WA 432	F	4	7	4	2	7	9	7	9	
5	Eructavit cor meum	gr	GR 65**	F	4	7	4	7	6	7	4	7	F
	Erue a framea Deus	sr	AR 31 LU 239 AM 385										
	Erue a framea Deus De ore leonis	rev	LA 172										
	Erue a framea Deus In proxima est tribulatio	rev	LA 169 WA 106										
2	Erue a framea Deus	re	LA 171 *WA 108	C	2	4	2	5	4	5	2	4	D
1	Erue Domine animas corum	of	OTT 177 SYG 236	F	-3	-5	-3	0	4	2	4	2	D
	Erue nos in mirabilibus Muro tuo	rev	LA 303 WA 184										
1	Eruisti Domine animam	an	WA 438	D	2	3	5	2	3	2	0	3	D
8	Erumpant montes	re	LA 10	D	3	5	7	5	7	5	7	9	G
7	Erumpant montes	an	WA 18 *LA 7	G	4	5	7	9	7	5	7	4	G
1	Erunt prava in directa	an	AR 251 LU 357 AM 227 WA 24 LA 21	C	2	9	10	9	7	9	7	9	D
1	Erunt primi novissimi	an	WA 76	a	-2	0	-2	-4	-2	0	-4	-5	D
	Est enim haec speciosior Nihil inquinatum	rev	LR 267 AM 1191										
4	Est secretum Valeriane	an	AR 924 LU 1754 *AM 1139 *WA 408 *LA 493	F	-3	-1	2	0	-3	-1	0	-5	E
	Est ubi vera quies Celebremus diem istum	rev	WA 248	a	-2	0	-2	-4	-5	-2	0	3	
	Esto fidelis usque ad mortem In illa die	rev	LA 52 WA 39										
	Esto igitur jam securus Agnosce O Vincenti	rev	WA 259										
	Esto mihi in Deum protectorem Deus in te speravi	rev	LA 97										
6	Esto mihi in Deum protectorem	int	GR 80 LU 511 *SYG 62 *GB 59 *GS 27	F	-3	0	-3	-1	0	-1	-5	0	F

	Incipit		References										
5	Esto mihi in Deum protectorem	gr	GR 339 LU 1013 SYG 103 GB 91 GS 64 149	F	2	0	2	0	2	0	2	4	F
	Esto nobis Domine turris	sr	LA 162 WA 104										
8	Esto nobis Domine turris	re	LA 162	a	1	3	1	0	1	3	0	-2	G
	Esto placabilis Genti peccatrici	rev	LA 306 WA 186										
	Esto tuis clemens cui Christus Apparuit Dominus	rev	PM 176	a	-2	0	1	0	-2	0	-2	-4	
1	Estote ergo misericordes	an	AR 521 LU 909 *AM 538 *WA 187 *LA 311	D	2	3	0	2	0	-2	0	3	D
1	Estote fortes in bello	an	AR [13] LU 1118 AM 628 *WA 410 LA 512	F	4	2	4	2	0	2	0	-3	D
7	Esuriente terra Aegypti	re	LR 306	G	5	4	5	7	5	7	5	4	G
7	Esurientes humiles implevit	an	LA 106	G	7	5	4	5	7	9	7	5	G
	Et abiit Ananias Saule frater	anv	LA 342										
	Et accepit angelus Stetit angelus	rev	LA 466										
1	Et accipiens Jesus	an	WA 188	C	2	9	11	9	12	9	7	5	D
	Et adorabunt eum omnes Descendet Dominus	rev	LA 14 380 WA 15										
	Et adorabunt eum omnes Orietur stella	rev	LA 23										
	Et adorabunt eum omnes Reges Tharsis	rev	LA 71										
	Et adorabunt eum omnes Dominabitur a mari	grv	GR 639 LU 1710	F	4	2	7	9	7	4	7	9	
	Et aedificavit turrim Vinea facta est	trv	SYG 150	F	4	7	6	2	4	2	0	2	
	Et ait ad illos quid est Dicit mater	rev	LR 315										
6	Et alias oves habeo	an	LA 235	c	-1	-3	-5	-3	0	2	0	2	c
	Et ambulabunt gentes Illuminare	rev	AM 1185 LR 75 LA 72 WA 53										
	Et animam sanctae Scholasticae In columbae specie	trv	SYG 56	D	5	9	7	5	0	5	7	10	
	Et apparuerunt apostoli Factus est repente	ofv	GB 192	a	-2	0	3	2	3	5	3	0	
	Et apparuerunt illis Cum complerentur	rev	WA 152										
8	Et audientes discipuli	an	AM 1002	a	-4	-2	0	-2	-4	0	3	5	G
8	Et audientes discipuli	an	AR 809 LU 1591	G	2	0	-2	0	2	0	-2	2	G
	Et audito eo multa Herodes enim	rev	LA 451 WA 362										

	Et audito eo multa Metuebat Herodes	rev	LA 451										
	Et benedicentur in semine Vocavit angelus	rev	LA 122										
	Et benedictum nomen Tibi laus tibi gloria	rev	WA 160	G	7	10	9	5	7	5	7	9	
	Et benedictus fructus ventri Ave Maria	trv	GB 55ᵛ	F	4	7	6	2	4	2	0	2	
	Et ceciderunt in conspectu Adoraverunt viventem	rev	LA 58 WA 46										
	Et clamans voce magna Cum esset plenus	rev	LA 42										
2	Et coegerunt illum dicentes	an	AR 476 *AM 490 *WA 132 LA *217 233	C	5	4	5	2	4	2	0	2	D
	Et coeperunt loqui Apparuerunt apostolis	rev	LR 112										
	Et completa oratione Domine non aspicias	trv	SYG 56	E	1	0	1	3	5	3	5	3	
	Et concupiscct rcx Diffusa est gratia	trv	SYG 49	D	-2	0	3	0	3	0	3	0	
	Et constituisti eum Gloria et honore	grv	GR [7] LU 1133 *SYG 201	c	2	0	-3	-2	-3	-5	-3	-5	
	Et convescens praecepit eis Post passionem	rev	LR 96 LA 245 WA 147										
	Et cum appropinquasset Cum audisset turba	rev	WA 112	D	7	5	7	5	3	5	7	5	
1	Et cum ejecisset Jesus daemonium	an	AR 389 LU 551 *AM 363 *LA 153	D	3	-2	0	7	8	7	5	8	D
	Et cum iter faceret Ibat igitur Saulus	anv	LA 340										
	Et cum iter faceret Saulus adhuc	anv	WA 262										
	Et cum jejunasset Ductus est Jesus	rev	LA 131 WA 87										
	Et cum recubuisset Dominus Jesus postquam	cov	SYG 129										
	Et dederunt in escam Insurrexerunt in me viri	rev	LA 180 WA 111										
	Et dederunt in escam Omnes amici mei	rev	LA 195 WA 122										
8	Et dicebant ad invicem	an	WA 131	F	2	4	2	0	2	4	2	7	G
8	Et dicebant ad invicem	an	LA 215	G	5	2	0	-2	2	0	5	4	G
8	Et dicebant unde huic	an	AR 325 LU 475	a	-2	-4	-2	0	-2	-4	0	-2	G
	Et dixit mihi nequaquam Vidi Dominum facie	rev	LA 141 **WA** 93										
	Ex dixit nequaquam		see Et dixit mihi nequaquam										
	Et dominabitur a mari Ecce veniet Dominus protector	rev	WA 10										

	Text	Type	Sources	Mode								
	Et dominabitur a mari Modo veniet dominator	rev	LA 20									
	Et dominabitur a mari Veniet nobis salus	rev	LA 27									
	Et domus impleta est In diebus illis mulier	anv	SYG 130									
	Et dum seminat Cum turba plurima	rev	LR 400	a	-2	0	-2	-4	-5	-2	0	1
4	Et ecce apparuerunt eis	an	AR 806 LU 1589 AM 998	F	-1	-3	-1	-3	-5	-3	-1	2	E
7	Et ecce terraemotus	an	AR 443 OHS 725 766 LU 782 AM 454 WA 127 *LA 214 232	d	-3	0	2	0	-2	0	2	0	G
7	Et ecce vox de nube	an	AR 807 LU 1000	G	4	5	7	9	5	9	10	9	G
	Et ego ad te Domine Domine Deus salutis	ofv	OTT 112 GB 74 SYG 84	G	2	-2	0	2	0	2	5	7
	Et ego dico tibi Beatus es Simon	rev	LR 367 *LA 418 WA 328									
	Et ego primogenitum Ipse invocabit	trv	GR 640 LU 1711	C	2	5	7	2	0	2	5	7
	Et ego vidi et testimonium Testimonium perhibuit	rev	LA 73	G	5	4	0	2	4	2	5	7
	Et elevabitur super omnes Egredietur Dominus et	rev	LA 24 WA 14									
1	Et erat ibi usque ad obitum	co	GR 7**	F	-1	0	-3	-5	-3	-1	-3	-1	D
	Et erat pater ejus et mater Cum inducerent	rev	LR 312									
	Et erat structura muri Vidi Jerusalem	rev	LA 228 WA 141									
	Et eripuisti animam Confitebor tibi	rev	LA 100 WA 69									
	Et eris corona gloriae Videbunt gentes	rev	LA 25 382 WA 23									
	Et eruisti animam		see Et eripuisti animam									
	Et erunt ut complaceant Justitiae Domini	ofv	OTT 94 GB 82v SYG 93	F	4	7	11	9	11	9	7	9
	Et esto ibi usque dum dicam Angelus Domini	trv	GR 6**	C	2	0	2	5	2	0	2	0
	Et ex corde diligamus Ubi caritas	anv	GR 204 OHS 451	F	2	0	2	4	0	2	0	-3
	Et exaltent eum in ecclesia Sacrificent Domino	grv	GR 89**	a	3	5	7	5	3	2	3	0
	Et exivit vox magna Audivi vocem ... angelorum	rev	WA 140									
	Et exsultavit spiritus meus Magnificat anima	trv	GR 50**	F	2	7	9	11	7	2	7	9
4	Et facta est comes	an	WA 389	F	-1	-3	-1	2	4	2	0	2	E
	Et factus est in pace Notus in Judaea	trv	GR [136] LU 1286	G	2	4	5	4	2	5	2	0

Incipit												
Et factus est in pace Terra tremuit	ofv	OTT 55 GB 128 SYG 153	D	3	7	5	7	8	7	5	7	
Et funes extenderunt Eripe me	trv	GR 208 OHS 534 LU 725 GS 99 GB 116v *SYG 137	F	2	4	2	4	2	0	2	0	
Et glorificatus sum De ventre	rev	LR 350										
Et gratia tua illis Absolve Domine	trv	GR 95* LU 1809	G	5	4	7	9	5	2	5	2	
Et hoc mandatum Diligamus nos	anv	SYG 131										
Et hoc vobis signum Ecce annuntio vobis	rev	LA 36	d	2	0	-2	-3	-5	-3	-2	0	
Et in omni loco Ab ortu solis	trv	GR [97] LU 1282	G	2	4	5	4	5	7	5	0	
4 Et in servis suis	an	WA 70 LA 104	F	-3	-1	0	2	-1	0	2	4	E
Et in terra		BOS #14	a	-7	-9	-7	-5	-4	-5	-7	-9	D
Et in terra		BOS #46	e	-5	-4	-2	-9	-12	-11	-7	-9	E
Et in terra		BOS #44	e	-5	-4	-2	-9	-7	-9	-4	-5	E
Et in terra		BOS #16	a	-4	-2	-5	-7	-5	-2	0	[0]	D
Et in terra		BOS #49	a	-4	-2	0	-2	-4	-5	-7	[0]	D
Et in terra		BOS #8	c	-3	-7	-3	0	[0	0	0	0]	F
Et in terra		BOS #38 GR 29* LU 37	c	-3	-5	-7	-5	-3	-5	-7	-5	F
Et in terra		BOS #40	F	-3	-5	0	2	4	0	-1	-3	F
Et in terra		BOS #34	c	-3	-1	-5	-3	-7	-5	-3	-1	F
Et in terra		BOS #53	d	-2	-3	-2	0	-2	-3	-5	-3	D
Et in terra		BOS #3	f	-1	-3	-5	-1	0	2	0	2	G
Et in terra		BOS #10	c	-1	-3	-1	4	2	4	2	0	E
Et in terra		BOS #5	f	-1	0	-1	-3	-5	-1	2	0	G
Et in terra		BOS #42	b	1	0	-2	-4	-2	-4	-2	0	E
Et in terra		BOS #9 *GR 36* *LU 43	E	1	3	5	7	5	3	1	0	G
Et in terra		BOS #23 GR 32* LU 40	d	2	-3	-2	0	-7	-5	-3	-2	G
Et in terra		BOS #37	c	2	-1	0	2	0	2	4	5	F
Et in terra		BOS #6	G	2	0	-2	-3	-5	0	-2	-3	G
Et in terra		BOS #20 *GR 12* LU 23	G	2	0	-2	-3	-2	0	-2	0	G
Et in terra		BOS #15	G	2	0	-2	0	2	4	2	0	E
Et in terra		BOS #30 GR 22* LU 32	G	2	0	-2	2	0	-2	0	-2	G
Et in terra		BOS #31	F	2	0	-1	-3	-1	0	2	6	E
Et in terra		BOS #36	c	2	0	-1	0	-1	-3	-5	-3	F
Et in terra		BOS #32	F	2	0	4	7	9	11	12	11	F
Et in terra		GR 87* LU 89	D	2	3	2	0	2	5	3	2	D

Et in terra	BOS #45	D	2	3	5	2	3	2	0	2	E
Et in terra	BOS #48 GR 42* LU 49	D	2	3	5	7	5	3	5	7	E
Et in terra	BOS #1 GR 25* LU 34	c	2	4	2	0	2	-3	-5	-3	D
Et in terra	BOS #29	F	2	4	2	0	2	4	2	0	D
Et in terra	BOS #28	F	2	4	2	0	2	4	7	4	D
Et in terra	BOS #47	G	2	4	5	4	2	0	-2	5	E
Et in terra	BOS #51 GR 39* LU 46	C	2	4	5	4	2	7	5	4	D
Et in terra	BOS #11	G	2	4	5	7	5	4	2	5	E
Et in terra	BOS #12 GR 48* LU 54	G	2	4	5	7	5	4	2	5	G
Et in terra	BOS #13 *GR 85* *LU 88	G	2	4	5	7	5	7	9	7	D
Et in terra	BOS #22	F	2	4	6	4	2	4	7	6	D
Et in terra	BOS #4	c	2	5	4	0	2	0	-2	-5	F
Et in terra	BOS #25	F	2	6	7	9	6	9	7	6	G
Et in terra	BOS #55	D	3	2	0	-2	0	5	7	10	C
Et in terra	BOS #54	D	3	2	0	-2	3	-2	0	[0]	D
Et in terra	BOS #52	D	3	2	3	5	7	5	3	5	G
Et in terra	BOS #19 GR 8* LU 19	a	3	5	3	0	-2	0	2	3	D
Et in terra	BOS #21	E	3	5	3	1	3	1	3	5	G
Et in terra	BOS #43 GR 51* LU 57	E	3	5	3	5	7	5	3	5	E
Et in terra	BOS #2	a	3	5	7	5	3	5	7	5	D
Et in terra	BOS #39	D	3	5	7	5	3	5	7	5	F
Et in terra	BOS #27	F	4	5	4	2	4	5	2	0	F
Et in terra	BOS #41	C	4	5	7	2	4	2	4	2	G
Et in terra	GR 18* LU 28	G	4	5	7	4	7	5	4	2	G
Et in terra	GR 5* LU 16	G	4	5	7	5	4	2	4	2	b
Et in terra	BOS #26	F	4	5	7	9	7	9	5	9	F
Et in terra	BOS #7	F	4	7	4	2	4	7	[0	0]	F
Et in terra	BOS #35	F	4	7	4	6	4	2	0	[0]	F
Et in terra	BOS #33	F	4	7	9	7	6	7	4	7	F
Et in terra	BOS #24 GR 83* LU 86	G	5	4	5	7	5	4	5	7	G
Et in terra	BOS #56 *GR 15* *LU 26	D	5	7	9	10	9	7	5	3	E
Et in terra	BOS #50	D	7	3	5	7	0	12	10	7	D
Et in terra	BOS #17	D	7	5	7	9	10	9	7	5	D
Et in terra	BOS #18 GR 45* LU 51	D	7	5	7	10	5	7	5	3	D
1 Et incipiens a Moyse et omnibus an	AR 475 AM 489	C	2	9	10	9	11	12	9	11	D

	Et incurventur ante te Det tibi Deus	rev	LA 137 WA 91										
7	Et ingressae non invenerunt	an	WA 138	c	-1	0	2	-1	2	4	2	0	G
3	Et ingressae non invenerunt	an	LA 223 *234	G	2	0	2	4	5	2	4	2	E
	Et intrantes domum Stella quam viderant	rev	LR 78 LA 71 WA 54										
3	Et intravit cum illis	an	AR 477 *AM 492 *WA 138	G	5	2	0	2	5	2	4	5	E
	Et introeuntes in monumentum Angelus Domini	rev	OHS 695 (nm) LR 84										
	Et invenietis requiem Tollite jugum	rev	LR 137 LA 506 WA 411										
7	Et ipse Jesus erat incipiens	an	AR 689 LU 1449 AM 887	G	7	4	5	7	9	7	9	7	G
	Et ipsi populus ejus Vidi civitatem	rev	LR 244										
7	Et ipsi vicerunt draconem	an	AR 764 LU 1529	G	4	5	7	4	5	7	9	7	G
2	Et Jesus proficiebat	an	AR 325 LU 474	C	2	5	4	7	9	5	7	5	D
	Et justitia oriatur Rorate caeli	intv	GS 5										
	Et lucis aeternae beatitudine Absolve, Domine	trv	GR 95* LU 1809	G	5	4	7	9	5	2	5	2	
	Et lux perpetua luceat Pro quorum memoria	cov	GS 233										
	Et maceriam circumdedit Vinea facta	trv	GR 230 OHS 654 LU 776^S *GS 111 *GB 120 *SYG 150	G	2	4	5	4	5	7	5	0	
7	Et me scitis	an	WA 104	d	-3	0	2	0	-2	-3	-7	-2	G
	Et meritis tanti Aemula prosequitur	rev	WA 284	D	7	9	7	5	7	5	3	2	
	Et misericordia ejus a progenie Beatam me dicent	rev	PM 258 LR 257 LA 444										
	Et mundus transit Nolite diligere	trv	GR 22**	G	2	5	4	2	5	2	0	2	
	Et ne avertas faciem Exaudi me	trv	GR 9**	D	-2	0	3	5	3	0	2	3	
	Et noluit consolari Vox in Rama	rev	LA 59										
	Et non erat qui sepeliret Effuderunt sanguinem sanctorum	trv	GR 42 LU 429 *GB 26^V *SYG 26	G	2	4	5	7	5	7	5	2	
	Et non poterant resistere Stephanus autem plenus	rev	WA 34										
	Et non revertetur oculus Memento mei	rev	LA 284										
	Et nos putavimus eum Vere languores	trv	GR [108]	F	2	4	2	4	2	0	2	0	
	Et nunc clamemus Dixit Judas Symoni	rev	WA 182										

	Incipit	Cat.	Sources	Mode									
8	Et nunc reges intelligite	an	AR 782 LU 1553	G	-2	2	5	4	0	4	5	2	G
	Et nunc sequimur Sicut in holocausto	ofv	OTT 92 *GB 250^V *SYG 243	C	2	5	2	5	4	5	7	4	
1	Et omnes angeli stabant	an	AR 898 LU 1729 AM 1103 WA 397	D	-2	3	5	3	5	7	10	7	D
1	Et omnis mansuetudinis	an	LA 93	a	-2	-4	-5	-4	-2	-5	-2	-5	D
ir	Et omnis mansuetudinis	an	AM 139 140	a	-2	-4	-2	0	1	-2	1	0	a
4	Et omnis mansuetudinis	an	WA 66	E	-2	-4	-2	1	-2	1	0	[0]	E
	Et omnis qui credit in me Ego sum resurrectio	cov	SYG 237										
	Et Parisiis Domino Beatissimus Dionysius	rev	WA 386										
	Et pascam illas in judicio Ego pascam	trv	GR 66**	a	3	0	3	2	-2	0	-2	0	
	Et pax Dei qui exsuperat Gaudete in Domino	intv	GS 4 SYG 6										
	Et Petrum lacrimantem suscepisti Tribularer si nescirem	rev	PM 48 VP 119 LA 130 WA 87										
	Et Petrus ad se Nunc scio vere	intv	GS 189 SYG 202										
	Et placuit Domino Visus est Gregorius	rev	PM 155										
	Et ponam in saeculum saeculi sedem Inveni David	ofv	OTT 147 *GB 28^V *SYG 27	G	2	5	7	5	4	7	9	5	
	Et ponam in saeculum saeculi semen Ipse invocabit	trv	GR 640 LU 1711	C	2	5	7	5	2	5	7	9	
	Et portae inferi non praevalebunt Tu es Petrus	intv	SYG 53										
	Et portae inferi non praevalebunt Tu es Petrus	trv	GR 409 LU 1332 GS 182 SYG 53	C	2	5	7	5	2	4	5	4	
	Et posuerunt adversum me Locuti sunt	rev	OHS 302 (nm)										
	Et praeparabitur in misericordia Egredietur Dominus	rev	LA 9 WA 11										
	Et qui inquirebant mala Tota die contristatus	rev	LA 168 WA 106										
7	Et qui praeibant increpabant	an	AR 356 LU 515 *AM 329 331 LA 125	G	4	5	7	5	9	7	5	7	G
	Et qui sitit veniat Ego sum radix	trv	GR 45**	G	-5	0	2	0	2	0	2	5	
	Et quod pingue et forte Ego pascam	trv	GR 66**	F	2	7	6	7	2	0	2	4	
	Et quodcumque ligaveris	see Quodcumque ligaveris											
	Et quodcumque solveris Tu es Petrus	trv	GR 409 LU 1332 GS 182 *SYG 53	F	2	4	2	4	2	4	5	2	
8	Et recordatae sunt verborum	an	LA 233	G	-2	-5	-2	0	2	-2	-5	-2	G

Incipit		Sources										
Et redde in hoc Domine non aspicias	trv	SYG 56	C	2	5	7	5	2	4	5	4	
Et regnum ejus Dabit illi	rev	WA 302										
Et regrediente anima Domine non aspicias	rcv	LR 322 LA 369 WA 298										
Et requiescet super eum Egredietur virga	rev	LR 395 LA 15										
Et requiescet super eum Egredietur virga	grv	GR 622[6] LU 1684	G	5	7	12	10	12	14	10	7	
3 Et respicientes viderunt	an	AR 446 OHS 730 LU 783 *AM 460 *WA 130 *LA 214	G	5	2	0	2	5	2	4	5	E
1 Et si coram hominibus ... Deus	co	GR [25] LU 1166 *SYG 200 GB 202 GS 219	D	3	0	3	5	7	5	3	5	D
Et si coram hominibus ... spes Justorum animae	ofv	OTT 144 SYG 223	C	2	4	5	7	9	7	9	5	
7 Et si ingenua es	an	WA 273	d	-7	0	-2	-3	-2	0	-2	0	G
8 Et si ingenua es	an	LA 357	F	2	4	7	6	4	2	7	9	G
Et si oportuerit	see Si oportuerit											
Et sicut cinnamomum Sicut cedrus	rev	PM 260 LR 252 LA 443 WA 355										
Et sicut dies verni Quae est ista	rev	PM 261 LR 253 WA 355										
Et sicut in Adam omnes Si enim credimus	grv	SYG 236										
Et sicut in Adam Si enim credimus	intv	SYG 236										
Et sicut in Adam Sicut portavimus imaginem	intv	SYG 237										
Et sicut nix super foenum Attende caelum	trv	GR 231 OHS 656 LU 776[V] *GS 112 GB 119[V] SYG 151	G	5	4	7	9	5	2	5	2	
Et sicut oculi ancillae Ad te levavi	trv	GR 124 LU 554 *GS 55 *GB 82[V] *SYG 93	G	2	5	4	2	5	4	2	0	
Et sicut per me civitas Lucia virgo	rev	LA 320 WA 243										
Et spiritus et sponsa Ego sum radix	trv	GR 45**	G	2	4	5	4	5	7	5	0	
4 Et subito circumfulsit	an	LA 340	F	-1	-5	-3	-1	0	-1	-3	-5	E
Et sustulit me Locutus est ad me	rev	LA 225 WA 140										
Et testes deposuerunt Exclamantes autem	rev	WA 35										
Et testes deposuerunt Impetum fecerunt	rev	LA 44										

	Et torcular fodit 　Vinea facta	trv	GR 230 OHS 654 LU 776[S] *GS 111 GB 120	G	5	4	7	9	5	2	5	2	
	Et tu Domine qui dicere 　Rogamus te Domine	rev	LA 557	c	-1	-5	-3	-1	-3	-1	0	-3	
	Et ubi vera quies 　Celebremus diem	rev	WA 248	a	-2	0	-2	-4	-5	-2	0	3	
	Et unumquodque eorum 　Similitudo aspectus	rev	WA 373										
	Et unus de senioribus 　Ecce vicit leo	rev	LA 209 WA 134										
	Et ut darent hostiam 　Postquam impleti	rev	LA 351										
1	Et ut perfecerunt omnia	an	LR 310	D	-2	3	5	3	5	7	10	7	D
	Et valde devote properantes 　Cum transisset	rev	WA 129	a	-2	0	-2	-5	-4	-2	2	-2	
	Et valde mane una sabbatorum 　Cum transisset	rev	OHS 696 (nm) LR 84 LA 213										
	Et valde mane una sabbatorum 　Maria Magdalene	rev	OHS 758 LR 85 WA 131										
7	Et valde mane una sabbatorum	an	LA 215 232	b	1	3	1	3	1	0	-2	-4	G
1	Et valde mane una sabbatorum	re	LA 211	C	2	5	2	4	5	7	5	2	D
8	Et valde mane una sabbatorum	an	AR 445 OHS 692 LU 776[KK] AM 456 WA 129	G	5	2	0	2	0	-2	0	2	G
3	Et venerunt festinantes	an	AM 887	G	5	2	0	2	4	5	7	4	E
7	Et venerunt festinantes	an	AR 689	G	7	5	7	10	9	7	9	10	G
	Et venit in spiritu 　Responsum accepit Simeon	cov	SYG 50										
	Et videas filios 　Ecce sic benedicetur	trv	GR [123] LU 1290	F	2	7	9	11	7	2	7	9	
	Et videbunt faciem ejus 　Vidi angelum	rev	LR 390										
	Et vim faciebant qui quaerebant 　Dominus mecum	rev	WA 111										
	Et virtutem terribilium tuorum 　Magnificentiam	trv	GR 99**	C	2	5	7	5	7	5	2	7	
	Et vocavit per gratiam 　Qui me segregavit	anv	WA 330										
	Et vox de throno exivit 　Audivi vocem in caelo	rev	LA 225 WA 140										
	Etenim non potuerunt mihi 　Saepe expugnaverunt	trv	GR 153 LU 571 GS 72 *GB 97[V] *SYG 110	G	2	5	2	5	7	5	4	0	
	Etenim pascha nostrum 　Surrexit pastor	rev	OHS 759 LR 86 415 LA 212										
	Etenim passer invenit 　Cor meum	trv	GR 626	G	2	5	2	5	7	5	4	0	

	Text		Sources									
1	Etenim sederunt principes	int	GR 36 LU 414 SYG 21 GB 21 GS 15	F	-3	-5	0	-3	0	2	0	2	D
	Etenim universi qui te De necessitatibus	trv	GR 102 LU 841^A *GS 39 *GB 69^V *SYG 78	C	2	5	2	4	5	2	0	2	
	Etsi oportuerit	see	Si oportuerit										
1	Euge nunc Dunstane	an	WA 313	D	2	0	3	5	2	0	3	2	D
	Euge serve bone et fidelis Iste homo perfecit	rev	WA 426										
1	Euge serve bone et fidelis ... dicit	an	AR 577^{15} [61] LU 262^5 1181 AM 661 740 LA 529	D	2	3	2	0	2	0	-2	0	D
4	Euge serve bone et fidelis ... intra	an	AR 577^{19} [82] LU 262^8 1200	E	1	0	-2	0	-2	0	1	3	E
7	Euge serve bone et fidelis ... intra	re	LR 193 LA 530 WA 425	G	7	9	7	5	7	5	4	5	G
1	Euge serve bone in modico fidelis	an	AR [74] LU 1195 *AM 670 *LA 540	D	-2	3	5	3	7	5	8	7	D
	Eum semper in caelis merearis O gloriosum praesulem	rev	PM 131										
	Euntes dicite discipulis ejus Angelus Domini	ofv	OTT 57 GB 132 *SYG 155	F	2	5	2	0	-3	-5	-3	0	
8	Euntes ibant et flebant	an	AR [11] LU 1114 *WA 394 415 LA 473 520	c	2	0	-1	0	-3	0	-1	-5	G
	Euntes ibant et flebant Qui seminant	trv	GR [24] LU 1164 GS 217 *GB 50 *SYG 51	G	2	5	4	2	5	2	0	2	
6	Euntes in mundum alleluia docete	an	AR 469 *AM 483	F	-1	2	4	-1	0	-3	-5	0	F
8	Euntes in mundum docete	an	AR 470 AM 484	a	-4	-2	0	-2	0	-2	-4	-2	G
1	Euntes in mundum docete ... baptizantes	an	LA 222 252	D	-2	3	5	3	5	7	5	7	D
	Euntes in mundum universum	alv	SYG 181	G	2	4	2	4	0	5	7	9	
1	Euntes in mundum universum	an	WA 146 *LA 253	C	2	5	4	2	4	2	0	5	D
5	Euntes praedicate evangelium	co	SYG 233	a	3	5	3	7	5	7	5	3	F
3	Euntibus animalibus ibant	re	WA 374	E	-2	3	5	8	7	8	7	5	E
1	Eutychius tulit filium	an	LR 274	C	2	9	10	9	12	9	7	9	D
8	Evangelista fulgidus	hy	ST 141	G	-2	-3	-2	0	-2	-5	-7	-3	G
	Evangelizare pauperibus misit	alv	GR 67**	C	2	4	2	0	2	4	5	4	
	Evangelizare pauperibus misit Spiritus Domini	grv	GR [100] LU 1283^A	F	4	2	7	9	7	4	7	9	
	Everte cor ejus in odium Recordare mei	ofv	OTT 125	G	2	0	2	0	-2	0	2	5	
4	Evigilia super nos	an	PM 108	C	2	5	4	2	4	2	0	2	E
4	Ex Aegypto vocavi	an	AR 222 LU 1083 AM 194 *WA 16 *LA 7	a	3	5	3	5	7	3	5	7	a

6 Ex altari tuo Domine	an	LR 126 LU 936	F	2	4	0	-3	-5	0	2	5	F
Ex die qua posuisti Docebo te	rev	LA 307										
6 Ex domo orationis	an	AM 779	F	-1	0	-3	-5	0	2	0	2	F
1 Ex ejus tumba marmorea	re	PM 118 VP 61 *WA 241	D	-2	0	3	0	2	0	-2	0	D
2 Ex more docti mystico	hy	ST 186 225 415	F	2	4	2	0	2	4	2	-1	D
2 Ex more docti mystico	hy	ST 282	F	2	4	2	0	2	4	2	0	D
6 Ex more docti mystico	hy	ST 338	C	2	5	9	0	4	5	2	0	F
2 Ex more docti mystico	hy	ST 379	E	3	5	3	1	3	5	3	0	D
7 Ex odoris mira	an	WA 346	G	5	4	5	7	9	7	5	4	G
3 Ex omni corde laudaverunt	an	WA 375	E	-2	3	5	8	7	8	7	3	E
Ex ore infantium	sr	LA 62 WA 47										
2 Ex ore infantium Deus	int	GR 40 LU 427 SYG 25 GB 26 GS 17	D	2	3	-2	2	0	3	2	3	D
1 Ex quo facta est vox	an	AR 248 772 LU 1541 AM 224 955 *WA 19 *LA 26	D	3	5	3	5	7	3	5	7	D
5 Ex quo omnia per quem omnia	an	AR 519 LU 915 AM 536 *WA 159	a	-2	-4	0	3	5	3	5	8	F
Ex quo omnia per quem omnia Unus est Dominus	rev	WA 161	G	5	4	0	2	4	2	5	7	
Ex Sion species decoris Paratus esto Israel	rev	WA 14										
5 Ex Sion species decoris	gr	GR 4 LU 328 SYG 3 GB 2^v GS 3	F	4	7	4	7	6	2	4	7	F
Ex te namque egredietur Dixit autem Dominus ad Abraham	rev	WA 80	g	-2	-3	-5	-7	-5	-3	0	2	
1 Ex utero senectutis	an	AR 733 LU 1496 AM 921 *WA 320	D	-2	3	5	3	7	5	8	7	D
Exaltabitur sicut unicornis Bonum est confiteri	ofv	OTT 26 GB 57 *SYG 59	G	5	7	9	7	4	5	7	10	
Exaltabo te Deus meus rex Confiteantur tibi	intv	GR 92**										
Exaltabo te Deus meus rex Sancti tui	intv	GR [18] LU 1149 GB 152^v SYG 169										
Exaltabo te Deus meus rex	alv	GR 54	a	-4	0	3	5	3	5	3	5	
Exaltabo te Domine quoniam suscepisti	an	OHS 183 (nm)										
Exaltabo te Domine quoniam suscepisti	sr	AR 589 LU 1320										
Exaltabo te Domine quoniam suscepisti Audivit Dominus	intv	GR 91 GS 33 GB 63^v SYG 68										
Exaltabo te Domine quoniam suscepisti Gaudens gaudebo	intv	GR 400 LU 1316										

	Exaltabo te Domine quoniam suscepisti Si diligis me	intv	GR [2¹] LU 1122¹										
8	Exaltabo te Domine quoniam suscepisti	an	LR 96 *WA 147 *LA 245	G	2	0	-2	0	2	0	-2	2	G
2	Exaltabo te Domine quoniam suscepisti ... Domine clamavi	of	GR 90 OTT 96 LU 528 SYG 66 GB 62ᵛ *GS 31 153	E	3	7	5	8	5	3	5	3	a
3	Exaltabo te Domine quoniam suscepisti ... Domine Deus	gr	GR 160 *SYG 113 *GB 101 GS 75	F	-5	-3	-1	0	-1	0	-3	0	E
2	Exaltabor in gentibus	an	LR 99	D	-2	3	2	3	5	7	5	7	D
6	Exaltabuntur cornua justi	an	LR 139 WA 412 LA 507	F	2	4	0	2	4	2	0	-1	F
7	Exaltare Domine alleluia in virtute	re	LR 98 *LA 246 *WA 147	a	3	5	3	5	3	2	5	8	G
4	Exaltare Domine in virtute	an	LR 96 WA 147 *LA 244	G	2	5	7	9	7	5	7	9	a
8	Exaltare Domine qui judicas	an	AR 197 LU 279ˢ	G	-2	-5	-3	-2	0	2	0	-2	G
8	Exaltare qui judicas	an	LA 100	F	2	4	2	0	4	6	7	4	G
6	Exaltare super caelos	an	WA 148	F	2	0	-1	2	4	0	-1	-3	F
3	Exaltasti Domine caput	an	WA 282	E	-2	3	5	8	7	5	8	7	E
1	Exaltata est gloriosa	an	PM 278	D	-2	3	5	7	8	7	5	3	D
	Exaltata est sancta Dei genitrix	sr	AR 822 LU 1601 LA 448 WA 7 310										
4	Exaltata est sancta Dei genitrix	an	LR 374 *LA 442	G	2	5	7	5	7	9	7	5	a
1	Exaltata est virgo Maria	re	LA 445	C	2	4	2	9	11	9	7	9	D
8	Exaltata est virgo Maria	an	AR 876 LU 1678 AM 1076	G	5	2	0	2	0	-2	0	2	G
6	Exaltate Dominum Deum ... in monte	an	AR 164	a	-2	0	-2	-4	0	1	0	-2	F
7	Exaltate Dominum Deum ... tabernaculum	an	LR 266	G	2	5	7	5	7	10	9	10	G
8	Exaltate qui judicas	an	WA 69	F	2	4	2	0	4	7	4	6	G
8	Exaltate regem regum	an	AR 492 LU 851 AM 509 LA 251	F	2	0	4	7	9	7	4	6	G
7	Exaltate regem saeculorum	an	AR 107 *AM 49	G	2	5	7	9	5	7	4	7	G
	Exaltent eum in ecclesia	sr	LA 365 WA 281										
2	Exaltent eum in ecclesia	gr	GB 244ᵛ *SYG 53	D	3	0	3	0	-2	2	-2	0	D
5	Exaltent eum in ecclesia	gr	GR 408 [2¹] LU 1122² *GB 244ᵛ GS 182	D	3	5	7	3	5	3	2	0	F
7	Exaudi Deus deprecationem meam	re	WA 66	G	5	4	5	7	5	7	9	7	G
	Exaudi Deus deprecationem nostram Miserere Domine populo	rev	WA 179										
	Exaudi Deus orationem meam cum Laetabitur justus	intv	GR [12] LU 1138 GS 205 GB 45ᵛ SYG 43										
	Exaudi Deus orationem meam cum Protexisti me	intv	GR [15] LU 1146 GS 205 GB 153										

#	Text		Sources										
4	Exaudi Deus orationem meam et clamor	of	SYG 129	C	2	4	5	7	4	2	9	11	E
	Exaudi Deus orationem meam et ne Dum clamarem	intv	GR 344 LU 1020 GS 32 151 GB 63 SYG 67										
5	Exaudi Deus orationem meam et ne	int	GR 143 SYG 103 GB 91^v GS 65	a	-2	0	-2	-4	0	3	2	0	F
8	Exaudi Deus orationem meam et ne	of	GR 129 OTT 36 SYG 95 GB 84 GS 56	a	-2	2	0	-2	0	-4	0	-2	G
	Exaudi Deus orationem meam et ne	alv	GB 246^v *SYG 243	G	2	5	7	9	7	9	10	9	
2	Exaudi Domine deprecationem servorum	an	WA 227	D	3	0	3	2	0	-2	0	5	D
	Exaudi Domine justitiam meam Ego autem cum justitia	intv	GR 121 GS 52 GB 80 SYG 91										
	Exaudi Domine justitiam meam Ego clamavi	intv	GR 130 GS 57 GB 84^v SYG 95										
	Exaudi Domine justitiam meam Probasti Domine	intv	GR 586 GS 195 GB 217^v SYG 217										
	Exaudi Domine justitiam meam Perfice gressus	ofv	OTT 90 *GB 58^v *SYG 61	a	-2	0	-5	-4	-2	0	1	-2	
7	[Exaudi Domine] ... multitudinem	an	WA 206 (inc lacking)										
8	Exaudi Domine orationem meam	an	AR [177] LU 1801 AM 1162 *WA 438 LA 559	a	-2	-4	-2	0	-2	0	-2	-4	G
3	Exaudi Domine populum tuum confitentem	an	GB 160^v	E	-2	3	5	7	5	7	8	7	E
3	Exaudi Domine populum tuum confitentem ... populi	an	WA 231	F	-1	0	-3	2	4	2	4	6	E
3	Exaudi Domine populum tuum toto tibi	an	GB 160^v	E	-2	3	5	7	5	7	8	7	E
4	Exaudi Domine vocem meam ... adjutor	int	GR 332 LU 1002 SYG 241 GS 145 *GB 249	F	2	0	-1	-3	-5	-3	-1	-3	E
1	Exaudi Domine vocem meam ... alleluia	int	GR 287 LU 854 SYG 181 GB 182 *GS 136	a	1	-2	3	5	7	5	7	8	a
2	Exaudi me Domine quoniam benigna	tr	GR 9**	D	-2	0	-2	-5	-2	0	-2	0	D
	Exaudi me in tua justitia Eripe me	ofv	OTT 51 *GB 111^v SYG 125	a	-2	0	3	0	-2	0	-2	0	
	Exaudi nos Deus salutaris	sr	LA 95 WA 67										
1	Exaudi nos Domine qui exaudisti	an	PM 49 VP 120 GB *161	D	-2	3	5	7	8	7	8	5	D
7	Exaudi nos Domine quoniam benigna	an	GR 84 *AM 821 LU 521 GB 61^v *SYG 64 *GS 29	G	5	7	9	7	5	7	2	5	G
	Exaudi orationem meam	alv	GR 21**	G	7	9	5	4	5	7	9	7	
	Exaudi orationem nostram Domine mi rex	rev	LR 425 LA 293 WA 179										

#	Text	Type	Sources	Start									End
	Exaudiat Dominus orationes / Adaperiat Dominus	rev	LR 425 WA 180 LA 295										
1	Exaudiat Dominus orationes	an	AR 551 LU 995 AM 589 LA 300	D	-2	3	5	3	5	7	5	2	D
1	Exaudiat Dominus orationes	an	WA 180	C	2	9	11	9	12	9	7	9	D
2	Exaudiat Dominus orationes	re	LA 299 *WA 180	A	3	5	7	5	8	7	8	5	D
	Exaudiat te Dominus	an	OHS 181 (nm)										
	Exaudiat te Dominus / Elegit te Dominus	intv	SYG 232										
4	Exaudisti Domine orationem	re	LA 271 *WA 166	E	5	3	5	7	8	3	0	1	E
7	Exaudisti Domine orationem	an	AR 541 LU 988 AM 578	G	5	4	5	7	9	7	5	4	G
4	Exaudivit de templo sancto	int	GR 282 LU 840 SYG 177 GB 161^v GS 132	D	3	5	7	5	7	5	7	5	E
4	Exaudivit ergo Deus	an	WA 287	G	2	0	-2	0	2	0	-2	-3	E
2	Excellenti prosapia	re	WA 282	A	3	5	3	8	7	8	10	8	D
1	Excelsi regis filium	an	WA 379	C	2	0	5	7	9	11	9	7	D
8	Excelsus super omnes	an	WA 63	a	-4	-2	0	-2	2	3	0	-2	G
	Excita Domine potentiam tuam / Aspiciens a longe	rev	LA 2										
	Excita Domine potentiam tuam / Veni Domine	rev	LA 14 WA 15										
	Excita Domine potentiam tuam	alv	GR 8 LU 336 GS 4 SYG 7 GB 5^v	a	-2	1	0	-2	0	-4	-5	-4	
1	Excita Domine potentiam tuam	an	AR 175 LU 279^Q	F	-1	-3	0	2	0	4	2	0	D
	Excita Domine potentiam tuam / Qui regis Israel	trv	GR 19 LU 351 GS 10 GB 10 *SYG 11	c	2	0	-5	0	2	4	-1	0	
	Excita Domine potentiam tuam / Domine Deus virtutum	grv	GR 15 LU 345 GS 8 GB 8 SYG 10	a	3	5	7	5	3	2	3	0	
2	Excita Domine potentiam tuam	gr	GR 15 LU 347 *SYG 10 *GS 9 *GB 9	G	4	2	5	2	4	5	2	0	a
	Exclamans Jesus voce magna / Tenebrae factae	rev	OHS 497 LU 703										
8	Exclamantes autem Judaei	re	WA 35	D	3	5	7	5	7	5	7	5	G
	Exclamantes autem turbae / Elegerunt apostoli	ofv	SYG 23	C	2	4	5	7	9	7	11	9	
1	Exclamaverunt ad te Domine	int	GR 488 LU 1465^A *SYG 172 *GB 163^v GS 185	F	-5	-3	4	5	4	2	0	2	D
	Exclamaverunt filii / Qui persequebantur	rev	WA 101										
8	Exclamemus omnes ad Dominum	an	WA 228 GB 154	G	5	7	9	7	5	7	5	4	G
8	Exemplo vitae venerabilis	re	LR 291	D	3	5	7	5	7	5	7	5	G

	Incipit		Sources										
4	Exemplum merear fieri	an	WA 352	F	-1	-3	-5	-3	-1	-3	-1	0	E
5	Exemplum veniae Mariam	an	WA 335	F	4	2	7	4	2	9	7	9	F
4	Exequie Martini	an	WA 404	G	-3	-2	0	-2	-3	-5	-2	0	E
7	Exhibeamus corpora nostra	an	AM 909	G	5	4	5	7	9	7	9	10	G
4	Exhortatus es in virtute	an	AR 433 OHS 403 LU 655 AM 417 418 WA 120 *LA 194	G	2	5	7	5	7	9	7	5	a
1	Exi cito in plateas	an	AR 538 LU 964 AM 558 *WA 187 *LA 310	a	-2	0	-2	-4	-2	-4	-2	-7	D
8	Exibant autem daemonia	an	AR 393 LU 1091 AM 368 LA 267	G	5	2	0	2	0	-2	0	2	G
4	Exibunt aquae vivae	an	AR 894^7 LU 1706 AM 1093	a	-2	0	3	7	5	3	5	7	a
1	Exiens Petrus apostolus	an	WA 340 LA 416	D	-2	3	5	3	5	7	5	3	D
4	Exiit qui seminat	an	WA 79	F	-3	-1	0	2	0	-1	0	-3	E
1	Exiit sermo inter fratres	an	AM 259	E	-4	-2	5	7	5	3	5	7	D
2	Exiit sermo inter fratres	co	GR 40 LU 423 *SYG 25 GS 17 GB 26	c	-3	-1	-5	-3	0	-1	0	-3	a
6	Exiit sermo inter fratres	an	AR 283 LU 426	F	-1	0	-3	-5	0	2	0	2	F
5	Exiit sermo inter fratres	gr	GR 39 LU 422 SYG 24 GB 24^v GS 16	F	2	0	2	0	2	4	0	2	F
8	Exiliit claudus	an	WA 340 LA 412	G	5	2	0	-2	0	2	0	4	G
	Existimantes autem illum Ibant parentes	rev	LR 314										
4	Existimo omnia detrimentum	an	AR 849 LU 1647	E	-2	0	1	-2	-4	0	1	3	E
	Exivi a patre et veni	alv	GR 272 LU 831	d	-2	0	2	3	5	2	5	3	
8	Exivi a patre et veni	an	WA 146	G	2	-2	-3	-5	-2	-3	-2	0	G
8	Exivi a patre et veni	an	AR 487 AM 503 *LA 243	G	5	2	0	-2	0	2	0	2	G
1	Exorta a Bethsaida	hy	ST 238	D	7	5	3	2	3	2	0	2	D
7	Exortum est in tenebris	an	AR 538^2 LU 965 *AM 561	G	4	5	7	9	12	7	9	7	G
7	Exortum est in tenebris ... corde	an	AR 271 LU 412 *AM 246 *WA 32 LA 38	b	3	0	3	5	3	5	3	1	G
8	Expandens manus suas	an	WA 39 *LA 51	G	5	4	5	4	2	5	7	5	G
4	Expandi manus meas	re	LA 502 *WA 236	F	-3	-1	0	2	4	2	4	6	E
	Expandi manus meas Eripe me ... Domine	ofv	SYG 125	E	-2	3	5	1	0	3	1	0	
	Expansis manibus beata	alv	GB 244	D	3	5	3	5	0	-2	3	5	
8	Expansis manibus orabat	an	WA 405 LA 488	G	5	2	0	-2	0	2	0	4	G
1	Expetitus a fratribus	an	WA 298 *LA 369	D	2	0	-2	0	3	2	0	-2	D

	Incipit	typ	Sources	M	1	2	3	4	5	6	7	8	F
	Expugna Domine impugnantes	an	OHS 234 (nm)										
1	Expugna impugnantes	an	WA 63 LA 87	a	-2	-5	-4	-2	-4	-5	-7	[0]	D
1	Expurgate vetus fermentum	re	OHS 814 LR 93 LA 212 WA 134	C	2	4	2	9	10	9	7	9	D
7	Exspecta Dominum viriliter	int	GR 158 SYG 112 GB 99^V GS 73	G	5	4	5	9	7	9	7	5	G
4	Exspectabo Dominum salvatorem	an	AR 222 LU 1080 AM 193 WA 4 20 LA 7	G	2	5	7	9	7	5	7	9	a
	Exspectans exspectavi Dominum Statuit Dominus	rev	LA 91 WA 65										
	Exspectans exspectavi Dominum Domine ad adjuvandum	ofv	GB 104^V	D	3	5	3	0	-2	0	3	2	
5	Exspectans exspectavi Dominum	of	GR 362 OTT 104 LU 1043 SYG 104 GB 92 *GS 66 159	a	3	5	3	5	3	5	8	5	F
	Exspectans exspectavi Dominum Domine ad adjuvandum	ofv	OTT 42 *SYG 106	F	4	5	2	0	2	4	2	4	
	Exspectans exspectavi Dominum Domine in auxilium	ofv	OTT 106 *GB 80^V *SYG 91	F	7	9	7	4	7	0	4	7	
	Exspectetur sicut pluvia	sr	WA 25										
	Exspectetur sicut pluvia Attende caelum	trv	GR 231 OHS 656 LU 776^U *GS 112 *GB 119^V *SYG 151	G	2	4	5	4	5	7	5	0	
4	Exspectetur sicut pluvia	an	AR 244 AM 218 WA 20 *LA 27	G	2	5	7	9	7	5	7	9	a
5	Exsulta et lauda Floriacum	re	LR 372	a	-2	0	-4	0	3	5	3	5	F
5	Exsulta et lauda habitatio	gr	GR 54**	D	3	5	3	0	2	3	5	3	F
4	Exsulta et lauda Jerusalem	an	WA 360	C	2	4	5	2	4	2	0	2	E
4	Exsulta filia Sion	co	GR 32 LU 406 SYG 17 *GB 16^V *GS F	D	2	3	-2	0	3	5	7	5	E
	Exsulta satis filia Sion Jerusalem plantabis	rev	LA 9 WA 11										
3	Exsulta satis filia Sion	of	GR 20 OTT 11 LU 352 SYG 12 *GB 10 GS 11	G	5	2	5	4	5	2	0	2	E
	Exsultabimus et laetabimur Inveni quem diligit	trv	GR (11)	G	5	7	9	5	0	5	7	9	
2	Exsultabit cor meum in salutari	gr	GR 587^1 LU 1612^1	E	3	7	5	8	5	7	8	5	a
	Exsultabo et laetabor	alv	GR [148] *LU 841^B	G	2	0	5	4	5	7	9	7	
3	Exsultabo in Jerusalem	int	GR 507 LU 1481	G	2	5	2	4	0	5	2	0	E
1	Exsultabunt Domino ossa	an	AR [176] GR 107* LU 1764 1799 *AM 1161 *WA 438 *LA 559	D	2	3	5	3	2	0	3	7	D
5	Exsultabunt omnia ligna	an	WA 29 *LA 64	a	3	0	-2	0	2	-2	-4	0	F

	Text	Type	Sources										
4	Exsultabunt sancti in gloria	an	WA 423	F	-1	-3	-1	0	2	0	-1	0	E
4	Exsultabunt sancti in gloria	of	GR [28] OTT 143 LU 1169 *SYG 191 *GB 195 GS 218	D	3	0	3	2	3	5	7	2	E
2	Exsultabunt sancti in gloria	gr	GR 646 SYG 205 *GB 210 *GS 214	E	3	7	5	8	5	7	8	5	a
	Exsultabunt sancti in gloria	alv	SYG 169 GS 216 (nm)	G	4	2	5	7	5	4	7	5	
7	Exsultans in praeconio	hy	ST 127	G	5	4	5	7	2	0	2	4	G
5	Exsultat in gloria	an	WA 286	F	4	7	9	7	5	7	9	7	F
	Exsultate Deo adjutori	sr	LA 97 WA 164										
	Exsultate Deo adjutori Cibavit eos	intv	GR [95] LU 1282										
	Exsultate Deo adjutori Cibavit eos	intv	GR 297 313 LU 887 943 GS 138 GB 191 SYG 184										
	Exsultate Deo adjutori Ego autem in Domino	intv	GR 467										
	Exsultate Deo adjutori Quasi modo geniti	intv	GR 261 LU 809 CS 124 CB 144^V										
6	Exsultate Deo adjutori	int	GR 368 *SYG 251 GB 257^V GS 168	a	-4	-2	0	-2	3	5	3	5	c
	Exsultate Deo adjutori	alv	GR 348 LU 1026 GS 150 SYG 244 GB 253	G	2	0	5	4	5	7	9	5	
4	Exsultate Deo adjutori	an	LA 98	E	1	3	1	-2	1	-2	1	3	E
6	Exsultate Deo adjutori	an	WA 68	F	2	4	0	2	0	2	0	-1	F
7	Exsultate justi et gloriamini	an	AR 96 LU 279^E	G	4	5	7	4	5	7	9	7	G
	Exsultate justi in Domino Cogitationes cordis ejus	intv	GR 324 [111] LU 970										
	Exsultate justi in Domino Ecce oculi Domini	intv	GR 494 GS 212 SYG 176										
	Exsultate justi in Domino Exclamaverunt ad te	intv	GR 488 LU 1465^A GS 185										
	Exsultate justi in Domino Gaudeamus ... Josaphat	intv	GR 653 LU 1751										
	Exsultate justi in Domino Gaudeamus ... monachorum	intv	GR (33)										
	Exsultate justi in Domino Gaudeamus ... sanctorum omnium	intv	GR 647 LU 1724										
	Exsultate justi in Domino Gaudeamus ... Thomae	intv	GR 46 LU 437										
	Exsultate justi in Domino Judicant sancti	intv	GR (8) GS 211 SYG 205										
	Exsultate justi in Domino Misericordia Domini	intv	GR 263 LU 816 GS 127 GB 146 SYG 164										

Mode	Incipit	Type	Sources	Pitch	1	2	3	4	5	6	7	8	End
	Exsultate justi in Domino Quasi modo geniti	intv	SYG 162										
	Exsultate justi in Domino Sancti tui	intv	GS 211										
	Exsultate justi in Domino Sapientiam sanctorum	intv	GR [25] LU 1166 GS 211 SYG 189										
1	Exsultavit cor ... et exaltatum	an	AR 826[1] LU 1612	C	2	9	10	9	7	9	7	5	D
7	Exsultavit cor ... qui humiliat	an	AR 131	G	4	5	7	9	7	5	9	7	G
	Exsultavit spiritus meus Quis Deus ... praeelegit	rev	LR 271										
5	Exsultavit spiritus meus	an	AR 123	a	-2	0	-4	0	3	2	0	3	F
8	Exsultavit spiritus meus	an	LA 93	F	2	4	2	0	4	6	4	2	G
8	Exsultavit spiritus meus	of	GR 587[5] LU 1612[3]	F	2	4	7	4	6	7	2	0	G
	Exsultavit ut gigas De illa occulta	rev	WA 25										
6	Exsultavit ut gigas	co	GR 20 LU 352 SYG 12 GB 10[v] GS 11	C	2	5	2	0	5	7	5	4	F
2	Exsultemus cuncti in Deo	gr	GB 227	A	3	5	8	5	7	5	3	7	D
3	Exsultemus Deo caeli	hy	ST 235	E	3	5	8	10	8	7	8	5	E
4	Exsultemus Domino regi	inv	WA 317	D	2	-2	2	3	5	3	2	0	E
	Exsultemus et in ipso Ubi caritas	anv	GR 204 OHS 451	F	2	4	2	4	5	4	2	4	
3	Exsultemus et laetemur hodie		AR 170*	D	5	7	10	9	7	5	3	5	E
4	Exsultemus et laetemur in Domino	re	WA 314	D	3	2	3	2	0	2	0	-2	E
7	Exsultemus in Domino	an	LA 40	d	-3	0	2	0	-2	0	2	0	G
6	Exsultent in Domino sancti	inv	LR 162 WA 304	D	3	5	3	5	3	2	3	5	F
	Exsultent justi Dei in conspectu	alv	GB 269[v]	C	2	4	5	7	5	7	11	7	
	Exsultent justi in conspectu	sr	AR [46] LU 1155 AM 645 984 1099 1100 1173 WA 423										
8	Exsultet caelum laudibus	hy	AM 257	G	-2	-3	-5	-2	2	0	-2	0	G
1	Exsultet caelum laudibus	hy	AM 621	D	-2	3	2	0	7	5	3	2	D
4	Exsultet caelum laudibus	hy	ST 195	F	-1	-3	-5	-3	-1	-3	-1	2	E
4	Exsultet caelum laudibus	hy	ST 241 AM 624	F	-1	-3	-5	-3	-1	2	4	2	E
4	Exsultet caelum laudibus	hy	ST 402	F	2	0	-3	-5	-3	-1	2	4	E
4	Exsultet caelum laudibus	hy	ST 100	F	2	0	-1	-3	-5	-3	-1	2	E
2	Exsultet caelum laudibus	hy	ST 337	C	2	0	2	5	4	2	0	2	D
2	Exsultet caelum laudibus	hy	ST 134	D	2	3	5	3	2	0	3	0	D
4	Exsultet caelum laudibus	hy	ST 59	C	2	5	4	2	0	2	4	7	E
2	Exsultet caelum laudibus	hy	ST 144	C	2	5	4	2	0	2	5	4	D
7	Exsultet gaudio pater justi	int	GR 59 LU 470	G	5	4	5	9	7	10	9	10	G

6 Exsultet in hac die	an	WA 316	c	2	5	4	0	2	0	-2	0	c
6 Exsultet jam angelica ... caelestis	hy	ST 345	F	7	9	7	4	2	4	5	4	F
3 Exsultet jam angelica ... caelorum	hy	WA 218 GS 105	G	2	5	4	5	7	5	4	2	E
1 Exsultet mentis jubilo	hy	VP 121	D	7	5	3	2	0	-2	3	2	D
1 Exsultet omnium turba ... Benedicti et eorum	an	AM 1120	D	-2	0	3	2	0	-2	2	3	D
1 Exsultet omnium turba ... Benedicti laetentur	an	AM 850 963 *LA 366	D	-2	0	3	2	0	-2	2	3	D
1 Exsultet omnium turba ... in transitu	an	WA 296	D	-2	0	3	2	0	-2	2	3	D
1 Exsultet omnium turba ... Scholasticae	an	AM 814	D	-2	0	3	2	0	-2	2	3	D
1 Exsultet orbis gaudiis	hy	AR [6] LU 1116	D	-2	3	2	0	7	5	3	2	D
4 Exsultet orbis gaudiis	hy	AR [5] LU 1115	F	2	0	-1	-3	-5	-3	-1	2	E
1 Exsultet orbis gaudiis	hy	AR 280 LU 425	C	2	4	7	5	4	2	4	5	D
5 Exsultet spiritus meus	an	AM 142 WA 66	a	-4	0	3	2	0	3	5	3	F
1 Exsultet spiritus noster	an	WA 281	C	2	5	7	5	4	2	5	2	D
Exsurgat Deus et dissipentur Benedictus Dominus	intv	SYG 238										
Exsurgat Deus et dissipentur Deus dum egredereris	intv	GR 300 LU 892 GS 139 GB 191^v SYG 186										
Exsurgat Deus et dissipentur Deus in loco sancto	intv	GR 347 LU 1024 GS 152 GB 253 SYG 245										
Exsurgat Deus et dissipentur Justi epulentur	intv	GR 412 GS 211 GB 219^v SYG 214										
Exsurgat Deus et dissipentur Spiritus Domini	intv	GR 292 [91] LU 878 1279 GS 234 M GB 185										
Exsurgat Deus et dissipentur Mirabilis Deus	ofv	OTT 141 GB 171 *SYG 175	F	2	4	2	4	9	7	4	6	
2 Exsurge Domine adjuva nos	an	GR 274 429 PM 133 LU 835 1358 *WA 226	A	3	5	7	3	2	0	3	7	D
2 Exsurge Domine adjuva nos	an	PM 69	C	4	5	7	4	2	0	4	7	D
Exsurge Domine Deus exaltetur Spiritus Domini	intv	GR 58**										
8 Exsurge Domine Deus exaltetur	tr	GR [101] LU 1283^B	E	3	5	8	5	7	8	10	8	G
Exsurge Domine Deus extolle	an	OHS 60 (nm)										
Exsurge Domine et intende	an	OHS 235 (nm)										
3 Exsurge Domine et intende	gr	GR 185 OHS 208 LU 607 SYG 124 GB 111^v GS 89	C	2	5	4	5	7	9	7	9	E
1 Exsurge Domine et judica	an	OHS 386 LU 641 *WA 118 *LA 191	F	4	2	4	0	2	-3	0	-1	D

	Exsurge Domine et judica 　　Respice Domine	grv	GR 354 LU 1033 GS 68 156 GB 94^v SYG 106	F	4	2	7	9	7	9	7	6	
3	Exsurge Domine fer opem	gr	GR 143 SYG 103 GB 91^v *GS 65	G	2	5	4	5	2	4	5	7	E
3	Exsurge Domine non praevaleat	gr	GR 123 LU 553 *SYG 93 *GB 82 GS 54	F	-5	-3	-1	0	-1	0	-3	0	E
1	Exsurge Domine non praevaleat	an	LA 95	D	3	2	0	2	3	0	-2	0	D
1	Exsurge Domine non praevaleat	an	AM 17 OHS 59 (nm) *WA 67	F	4	2	4	0	2	0	2	-1	D
	Exsurge Domine salvum me fac	an	OHS 57 (nm)										
	Exsurge gloria mea 　　Paratum cor meum	rev	LA 94 WA 66										
	Exsurge quare obdormis 　　Exsurge Domine adjuva nos	anv	GB 61										
1	Exsurge quare obdormis	int	GR 77 LU 504 SYG 60 GB 57^v *GS 26	D	3	2	0	-2	0	3	5	3	D
1	Exsurgens Joseph a somno	an	AR 652 LU 1402 AM 840	F	4	2	4	2	0	2	0	-3	D
8	Exsurgens Maria abiit	an	AR 771 LU 1540 AM 954	G	-5	-2	2	0	2	0	2	4	G
	Exsurget rex immensae 　　Ecce radix	rev	WA 15										
	Extendens caelum sicut pellem 　　Emitte spiritum	ofv	OTT 77 GB 184 SYG 182	D	5	7	5	7	5	7	5	7	
8	Extollens quaedam mulier	an	AR 390 LU 557 AM 365 WA 99 *LA 154	G	5	2	0	-2	0	2	0	2	G
1	Extrahentes Joseph de lacu	re	LA 147	D	2	0	2	0	2	-2	2	5	D
3	Extuli electum de populo	int	LU 1623^A	E	1	-2	3	0	3	5	3	5	E
3	Fac benigne in bona voluntate	an	AR 387 AM 361 *WA 98 LA 152	G	2	0	4	7	5	4	2	4	E
	Fac cum servo tuo Domine 　　Domine vivifica	ofv	OTT 31 *GB 64 *SYG 68	G	4	7	5	9	7	5	4	5	
7	Fac Deus potentiam	an	AM 154 *LA 99	d	-2	-3	-2	0	2	0	-2	0	G
5	Fac Domine judicium injuriam	an	AR 431 OHS 309 350	c	-1	-3	-5	-3	-7	-3	0	2	F
2	Fac mecum Domine signum	int	GR 134 SYG 98 GB 87^v *GS 60	D	2	3	5	3	0	3	2	-2	D

#	Incipit		Refs										
	Fac nos innocuam Joseph	alv	GR 486 LU 1441	G	-2	-3	-2	0	-2	2	0	2	
	Fac tibi arcam de lignis Dixit Dominus ad Noe	rev	LR 399 LA 116 WA 76										
	Fac ut amor Christi Solve jubente	rev	WA 279										
8	Faciam te in gentem magnam	int	GR (24)	G	5	2	0	2	-2	0	2	0	G
4	Faciamus hic tria tabernacula	an	AR 381 LU 549 AM 354	G	2	5	7	5	7	9	7	5	a
4	Faciem meam non averti	an	AR 426 OHS 186 198 AM 404 *WA 114 LA 184	a	-2	0	3	5	3	5	7	3	a
4	Facies et pennas	re	WA 373	E	-2	-4	-2	0	-4	-2	1	3	E
	Facies mea intumuit	sr	AR 678										
2	Facies unctionis	int	OHS 413 LU 661	C	2	5	2	0	2	5	4	5	D
8	Facite vobis amicos	an	WA 188	F	2	4	2	4	2	4	2	4	G
7	Facta autem hac voce	re	LA 260 WA 155	G	2	0	2	0	2	5	4	5	G
7	Facta est cum angelo	an	AR 265 LU 398 *AM 241 *WA 32 *LA 37	G	7	5	4	7	9	7	5	7	G
8	Facta est Judaea	an	LA 90	F	2	4	6	7	4	6	7	4	G
	Facta est Judaea In exitu Israel	alv	SYG 248	D	3	5	7	5	7	5	3	5	
8	Facta sunt enim haec	an	AR 538^{9} LU 969 *AM 567	G	5	2	-2	0	2	0	-2	2	G
1	Facti sumus sicut consolati	an	WA 66 LA 93	a	-2	0	-2	-5	-4	-2	-4	-5	D
2	Facto diluvio super terram	re	WA 76	D	2	0	-2	3	2	0	2	3	D
	Factum est cor meum tamquam cera Foderunt manus	intv	GR 16**										
3	Factum est cor meum tamquam cera	int	GR 505 LU 1477	E	1	0	-2	3	5	3	5	8	E
1	Factum est dum tolleret	re	LA 272 WA 167	F	-1	0	-3	-1	-3	-1	0	2	D
8	Factum est in die	an	WA 332	F	2	4	7	4	6	4	2	4	G
4	Factum est in una	an	WA 157	F	-1	-3	-1	0	2	0	-1	-3	E
	Factum est proelium in caelo Michael et angeli	rev	PM 191										
	Factum est silentium ... committeret Fidelis sermo	rev	WA 381										
1	Factum est silentium ... committeret	re	LA 465 WA 380	C	2	0	2	0	2	5	7	5	D
8	Factum est silentium ... draco	an	AR 859 AM 1062 *WA 384 *LA 472	F	2	4	6	7	6	7	9	7	G
	Factum est silentium ... et accepit Stetit angelus	rev	WA 380										
4	Factum est ut quaedam	an	WA 326	E	-2	-4	-2	0	-4	-2	1	0	
	Factumque est et reverentissimum Pater sanctus dum intentam	rev	LA 371 WA 298										E

	Factus es adjutor	see	Factus est adjutor										
8	Factus es spes mea Domine	tr	GR 424 LU 1353	G	2	4	2	0	2	0	5	7	G
1	Factus est adjutor	an	AR 379 *AM 352 *WA 93 *LA 142	F	2	4	2	4	0	4	2	-1	D
4	Factus est Dominus firmamentum	of	GR 150 OTT 42 LU 567 SYG 108 GB 96ᵛ GS 70	D	3	5	3	0	-2	0	-2	3	E
1	Factus est Dominus protector	int	GR 320 LU 961 SYG 239 GB 247ᵛ GS 142	D	7	8	7	5	3	5	3	5	D
7	Factus est mihi Dominus	re	LA 101 *WA 69	G	2	0	2	4	5	7	5	4	G
8	Factus est repente de caelo	an	LR 108 LU 868 *WA 152 LA 255	c	2	0	-1	0	-3	0	-1	-3	G
8	Factus est repente de caelo	of	GB 192	D	2	5	7	5	7	10	5	3	G
	Factus est repente de caelo	alv	SYG 183 *GS 140	F	4	2	-1	0	2	0	2	-3	F
7	Factus est repente de caelo	co	GR 296 [94] LU 882 1281 GS 137 234 SYG 184 *GB 191	G	7	0	7	5	10	9	10	7	G
	Factus sum in derisu / Conclusit vias meas	rev	LA 176 WA 115										
	Factus sum infirmis infirmus / Ego autem cum mihi	trv	GR 566	G	-5	0	2	5	2	5	7	5	
4	Factus sum sicut homo	an	OHS 613 LU 770 *WA 126 LA 204	c	2	0	2	4	0	2	-3	2	a
	Factus sum sicut homo ... traditus / Domine Deus salutis	ofv	OTT 112 GB 74 SYG 84	d	2	-2	0	2	0	2	0	-3	
7	Fallax ad patibulum	hy	ST 44	G	-2	2	0	2	4	5	4	2	G
8	Fallax gratia et vana	re	LR 222	G	-2	0	-7	-5	-2	0	2	0	G
	Famulos respice Christe / Beatam Aredii animam	grv	SYG 219	a	3	5	7	5	3	2	0	3	
	Fantasticum quidem / Igne fervoris	rev	WA 294										
	Fasciculus myrrhae dilectus	sr	AR 846 LU 1638 AM 1044										
4	Fasciculus myrrhae dilectus	an	AR 675 LU 1423	G	2	5	9	7	5	7	9	7	a
7	Fatiscens corpus febribus	an	WA 252	G	7	9	7	5	4	5	7	5	G
	Favus distillans labia ejus / Veniens a Libano	rev	PM 235 WA 140										
3	Favus distillans labia tua	an	PM 274 LR 247 375 WA 354 LA 456	E	-2	3	5	8	7	8	7	5	E
8	Febres fugat tactu	an	WA 249	G	-5	-2	-3	-2	0	2	0	-2	G
7	Febus et Cornelius	re	WA 409	G	2	0	5	4	5	7	9	5	G
4	Feci judicium et justitiam	co	GR [59] LU 1224 *SYG 40 GB 43ᵛ GS 230	G	-2	-3	0	2	0	2	-2	0	E

	Incipit		Source										
	Fecique tibi nomen / Ego te tuli	rev	LA 270 WA 166										
	Fecisti enim nos		see Fecisti nos enim										
	Fecisti nos enim Deo / Dignus es	rev	LR 416 AM 1199 / LA 224 WA 139										
	Fecisti viriliter et confortatum	alv	GR 39**	a	-2	1	0	-2	0	-4	-5	-4	
7	Fecit Deus potentiam	an	AR 162	d	-2	-3	-2	0	2	0	-2	0	G
6	Fecit Joas rectum	an	AR 542 LU 988 / AM 579	F	2	4	2	0	-3	-5	-3	0	F
3	Fecit me Dominus quasi patrem	re	LR 306	G	5	2	0	5	4	5	7	5	E
8	Fecit mihi magna	an	AR 301 LU 445 / AM 278	F	2	0	4	7	6	2	-1	0	G
5	Fecit nos Deo et patri suo	an	AR 894^9 LU 1708 / AM 1095	a	-4	0	3	5	3	5	3	2	F
	Fecit Salomon solemnitatem / Domine Deus in simplicitate	ofv	OTT 159 *GB 175^v / *SYG 264	c	2	0	-3	0	-5	-3	0	2	
	Fecit sibi arcam / Noe vir justus	rev	LA 116										
1	Felices sensus beatae Mariae	co	GR 601 LU 1637	D	3	2	3	5	2	3	2	0	D
	Felici commercis pro terrenis / Gloriosus Dei	rev	VP 254 WA 260										
2	Feliciter virgines vincunt	re	WA 394	D	-2	-5	-2	0	2	0	-2	0	D
	Felix certe et omni / Beata progenies	rev	WA 367	c	-1	0	2	0	-1	0	-1	-3	
1	Felix es dilecte Deo	an	WA 316	C	2	5	2	0	2	7	5	4	D
	Felix es sacra virgo Maria / Tu gloria	trv	GR 441 LU 1378	D	3	0	3	7	3	5	3	5	
	Felix es sacra virgo Maria	alv	GR 542 LU 1539	G	5	4	5	7	5	2	0	2	
2	Felix Maria unxit	re	PM 169	D	-2	0	2	0	3	2	3	5	D
1	Felix Maria unxit	re	WA 337	D	3	2	0	3	0	-2	0	3	D
4	Felix namque es beata virgo	an	WA 366	E	3	5	3	0	-2	3	5	8	E
	Felix namque es nimium beate / Stephane	alv	SYG 211	E	3	0	-2	3	5	3	7	8	
	Felix namque es quae et genitricis / Nativitas tua	rev	WA 366										
1	Felix namque es sacra virgo et omni	an	LA 459	D	2	3	0	2	0	-2	0	3	D
	Felix namque es sacra virgo Maria / Beata progenies	re	PM 262 LR 249 / LA 459										
1	Felix namque es sacra virgo Maria	re	AR 127* *PM 242 / *LR 255 LA 447 / *WA 357	C	2	4	5	0	4	2	5	2	D
8	Felix namque es sacra virgo Maria	of	OTT 188	F	2	4	7	4	2	0	2	4	G
1	Felix namque es sacra virgo Maria	of	GR [82] LU 1271 / *GB 233 *GS r	D	3	5	3	0	-2	3	5	7	D
	Felix pater felicioris filiae / O felix Joachim	rev	PM 182										

4	Felix per omnes festum mundi cardines	hy	ST 393	F	-3	-5	-3	0	-1	0	2	0	E
4	Felix per omnes festum mundi cardines	hy	ST 297	F	-1	-3	-5	-3	-1	0	-1	0	E
4	Felix per omnes festum mundi cardines	hy	ST 54 95 431	F	-1	-3	-5	-3	0	-1	0	2	E
8	Felix per omnes festum mundi cardines	hy	ST 430	G	2	0	-2	2	4	0	7	5	G
1	Felix per omnes festum mundi cardines	hy	ST 54	C	2	4	5	7	9	7	5	4	D
8	Felix per omnes festum mundi cardines	hy	ST 447	D	5	3	5	7	9	7	5	3	G
6	Felix per omnes festum mundi cardines	hy	ST 455	C	5	4	2	5	7	5	4	2	C
2	Felix Vedastus pontifex	hy	ST 146	C	2	5	4	2	4	0	2	4	D
7	Ferculum fecit sibi	an	WA 163	G	7	5	7	5	2	0	5	7	G
7	Festa celebria militans hodie	hy	ST 308	G	2	4	2	4	5	4	2	0	G
6	Festa dies mundo	re	WA 350	G	5	7	5	7	9	5	2	3	c
3	Festa patris Augustini	hy	ST 235	E	3	5	8	10	8	7	8	5	E
2	Festa praesentis celebret diei	hy	ST 152	a	-2	0	-4	-2	-7	-2	0	-2	D
1	Festa praesentis celebret diei	hy	ST 151	D	3	-2	0	3	5	3	5	3	D
2	Festi sacrati praesulis	hy	ST 432	G	-3	-2	0	-2	-3	-5	0	-2	D
2	Festina ne tardaveris	re	LA 10 WA 15	A	3	5	8	5	3	5	8	7	D
	Festinet justus non vereatur Sanguinis et aquae	rev	PM 156 LR 344										
8	Festiva saeclis colitur	hy	ST 98	G	2	0	-2	2	5	4	0	2	G
8	Festivis resonent compita vocibus	hy	AM 947	G	-3	-2	-5	0	2	0	-2	-3	G
8	Festivis resonent compita vocibus	hy	AR 760 LU 1537^v	G	-3	-2	-3	-5	0	2	0	-2	G
8	Festum colentes annuum	hy	ST 402	G	-5	-2	0	2	0	-2	0	5	G
6	Festum colentes celebre	hy	ST 192	F	-1	0	-1	-3	-5	0	2	0	F
8	Festum nunc celebre magnaque gaudia	hy	ST 231	G	-3	-2	-5	0	2	0	-2	-3	G
8	Festum nunc celebre magnaque gaudia	hy	ST 292	G	-3	-2	-5	0	2	0	-2	0	G
8	Festum nunc celebre magnaque gaudia	hy	ST 292 (var)	G	-3	-2	-3	-5	0	2	0	-2	G
8	Festum nunc celebre magnaque gaudia	hy	ST 389	G	-2	-5	0	2	0	-2	-3	-5	G
8	Festum nunc celebre magnaque gaudia	hy	ST 259	G	2	-3	-2	-5	0	2	0	-2	G
6	Festum nunc celebre magnaque gaudia	hy	ST 453	C	2	4	2	0	5	7	9	7	C
2	Festum nunc celebre magnaque gaudia	hy	ST 420	C	2	4	5	7	5	2	4	5	D
2	Festum nunc celebre magnaque gaudia	hy	ST 293	C	2	4	5	7	5	2	5	4	D
	Fiant aures tuae intendentes De profundis	ofv	OTT 126 *GB 265 *SYG 258	D	-2	-5	0	-2	3	0	2	0	
	Fiant aures tuae intendentes De profundis clamavi ad te	trv	GR 75 LU 499 GS 25 *GB 56^v *SYG 59	G	2	4	5	4	2	5	7	0	
	Fiant in capite Joseph Benedictiones patris	rev	LR 307										
7	Fiat Domine cor meum	an	WA 406 *LA 489	d	-3	0	2	0	-3	-2	-3	-7	G

1 Fiat manus tua	an	AM 106 LA 89	D	7	9	7	5	7	5	3	5	D
Fiat pax in virtute tua Laetatus sum	grv	GR 139 LU 560 GS 63 162 GB 89^v SYG 100	d	-2	0	5	7	5	0	3	2	
Fiat pax in virtute tua Rogate quae	grv	GR [135] LU 1285	d	-2	0	5	7	5	0	3	2	
Fiat pax in virtute tua Laetatus sum in his	trv	SYG 101	C	2	0	2	5	2	0	2	0	
4 Fidelia omnia mandata	an	AM 125 WA 63 *LA 87	E	3	5	3	1	0	1	3	1	E
4 Fidelis Dominus in omnibus	an	AR 205 OHS 44 LU 312	E	3	5	3	5	3	0	1	3	E
4 Fidelis namque et prudens dispensator	re	PM 309	C	2	5	4	5	2	5	7	5	E
1 Fidelis sermo et omni	re	LA 471 *WA 381	C	2	5	7	5	4	0	2	0	D
3 Fidelis servus et prudens	an	AR [74] LU 1196 1446 *AM 671 *WA 427 LA 540	G	2	5	2	5	4	0	2	4	E
4 Fidelis servus et prudens ... amen	re	AM 1193 *LR 316	E	3	0	1	-2	0	1	0	3	E
7 Fidelis servus et prudens ... ut det	co	GR 570 [34][41][50] LU 1185 GB 52^v *SYG 56 *GS 224	G	2	4	0	2	5	4	5	7	G
Fiducia magna erit Memor esto fili	rev	LA 289 WA 176										
4 Fiebat interea praediorum	an	WA 244	F	-1	-3	-1	-3	-5	-3	-1	2	E
8 Fili a juventute tua	an	LA 281	G	2	4	5	2	0	-2	2	0	G
4 Fili noli deficere	re	WA 170	F	-1	0	-3	0	2	0	-1	0	E
1 Fili praebe mihi cor tuum	an	AM 566	F	2	0	2	4	2	0	2	4	D
5 Fili praebe mihi cor tuum	an	AR 538^7 LU 977	F	4	7	6	4	7	9	7	9	F
3 Fili quid fecisti ... ecce	an	AR 693 *AM 891	G	5	4	0	2	-3	0	2	0	E
1 Fili quid fecisti ... ego	co	GR 66 LU 481 SYG 33 *GB 37 GS 21	F	-3	0	-1	2	4	0	2	-1	D
8 Fili quid fecisti ... ego	an	WA 58	F	2	4	2	0	2	4	2	4	G
8 Fili quid fecisti ... quid	an	AR 330 LU 477 *LA 106	F	2	4	7	4	2	0	2	4	G
8 Fili recordare quia recepisti	an	AR 384 LU 1087 *AM 358 WA 187 *LA 145	G	5	2	0	-2	0	2	0	4	G
1 Filiae Jerusalem venite	re	LR 169 *LA 389 *WA 304	a	2	3	-2	0	-2	-4	-2	0	D
1 Filiae Jerusalem venite	an	AR 577^11 [33] LU 262^1 1145 AM 636 735 WA 304 LA 385	C	2	5	7	5	2	0	2	0	D
Filiae regum in honore tuo Speciosus forma	grv	GR 103**	G	2	4	5	4	5	4	5	7	

3 Filiae regum in honore tuo	of	GR [63] OTT 157 LU 1228 *SYG 39 *GB 43 GS 229	G	5	7	5	7	5	7	5	2	E
8 Filii hominum in tegmine	tr	GR 55**	D	3	5	2	3	5	0	-2	0	G
1 2 Filii hominum scitote	an	LR 149 WA 416 *LA 522	C	2	5	4	2	0	5	9	7	D
Filii qui nascentur / Docete filios	rev	LA 387 WA 142										
8 Filii Sion exsultent	an	AR 186	c	2	0	-1	0	-3	-7	-5	-3	G
Filii tui de longe venient / Venit lumen	rev	LR 80										
Filii tui de longe venient	alv	GR 46**	G	5	4	5	7	9	5	4	5	
Filii tui sicut novellae / Uxor tua	grv	GR [122] LU 1289	a	3	5	7	5	3	2	3	0	
1 Firmamentum meum et refugium	re	LA 82	F	2	4	2	0	4	2	0	2	D
8 Fit porta Christi pervia	hy	ST 223	G	-5	0	2	0	-3	-2	0	2	G
8 Fit porta Christi pervia	hy	ST 375	G	-5	0	2	0	-2	0	2	5	G
8 Fit porta Christi pervia	hy	ST 280	G	-2	0	2	5	4	5	7	5	G
8 Fit porta Christi pervia	hy	ST 433	G	2	0	-2	0	2	4	0	-2	G
4 Flabit spiritus ejus	an	WA 60	F	-1	-3	-1	0	2	4	2	0	E
1 Flagrabat in beatissimis	an	WA 377	C	2	9	10	9	7	9	7	5	D
Fletum deduxerunt oculi / Qui consolabatur	rev	WA 175										
4 Florem mundi adolescens	an	WA 248	F	-3	-5	-3	-1	2	4	2	4	E
3 Florem mundus protulit	hy	ST 309	D	5	7	5	7	10	9	7	9	E
5 Flores apparuerunt in terra	gr	GR 439 LU 1376	F	2	0	2	4	2	4	0	2	F
Flores apparuerunt in terra / Jam hiems	trv	GR 615	D	3	2	3	5	3	5	7	5	
Flores apparuerunt in terra	alv	GR 442	D	7	5	7	9	10	9	7	5	
1 Florete flores quasi lilium	co	GR 622 LU 1677	F	-1	2	4	0	-1	-3	-5	-3	D
Floribus ejus nec rosae / Beata vere mater	rev	LR 388	a	-2	0	-2	-4	-5	-2	0	1	
5 Floro primariisque regni	an	LR 280	c	2	-3	-7	-3	0	-1	2	0	F
7 Fluctus tui super me	re	LA 305 *WA 186	c	-1	0	2	0	2	4	2	4	G
Fluenta evangelii de ipso / Hic est discipulus qui	rev	LA 50 WA 40										
Fluenta evangelii de ipso / Iste est Joannes	rev	PM 33										
6 Fluminis impetus ... alleluia	an	LR 69 *WA 53 *LA 66	F	2	0	-1	2	4	-1	0	-3	F
Fluminis impetus ... civitatem / Adjuvabit eam	grv	GR [56] LU 1221 GS 181 *GB 50 SYG 50	c	2	0	2	0	-3	0	2	4	

4 Fluminis impetus ... Scholasticam	an	LR 290	D	-2	0	3	0	2	-2	2	5	E
2 Foderunt manus meas	co	GR [111]	D	-2	0	2	3	2	0	-2	3	D
6 Foderunt manus meas	int	GR 16**	F	2	0	-3	-1	0	-5	-3	-5	F
5 Fons hortorum puteus aquarum	an	PM 275 LR 250 *WA 354 *LA 456	b^b	-3	-1	-3	-5	-1	-3	2	4	F
8 Fontes aquarum sanctificati	an	WA 59 *LA 76	G	-2	0	2	0	-3	-2	0	2	G
1 Fontes et omnia quae moventur	an	AR 504 LU 884 AM 521 *WA 153 LA 261	D	7	10	7	5	7	5	2	3	D
8 Formans me ex utero	an	LR 351 WA 321 *LA 403	G	-2	-5	-3	-2	0	2	0	2	G
Formavit igitur Deus hominem In principio creavit	rev	LR 398 WA 72										
Formavit igitur Dominus hominem In principio fecit	rev	LA 108 WA 72										
8 Formavit igitur Dominus hominem	re	LA 109 *WA 72	G	2	0	2	0	2	0	2	4	G
4 Fortem virili pectore	hy	AR [100] LU 1234	E	-2	-4	0	3	1	-2	-4	-2	E
3 Fortem virili pectore	hy	AM 685	E	1	3	1	0	-2	0	-2	-4	E
2 Fortem virili pectore	hy	AR [99] LU 1234 AM 684	D	3	2	5	3	0	2	5	3	D
4 Forti animo esto Tobia	an	AR 891 LU 1701	G	-2	0	-2	-3	-2	0	2	0	E
8 Fortis en praesul	hy	AM 870	G	2	0	-3	-2	-3	-5	-3	-7	G
4 Fortitudo mea et laus	an	AR 152	F	-3	-1	0	2	0	-1	-3	-1	E
6 Fortitudo mea et laus	an	WA 82	c	-1	0	-3	-5	0	2	0	2	c
8 Fortitudo mea et laus ... iste	tr	GR 468	D	3	5	2	3	5	0	-2	0	G
2 Framea suscitare adversus eos	an	AR 426 OHS 188 203 AM 405 *WA 114 LA 184	F	-1	-3	-1	0	-5	-3	0	2	D
2 Francicae lumen columenque gentis	hy	LR 273	A	5	3	5	8	7	5	7	8	D
Franciscus pauper et humilis	alv	GR 602 LU 1643	C	2	5	7	4	2	5	4	5	
1 Frange esurienti panem	re	LA 131	D	2	3	5	3	0	3	5	7	D
8 Fratres alacri pectore	hy	ST 428	G	2	0	-2	0	2	4	0	-2	G
8 Fratres existimo	an	WA 71	F	2	4	7	6	4	2	4	2	G
8 Fratres mei elongaverunt	re	LA 176 WA 110	F	2	4	2	4	6	2	0	4	G
1 Fructum salutiferum	an	LR 120 LU 922	C	2	0	5	4	2	0	5	7	D
3 Frumentum Christi sum	co	GR 427 LU 1354^V	G	4	2	5	4	2	0	5	2	E
Fuerunt mihi lacrimae meae Sicut cervus	trv	GR 232 OHS 673 LU 776^{BB} *GS 112 *GB 120 *SYG 151	G	2	4	5	4	5	7	5	0	
Fuerunt sine querela Propter testamentum	rev	WA 422										
2 Fuerunt sine querela	re	LR 138 *LA 509 *WA 413	A	3	7	5	3	5	8	7	8	D

	Incipit	Type	Sources										
	Fuit autem cum discipulis Sub manu	anv	LA 342 WA 264											
1	Fuit Dominus cum Joseph	re	LR 305	a	-2	0	-2	-4	0	-4	-5	-7	D
	Fuit homo missus a Deo	sr	AR 740 LU 1499 AM 925 WA 323											
	Fuit homo missus a Deo Elisabeth Zachariae	rev	PM 158 LR 348 LA 401 WA 321											
	Fuit homo missus a Deo Inter natos	rev	LA 406											
5	Fuit homo missus a Deo	gr	GR 522 *SYG 195 *GB 196ᵛ GS 1 188	F	2	0	-3	0	2	-1	0	2	F
7 8	Fuit homo missus a Deo	re	LR 348 LA 401 *WA 320	G	2	5	2	-2	0	2	0	-2	G
	Fuit in deserto Hic praecursor	rev	WA 323											
7	Fuit sacra virgo	re	WA 433	G	-2	0	-2	0	3	2	3	7	G
8	Fuit vir vitae venerabilis	an	LR 318	c	-3	0	2	0	-1	0	-1	-3	G
1	Fuit vir vitae venerabilis	an	WA 296 LA 366	D	-2	0	2	3	5	3	2	0	D
8	Fuit vir vitae venerabilis	re	LR 320	F	2	4	2	4	2	4	6	4	G
7	Fuit vir vitae venerabilis ... qui ab ipso	re	LA 367 WA 297	G	2	5	2	-2	0	4	0	2	G
8	Fuit vir vitae venerabilis ... qui ab ipso	an	AM 851	F	2	7	6	4	6	7	4	2	G
1	Fulcite me floribus	an	AR 675 844 LU 1423 1639 AM 1048	D	2	3	5	2	3	2	0	3	D
8	Fulgebat in eo canities morum	an	PM 150	c	-3	0	-1	-3	-5	-3	-7	-3	G
1	Fulgebat in venerando	re	WA 287	D	-2	3	5	7	5	3	5	7	D
1	Fulgebunt justi et tamquam	an	AM 880 WA 393 *LA 520	D	-2	3	2	0	2	0	-2	0	D
7	Fulgebunt justi et tanquam	re	WA 429	G	2	0	2	0	2	5	4	2	G
	Fulgebunt justi et tamquam	alv	GR 575 SYG 193 GB 268ᵛ *GS 225	C	2	4	5	4	2	0	4	5	
7	Fulgebunt justi sicut lilium	re	LR 173	G	5	4	5	7	9	5	4	5	G
2	Fulgebunt justi sicut sol in conspectu	an	LR 167 AR [30] AM 633 800 811 LU 1121	D	3	0	2	0	-2	3	5	7	D
2	Fulgebunt justi sicut sol in regno	an	AM 1121	D	3	0	2	0	-2	3	5	7	D
8	Fulgentibus palmis prosternimur	an	OHS 102 LU 589	D	5	7	3	2	3	0	3	5	G
	Fulget ideo sicut sol Gloriosi Domine	rev	WA 260	a	1	3	1	0	-2	0	-2	-4	
8	Fundamenta ejus in montibus	tr	GR 402	D	3	5	2	3	5	0	-2	0	G
	Fundamenta ejus in montibus Sapientia aedificavit	grv	GR 398	D	7	3	5	7	5	3	0	-2	
	Fundamenta ejus in montibus	alv	SYG 263	G	7	9	7	5	7	9	10	12	

Fundata est domus Domini In dedicatione	rev	LR 233										
2 Fundata est domus Domini	re	PM 239 LR 234 AM 1190 LA 549	A	3	5	7	5	8	7	8	5	D
Fundata est domus Domini ... super	alv	SYG 264	D	7	9	7	5	7	0	3	5	
Fundata est domus Domini ... supra	alv	SYG 264	G	5	7	9	10	9	7	5	4	
7 Fundatur exsultatione universae	an	LR 261	b	3	0	3	5	3	1	3	6	G
Futurum est enim ut Herodes Angelus Domini	trv	GR 6**	F	2	0	2	0	-3	0	-1	0	
8 Gabriel angelus apparuit Zachariae	re	LA 407	G	-2	0	-7	-5	-2	0	2	0	G
5 Gabriel angelus apparuit Zachariae	re	LR 356 *WA 321	F	7	5	4	5	4	7	9	7	F
7 Gabriel angelus descendit ad Zachariam	an	AR 664	G	4	5	7	9	7	9	5	7	G
7 Gabriel angelus locutus ... ave	an	AR 670 LU 1417 AM 866	G	7	5	4	5	7	9	10	9	G
4 Gabriel angelus locutus ... ecce	an	AR 662 LU 1408	G	-3	-2	-3	-5	-3	-2	0	-2	E
Gabrielem archangelum scimus Gaude Maria	rev	PM 146 *AM 1195 VP 130 *LA 354 *WA 271	c	2	0	2	5	4	2	7	5	
4 Gaude Dei genitrix virgo	an	AR 125* PM 167 VP 48	C	2	5	4	2	4	2	0	2	E
1 Gaude et laetare filia Sion	an	LA 18	D	3	0	-2	3	5	7	9	7	D
2 Gaude Maria virgo	tr	GR [78] LU 1266	D	-2	-5	-3	-7	-5	-3	-2	0	D
4 Gaude Maria virgo	an	LR 251 *WA 268 LA 350 383	a	-2	0	3	7	5	3	5	7	a
6 Gaude Maria virgo	re	PM 146 AM 1195 VP 130 *LA 354 WA 271	a	-2	3	5	7	5	7	8	7	c
8 Gaude mater Anna	hy	AM 985	G	2	0	-2	-3	-2	0	2	5	G
7 Gaude mater ecclesia	hy	ST 123	G	2	0	-2	0	2	0	2	4	G
5 Gaude mater ecclesia	hy	ST 138	F	2	4	7	9	7	5	7	9	F
5 Gaude mater ecclesia	hy	VP 206	F	4	7	9	7	6	7	9	11	F
8 Gaude sacrata meritis	hy	ST 401	G	-2	0	2	5	4	5	7	5	G
8 Gaude sacrata meritis	hy	ST 145	G	2	0	2	0	-2	2	0	5	G
3 Gaude virgo Maria	an	WA 359	G	2	5	4	5	4	2	0	2	E
6 Gaude visceribus mater in intimis	hy	ST 434	F	-5	-3	0	2	0	2	4	2	F

3	Gaude visceribus mater in intimis	hy	ST 339	D	2	3	5	3	2	5	7	10	E
3	Gaude visceribus mater in intimis	hy	ST 299 (var)	D	2	3	5	7	5	7	5	10	E
3	Gaude visceribus mater in intimis	hy	ST 299 397	D	2	3	5	7	5	10	12	10	E
2	Gaude visceribus mater in intimis	hy	ST 96	C	2	5	7	9	7	4	2	0	D
3	Gaude visceribus mater in intimis	hy	ST 236	D	3	5	7	5	7	5	10	12	E
6	Gaudeamus omnes fideles	an	PM 37 *WA 32 *LA 38	F	2	0	2	4	0	2	0	4	F
1	Gaudeamus omnes in ... Agathae	int	GR 436 LU 1368 *SYG 50 GB 49^v	C	2	9	10	9	7	9	7	5	D
7	Gaudeamus omnes in ... Agathae	re	WA 275	G	5	4	5	7	5	7	9	7	G
1	Gaudeamus omnes in ... Annae	int	GR 559 LU 1571	C	2	9	10	9	7	9	7	5	D
1	Gaudeamus omnes in ... assumptione	int	GR (30) *SYG 215 GS s	C	2	9	10	9	7	9	7	5	D
4	Gaudeamus omnes in ... Bartholomaei	int	GB 226^v	D	3	0	2	3	2	3	2	3	E
1	Gaudeamus omnes in ... Benedicti	int	GR (16)	C	2	9	10	9	7	9	7	5	D
1	Gaudeamus omnes in ... boni consilii	int	GR 24**	C	2	9	10	9	7	9	7	5	D
1	Gaudeamus omnes in ... Joachim	int	GR (28)	C	2	9	10	9	7	9	7	5	D
1	Gaudeamus omnes in ... Josaphat	int	GR 653 LU 1751	C	2	9	10	9	7	9	7	5	D
1	Gaudeamus omnes in ... monachorum	int	GR (33)	C	2	9	10	9	7	9	7	5	D
1	Gaudeamus omnes in ... reginae	int	LU 1476^B	C	2	9	10	9	7	9	7	5	D
1	Gaudeamus omnes in ... sanctorum	int	GR 647 LU 1724 GB 237	C	2	9	10	9	7	9	7	5	D
1	Gaudeamus omnes in ... solemnitate	int	GR 619 LU 1556 1675	C	2	9	10	9	7	9	7	5	D
1	Gaudeamus omnes in ... Thomae	int	GR 46 LU 437	C	2	9	10	9	7	9	7	5	D
8	Gaudeamus universi ecclesiae	an	WA 287	G	-2	-3	-2	0	2	0	-2	2	G
2	Gaudeat ecclesia festa colens annua	hy	ST 159	D	-2	0	3	2	0	2	0	-2	D
	Gaudebunt labia mea Repleatur os meum	rev	LA 97 WA 67										
5	Gaudebunt labia mea	re	LA 98 WA 68	a	-4	0	3	2	3	0	-2	0	F
5	Gaudens gaudebo in Domino	int	GR 77**	c	-3	0	-3	-7	-3	-5	-3	-2	F
3	Gaudens gaudebo in Domino	int	GR 400 LU 1316	E	1	-2	3	0	3	5	3	5	E
1	Gaudens in verbo sed turbata virgo	hy	ST 378	D	-2	0	2	3	5	7	5	3	D
2	Gaudens perenniter felicitas	tr	SYG 238	D	-2	0	-2	-5	-2	0	-2	0	D
	Gaudent angeli et exsultant Fidelis sermo	rev	LA 471										
	Gaudent angeli et laetantur Celebremus conversionem	rev	LA 345 WA 266										
6	Gaudent in caelis animae	an	AR 577^{14} [48] LU 262^3 1160 *AM 653 739 1122 *WA 351 *LA 479	F	2	0	-1	-3	0	2	4	2	F

	Incipit		Source										
8	Gaudeo in passionibus	of	GR 68**	F	-3	0	4	2	0	2	4	2	G
	Gaudeo plane quia hostia 　　Beatus Laurentius dixit ego	rev	LA 438 WA 349										
8	Gaudeo plane quia hostia	re	LA 439 WA 349	G	5	3	5	7	5	7	5	7	G
	Gaudete et exsultate 　　Beati estis sancti	rev	LR 389 WA 396										
8	Gaudete et exsultate	an	LR 144 *LA 509	a	-4	-2	0	3	0	2	-2	0	G
1	Gaudete in Domino semper	int	GR 6 LU 334 SYG 6 GB 5 GS 4	D	-2	2	-2	2	0	2	3	5	D
	Gaudete justi in Domino 　　Ecce oculi Domini	intv	GB 171^v										
	Gaudete justi in Domino 　　Exclamaverunt ad te	intv	GB 163^v										
	Gaudete justi in Domino 　　Gaudeamus omnes ... sanctorum	intv	GB 237										
	Gaudete justi in Domino 　　Judicant sancti gentes	intv	GB 210										
	Gaudete justi in Domino 　　Misericordia Domini	inv	GB 146										
	Gaudete justi in Domino 　　Sapientiam sanctorum	intv	GB 194^v										
	Gaudete justi in Domino	alv	GR 406 LU 1327 *SYG 169	F	2	-3	2	4	2	4	5	4	
	Gaudete justi in Domino 　　Vox exsultationis	rev	LA 390	G	4	2	4	5	4	2	0	2	
1	Gaudete justi in Domino alleluia	co	GR [20] LU 1152 *GS 218 *GB 153 SYG 169	D	-2	0	3	2	0	2	3	0	D
1	Gaudete justi in Domino alleluia	re	LR 174	D	-2	0	3	2	0	3	0	7	D
4	Gaudium mundi nova stella caeli	hy	ST 467	G	2	4	2	4	5	4	2	0	b
	Gavisi sunt discipuli	sr	AR 43 LU 249 LA 241										
	Gavisi sunt discipuli	alv	SYG 163	F	-1	-3	-5	-3	-1	0	2	0	
6	Gavisi sunt discipuli	an	LA 230	F	-1	2	4	0	-3	-5	0	-1	F
1	Gemma caelestis pretiosa regis	hy	AM 961	D	2	3	0	-2	0	3	2	0	D
	Gemma lucens 　　Rosa vernans	alv	VP 52	G	2	0	5	0	2	0	-3	-5	
	Gemma virginum lux	sr	WA 310										
8	Generatio haec prava	an	AR 375 AM 348 *WA 89 *LA 135	G	5	2	-2	0	4	7	5	4	G
6	Gens et regnum quod non servierit	an	AR 894^7 LU 1706 AM 1093	F	-3	-5	0	2	0	2	4	7	F
1	Gens fidelis jucundetur	hy	ST 315	D	3	7	8	7	5	3	5	3	D
7 8	Genti peccatrici populo	re	LA 306 *WA 186	c	-1	-3	-1	0	2	0	2	0	G
8	Gentis Polonae gloria	hy	AR 886 LU 1697	G	-2	-3	-2	0	-2	0	2	5	G

6	Genuisti qui te fecit	an	AR 882[3] LU 1686	F	2	0	2	4	0	-1	2	-1	F
1	Genuisti qui te fecit	an	AM 1082	D	2	3	5	2	5	7	3	2	D
2	Genuit puerpera regem	an	AR 264 LU 396 AM 240 WA 31 *LA 37	F	-1	0	-3	-1	-3	-5	-1	-3	D
	Genus electum gens sancta Laudem dicite	rev	WA 396	G	5	4	0	2	4	2	5	7	
1 2	Germinaverunt campi	re	LA 26 WA 18	D	2	0	-2	0	3	5	3	5	D
1	Germinavit radix Jesse	an	AR 295 LU 443 *AM 272 WA 50 LA 65	D	2	3	5	2	5	7	3	2	D
8	Gertrudis arca numinis	hy	AM 1129	G	2	4	5	4	2	0	2	-2	G
1	Gesta sanctorum martyrum	hy	ST 10	F	2	5	7	5	2	5	4	2	D
1	Gloria Christe tuo	re	WA 300	D	-2	0	3	5	7	0	-2	-5	D
	Gloria claritas decus Te laudant angeli	rev	WA 28	a	-2	-5	-4	-2	2	-2	0	-5	
	Gloria creatori omnipotenti Ecce Adam quasi unus	rev	LA 112	G	5	2	4	5	7	5	4	5	
	Gloria Deo patri cuncta Impetum fecerunt	rev	WA 34	a	-2	-4	-5	-7	-4	-5	-7	-9	
	Gloria Deo patri sit Benedicamus patrem	rev	LA 477	G	5	4	0	2	4	2	4	5	
2	Gloria dignos colimus triumphos	hy	ST 393	D	-2	0	2	3	0	3	0	-2	D
	Gloria et divitiae Beatus vir qui metuit	rev	LR 165										
6	Gloria et divitiae	of	GR 572 LU 1587	F	2	0	4	2	4	2	0	2	F
	Gloria et divitiae Beatus vir qui timet	trv	GR [8] LU 1134 *GS 203 *GB 52[v] *SYG 55	G	2	4	5	4	5	7	5	0	
1	Gloria et honor Deo	an	WA 160	F	-3	-5	-3	4	5	4	2	4	D
	Gloria et honore coronasti	sr	AR 809 [20] LU 1124 1587 AM 641 995										
5	Gloria et honore coronasti	gr	GR [7] LU 1133 SYG 201	F	4	5	4	2	4	2	0	2	F
2	Gloria et honore coronasti ... Domine Deus	co	SYG 214	D	-5	-2	0	-2	0	-2	0	2	D
	Gloria et honore coronasti ... Domine et constituisti Egredimini et videte	intv	GR 11**										
	Gloria et honore coronasti ... Domine et constituisti	alv	GS 208	D	-2	0	3	5	7	5	3	5	
7	Gloria et honore coronasti ... Domine et constituisti	re	LR 160 LA 526 WA 418	G	2	0	2	5	4	5	7	5	G
	Gloria et honore coronasti ... Domine et constituisti	alv	GB 23 *SYG 201	G	2	0	5	7	9	5	4	5	
6	Gloria et honore coronasti ... et constituisti	gr	SYG 217	F	2	0	-1	2	4	5	2	0	F

1 Gloria et honore coronasti ... et constituisti	of	GR [2] OTT 133 LU 1137 SYG 34 GB 23^V *GS 202 W	F	2	4	5	4	5	4	7	6	D
7 Gloria et honore coronasti ... et constituisti	int	SYG 200 GB 233^V *GS 204	G	7	10	12	10	7	5	7	4	G
Gloria in excelsis Deo		BOS #4 (nm)										
Gloria		BOS #14 (nm)										
Gloria		BOS #33 (nm)										
Gloria		BOS #40 (nm)										
Gloria		BOS #50 (nm)										
8 Gloria X		GR 36* BOS #9 LU 43	c	-3	-5	-8	-7	-5	-3	-1	-3	G
5 Gloria VIII		GR 29* LU 37	c	-3	-5	-7	-5	-3	-5	-7	0	F
III Gloria		BOS #8	c	-3	-5	-7	-3	0	2	0	-1	F
III Gloria		BOS #7	c	-3	-5	-3	-1	0	-3	-7	-5	F
IV Gloria		BOS #6	c	-3	-5	-3	-1	0	-3	-5	-7	G
3 Gloria XIV		GR 48* LU 54	c	-3	-5	-3	-1	0	-3	-5	-3	E
8 Gloria ad lib I		GR 83* LU 86	G	-3	0	2	4	5	2	0	2	G
1 Gloria XIII		GR 45* LU 51	a	-2	-4	-2	0	-2	-5	-4	-7	D
I Gloria		BOS #18	a	-2	-4	-2	0	-2	-4	-5	-4	D
4 Gloria I		BOS #12 GR 5* LU 16	b	-2	-4	-2	0	-2	0	1	0	b
I Gloria		BOS #19	a	-2	-4	-2	0	-2	0	2	0	D
1 Gloria II		GR 8* LU 19	a	-2	-4	-2	0	-2	1	0	3	D
8 Gloria V		GR 18* LU 28	G	-2	-3	-5	-3	-2	0	-2	2	G
IV Gloria		BOS #25	G	-2	-3	-5	-3	-2	0	2	0	G
I Gloria		BOS #16	a	-2	0	-7	-9	-5	-4	-5	-7	D
6 Gloria VII		BOS #1 GR 25* LU 34	e	-2	0	-2	-4	-2	0	-2	0	F
II Gloria		BOS #15	a	-2	0	-2	-4	0	2	0	-2	E
I Gloria		BOS #17	a	-2	0	-2	0	-2	-4	-5	-4	D
4 Gloria ad lib IV		GR 89* LU 88	a	-2	0	2	0	-2	0	-2	0	E
IV Gloria		BOS #24	G	-2	0	2	4	5	2	0	-3	G
IV Gloria		BOS #5	c	-1	-3	-5	0	2	0	2	-3	G
IV Gloria		BOS #41	F	-1	-3	-1	-3	-1	-3	-5	-1	G
II Gloria		BOS #11	b	1	-2	-4	-2	0	1	-2	-4	E
II Gloria		BOS #47	E	1	0	-2	0	3	1	0	-2	E
II Gloria		BOS #44	E	1	0	-2	3	5	7	8	7	E
II Gloria		BOS #45	E	1	0	-2	3	5	7	8	7	E
II Gloria		BOS #46	E	1	0	-2	3	5	7	8	7	E

II Gloria	BOS #10	b	1	0	1	-2	0	-7	-4	-2	E
II Gloria	BOS #42	E	1	3	0	1	0	-2	3	5	E
8 Gloria III	BOS #20 GR 12* LU 23	G	2	0	-2	0	2	0	5	0	G
IV Gloria	BOS #21	G	2	0	-2	0	2	0	5	0	G
IV Gloria	BOS #23	G	2	0	-2	0	2	4	5	2	G
7 Gloria IX	GR 32* LU 40	G	2	0	-2	0	2	4	5	4	G
2 Gloria ad lib III	BOS #22 GR 87* LU 89	G	2	0	-2	0	3	2	3	5	D
II Gloria	BOS #31	F	2	0	-1	0	2	0	6	0	E
IV Gloria	BOS #3	c	2	0	2	-2	-3	-2	-3	-5	G
I Gloria	BOS #2	c	2	0	2	4	5	4	2	-3	D
III Gloria	BOS #38	F	2	0	2	4	5	4	2	0	F
III Gloria	BOS #27	F	2	0	2	4	5	4	2	7	F
I Gloria	BOS #53	D	2	3	5	2	3	2	0	5	D
I Gloria	BOS #29	F	2	4	0	2	4	2	0	2	D
8 Gloria VI	BOS #30 GR 22* LU 32	F	2	4	0	2	4	6	4	2	G
III Gloria	BOS #37	F	2	4	0	4	6	7	6	4	F
III Gloria	BOS #36	F	2	4	0	5	4	2	4	0	F
III Gloria	BOS #39	F	2	4	2	0	-3	-1	0	2	F
I Gloria	BOS #28	F	2	4	2	0	2	4	2	4	D
4 Gloria IV	BOS #56 GR 15* LU 26	C	2	5	4	5	7	4	7	5	E
I Gloria	BOS #54	D	3	0	-2	3	5	7	0	3	D
IV Gloria	BOS #52	D	3	2	3	5	3	0	2	3	G
4 Gloria XV	BOS #43 GR 51* LU 57	E	3	5	3	5	3	0	3	5	E
2 Gloria ad lib II	BOS #13 GR 85* LU 88	a	3	5	7	5	3	7	5	7	D
III Gloria	BOS #26	F	4	5	7	9	12	7	9	7	F
III Gloria	BOS #32	F	4	6	7	9	11	12	11	9	F
III Gloria	BOS #35	F	4	7	4	6	4	2	0	4	F
III Gloria	BOS #34	F	4	7	9	6	7	4	7	4	F
2 Gloria XI	BOS #51 GR 39* LU 46	D	5	3	2	3	5	3	2	0	D
I Gloria	BOS #49	D	7	3	2	0	2	5	2	3	D
4 Gloria XII	GR 42* LU 49	D	7	5	3	2	0	2	3	5	E
II Gloria	BOS #48	D	7	5	3	2	0	2	3	7	E
III Gloria	BOS #55	C	7	9	7	5	4	2	0	2	C

	Gloria in excelsis Deo Hodie nobis caelorum	rev	LR 56 LU 375 LA 32 WA 27										
8	Gloria in excelsis Deo ... alleluia	an	AR 267 LU 402 AM 243 *WA 32 LA 38	F	2	4	2	0	2	4	2	4	G
3	Gloria laudis resonet in ore	an	AR 518 LU 914 *AM 536 *WA 158	E	-2	3	5	8	7	8	7	5	E
1	Gloria laus et honor	hy	ST 484	a	-2	-4	-2	0	-2	-4	-2	0	D
1	Gloria laus et honor	hy	GR 176 OHS 99 LU 586 *WA 210	a	-2	0	-2	-4	-2	0	-4	-5	D
2	Gloria laus et honor	hy	ST 485 GB 107^v	A	5	8	7	5	3	5	8	10	D
1	Gloria laus et honor	hy	PM 59 *GS 83	D	7	5	7	5	3	5	7	5	D
8	Gloria Libani data	an	AR 787 LU 1558	G	5	2	0	-2	0	2	0	2	G
1	Gloria Libani data	an	AM 971	D	7	5	7	9	7	5	7	10	D
5	Gloria patri genitoque	re	WA 160	a	-4	0	3	5	3	5	3	5	F
	Gloria sit altissimo Iste est Joannes	rev	PM 33	F	2	0	-1	-3	0	2	0	4	
	Gloria sit Deo patri Haec est vera fraternitas	rev	LA 517	G	5	4	2	4	2	0	-3	0	
	Gloria sit Deo qui omnia Cum transisset	rev	WA 129										
	Gloria sit patri summo creatori Impii super justum	rev	WA 38(35)	G	7	9	10	7	9	5	7	9	
8	Gloria tibi Domine	hy	AM 997	F	2	4	7	2	4	0	2	7	G
1	Gloria tibi trinitas	an	AR 518 LU 914 AM 535 *WA 158	D	2	3	0	-2	3	5	3	5	D
	Gloriabuntur in te omnes In nomine Jesu	intv	GR 561 LU 1574										
6	Gloriabuntur in te omnes	of	GR 526 LU 1508 OTT 135 SYG 200 GB 201^v GS 218	D	3	5	3	0	3	5	3	-2	F
1	Gloriam concinunt Deo	an	WA 359	D	3	0	-2	3	5	3	5	7	D
	Gloriam et magnum decorem Domine praevenisti Saturninum	intv	SYG 229										
6	Gloriam martyrum recolamus	an	LA 392	c	-3	-5	0	4	2	4	5	4	c
6	Gloriam mundi	an	WA 240	c	2	4	0	-2	-3	-2	0	2	c
7	Glorificati hominis viderunt	an	WA 404	G	5	4	5	7	9	7	5	4	G
	Glorificavit eum in conspectu regum Elegit eum	rev	PM 311										
	Gloriosa dicta sunt	sr	WA 359										
8	Gloriosa dicta sunt	an	LR 265	c	-3	0	-1	-5	-3	-5	-7	-5	G
8	Gloriosa dicta sunt	co	GR 404 LU 1319	G	2	0	-2	0	2	4	5	0	G
	Gloriosa dicta sunt Fundamenta ejus	trv	GR 402	G	2	4	5	7	5	0	2	0	
1	Gloriosa es Maria Magdalene	re	WA 335	C	2	0	2	4	5	4	2	4	D

4	Gloriosa festivitas	hy	ST 458	D	2	7	5	2	0	3	2	0	E
1	Gloriosa magnifici voluntas	an	WA 287	a	-2	-4	-2	0	-7	-4	-5	-7	D
	Gloriosae Mariae virginis nativitatem / Cum jucunditate	rev	WA 367										
	Gloriosae Virginis Mariae nativitatem	alv	GB 231^v	F	2	4	2	-1	0	2	0	2	
	Gloriosae virginis Mariae ortum / Hodie nata est ... gloriosa	rev	WA 365										
7	Gloriosae virginis Mariae ortum	re	LA 457 *WA 365	c	-1	0	2	0	2	4	2	4	G
3	Gloriosae virginis Mariae ortum	an	WA 368	G	2	0	2	4	5	2	4	2	E
1	Gloriosae virginis Mariae ortum	an	AR 833 LU 1623^F AM 1031	C	2	5	7	5	4	2	0	4	D
1	Gloriosi Domine testis	re	WA 260	D	-2	0	3	2	0	-2	3	5	D
3	Gloriosi principes terrae	an	LA 418	G	2	0	2	4	5	4	2	4	E
6	Gloriosi principes terrae	an	AR 774 *AM 958 *WA 325	F	2	0	2	5	4	2	4	2	F
	Gloriosus apparuisti in conspectu	sr	AR 808 LU 1585 AM 999										
4	Gloriosus apparuisti in conspectu	an	WA 380 *LA 465	G	2	5	7	5	7	9	7	5	a
8	Gloriosus confessor ... Benedictus	an	AM 852 WA 334 LA 374	G	-2	-5	-2	0	2	0	-2	2	G
3	Gloriosus confessor ... orationem	an	AM 964	G	2	0	4	5	4	5	7	5	E
1	Gloriosus Dei amicus	re	VP 254 *WA 260	D	3	5	3	0	2	3	2	0	D
1	Gloriosus Dei martyr	re	VP 199	D	-2	0	3	5	3	2	0	2	D
1	Gloriosus Deus in sanctis	gr	GR [22] LU 1163 *SYG 40 GB 43^v *GS 212	A	3	5	8	5	7	5	3	7	D
7	Gloriosus es Oswaldus	re	WA 390	G	2	0	2	0	2	0	7	5	G
6	Grata facta est a Domino	re	LA 321 *WA 244	C	2	0	2	0	2	4	0	-3	C
4	Grates tibi Jesu novas	hy	ST 11	F	-3	-1	-3	-5	-3	-1	2	4	E
	Gratia Dei in me vacua / Qui operatus	rev	LA 424 WA 330										
4	Gratia Dei in me vacua	an	AR 609 756 LU 1348 AM 793 941 *WA 266 *LA 431	a	-2	0	3	5	3	5	7	3	a
	Gratia Dei in me vacua / Qui operatus est	grv	GR 418 LU 1345 GB 208 *GS 178 SYG 204	c	2	0	-1	0	-3	0	2	0	
	Gratia Dei sum id quod sum / Gratia Dei	anv	WA 266 LA 431										
8	Gratia Dei sum id quod sum	re	LA 429	G	2	5	4	2	5	4	5	2	G
4	Gratias ago Deo	an	WA 349	G	-3	-2	0	-3	-2	0	2	0	E
	Gratias ago tibi	see also Gratias tibi ago											
	Gratias ago tibi Domine Jesu / Interrogatus te	alv	WA 348 LA 436										

Gratias Domini in aeternum Extuli electum		intv	LU 1623[A]									
Gratias Domini in aeternum Facies unctionis		intv	OHS 413 LU 661									
Gratias tibi ago			<u>see also</u> Gratias ago tibi									
Gratias tibi ago Domine Jesu Beatus Laurentius oravit		rev	LA 440 WA 350									
Gratias tibi ago Domine Jesu Ego autem adjuvata		rev	LA 361 WA 274									
2	Gratias tibi ago Domine Jesu	an	WA 349	D	2	0	-2	0	3	2	-2	0 [D]
7	Gratias tibi ago Domine quia	an	AR 625 LU 1371 *AM 807 WA 276 *LA 363	d	-3	0	2	0	-2	0	-3 -2	G
1	Gratias tibi Deus gratias	an	AR 517 LU 907 AM 534	C	2	0	4	2	5	4	0	2 D
6	Gratias tibi Domine	re	WA 385	D	-2	3	5	7	5	7	10	5 F
2	Gratificavit nos Deus	tr	GR 538	D	-2	0	-2	-5	-2	0	-2	0 D
2	Gratuletur omnis caro	hy	ST 446	D	2	-2	0	3	5	7	5	3 D
8	Gratuletur omnis caro	hy	ST 221	C	2	4	5	7	9	7	5	12 G
	Gravis quidem est Domine si adhuc	rev	LA 481									
8	Gregem tuum Domine	an	VP 30	G	2	5	2	5	4	0	7	5 G
1	Gregorius monachorum	an	AM 833	C	2	9	11	9	7	9	7	5 D
3	Gregorius praesul meritis	re	PM 140 VP 123	E	-2	3	5	8	7	5	7	8 E
6	Gregorius respiciens	an	AM 834	F	-1	-3	-1	0	-5	-3	0	2 F
8	Gressus meos dirige Domine	of	GR 137 OTT 39 *SYG 99 *GB 88[v] *GS 62	F	2	4	2	-1	0	-3	0	4 G
	Gressus meos dirige secundum	alv	GR [143]	c	2	0	4	2	0	-3	-1 -3	
	Gustate et videte quoniam	alv	GR 616	D	-2	0	2	3	5	7	5	3
3	Gustate et videte quoniam	co	GR 341 LU 1015 GS 150 *SYG 244 *GB 251[v]	G	2	5	2	5	0	2	0	-2 E
8	Gustate et videte quoniam	tr	GR 95**	D	3	5	3	0	2	-2	0	3 G
	Gustavit et vidit Os suum	rev	LR 226									
6	Gyrum caeli circuivi	re	LA 277 *WA 168	G	2	5	2	4	2	0	2	0 G

1	Habebitis autem hunc diem	an	AM 953	D	-2	3	5	3	7	5	3	2	D
1	Habebitis autem hunc diem	an	AR 769 LU 1538^v	C	2	5	2	0	5	7	9	10	D
	Habet in vestimento	alv	GR 641 LU 1712	D	-2	0	3	0	-2	2	3	5	
7	Habet in vestimento	an	AR 894^{13} OHS 832 LU 1718 AM 1097	G	5	4	5	7	9	7	5	9	G
4	Habitabit in tabernaculo	an	OHS 592 LR 153 LU 752 WA 124 416 *LA 201 523	F	-1	-3	0	-1	-3	-1	0	2	E
4	Habitare fratres	an	WA 66	E	-2	0	-2	-4	-2	1	-2	1	E
8	Habitat Deus Oswaldus	an	WA 283	F	2	4	2	0	4	7	6	2	G
1	Habuit Gertrudis potestatem	an	AM 1131	D	2	-2	0	7	9	7	5	3	D
8	Haec accepit benedictionem	an	LR 289	G	2	5	4	5	2	0	4	5	G
6	Haec aula accipiet	an	WA 317	E	1	-2	-4	-2	1	3	1	3	F
8	Haec autem scripta sunt	an	LA 230	G	-2	0	2	0	-2	-3	-2	-5	G
	Haec cogitaverunt et erraverunt Dixerunt impii	rev	WA 116										
	Haec cogitaverunt et erraverunt Viri impii	rev	OHS 184 (nm)										
	Haec dies quam fecit Vidi aquam	anv	SYG 145										
	Haec dies quam fecit Pascha nostrum	cov	SYG 154										
2	Haec dies quam fecit	an	AR 445 OHS 730 771 LU 783	a	-2	1	0	-2	0	-4	0	3	a
2	Haec dies quam fecit	gr	GR 241 LU 778 OHS 709 SYG 152 *GB 125 GS 117	a	-2	1	0	-2	0	-4	0	3	a
	Haec dies quam fecit	alv	GR 259 OHS 827 LU 805 GS 123 SYG 161 GB 142^v	c	-1	2	0	-1	0	2	0	-3	
	Haec dies quam fecit Benedictus qui venit	ofv	OTT 64 GB 144 SYG 161	F	2	4	2	4	2	0	2	4	
2	Haec est clara dies	hy	ST 496	D	7	9	7	5	7	5	3	5	D
8	Haec est dies qua candidae	hy	AR 884 AM 1086	G	2	4	5	4	2	0	2	-2	G
	Haec est dies quam fecit	sr	LA 86 WA 62										
4	Haec est dies quam fecit	an	PM 147	E	1	0	-2	3	1	0	-2	0	E
	Haec est domus Domini	sr	AR [112] [113] LU 1246										
	Haec est domus Domini O quam metuendus	rev	LR 239										
	Haec est domus Domini Domus mea	trv	SYG 264 (nm)										
1	Haec est domus Domini	an	AR [107] LU 1247 AM 697 *WA 319 *LA 552	D	3	2	0	-2	3	7	5	7	D

3 Haec est generatio	an	WA 421	E	-2	3	5	3	5	8	7	8	E
Haec est generatio	alv	GR 114**	G	2	0	5	4	5	7	9	5	
3 Haec est generatio	an	LR 383	G	5	4	2	0	4	2	5	4	E
1 Haec est Jerusalem civitas	re	LA 228 *WA 142	G	-2	0	-2	-3	0	4	0	2	D
3 Haec est quae nescivit	an	AR [88] LU 1211 *AM 679 WA 353 *LA 347	E	1	0	1	-2	3	5	8	7	E
1 Haec est regina virginum	an	PM 271 *WA 354	C	2	4	5	7	4	5	7	5	D
1 Haec est vera fraternitas	re	PM 222 LR 187 LA 409 WA 422	a	-2	0	-2	0	-2	0	-2	-4	D
Haec est vera fraternitas	alv	GR 495 LU 1492^A 1508 GB 231^V	G	2	0	5	4	5	7	5	4	
8 Haec est vera fraternitas	re	LA 517	G	2	4	2	0	-2	0	2	0	G
1 Haec est vera fraternitas	an	LA 521	D	3	0	-2	3	5	3	5	7	D
1 Haec est virgo prudens	re	LR 217 LA 545	D	2	3	5	3	0	3	5	3	D
Haec est virgo sapiens et una Haec est virgo prudens	rev	LR 217										
1 Haec est virgo sapiens et una	an	AR [87] LU 1210 AM 678 *WA 434 *LA 545	D	-2	3	5	3	5	7	5	8	D
Haec est virgo sapiens et una	alv	GR [57] LU 1222	C	2	4	2	4	2	0	7	9	
Haec est virgo sapiens quam	alv	GS 228	a	-2	-4	-5	-9	-5	-2	-4	-5	
7 Haec est virgo sapiens quam	re	LR 225 *LA 544 WA 432	G	2	0	2	5	7	5	4	5	G
1 Haec est virgo sapiens quam	an	AR [87] LU 1210 AM 678 *WA 434 *LA 546	D	3	2	0	-2	3	7	5	7	D
Haec forma prae filiis Exaltata est virgo	rev	LA 445										
8 Haec locutus sum vobis	an	AR 498 AM 515 LU 858 LA 254	G	-2	-5	-3	-2	0	2	0	-2	G
4 Haec locutus sum vobis	an	WA 151	E	-2	0	-2	-4	-2	0	-4	0	E
2 Haec mulier sancta	an	WA 335	D	-2	0	-2	0	2	0	3	2	D
Haec requies ejus in saeculum Exsulta et lauda	rev	LR 372	c	2	0	-1	-3	-5	-7	-3	-7	
7 Haec requies mea	an	WA 439	d	-3	0	2	0	-3	-2	0	-2	G
Haec speciosum forma Videte miraculum	rev	WA 268(271)	c	2	0	-1	-3	-5	-3	0	-5	
4 Haec tua sunt Christe	re	WA 316	C	2	5	2	4	5	4	2	5	E
1 Haec tua virgo monimenta laudis	hy	ST 354	D	7	3	5	3	2	0	-2	0	D
2 Haec virgo sancta	an	WA 435	D	-5	-2	0	3	0	-2	0	3	D
7 Haec virgo sancta	re	WA 433	d	-2	0	-2	0	3	2	0	-2	G
4 Hanc ergo salvator	an	WA 359	F	-3	-5	-3	-1	2	4	2	0	E

	Incipit	Type	Sources	Mode									Final
6	Hanc ergo toto corde	an	WA 335	F	-3	-5	-3	0	2	5	4	2	F
5	Haurietis aquas	an	AR 238 *AM 213 WA 17 LA 22	F	4	7	6	4	7	9	7	4	F
	Hebraeorum gens perfida Impii super justum	rev	WA 38(35)	G	7	9	10	9	7	9	5	7	
	Hei	see also Heu											
2	Hei mihi Domine quia peccavi	re	AR [165] LU 1791 *WA 436 *LA 555	C	2	4	5	4	2	4	2	0	D
7	Helena Constantini mater	an	WA 309 *LA 397	G	7	4	7	9	7	4	7	9	G
7	Helena sancta dixit	an	WA 309 *LA 398	G	4	5	7	4	5	7	5	2	G
	Heri enim rex noster Hesterna die	rev	LA 46										
1	Herodes enim metuebat Joannem	re	LA 451	D	-2	0	3	2	3	0	-2	0	D
8	Herodes enim metuebat Joannem	an	PM 184	G	2	0	-2	0	2	0	2	0	G
3	Herodes enim tenuit	an	WA 363	G	-3	-2	0	-2	-3	-5	0	4	E
3	Herodes enim tenuit	an	AR 829 LU 1620 AM 1026 *LA 454	G	2	5	2	5	4	0	2	5	E
1	Herodes enim tenuit	re	WA 362	D	3	0	-2	3	5	7	5	3	D
1	Herodes iratus occidit	an	AR 283 LU 427 *AM 260 *WA 46 *LA 61	D	-2	3	5	3	7	5	8	7	D
8	Herodes rex apposuit	an	AR 799 LU 1577 *AM 989	G	5	2	0	2	0	2	0	2	G
1	Herodes videns	an	WA 43	D	-2	3	5	3	5	7	5	7	D
6	Herodis insanus furor	hy	ST 20	C	2	5	4	2	-1	0	5	4	C
1	Hesterna die Dominus	an	LA 43	D	-2	3	5	3	5	7	9	7	D
7	Hesterna die Dominus	re	LA 46 *WA 36	G	2	-2	0	2	4	5	7	5	G
	Heu	see also Hei											
	Heu me fili mi Sufficiebat nobis	rev	LA 289 WA 176										
2	Heu me quia incolatus meus	an	AR [143] LU 1773 AM 1151 *WA 435 *LA 560	F	-1	-3	-5	-3	-5	-3	0	-1	D
7	Hi accipient benedictionem	an	PM 329 LU 1846 VP 274	G	2	5	7	5	7	9	10	12	G
	Hi empti sunt ex omnibus Centum quadraginta	rev	LA 60 WA 45										
1	Hi novissimi una hora	an	AR 346 AM 316 LA 115	D	7	10	7	5	7	8	7	5	D
1	Hi qui amicti sunt	an	AR 763 LU 1528 *AM 948^B	D	-2	0	3	0	2	0	-2	3	D
1	Hi qui linguis loquuntur	an	LA 266	D	7	10	7	5	7	3	5	9	D
8	Hi sancti viri ... Dionysii	re	WA 388	G	-2	0	-7	-5	-2	0	2	0	G
1	Hi sancti viri ... Eleutherii	an	WA 389	D	-2	3	5	3	5	7	5	3	D

1 Hi sunt ecclesiarum	an	WA 325		C	2	4	5	2	5	4	5	7	D
Hi sunt qui cum mulieribus Ambulabunt mecum	rev	LA 57											
Hi sunt qui cum mulieribus Isti sunt sancti qui non	rev	LA 59 WA 45											
1 Hi sunt qui cum mulieribus	an	AR 286 LU 426 AM 262 WA 47 LA 62		D	7	8	7	5	7	8	7	5	D
Hi sunt qui tollentes Ecce vidi agnum	rev	LA 59											
1 Hi sunt qui venerunt	an	AR 763 LU 1528 AM 949		D	7	10	7	9	7	5	7	5	D
Hic accipiet benedictionem Beatus vir qui suffert	rev	LR 160											
6 Hic accipiet benedictionem	an	LU 1827		F	2	4	0	-1	-3	-5	0	2	F
7 Hic accipiet benedictionem	an	PM 329 LR 153 197 WA 416 425 LA 523		G	2	5	7	5	7	9	10	12	G
8 Hic caeli terraeque Petro	an	WA 278		G	-5	-2	0	2	0	2	0	-2	G
Hic Deus meus et honorabo eum Cantemus Domino	trv	GR 229 OHS 652 LU 776^R *GS 111 *GB 119 *SYG 150		G	2	4	5	4	5	4	5	7	
2 Hic dum matris adhuc	an	WA 238		D	-2	0	3	2	3	5	3	2	D
Hic erit magnus Ecce concipies	rev	WA 302		c	-1	-5	-3	0	-1	-3	0	2	
8 Hic est beatissimus evangelista	an	VP 84		F	2	0	4	7	6	2	4	2	G
8 Hic est beatissimus evangelista	re	LA 50 WA 40		F	2	4	2	4	6	4	2	4	G
1 Hic est dies praeclarus in quo decus	re	LR 370		D	7	10	12	10	7	3	7	5	D
8 Hic est dies praeclarus in quo salvator	re	LR 81 LA 68 *WA 55		F	2	4	2	4	2	4	6	4	G
2 Hic est dies verus Dei	hy	ST 278		D	-2	0	3	5	3	0	5	3	D
7 Hic est dies verus Dei	hy	ST 35		G	2	0	-2	0	2	0	5	7	G
7 Hic est dies verus Dei	hy	ST 9		G	2	0	-2	0	2	5	7	5	G
6 Hic est dies verus Dei	hy	ST 418		F	2	4	2	4	2	0	4	7	F
Hic est discipulus ille quem diligebat Hic est beatissimus	rev	LA 50 WA 40											
Hic est discipulus ille qui testimonium	alv	GR 39 LU 422 *GS 17 GB 24^V SYG 24		D	-2	0	2	3	5	7	5	3	
3 Hic est discipulus ille qui testimonium	an	AR 279 LU 421 *AM 255 WA 42 LA 55		G	2	5	2	5	4	2	0	2	E
3 Hic est discipulus meus	an	AR 279 LU 424 *AM 256 *WA 42 *LA 55		G	2	5	2	5	4	0	2	4	E
7 Hic est discipulus qui testimonium	re	LA 50 *WA 40		c	2	0	4	5	7	2	0	2	G

	Hic est enim propheta Praecursor	rev	LR 356 384 AM 1197 LA 405 WA 322										
7	Hic est fratrum amator	re	LA 298 WA 182	G	2	0	2	0	2	5	4	5	G
	Hic est Gregorius Iste est de	rev	WA 290										
7	Hic est Martinus electus	re	PM 343 *LA 481 WA 399	G	2	0	2	5	7	5	4	5	G
8	Hic est Michael archangelus	re	PM 153 LA 468 *WA 382	F	2	4	2	4	2	4	6	4	G
7	Hic est praecursor dilectus	re	LR 353 VP 177	G	2	0	2	5	4	5	7	5	G
4	Hic est praepositus paradisi	an	LA 467	E	-2	0	3	7	5	3	5	7	E
7	Hic est praepositus paradisi	re	WA 383	G	2	0	2	0	2	5	4	5	G
	Hic est propheta	see	Hic est enim propheta										
5	Hic est qui venit per aquam	re	PM 163	a	-1	-3	0	-5	-3	-5	-7	-3	F
3	Hic est qui venit per aquam	gr	GR 537 LU 1533	G	2	5	4	5	2	4	5	7	E
7	Hic est sacerdos magnus	an	PM 224	G	7	5	4	5	9	7	9	5	G
	Hic est sacerdos quem coronavit	alv	GR [8] [34] LU 1184	D	-2	0	2	3	5	7	5	3	
	Hic est vere martyr quem coronavit	alv	SYG 226	D	-2	0	2	3	5	7	5	3	
7	Hic est vere martyr qui pro Christi	re	PM 218 LR 158 *WA 417	G	5	4	5	7	5	9	7	5	G
7	Hic est vere martyr qui pro Christi	an	WA 419 *LA 528	G	5	4	5	7	9	7	9	10	G
	Hic est vere martyr qui pro Christo	alv	SYG 229	D	3	2	5	3	2	3	0	3	
8	Hic est vir qui non est derelictus	an	PM 220	G	-2	-5	-2	0	2	0	2	0	G
8	Hic est vir qui non est derelictus	an	LA 528 WA 415	G	-2	0	-7	-5	-2	0	2	0	G
8	Hic est vir qui non est derelictus	re	WA 418	F	2	4	7	2	0	2	4	2	G
1	Hic est verus christicola	hy	ST 340	D	3	0	3	0	-2	3	5	7	D
8	Hic in annis adolescentiae	re	WA 290	G	-2	0	-7	-5	-2	0	2	0	G
2	Hic itaque cum jam relictis	an	LA 369	F	-3	2	-1	-5	-3	0	-1	-5	D
	Hic itaque non solum Hic in annis	rev	WA 290										
4	Hic locus nempe vocitatur aula	hy	ST 44	E	-2	0	3	5	3	5	3	1	E
	Hic Martinus pauper	alv	SYG 227 GS 200	C	2	5	7	4	2	5	4	5	
	Hic martyr Domini pro lege	alv	SYG 223	D	3	0	-2	3	5	3	5	7	
7	Hic praecursor directus	re	LA 404 *WA 323	G	2	0	-2	2	5	4	5	7	G
5	Hic summista vatidicus	an	WA 311	F	4	7	4	2	7	9	7	9	F
2	Hic super excelsae	an	WA 277	D	-2	0	3	5	3	2	0	-2	D
5	Hic tanguntur	an	WA 295	F	4	7	6	4	6	4	2	7	F
	Hic venit in testimonium Inter natos	rev	LR 355 *WA 323	a	-2	0	3	2	-2	3	0	2	

8	Hic vir despiciens mundum	an	AR 577[19] [85] LU 2627 1199 AM 675 744 WA 417 LA 528	G	5	2	0	-2	0	2	0	4	G
4	Hinc horrendo carceris	an	WA 261	F	-1	-3	-1	-3	0	-1	0	2	E
1	Hinc tota Teutonia	hy	ST 312	c	-1	-3	-5	-3	-7	-8	-10	-3	D
2	Hoc audito furore	an	WA 378	D	-2	0	3	2	0	3	7	5	D
8	Hoc corpus quod pro vobis	co	GR 155 [104] LU 573 SYG 111 GB 98[v] GS 72	G	2	-2	2	0	2	-3	-2	0	G
	Hoc Domine ad laudem Dedisti Domine	rev	LA 495 WA 409										
	Hoc erit signum Benedicens ergo Deus	rev	WA 78	c	2	5	4	5	4	2	4	2	
	Hoc est praeceptum meum	alv	SYG 194	c	-3	-1	-3	-5	-7	-3	-1	-3	
8	Hoc est praeceptum meum	re	LA 510	G	-2	0	-7	-5	-2	0	2	0	G
8	Hoc est praeceptum meum	an	AR [2] LU 1111 AM 622 *WA 414 *LA 511	c	-1	-3	-5	-3	-1	-3	-5	-8	G
	Hoc est testimonium Ecce agnus Dei	rev	LA 36										
	Hoc est testimonium Me oportet	rev	WA 11										
1	Hoc est testimonium	an	AR 249 AM 224 WA 23 *LA 16	D	-2	3	5	3	5	7	10	7	D
1	Hoc genus daemoniorum	an	AR 547 AM 584	D	-2	0	2	3	5	3	2	0	D
4	Hoc in templo summe Deus	hy	ST 107	F	-3	0	-3	-5	-3	-1	0	-1	E
7	Hoc jam tertio	an	LA 220	d	-3	0	2	0	-2	0	-3	-2	G
	Hoc jam tertio	alv	SYG 160	D	2	0	2	0	-2	2	3	5	
3	Hoc jam tertio	an	WA 135	G	4	5	2	5	4	0	2	4	E
	Hoc nunc os ex ossibus Immisit Dominus soporem	rev	LA 110 WA 73										
	Hoc signum crucis erit	sr	AR 702 703 LU 1454 LA 398 WA 309										
	Hoc signum crucis erit Dulce lignum	rev	LA 396 WA 308										
4	Hoc signum crucis erit	re	LA 396 *WA 308	F	-3	0	2	0	-1	0	-1	0	E
8	Hodie afflictus sum valde	an	OHS 625 LU 776[c]	F	2	0	2	4	0	-1	-3	0	G
8	Hodie beata virgo Maria	an	AR 622 LU 1367 AM 805 *LA 356	F	2	4	7	4	6	4	2	0	G
	Hodie beata virgo Maria Responsum accepit Simeon	anv	SYG 47 *GS i	D	3	2	0	2	0	-2	2	3	
8	Hodie caelesti sponso	an	AR 315 LU 457 AM 293 *WA 56 *LA 74	F	2	4	6	7	2	4	2	6	G

6 Hodie caelistis porta	an	WA 319	c	2	4	2	5	4	2	4	0	c
1 Hodie Christus natus est	an	AR 272 LU 413 AM 249 *WA 42 LA 39	F	2	4	2	4	5	4	2	0	D
1 Hodie completi sunt dies	an	AR 509 LU 886 *AM 524 *WA 154 (inc illeg) *LA 263	C	2	4	5	4	2	4	2	0	D
8 Hodie devicta morte	an	WA 130	D	3	7	5	3	5	12	10	9	G
6 Hodie dies illuxit	an	WA 153	c	2	0	2	4	0	-3	-5	0	c
3 Hodie dilectus Domini	co	SYG 57	c	-1	0	-3	-1	-3	-5	-3	-1	E
4 Hodie dilectus Domini	co	GB 55	F	2	-1	0	-3	-1	-3	-5	-3	4
1 Hodie egressa est virga	an	AR 590 LU 1321 AM 767	D	2	3	0	-2	3	5	7	5	D
8 Hodie electorum omnium caput	an	PM 130 *WA 267 (inc illeg)	G	-2	-5	-2	0	2	0	2	-2	G
8 Hodie gloriosa caeli regina	an	AR 637 LU 1383	F	2	4	2	0	4	6	7	2	G
8 Hodie huic domui salus	an	LA 551	F	2	4	6	7	6	4	6	7	G
Hodie illuxit nobis dies redemptionis Hodie nobis de caelo	rev	LU 376 LR 57 LA 32 WA 28										
1 Hodie illuxit nobis laetus dies	an	PM 161 WA 329	C	2	4	5	2	0	5	7	9	D
3 Hodie in Jordane baptizato	re	LR 71 *LA 67 WA 53	G	2	5	4	2	5	4	0	2	E
6 Hodie intacta virgo	an	VP 73 *WA 32 *LA 38	F	-1	0	-3	-5	0	2	4	0	F
Hodie Maria virgo caelos ascendit	alv	SYG 216 *GS 195	G	-2	-3	-2	0	2	0	2	4	
1 Hodie Maria virgo caelos ascendit	re	LR 379	D	2	0	-2	3	2	0	2	0	D
8 Hodie Maria virgo caelos ascendit	an	AR 824 LU 1607 AM 1018 *WA 360 LA 449	F	2	4	6	7	6	4	2	4	G
4 Hodie Maria virgo puerum	re	LA 353	F	-3	0	-1	0	2	0	-1	0	E
8 Hodie Maria virgo puerum	an	WA 272	F	2	4	7	6	4	2	4	2	G
1 Hodie martyrum flores	re	WA 46	C	2	5	2	4	2	0	2	5	D
Hodie nata est beata Gloriosae virginis	rev	LA 457										
1 Hodie nata est beata	an	WA 364	C	2	5	7	5	4	2	0	5	D
3 Hodie nata est beata ... cujus vita gloriosa	re	LA 456 WA 365	G	2	5	4	2	4	2	0	2	E
8 Hodie nata est beata ... cujus vita inclita	an	LA 462	F	2	4	6	7	6	4	2	6	G
4 Hodie nata est virgo	an	WA 364	D	3	2	0	2	5	3	0	3	E
Hodie natus est nobis rex Beata Dei genitrix	rev	WA 29										
1 Hodie nobis beata illuxit	an	PM 41	D	-2	0	3	2	0	2	3	0	D
5 Hodie nobis caelorum rex	re	LR 56 LU 375 LA 32 WA 27	c	-3	0	-3	0	-5	-3	-5	-7	F

	Title	Type	Sources										
8	Hodie nobis de caelo pax	re	LU 376 *LR 57 *LA 32 *WA 28	G	-2	2	4	5	4	5	7	5	G
8	Hodie nomen tuum ita	an	AR 631 LU 1381	G	-2	-5	-3	-2	0	2	0	2	G
8	Hodie praeclarissimus Deo	re	WA 289	G	2	0	-2	-3	-2	0	2	0	G
8	Hodie sacra virgo	an	AM 819	F	2	4	7	6	7	4	2	0	G
8	Hodie sacratissima	hy	ST 427	G	-2	-5	-3	-2	0	2	0	-2	G
2	Hodie sanctus Benedictus	an	AM 857 *LA 376	C	5	4	2	4	0	2	4	2	D
8	Hodie sanctus Joannes	an	WA 346	F	2	4	2	4	2	4	2	0	G
1	Hodie sanctus Maurus	an	AM 782	C	2	0	4	5	2	5	7	9	D
	Hodie scietis quia veniet	sr	AR 257 LU 359 AM 234 237 LA 30										
	Hodie scietis quia veniet Sanctificamini hodie	rev	LA 29 WA 25										
8	Hodie scietis quia veniet	an	AR 255 LU 358 AM 232 *WA 26 LA 30	c	-1	-3	-1	0	-1	-3	-5	-3	G
4	Hodie scietis quia veniet	inv	LA 29 *WA 25	C	2	5	4	5	2	5	2	5	E
6	Hodie scietis quia veniet ... salvabit	int	GR 24 LU 359 SYG 13 GB 12^v *GS 12	D	3	5	8	7	5	3	0	3	F
2	Hodie scietis quia veniet ... salvabit	gr	GR 24 LU 360 SYG 13 *GB 12^v *GS 12	G	4	2	5	2	4	5	2	0	a
4	Hodie si vocem Domini	inv	LA 156 *WA 105	C	2	5	4	5	2	5	2	5	E
8	Hodie Simon Petrus ascendit	an	WA 333 (inc illeg)										G
1	Hodie Simon Petrus ascendit	an	AR 754 LU 1525 AM 939 LA 421	C	2	4	5	4	2	4	2	0	D
6	Hodie summi consules	an	WA 329	d	2	3	2	0	-2	0	-2	-5	C
4	Hodie vas electionis	an	WA 291	C	2	4	5	4	5	7	9	7	E
6	Hodie veri solis	an	WA 323	c	2	4	0	4	7	5	7	4	c
2	Hodie virgo Maria elevatur	an	WA 358	D	-5	-2	0	2	0	3	0	-2	D
2	Holocausta medullata laudationis	of	SYG 230	D	-2	0	3	-2	2	0	-2	0	D
6	Holocaustum et pro peccato	of	GR [115] LU 974	F	2	0	2	4	2	0	2	0	F
	Holocaustum et pro peccato Hostiam et oblationem	trv	GR 61	C	2	5	7	5	2	4	5	4	
1	Hominis superne conditor	hy	AR 183	F	2	4	2	0	-1	2	-1	0	D
2	Homo Dei ducebatur	re	PM 117 *LA 500 WA 233	E	3	7	5	3	5	8	7	5	a
8	Homo erat in Jerusalem	an	WA 270	G	-2	-5	-2	0	2	0	-2	2	G
4	Homo erat in Jerusalem	an	LA 352	C	2	0	2	4	5	4	2	4	E
7	Homo natus est in ea	an	LR 74 WA 29 LA 64	d	-3	0	2	0	2	0	-2	-3	G
	Homo natus est in ea Fundamenta ejus	trv	GR 402	G	2	4	5	4	5	4	7	9	

7	Homo peregre profectus	co	GR 92**	G	2	0	2	5	4	5	7	5	G
8	Homo quidam descendebat	an	AR 564 LU 1032 AM 603 *WA 189 LA 315	G	-5	-2	0	2	0	-2	0	2	G
4	Homo quidam erat dives qui ... factum	an	WA 187	C	2	5	4	5	7	5	4	2	E
1	Homo quidam erat dives qui ... qui jacebat	an	LA 309	D	-2	0	3	2	3	2	0	2	D
6	Homo quidam fecit ... et misit	re	AR 112* PM 105 LR 419 LU 1856 AM 1189 VP 15	F	2	0	2	4	0	2	0	5	F
3	Homo quidam fecit ... et vocavit	an	AR 537 LU 1101 AM 557 *WA 187 *LA 310	G	2	0	2	4	5	2	0	2	E
1	Homo quidem erat dives valde	hy	ST 487	D	2	5	7	10	12	10	7	10	D
7	Honestum fecit illum	re	LR 154 206 *LA 526	G	2	0	2	0	2	0	2	5	G
6	Honor virtus et potestas	re	WA 160	c	2	0	2	4	0	2	0	2	c
	Honora Dominum de tua substantia Audi fili	rev	WA 171										
4	Honora Dominum de tua substantia	of	GR 569 LU 1582	D	3	0	2	3	0	5	3	0	E
6	Honora Dominum de tua substantia	co	GR 349 LU 1026 *SYG 246 GB 253v GS 153	D	3	5	3	5	7	5	7	5	F
6	Hora consurgit aurea	hy	ST 327	F	2	4	5	4	2	4	2	0	F
4	Hortus conclusus amica mea	an	WA 356	G	2	0	2	5	4	2	4	2	E
8	Hortus conclusus es ... hortus	an	WA 353	G	5	2	0	-2	0	2	0	4	G
2	Hortus conclusus es ... hortus ... surge	an	LA 446 *86	D	-2	0	3	2	0	3	2	0	D
1	Hortus conclusus es ... quam pulchra	an	WA 361	D	-2	0	3	2	0	3	0	-2	D
1	Hortus conclusus es ... surge	an	LR 255	D	-2	0	3	2	3	5	3	2	D
	Hortus conclusus est	alv	GB 232	D	-2	2	3	5	2	0	3	2	
7	Hortus conclusus soror mea	re	LR 270	G	2	0	2	5	4	5	7	5	G
	Hosanna filio David	alv	SYG 2	E	1	0	-2	3	5	7	8	5	
7	Hosanna filio David	an	GR 166 OHS 91 LU 580 *WA 112 209 LA 179	G	7	5	4	5	7	9	7	4	G
2	Hostiam et oblationem	tr	GR 61	D	-2	0	-2	-5	-2	0	-2	0	D
	Hostiam sanctam viventem Lucia virgo judici	rev	WA 245										
	Hostias et preces tibi Domine laudis Domine Jesu Christe	ofv	GR 100* LU 1813 GS 232 *GB 266	C	2	5	4	2	0	2	5	4	
	Hostias et preces tibi Domine offerimus Domine Jesu Christe	ofv	SYG 235	F	-1	0	2	0	-1	-3	0	-1	
8	Hostis Herodes impie	hy	ST 180	G	-2	-3	-5	-2	2	0	-2	0	G

3	Hostis Herodes impie	hy	ST 256 275	E	-2	3	5	8	5	8	5	8	E
3	Hostis Herodes impie	hy	ST 221	E	-2	3	5	8	7	5	8	7	E
3	Hostis Herodes impie	hy	LR 69 AM 288	D	2	3	5	7	0	2	3	5	E
3	Hostis Herodes impie	hy	ST 180	D	2	3	5	7	0	2	5	3	E
5	Hostis Herodes impie	hy	ST 72	F	2	4	2	0	2	4	6	4	F
8	Hostis Herodes impie	hy	ST 413	F	2	4	7	2	4	0	2	7	G
3	Hostis Herodes impie	hy	ST 156	G	2	5	4	5	4	2	4	2	E
4	Hostis Herodes impie	hy	ST 276	C	4	5	7	5	2	4	5	7	E
1	Huic dum eremum	an	LR 324	D	3	0	-2	3	5	3	5	7	D
4	Hujus amore	an	WA 277	F	-3	0	-3	-1	2	4	2	0	E
2	Hujus diei gloria	hy	ST 327	D	-2	0	3	5	3	2	0	-2	D
3	Hujus diei gloria	hy	ST 234	D	2	3	5	7	0	2	3	5	E
8	Hujus diei gratia	hy	ST 396	G	2	4	5	4	2	0	5	7	G
4	Hujus obtentu Deus alme nostris	hy	LR 213	F	-1	0	2	4	2	0	-3	-1	E
2	Humili prece et sincera devotione	hy	ST 492	D	7	5	3	5	7	3	2	0	a
	Humiliaverunt in compedibus Joseph cum intraret	rev	WA 96										
3	Humiliavit semetipsum Dominus	int	GR [106]	E	-2	3	5	8	7	8	5	7	E
	Hunc ergo cum vidisset Sic eum volo manere	rev	LA 53 WA 41										
	Hunc ergo locum Dei In hoc ergo loco	rev	WA 388										
2	Hymnis angelicis ora resolvimus	hy	LR 288	D	3	2	3	5	7	0	-2	3	D
8	Hymnizemus regi Christo	hy	ST 310	G	2	0	5	4	2	0	2	0	G
8	Hymnos dulces personemus	hy	ST 50	c	2	4	5	4	2	0	2	0	c
2	Hymnum canamus gloriae	hy	ST 390	D	-2	-5	-7	-2	0	2	3	2	D
8	Hymnum cantate nobis	an	LA 96 WA 67	a	-2	-4	-2	0	-2	-4	0	2	G
8	Hymnum cantate nobis alleluia	re	LA 239 *WA 145	D	5	7	5	3	0	2	3	2	G
8	Hymnum cantemus Domino	hy	ST 369	G	-5	-2	0	2	0	-2	0	5	G
2	Hymnum dicamus Domino	hy	ST 9	E	-2	0	-2	-4	-2	0	1	3	D
2	Hymnum dicamus Domino	hy	ST 33 386	E	-2	0	-2	-4	-2	0	3	5	D
8	Hymnum dicamus Domino	an	AR 349 AM 320 *WA 62	G	2	0	-2	2	4	5	4	2	G
	Hymnum dicite et superexaltate Benedictus es	trv	GS 44	c	-1	0	-1	-5	0	-3	-5	-8	
4	Hymnum dicite et superexaltate	an	AR 354 AM 327 *WA 79 LA 124	F	-1	0	-1	-3	-5	0	2	4	E
8	Hymnum novae laetitiae	hy	ST 139	G	2	5	4	2	3	2	0	-2	G
8	Hymnus omnibus sanctis ejus	an	AR 899 LU 1729 *AM 1104 *WA 397	G	5	2	0	-2	0	2	0	4	G

7	Ibant apostoli gaudentes	re	LR 166 LA 393 *WA 411	G	5	4	5	7	5	7	9	7	G
	Ibant gaudentes a conspectu	see	Ibant apostoli										
6	Ibant parentes Jesu	re	LR 314	F	2	0	2	4	2	4	2	0	F
1	Ibant parentes Jesu	an	AR 652 LU 1405	D	7	8	7	5	3	5	7	3	D
7	Ibant parentes Jesu	an	AM 841	G	7	9	5	9	10	7	4	7	G
	Ibat igitur Saulus / Saulus adhuc spirans	rev	LA 341 WA 263										
7	Ibat igitur Saulus	re	LA 344 *WA 263	G	2	0	2	0	2	4	5	7	G
1	Ibat igitur Saulus	an	LA 340 WA 262 (inc illeg)	D	2	3	2	0	2	0	2	0	D
1	Ibat Jesus in civitatem	an	AR 403 566 LU 1095 *AM 379 606 *LA 164	C	2	5	2	0	2	5	2	4	D
	Ibi confregit cornu arcum / Terra tremuit	ofv	OTT 55 *GB 128 *SYG 153	G	4	7	4	5	7	2	4	0	
	Ibi confregit potentias / Notus in Judaea	trv	GR [136] LU 1286	G	2	5	2	5	7	5	0	2	
4	Ibi olim positi fuimus	an	WA 346	F	-3	-1	0	-1	-3	-5	-3	-1	E
7	Ibo mihi ad montem	an	WA 361	G	5	4	5	7	10	9	10	7	G
8	Ideo jurejurando fecit	an	AR [56] LU 1176 AM 658 *LA 536	F	2	4	7	6	7	4	2	4	G
5	Ideo petivi inducias	an	WA 247	a	-2	-4	0	3	5	3	1	3	F
6	Ideo sunt ante thronum	an	AR 764 LU 1529 *AM 949	F	2	0	2	5	2	4	5	4	F
5	Ideoque dico tibi	an	WA 338	F	4	7	5	4	7	9	7	9	F
	Ideoque et quod nascetur ex te / Quomodo fiet ... respondens	rev	WA 302	D	7	5	3	5	7	5	7	8	
	Ideoque quod nascetur ex te / Ave Maria	trv	GR 459 LU 1412 GS 183 *SYG 57	C	2	5	7	5	2	5	7	9	
	Ideoque quod nascetur ex te / Ave Maria	ofv	OTT 13 *SYG 12	F	2	9	11	6	9	7	9	12	
6	Igitur Abraham de nocte	re	WA 82	c	-3	-5	0	2	0	2	4	5	c
2	Igitur dissimulata	re	WA 342	C	2	4	2	5	4	5	7	2	D
2	Igitur Joseph ductus	re	WA 95	A	3	5	3	5	7	8	7	5	D
8	Igitur Lucianus de revelatione	re	WA 345	G	-2	0	-2	0	2	5	2	5	G
	Igitur perfecti sunt caeli / In principio Deus creavit	rev	LA 108 WA 72										
1	Igitur perfecti sunt caeli	re	LA 112	D	3	0	-2	3	5	7	5	3	D
	Igitur puella cui dixero / Veni hodie	rev	LA 122 WA 83										
6	Igne fervoris divini	re	WA 294	c	2	0	2	4	0	-3	-1	0	c

	Incipit	Type	Source		1	2	3	4	5	6	7	8	
	Igne me examinasti 　In craticula	rev	WA 346	a	1	0	-2	-4	0	3	5	3	
8	Igne me examinasti	an	WA 348 *LA 436	G	2	0	-2	2	5	4	2	5	G
	Igne me examinasti 　Probasti Domine	grv	GR 579 LU 1594 GS 194 GB 217^v SYG 213	c	2	0	2	0	-1	0	2	0	
1	Ignem veni mittere	an	AR 538^5 LU 966 AM 564	D	2	3	0	2	0	-2	0	3	D
1	Ignem veni mittere	co	GR 562 LU 1575	F	4	2	4	0	-1	0	-1	-3	D
1	Ille homo qui dicitur Jesus	an	AR 403 LU 1095 AM 378 *LA 164 *WA 105	a	-2	2	0	-4	-2	0	-2	-4	D
1	Ille me clarificabit	an	LA 242	D	3	0	-2	3	5	3	7	10	D
	Ille namque tenet 　Caritas est summum	anv	SYG 132	c	-1	-5	-3	0	-1	-5	-3	0	
4	Ille nempe Daciani	hy	ST 466	G	4	2	4	5	2	4	2	0	E
1	Illi autem profecti	an	LR 104 *WA 150 *LA 252 253	D	-2	3	5	3	5	7	5	7	D
	Illi enim conjuncta es 　Gaudens perenniter	trv	SYG 238	C	2	4	5	7	5	2	4	5	
1	Illi ergo homines	an	AR 399 LU 564 AM 375	C	2	5	4	2	0	2	5	2	D
1	Illi homines cum signum	an	WA 104	C	2	4	5	7	5	4	2	0	D
1	Illi homines cum vidissent	an	LA 163	C	2	9	11	9	7	9	11	9	D
	Illic David suscitabo cornu 　Sacerdotes	trv	LU 1623^C	G	2	4	5	4	5	7	5	2	
	Illic interrogaverunt nos 　Hymnum cantate	rev	LA 239 WA 145										
	Illic producam	see	Illuc producam										
1	Illo quoque negante	an	WA 404	C	2	9	11	9	7	9	11	9	D
	Illuc enim ascenderunt 　Laetatus sum in his	trv	SYG 101	F	-3	0	-3	0	2	0	2	4	
	Illuc producam cornu David 　Sacerdotes ejus	grv	GR [36] LU 1187 *GS 225 *GB 212 SYG 209	D	7	5	7	10	7	9	5	3	
8	Illumina Domine hiis	an	WA 70	G	5	2	0	-2	0	2	0	-2	G
8	Illumina Domine sedentes	an	AR 191	G	5	2	0	-2	0	2	0	-2	G
1	Illumina Domine vultum	an	AR 107	a	-2	0	-2	-4	-2	1	-2	1	a
1	Illumina faciem tuam super servum	co	GR 76 LU 501 SYG 60 GB 57^v GS 25	D	3	2	3	0	-2	3	5	3	D
	Illumina faciem tuam super servum 　In te speravi	ofv	OTT 101 *GB 68^v SYG 76	D	3	5	3	0	3	0	-2	0	
8	Illumina nos Domine	an	AR 327	G	2	0	-2	0	2	0	5	4	G
4	Illumina oculos meos ne unquam	int	GR [147]	F	4	2	4	0	-3	-1	0	-1	E

#	Title		Source										
4	Illumina oculos meos nequando	of	GR 331 OTT 87 LU 1000 SYG 92 GB 81 GS 54 145	F	4	2	4	0	-3	2	0	-1	E
7	Illuminans altissimus	hy	ST 372	G	2	0	-2	0	-2	2	5	7	G
2	Illuminans altissimus	hy	ST 31	G	2	4	5	2	4	2	0	2	a
2	Illuminans altissimus	hy	ST 414	C	2	5	4	2	4	2	4	5	D
8	Illuminare Domine his qui	an	AM 81 586	G	5	2	0	-2	0	2	0	-2	G
5	Illuminare illuminare Jerusalem	re	AM 1185 *LR 75 *LA 72 *WA 53	F	2	4	2	0	2	0	2	-3	F
8	Illuminatio mea et salus mea	an	AR 86 LU 279^B LA 82	c	-1	-5	-3	-1	-3	-1	0	-3	G
8	Illuminator omnium	hy	ST 391	G	-5	-2	0	2	0	-2	0	5	G
8	Illuminator omnium	hy	ST 131	G	2	0	-2	-3	-5	-2	2	0	G
8	Illuminavit hunc diem rerum	hy	ST 400	G	-5	-2	0	2	0	-2	0	5	G
2	Illuminavit hunc diem rerum	hy	ST 434	C	2	5	4	2	4	2	4	5	D
	Illusionem regis cognoscens Repletus sancto spiritus	grv	GB 54	a	3	5	7	8	5	3	5	8	
	Illusionem regis cognoscens Repletus sancto spiritu	grv	SYG 56	F	4	2	7	9	7	9	7	11	
	Illuxerunt coruscationes In mari via tua	rev	LA 157										
	Illuxerunt coruscationes Viderunt te aquae	rev	LA 237 WA 144										
3	Illuxerunt coruscationes	int	GR 571 LU 1585	E	-2	3	5	8	5	3	5	7	E
8	Illuxerunt fulgura Dei	an	LR 294	c	2	0	-1	0	-3	0	-1	-3	G
8	Illuxit nobis dies	an	LA 39	G	5	2	0	-2	0	2	0	2	G
7	Imitator Domini Oswaldus	an	WA 286	G	4	5	7	9	7	5	4	2	G
6	Imitatores mei estote	co	GR 548 LU 1546	D	3	2	3	5	7	5	3	5	F
1	Immaculatam conceptionem virginis	an	PM 121	D	-2	0	3	3	0	3	5	7	D
2	Immaculatam conceptionem virginis	inv	LR 259	C	2	4	5	2	0	2	0	2	D
2	Immaculatas hostiarum preces	of	SYG 220	D	-5	0	-2	0	-2	0	3	0	D
	Immaculatus Dominus Gaudeamus omnes ... Agathe	rev	WA 275										
	Immania enim pro Christo Candidi facti	rev	LA 387										
	Immania enim pro Christo Certamen magnum	rev	LR 185 LA 518										
	Immania enim pro Christo Verbera carnificum	rev	WA 421										
2	Immense caeli conditor	hy	ST 253	D	-2	3	5	7	5	3	2	5	D
2	Immense caeli conditor	hy	ST 183	D	-2	3	5	7	5	3	5	3	D
2	Immense caeli conditor	hy	ST 271	D	-2	3	5	7	5	3	5	7	D

2	Immense caeli conditor	hy	ST 362 AM 137	F	2	4	0	2	0	-1	2	0	D
1	Immense caeli conditor	hy	AR 101 LU 517	F	2	4	2	0	-1	2	-1	0	D
2	Immense caeli conditor	hy	ST 86	F	2	4	2	0	-1	2	0	-1	D
2	Immense caeli conditor	hy	ST 271	F	2	4	2	0	2	4	0	-3	D
8	Immense caeli conditor	hy	AM 136	D	3	5	3	7	5	0	3	5	G
2	Immense caeli conditor	hy	ST 213	D	3	5	7	3	5	3	5	2	D
7	Immisit Dominus soporem ... et cum	re	LR 343	G	2	0	2	0	2	5	7	5	G
5	Immisit Dominus soporem ... et tulit	re	LA 110 WA 73	F	4	7	4	7	9	7	9	6	F
8	Immittet angelus Domini	of	GR 359 OTT 102 LU 1039 SYG 79 GB 71 GS 41 157	G	2	-2	2	0	5	2	0	2	G
3	Immittet angelus Domini	an	AR 144 OHS 362 LU 293	G	2	4	2	5	2	0	2	5	E
	Immola Deo sacrificium	an	OHS 300 (nm)										
	Immola Deo sacrificium Elegit te	rev	LR 204										
	Immola Deo sacrificium Temptavit Deus	rev	LA 121										
6	Immola Deo sacrificium	gr	SYG 233	F	2	0	-3	0	2	0	2	-3	F
1	Immolabit haedum multitudo	re	AR 114* LR 122 LU 926	D	-2	0	-2	0	2	3	0	-2	D
1	Immutemur habitu in cinere	an	GR 85 LU 523 *GS 30	G	-5	-2	0	2	0	2	0	5	D
	Impellunt plurimi nec movetur Jussu impii	rev	WA 245										
	Imperat ubi Jesus Scande thronum	rev	WA 355	a	1	3	8	7	5	7	3	0	
8	Imperatoris filium	hy	ST 392	G	-5	-2	0	2	0	-2	0	5	G
	Imperatrix reginarum	alv	VP 51	D	5	7	9	10	9	7	5	3	
	Impetra quaesumus veniam O beate Joannes	rev	VP 210										
1	Impetum fecerunt unanimiter	an	LA 41	G	-7	-5	2	4	2	0	2	4	D
1	Impetum fecerunt unanimiter	re	LA 44 *WA 34	D	2	3	5	3	0	3	5	3	D
2	Impetum inimicorum	re	LA 296 *WA 181	D	-2	0	-2	-5	-2	0	2	3	D
4	Impietatibus nostris	an	AR 130	D	2	3	5	3	2	3	0	-2	E
7	Impii super justum	re	LA 45 *WA 35	G	2	0	2	4	5	7	5	4	G
8	Impii super justum	an	WA 37 *LA 41	F	2	4	7	6	4	2	4	2	G
7	Impleta gaudent viscera	hy	ST 38	G	-2	2	0	2	4	5	4	2	G
1	Impleta gaudent viscera	hy	ST 94	a	3	0	-2	-4	-2	0	-5	-7	D
4	Implevit eos Dominus	an	WA 375	E	-2	1	0	1	3	1	0	-2	E
7	Imposita manu puero	an	WA 400 LA 485	d	-3	0	2	0	-2	0	-3	-2	G
	Improperia improperantium Deus Israel	rev	WA 114										

#	Title	Type	Sources	Mode	1	2	3	4	5	6	7	8	End
8	Improperium exspectavit cor meum	of	GR 184 326 [115] OHS 142 OTT 49 LU 602 974 *SYG 123 *GS 88 *GB 110^v	F	2	0	-1	-5	-3	0	2	4	G
2	Improperium exspectavit cor meum	gr	GR [107]	A	3	5	8	5	7	8	7	5	D
	Impulsus versatus sum / Dextera Domini	ofv	OTT 25 GB 39^v SYG 43	C	2	9	10	9	12	11	9	7	
4	In adventu summi regis	an	PM 22	C	2	0	2	5	4	5	7	5	E
	In aeternum Domine permanet	sr	AR 35 LU 243										
4	In aeternum Dominus regnabit	an	WA 68 *LA 98	F	-3	-1	0	2	0	-1	-3	0	E
8	In aeternum et in saeculum	an	WA 70	c	-1	0	-1	-3	-5	-7	-5	-3	G
1	In aeternum misericordia ejus	an	AR 2 (sup)	D	2	3	5	3	5	7	3	2	D
	In auro venerantes / Rex magnus	rev	WA 56										
4	In caelesti collegio	hy	VP 226	E	3	5	3	5	8	7	5	7	E
8	In caelesti regno	an	WA 393	G	5	2	0	-2	0	2	0	4	G
8	In caelestibus regnis	an	AR [48] LU 1157 AM 799 811 LA 390 391	C	5	2	0	-2	0	2	0	4	G
7	In caelestibus regnis ... alleluia	an	AR [29] LU 1120 AM 633	G	5	4	5	7	9	7	5	9	G
4	In caelis gaudent	an	WA 432	F	-1	-3	-1	0	-1	-3	-5	0	E
	In capite libri scriptum / Hostiam et oblationem	trv	GR 61	F	2	0	2	0	-3	-1	0	2	
	In caritate perpetua dilexi te / Virgo Israel	rev	LA 19 381 WA 23										
	In caritate perpetua dilexi te / Jam hiems	trv	GR 615	D	-2	0	3	5	3	0	3	5	
3	In caritate perpetua dilexit nos	an	AR 5387 LU 977	E	1	0	-2	3	5	3	5	8	E
8	In caritate perpetua dilexit nos	an	AM 565	G	5	2	0	-2	0	2	0	2	G
4	In choro confessorum	an	WA 315	E	-2	1	0	-2	0	3	5	3	E
1	In circuitu populi	an	AR 120 OHS 288 LU 286	D	2	3	5	2	5	7	3	2	D
6	In circuitu tuo	an	WA 392	c	2	0	2	4	0	-2	0	5	c
2	In circuitu tuo ... ubi constituisti	re	WA 423	D	-2	0	-2	0	3	0	-2	0	D
5	In circuitu tuo ... ubi constituisti	re	VP 256 *LA 518 *WA 429	F	4	7	9		4	7	9	11	F
7	In civitate Domini clare sonant	an	PM 203	G	4	5	7	5	4	5	7	9	G
	In columbae specie Scholasticae	sr	AM 812										
2	In columbae specie Scholasticae	re	AM 1192 *LR 299	D	-5	-2	2	0	3	2	3	2	D
	In columbae specie spiritus	sr	WA 58										
2	In columbae specie spiritus	re	PM 43 LR 71 *LA 68 *WA 58	D	-5	-2	0	2	0	3	2	3	D

	Incipit	genre	Sources										
8	In columbae specie vidit	tr	SYG 56	G	2	4	2	0	2	0	5	7	G
8	In columbae specie vidit	tr	GB 54^v	E	3	5	8	5	7	8	10	8	G
	In commisso quoque fidelis Erat namque	rev	LA 325										
1	In conceptione sua	an	LR 261	D	3	2	3	5	2	0	3	2	D
8	In consilio justorum	an	WA 394	G	2	0	-2	0	2	5	4	2	G
2	In consilio justorum	an	LA 473	D	3	2	0	-2	3	5	7	5	D
	In conspectu agni amicti Isti sunt agni	rev	OHS 823 LR 169 LA 212 WA 134 305										
	In conspectu angelorum	sr	AR 861 LU 1658 1659 AM 1060										
5	In conspectu angelorum	an	AM 146 147 *WA 67 384 *LA 96	a	-2	0	-2	-4	3	5	3	2	F
	In conspectu angelorum	alv	GR [87] LU 1276 GS 197	C	2	5	2	4	0	2	5	4	
1	In conspectu angelorum ... adorabo	of	GR 548 LU 1546	C	2	9	10	9	12	9	7	9	D
	In conspectu angelorum ... adorabo	alv	GR 635 LU 1700	C	2	5	2	4	0	2	5	4	
	In conspectu angelorum ... et adorabo Stetit angelus	ofv	OTT 170 GB 170^v	C	2	4	5	7	9	7	9	5	
8	In conspectu angelorum ... et adorabo	re	AM 1202 *LR 384 *VP 216 LA 466 WA 381	D	3	5	7	5	7	5	7	9	G
1	In conspectu gentium	re	LA 467 *WA 380	D	2	3	5	3	0	3	5	3	D
	In conspectu omnis populi Pretiosa in conspectu	rev	LA 386 WA 307										
	In conspectu tuo Domine Protege Domine plebem	ofv	SYG 174	C	2	5	2	4	0	2	4	5	
	In convertendo inimicum meum Exsurge Domine	grv	GR 123 LU 553 GS 54 GB 82 SYG 93	E	1	-2	3	5	3	5	7	8	
1	In corde Gertrudis	an	AM 1127	D	-2	3	5	3	7	10	12	10	D
2	In corde laetitia	an	WA 285	D	-2	0	3	5	3	2	0	3	D
	In craticula positus Meruit esse	rev	LA 439 WA 350										
	In craticula te Deum Beatus Laurentius orabat	anv	LA 437										
4	In craticula te Deum	re	LA 439 *WA 349	F	-3	0	2	0	-3	-1	-3	0	E
1	In craticula te Deum	an	AR 815 AM 1007 *WA 350 LA 441	C	2	5	4	2	5	7	5	7	D
5	In craticula te Deum ... affatus	re	WA 346	F	4	5	7	9	11	9	7	4	F
	In cruce denique moriturus Diligebat autem eum	rev	LA 55 WA 40										
	In cujus adventu asportabuntur tibi Quam felix es Gallia	rev	PM 347	G	5	4	0	2	4	2	5	7	

8 In cujus nomine	an	WA 258	D	3	2	3	5	7	5	7	5	G
4 In cymbalis benesonantibus	an	AM 79 *WA 70 *LA 105	E	1	-2	0	1	3	1	0	1	E
1 In dedicatione hujus templi	an	WA 319	F	-1	-3	-1	0	2	-1	2	4	D
1 In dedicatione templi	re	LR 233 LA 548	D	2	3	5	3	0	3	5	3	D
5 In Deo confisum est	gr	OHS 416 LU 662	D	3	5	3	5	3	5	7	5	F
In Deo faciemus virtutem Da nobis Deus	grv	GR 107**	F	4	7	9	11	7	9	7	6	
In Deo laudabimur Libera nos Domine	grv	GB 264^v	G	7	5	7	9	5	2	7	4	
In Deo laudabimur Liberasti nos	grv	GR 387 LU 1075 GS e *SYG 258	G	7	5	7	9	5	2	7	5	
In Deo laudabimur Salvasti enim nos	grv	GR 98**	G	7	5	7	9	5	2	7	5	
3 In Deo laudabo verbum	int	GR 127 GS 56 SYG 94 *GB 83^v	G	2	5	4	5	2	5	2	0	E
1 In Deo raptus	re	LR 281	C	2	5	4	7	5	7	5	2	D
In Deo salutare meum	alv	GR 622^4	D	-2	0	3	2	3	5	2	0	
1 In Deo speravi non timebo	an	AR 137 LU 279^K	D	-2	3	5	3	7	5	7	8	D
In Deo speravit cor meum	alv	GR [146]	C	2	4	5	4	2	0	2	0	
5 In Deo speravit cor meum	gr	GR 348 LU 1025 *SYG 98 GB 87^v GS 60. 152	D	3	5	3	5	3	5	7	5	F
3 In diademate capitis Aaron	re	PM 225 *LA 229 385 *WA 141	E	-2	3	5	8	7	8	7	5	E
In die illa erit fons Hic est qui venit	rev	PM 163										
8 In die magno festivitatis	an	AR 416 LU 1098 AM 393 *WA 109 *LA 173	G	5	2	0	-2	0	2	0	7	G
1 In die qua invocavi te	re	OHS 62 (nm) LR 339 *LA 175 *WA 110	C	2	4	5	2	5	2	5	7	D
1 In die quando venerit	an	SYG 71	C	2	0	5	7	9	7	5	4	D
8 In die resurrectionis ... congregabo	an	SYG 146	D	3	5	3	5	7	5	7	5	G
In die resurrectionis ... praecedam	alv	GR 262 LU 809 *GS 121 *SYG 169 GB 140	G	7	5	2	5	7	0	-2	2	
1 In die solemnitatis vestrae	of	GR 254 OHS 809 OTT 61 LU 798 SYG 159 GB 139^v GS 122	C	2	5	4	5	4	7	5	7	D
In die tribulationis meae clamavi In die qua invocavi	rev	OHS 62 (nm) LR 339 LA 175 WA 110										
7 In die tribulationis meae Deum	an	OHS 393 LU 647 *WA 119 *LA 192	G	4	5	7	10	9	10	9	5	G

	In die tribulationis nostrae Angeli Dei qui	rev	VP 225	D	7	5	3	5	7	5	7	10	
7	In diebus illis mulier quae erat	an	AR 791 LU 1566 AM 975 WA 338 *GS 96	G	5	4	5	7	9	7	5	7	G
	In diebus illis salvabitur Juda Ecce dies	rev	PM 20 LA 10 WA *11 13										
	In diem perditionis Revelabunt caeli	rev	WA 120										
5	In Domino Deo suo	an	WA 34	F	5	4	5	7	9	7	9	11	F
5	In Domino justificabitur	an	AR 167 *AM 70 71	a	-4	0	3	0	2	3	5	3	F
	In Domino laudabitur anima Benedicam Dominum	rev	LA 88 WA 63										
	In Domino laudabitur anima Immittet angelus	ofv	OTT 102 GB 71 SYG 79	G	2	-2	2	0	2	5	7	5	
	In Domino laudabitur anima Benedicam Dominum	grv	GR 350 LU 1028 GS 154 GB 253^V SYG 246	G	2	5	7	9	5	2	0	5	
4	In domum Domini laetantes	an	LA 102	E	3	7	5	7	3	0	1	3	E
	In ea omnis qui petit Domus mea	trv	SYG 264 (nm)										
4	In ecclesiis benedicite	re	LA 238 *WA 143	F	-3	0	2	0	-3	-1	-3	-1	E
8	In ecclesiis benedicite	an	WA 66 *LA 93	G	-2	0	2	5	2	0	-2	0	G
	In ecclesiis benedicite Confirma hoc	ofv	OTT 79 *GB 189^V SYG 183	F	2	0	2	5	4	2	0	2	
	In eo dum conturbata Domine audivi	trv	GR 206 OHS 529 LU 721 *GS 98 GB 116 SYG 136	C	2	5	7	5	2	5	2	0	
4	In episccpatu suo	an	WA 295	C	2	5	4	5	7	5	2	5	E
1	In excelsis laudate Deum	an	LA 89	a	-2	0	-2	-5	-4	-2	-4	-5	D
6	In excelsis laudate Deum	an	AR 349 *WA 64	F	2	4	2	0	-3	0	2	0	F
8	In excelso throno vidi sedere	int	GR 64 LU 477 SYG 32 GB 36 GS 20	G	2	-2	2	-2	2	5	0	2	G
3	In excessu	an	WA 327	E	-2	3	5	7	5	3	5	8	E
	In exitu Israel ex Aegypto	alv	GR 381 LU 1068 GB 261	C	2	4	2	4	5	4	2	5	
	In exitu Israel ex Aegypto	alv	SYG 248	D	3	5	7	5	7	5	7	3	
	In factis manuum tuarum Eripe me de inimicis	ofv	GB 111^V	F	2	4	2	4	6	4	7	2	
4	In ferventis olei dolium	an	AR 706 LU 1462 AM 904 *WA 38 *LA 49	F	-3	-1	0	-1	0	-1	-3	-1	E
7	In fide et lenitate ipsius	an	PM 232 LR 197 *WA 429	G	4	5	7	9	7	9	7	5	G
8	In Franciam missus	an	LR 279	G	5	2	0	-2	0	2	0	5	G
7	In Galilaea Jesum	an	WA 138 *LA 222	G	4	5	7	9	5	7	5	4	G

	Incipit	Type	Sources	Mode									Final
6	In hac ergo fidei	an	WA 389	F	-1	0	-3	-5	0	2	0	2	F
7	In hoc cognoscent omnes	an	GR 202 OHS 450 LU 674 *SYG 131	d	-3	0	2	0	2	0	-3	-2	G
	In hoc cognovi	sr	AR 589 LU 1319 AM 761 762										
8	In hoc ergo loco	re	WA 388	D	3	5	7	5	7	5	7	9	G
4	In honore beatissimae Mariae	inv	WA 353	C	2	0	2	4	5	4	2	5	E
4	In honore beatissimae matronae	inv	WA 339	C	2	0	2	4	5	4	2	5	E
	In hymnis et confessionibus Ornaverunt faciem	rev	LA 296 WA 181										
8	In hymnis et confessionibus	re	PM 115 LA 296 *WA 181	D	3	5	7	5	0	3	2	3	G
8	In illa die stillabunt	an	AR 213 LU 323 AM 187 WA 6 LA 6	G	-2	0	2	0	2	4	0	2	G
6	In illa die suscipiam	re	WA 39 *LA 52	F	5	4	5	2	5	2	0	2	F
	In illa die vos cognoscetis Non vos relinquam	rev	WA 148										
	In illo die vos cognoscetis Non relinquam	rev	LR 98										
	In illo loco quidam Dum beatus vir	rev	WA 333										
8	In illo tempore exauditae	re	PM 198	D	3	5	7	5	7	9	7	5	G
	In illum diem	see In illa die											
8	In innocentia cordis	an	AR 130	G	2	0	4	2	5	4	2	5	G
8	In Israel magnum nomen	an	AM 66 67 *WA 69 *LA 101	c	-1	-3	-5	-3	-5	-7	-5	-3	G
8	In isto loco promissio	re	LA 330	D	3	5	7	5	7	5	7	9	G
7	In jejuniis et orationibus	an	WA 343	G	5	4	5	7	9	7	5	7	G
5	In jejunio et fletu orabunt	re	PM 49 LA 128 *WA 86	F	4	7	9	7	6	4	7	9	F
2	In laude Martini decus	hy	ST 434	D	2	0	-2	0	3	2	3	5	D
	In laetitia et exsultatione Adducentur regi	trv	GB 45	a	-2	-4	0	-2	0	2	3	0	
1	In lege Domini fuit	an	LR 149 *WA 416 *LA 521	D	3	0	2	3	2	-2	3	7	D
1	In lege Domini Oswaldus	an	WA 282	D	-2	3	5	3	5	7	5	7	D
7	In loco pascuae ibi Dominus	an	AR 153 LU 279^M *LA 555	G	4	5	7	9	7	9	5	4	G
7	In loco pascuae ibi me	an	WA 437	d	-3	0	2	0	-2	0	-3	-2	G
8	In loco pascuae ibi me	an	AR [161] LU 1787	G	-2	2	5	4	0	4	5	2	G
6	In loco viridi Domine	re	VP 242	a	3	5	8	7	5	7	3	5	c
4	In mandatis ejus	an	LA 87	G	2	0	-3	-2	0	-2	-3	2	E

	In manibus portabunt te Angelis suis	trv	GR [144]	F	2	4	2	0	2	0	-3	-1	
	In manibus portabunt te Qui habitat	trv	GR 95 LU 533 GS 35 GB 65 SYG 73	F	2	4	2	0	2	0	-3	-1	
	In manibus portabunt te Angelis suis	grv	GR 94 LU 533 GS 34 GB 65 SYG 72	a	3	5	7	5	3	2	3	0	
5	In manu tua Domine	inv	LA 80 *WA 76	a	-4	0	3	5	3	5	3	0	F
6	In manu tua Domine	inv	LA 93 *WA 66	F	2	0	2	4	2	0	2	4	F
	In manus tuas Domine	sr	AR 62 63 LU 269 270										
5	In mari via tua	int	GR (3)	F	2	4	5	4	2	4	2	0	F
2	In mari via tua	re	LA 157 WA 101	A	3	5	7	5	8	7	8	10	D
ir	In matutinis Domine	an	AM 372	a	-2	0	-2	-4	-2	0	1	-2	a
7	In matutinis Domine	an	WA 82	G	5	4	5	7	9	7	9	10	G
	In matutinis meditabor Deus Deus meus	ofv	OTT 66 GB 147V SYG 165	D	2	-2	0	7	5	7	8	7	
5	In me gratia omnis viae	gr	GR 43**	F	2	0	-1	0	2	4	5	2	F
8	In me gratia omnis viae	of	GR 621 LU 1676B	D	3	2	3	5	7	5	7	10	G
	In me omnis gratia viae Ego sicut vitis	rev	PM 256 LA 225 WA 139 305										
3	In mediis flammis	an	WA 247	E	-2	3	5	8	7	8	10	8	E
1	In medio carceris stabat	an	LA 455	D	-2	0	2	3	0	2	0	-2	D
	In medio duorum animalium Domine audivi	trv	GR 206 OHS 529 LU 721 GS 98 GB 116 SYG 136	C	2	5	7	5	2	4	5	4	
	In medio ecclesiae Cibavit illum Dominus pane	rev	LA 54										
	In medio ecclesiae Cibavit illum pane	rev	WA 41										
8	In medio ecclesiae	an	WA 52 *LA 56	G	-5	-2	0	2	0	-3	-2	0	G
1	In medio ecclesiae	re	PM 226 227 LR 203 LA 55	C	2	5	7	9	7	4	5	2	D
6	In medio ecclesiae	int	GR [38] LU 1190 *SYG 24 GS 16 *GB 24	D	3	5	3	5	3	-2	0	3	F
8	In medio et in circuitu	an	WA 376	D	5	3	5	7	5	3	2	-2	G
	In memoria aeterna Requiem aeternam	grv	GR 95* LU 1808 SYG 235	a	3	5	7	5	3	2	3	0	
	In mente habete diem Erit vobis	ofv	OTT 63 GB 141V SYG 160	a	3	5	3	5	3	5	3	5	
8	In monte Oliveti oravit	re	GR 168 *OHS 375 *LU 633 LA 189 WA 118	G	2	0	2	0	-2	0	2	5	G
2	In monte olivis consito	hy	LR 448	a	-2	-5	-7	-2	0	3	2	0	a

	Text	Type	Sources	Mode	1	2	3	4	5	6	7	8	End
	In multitudine presbyterorum	alv	GR 528 LU 1513	G	2	0	5	7	5	4	0	2	
	In multitudine virtutis Benedicite gentes	ofv	OTT 71 SYG 105 GB 93^V	D	2	-2	0	7	5	7	8	7	
6	In Niniven civitate	an	WA 229	D	3	2	-2	2	5	2	3	2	F
3	In nomine Domini Dei nostri	an	WA 227	D	-2	3	5	8	7	5	7	10	a
3	In nomine Domini omne genu	int	GR 190 OHS 320 LU 616 *SYG 126 *GB 113^V *GS 91	E	-2	3	5	8	7	8	7	8	E
2	In nomine Jesu Christi	an	WA 340 LA 412	D	-2	0	2	3	5	3	2	0	D
3	In nomine Jesu omne genu	int	GR 50 561 LU 446 1574	E	-2	3	5	8	7	8	7	8	E
	In nomine meo daemonia Ite in orbem	rev	LR 114										
	In nomine patris Ite in orbem	rev	WA 148										
4	In occursum salvatoris	inv	WA 22	C	2	5	2	4	5	4	2	0	E
4	In odorem unguentorum	an	AR 821 [98] LU 1233 1606 AM 687 1014 WA 358 LA 448	G	2	5	7	5	7	9	7	5	a
	In omnem terram exivit sonus apostolorum	alv	SYG 209	D	7	9	7	5	3	5	7	5	
	In omnem terram exivit sonus eorum	sr	AR [9] LU 1113 1518 AM 623 935 LA 505 WA 410										
	In omnem terram exivit sonus eorum Petrus apostolus	anv	LA 426										
	In omnem terram exivit sonus eorum Isti sunt qui	rev	LR 145										
	In omnem terram exivit sonus eorum Isti sunt viri sancti quos	rev	WA 413										
	In omnem terram exivit sonus eorum Isti viventes	rev	LA 508										
	In omnem terram exivit sonus eorum Qui sunt isti	rev	LA 510										
	In omnem terram exivit sonus eorum O quam pulchri	rev	VP 252	a	-2	0	3	2	0	-2	0	-7	
1	In omnem terram exivit sonus eorum	re	LA 510	D	-2	0	3	5	3	5	0	2	D
	In omnem terram exivit sonus eorum	alv	GB 267	c	-1	2	0	-1	0	2	0	-3	
8	In omnem terram exivit sonus eorum	co	GR [90]	G	2	5	2	5	4	0	2	5	G
2	In omnem terram exivit sonus eorum	an	LR 135 *WA 411 LA 505	D	3	2	3	5	0	3	2	3	D
	In omnem terram exivit sonus eorum	alv	GS x	D	3	5	3	8	7	5	7	3	
2	In omnem terram exivit sonus eorum	of	GR 406 LU 1327 OTT 130 SYG 54 GB 236 GS z 203	E	3	5	7	5	3	5	7	5	a

	Incipit	Type	Sources										
2	In omnem terram exivit sonus eorum	gr	GR 629 LU 1486 *GS x *GB 202^v	E	3	5	8	5	7	8	5	3	a
	In omnem terram exivit sonus eorum / Qui sont isti	rev	LR 146	D	7	5	7	5	3	2	5	7	
	In omnem terram exivit sonus eorum	alv	GB 267	D	7	10	7	5	7	5	2	3	
	In omnibus exhibeamus / Ecce nunc tempus	rev	LR 403 LA 127 WA 85										
	In omnibus exhibeamus / Paradisi portas	rev	PM 51										
1	In omnibus exhibeamus	re	LA 127 *WA 85	D	7	9	7	3	5	7	5	7	D
	In omnibus his non peccavit / Si bona suscepimus	rev	LA 282 WA 171										
1	In omnibus his non peccavit	an	AR 546 LU 992 AM 583 *WA 171 *LA 287	C	2	9	10	9	11	12	9	7	D
	In pace factus est locus / Ecce quomodo	rev	WA 126										
7	In pace factus est locus	an	OHS 612 LU 769 WA 126 *LA 204	G	4	5	7	9	7	5	4	2	G
8	In pace in idipsum dormiam	an	OHS 591 LU 752 WA 124 LA 201	G	5	4	0	4	5	2	0	2	G
6	In paradiso ecclesiae	an	WA 311	c	2	5	2	0	2	4	2	0	c
8	In paradisum deducant	an	WA 439	G	4	5	7	9	7	5	4	5	G
7	In paradisum deducant ... chorus	an	AR [185] GR 109* LU 1768	G	4	5	7	9	7	5	4	5	G
1	In patientia vestra	an	AR [4] LU 1112 AM 623 WA 414 LA 511	D	-2	0	2	3	5	3	2	0	D
3	In patre manet	an	WA 159	G	2	5	4	2	4	5	7	5	E
2	In patre manet	re	WA 50	A	3	5	7	5	7	5	8	7	D
1	In plateis ponebantur	an	WA 325	C	2	9	7	9	11	9	7	5	[D]
1	In principio creavit Deus	re	LR 398 LA 108 WA 72	C	2	5	7	9	7	9	5	7	D
1	In principio Deus antequam terram	re	LR 421 *LA 276 *WA 168	F	2	4	2	4	2	0	2	5	D
1	In principio Deus creavit	re	LA 108 *WA 72	C	2	9	7	9	7	5	7	11	D
2	In principio erat verbum	hy	ST 39	a	-2	-5	-7	-2	0	3	2	0	a
7	In principio erat verbum	re	LR 66	G	2	0	2	0	2	5	4	5	G
	In principio erat verbum / Verbum caro	rev	LR 67 *LA 34 WA 30	G	5	4	0	2	4	2	5	7	
7	In principio erat verbum ... omnia	re	WA 30	G	2	0	2	0	2	5	4	5	G
8	In principio et ante saecula	an	LR 60 WA 29 *LA 64	G	5	2	0	-2	0	2	5	4	G
	In principio fecit Deus / Formavit igitur	rev	LA 109 WA 72										
1	In principio fecit Deus	re	LA 108 WA 72	C	2	5	7	9	7	9	5	7	D

4	In prole mater	an	PM 251 *WA 268 *LA 348	F	4	2	-1	0	2	-1	0	-3	E
7	In proxima est tribulatio	re	LA 169 WA 106	b	1	3	1	0	1	3	5	3	G
1	In psalterio et cithara	an	WA 69	C	2	5	7	5	4	5	4	2	D
	In quacumque die invocavero / Domine exaudi	trv	GR 191 OHS 324 LU 619 *GS 92 GB 114 SYG 127	C	2	5	7	2	0	2	4	5	
	In quacumque die invocavero / Si ambulavero	ofv	OTT 118 GB 86[v] *SYG 97	F	2	9	11	9	12	9	7	11	
	In quibus una cum filiis / Nolite timere non	rev	LA 327										
	In quo lux caelestis / Tantas per illum	rev	WA 387										
	In regeneratione cum sederit / Magnus sanctus Paulus	anv	LA 423 WA 330										
	In regeneratione cum sederit / Amen dico vobis	cov	SYG 205										
	In regeneratione cum sederit / Vos qui secuti	rev	WA 413										
1	In regeneratione cum sederit	an	AM 1125 WA 332 LA 432	D	-2	0	3	2	0	2	0	-2	D
	In resurrectione tua Christe	alv	GB 146[v]	C	4	5	4	2	0	2	4	2	
	In salicibus in medio ejus / Super flumina	ofv	OTT 119 GB 102[v] *SYG 115	D	2	3	5	7	5	7	10	12	
1	In salutari tuo anima mea	co	GR 383 LU 1069 *SYG 258 GB 263 *GS d 166	D	3	2	3	5	2	3	2	3	D
2	In sanctis crescens	re	WA 293	A	3	5	7	5	3	5	8	5	D
6	In sanctis ejus	an	AM 64 *WA 68 *LA 99	F	2	4	2	0	-3	0	2	0	F
1	In sanctis gloriosus	an	PM 208	D	3	0	2	3	2	0	-2	0	D
7	In sanctis suis alleluia	re	LA 387	G	5	4	5	7	5	9	7	9	G
8	In sanctitate et justitia	an	AR 780	c	-1	-5	-1	0	-3	-5	-7	-5	G
8	In sanctitate fulgida	re	WA 431	G	2	0	7	5	4	5	2	0	G
7	In sanctitate serviamus	an	AR 149 AM 65 LA 99	G	4	5	7	9	5	7	5	4	G
6	In sermonibus Domini opera	int	GR 622[1] LU 1681[1]	D	-4	-2	0	-2	3	5	3	7	F
8	In servis suis alleluia	re	WA 307	G	2	0	-2	2	5	7	9	5	G
1	In servis suis alleluia	re	LR 168	D	3	2	3	5	3	7	5	7	D
5	In servis suis miserebitur	an	AR 194	a	-4	0	3	2	3	5	3	5	F
8	In sole posuit Deus	an	LR 260	c	-3	0	-5	-3	-5	-7	-5	-10	G
5	In sole posuit tabernaculum	an	WA 27 *LA 63	a	3	2	0	3	2	0	-4	0	F
2	In sole posuit tabernaculum	gr	GR 14 LU 344 SYG 10 *GB 8[v] *GS 8	E	3	5	8	5	7	8	5	3	a

2 In spiritu humilitatis	an	AR 365 AM 342 WA 88 LA 132	C	2	5	4	2	0	2	5	2	D
In spiritu humilitatis Sicut in holocaustum	ofv	SYG 243	C	4	2	4	5	4	5	7	4	
2 In splendenti nube	re	PM 173	D	-5	-2	0	3	2	3	5	3	D
6 In splendoribus sanctorum	co	GR 30 LU 395 SYG 15 GB 15 GS E 14	F	-3	0	-3	0	2	0	2	0	F
6 In sudore vultus tui	an	WA 206	c	-2	0	2	0	2	0	-2	2	c
7 In sudore vultus tui	re	LA 111 *WA 74	G	2	5	2	4	2	0	5	4	G
In te confirmatus sum Spes mea Domine	rev	LA 115	F	-1	0	4	6	4	2	4	2	
In te Domine speravi non confundar	sr	WA 164 LA 94										
In te Domine speravi non confundar Illumina faciem tuam	cov	SYG 60 GB 57^v										
In te Domine speravi non confundar Inclina aurem tuam	cov	SYG 244										
In te Domine speravi non confundar Ego autem in Domino speravi	intv	GR 132 GS 58 SYG 96 GB 85										
In te Domine speravi non confundar Esto mihi	intv	GR 80 LU 511 GS 27 GB 59 SYG 62										
In te Domine speravi non confundar Mihi absit gloriari	intv	GR 65**										
In te Domine speravi non confundar Miserere mihi Domine	intv	GR 163 GS 76 GB 103^v SYG 116										
In te Domine speravi non confundar Repleatur os meum	intv	GR 302 LU 897 GS 140 SYG 186										
In te Domine speravi non confundar	alv	GR 335 LU 1008 GS 146 *GB 250 *SYG 241	G	2	5	4	5	2	5	2	0	
5 In te Domine sperent	re	WA 86	F	4	7	9	7	9	7	9	4	F
2 In te jactatus sum	re	LA 169 *WA 106	A	3	5	8	7	8	5	7	5	D
In te speraverunt patres Deus Deus meus	trv	GR 180 OHS 109 LU 594 GS 86 *GB 109 SYG 122	C	2	5	4	5	2	5	2	4	
In te speraverunt patres Media vita	rev	PM 45 AR 152* VP 106	D	7	5	7	8	7	5	7	8	
2 In te speravi Domine	of	GR 356 [125] LU 1035 OTT 101 SYG 76 *GB 68^v *GS 38 156	A	3	5	7	5	8	5	7	8	D
8 In tempore illo consurget	re	LA 469 WA 382	D	3	5	7	5	7	5	7	9	G
In tempore illo salvabitur In tempore illo consurget	rev	LA 469 WA 382										
3 4 In toto corde meo alleluia	re	LA 239 *WA 144	D	2	3	0	2	3	5	7	5	E
4 In tribulatione clamamus	an	GB 156^v	C	4	5	4	2	4	5	4	2	E

	Incipit		Sources										
7	In tribulatione invocavi Dominum	an	AR 409 AM 389 WA 108 LA 171	d	-2	-3	-2	0	2	-2	0	-2	G
	In tribulatione invocavi Dominum Dextera Domini	ofv	OTT 25 SYG 43	A	3	7	5	7	5	3	5	3	
3	In tribulatione lapidum	an	WA 33	E	-2	3	5	8	7	3	7	8	E
7	In tribulationibus exaudi	an	GB 157	b	1	3	1	0	1	3	5	3	G
8	In tua justitia	an	AR 91 LU 279^c WA 61 *LA 82	c	-1	0	-3	-5	-1	0	-3	-5	G
	In tua patientia possedisti	alv	SYG 5										
1	In tua patientia possedisti	an	AR 591 LU 1322 AM 769 WA 242 LA 320	D	-2	3	5	3	5	7	10	7	D
1	In tuo adventu	an	WA 8	D	-2	3	5	3	5	7	5	2	D
1	In tympano et choro	an	AM 71 320 *LA 102	D	3	2	0	-2	3	5	7	5	D
2	In universa terra gloria	an	LR 150 *WA 416 *LA 522	D	5	3	2	-2	0	-2	0	3	D
6	In universa terra nomen	an	WA 282	F	2	4	2	0	2	0	2	4	F
7	In vasta solitudine	hy	ST 128	G	2	5	0	2	0	-2	0	7	G
2	In velamento clamabant	an	AR [29] LU 1120 AM 633 *LA 386 391	D	-2	0	3	2	0	3	2	-2	D
2	In velamento clamavi	an	AR 348 *AM 320	D	-2	0	3	0	2	0	-2	0	D
8	In veritate tua	an	AM 74 WA 70 *LA 104	a	-4	-2	0	-2	-4	0	3	2	G
8	In vesperi dictamine	hy	ST 379	G	2	4	5	4	2	0	2	4	G
	In veste enim poderis In diademate	rev	LA 229										
	In via testimoniorum Benedictus ... in labiis	ofv	OTT 28 *GB 60 *SYG 63	G	2	5	4	5	4	5	2	4	
1	In viam pacis dirige	an	LA 105	F	2	4	2	4	2	-1	0	2	D
7	In viam pacis et prosperitatis	an	PM 308	G	4	5	7	9	7	5	9	7	G
	In viis justitiae ambulo Meum est consilium	trv	GR 26**	G	-5	0	2	5	4	5	0	-2	
1	In virtute tua Domine Deus	an	WA 283	C	2	5	4	2	4	2	0	2	D
7	In virtute tua Domine laetabitur	int	GR [10] LU 1135 SYG 51 *GB 51 *GS 205	G	2	-2	2	0	2	5	4	5	G
6	In virtute tua Domine laetabitur	of	GR [46] OTT 152 LU 1205 *SYG 52 GB 51^v *GS 209	G	2	5	7	5	3	0	3	0	c
1	In visione Dei	re	WA 372	D	-2	0	3	2	0	3	0	-2	D
4	In visione sancta	re	WA 312	E	1	-2	0	-2	-4	-2	1	0	E
6	In voce exsultationis	an	LR 122 LU 930	E	1	-2	-4	-2	1	3	1	3	F
4	In voluntate tua Domine	int	GR 380 LU 1066 *SYG 256 *GB 261^v *GS 165	D	3	0	3	2	3	2	3	2	E

#	Text	Type	Sources		1	2	3	4	5	6	7	8	
2	In wulstano cujus aetas	an	WA 248	D	-2	0	2	3	0	3	0	2	D
	Incessanter pro nobis supplica / Pater insignis	rev	VP 128	D	7	5	3	7	5	3	2	0	
4	Inclina aurem tuam accelera	co	GR 338 LU 1012 / *SYG 244 *GB 251 / GS 149	F	2	0	-3	0	-1	0	2	4	E
	Inclina aurem tuam ad precem / Domine Deus salutis	ofv	OTT 112 *GB 74 / SYG 84	c	2	0	2	0	2	-3	2	0	
	Inclina cor meum Deus	sr	AR 29 LU 237 / AM 33										
	Inclina Domine aurem ... aperi / Qui caelorum contines	rev	WA 185										
	Inclina Domine aurem ... et exaudi me / Fac mecum Domine	intv	GR 134 GS 60 / GB 87^V SYG 98										
	Inclina Domine aurem ... et exaudi me / Miserere mihi	intv	GR 363 LU 1044 / GS 159 GB 256 / SYG 249										
2	Inclina Domine aurem ... et exaudi me	an	WA 69 LA 100	D	3	2	0	3	2	0	-2	0	D
1	Inclina Domine aurem ... et exaudi / me salvum	int	GR 360 LU 1040 / *SYG 249 GB 255^V / GS 158	C	2	9	10	9	12	9	7	5	D
	Inclina Domine aurem ... et exaudi / verba	an	OHS 178 (nm)										
2	Inclinans faciem meam	re	WA 175	A	3	5	7	5	8	7	8	10	D
1	Inclinate aurem vestram	an	WA 67 LA 97	F	2	4	2	0	2	4	2	0	D
1	Inclinavit Dominus aurem	an	AR 98 OHS 222 / LU 280 AM 133 134 / *WA 64 LA 90	F	2	4	2	4	2	-1	0	2	D
1	Inclinavit se Jesus	an	AR 395 LU 1092 / AM 370 WA 100 / LA 155	D	2	3	5	2	5	7	3	2	D
1	Inclyta stirps Jesse	an	PM 183	D	-2	0	3	2	0	3	0	-2	D
1	Inclyta stirps Jesse	an	AM 985	C	2	4	5	2	0	2	5	7	D
5	Indicabo tibi homo	re	LA 306 WA 186 (inc / illeg)	F	4	7	9	7	6	4	7	9	F
7	Induere vestimentis	an	WA 269	G	4	5	7	4	7	9	7	5	G
	Induit eam Dominus vestimentis / Signum magnum	rev	PM 120 LR 268										
	Induit eum Dominus loricam / Amavit eum Dominus	rev	PM 223 LR 201 / LA 532 WA 427										
7	Induit eum Dominus stola	an	LR 275	d	-3	0	2	0	-2	0	2	0	G
8	Induit eum Dominus vestimentis	tr	GR 13**	D	3	5	2	3	5	0	-2	0	G
7	Induit me Dominus cyclade	an	WA 253 *LA 332	d	-3	0	2	0	-2	0	-3	-2	G
6	Induit me Dominus vestimento	re	LR 228 LA 335 / *WA 253	F	2	0	-1	0	2	-3	-1	0	F
	Induit te Dominus vestimento / Audi filia	rev	VP 250 *WA 433	D	7	5	7	5	3	2	5	7	

	Incipit		Source									
	Indulgentiam ejus	see	Indulgentiam illius									
	Indulgentiam illius fusis 　Nos alium Deum	rev	LA 291 WA 177									
8	Induta est caro mea	re	LA 283 WA 172	G	2	-2	0	4	0	-2	2	5	G
3	Induxerunt puerum Jesum	an	LR 309	E	-2	3	5	8	10	8	7	5	E
	Induxisti nos in laqueum 　Probasti nos	trv	GR 108**	G	2	4	5	7	5	0	2	0	
	Inebriabo animam sacerdotum	sr	AR 8 (sup 2)									
	Inebriabuntur ab ubertate	sr	AR 7 (sup 2)									
	Inebriabuntur ab ubertate 　Filii hominum	trv	GR 55**	G	-5	0	2	4	2	5	4	0	
	Inebriabuntur ab ubertate	alv	GR 425	c	-1	2	0	-1	0	2	0	-3	
	Infantia quidem computabatur 　Diem festum sacratissimae	rev	LA 332 WA 253									
2	Infantiae primordia	an	WA 311	D	-5	-2	0	-2	0	2	3	0	D
8	Infantum diem martyrum	hy	ST 413	G	2	0	-2	0	2	4	0	-2	G
	Infirmata est in paupertate 　Miserere mei	trv	GR [145]	D	3	2	3	5	7	5	3	5	
4	Infirmata est virtus	an	LA 185	D	2	5	7	5	7	9	5	7	E
1	Infirmus fui et visitastis	co	GR 553 LU 1560	D	-2	0	2	3	2	0	2	3	D
1	Inflammatum est cor meum	gr	GR 622[1] LU 1681[2]	C	2	5	7	9	7	5	7	2	D
3	Infra annus adolescentiae	an	LR 274	G	2	0	2	5	4	2	4	2	E
6	Infunde precamur Domine	an	LA 538	c	2	4	0	-1	-3	-5	0	2	c
7	Ingenua sum et exspectabilis	an	WA 273 *LA 356	G	7	4	7	9	7	5	4	5	G
2	Ingrediar in locum	an	WA 439	F	-1	0	-3	-5	-3	0	-1	-5	D
2	Ingrediente Domino	re	GR 177 PM 60 OHS 104 LU 590 LA 181 *WA 112 GS 85	D	-2	0	3	2	3	0	2	0	D
7	Ingressa Agnes turpitudinis	an	AR 603 LU 1340 *AM 786 *WA 255 *LA 338	d	-3	0	2	0	-3	-2	0	-5	G
	Ingressa Agnes turpitudinis	alv	GB 45	D	2	3	5	7	5	7	10	7	
8	Ingresso Zacharia templum	an	AR 661 735 LU 1408 1497 AM 923 WA 320 *LA 400	G	5	2	0	2	0	-2	0	2	G
6	Ingressus Aaron tabernaculum	of	GR 17**	F	4	2	5	4	0	2	0	2	F
4	Ingressus angelus ad Mariam	an	WA 301	F	-1	-3	-1	-3	0	-1	0	2	E
1	Ingressus angelus ad Mariam	re	WA 301	C	2	0	2	5	2	4	0	2	D
7	Ingressus angelus ad Tobiam	an	AR 891 LU 1701	G	7	9	5	2	4	5	4	2	G
7	Ingressus est Raphael angelus	an	PM 199	G	2	0	5	7	9	7	4	7	G
7	Ingressus Paulus in synagogam	an	WA 264 LA 343	b	1	3	1	3	1	0	-2	-4	G

	Incipit		Source	M									
7	Ingressus Paulus in synagogam	re	LA 345 *WA 265	G	2	0	2	4	5	7	5	4	G
4	Ingressus Paulus in synagogam	of	SYG 45	C	2	4	5	7	2	7	5	4	E
7	Ingressus Raphael archangelus	an	LA 293	G	7	5	4	5	7	9	7	5	G
	Ingressus Zacharias templum	alv	SYG 198	D	7	9	7	5	3	5	7	5	
	Inhabitabo in tabernaculo tuo — Factus es spes	trv	GR 424 LU 1353	G	2	4	5	4	5	4	5	7	
2	Inimicitias ponam inter te	of	GR 584 LU 1603	a	-5	-2	2	0	3	0	-2	0	a
	Inimicos eos induam confusione — Sacerdotes	trv	LU 1623^C	G	2	5	4	2	5	2	0	2	
1	Iniquitates nostrae Domine	an	GB 156^v *WA 228	D	3	5	3	0	2	3	2	0	D
	Iniquos odio habui — Adjutor et susceptor	rev	LR 414 LA 168 WA 108										
	Initio cognovi de testimoniis	alv	GR 82**	D	-2	0	2	0	-2	0	2	3	
	Initium sapientiae timor	alv	GR 112**	D	-2	-5	-2	0	-2	2	5	2	
2	Initium sapientiae timor	re	LA 278 *WA 170	A	3	5	7	5	8	7	8	5	D
2	Inito consilio fratres	an	LR 325 *LA 370	C	5	4	5	2	4	0	2	4	D
2	Inito consilio venenum	re	WA 297	G	-2	-5	-2	-3	-5	-7	-2	0	G
2	Inito consilio venenum	an	WA 300	F	-1	-3	-1	-3	-5	-3	-1	-3	D
2	Inito consilio venenum	re	LR 321 *LA 368	C	2	5	2	5	4	5	2	4	D
4	Innocens manibus et mundo corde	an	AR 81 LU 279^A	F	-3	-1	0	2	0	2	4	2	E
6	Innocens manibus et mundo corde	co	GR (37)	F	-3	0	2	4	2	4	2	0	F
5	Innocenter puerilia	an	WA 240	F	4	7	5	4	7	9	7	9	F
2	Innocentes pro Christo	an	AR 287 LU 432 AM 264 *WA 44 *LA 62	C	2	5	7	4	5	2	0	2	D
8	Innova signa et immuta mirabilia	co	GR 87**	F	2	4	2	0	2	-3	2	0	G
4	Innuebant patri ejus	an	AR 736 LU 1503 AM 924 WA 323 LA 86 407	D	2	3	5	2	5	7	3	2	E
2	Innuebant patri ejus	re	LR 354 *LA 406 WA 322	A	3	7	5	8	10	8	7	5	D
	Inquire ut facias — Omni tempore benedic	rev	LA 288										
	Inquirentes autem Dominum — Timete Dominum	grv	GR 648 LU 1726 *GS 213 *GB 216 *SYG 192	D	3	0	-2	0	2	0	7	8	
3	Inseparabilis fides passioque	an	LA 427	G	5	2	0	2	4	5	2	4	E
8	Insidens nostris peramanter	hy	AR 8 (sup 2)	G	2	-2	0	2	0	-2	2	5	G
8	Insigne praeconium alme	an	WA 384	D	3	5	7	3	2	0	5	7	G
	Inspexit et fecit secundum exemplar — Maurus a teneris	rev	PM 124 LR 275										
2	Instabat enim precibus	an	WA 287	D	-2	0	-2	0	3	2	3	5	D

	Text	Type	Sources										
1	Instet clara dies quo recolendus	hy	ST 147	D	7	8	7	5	3	5	7	0	D
	Insurge ergo et toto 　　Ecce jam in sublime	rev	WA 258										
8	Insurrexerunt in me testes iniqui	an	OHS 481 LU 690 *WA 122 *LA 195	G	2	0	4	5	4	2	5	7	G
	Insurrexerunt in me viri absque 　　Animam meam	rev	OHS 499 LU 704 LA 197										
5	Insurrexerunt in me viri iniqui	of	GR [110]	a	-4	0	3	5	3	0	-2	2	F
3	Insurrexerunt in me viri iniqui	re	OHS 185 (nm) LA 180 *WA 111	F	-3	0	-1	0	-1	0	2	0	E
	Intactae matri reseratur janua 　　Porta Sion	rev	PM 268	a	-2	-5	-4	-7	-9	-7	-4	-7	
	Intellexisti cogitationes meas 　　Mihi autem	ofv	OTT 128 GB 203 SYG 201	D	5	7	10	5	10	7	5	9	
5	Intellexit Deus clamorem	an	WA 282	F	4	7	6	4	2	7	9	7	F
	Intellexit protinus vir Dei 　　Inito consilio	rev	LR 321 LA 368 WA 297										
8	Intellige clamorem meum	an	WA 64 *LA 89	c	-1	-3	-5	-3	-5	-3	-5	[0]	G
5	Intellige clamorem meum	co	GR 114 LU 549 SYG 78 GB 70v *GS 40 48	F	4	6	7	9	7	9	7	9	F
	Intelligite qui obliviscimini	an	OHS 300 (nm)										
4	Intemerata virgo quae redemptorem	an	PM 270	D	2	3	5	3	0	2	3	2	E
1	Intempesta nocte cuncta	an	WA 299	C	2	9	7	5	7	11	9	7	D
1	Intempestae noctis hora	re	LR 328 LA 371 WA 334	D	-2	0	3	2	0	-2	0	-2	D
6	Intempestae noctis hora	of	GB 55	G	2	4	5	7	9	5	7	5	c
3	Intempestae noctis hora	of	SYG 57	D	3	2	5	3	5	2	3	5	E
	Intende animae meae 　　Deus Israel	rev	OHS 241 (nm)										
	Intende animae meae 　　Ne avertas	rev	WA 107										
	Intende animae meae 　　Salvum me fac	rev	LA 177 WA 111										
	Intende in adjutorium meum	an	OHS 238 (nm)										
6	Intende in me	an	WA 65	F	-1	-3	0	2	0	2	0	[0]	F
8	Intende in me	an	LA 92	G	5	4	2	4	5	4	2	0	G
8	Intende qui regis Israel	hy	ST 30	G	-2	-3	-5	-2	2	0	-2	0	G
2	Intende qui regis Israel	hy	ST 8	D	-2	-3	-2	0	2	0	-2	0	D
8	Intende voci orationis meae	an	AR 70	G	-5	-2	0	2	0	2	0	-2	G
5	Intende voci orationis meae	of	GR 135 OTT 83 SYG 98 *GB 87v *GS 60 142	a	-2	1	0	-4	-2	-4	-2	-4	F
	Intente vigilans 　　Auditor legis	rev	WA 282	c	-1	0	2	0	-3	-5	-3	0	

	Incipit		Source										
1	Inter aeternas superum	hy	AM 854	D	2	3	0	-2	0	3	2	0	D
	Inter apostolos novissimus A Christo de caelo	rev	WA 263										
	Inter apostolos vocatione Prostratus est	anv	LA 343										
	Inter apostolos vocatione A Christo de caelo	grv	SYG 44	D	3	2	7	9	7	9	7	10	
	Inter apostolos vocatione Ingressus Paulus	ofv	SYG 45	D	5	7	9	7	5	10	7	3	
	Inter choros confessorum O laudanda	rev	LR 326	a	3	2	-2	-4	-2	0	-7	-4	
	Inter haec manet Christi miles	rev	WA 259	D	7	8	10	8	7	5	3	2	
	Inter iniquos projecerunt Omnes amici	rev	OHS 485 LU 693										
	Inter natos mulierum	sr	AR 740 LU 1502 AM 921 922										
1	Inter natos mulierum	re	LR 355 LA 406 *WA 323	D	-2	0	3	2	0	-2	0	-2	D
	Inter natos mulierum	alv	GS m	C	2	5	2	4	0	2	7	4	
	Inter natos mulierum	alv	SYG 196	G	2	5	4	5	7	5	2	5	
3	Inter natos mulierum	an	AR 736 LU 1504 *AM 925 *WA 321 *LA 86 407	G	5	4	2	5	4	0	2	4	E
	Inter vestibulum et altare In jejunio	rev	PM 49 LA 128 WA 86										
	Intercede pia pro nobis Virgo parens Christi	rev	AR 131* VP 39 LU 1862	F	2	4	5	4	5	4	2	0	
	Intercede pro nobis ad Deum Tu es vas	rev	PM 162 WA 263										
	Intercede pro nobis ad Deum Tu es vas	trv	GR 420 LU 1346 *GS 178 SYG 44	F	2	4	2	0	2	4	2	4	
	Intercede pro nobis summe Sancte Michael archangelorum	rev	LA 470										
	Intercedite pro nobis Omnes sancti qui	rev	WA 397										
	Interiora mea efferbuerunt Adesto dolori	rev	LA 286										
4	Interrogabat Magos Herodes	re	PM 42 LR 77 *LA 70 *WA 54	F	-3	0	-1	0	-1	2	0	-1	E
8	Interrogabat Magos Herodes	an	AR 333 LU 482 AM 299 *LA 74	G	-2	-5	-3	-2	0	2	0	2	G
	Interrogabat Magos Herodes	alv	SYG 31 GB 33^v	a	-2	0	2	0	-2	0	-2	-4	
1	Interrogatus a Judaeis	an	WA 191	D	-2	0	3	2	3	5	7	5	D
1	Interrogatus Joannes	re	LA 451	D	-2	0	3	2	0	-2	0	-2	D
7	Interrogatus te Dominum	an	WA 348 *LA 436	G	4	5	7	5	9	7	4	7	G

4	Intonuit de caelo Dominus	of	GR 249 OTT 58 LU 791 OHS 786 SYG 156 GB 134ᵛ GS 119 138	D	3	5	7	5	7	5	8	7	E
4	Intonuit Dominus de caelo	of	GR (14)	D	3	5	7	5	7	5	8	7	E
	Intrate in conspectu ejus Jubilate Domino omnis terra	trv	GR 82 LU 513 GS 28 *GB 59ᵛ *SYG 62	G	2	4	5	4	0	2	0	2	
3	Intravit autem rex	an	AR 570 LU 1062 *AM 611	G	5	2	0	2	5	2	4	5	E
1	Intravit Jesus in templum	an	AR 374 AM 347 LA 135	C	2	9	10	9	12	9	7	9	D
1	Intravit Maria in domum Symonis	an	WA 338	D	-2	3	5	7	5	3	5	7	D
2	Intravit Maria in domum Zachariae	an	AR 771 LU 1541 AM 954	D	-5	-2	0	-2	0	2	3	0	D
1	Intrepidus itaque candentis	an	WA 261	D	-2	3	5	3	5	7	9	7	D
	Intrepidus itaque Dei Assumptus ex eculeo	rev	WA 258										
4	Intret in conspectu tuo	int	GR [21] LU 1162 *SYG 40 *GB 43ᵛ GS 210	F	-3	-1	-3	0	2	4	2	4	E
5	Intret oratio mea ... Domine	an	AR 209 OHS 50 LU 316 *AM 59 60 *WA 68 *LA 98	a	-4	0	3	2	0	2	3	-2	F
3	Intret oratio mea ... inclina	int	GR 106 LU 541 SYG 81 *GB 73 GS 42	G	5	7	5	2	5	7	5	2	E
5	Introduxit me rex	an	WA 360	F	4	5	7	9	11	7	5	4	F
	Introduxit nos Dominus		see Introduxit vos Dominus										
8	Introduxit vos Dominus	int	GR 244 OHS 773 LU 785 SYG 154 GD 129 *GS 118	D	3	5	3	7	9	10	7	5	G
3	Introeuntem te Domine	an	SYG 120	G	2	5	2	0	5	4	5	7	E
	Introgressus ostium Vides o frater	rev	WA 344										
4	Introibo ad altare Dei ad Deum	of	GR 83**	D	3	0	3	2	3	5	7	5	E
8	Introibo ad altare Dei ad Deum	co	GR 80 LU 508 *GS 27 *SYG 61 *GB 59	G	5	2	5	4	0	2	5	4	G
4	Introibo ad altare Dei ad Dominum	an	WA 318	G	2	5	7	5	7	9	7	5	a
7	Introibo ad altare Dei sumam	an	LR 125 LU 934	G	4	5	7	9	12	7	9	7	G
5	Introibo in domum tuam	of	GR 2**	F	2	0	2	4	5	4	5	4	F
4	Introibo in domum tuam	an	LR 232	G	2	5	7	5	7	9	7	5	a
4	Intuemini quam sit	an	AR 243	G	2	5	7	5	7	9	7	5	a
3	Intuemini quantus sit	re	LA 20 381 *WA 24	G	2	4	5	4	5	4	2	0	E
4	Intuemini quantus sit	an	WA 26 LA 26	G	2	5	7	5	7	5	7	9	a

	Incipit		Sources										
	Intuens in caelum Stephanus servus	rev	WA 36										
4	Intuens in caelum	an	WA 51 *LA 43	E	-2	1	0	1	0	-2	-4	-2	E
4	Intuens in caelum	re	LA 43 *WA 34	D	3	0	3	2	3	5	3	2	E
1	Inundaverunt aquae Domine	an	GB 159^v	D	3	5	3	0	2	3	2	0	D
8	Inundaverunt aquae super caput	an	AR 426 OHS 190 AM 405 *WA 114 *LA 184	G	-2	0	2	4	0	2	0	2	G
	Invadent enim gregem Dixerunt discipuli	grv	GB 242	F	4	2	7	9	7	9	7	11	
1	Invenerunt in modum	an	WA 410 LA 494	D	-2	3	5	3	5	7	9	7	D
1	Invenerunt in modum	re	WA 409	D	3	5	3	2	3	5	3	5	D
	Inveni David servum meum Statuit ei Dominus	intv	SYG 37										
	Inveni David servum meum Posui adjutorium	rev	PM 314 LR 199 LA 531 WA 425										
4	Inveni David servum meum	re	LR 198 *LA 532	F	-3	0	-1	2	0	-1	0	-1	E
1	Inveni David servum meum	gr	GR [3] LU 1130 SYG 37 GB 41 GS 221	D	-2	0	2	0	-2	0	2	0	D
	Inveni David servum meum	alv	GR 514 LU 1489 *GS 222 *SYG 38	D	-2	0	2	3	5	7	5	3	
8	Inveni David servum meum	of	GR [9] [34] OTT 147 LU 1185 *SYG 27 GB 28^v *GS 223	E	3	5	7	5	8	5	3	5	G
8	Inveni quem diligit anima	tr	GR (11)	G	2	4	2	0	2	0	-2	0	G
	Inveniatur manus tua omnibus Desiderium animae	ofv	OTT 153 *GB 53^v *SYG 215	a	-4	0	3	5	3	5	3	5	
	Invenietis infantem pannis Angelus ad pastores	rev	LR 63 LA 32										
	Invenimus locum Domino Alleluia audivimus	rev	LA 238										
	Invenit eos concordes Advenit ignis	rev	LR 116 LA 259 WA 153										
1	Invenit Philippus Nathanael	an	LR 313	D	-2	3	5	3	5	7	5	7	D
	Inventa bona margarita Haec est virgo sapiens quam	rev	WA 432										
8	Inventa bona margarita	an	LR 225 *LA 545	G	5	2	0	-2	0	2	0	7	G
2	Inventor rutili dux bone luminis	hy	ST 479	D	-2	0	3	2	0	-2	0	3	D
2	Inventor rutili dux bone luminis	hy	GS 104	G	2	4	2	0	2	5	2	0	a
2	Inventor rutili dux bone luminis	hy	ST 478	C	2	5	2	0	2	4	5	2	D
2	Inventor rutili dux bone luminis	hy	WA 217	C	2	5	4	0	2	5	4	0	D
4	Inventor rutili dux bone luminis	hy	ST 478	D	7	8	7	5	7	2	3	5	E

	Title	Type	Sources										
4	Invicte martyr unicum	hy	AR [32]	E	-2	-4	0	3	1	-2	-4	-2	E
3	Invicte martyr unicum	hy	AR [31]	E	1	3	1	0	-2	0	-2	-4	E
3	Invicte martyr unicum	hy	AR [18]	a	2	0	-2	-5	-7	-2	0	3	E
6	Invicte martyr unicum	hy	AR [17]	F	2	4	2	4	2	0	4	7	F
1	Invicte martyr unicum	hy	AR 274	C	2	4	7	5	4	2	4	5	D
	Invoca me in die / In te Domine sperent	rev	WA 86										
2	Invocabat Scholastica Dominum	an	LR 294	F	-1	-3	-1	-3	-5	-3	0	-1	D
6	Invocabimus nomen tuum	an	AR 157 LU 279°	F	2	4	5	4	2	0	2	4	F
8	Invocabit me et ego exaudiam	int	GR 93 LU 532 *SYG 72 *GB 64v *GS 34	G	-2	0	5	4	5	2	-2	0	G
	Invocabit me et ego exaudiam / Qui habitat	trv	GR 95 LU 533 GS 35 *GB 65 *SYG 73	D	3	2	3	5	7	5	3	5	
4	Invocabo nomen tuum Domine	an	AR 425 OHS 152 LU 604 AM 403 *LA 185	G	2	5	7	5	7	9	7	5	a
1	Invocantem Dominum exclamemus	an	WA 227	C	2	9	11	9	12	9	11	12	D
2	Invocantem exaudivit Dominus	an	LR 192 *WA 424 LA 529	C	2	5	2	0	2	5	4	5	D
	Invocavi Dominum patrem	sr	AM 838										
7	Invocavi Dominum patrem	an	WA 435	G	5	4	5	7	9	7	9	12	G
6	Invocavit altissimum potentem	of	GR 470	C	2	9	10	9	10	9	12	9	F
	Invocavit me et ego	see	Invocabit me et ego										
	Ipse autem vulneratus / Sicut ovis	rev	WA 126										
	Ipse autem vulneratus / Vere languores	trv	GR [108]	F	-3	0	-3	0	-3	0	2	0	
8	Ipse enim pater amat vos	an	AR 486 *AM 502	F	2	4	2	4	2	4	2	0	G
	Ipse est directus divinitus	alv	GR 566 LU 1581	a	-4	0	-2	-5	-4	-5	-7	-9	
8	Ipse est Dominus meus	an	WA 343	F	2	4	7	6	4	2	4	2	G
	Ipse est rex justitiae / Praecursor pro nobis	rev	LA 25 WA 22										
	Ipse fecit nos et non ipsi nos / Jubilate Domino	trv	GR 82 LU 513 *GS 28 *GB 59v *SYG 62	c	-1	0	-1	-5	0	-1	0	-1	
	Ipse fecit nos et non ipsi nos / Jubilate Deo	ofv	OTT 23 *GB 36v *SYG 32	c	-1	0	4	0	-1	2	4	0	
1	Ipse habet in vestimento	gr	LU 1476D	C	2	9	10	9	10	9	7	9	D
6	Ipse invocabit me alleluia	an	LU 384 *LR 60 *WA 49 LA 33	F	-1	2	4	0	-3	-5	0	-1	F
2	Ipse invocabit me pater meus	tr	GR 640 LU 1711	D	-2	0	-2	-5	-2	0	-2	0	D
7	Ipse Jesus erat incipiens	an	AR 655 AM 844	G	7	4	5	7	9	7	9	7	G

	Incipit	Type	References	Mode									Final
	Ipse liberavit me de laqueo	sr	AR 30 LU 238 AM 338										
8	Ipse me coronavit	re	LA 360 WA 274	F	2	4	2	4	2	4	6	2	G
	Ipse per hunc nostros Qui regni	rev	LR 367 LA 418 *WA 328										
	Ipse praeibit ante illum Hic est praecursor	rev	LR 353 VP 177										
	Ipse praeibit ante illum Joannes vocabitur	rev	WA 322										
7	Ipse praeibit ante illum	an	AR 732 LU 1496 *AM 920 *WA 321 *LA 403	b	-4	-2	1	3	5	3	1	3	G
8	Ipse praeibit ante illum	re	LR 357 *LA 404 WA 321	F	2	4	2	4	2	4	2	4	G
7	Ipse praeibit ante illum	an	LR 352	G	2	5	9	7	5	7	10	9	G
	Ipse super maria fundavit Domini est terra	rev	LA 83 WA 61										
	Ipse super maria fundavit Tollite portas	ofv	OTT 14 SYG 14 GB 13	GG	7	5	7	10	7	5	7	5	
1	Ipsi soli servo fidem	an	LA 335 *WA 254	F	2	0	-3	-1	0	-1	-5	0	D
	Ipsi sum desponsata Jam corpus ejus	rev	LA 336 WA 254										
7	Ipsi sum desponsata	an	LA 334 *WA 254	d	-3	0	2	0	2	0	-3	-2	G
8	Ipsi sum desponsata	re	LA 335 WA 255	F	2	4	2	4	2	4	6	2	C
	Ipsi vero consideraverunt Deus Deus meus	trv	GR 180 OHS 109 LU 594 GS 86 GB 109 *SYG 122	F	-3	0	-3	0	-3	2	0	-1	
7	Ipsi vero in vanum	an	LA 187	G	2	5	7	5	7	9	10	7	G
2	Ipsi vero in vanum	an	AM 410 WA 117	C	2	5	7	5	7	9	11	7	D
4	Ipsi vero non cognoverunt	inv	LA 175 *WA 110	C	2	5	2	5	4	5	7	5	E
8	Ipsius quoque gloriae	an	WA 291	G	2	0	-2	0	2	0	2	5	G
	Ipso anno	see also Eodem vero anno											
4	Ipso anno quo de hac vita	re	LR 331	F	-3	0	-1	2	0	-1	0	-1	E
	Ipsum benedicite et cantate illi Benedicite Deum	rev	PM 113 LA 289										
	Ipsum unicum Dei patris Te laudant angeli	rev	WA 28	a	-2	-5	-4	-2	2	-2	0	-5	
3	Ira justa conditoris	hy	LR 442	E	1	0	-2	3	5	8	10	8	E
	Iratus Herodes jussit Vox in Rama	rev	WA 46										
8	Iratus rex Saul	an	WA 164 LA 273	G	5	2	0	-2	2	0	4	5	G
	Israel si me audieris Ecce mitto angelum	rev	LA 157 *WA 102	a	3	0	-2	0	-4	-5	-2	-4	
	Israel si me audieris Jerusalem cito veniet	rev	LA 8 *WA 9	a	3	0	-2	0	-4	-5	-2	-4	

	Incipit		Sources										
3	Ista est columba mea	an	AR 630 LU 1375	G	2	5	4	0	2	4	5	7	E
	Ista est quae ascendit Ista est speciosa	rev	LR 378 PM 312 WA 356										
8	Ista est speciosa electa	an	WA 365	G	-2	-5	-2	2	-2	0	2	4	G
	Ista est speciosa inter filias Haec virgo sancta	rev	WA 433	d	-2	0	3	0	2	3	5	3	
2	Ista est speciosa inter filias	re	PM 312 LR 378 *WA 356	F	-1	2	0	-3	-1	-3	-1	0	D
8	Ista est speciosa inter filias	an	AR [98] LU 1233	F	2	4	2	4	2	0	4	7	G
3	Ista est speciosa inter filias	an	AR [88] LU 1211 *AM 679 688	G	2	5	2	5	4	0	2	5	E
	Ista est speciosa quae ascendit Ista est speciosa	rev	PM 312										
8	Ista est virgo sapiens	an	WA 434	G	2	0	-2	0	5	4	2	5	G
8	Istarum est enim regnum	an	AR 645 LU 262[11] 1237 AM 691 748	G	5	2	0	2	0	-2	0	2	G
4	Iste cognovit justitiam	an	WA 428 *LA 528	F	-1	-3	0	-1	-3	-5	-3	-1	E
	Iste cognovit justitiam	alv	SYG 189	C	2	4	5	4	2	0	4	5	
3	Iste cognovit justitiam	re	LR 151 LA 523 WA 417	G	5	4	2	5	4	2	0	2	E
4	Iste confessor Domini colentes	hy	AR [72]	F	-3	-1	2	4	2	4	6	4	E
1	Iste confessor Domini colentes	hy	AR [53] LU 1179 AM 656 669	a	-2	0	-2	-4	-7	-9	-2	-4	D
2	Iste confessor Domini colentes	hy	AM 668	D	-2	0	2	3	2	0	2	0	D
2	Iste confessor Domini colentes	hy	AR [68] LU 1196	D	-2	0	3	2	0	2	0	-2	D
8	Iste confessor Domini colentes	hy	AR [52]	G	2	-2	0	2	0	-2	2	5	G
8	Iste confessor Domini colentes	hy	AR [51] LU 1178 AM 664	G	2	0	-3	-2	-3	-5	-3	-7	G
8	Iste confessor Domini colentes	hy	AR [49] LU 1177 AM 655	G	2	0	-3	-2	0	2	-2	2	G
1	Iste confessor Domini colentes	hy	AR [69] LU 1198	D	2	3	0	-2	0	3	2	0	D
1	Iste confessor Domini colentes	hy	AR [71]	D	3	0	3	2	0	2	-2	2	D
1	Iste confessor Domini sacratus	hy	LR 190	a	-2	0	-2	-4	-5	-7	-2	-4	D
1	Iste confessor Domini sacratus	hy	ST 104	a	-2	0	-2	-4	-5	-2	-4	-5	D
1	Iste confessor Domini sacratus	hy	ST 200	E	-2	1	0	-2	0	-4	0	3	D
8	Iste confessor Domini sacratus	hy	ST 103	G	2	0	-3	-2	-5	-7	-3	0	G
8	Iste confessor Domini sacratus	hy	ST 62	G	2	0	-3	-2	-5	-3	-5	-7	G
8	Iste confessor Domini sacratus	hy	ST 243	G	2	0	-3	-2	0	2	0	-2	G
8	Iste confessor Domini sacratus	hy	ST 404	G	2	0	-3	-2	0	2	0	2	G
1	Iste confessor Domini sacratus	hy	ST 200	G	2	0	-2	-5	-7	0	-2	0	D
8	Iste confessor Domini sacratus	hy	ST 104	G	2	0	-2	0	2	-2	2	5	G

8	Iste confessor Domini sacratus	hy	ST 135		G	2	4	2	4	5	4	2	0	G
6	Iste confessor Domini sacratus	hy	ST 153		D	3	5	3	2	0	3	-2	0	F
2	Iste confessor Domini sacratus	hy	ST 104		G	7	9	7	5	7	10	9	7	d
2	Iste dilectus Joannis	hy	ST 412		C	2	0	5	4	2	0	5	7	D
8	Iste est de primoribus theologis	an	WA 291		G	-2	-5	-2	2	0	2	0	2	G
1	Iste est de prioribus theologis	re	VP 122 *WA 290		D	-2	0	3	5	3	2	3	0	D
8	Iste est de sublimibus caelorum	re	VP 259 LA 405		G	-2	0	-7	-5	-2	0	2	0	G
2	Iste est discipulus	an	WA 43		F	-1	-3	-1	-3	-5	-3	-1	-3	D
	Iste est enim Joannes Iste est de sublimibus	rev	LA 405		G	5	4	0	2	4	2	5	7	
7	Iste est frater vester	re	LA 150 WA 97		G	7	5	4	5	7	9	7	9	G
	Iste est Gregorius praesul Iste est de prioribus	rev	VP 122											
8	Iste est Gregorius qui simoniacam	an	PM 156		G	5	2	0	-2	0	2	-2	-3	G
1	Iste est Joannes	an	AR 282 LU 420 *AM 257 *WA 42 *LA 56		F	-5	-3	4	5	4	2	4	5	D
1	Iste est Joannes	re	PM 33 *LA 53 WA 41		D	7	8	7	5	3	5	8	7	D
3	Iste est Odo abbas mirabilis	re	PM 210		E	-2	3	5	8	5	8	3	5	E
	Iste est qui ante Deum ... et de omni Iste est de sublimibus	rev	VP 259											
8	Iste est qui ante Deum ... et de omni	re	LR 208		F	2	4	2	4	6	4	2	4	G
	Iste est qui ante Deum ... et est	alv	SYG 211		E	1	3	5	3	0	1	-2	-4	
8	Iste est qui ante Deum ... et omnis	an	WA 294 LA 539		G	-2	-5	-2	0	2	0	2	0	G
8	Iste est qui ante Deum ... et omnis	re	LR 199 *LA 535 *WA 426		F	2	4	2	4	6	4	2	4	G
	Iste est qui contempsit Iste cognovit	rev	LR 151 LA 523 WA 417											
	Iste est qui contempsit Iste est	rev	LR 199 LA 535 WA 426											
	Iste est qui contempsit Iste homo	rev	LR 207											
	Iste est qui contempsit Iste sanctus pro lege	rev	LR 150											
8	Iste est qui contempsit	an	WA 426		F	2	4	7	6	4	2	4	6	G
	Iste est qui pro lege Dei	alv	SYG 210		D	3	2	5	3	2	3	0	-2	
8	Iste homo ab adolescentia	re	LA 534 WA 426		D	3	5	7	5	7	3	5	7	G
8	Iste homo perfecit omnia	re	LR 207 WA 426		D	3	5	7	5	7	5	7	10	G
	Iste puer magnus coram Domino Descendit angelus	rev	LR 352											
4	Iste puer magnus coram Domino	an	AR 733 LU 1496		G	2	5	7	9	5	7	9	7	a

Mode	Incipit	Type	Source										
7	Iste puer magnus coram Domino	an	AM 921	G	2	5	7	9	5	7	9	7	G
1	Iste puer magnus coram Domino	an	WA 323	C	2	5	7	9	7	5	7	9	D
8	Iste quem laeti colimus fideles	hy	AR 654 181* AM 844 VP 126	a	-2	0	2	3	2	0	2	3	G
	Iste sanctus digne in memoriam	alv	SYG 226 *GS 207	G	-2	0	2	0	-2	2	4	5	
1	Iste sanctus digne in memoriam	re	LR 203 WA 391 (inc illeg)	D	3	0	-2	3	5	7	5	3	D
8	Iste sanctus fecit mirabilia	an	PM 229	G	-5	-2	2	0	2	5	4	5	G
	Iste sanctus pro lege Dei Hic est vir qui non est derelictus	rev	WA 418										
5	Iste sanctus pro lege Dei	re	LR 150 LA 522 *WA 416	c	-3	0	2	0	-3	0	-5	-3	F
8	Iste sanctus pro lege Dei	an	AR 334 577[12] [15] LU 262 1123 AM 639 736 LA 521	a	-2	-4	-2	0	-2	-4	0	3	G
5	Isti etenim maximo	an	WA 342	F	4	7	4	2	7	9	7	9	F
7	Isti sunt agni novelli	re	OHS 823 LR 169 LA 212 WA 134 305	G	2	0	2	0	2	5	4	5	G
7	Isti sunt dies quos observare	re	LA 166 WA 105	G	7	9	7	5	7	5	7	5	G
	Isti sunt duae olivae Isti sunt duo viri	rev	LA 409 WA 324										
	Isti sunt duae olivae	alv	SYG 199 *GS n	a	-4	0	-2	-5	-4	-7	-9	-7	
7	Isti sunt duae olivae	re	WA 329	G	2	0	2	0	2	5	4	5	G
1	Isti sunt duae olivae	an	AR 745 LU 1510 *WA 333	C	5	4	2	4	2	0	2	4	D
	Isti sunt duo filii Isti sunt duae olivae	rev	WA 329										
	Isti sunt duo viri	alv	SYG 208	D	2	-2	0	2	3	5	3	2	
7	Isti sunt duo viri	re	LA 409 *WA 324	G	7	4	7	5	7	9	5	4	G
	Isti sunt qui non inclinaverunt Isti sunt qui passi	rev	WA 45										
	Isti sunt qui ut nubes Candidi facti	rev	WA 306										
	Isti sunt qui venerunt Isti sunt triumphatores	rev	LR 143 LA 508										
	Isti sunt qui venerunt Laverunt stolas	rev	WA 44										
	Isti sunt qui venerunt Tradiderunt corpora ... et	rev	LR 179 LA 515 WA 421										
	Isti sunt qui venerunt Tradiderunt corpora ... ideo	rev	LA 388										
	Isti sunt qui venerunt	alv	SYG 194	C	2	4	5	7	9	7	5	7	
8	Isti sunt qui viventes	re	LR 145	F	2	4	2	0	4	7	6	7	G
2	Isti sunt sancti martyres	an	LA 521	C	2	5	4	5	2	0	2	5	D

8	Isti sunt sancti qui non inquinaverunt	re	LA 59 *WA 45	G	-2	-5	-3	-2	-3	-5	-7	-5	G
3	Isti sunt sancti qui passi	re	LA 60 *WA 45	c	-1	0	-3	-5	-3	-1	0	-1	E
1	Isti sunt sancti qui pro Dei	an	AR 744 *AM 929 *LA 513	F	-5	-3	4	5	4	2	4	5	D
2	Isti sunt sancti qui pro testamento	an	AR [46] LU 1156 AM 651 *WA 424 LA 520	F	-1	-5	-1	0	-3	-5	-3	0	D
2	Isti sunt sancti qui pro testamento	re	LA 390	G	2	0	2	4	5	4	2	0	D
7	Isti sunt sancti qui pro testamento	re	WA 422	G	5	4	5	7	5	7	9	7	G
8	Isti sunt sermones	an	AR 483 *AM 498 *WA 134 *LA 219	F	2	0	2	4	2	4	2	0	G
4	Isti sunt triumphatores	re	LR 143 LA 508 WA 412	F	-3	0	-1	0	2	0	2	4	E
1	Isti sunt viri sancti facti	an	AR 781 LU 1552	C	5	4	2	4	2	0	2	4	D
4	Isti sunt viri sancti quos	an	WA 325	E	-2	1	0	-2	-4	-2	0	-2	E
8	Isti sunt viri sancti quos	re	LR 145 LA 509 *WA 413	F	2	4	2	4	6	4	2	4	G
4	Isti viventes in carne	re	WA 413 *LA 508	F	2	4	2	0	4	7	6	9	E
	Istorum est enim regnum Isti sunt sancti qui pro	rev	WA 422										
8	Istorum est enim regnum	an	AR 577[14] [40] LR 181 LU 262[2] 1154 AM 647 738 WA 422 *LA 516	G	5	2	0	2	0	-2	0	2	G
	Ita oculi nostri ad Dominum Ad te levavi	trv	GR 124 LU 554 GS 55 GB 82[v] SYG 93	D	3	0	3	7	3	5	3	5	
	Ita ut in sublime Dum sacramenta	rev	WA 399										
1	Ite dicite Joanni	an	WA 15 *LA 10	a	-2	0	-2	-4	-2	3	0	-2	D
8	Ite et vos in vineam	an	AR 344 LU 497 AM 314 WA 75 LA 114	c	-1	-3	-5	-3	-5	-7	-5	-3	G
6	Ite in orbem universum	re	LR 114 *LA 258 *WA 148	F	2	0	-3	-1	0	-1	-3	0	F
1	Ite missa est XIII		GR 47* LU 53	D	-2	0	3	2	-2	2	0	3	D
1	Ite missa est IV		GR 18* LU 28	a	-2	0	3	2	0	-2	0	-2	D
5	Ite missa est II[b]		GR 11* LU 22	c	-1	-5	-3	-5	-8	-7	-5	-10	C
8	Ite missa est VII		GR 28* LU 37	c	-1	-3	-5	-7	-3	0	-1	-5	G
1	Ite missa est XI		GR 41* LU 48	a	1	0	-2	0	-7	-4	-2	0	D
8	Ite missa est Ia		GR 7* LU 19	G	2	0	-2	0	2	0	5	4	G
8	Ite missa est XIV		GR 50* LU 56	G	2	0	2	0	-5	0	-2	0	G
8	Ite missa est XII		GR 44* LU 51	G	2	4	0	7	5	4	2	0	G
8	Ite missa est VI		GR 25* LU 34	G	2	4	2	5	4	0	2	0	G

3	Ite missa est IIa		GR 11* LU 22	G	2	4	2	5	4	2	0	2	E
8	Ite missa est V		GR 21* LU 31	G	2	4	5	4	2	0	2	4	G
4	Ite missa est XV		GR 53* LU 59	C	2	5	4	2	4	[0	0	0]	E
1	Ite missa est IX		GR 35* LU 43	D	3	5	7	5	3	2	0	3	D
7	Ite missa est Ib		GR 7* LU 19	G	4	5	7	5	7	9	7	4	G
5	Ite missa est VIII		GR 31* LU 39	F	4	5	7	9	7	5	7	12	F
4	Ite nuntiate fratribus meis	an	AM 485 *AR 471 LA 233 234	F	-1	-3	-1	0	2	0	2	-3	E
	Ite nuntiate fratribus meis	alv	SYG 163	E	5	7	5	3	5	3	0	1	
1	Iter faciente Jesu	an	AR 355 LU 510 AM 329 *WA 83 *LA 124	C	2	0	2	5	2	4	2	0	D
8	Iterum autem videbo vos	an	LA 237	G	2	0	2	0	2	0	2	0	G
	Iterum autem videbo vos	alv	GS 129 *SYG 166	F	4	2	0	4	-1	0	-1	-3	
8	Iterum videbo vos alleluia	an	WA 143	G	2	5	4	0	2	5	4	0	G
1	Iterum videbo vos alleluia	an	LA 236 *231	F	4	2	4	0	2	5	2	4	D
	Iterum videbo vos et gaudebit	alv	SYG 166	a	-2	-4	-5	-2	-4	-5	-7	-9	
8	Iterum autem videbo vos et gaudebit	an	AM 492 LA 237	F	2	4	2	4	2	4	2	4	G
8	Jacebant sancta corpora	hy	ST 396	G	-2	0	2	5	4	5	7	5	G
8	Jacob autem genuit Joseph	co	GR 487 LU 1277^B	c	-1	0	-3	-5	0	2	0	-1	G
1	Jacob autem genuit Joseph	an	AR 319 648 688 LU 467 1400 AM 836 886	C	2	9	10	9	12	9	7	9	D
4	Jacobe juste	hy	ST 402	F	-3	-5	-3	0	-3	-5	0	2	E
4	Jacobe juste	hy	ST 241	F	-1	-3	-5	-3	0	-3	-1	0	E
7	Jacta cogitatum tuum	gr	GR 328 LU 982 SYG 67 GB 63^v *GS 32 49 143	G	5	2	0	2	0	-2	0	2	G
4	Jam bone pastor Petre	hy	AM 824 936 990	E	1	0	-2	-4	-2	1	-2	0	E
7	Jam carmine mellifluo	hy	ST 158	G	2	0	-2	2	0	2	4	0	G
8	Jam Christe sol justitiae	hy	ST 89	G	-2	-3	-5	-2	2	-2	0	2	G
8	Jam Christe sol justitiae	hy	ST 380	G	-2	-3	-2	0	2	0	-2	0	G
4	Jam Christus ascendit polum	hy	ST 419	D	7	5	0	2	3	5	7	5	E

7 Jam Christus astra ascenderat	hy	ST 38	G	-2	2	0	2	4	5	4	2	G
8 Jam Christus astra ascenderat	hy	ST 453	G	2	-2	0	2	4	5	4	2	G
7 Jam Christus astra ascenderat	hy	ST 10	G	2	0	-2	0	2	5	7	5	G
1 Jam Christus astra ascenderat	hy	ST 94	a	3	0	-2	-4	-2	0	-5	-7	D
1 Jam Christus astra ascenderat	hy	LR 107 ST 391	D	3	0	-2	3	5	7	5	10	D
1 Jam Christus astra ascenderat	hy	ST 421	D	5	3	-2	0	2	3	5	3	D
2 Jam Christus sol justitiae	hy	AM 338	A	3	5	7	5	3	5	3	7	D
7 Jam corpus ejus corpori meo	an	LA 334	d	-3	0	2	0	2	0	-3	-2	G
8 Jam corpus ejus corpori meo	an	WA 254	G	-2	-5	-2	-3	-2	0	2	0	G
8 Jam corpus ejus corpori meo	re	LA 336 WA 254	F	2	4	2	4	2	4	6	2	G
2 Jam decus lactentium	an	WA 238	C	2	5	4	2	4	0	4	2	D
4 Jam enim hiems	an	WA 434 *LA 543	G	2	5	7	5	7	9	7	5	a
5 Jam fulget oriens	an	PM 26	C	2	4	5	7	9	7	9	12	C
2 Jam hiems transiit ... flores	tr	GR 615	D	-2	0	-2	-5	-2	0	-2	0	D
8 Jam hiems transiit ... surge	an	AR [98] [116] LU 1233 1259 *AM 687 707	G	5	2	0	-2	0	2	0	4	G
6 Jam laetus moriar quia vidi	re	PM 142	F	5	2	0	2	5	4	7	5	F
8 Jam lucis orto sidere	hy	AM 2 81	G	-5	-2	0	2	0	-2	0	5	G
4 Jam lucis orto sidere	hy	ST 71	a	-2	-5	-7	-2	0	2	0	-2	E
7 Jam lucis orto sidere	hy	ST 203	d	-2	-5	-7	-2	0	2	0	-2	G
2 Jam lucis orto sidere	hy	ST 172	G	-2	-5	-2	0	-2	3	5	3	G
1 Jam lucis orto sidere	hy	ST 142	d	-2	-3	-5	-7	-3	-5	-7	-9	D
2 Jam lucis orto sidere	hy	ST 73	D	-2	0	2	0	-2	-3	-2	0	D
1 Jam lucis orto sidere	hy	ST 148	D	-2	0	3	0	-2	3	5	3	D
2 Jam lucis orto sidere	hy	AR 13 LU 224 AM 81 ST 3 264	D	-2	0	3	5	3	2	0	5	D
2 Jam lucis orto sidere	hy	ST 142	e	-2	1	0	-2	0	-2	-3	-5	a
2 Jam lucis orto sidere	hy	ST 73	D	-2	3	2	0	7	5	3	2	D
5 Jam lucis orto sidere	hy	ST 74	f	-1	-3	-6	-5	-3	-5	-8	-10	f
4 Jam lucis orto sidere	hy	ST 154	E	1	3	1	0	-2	-4	-2	0	E
4 Jam lucis orto sidere	hy	ST 71	E	1	3	1	0	-2	0	-2	-4	E
2 Jam lucis orto sidere	hy	ST 75	D	2	-2	0	2	5	3	2	0	D
8 Jam lucis orto sidere	hy	ST 265	G	2	0	-3	-2	0	2	0	2	G
1 Jam lucis orto sidere	hy	ST 72	G	2	0	-2	-3	-2	0	2	0	D
8 Jam lucis orto sidere	hy	AM 2 ST 266	G	2	0	-2	0	2	0	2	5	G
8 Jam lucis orto sidere	hy	ST 77 172	G	2	0	-2	0	2	0	2	5	G
6 Jam lucis orto sidere	hy	AR 78 AM 1	F	2	0	-1	2	4	2	0	2	F

8	Jam lucis orto sidere	hy	AR 14 LU 224	G	2	4	0	2	5	4	2	4	G
6	Jam lucis orto sidere	hy	ST 67 167	F	2	4	2	0	2	0	2	4	F
2	Jam lucis orto sidere	hy	ST 73	C	2	4	2	0	2	0	4	2	D
8	Jam lucis orto sidere	hy	AM 2 82	G	2	4	2	0	2	4	5	4	G
5	Jam lucis orto sidere	hy	ST 72	F	2	4	2	0	2	4	6	4	F
1	Jam lucis orto sidere	hy	ST 76	F	2	4	5	4	2	0	2	4	D
2	Jam lucis orto sidere	hy	OHS 76 198 (nm)	C	2	4	5	4	2	0	2	4	D
5	Jam lucis orto sidere	hy	ST 74	F	2	4	5	4	2	0	7	9	F
5	Jam lucis orto sidere	hy	ST 451	c	2	5	2	4	5	7	5	4	F
1	Jam lucis orto sidere	hy	ST 76	C	2	9	10	9	7	9	7	5	D
1	Jam lucis orto sidere	hy	ST 75	a	3	0	-2	-4	-2	0	-5	-7	D
1	Jam lucis orto sidere	hy	ST 3 26 75 360	D	3	0	-2	3	5	7	5	10	D
2	Jam lucis orto sidere	hy	ST 206	E	3	5	3	1	3	5	3	0	D
2	Jam lucis orto sidere	hy	ST 172	A	3	5	8	7	5	3	5	3	D
7	Jam lucis orto sidere	hy	ST 265	G	4	5	4	2	0	2	4	5	G
6	Jam lucis orto sidere	hy	ST 245	C	4	5	7	5	4	2	0	2	C
8	Jam lucis orto sidere	hy	ST 206	G	5	4	2	0	2	-2	2	5	G
8	Jam lucis orto sidere	hy	ST 121	C	5	4	5	7	9	7	5	7	G
8	Jam lucis orto sidere fulget dies	hy	ST 116	G	2	4	2	5	4	2	0	-2	G
8	Jam lucis splendor rutilat	hy	ST 367	G	-5	-2	0	2	0	-2	0	5	G
2	Jam lucis splendor rutilat	hy	ST 415	D	-2	0	3	5	3	2	0	5	D
2	Jam morte victor obruta	hy	AR 876 AM 1077	a	-2	-5	-7	-2	0	3	2	0	a
8	Jam noctis umbrae concidunt	hy	AM 816	G	2	4	5	4	2	0	2	-2	G
8	Jam non dicam vos	re	PM 330 LR 110 LU 1847 VP 275 LA 257 *WA 154	F	2	4	2	4	2	4	6	4	G
	Jam per terras Magne pater Nicholae	rev	WA 241	d	-2	-3	-5	-7	-2	0	2	0	
	Jam quodammodo Dum vero adhuc	rev	WA 239	D	7	5	7	5	3	2	5	7	
2	Jam regina discubuit	hy	AM 1020	a	-2	-5	-7	-2	0	3	2	0	a
8	Jam sol recedit igneus	hy	AR 206 516 LU 312 915	a	-2	-4	-7	-5	-4	-2	0	-2	G
2	Jam surgit hora tertia	hy	ST 35	D	-2	-3	-2	0	-2	0	2	5	D
8	Jam surgit hora tertia	hy	ST 4	G	-2	-3	-2	0	2	0	2	5	G
8	Jam ter quaternis trahitur	hy	ST 88	G	-2	-3	-5	-2	2	0	-2	0	G
6	Jam tibi fili	an	WA 256	F	2	4	2	0	2	0	2	4	F
4	Jam toto subitus vesper eat polo	hy	AR 840 LU 1640 AM 1045	D	2	3	5	7	5	2	3	5	E
4	Janitor caeli doctor orbis pariter	hy	ST 234	F	-1	-3	-5	-3	0	-3	-1	0	E

4	Jerusalem cito veniet salus	re	LR 392 *LA 8 *WA 9	E	1	-4	-2	1	-2	0	1	3	E
7	Jerusalem gaude gaudio	an	AR 231 *LA 16 LU 338 AM 204	a	2	3	5	3	2	0	3	2	G
5	Jerusalem gaude gaudio	an	WA 16	F	4	5	7	5	4	5	2	4	F
7	Jerusalem Jerusalem quae occidis	an	LA 45	G	4	5	2	5	4	7	4	5	G
	Jerusalem luge	see also Jerusalem surge											
5	Jerusalem luge et exue	re	LA 202 *WA 125	a	-4	0	3	2	3	5	7	5	F
8	Jerusalem plantabis vineam	re	LA 9 *WA 11	G	-2	-5	-3	-2	-3	-5	-7	-5	G
	Jerusalem quae aedificatur Laetatus sum in his	trv	SYG 101	D	-2	0	3	5	3	0	3	5	
4	Jerusalem quae aedificatur	co	GR 141 LU 563 SYG 102 GB 91 GS 64	E	1	-2	0	-4	-2	3	5	1	E
7	Jerusalem respice	an	WA 8 *LA 22	G	2	5	4	5	7	5	7	9	G
	Jerusalem surge	see also Jerusalem luge											
5	Jerusalem surge et exue	re	OHS 598 LU 757	a	-4	0	3	2	3	5	7	5	F
2	Jerusalem surge et sta	co	GR 6 LU 330 SYG 5 *GB 4 GS 3	D	2	-2	0	3	2	3	2	3	D
6	Jesu amor unice	hy	ST 48	c	4	5	7	9	7	2	5	4	c
4	Jesu Christe auctor vitae	hy	ST 234	E	-2	1	-2	-4	-2	0	-2	0	E
4	Jesu Christe auctor vitae	hy	ST 394	E	-2	1	-2	-4	-2	1	-2	0	E
	Jesu Christe fili Dei	sr	WA 7 310										
4	Jesu Christe patris unigenite	hy	ST 48	E	1	3	1	0	-2	0	3	5	E
3	Jesu Christi Domini	an	WA 372	F	-3	-1	-5	-3	0	-3	0	2	E
8	Jesu corona caelitum	hy	LR 455	G	2	0	-2	2	5	4	0	2	G
8	Jesu corona celsior	hy	AR [78] AM 780	G	-5	0	2	0	-3	-2	0	2	G
4	Jesu corona celsior	hy	AR [80]	E	-2	-4	0	3	1	-2	-4	-2	E
8	Jesu corona celsior	hy	AR [75] AM 672	G	-2	-3	-2	0	-2	0	2	5	G
3	Jesu corona celsior	hy	AR [77]	E	-2	3	5	8	7	8	10	8	E
3	Jesu corona celsior	hy	AM 673	E	1	3	1	0	-2	0	-2	-4	E
1	Jesu corona celsior	hy	ST 44	C	2	4	7	5	4	2	5	4	D
8	Jesu corona celsior	hy	ST 371	D	3	5	3	5	7	5	0	3	G
8	Jesu corona celsior	hy	ST 16	D	3	5	3	7	5	0	3	5	G
4	Jesu corona virginum	hy	ST 105	E	-4	-2	1	0	1	3	1	0	E
4	Jesu corona virginum	hy	AR [91] LU 1213	E	-2	-4	0	3	1	-2	-4	-2	E
8	Jesu corona virginum	hy	ST 16	G	-2	0	2	4	5	4	5	7	G
8	Jesu corona virginum	hy	ST 44	G	-2	0	2	5	4	5	7	5	G
2	Jesu corona virginum	hy	ST 203	D	-2	2	3	5	7	5	3	2	D

3 Jesu corona virginum	hy	ST 405	E	-2	3	5	8	7	5	3	5	E
3 Jesu corona virginum	hy	ST 63	E	-2	3	5	8	7	5	8	7	E
3 Jesu corona virginum	hy	AM 677	E	1	3	1	0	-2	0	-2	-4	E
8 Jesu corona virginum	hy	AR [89] LU 1211 AM 677 771	G	2	4	5	4	2	0	2	-2	G
2 Jesu corona virginum	hy	ST 442	D	2	5	3	2	5	3	0	2	D
6 Jesu corona virginum	hy	ST 313	C	2	5	4	2	0	2	4	5	C
2 Jesu corona virginum	hy	AR [90]	D	3	2	5	3	0	2	5	3	D
2 Jesu corona virginum	hy	ST 244	A	3	5	3	5	8	5	8	3	D
1 Jesu decus angelicum	hy	AR 302 AM 281	a	-7	-4	-5	-7	0	2	-2	0	a
1 Jesu dulcis memoria	hy	AR 300 LU 452 AM 278	a	-7	-4	-5	-7	0	2	-2	0	a
2 Jesu nostra redemptio	hy	ST 93	d	-2	-5	-7	-2	0	3	2	0	d
4 Jesu nostra redemptio	hy	ST 231	F	-1	0	2	4	2	-1	-3	-1	E
4 Jesu nostra redemptio	hy	GR 156* AM 506	F	-1	0	2	4	2	0	-3	-1	E
4 Jesu nostra redemptio	hy	PM 95	F	-1	2	3	2	0	-3	0	-1	E
4 Jesu nostra redemptio	hy	ST 390	D	2	3	5	7	5	3	0	2	E
8 Jesu nostra redemptio	hy	ST 190	G	2	4	2	0	2	0	5	4	G
3 Jesu nostra redemptio	hy	ST 37	G	2	4	2	5	4	2	0	2	E
4 Jesu nostra redemptio	hy	ST 293	C	4	5	7	9	7	5	2	4	E
4 Jesu nostra redemptio	hy	ST 293	C	4	5	7	9	7	5	4	5	E
1 Jesu nostra redemptio	hy	ST 112	D	7	8	7	5	7	8	10	8	D
4 Jesu quadragenariae	hy	ST 112	E	-2	1	0	1	3	5	8	5	E
7 Jesu quadragenariae	hy	ST 226	G	2	0	-3	-2	0	2	0	2	G
8 Jesu quadragenariae	hy	ST 282	G	2	0	-3	-2	0	2	5	2	G
1 Jesu quadragenariae	hy	ST 383	D	2	0	-2	0	2	0	2	0	D
7 Jesu redemptor omnium	hy	ST 201 (inc lacking)										
4 Jesu redemptor omnium	hy	AR [60]	E	-2	-4	0	3	1	-2	-4	-2	E
4 Jesu redemptor omnium	hy	ST 387	E	-2	-4	0	3	5	3	1	3	E
8 Jesu redemptor omnium	hy	AM 268	G	-2	-3	-5	-2	2	0	-2	0	G
3 Jesu redemptor omnium	hy	ST 244	E	-2	3	5	8	7	5	8	7	E
4 Jesu redemptor omnium	hy	AR [59] AM 660	F	-1	-3	-1	2	4	0	-1	2	E
3 Jesu redemptor omnium	hy	AM 660	E	1	3	1	0	-2	0	-2	-4	E
4 Jesu redemptor omnium	hy	AR [57]	G	2	0	2	4	2	0	2	4	b
8 Jesu redemptor omnium	hy	ST 119	F	2	4	2	0	4	7	6	4	G
1 Jesu redemptor omnium	hy	AR 260 291 LU 365	C	2	4	7	5	4	2	4	5	D
7 Jesu redemptor omnium	hy	ST 104	F	2	4	7	6	4	2	0	4	G

7	Jesu redemptor omnium	hy	ST 201	G	2	5	4	2	0	2	5	7	G
3	Jesu redemptor omnium	hy	ST 62	E	3	5	8	7	5	3	5	3	E
8	Jesu redemptor omnium	hy	ST 404	G	4	2	5	4	2	0	2	5	G
7	Jesu redemptor omnium	hy	AR [58]	G	4	5	7	9	7	5	4	5	G
4	Jesu redemptor omnium	hy	ST 342	D	7	8	7	5	3	2	0	2	E
6	Jesu redemptor saeculi	hy	ST 325	F	-3	0	2	4	5	4	0	2	F
8	Jesu redemptor saeculi	hy	ST 93	a	3	0	3	2	3	0	3	2	G
8	Jesu redemptor saeculi	hy	ST 382	G	4	2	5	4	2	0	2	5	G
8	Jesu redemptor saeculi	hy	ST 215	G	5	2	5	4	2	5	4	2	G
1	Jesu rex admirabilis	hy	LR 431	C	2	4	7	5	4	2	4	5	D
7	Jesu rex regum omnium	hy	ST 392	F	2	4	6	7	6	4	2	4	G
8	Jesu sacrator mentium	hy	ST 382	G	-2	0	2	5	4	5	7	5	G
4	Jesu sacrator mentium	hy	ST 164	E	1	-2	-4	-2	1	0	-2	0	E
8	Jesu salvator saeculi	hy	ST 144	a	-2	0	3	-2	-4	-7	-5	-4	G
1	Jesu salvator saeculi	hy	ST 237	D	2	-2	2	5	7	5	2	3	D
8	Jesu salvator saeculi	hy	AM 1105	G	2	0	-2	2	5	4	0	2	G
7	Jesu salvator saeculi	hy	ST 400	F	2	4	6	7	6	4	2	4	G
8	Jesu salvator saeculi	hy	ST 194	C	2	5	4	5	7	9	7	5	G
1	Jesu salvator saeculi	hy	ST 42	G	2	9	10	9	7	9	7	5	a
4	Jesum de Maria	inv	LR 444	D	3	0	3	2	3	5	0	5	E
	Jesum quaeritis Nazaraenum Angelus Domini locutus	rev	LA 208										
6	Jesum quem quaeris	an	WA 134	F	2	0	2	6	4	2	4	2	F
6	Jesum quem quaeritis	an	LA 216 *234	c	2	0	2	5	4	5	4	2	c
8	Jesum qui crucifixus est	an	LA 223	G	-2	0	2	5	4	0	4	5	G
6 8	Jesum tradidit impius	re	OHS 507 LU 711 *LA 199	e	3	0	3	0	3	5	3	0	c
1	Jesus autem cum jejunasset	an	AR 369 LU 530 AM 343 *WA 88 *LA 133	D	3	0	-2	3	5	3	7	5	D
	Jesus autem eo quod maneat	alv	GR [101] LU 1283[B]	G	5	4	5	7	9	5	4	5	
1	Jesus autem transiens	an	AR 391 LU 1089 AM 366 WA 99 LA 154	D	-2	3	5	3	5	7	5	7	D
	Jesus Christus qui est lux Adducunt beato Mauro	rev	LR 278										
1	Jesus haec dicens	an	WA 79 *LA 119	D	2	3	5	3	2	0	3	5	D
8	Jesus junxit se discipulis	an	AR 448 OHS 771 AM 460 *LA 217	G	-5	-2	0	2	0	2	0	2	G
8	Jesus refulsit omnium	hy	ST 257	G	2	-3	-2	0	2	0	-3	-2	G

8 Jesus refulsit omnium	hy	ST 413	G	2	-2	0	2	-2	0	2	4	G
3 Jesus refulsit omnium	hy	VP 93	D	2	3	5	7	0	2	3	5	E
3 Jesus refulsit omnium	hy	ST 372	D	2	3	5	7	5	3	0	2	E
1 Jesus refulsit omnium	hy	ST 63	C	2	4	7	4	2	5	4	2	D
8 Jesus respondens mulieri	an	WA 94	F	2	4	7	6	7	9	4	2	G
Jesus stetit in medio Angelus Domini	ofv	OTT 57 SYG 155 *GB 132	F	2	4	7	4	2	0	2	4	
1 Joannes apostolus ... a Christo	an	LA 52	D	-2	3	5	3	5	7	9	7	D
1 Joannes apostolus ... virgo	an	WA 38 *LA 48	D	3	2	0	2	0	-2	3	5	D
1 Joannes autem cum audisset	an	AR 226 LU 1081 AM 197 *WA 16 LA 11	D	3	0	-2	3	5	3	7	5	D
Joannes baptista arguebat Misit Herodes	rev	WA 362										
4 Joannes baptista arguebat	re	LA 451	F	-3	0	-1	0	2	0	-1	0	E
2 Joannes baptista arguebat	re	WA 362	A	3	5	7	5	8	7	8	10	D
8 Joannes est nomen ejus	an	AR 732 LU 1496 AM 920 WA 323	a	-4	-2	0	-2	3	2	0	-4	G
Joannes est nomen ejus	alv	GB 198^V	C	2	5	2	0	5	7	5	7	
1 Joannes et Paulus agnoscentes	an	AR 743 LU 1510 *WA 324	D	-2	3	5	3	7	10	7	5	D
8 Joannes et Paulus cognoscentes	an	LA 411	G	5	2	0	-2	0	2	0	4	G
1 Joannes et Paulus dixerunt ad Gallicanum	an	AR 744 LU 1510 *WA 325 *LA 411	D	-2	3	5	3	7	5	2	3	D
Joannes hic theologus Iste est Joannes	rev	PM 33 WA 38(41)	F	2	0	-1	-3	0	2	0	4	
3 Joannes in principio	hy	ST 369	D	2	3	5	7	0	2	3	5	E
4 Joannes virgo	hy	ST 402	F	-3	-5	-3	0	-3	-5	0	2	E
4 Joannes vocabitur nomen	re	WA 322	F	-3	0	2	0	-1	0	-1	0	E
1 Joannes vocabitur nomen	an	AR 736 LU 1504 AM 924 WA 323 LA 408	D	-2	3	5	3	5	7	8	7	D
Jocundare, jocundus		see Jucundare, jucundus										
8 Joseph autem mercatus sindonem	co	GR 18**	F	2	4	2	0	4	7	6	7	G
5 Joseph cum intraret	re	LA 148 *WA 96	F	4	7	9	11	7	4	7	9	F
Joseph dum intraret		see Joseph cum intraret										
7 Joseph fili David noli timere	an	AR 691 AM 889 WA 25 *LA 30	G	4	5	7	5	9	7	10	9	G
7 Joseph fili David noli timere	co	GR 458 LU 1403	G	5	4	5	2	5	7	5	7	G
4 Joseph opifex sancte	an	LU 1447	c	2	0	2	4	2	0	2	-3	a
4 Joseph vir ejus cum esset	an	AR 649 LU 1401 *AM 837	F	-1	0	-3	-5	-3	-1	2	4	E
7 Jubilate Deo in voce	an	AR 70	G	4	5	7	9	7	5	2	4	G

	Jubilate Deo omnis terra In excelso throno	intv	GR 64 LU 477 GS 20 GB 36 SYG 32										
	Jubilate Deo omnis terra Omnis terra	intv	GR 67 LU 484 GS 21 GB 37 SYG 35										
	Jubilate Deo omnis terra Venite audite	intv	GR 398										
	Jubilate Deo omnis terra Vocem jucunditatis	intv	GR 270 LU 830 GS 130 GB 151 SYG 168										
	Jubilate Deo omnis terra	alv	GB 148	D	-2	2	5	3	2	3	2	0	
4	Jubilate Deo omnis terra	an	AR 3 *WA 69 *LA 101	E	1	3	1	-2	1	0	1	-2	E
8	Jubilate Deo omnis terra	int	GR 265 LU 821 *SYG 165 *GB 148 *GS 128	G	2	5	0	-2	0	2	5	0	G
	Jubilate Deo omnis terra Benedicite gentes	ofv	OTT 71 *GB 93^V *SYG 105	C	2	5	7	2	5	2	4	0	
	Jubilate Deo omnis terra	alv	GR 65 LU 479 SYG 32 GB 256 GS 20	G	4	2	4	5	4	2	4	2	
5	Jubilate Deo omnis terra	of	GR 66 OTT 23 LU 480 SYG 32 GB 36^V GS 20 65	F	4	7	4	2	4	5	2	0	F
	Jubilate Deo omnis terra	alv	GR [127] LU 1294	G	5	4	5	7	9	5	4	5	
1	Jubilate Deo universa terra	of	GR 69 OTT 69 LU 486 SYG 36 GB 38 GS 22	C	2	9	10	9	12	9	7	9	D
	Jubilate Domino omnis terra Revelabitur gloria Domini	cov	SYG 14										
	Jubilate Domino omnis terra Viderunt omnes fines	cov	SYG 21										
8	Jubilate Domino omnis terra	tr	GR 82 LU 513 SYG 62 GB 59^V GS 28	G	2	4	2	0	2	0	5	7	G
8	Jubilate in conspectu	an	AR 145	a	-2	0	-2	-4	-2	0	2	3	G
6	Jubilemus Deo salutari	inv	LA 90 WA 65	c	2	0	2	4	2	4	2	0	c
3	Jucunda patrum rediit	hy	AM 876	E	1	3	1	0	-2	0	-2	-4	E
5	Jucundantur et laetantur	hy	ST 464	F	4	7	9	7	11	9	7	12	F
8	Jucundare filia Sion	an	AR 213 LU 323 AM 187 *WA 6 *LA 6	F	4	6	7	9	7	6	7	9	G
1	Jucundetur et laetetur augmentetur	hy	ST 110	D	7	9	5	7	9	10	9	7	D
1	Jucundis pangat mentibus	hy	ST 125	D	2	3	0	-2	3	5	7	5	D
	Jucunditatem et exsultationem In medio ecclesiae	rev	PM 226 LR 203 LA 55										
	Jucundus homo qui miseretur Deriventur fontes	grv	GR 555 LU 1562	a	3	5	3	5	7	8	7	3	
4	Judaea et Jerusalem	re	AM 1183 *PM 25 *WA 27	F	-3	-1	0	-1	-3	-1	2	4	E

8	Judaea et Jerusalem	an	AR 255 LU 358 AM 232 WA 26 *LA 30	G	-2	-5	-3	-2	0	2	0	2	G
2	Judas mercator pessimus	re	OHS 389 LU 644	C	2	4	2	5	4	5	2	4	D
8	Judica causam meam defende	an	AR 422 OHS 68 AM 400 WA 113 *LA 181	a	-4	-2	-4	-2	0	-2	-4	0	G
	Judica Domine causam animae Contumelias	rev	OHS 241 (nm)										
	Judica Domine nocentes me Posuit coronam	rev	LR 152 LA 525 WA 418										
	Judica Domine nocentes me Ego autem dum mihi	grv	GR 187 OHS 258 LU 610 *GS 90 *GB 112ᵛ *SYG 125	E	1	-2	3	7	3	5	8	7	
3	Judica Domine nocentes me	co	GB 105	E	1	3	5	7	5	3	5	1	E
4	Judica Domine nocentes me	int	GR 185 OHS 206 LU 606 SYG 124 *GB 111 *GS 89	D	3	2	3	0	3	5	7	5	E
4	Judica me Deus et discerne	int	GR 151 LU 569 *SYG 109 *GS 71 *GB 97	E	3	1	0	1	3	6	5	3	E
	Judica me Domine quoniam ego Domine dilexi	intv	SYG 85										
	Judica me Domine quoniam ego Redime me	intv	GR 115 GS 48 GB 76 SYG 87										
	Judica me Domine secundum justitiam Synagoga populorum	rev	OHS 242 (nm)										
	Judicabit Dominus populum In servis suis	rev	LR 168 WA 307										
	Judicabunt sancti nationes	alv	SYG 188 *GS 199	C	2	5	2	0	2	4	5	7	
7	Judicant sancti gentes	int	GR 645 (8) SYG 205 GB 210 GS 211	G	5	7	9	7	5	7	5	9	G
	Judicasti Domine causam Contumelias	rev	WA 116										
4	Judicasti Domine causam	an	AR 88 409 AM 97 112 389 *WA 108 *LA 171	G	2	5	7	9	7	5	7	9	a
	Judice confuso et cuncto Lucia martyr	rev	WA 246										
1	Judicii signum tellus sudore madescit	hy	ST 494	D	2	3	5	2	3	2	0	2	D
7	Jugum enim meum	an	WA 412 *LA 507	G	4	5	7	9	5	7	4	5	G
8	Juravi dicit Dominus	re	LA 19 WA 23	a	-2	-4	0	3	2	-2	0	-2	G
	Juravi et statui custodire	alv	GR 73**	G	-2	-3	-2	-5	-3	0	2	4	
3	Juravit Dominus et non paenitebit	gr	SYG 33 GB 40ᵛ *GS 221	E	1	-4	-2	0	1	0	1	-2	E
7	Juravit Dominus et non paenitebit	int	GR [100] LU 1283	G	2	-2	2	0	2	5	2	5	G
8	Juravit Dominus et non paenitebit	re	LR 195 *LA 531 WA 425	D	3	5	7	5	7	5	7	3	G

8	Juravit Dominus et non paenitebit	an	AR [10] LU 1114 *AM 626 *WA 415 LA 421	G	4	7	5	7	5	4	2	5	G
	Juravit Dominus et non paenitebit	alv	GR [37] LU 1187 *SYG 189 *GB 41^V	D	7	5	7	8	7	5	7	3	
2	Jure Petro ecclesiae	an	WA 278	a	-2	0	3	5	7	5	3	0	a
7	Jussit Valerianus	re	WA 351	G	2	0	2	0	2	5	4	5	c
7	Jussu impii Paschasii	re	WA 245	a	-2	-4	0	-2	-4	-2	0	3	G
	Jussu regis amputatum Accedentes discipuli	rev	LA 453										
2	Juste et pie vivamus	an	AR 232 LU 339 AM 205 WA 16 62 LA 16	D	-2	0	2	3	5	3	2	0	D
4	Juste et sancte vivendo	an	WA 242	F	-1	-3	0	2	4	2	0	2	E
1	Juste judex Jesu Christe	hy	ST 498	d	-2	-3	-5	-3	0	-7	-2	-3	D
8	Juste judicate filii	an	WA 65 *LA 92	c	-1	-5	-3	-1	0	-1	-3	-5	G
	Justi autem in perpetuum vivent	sr	AR [46]										
	Justi autem in perpetuum vivent Fulgebunt justi et tamquam	rev	WA 429										
	Justi autem in perpetuum vivent Fulgebunt justi sicut lilium	rev	LR 173										
4	Justi autem in perpetuum vivent	an	LR 180 *WA 421 *LA 516	F	-3	-1	0	-1	0	2	0	-1	E
8	Justi autem in perpetuum vivent	re	LA 478	G	2	4	2	0	2	4	2	4	G
	Justi confitebuntur ... alleluia	sr	AR [46] LU 1155										
1	Justi confitebuntur ... et habitabunt	an	AM 980 WA 394 LA 473	D	-2	0	3	2	0	-2	3	5	D
	Justi confitebuntur ... et habitabunt	alv	SYG 190	C	2	4	5	4	2	5	2	5	
	Justi confitebuntur ... et habitabunt	alv	GR 96**	D	7	8	7	5	7	5	2	3	
5	Justi decantaverunt Domine	int	GR 444 LU 1384	F	2	0	4	2	4	0	4	7	F
6	Justi epulentur ... delectentur	int	GR 412 SYG 214 GB 219^V GS 211	F	2	0	2	4	0	2	0	2	F
1	Justi epulentur ... delectentur	of	GR 96**	D	3	0	-2	0	2	3	5	3	D
	Justi epulentur ... delectentur	alv	GR [27] 190 *GB 269^V GS 216 SYG 190	D	3	2	5	3	2	3	0	7	
	Justi epulentur ... parasti	alv	GR 56**	D	3	2	5	3	2	3	0	7	
8	Justi fulgebunt sicut sol	an	LA 518	c	2	0	-1	0	-3	0	-1	-5	G
	Justi fulgebunt sicut sol	alv	GB 268^V	c	4	5	4	2	0	2	4	2	
	Justi quasi virens folium	alv	GR (21)	G	5	7	5	0	2	0	-2	2	
	Justificati gratis per gratiam Gratificavit nos	trv	GR 538	D	-2	0	3	5	0	2	3	5	
8	Justificeris Domine in sermonibus	an	AR 432 OHS 399 LU 652 *AM 413 WA 120 LA 193	G	2	0	-2	0	2	0	-2	2	G

	Incipit		Sources										
	Justitia ejus super filios Benedic anima mea	ofv	OTT 110 *SYG 80 GB 72	G	5	7	5	7	5	7	5	9	
4	Justitia indutus sum	of	GR 633 LU 1696	C	2	5	4	5	2	0	2	5	E
4	Justitiae Domini rectae	of	GR 126 OTT 94 LU 555 SYG 93 GB 82^V GS 55 151	D	3	5	7	5	7	5	3	5	E
	Justitiam tuam non abscondi Memor fui	grv	GR 564 LU 1580	E	1	-2	3	5	3	5	6	5	
	Justitiam tuam non abscondi Annuntiavi	trv	GR [2^2] LU 1122^4	G	2	4	5	4	5	7	5	0	
	Justitiam tuam non abscondi Annuntiavi	grv	LU 1623^B	F	4	7	9	11	7	6	9	11	
7	Justorum animae in manu ... malitiae	an	LA 519	d	-3	0	2	0	-3	-2	0	-2	G
8	Justorum animae in manu ... malitiae	re	WA 422	G	2	-2	0	2	-3	-5	-7	0	G
7	Justorum animae in manu ... malitiae	int	SYG 224	G	2	-2	2	0	2	5	7	5	G
	Justorum animae in manu ... malitiae	alv	GR 561 GB 268	D	3	0	-2	3	5	7	5	3	
5	Justorum animae in manu ... malitiae	gr	GR 413 LU 1547 SYG 194 GB 171 GS 213	D	3	7	8	7	5	7	5	3	F
3	Justorum animae in manu ... malitiae	co	GR 505 LU 1549 *SYG 173 *GB 167^V *GS 219	G	4	2	5	4	2	0	5	2	E
1	Justorum animae in manu ... mortis	re	LR 189	D	2	3	0	2	0	2	3	0	D
1	Justorum animae in manu ... mortis	of	GR 649^V[30] OTT 144 LU 1172 SYG 223	D	3	0	-2	0	3	7	5	7	D
	Justorum semita quasi lux In Deo raptus	rev	LR 281	D	7	5	7	5	3	2	5	7	
4	Justum deduxit ... et dedit	an	LA 538	F	-3	-1	0	2	0	2	-1	0	E
7	Justum deduxit ... et dedit	re	LR 200 *LA 525 ×WA 427	G	2	5	4	2	5	0	2	0	G
	Justum deduxit ... et ostendit ... gloriam	alv	SYG 229	G	2	0	-2	0	2	0	-2	2	
	Justum deduxit ... et ostendit ... regnum	sr	WA 428 LA 536										
	Justum deduxit ... et ostendit ... regnum Hic est vere martyr	rev	PM 218 LR 158 WA 417										
	Justum deduxit ... et ostendit ... regnum Honestum fecit	rev	LR 206										
	Justum deduxit ... et ostendit ... regnum Magnificavit eum	rev	LA 534 WA 427										
	Justum deduxit ... et ostendit ... regnum	alv	GB 271	b	-4	-2	1	0	-2	-4	0	-4	
7	Justum deduxit ... et ostendit ... regnum	an	WA 428 LA 538	d	-3	0	2	0	-2	0	-3	-2	G

	Justum deduxit ... et ostendit ... regnum	alv	GB 271	D	-2	0	2	3	5	7	5	3	
	Justum deduxit ... et ostendit ... regnum	alv	SYG 214	G	2	4	5	4	5	4	2	0	
5	Justus cum ceciderit	gr	GR [13] LU 1139	F	2	4	2	-1	0	2	0	2	F
	Justus Dominus et justitiam	an	OHS 61 (nm)										
7	Justus Dominus et justitiam ... aequitatem	an	LR 150 193 *WA 416 424 *LA 522	d	-3	0	2	0	-3	-2	0	-2	G
5	Justus Dominus et justitias	co	GR 120 *SYG 89 *GB 78^V *GS 51	c	-3	0	-1	0	-3	2	0	-3	F
1	Justus es Domine et rectum	int	GR 365 LU 1047 SYG 250 GB 256 GS 160	D	7	8	7	5	3	5	7	10	D
4	Justus florebit in domo	inv	WA 415	D	3	0	3	2	3	5	3	0	E
	Justus germinabit sicut lilium	sr	AR 657 658 692 LU 1405 1443 WA 428										
	Justus germinabit sicut lilium	alv	GR [40](42) LU 1192 *SYG 207 *GB 270^V GS 222	a	-4	0	-2	-5	-4	-7	-4	-7	
1	Justus germinabit sicut lilium	re	LR 151 LA 522 *WA 416	D	7	8	7	5	3	5	7	10	D
	Justus non conturbabitur	alv	GR 573 *GS 208 SYG 34 GB 270	D	-2	0	2	3	5	7	5	3	
5	Justus non conturbabitur	gr	GB 162^V GS 206	F	2	4	2	-1	0	2	0	2	F
1	Justus non conturbabitur	int	GB 229 GS 205	D	3	0	3	2	0	-2	0	-2	D
8	Justus ut palma florebit	an	LR 154 *WA 417	a	-4	-2	0	-2	-4	0	2	3	G
2	Justus ut palma florebit	an	LA 524	D	-2	0	2	3	5	3	2	0	D
4	Justus ut palma florebit	of	GR [41] OTT 150 LU 1193 SYG 24 GB 25^V GS m 17	E	1	3	5	3	1	-2	3	1	E
1	Justus ut palma florebit	int	GR [45] LU 1204 SYG 195 GB 197^V GS 205	D	3	0	3	2	0	-2	0	-2	D
	Justus ut palma florebit	alv	GR [49](41) LU 1207 *GS 207 SYG 198 *GB 230	F	4	2	-1	0	2	0	2	-3	
2	Justus ut palma florebit	gr	GR [42] LU 1201 SYG 195 GB 23 *GS 202	G	4	2	5	2	4	5	2	0	a
	Juvenem quoque jam Caelestium minister	rev	WA 294	G	5	4	0	2	4	2	5	7	
4	Juvenes et virgines	an	WA 82	F	-1	-3	-1	-3	-5	-3	-1	0	E
4	Juvenes et virgines	an	LU 1829	E	1	3	0	3	1	0	-2	0	E
1	Juvenes et virgines ... quia	an	AR 302 LU 450 AM 280	D	7	10	7	5	7	5	2	3	D

Juxta est Dominus his Clamaverunt justi	grv	GR [29] LU 1170 *GS 213 GB 194 SYG 188	G	4	7	10	7	5	9	7	5
Juxta est salus mea Juravi dicit Dominus	rev	LA 19 WA 23									
4 Juxta vestibulum et altare	an	GR 85 LU 523 WA 206 GS 30	F	2	0	2	4	2	4	2	0 E
5 Katherinae solemnia sancta colat ecclesia	hy	ST 49	F	7	9	11	9	11	12	11	9 F
Kyrie eleison as used in litanies		see Kyrie ... pater de caelis, following main Kyrie section									
Kyrie eleison		MEL #89	G	-5	-2	-3	-5	0	7	5	4 G
Kyrie		MEL #206	D	-5	-2	0	-2	0	2	3	0 D
Kyrie		MEL #1	d	-5	0	-2	0	-2	-5	-4	-5 D
Kyrie		MEL #139	F	-5	0	4	2	0	7	0	-1 F
Kyrie		MEL #138	F	-5	0	5	4	2	0	7	9 F
Kyrie		MEL #25	a	-4	0	-2	-4	-5	-7	-2	-4 D
Kyrie		MEL #5	c	-3	-5	-7	-3	-2	0	2	4 F
Kyrie		MEL #11	c	-3	-5	-7	0	5	4	2	0 F
Kyrie		MEL #4	c	-3	-5	-3	-2	-3	-5	-7	-5 F
Kyrie		MEL #136	F	-3	-5	-3	0	[0	0	0	0] F
Kyrie		MEL #10	c	-3	-5	-1	0	2	0	-1	-3 G
Kyrie		MEL #88	G	-3	-5	0	2	4	2	0	2 G
Kyrie		MEL #137	F	-3	-5	0	2	4	2	4	6 F
Kyrie		MEL #3	c	-3	-5	0	2	4	5	4	2 G
Kyrie		MEL #91	G	-3	-2	-3	-5	0	2	4	2 G
Kyrie		MEL #87	G	-3	-2	0	-2	-3	-5	0	2 G
Kyrie rex regum*		MEL #9	c	-3	-1	-3	-5	0	2	4	0 G
Kyrie		MEL #134	F	-3	-1	-3	-5	0	2	4	6 F
Kyrie		MEL #135	F	-3	-1	[0	0	0	0	0	0] E
Kyrie		MEL #122	F	-3	0	-1	-3	-5	-3	-1	0 E
Kyrie		MEL #133	F	-3	0	-1	0	2	-1	[0	0] E
6 Kyrie VIII amator sancte (etc)**		MEL #132 GR 81* LU 84	F	-3	0	2	4	5	4	2	0 F

---

 * Trope texts are given for identification only, and do not affect the order of the melodies.
** (etc) indicates that more than one trope was used with this melody.

Kyrie	MEL #199	D	-2	-5	-3	-5	-7	-2	0	5	D
Kyrie	MEL #205	D	-2	-5	-3	-5	-2	2	0	-2	D
Kyrie alpha et O	MEL #204	D	-2	-5	-2	0	-2	-5	-2	0	E
8 Kyrie ad lib IX O pater excelse	MEL #86 GR 82* LU 85	G	-2	-5	-2	0	2	0	5	4	G
Kyrie	MEL #19	a	-2	-5	-2	0	3	2	0	2	D
1 Kyrie ad lib VII splendor aeternae	MEL #192 GR 81** LU 84	D	-2	-5	-2	0	5	7	3	2	D
Kyrie puerorum caterva (etc)	MEL #24	a	-2	-4	-2	0	-7	-5	-4	-2	G
8 Kyrie VII rex splendens	GR 25* LU 34	a	-2	-4	-2	0	-7	-5	-4	-2	G
Kyrie	MEL #23	a	-2	-4	-2	0	-2	-4	-2	-7	D
Kyrie	MEL #17	a	-2	-4	0	3	1	0	1	0	F
Kyrie	MEL #156	E	-2	-4	3	1	0	8	3	1	C
Kyrie	MEL #7	c	-2	-3	-5	-3	[0	0	0	0]	E
Kyrie summe pater rerum	MEL #22	a	-2	0	-7	-4	-2	2	3	0	D
Kyrie	MEL #21	a	-2	0	-7	-4	0	-2	-5	-7	D
Kyrie	MEL #203	D	-2	0	-2	-5	-3	-5	-7	-2	D
Kyrie miserere rex (etc)	MEL #155	E	-2	0	-2	-4	-2	0	[0	0]	E
Kyrie	MEL #202	D	-2	0	-2	5	7	5	7	9	G
Kyrie	MEL #159	E	-2	0	1	0	-2	0	3	5	E
Kyrie	MEL #20	a	-2	0	2	3	-2	0	2	3	D
Kyrie	MEL #197	D	-2	0	2	3	0	[0	0	0]	D
Kyrie	MEL #195	D	-2	0	2	3	2	0	2	-2	D
Kyrie conditor rerum alme	MEL #191	D	-2	0	2	3	2	0	2	3	D
Kyrie	MEL #158	E	-2	0	3	1	0	-2	0	-4	E
1 Kyrie XIII stelliferi conditor	MEL #194 GR 44* LU 51	D	-2	0	3	2	-2	2	0	3	D
1 Kyrie IV cunctipotens genitor (etc)	MEL #18 LU 25 GR 15*	a	-2	0	3	2	0	-2	0	-2	a
2 Kyrie ad lib III rector cosmi pie	GR 77* LU 81	D	-2	0	3	2	0	-2	2	5	D
Kyrie unus omnipotens (etc)	MEL #198	D	-2	0	3	2	0	-2	2	5	D
Kyrie	MEL #157	E	-2	0	3	5	0	1	0	-2	E
Kyrie	MEL #201	D	-2	0	3	5	0	7	5	3	D
Kyrie	MEL #196	D	-2	0	3	5	3	2	0	-3	D
Kyrie	MEL #200	D	-2	0	3	5	7	3	5	7	D
Kyrie laudes pangamus	MEL #2	d	-2	2	0	-2	-3	-2	-3	-5	G
Kyrie	MEL #90	G	-2	2	0	5	7	5	4	2	G
Kyrie	MEL #193	D	-2	3	0	-2	0	2	[0	0]	E

	Kyrie	MEL #8	c	-1	-3	-5	-7	-3	0	2	0	F
	Kyrie	MEL #126	F	-1	-3	-5	-3	-1	0	2	4	F
	Kyrie alme pater Jesu	MEL #125	F	-1	-3	-5	0	2	4	5	4	F
	Kyrie	MEL #221	C	-1	-3	-5	0	2	4	5	4	C
4	Kyrie XVIII Deus genitor	GR 58* LU 62	c	-1	-3	-1	-3	-5	-3	-1	2	b
	Kyrie o summe rex (etc)	MEL #124	F	-1	-3	-1	-3	-5	-3	0	-3	E
	Kyrie	MEL #14	b^b	-1	-3	-1	0	-1	-5	-3	[0]	F
	Kyrie	MEL #123	F	-1	-3	-1	0	2	0	-1	[0]	E
	Kyrie	MEL #6	c	-1	-3	0	-1	-5	-3	-1	0	F
	Kyrie	MEL #131	F	-1	-3	4	-3	-1	0	4	2	F
	Kyrie	MEL #130	F	-1	0	-3	4	2	4	0	2	D
	Kyrie	MEL #129	F	-1	0	-1	0	-1	-3	-1	0	D
	Kyrie	MEL #128	F	-1	0	2	0	-1	-3	2	-3	D
	Kyrie	MEL #127	F	-1	0	2	4	2	0	4	6	F
	Kyrie	MEL #13	b	1	-2	-4	1	0	-2	-4	-2	E
	Kyrie	MEL #12	b	1	0	-2	-4	-2	-7	-4	-9	E
1	Kyrie XI orbis factor	MEL #16 GR 38* LU 46	a	1	0	-2	0	-7	-4	-2	0	D
1	Kyrie ad lib X orbis factor	GR 82* LU 85	a	1	0	-2	0	-7	-4	0	-2	D
4	Kyrie XV dominator Deus	GR 51* LU 56	b	1	0	-2	0	-2	-4	-2	0	b
	Kyrie	MEL #152	E	1	0	-2	0	1	-2	-4	-2	E
	Kyrie Deus genitor alme	MEL #151	E	1	0	-2	0	1	0	-2	-4	E
	Kyrie genitor ingenite	MEL #150	E	1	0	-2	0	3	5	0	1	E
	Kyrie	MEL #148	E	1	0	-2	0	3	5	7	8	E
	Kyrie immense conditor	MEL #149	E	1	0	-2	0	3	5	7	8	E
	Kyrie	MEL #147	E	1	0	-2	3	5	3	1	0	E
	Kyrie	MEL #146	E	1	0	-2	3	5	7	8	7	E
	Kyrie	MEL #145	E	1	3	0	1	0	-2	3	5	E
	Kyrie	MEL #141	E	1	3	1	0	-2	-5	-4	[0]	E
	Kyrie	MEL #144	E	1	3	1	0	-2	-4	-2	0	E
	Kyrie	MEL #143	E	1	3	1	0	-2	0	3	5	E
4	Kyrie III Deus sempiterne	MEL #142 GR 11* LU 22	E	1	3	1	0	-2	0	3	5	E
	Kyrie	MEL #140	E	1	3	1	0	1	0	-2	0	E
	Kyrie Deus excelse pater	MEL #76	G	2	-2	0	2	4	5	4	2	G
	Kyrie devote canentes	MEL #77	G	2	-2	0	2	5	2	5	2	G

Kyrie regum summe caeli	MEL #184	D	2	-2	0	3	5	3	2	0	D
Kyrie nesciens principium	MEL #75	G	2	0	-3	-2	-3	-5	-3	-2	G
Kyrie	MEL #74	G	2	0	-2	-3	-2	-5	-3	-2	G
Kyrie	MEL #15	a	2	0	-2	0	-2	[0	0	0]	F
7 Kyrie ad lib V conditor omnium	GR 79* LU 82	G	2	0	-2	0	-2	2	5	4	G
Kyrie suavis tu Deus (etc)	MEL #70	G	2	0	-2	0	-2	2	5	4	G
Kyrie rex celse	MEL #82	G	2	0	-2	0	2	-2	2	0	G
Kyrie	MEL #73	G	2	0	-2	0	2	0	4	2	E
Kyrie	MEL #72	G	2	0	-2	0	2	4	5	4	G
Kyrie	MEL #69	G	2	0	-2	0	2	5	4	2	G
Kyrie kyrion o theos pater	MEL #189	D	2	0	-2	0	3	2	3	5	D
Kyrie in praesepe Christus	MEL #183	D	2	0	-2	2	3	2	0	2	D
Kyrie	MEL #71	G	2	0	-2	2	4	2	0	2	G
Kyrie	MEL #117	F	2	0	-1	0	5	4	2	4	F
Kyrie	MEL #84	G	2	0	[0	0	0	0	0	0]	G
Kyrie	MEL #85	G	2	[0	0	0	0	0	0	0]	E
8 Kyrie XIV Jesu redemptor	GR 47* LU 54	G	2	0	2	0	-5	0	-2	0	G
Kyrie o theos generis (etc)	MEL #68	G	2	0	2	0	-5	0	-2	0	D
Kyrie	MEL #81	G	2	0	2	0	-2	0	-2	2	G
Kyrie	MEL #182	D	2	0	2	0	-2	0	3	2	D
Kyrie	MEL #80	G	2	0	2	0	-2	5	4	2	G
Kyrie	MEL #116	F	2	0	2	4	2	-1	0	5	F
Kyrie Jesu redemptor (etc)	MEL #64	G	2	0	2	4	2	0	-3	-2	G
Kyrie	MEL #121	F	2	0	2	4	2	0	5	4	F
Kyrie omnipotens pater	MEL #67	G	2	0	2	4	5	4	2	4	G
6 Kyrie XVIIb	GR 56* LU 61	F	2	0	2	4	7	5	4	2	F
Kyrie	MEL #114	F	2	0	2	4	7	5	4	2	F
Kyrie creator	MEL #62	G	2	0	2	5	0	2	0	-2	D
Kyrie	MEL #181	D	2	0	3	5	7	9	10	12	D
Kyrie immense conditor	MEL #61	G	2	0	4	5	4	2	0	2	G
Kyrie	MEL #190	D	2	0	5	0	3	2	0	7	D
Kyrie	MEL #63	G	2	0	5	4	2	0	-5	0	G
Kyrie	MEL #66	G	2	0	5	4	2	0	4	5	G
Kyrie	MEL #115	F	2	0	5	4	2	4	0	-3	F
Kyrie	MEL #65	G	2	0	5	4	5	7	[0	0]	G
Kyrie	MEL #180	D	2	3	2	3	0	7	3	0	D

	Title	Source										
	Kyrie	MEL #179	D	2	3	5	2	3	2	0	5	D
	Kyrie	MEL #178	D	2	3	5	3	2	0	2	0	D
	Kyrie	MEL #176	D	2	3	5	3	2	0	5	0	D
	Kyrie	MEL #177	D	2	3	5	3	2	0	5	3	D
	Kyrie Jesu rex caeli	MEL #53	G	2	4	0	2	0	[0	0	0]	G
	Kyrie genitor eleison	MEL #217	C	2	4	0	2	4	[0	0	0]	D E
	Kyrie	MEL #106	F	2	4	0	2	4	2	0	-1	D
	Kyrie auctor caelorum (etc)	MEL #52	G	2	4	0	2	4	5	4	5	G
3	Kyrie XVI	GR 54* LU 59	G	2	4	0	2	4	7	4	5	E
	Kyrie	MEL #110	F	2	4	0	5	4	2	0	-1	F
	Kyrie clementissime (etc)	MEL #111	F	2	4	0	5	4	2	4	0	F
8	Kyrie XII pater cuncta (etc)	GR 42* LU 48 MEL #58	G	2	4	0	7	5	4	2	0	G
	Kyrie	MEL #79	G	2	4	2	-5	-2	-3	-5	-3	G
	Kyrie	MEL #109	F	2	4	2	-3	0	-1	-3	-1	D
	Kyrie	MEL #51	G	2	4	2	0	2	0	-2	0	G
	Kyrie	MEL #120	F	2	4	2	0	2	0	-1	[0]	F
	Kyrie	MEL #103	F	2	4	2	0	2	0	[0	0]	F
	Kyrie	MEL #57	G	2	4	2	0	2	0	2	-3	G
	Kyrie omnipotens genitor lumenque	MEL #56	G	2	4	2	0	2	0	4	5	G
	Kyrie	MEL #50	G	2	4	2	0	2	5	4	5	D
	Kyrie	MEL #112	F	2	4	2	0	4	2	[0	0]	G
	Kyrie o theos yschyros	MEL #219	C	2	4	2	0	4	2	5	4	D
	Kyrie	MEL #104	F	2	4	2	4	2	0	[0	0]	E
	Kyrie	MEL #105	F	2	4	2	4	2	0	2	4	F
	Kyrie	MEL #216	C	2	4	2	4	2	0	4	5	D
	Kyrie Christe caelorum	MEL #215	C	2	4	2	4	2	7	4	5	E
	Kyrie	MEL #107	F	2	4	2	4	5	4	2	0	F
	Kyrie	MEL #108	F	2	4	2	4	5	4	2	0	F
	Kyrie adest reducta	MEL #49	G	2	4	2	4	5	4	2	0	G
	Kyrie caelum terramque	MEL #54	G	2	4	2	4	5	4	2	4	G
	Kyrie qui dignasti	MEL #218	C	2	4	2	4	5	4	2	4	E
	Kyrie	MEL #113	F	2	4	2	4	6	4	2	4	G
	Kyrie archangeli laetantur (etc)	MEL #55	G	2	4	2	5	4	0	2	0	G D
7	Kyrie VI rex genitor	GR 21* LU 34	G	2	4	2	5	4	0	2	0	G
3	Kyrie II fons bonitatis (etc)	MEL #48 GR 8* LU 19 VP 165	G	2	4	2	5	4	2	0	2	E

	Kyrie theoricam practicamque (etc)	MEL #47	G	2	4	2	5	4	2	4	0	G
	Kyrie	MEL #214	C	2	4	2	5	4	2	4	2	E
	Kyrie	MEL #226	GG	2	4	2	5	7	5	4	2	D
	Kyrie	MEL #225	GG	2	4	2	5	7	9	7	5	D
	Kyrie	MEL #44	G	2	4	5	2	0	2	0	-3	G
	Kyrie	MEL #213	C	2	4	5	2	0	2	5	7	D
	Kyrie summe sophie	MEL #43	G	2	4	5	2	4	2	0	2	G
	Kyrie	MEL #211	C	2	4	5	2	4	2	0	5	C
	Kyrie	MEL #42	G	2	4	5	2	5	4	0	2	F
	Kyrie	MEL #60	G	2	4	5	4	0	-2	2	0	G
	Kyrie summe pater summum	MEL #59	G	2	4	5	4	2	0	[0	0]	G
	Kyrie	MEL #41	G	2	4	5	4	2	0	2	-2	G
	Kyrie	MEL #99	F	2	4	5	4	2	0	2	4	F
8	Kyrie V magnae Deus	MEL #78 GR 18* LU 28	G	2	4	5	4	2	0	2	4	G
	Kyrie rex Deus immense	MEL #83	G	2	4	5	4	2	0	7	5	G
1	Kyrie ad lib I clemens rector	MEL #102 GR 75* LU 79	F	2	4	5	4	2	4	0	-3	D
6	Kyrie	GR 94* LU 1807	F	2	4	5	4	2	4	2	0	F
	Kyrie	MEL #101	F	2	4	5	4	2	4	2	0	F
	Kyrie omnipotens stelligeri	MEL #46	G	2	4	5	4	2	4	2	0	G
	Kyrie	MEL #100	F	2	4	5	4	2	4	5	4	F
8	Kyrie ad lib VI te Christe rex	GR 80* LU 83	G	2	4	5	4	2	4	5	4	G
	Kyrie incarnatum quoque	MEL #45	G	2	4	5	4	2	5	7	5	G
	Kyrie	MEL #212	C	2	4	5	4	2	7	5	7	E
	Kyrie ad laudem summae	MEL #98	F	2	4	7	6	4	9	7	6	G
	Kyrie hagie atque benigne	MEL #119	F	2	4	7	6	7	4	6	7	G
	Kyrie	MEL #97	F	2	4	7	9	7	9	12	11	F
	Kyrie princeps astrigeram	MEL #36	G	2	5	0	2	-3	-2	0	2	G
	Kyrie rex Deus aeterne (etc)	MEL #96	F	2	5	0	2	0	-1	-3	-5	F
	Kyrie	MEL #40	G	2	5	2	0	-2	-3	-5	-3	G
	Kyrie	MEL #220	C	2	5	2	0	5	7	9	12	D
	Kyrie	MEL #35	G	2	5	2	4	0	2	4	0	G
	Kyrie Christe redemptor (etc)	MEL #39	G	2	5	2	5	4	0	2	0	G
8	Kyrie I lux et origo	GR 4* LU 16	G	2	5	2	5	4	0	2	0	G
	Kyrie rex pie	MEL #38	G	2	5	4	2	0	-2	2	5	G
	Kyrie	MEL #210	C	2	5	4	2	0	2	5	2	D

1 Kyrie XVIIa	GR 55* LU 60	C	2	5	4	2	0	2	5	2	D
1 Kyrie ad lib XI salve	GR 83* LU 86	C	2	5	4	2	0	2	5	4	D
Kyrie	MEL #33	G	2	5	4	2	4	5	4	[0]	G
Kyrie	MEL #34	G	2	5	4	2	5	7	4	2	G
Kyrie	MEL #37	G	2	5	4	5	7	9	7	5	G
Kyrie	MEL #32	G	2	5	7	5	4	2	0	2	G
Kyrie	MEL #175	D	3	-2	0	3	5	3	2	0	D
Kyrie	MEL #153	E	3	-2	3	1	0	8	5	3	E
Kyrie	MEL #154	E	3	-2	3	1	0	8	5	3	E
Kyrie	MEL #188	D	3	2	0	-2	0	-2	3	2	D
Kyrie	MEL #173	D	3	2	0	-2	0	3	7	5	D
Kyrie	MEL #172	D	3	2	0	-2	3	5	3	5	F
Kyrie Deus pater auctor	MEL #174	D	3	2	0	2	5	3	2	0	D
Kyrie	MEL #187	D	3	2	0	3	0	-2	3	5	D
Kyrie	MEL #186	D	3	2	3	7	2	5	3	2	D
Kyrie virginis odas	MEL #224	A	3	5	3	5	7	3	5	3	D
Kyrie o pater immense	MEL #223	A	3	5	3	5	7	8	5	8	D
Kyrie alme pater fili (etc)	MEL #171	D	3	5	7	5	3	2	0	3	D
1 Kyrie IX cum jubilo	GR 32* LU 40	D	3	5	7	5	3	2	0	3	D
Kyrie	MEL #170	D	3	5	7	5	7	9	7	5	D
Kyrie	MEL #222	A	3	5	8	5	3	5	3	5	D
Kyrie X alme pater	GR 35* LU 43	D	3	7	5	3	2	0	2	0	D
Kyrie ad monumentum (etc)	MEL #209	C	4	2	4	9	7	5	4	2	D
5 Kyrie VIII de angelis	MEL #95 GR 28* LU 37	F	4	5	7	9	7	5	7	12	F
Kyrie	MEL #94	F	4	7	4	7	9	7	11	9	F
5 Kyrie ad lib IV altissime	GR 78* LU 81	F	4	7	4	7	9	7	11	9	F
Kyrie	MEL #93	F	4	7	9	11	12	11	9	7	F
Kyrie	MEL #208	C	5	2	0	5	7	2	5	7	F
Kyrie pater excelse	MEL #27	G	5	2	0	5	7	9	7	5	G
Kyrie	MEL #169	D	5	3	2	0	5	7	5	7	G
Kyrie alme domine (etc)	MEL #31	G	5	4	2	0	2	4	2	4	G
Kyrie eleison	MEL #207	C	5	4	2	4	2	0	2	4	C
Kyrie magne Michaele	MEL #30	G	5	4	2	4	5	4	2	0	G
Kyrie	MEL #118	F	5	4	2	4	7	9	7	4	F
Kyrie	MEL #29	G	5	4	5	2	4	5	4	2	G

	Kyrie	MEL #28	G	5	4	7	5	4	2	0	5	G
	Kyrie	MEL #168	D	5	7	5	10	9	10	7	5	G
	Kyrie	MEL #167	D	7	5	2	3	2	0	[0	0]	D
	Kyrie	MEL #165	D	7	5	3	5	7	0	3	5	D
	Kyrie	MEL #164	D	7	5	3	5	7	10	12	10	D
	Kyrie	MEL #92	F	7	5	4	2	4	7	4	2	F
	Kyrie o Deus pater ingenite	MEL #163	D	7	5	7	3	2	0	2	0	D
	Kyrie	MEL #166	D	7	5	7	3	5	7	5	3	D
	Kyrie rex saeculorum	MEL #162	D	7	5	7	8	7	5	7	5	D
	Kyrie	MEL #160	D	7	8	7	5	7	5	3	2	D
	Kyrie theoricam practicamque (etc)	MEL #185	D	7	9	7	5	3	5	7	5	D
	Kyrie pater summe qui	MEL #26	G	7	9	7	5	4	7	9	10	G
1	Kyrie ad lib II summe Deus qui cuncta	MEL #161 GR 76* LU 80	D	7	10	7	5	7	3	5	3	D
	Kyrie ... pater de caelis	AR 212* GR 233 274	c	-3	-5	-3	0	-3	-5	-3	0	
	Kyrie ... pater de caelis	PM 284 VP 34	a	-2	1	0	-2	0	-2	1	0	
	Kyrie ... pater de caelis	AR 183* LU 1876	a	-2	2	0	-2	2	0	-2	2	
	Kyrie ... pater de caelis	PM 286 VP 36	c	-1	-3	-1	-5	-3	0	-1	-3	
	Kyrie ... pater de caelis	PM 281 283 VP 31 33	a	1	-2	-4	-2	0	1	-2	-4	
	Kyrie ... pater de caelis	PM 77	a	1	0	-2	-4	-2	0	-4	-7	
	Kyrie ... pater de caelis	VP 171	E	3	1	0	3	1	0	3	1	
	Kyrie ... pater de caelis	PM 284 VP 34	F	4	2	-1	0	-3	-5	-3	0	
	Kyrie ... pater de caelis	AR 185* LU 1878 AM 125	G	4	2	0	4	2	0	4	2	
	Kyrie ... pater de caelis	PM 285 VP 35	D	7	5	3	0	2	3	2	0	
5	Labia eorum salutarem	an	WA 372	a	-2	-4	0	3	5	3	0	3	F
8	Labia insurgentium et cogitationes	an	AR 427 OHS 191 219 AM 406 WA 114 LA 185	G	2	0	2	0	-2	0	2	5	G
8	Labia mea laudabunt	an	AM 362	G	-2	2	5	4	0	4	5	2	G
	Laborem manuum tuarum Beatus quicumque	grv	LU 1442	F	4	7	9	11	7	9	7	6	

	Labores manuum tuarum Beati omnes qui timent	grv	SYG 234	F	4	2	7	9	7	9	7	11	
	Lacrimosa dies illa Libera me de morte	rev	WA 438	a	-2	-4	-5	-7	-5	-4	-7	-9	
2	Lacte quondam profluentes	hy	AM 1021	C	2	0	5	4	2	0	5	7	D
2	Laetabimur in salutari tuo	co	GR 144 SYG 104 GB 92^v GS 66	D	-2	0	-2	-3	-2	0	-2	0	D
	Laetabitur justus in Domino	sr	WA 304 305										
7	Laetabitur justus in Domino	an	AR 188	d	-2	-3	0	2	-2	0	-2	0	G
8	Laetabitur justus in Domino ... laudabuntur	an	WA 417	G	-2	-5	-3	-2	0	2	0	2	G
7	Laetabitur justus in Domino ... laudabuntur	an	LR 153	d	-2	-3	0	2	-2	0	-2	0	G
5	Laetabitur justus in Domino ... laudabuntur	co	GR [18] LU 1149 SYG 170 GB 53^v GS 210	F	2	4	2	0	-1	0	2	0	F
5	Laetabitur justus in Domino ... laudabuntur	re	LR 171 *WA 304	F	2	4	2	0	-1	0	2	0	F
	Laetabitur justus in Domino ... laudabuntur	alv	SYG 209 *GS 207	a	3	2	0	2	-2	0	-2	-4	
7	Laetabitur justus in Domino ... laudabuntur	an	LA 524	G	4	5	7	5	9	7	9	7	G
8	Laetabitur justus in Domino ... laudabuntur	int	GR [12] LU 1138 SYG 43 GB 45^v GS z 205	G	5	2	-2	0	2	0	5	2	G
3	Laetabor super populo meo	an	AR 4 (Sup 2)	G	2	5	2	4	5	4	5	4	E
7	Laetamini caeli et exsultet terra	an	LR 341	E	-4	0	3	5	1	3	0	3	E
	Laetamini cum Jerusalem	alv	GR 510 LU 1483	a	-2	0	-2	-5	-2	-4	-5	-7	
5	Laetamini cum Jerusalem	an	AR 248 *AM 223 *WA 19 *LA 17	c	-1	-5	-3	-5	-3	0	2	0	F
	Laetamini in Domino et exsultate	sr	AR [45] LU 1154 AM 649 982 1104										
	Laetamini in Domino et exsultate Laetabitur justus	rev	LR 171 WA 304										
1	Laetamini in Domino et exsultate	of	GR 415 456 [20] OTT 140 LU 1151 1337 SYG 41 GB 44 *GS 218	D	2	3	5	3	0	2	3	-2	D
	Laetamini in Domino et exsultate	alv	GB 269 GS 217 (nm)	F	2	4	0	2	4	7	6	7	
8	Laetamini in Domino et exsultate	an	WA 421	G	5	2	0	2	0	-2	0	2	G
3	Laetamini in Domino et exsultate	an	LR 385 *WA 395 *LA 475	G	5	2	0	2	4	5	4	2	E
5	Laetamini omnes in Domino	an	LR 266	c	-1	0	-3	-7	-3	0	2	0	F
7	Laetare alma mater ecclesia	an	PM 150	G	5	4	5	7	5	2	5	4	G
5	Laetare Jerusalem et conventum	int	GR 138 LU 559 *SYG 100 GB 89^v *GS 63	F	5	2	4	2	0	2	4	7	F

	Text	Type	Sources										
2	Laetare mater nostra	co	GR 16**	D	2	-2	0	3	2	3	2	3	D
3	Laetare virgo Maria de te	an	PM 257 *SYG 18	G	5	4	5	7	5	4	5	2	E
7	Laetare virgo mater alleluia	an	AR 875 LU 1674	d	-2	0	-5	-2	-3	-5	-2	-3	G
7	Laetare virgo mater alleluia	an	AM 1075	G	4	5	7	5	4	5	7	9	G
	Laetatus sum in his Jerusalem quae aedificatur	cov	SYG 102										
	Laetatus sum in his Da pacem	intv	GR 372 [135] LU 1056 GS 161 GB 259^V										
	Laetatus sum in his Laetare Jerusalem	intv	GR 138 LU 559 GS 63 GB 89^V SYG 100										
2	Laetatus sum in his	tr	SYG 101	D	-2	0	-2	-5	-2	0	-2	0	D
7	Laetatus sum in his	gr	GR 139 LU 560 SYG 100 *GB 89^V *GS 63 162	c	2	0	2	0	-3	2	0	2	G
	Laetatus sum in his	alv	GR 5 LU 329 SYG 3 GB 3 GS 162	D	3	0	-2	3	5	3	7	5	
4	Laetatus sum in his	an	AR 100 OHS 225 LU 282	E	3	5	7	3	0	1	3	1	E
8	Laetatus sum in his	an	LA 99	G	5	4	5	2	0	2	0	-2	G
1	Laetemur hodie cum ingenti	in	SYG 227	C	2	9	11	9	12	9	11	9	D
7	Laetemur omnes in Domino	int	SYG 44 *GS h 177	G	5	7	9	7	5	7	5	4	G
	Laetentur caeli ... ante faciem Surrexit Dominus de sepulchro	rev	LA 213										
4	Laetentur caeli ... ante faciem	an	LR 60 LU 387 *WA 49 *LA 33	a	-2	0	3	5	3	5	7	5	a
4	Laetentur caeli ... ante faciem	of	GR 29 OTT 15 LU 394 *SYG 15 *GB 15 GS 14	C	2	5	4	5	7	2	7	5	E
2	Laetentur caeli ... jubilate	re	LA 5 *WA 5	A	3	5	7	8	7	8	10	5	D
4	Laetentur caeli ... quia venit	an	LR 100	a	-2	0	3	5	3	5	7	5	a
2	Laetentur omne saeculum	hy	ST 440	C	2	5	7	4	5	2	0	2	D
1	Laetentur omnes qui sperant ... in aeternum	an	LR 381 *WA 395 *LA 474	D	-2	3	0	2	0	-2	3	5	D
6	Laetentur omnes qui sperant ... in aeternum	re	PM 122 VP 97	c	2	0	2	4	0	-3	-5	0	c
8	Laetentur omnes qui sperant ... quoniam	an	LR 192 *WA 424 *LA 529	G	2	0	2	5	4	2	4	5	G
8	Laetetur cor quaerentium	an	WA 70 *LA 103	a	-4	-2	0	3	2	0	2	0	G
2	Laetetur cor quaerentium	int	GR 146 SYG 106 GB 94^V GS 68 169	A	3	5	8	5	3	5	8	7	D
	Laetetur mons Sion Suscepimus Deus	trv	GR 113**	G	2	4	5	4	2	5	2	0	

Laetifica animam servi tui Inclina Domine	intv	GR 360 LU 1040 GS 158 GB 255[V]									
Laetificabis eum in gaudio Desiderium animae	ofv	OTT 153 SYG 215 *GB 53[V]	F	-5	-3	0	2	0	2	0	-5
Laetitia sempiterna erit Lux perpetua	rev	LR 168									
Laetitia sempiterna super capita	sr	AR [35] LU 1120									
2 Laetus hoc festum colat universus	hy	ST 192	D	-2	0	3	2	0	2	0	-2 D
4 Laeva ejus sub capite meo	an	AR [114] LR 214 LU 1258 AM 707 *LA 541 WA 434	G	2	5	7	5	7	9	7	5 a
Lancea militis aperuit latus Immisit Dominus	rev	LR 343									
6 Languentibus in purgatorio	hy	AR 198*	D	3	5	3	8	7	5	3	2 F
7 Languor accrescens in dies	an	WA 296	G	7	9	7	5	4	5	7	5 G
Lapidabant Stephanum	see also	Lapidaverunt									
4 Lapidabant Stephanum invocantem	re	LA 44 *WA 35	F	-3	0	-1	0	2	0	-1	0 E
Lapidaverunt Stephanum et ipse Lapides torrentes	rev	WA 51(36)									
8 Lapidaverunt Stephanum et ipse	an	AR 273 LU 414 1583[A] AM 250 *WA 37 *LA 47	G	-2	2	5	4	0	4	5	2 G
Lapidem quem reprobaverunt Benedictus qui venit	rev	LA 37 WA 49									
8 Lapidem quem reprobaverunt	an	SYG 149	G	2	0	-2	0	2	4	2	0 G
Lapidem quem reprobaverunt	alv	SYG 161	F	2	4	2	0	2	0	-3	-1
Lapidem quem reprobaverunt Benedictus qui venit	ofv	OTT 64 GB 144 SYG 161	G	2	5	7	5	7	5	7	9
Lapidem quem reprobaverunt Haec dies	grv	GR 253(241) LU 797(778) OHS 807(709) *SYG 158(152) *GB 137(125) *GS 121(117)	a	5	7	5	7	5	0	5	3
1 Lapides pretiosi omnes	an	AR [107] LU 1247 AM 698 *WA 319 LA 552	D	-2	0	3	2	0	2	3	-2 D
7 Lapides pretiosi omnes	re	PM 239 LR 242 LA 550	G	2	0	5	4	5	7	9	5 G
7 Lapides torrentes illi	re	WA 36	G	2	0	7	5	7	10	7	9 G
7 Lapides torrentes illi	an	AR 273 LU 414 1583[A] *AM 250 *WA 37 LA 47	G	4	5	7	4	5	7	9	7 G
Laqueus contritus est Anima nostra	grv	GR 41 [26] LU 1167 GS 17 GB 26 SYG 25	F	4	7	9	7	9	7	9	4

	Lauda anima mea Dominum Redemptor meus vivit	rev	LA 560	a	-2	0	1	0	-2	0	-2	-4	
1	Lauda anima mea Dominum	an	AR 131	D	-2	3	5	3	2	5	7	5	D
	Lauda anima mea Dominum	alv	SYG 256 *GS 166	c	-1	2	0	-1	0	2	0	-3	
4	Lauda anima mea Dominum	of	GR 267 OTT 67 LU 823 899 SYG 166 *GB 149 GS K a 129	C	4	7	4	7	9	7	5	4	E
8	Lauda Deum tuum Sion	an	AR 172	F	2	4	2	0	2	4	0	4	G
1	Lauda et laetare	an	AM 1130	D	7	9	7	10	7	5	7	9	D
1	Lauda Jerusalem Dominum	an	LA 105	a	-2	0	-2	-5	-4	-2	-4	-7	D
1	Lauda Jerusalem Dominum	an	AR 167 *AM 162	a	-2	0	-2	-4	-2	1	-2	1	a
	Lauda Jerusalem Dominum lauda	alv	GR [136] LU 1285 SYG 259	a	-2	1	0	-2	0	-4	-5	-4	
3	Lauda Jerusalem Dominum quoniam	of	GR 487 LU 1277^B	F	-3	0	4	2	-1	0	2	0	E
3	Lauda mater ecclesia	hy	VP 191	a	-2	-5	-4	-5	-7	-2	0	3	E
2	Lauda mater ecclesia	hy	ST 123	C	2	4	0	2	5	4	2	5	D
7	Laudabile miraculum	re	WA 289	G	2	0	5	4	5	7	5	7	G
8	Laudabilis populus quem Dominus	re	LA 304 WA 184	b	1	3	1	3	1	3	1	-2	G
4	Laudabo Deum meum	an	AR 127 AM 160 WA 60 LA 105	F	-1	-3	-1	0	2	4	2	0	E
8	Laudamini in nomine sancto	of	GR 114**	D	3	7	5	0	5	7	10	7	G
1	Laudamus nomen tuum	an	AR 72 *AM 42	D	-2	3	5	7	5	3	2	3	D
	Laudanda tremenda	alv	GB 213^V	G	4	5	4	2	0	2	4	2	
	Laudans invocabo Dominum Diligam te Domine	rev	LA 82 WA 61										
2	Laudate Deum caeli caelorum	an	AR 366 AM 342 *WA 88 *LA 132	E	-4	-2	0	-4	-2	0	3	0	D
	Laudate Deum omnes angeli	alv	GR 68 LU 486 GS 22 *SYG 35 *GB 168^V	a	-2	0	-2	-5	-4	-2	-4	-2	
3	Laudate Deum omnes angeli	an	AR 866 LU 1666 *AM 1068	E	-2	3	5	3	5	8	7	8	E
	Laudate Dominum de caelis Virgines laudent	intv	GR 102**										
1	Laudate Dominum de caelis	an	AR 342 AM 43 313 *LA 114 *WA 75	a	-2	-5	-4	-2	-4	-5	-7	[0]	D
3	Laudate Dominum de caelis	gr	GR [86] LU 1275	G	4	7	5	2	0	5	4	7	E
	Laudate Dominum Deum nostrum Vos qui in turribus	rev	WA 178										
	Laudate Dominum Deum nostrum	alv	GR 41**	E	-2	3	5	3	5	8	7	8	
2	Laudate Dominum Deum nostrum	re	WA 178	A	3	5	3	5	8	5	3	8	D
	Laudate Dominum in sanctis	alv	SYG 224	a	-2	2	0	-2	0	-4	-5	-4	

Mode	Text	Type	Sources										
	Laudate Dominum omnes angeli Minuisti eum	intv	GR 517 LU 1493										
8	Laudate Dominum omnes angeli	tr	GR 636 SYG 83 GS 46	G	2	4	2	0	2	0	5	7	G
	Laudate Dominum omnes gentes Loquebar de testimoniis	intv	GR 395 LU 1309										
8	Laudate Dominum omnes gentes	tr	GR 110 237 OHS 683 LU 776^{II} SYG 83 GB 74 GS 46 115 173	G	2	4	2	0	2	0	5	7	G
4	Laudate Dominum omnes gentes	an	LA 90	G	2	5	2	5	2	0	-2	0	E
5	Laudate Dominum omnes gentes	co	GR [130] LU 1297	a	3	2	3	0	-4	-2	0	-2	F
	Laudate Dominum omnes gentes	alv	SYG 256 *GB 263^{V} *GS b	A	3	5	8	5	7	5	3	5	
1	Laudate Dominum omnes gentes	an	AR 72	F	4	5	2	4	2	0	2	5	a
7	Laudate Dominum qui sanat	an	AR 152	G	4	5	7	9	7	9	7	5	G
2	Laudate Dominum quia benignus	of	GR 140 [138] OTT 40 LU 562 SYG 102 *GB 90 *GS 64	D	-5	-2	0	2	3	2	0	2	D
3	Laudate Dominum quia benignus	an	AR 112	G	4	5	2	0	2	0	-3	-2	E
7	Laudate Dominum quoniam confirmata	an	AR 76	G	7	9	5	4	2	4	0	2	G
8	Laudate Dominum secundum multitudinem	an	AR 195	G	-2	2	5	4	0	4	5	2	G
	Laudate eum omnes angeli ejus Laudate Dominum	grv	GR [86] LU 1275	G	4	5	7	5	9	7	9	7	
2	Laudate nomen Domini	an	AR 108	E	-4	-2	-4	-2	1	3	1	3	D
	Laudate nomen ejus Jubilate Deo	ofv	OTT 23 *GB 36^{V} *SYG 32	F	4	7	9	7	11	9	7	6	
	Laudate pueri Dominum Consummatus in brevi	intv	GR 81**										
	Laudate pueri Dominum Dedit illi Deus	intv	GR 422 LU 1352										
	Laudate pueri Dominum Effusum est in terra	intv	GR 554 LU 1561										
	Laudate pueri Dominum Veni de Libano	intv	GR 613 LU 1668										
	Laudate pueri Dominum Alma Scholastica	rev	LR 290										
1	Laudate pueri Dominum	int	GR 550 *SYG 206 *GB 211 GS 190	D	-2	0	3	2	0	3	-2	3	D
	Laudate pueri Dominum	alv	GR 42 260 OHS 827 LU 428 805 GS p 123 216 SYG 161 GB 142^{V}	a	-2	1	0	-2	0	-4	-5	-4	
	Laudate pueri Dominum Resurrexit tamquam dormiens	alv	GB 126	D	2	-2	0	2	3	5	3	2	
8	Laudem dicite Deo nostro	re	WA 396	G	-7	0	-2	0	-7	-5	-2	0	G

5	Laudem dicite Deo nostro	an	LR 388 *WA 397 *LA 476	F	4	7	6	4	9	7	6	7	F
	Laudem Domini loquetur	alv	GR 52 LU 448	a	-2	0	-2	-5	-4	-5	-4	-2	
	Laudem Domini loquetur Prope est Dominus	grv	LU 354 GR 21 GB 7 SYG 8 GS 6	C	2	0	-3	0	-3	0	-5	-3	
2	Laudemus Christum regem	inv	WA 256	C	2	5	4	2	0	2	9	7	D
2	Laudemus Deum nostrum ... beatae N.	inv	LR 211	C	2	4	5	2	0	2	5	4	D
2	Laudemus Deum nostrum ... Benedicti	inv	LR 443	C	2	4	5	2	0	2	5	4	D
2	Laudemus Deum nostrum ... doctoris	inv	LR 432	C	2	4	5	2	0	2	5	4	D
2	Laudemus Deum nostrum ... Joseph	inv	LR 435	C	2	4	5	2	0	2	5	4	D
2	Laudemus Deum nostrum ... Martini	inv	LR 454	C	2	4	5	2	0	2	5	4	D
6	Laudemus Deum virginis	inv	WA 310 *59	C	5	7	5	7	5	7	5	4	F
1	[Laudemus Dominum]	re	WA 391	D	3	0	-2	3	5	7	5	3	D
2	Laudemus Dominum quem laudant	an	AR 865 LU 1665 AM 1067 *WA 381 *LA 467 477	D	-2	0	3	2	0	2	3	0	D
4	Laudemus Dominum quod doctrinis	an	WA 291	E	-2	1	3	1	0	-2	0	-2	E
	Laudemus et superexaltemus Benedicamus patrem	trv	GB 214ᵛ	G	2	4	5	4	5	4	5	4	
8	Laudemus virum gloriosum	an	AR 824 LU 1610	G	5	2	0	4	7	5	4	2	G
2	Laudes magnificas altithrono Deo	hy	ST 55	G	2	4	0	2	5	4	2	0	a
4	Laudes omnipotens ferimus tibi	hy	ST 490	D	3	-2	0	2	3	5	3	2	E
4	Laudibus cives resonent canoris	hy	PM 339	a	-2	0	-2	-4	-5	-4	-2	-5	E
1	Laudibus cives resonent canoris	hy	AM 848	D	2	3	0	-2	0	3	2	0	D
	Laudibus gloriosus es O quam admirabilis vir	rev	WA 390	a	7	5	7	8	7	5	7	5	
8	Laurentius bonum opus	an	AR 814 LU 1597 AM 1006 WA 350 *LA 440	a	-4	-2	0	2	0	-2	0	-2	G
	Laurentius bonum opus	alv	GB 218	F	2	4	0	2	4	7	6	7	
1	Laurentius ingressus est	an	AR 813 LU 1596 *AM 1005 *WA 350 *LA 440	D	2	3	5	2	3	5	2	3	D
7	Laus angelorum inclita	hy	ST 401	c	-3	0	-5	0	-3	-1	-3	-5	G
2	Laus angelorum inclita	hy	ST 340	a	-2	0	3	2	0	3	0	-2	a
4	Laus Deo patri parilique proli	an	AR 519 LU 914 *AM 536 *WA 158	E	-2	1	-2	-4	-2	0	-2	-4	E
2	Laus et perennis gloria Deo	an	AR 518 LU 914 AM 535 *WA 158	D	-2	0	3	5	3	0	-2	0	D
8	Laus trinitati resonet perennis	hy	ST 391	G	2	0	-3	-2	-3	-5	-3	0	G
3	Lavabo inter innocentes	of	SYG 86	D	2	3	5	3	5	7	5	7	E

8 Lavabo inter innocentes	co	GR 162 *SYG 114 *GB 102 GS 75	D	3	7	5	7	5	7	5	3	G
1 Laverunt stolas suas	re	WA 44	G	2	0	-2	2	5	9	7	0	G
7 Lavit Maria lacrimis	an	WA 336	G	5	4	5	7	9	7	5	4	G
1 Lazarus amicus noster dormit	an	AR 404 LU 1096 AM 380 WA 105 LA 165	F	2	4	2	4	2	-1	0	2	D
Legem pone mihi Domine et viam Levabo oculos	ofv	OTT 34 GB 67^v SYG 76	D	3	5	7	5	7	5	3	5	
Leva in circuitu Jerusalem surge	cov	SYG 5										
Leva in circuitu Leva Jerusalem	rev	LA 9										
Leva in circuitu	alv	GR 45**	D	3	2	5	3	2	3	0	2	
8 Leva Jerusalem oculos	re	LA 9	F	2	4	2	4	6	4	2	4	G
1 Leva Jerusalem oculos	an	AR 220 AM 191 LA 7	D	7	9	7	10	7	5	7	5	D
1 Levabit Dominus signum	an	AR 230 AM 203 WA 11 LA 12	D	-2	0	2	3	5	3	2	0	D
8 Levabo oculos meos et considerabo	of	GR 100 OTT 34 *SYG 76 GB 67^v GS 38	D	3	5	7	5	7	5	3	5	G
1 Levate capita vestra	an	AR 260 LU 365 AM 237 WA 26 LA 30	D	-2	0	2	3	5	3	2	0	D
Levavi oculos meos in montes Adeamus cum fiducia	intv	GR 43**										
2 Levita Laurentius bonum opus	re	PM 174 LA 434 *WA 347	A	3	5	7	5	8	7	8	5	D
8 Levita Laurentius bonum opus	an	AR 813 LU 1593 AM 1005 WA 346 LA 437	G	5	2	0	-2	0	2	0	-2	G
Levita Laurentius bonum opus	alv	GR 579 LU 1595 *GS 194	G	5	4	2	4	0	2	0	-2	
Levita Laurentius bonum opus	alv	SYG 213	G	7	5	4	2	5	7	0	-2	
1 Levita Vincentius dixit	re	WA 257	D	3	5	3	0	-2	3	5	7	D
5 Levita Vincentius dixit	an	WA 256	F	4	7	5	7	·5	4	2	5	F
Lex Dei ejus in corde	sr	AR [85] LU 1195										
Lex Dei ejus in corde Apud Dominum	trv	GR 528	F	2	0	2	0	-3	0	-1	0	
Lex Dei ejus in corde Os justi	grv	GR [38] LU 1191 *GS 204 *GB 53 *SYG 206	D	7	5	7	10	9	10	7	5	
1 Lex Domini irreprehensibilis	int	GR 122 SYG 91 GB 81 GS 53	a	-2	1	0	-2	0	-2	-4	-2	D
1 Lex per Moysen data	an	AR 239 AM 214 *WA 17 *LA 23	D	-2	0	2	3	5	3	2	0	D
8 Lex veritatis fuit in ore ejus	int	GR 526 LU 1511	D	3	5	7	3	7	10	9	7	G

#	Text	Type	Sources	Mode	n1	n2	n3	n4	n5	n6	n7	n8	Final
1	Libenter gloriabor	re	WA 265	D	-2	0	3	2	3	0	2	0	D
8	Libenter gloriabor	an	AR 609 756 LU 1348 AM 793 941 WA 266 LA 430	G	5	2	0	-2	0	2	0	4	G
3	Libera Domine populum	an	GB 154^v	E	-2	3	5	7	5	7	8	7	E
	Libera me ab hiis / Vide quia tribulor	rev	WA 107										
	Libera me de ore leonis / Deus Deus meus	trv	GR 180 OHS 109 LU 594 GS 86 GB 109 SYG 122	F	2	4	2	4	2	0	2	4	
8	Libera me de sanguinibus	an	AR 430 OHS 304 *AM 409 WA 117 LA 187	a	-4	-2	0	-2	-4	0	3	5	G
1	Libera me Domine de morte aeterna	re	AR [174] GR 102* LU 1767 PM 321 *LA 557 *WA 438	D	-2	0	3	2	0	2	3	0	D
1	Libera me Domine de viis inferni	re	AR [173] LU 1798 *PM 317 *LA 556	D	-2	3	5	8	7	8	7	5	D
1	Libera me Domine et pone me	an	AM 6 *AR 82 WA 109	D	7	10	7	5	7	5	3	2	D
	Libera nos Domine de affligentibus	see Liberasti nos Domine ex ...											
6	Libera nos salva nos	an	WA 158	D	2	0	2	3	5	3	5	8	F
	Liberabo te de manu / Puer meus noli	rev	LA 434 WA 349										
	Liberasti in brachio tuo / Tu es Deus qui facis mirabilia	grv	GR 81 LU 512 *GB 59^v *SYG 62 *GS 28	G	5	7	4	5	4	2	4	5	
7	Liberasti nos Domine ex affligentibus	gr	GR 387 LU 1075 GS e *SYG 258 GB 264^v	a	3	5	3	5	7	3	2	3	G
8	Liberasti virgam	an	WA 67 *LA 96	G	2	0	-2	2	5	2	4	2	G
3	Liberator meus de gentibus	int	GR 159 *SYG 113 *GB 100^v GS 74	G	2	5	2	5	0	2	-2	-3	E
	Liberator meus de gentibus / Intonuit de caelo	ofv	OTT 58 GB 134^v *SYG 156	G	2	5	7	5	4	5	4	0	
	Liberator meus de gentibus / Populum humilem	ofv	OTT 93 GB 95^v SYG 107	F	4	7	9	7	4	7	4	7	
	Liberator meus Deus / Diligam te	rev	LR 342	D	7	5	7	5	3	2	3	5	
	Liberator meus Domine / Eripe me Domine	grv	GR 152 LU 570 GS 71 *GB 97^v *SYG 109	G	2	5	4	5	7	2	5	4	
7	Liberavit Dominus pauperem	an	OHS 382 LU 638 WA 118 *LA 190	d	-3	0	2	3	0	-2	-3	-7	G
8	Liberiori generi	an	LR 319 WA 296 LA 367	G	5	2	0	2	0	2	0	-2	G
8	Licuit sanguine loqui	an	WA 44	F	2	4	2	4	2	0	4	7	G
6	Lignum habet spem	of	GR 466 LU 1421	F	4	2	0	2	0	4	7	4	F
1	Lignum vitae crucem	an	SYG 141	G	2	0	2	4	5	4	2	0	D

	Incipit		Sources										
	Lingua mea calamus scribae Constitues eos	ofv	OTT 131 GB 206^v SYG 203	G	5	2	0	5	4	5	2	4	
5	Lingua pangat et cor tangat	hy	ST 322	F	4	7	4	7	9	7	12	9	F
	Lingua pravorum peribit	alv	GR 29**	G	2	4	5	4	0	2	0	5	
8	Linguam refrenans temperet	hy	ST 474	G	-2	2	0	2	4	0	2	5	G
5	Locus iste a Deo factus	gr	GR [72] LU 1251 *SYG 263 GB 173^v GS 175	F	2	0	2	4	5	4	7	4	F
	Locus iste sanctus est	sr	AR [111] [112] LU 1245 AM 692 693 694										
	Locuti sunt adversum me	re	OHS 302 (nm)										
	Locuti sunt adversum me Opprobrium factus	rev	OHS 185 (nm) LA 180										
	Locuti sunt adversum me Domine fac mecum	ofv	OTT 37 GB 85^v *SYG 96	C	2	9	10	9	12	9	7	9	
	Locutum est os meum Jubilate Deo	ofv	OTT 69 GB 38 SYG 36	C	2	9	10	9	12	9	7	9	
2	Locutus est ad me unus	re	LA 225 *WA 140	D	3	2	3	0	-2	0	2	3	D
2	Locutus est Dominus ad Abraham	re	LR 402 LA 120 WA 80	a	3	2	3	0	3	2	3	0	a
	Locutus est Dominus ad Moysen Isti sunt dies	rev	LA 166 WA 105										
4	Locutus est Dominus ad Moysen	re	LR 411 *LA 156 *WA 100	F	-3	0	-1	2	0	-1	0	-1	E
	Locutus est Dominus ad Moysen Sanctificavit Moyses	ofv	OTT 114 GB 259^v SYG 254	F	4	7	4	7	9	7	9	7	
	Locutus est populus Panis quem ego dabo	rev	LR 124										
	Longe a salute mea Deus Deus meus	trv	GR 180 OHS 109 LU 594 GS 86 GB 109 SYG 122	D	3	5	3	0	2	3	2	0	
8	Longe fecisti notos meos	an	OHS 502 LU 707 *WA 123 LA 198	G	2	0	4	2	5	4	2	5	G
8	Longo contritus carcere	an	SYG 148	F	2	4	2	0	2	0	4	6	G
8	Loquamur nunc usque mane	an	AM 815	c	-1	-3	-1	-3	-5	-3	-1	0	G
	Loquebantur variis linguis	sr	WA 155										
	Loquebantur variis linguis Apparuerunt apostolis	rev	LA 260 WA 156										
	Loquebantur variis linguis Repleti sunt	rev	LU 875 AM 1187 PM 90 LR 110 LA 256 WA 152										
2	Loquebantur variis linguis	re	WA 156	D	-5	-2	0	3	5	3	2	0	D
7	Loquebantur variis linguis	an	AR 504 LU 884 AM 521 WA 153 LA 262 265	c	-1	-3	0	2	4	0	-1	-3	G

	Loquebantur variis linguis	alv	GR 297 LU 888 *GS 139 *GB 193 SYG 184	C	2	4	5	7	5	4	2	5	
2	Loquebantur variis linguis ... prout	re	LR 113	D	-2	-5	-2	0	-2	0	3	5	D
2	Loquebantur variis linguis ... prout	re	LA 259	A	3	5	7	5	3	8	10	8	D
	Loquebar de testimoniis tuis	alv	GS 228	C	2	4	5	2	4	0	2	4	
5	Loquebar de testimoniis tuis	int	GR 395 591 [51] LU 1309 1618 1215 SYG 39 GB 42v *GS 225	F	4	7	9	7	9	7	4	6	F
	Loquebar Domine de testimoniis	alv	GR 437 LU 1369	D	-2	-5	-2	0	-2	0	2	3	
	Loquebar Domine de testimoniis	alv	SYG 39 GB 244	F	-1	0	2	-3	-1	0	-1	-3	
4	Loquebatur Christus ad dilectam	an	AM 1135	D	2	3	5	7	5	0	2	3	E
6	Loquens Dominus ad Noe	an	WA 76	c	2	0	2	4	5	4	2	4	c
1	Loquere Domine quia audit	an	AR 517 LU 907 AM 534 WA 164 *LA 273	D	-2	2	3	5	3	0	-2	3	D
3	Loquetur Dominus pacem	int	GR 516 LU 1492 *SYG 193 *GB 196 *GS 212	G	5	2	0	5	4	2	5	4	E
	Loquetur pacem gentibus Bethlehem civitas	rev	LA 13 WA 14										
	Loquetur pacem gentibus Exsulta satis	ofv	OTT 11 GB 10 SYG 12	G	4	5	2	5	2	5	2	0	
	Loquimur Dei sapientiam Non judicavi	trv	GR 476	G	-2	0	-2	-5	-3	-2	0	-2	
4	Luca fidelis	hy	ST 403	F	-3	-5	-3	0	-3	-5	0	2	E
4	Luca fidelis	hy	ST 241	F	-1	-3	-5	-3	0	-3	-1	0	E
4	Luca sancte	hy	ST 403	F	-3	-5	-3	0	-3	-5	0	2	E
	Luce splendida fulgebis Plateae tuae	rev	WA 141										
4	Lucem tuam Domine nobis concede	an	VP 30	C	2	0	2	5	7	5	4	2	E
1	Lucia martyr invictissima	re	WA 246	C	2	5	4	5	7	5	4	2	D
4	Lucia virgo judici	re	WA 245	F	-3	-1	-3	-5	-3	0	-1	0	E
7	Lucia virgo quid a me	an	AR 592 LU 1324 *AM 770 *WA 243 *LA 322	G	4	5	7	9	7	4	7	5	G
7	Lucia virgo quid a me	re	LA 320 WA 243	G	5	4	5	7	5	7	9	7	G
1	Lucia virgo venerabilis	an	WA 243	a	-2	0	-2	-4	0	3	0	-2	D
1	Luciano venerabili	an	WA 341	C	2	9	11	9	7	9	7	5	D
4	Lucianus presbyter dixit	re	WA 343	F	-3	0	-3	0	2	0	-1	0	E
7	Lucifer diem inchoat	hy	ST 374 388 404	c	-3	0	-5	0	-3	-1	-3	-5	G
2	Lucis beatae gaudiis	hy	LR 444	a	-2	-5	-7	-2	0	3	2	0	a

8	Lucis creator optime	hy	ST 86		a	-2	-4	-7	-4	-5	-4	-2	0	G
2	Lucis creator optime	hy	ST 438		D	-2	3	5	7	5	3	5	3	D
1	Lucis creator optime	hy	ST 156		E	-2	3	5	8	5	7	10	8	D
8	Lucis creator optime	hy	ST 252 268		G	2	-3	-2	0	2	0	-3	-2	G
8	Lucis creator optime	hy	ST 268		G	2	-2	0	2	0	-2	0	2	G
8	Lucis creator optime	hy	ST 182		G	2	0	-2	2	5	0	2	0	G
8	Lucis creator optime	hy	AR 49 LU 257		D	2	3	5	3	5	7	5	3	G
7	Lucis creator optime	hy	ST 361		G	2	4	5	4	2	0	5	7	G
7	Lucis creator optime	hy	ST 471		c	2	4	5	4	2	4	5	4	G
8	Lucis creator optime	hy	AR 48 LU 256 *AM 128		G	2	5	4	2	0	5	7	4	G
7	Lucis creator optime	hy	ST 212		G	2	5	4	2	4	5	7	4	G
1	Lucis creator optime	hy	AR 51 LU 258		D	7	9	7	5	7	10	9	7	D
6	Lucis hujus festa colat plebs honesta	hy	ST 129		F	-3	-5	0	-1	-3	0	2	0	F
1	Lucis hujus festa colat plebs honesta	hy	ST 107		D	7	9	5	7	9	12	10	9	D
1	Lugebat autem Judam	an	AR 550 LU 994 *AM 588		C	2	0	5	2	4	2	0	5	D
	Lumen ad revelationem Responsum acceperat	rev	LA 349											
8	Lumen ad revelationem	an	AR 620 GR 428 PM 132 LU 1357 1366 AM 803 *LA 350 SYG 47 GS 180		c	-1	-5	-1	0	-3	-5	-3	-5	G
	Lumen ad revelationem Nunc dimittis	trv	GB 49		G	2	4	5	4	2	5	7	0	
	Lumen ad revelationem Nunc dimittis	trv	GR 434 LU 1363 GS k SYG 50		D	3	0	3	7	3	5	3	5	
3	Lumen clarum rite fulget	hy	ST 485		G	2	-3	-5	0	2	0	2	5	E
4	Lumine vultus tui	an	WA 33		F	-1	-3	-1	0	2	0	-1	2	E
	Lustra sex qui jam peracta	hy	ST 385											
3	Lustra sex qui jam peracta	hy	ST 91		E	-2	3	5	8	10	8	5	8	E
1	Lustra sex qui jam peregit	hy	AR 410 OHS 71 192		D	2	5	7	5	7	10	9	7	D
	Lustris sex		see also Lustra sex											
1	Lustris sex qui jam peractis	hy	AM 386		D	2	5	7	5	7	10	9	7	D
1	Lutum ex sputo Dominus	co	SYG 106		C	2	5	2	0	5	7	9	7	D
6	Lutum fecit ex sputo	co	GR 146 GS 68		F	-1	0	-3	-5	0	2	4	2	F
8	Lutum fecit ex sputo	co	GB 94		G	2	4	5	4	0	2	0	-2	G
8	Lux aeterna luceat eis	co	GR 102* LU 1815 SYG 236 GB 266[v] GS 233		a	-2	-4	-2	0	-2	0	3	2	G
8	Lux alma Jesu mentium	hy	AR 806		G	2	5	4	2	0	-2	2	0	G

	Incipit		Sources										
8	Lux de luce apparuisti	an	AR 332 LU 482 AM 298 *WA 54 *LA 69	c	-1	-3	-1	0	-1	-5	-7	-5	G
4	Lux ecce surgit aurea	hy	AR 148 AM 65	E	-4	-2	1	0	1	3	1	0	E
1	Lux ecce surgit aurea	hy	ST 318	F	-1	0	2	4	2	4	2	9	D
4	Lux ecce surgit aurea	hy	ST 279	E	1	0	-2	-4	-2	0	1	0	E
1	Lux ecce surgit aurea	hy	AM 65	a	2	0	-2	-4	-2	0	-2	-4	D
3	Lux ecce surgit aurea	hy	ST 214	D	2	3	5	3	5	3	2	3	E
8	Lux ecce surgit aurea	hy	ST 363	D	2	3	5	7	3	5	0	2	G
8	Lux fulgebit hodie super nos	int	GR 30 LU 403 SYG 15 GB 15 GS E	D	3	5	7	3	7	10	9	7	G
1	Lux hodierna fulget in arva	hy	ST 82	a	1	0	-2	-4	0	-2	-4	-5	D
	Lux maris gaude	hy	ST 305	D	2	3	0	-2	5	7	5	3	
8	Lux mundi beatissima	hy	ST 378	G	2	4	2	0	-2	0	2	0	G
7	Lux o decora patriae	hy	AR 778	G	4	5	7	9	7	5	4	5	G
6	Lux orta est justo	an	LR 140 *WA 412 *LA 43 507	F	-1	2	4	-1	0	-3	-5	0	F
1	Lux orta est super nos	an	WA 32 *LA 38	F	-1	-3	0	-1	-3	-5	-3	0	D
	Lux perpetua lucebit sanctis	sr	AR [35] LU 1119 AM 629 1171										
4	Lux perpetua lucebit sanctis	an	LA 387 391	F	-3	-1	0	2	-1	-3	0	2	E
	Lux perpetua lucebit sanctis In circuitu tuo	rev	WA 423	D	-2	0	3	5	3	5	7	5	
3	Lux perpetua lucebit sanctis	re	LR 168 LA 387 WA 306	c	-1	0	-3	-5	-1	-5	-3	0	E
	Lux perpetua lucebit sanctis	alv	GB 163^{v}	G	2	5	4	2	4	2	0	2	
1	Lux perpetua lucebit sanctis	an	WA 305	C	2	9	11	9	7	9	7	4	D
1	Lux perpetua lucebit sanctis	an	AR 577^{11} [28] LU 262^{1} 1118 AM 632 735 907 WA 306	D	3	0	-2	0	2	0	5	7	D
4	Lux perpetua lucebit sanctis	an	LR 172	D	3	0	-2	0	2	0	5	7	E
1	Lux vera lucis radium	hy	ST 337	D	-2	0	3	5	3	2	3	0	D
8	Lux visa per caliginem	hy	ST 333	G	2	0	-3	-5	-3	-2	0	2	G

1	Magdalenam sua crimina	an	WA 336	C	2	9	11	9	7	9	7	5	D
2	Magi intrantes domum	an	AR 320 LU 468	D	2	-2	0	5	7	3	2	-2	D
	Magi veniunt ab Oriente Interrogabat Magos	rev	PM 42 LR 77 LA 70 WA 54										
8	Magi veniunt ab Oriente	re	LR 76 LA 68 *WA 53	F	2	4	2	4	2	4	6	4	G
8	Magi videntes stellam dixerunt	an	AR 311 LU 455 AM 289 WA 52 *LA 66	F	2	4	2	4	2	0	2	4	G
1	Magi videntes stellam obtulerunt	an	WA 57	D	-2	0	2	3	5	3	0	-2	D
4	Magister dicit tempus meum	an	AR 418 LU 1100 AM 396 *WA 114 LA 174	a	-2	0	3	5	3	5	7	5	a
8	Magister quid faciendo vitam	an	AM 602 *AR 563 *LU 1106 LA 315	a	-4	-2	0	2	3	2	0	-2	G
8	Magister quod est mandatum	an	AR 568 AM 608 *WA 190 LA 317	a	-4	-2	0	3	2	3	0	-2	G
8	Magister scimus quia verax es	an	AR 573 LU 1107 *AM 614 *WA 191 *LA 319	a	-4	-2	0	2	3	0	-2	-4	G
3	Magna enim sunt judicia	re	LA 279 *WA 170	G	2	4	2	0	2	4	5	4	E
	Magna est gloria ejus	sr	AR 657 809 [21] LU 1404 1405 1125 1588										
	Magna est gloria ejus In virtute	ofv	OTT 152 *GB 51^v *SYG 52	F	2	4	2	0	2	7	9	7	
	Magna est gloria ejus Posuisti Domine	ofv	OTT 136 GB 233^v	F	2	4	7	4	2	0	2	4	
4	Magna est gloria ejus	co	GR [2] LU 1649 SYG 171 *GB 24 ×GS w 202	G	2	5	2	0	2	0	2	-2	E
8	Magna et mirabilia	an	WA 143	F	2	4	2	4	2	-1	0	2	G
1	Magna magnalia de Michael	an	LA 465	D	7	10	7	5	7	5	2	3	D
3	Magna opera Domini	an	AR 45 OHS 157 LU 253	G	5	4	2	0	2	4	2	0	E
1	Magnae dies laetitiae	hy	ST 122	D	7	9	7	5	3	2	0	-2	D
1	Magnae Deus potentiae	hy	AM 153 ST 363	F	2	4	0	2	0	-1	2	0	D
1	Magnae Deus potentiae	hy	AR 161	F	2	4	2	0	-1	2	-1	0	D
8	Magnae Deus potentiae	hy	AM 153	D	3	5	3	7	5	0	3	5	G
2	Magnae Deus potentiae	hy	ST 214	D	3	5	7	3	5	3	5	2	D
6	Magne Deus nostrae laudis	re	WA 318	c	2	0	2	4	0	-2	-3	-2	c
7	Magne pater Augustine	hy	ST 133	G	2	0	5	4	2	4	2	0	G
1	Magne pater Augustine	hy	VP 208	D	7	8	7	5	3	5	0	3	D
7	Magne pater Nicholae	re	WA 241	c	2	0	-1	-3	0	-5	-3	-5	G

4 Magni palmam certaminis	hy	ST 13	D	2	0	-2	2	3	5	7	5	E
7 Magnificabitur usque ad terminos	an	AR 894[7] LU 1706 AM 1093	G	4	5	7	5	2	5	4	5	G
5 Magnificat anima mea	an	WA 64	c	-1	-3	-5	-3	-5	-3	-5	-7	F
8 Magnificat anima mea	tr	GR 50**	E	3	5	8	5	7	8	10	8	G
Magnificat anima mea ... et exsultavit Beatam me dicent	rev	WA 356										
Magnificat anima mea ... et exsultavit	alv	GR 587[3] 49** LU 1612[2]	F	2	0	5	4	2	4	0	2	
1 Magnificat anima mea ... et exsultavit	of	GR 617 LU 1670	C	2	9	10	9	12	9	7	9	D
5 Magnificat anima mea ... quia fecit	re	LR 270	F	4	2	4	5	4	2	0	4	F
8 Magnificat anima mea ... quia respexit	an	AR 103 AM 137 *PM 165	G	5	2	0	2	0	2	0	-2	G
Magnificate Dominum mecum	sr	AR 305 LU 451										
7 Magnificate Dominum mecum	re	LR 269	G	5	4	5	7	5	7	5	4	G
7 Magnificatus est rex pacificus	an	AR 259 LU 364 AM 236 *WA 26 LA 31	G	4	5	7	5	2	5	4	0	G
7 Magnificavit Dominus facere	an	AR 121 OHS 289 LU 286	G	4	5	7	4	5	7	9	7	G
Magnificavit eum in conspectu Justum deduxit	rev	LA 525 WA 427										
1 Magnificavit eum in conspectu	re	LA 534 *WA 427	D	-2	0	-2	0	3	0	-2	0	D
7 Magnificemus Christum regem	an	LA 90	G	4	5	7	9	7	9	10	9	G
2 Magnificentiam gloriae sanctitatis	tr	GR 99**	D	-2	0	-2	-5	-2	0	-2	0	D
2 Magno canentes annua	hy	ST 428	G	-3	-2	0	-2	-3	-5	0	-2	D
2 Magno canentes annua	hy	ST 285	D	-2	-5	-2	0	3	0	3	2	D
2 Magno canentes annua	hy	ST 285	D	-2	-3	-2	-5	-7	-2	0	3	D
2 Magnum haereditatis mysterium	an	AR 297 LU 444 AM 275 716 *WA 51 LA 66	a	-2	0	2	3	5	3	2	0	a
7 Magnum mysterium declaratur	an	WA 59 LA 78 *VP 96	G	7	5	4	7	9	5	7	5	G
2 Magnum salutis gaudium	hy	ST 145	c	-3	-5	-1	0	-1	-3	0	-1	a
6 Magnum salutis gaudium	hy	ST 418	D	-2	0	3	0	2	0	-2	3	C
2 Magnum salutis gaudium	hy	ST 118	D	2	0	2	3	0	-2	0	3	D
1 Magnum salutis gaudium	hy	ST 9	D	2	3	-2	0	2	3	-2	0	D
2 Magnum salutis gaudium	hy	ST 448	C	2	4	5	4	2	4	2	0	D
7 Magnum salutis gaudium	hy	ST 34 42	G	4	5	7	9	7	5	4	5	G
2 8 Magnum salutis gaudium	hy	ST 439	D	5	3	5	7	8	7	5	3	G
2 Magnum salutis gaudium	hy	ST 500	D	5	3	7	3	5	7	3	0	D

	Incipit		Sources										
	Magnus Dominus et magna virtus Magnus Dominus	rev	LR 340										
4	Magnus Dominus et magna virtus	re	WA 159	E	-2	-4	-2	1	0	1	-2	0	E
	Magnus Dominus ... et magna virtus Angelus Domini	grv	GR 634 LU 1699	c	2	0	-3	0	-7	-3	0	2	
	Magnus Dominus ... et magnitudinis Magnus Dominus et magna	rev	WA 159										
1	Magnus Dominus ... et magnitudinis	an	AR 204 OHS 43 LU 310	D	7	10	7	5	7	5	3	5	D
4	Magnus Dominus ... et sapientiae	re	LR 340	E	-2	-4	-2	0	1	-2	0	-2	E
	Magnus Dominus ... in civitate	an	OHS 298 (nm)										
	Magnus Dominus ... in civitate Gaudeamus ... Agathae	intv	SYG 50										
	Magnus Dominus ... in civitate Gaudeamus ... Benedicti	intv	GR (16)										
	Magnus Dominus ... in civitate Gaudeamus ... Mariae virginis	intv	SYG 215										
	Magnus Dominus ... in civitate Laetemur omnes	intv	SYG 44										
	Magnus Dominus ... in civitate Omnia quae fecisti	intv	GS 76 164 GB 102 SYG 114										
	Magnus Dominus ... in civitate Suscepimus Deus	intv	GR 339 432 LU 1361 GS j 149 GB 47 SYG 48										
	Magnus Dominus ... in civitate In circuitu	rev	VP 256 LA 518 WA 429										
	Magnus Dominus ... in civitate Vidi civitatem ... ornatam	rev	LA 388										
	Magnus Dominus ... in civitate	alv	GR 340 LU 1014 *SYG 242	d	-2	-5	-2	0	3	2	3	5	
	Magnus Dominus noster	sr	AM 162 LA 105 WA 70										
8	Magnus Dominus ... valde	an	LA 90	F	2	4	2	0	4	2	4	6	G
	Magnus et metuendus Tui sunt caeli	ofv	OTT 18 *GB 19^v *SYG 20	c	-1	2	0	-3	-5	-7	-5	-3	
	Magnus sanctus Paulus Tu es vas	rev	LA 429										
	Magnus sanctus Paulus	alv	GB 208	a	-4	0	-2	-5	-7	-4	-7	0	
1	Magnus sanctus Paulus	re	PM 129 LA 430 WA 265	D	-2	0	3	5	3	5	0	2	D
8	Magnus sanctus Paulus	an	PM 163 *WA 330 *LA 423	c	-1	0	-3	0	-5	-3	-5	-3	G
	Magnus sanctus Paulus	alv	GR 419 LU 1346	D	2	0	2	0	-2	0	2	3	
	Magnus sanctus Paulus	alv	GS 178 189	D	3	2	5	3	2	3	0	7	
8	Maiolus caritate redundans	an	AM 875	F	2	4	2	4	2	4	2	0	G

	Majestas Domini aedificavit Domine Deus in simplicitate	ofv	OTT 159 *SYG 264 *GB 175^v	a	3	0	3	0	2	3	-4	-2	
1	Majorem caritatem nemo habet	an	AR [2] LU 1111 AM 622 WA 414 LA 511	D	-2	0	3	2	0	-2	3	5	D
2	Majorem caritatem nemo habet	of	GR 654 LU 1752	A	3	7	5	3	5	8	5	8	D
5	Majorem hac dilectionem	int	GR 553 LU 1559	F	4	5	2	0	2	4	2	4	F
	Maledictus eris super terram Ubi est Abel	rev	LA 112 WA 74										
8	Malos male perdet ... agricolis	an	AM 359 WA 95 (inc illeg)	G	2	4	5	4	2	0	2	0	G
3	Malos male perdet ... aliis	an	AR 385 LU 1088 WA 95 *LA 145	G	2	5	4	2	0	2	0	-3	E
	Mandatum novum do vobis Ubi est caritas	anv	SYG 131										
3	Mandatum novum do vobis	an	GR 200 OHS 446 LU 671 WA 214 *GS 96 SYG 130	G	2	5	2	5	4	2	0	2	E
1	Mandavit Dominus benedictionem	an	LR 338	F	4	2	4	2	-1	0	2	0	D
	Mandavit Dominus benedictionem Ecce quam bonum	grv	GB 201 *SYG 199 GS *n 214	D	7	3	5	7	5	2	3	0	
1	Manducaverunt et saturati sunt	co	GR 84 LU 515 SYG 64 GB 61 GS 29	D	2	-2	0	3	5	7	3	5	D
	Mane nobiscum Domine	sr	WA 138										
	Mane nobiscum Domine	alv	SYG 156	G	2	0	5	7	9	7	10	7	
	Mane nobiscum Domine	alv	GS 126	D	3	2	0	-2	2	3	0	7	
7	Mane nobiscum quoniam	an	AR 476 AM 491 *WA 138 *LA 218 234	G	4	5	7	9	7	9	10	9	G
4	Mane surgens Jacob	an	LA 553	E	-2	0	1	0	-4	-2	0	-2	E
4	Mane surgens Jacob	re	LR 240 LA 552	F	-1	0	2	4	2	-1	0	2	E
	Maneant in nobis	see	Maneant in vobis										
7	Maneant in vobis fides	an	GR 203 OHS 450 LU 674 *WA 214 SYG 131	G	2	4	5	4	2	0	2	4	G
	Manete in dilectione Ego sum vitis	rev	WA 305										
1	Manifestavit se Jesus	an	WA 135	D	2	3	5	7	5	3	2	0	D
8	Manifeste magnum est	an	AR 335	G	-2	-5	-3	-2	0	2	0	-2	G
8	Manum suam aperuit inopi	an	AR 577^{22}[103] LU 262^{10} 1236	G	-2	-5	-2	0	2	0	2	0	G
4	Manum suam aperuit inopi	an	AM 690 747	C	2	4	5	4	5	7	5	4	E
	Manum suam aperuit inopi	alv	GR 632 LU 1695	C	2	9	10	9	7	9	5	4	
	Manus quidem manus sunt Surge pater	rev	LA 137										
	Manus tuae Domine	see	Manus tuae fecerunt										

	Manus tuae fecerunt me Bonum mihi Domine	rev	LA 142 WA 93									
8	Marcellini atque Petri	hy	ST 17	C	7	5	7	9	11	9	7	9	G
7	Marcellinum atque Petrum	hy	ST 17	G	2	4	0	2	4	5	4	2	G
8	Maria autem conservabat	an	AR 329 LU 476 WA 47	G	4	2	5	4	0	2	-2	2	G
7	Maria decus hominum	hy	ST 398	G	2	4	5	4	2	0	5	7	G
6	Maria ergo unxit pedes	an	AM 977 *AR 793 *GS 96 SYG 132	F	2	0	2	4	5	2	0	2	F
4	Maria et flumina	an	AR 313 LU 464 AM 291 *WA 56 LA 74	F	-3	-1	0	2	0	-1	0	2	E
8	Maria Magdalene et altera	re	OHS 758 LA 209 WA 131	D	3	5	7	5	7	5	7	9	G
	Maria Magdalene et Maria Jacobi Et valde mane	rev	LA 211									
6	Maria Magdalene ut cognovit	re	WA 336	c	-3	-2	0	-2	-3	-5	0	2	c
8	Maria quae mortalium	hy	AR 4(sup 1)	E	3	5	3	5	8	7	8	10	G
7	Maria stabat ad monumentum	an	AR 450 OHS 804 AM 463 WA 135 *LA 220	G	4	5	7	9	5	2	5	4	G
7	Maria templum Domini	hy	ST 398	G	2	4	5	4	2	0	5	7	G
7	Maria ut audivit	re	WA 302	G	2	5	4	2	4	0	2	0	G
	Maria virgo assumpta est	sr	AR 823 LU 1605 AM 1015									
8	Maria virgo assumpta est	an	AR 820 LU 1606 AM 1014 WA 358 *LA 448	G	-2	-5	-3	-2	0	2	0	4	G
7	Maria virgo regia	hy	ST 399	G	2	4	5	4	2	0	5	7	G
1	Maria virgo semper laetare	an	PM 258	D	3	0	-2	3	5	7	8	7	D
7	Maria virgo semper laetare	an	WA 353 366	G	4	5	7	9	7	5	4	5	G
8	Mariae Magdalenae festum	an	WA 338	G	2	0	-2	0	5	4	2	5	G
	Martialis magnus precibus	alv	SYG 208	D	-2	0	2	3	5	7	5	3	
7	Martinae celebri plaudite nomini	hy	AR 614	G	4	5	7	9	7	5	7	0	G
8	Martine confessor Dei	hy	ST 401	G	-5	-2	0	2	0	-2	0	5	G
8	Martine confessor Dei	hy	ST 237	G	2	-2	0	2	0	2	0	5	G
2	Martine confessor Dei	hy	ST 434	D	2	0	-2	0	3	2	3	5	D
7	Martine misit nos Dominus	an	WA 399 *LA 483	G	4	5	7	5	2	5	4	0	G
6	Martine par apostolis	hy	ST 401	c	2	4	5	4	2	0	2	4	c
8	Martine par apostolis	hy	ST 462	G	2	5	4	2	0	2	0	-3	G
8	Martine par apostolis	hy	ST 99	G	2	5	4	2	0	2	4	5	G
	Martinum Maria suscepit Ecclesia virtute	rev	WA 401									

8	Martinus Abrahae sinu	an	AR 918 LU 1749 AM 1116 WA 398 *LA 487	G	-5	-2	0	2	0	2	0	2	G
	Martinus Abrahae sinu	alv	SYG 226	G	2	0	-2	2	5	4	2	0	
1	Martinus Abrahae sinu	re	PM 206 LA 485 WA 401	D	3	0	-2	3	5	3	5	7	D
7	Martinus Abrahae sinu	co	SYG 225	G	5	2	0	5	4	5	7	9	G
7	Martinus adhuc catechumenus	an	WA 398 *LA 480	G	4	5	7	5	2	5	4	0	G
2	Martinus ecce migrat	inv	WA 398	D	-2	0	3	0	3	5	3	2	D
	Martinus episcopus migravit / Martinus Abrahae	rev	PM 206 LA 485 WA 401										
	Martinus episcopus migravit / Martinus igitur obitum	ofv	SYG 225	D	-2	0	3	5	7	5	7	3	
8	Martinus episcopus migravit	an	WA 401	G	5	2	0	-2	0	2	0	4	G
	Martinus hic pauper	alv	SYG 227	F	4	2	-1	0	2	0	2	-3	
1	Martinus igitur obitum	of	SYG 225	D	-2	0	-2	0	3	0	3	2	D
1	Martinus signipotens	an	WA 405	D	-2	0	3	2	0	-2	0	3	D
	Martinus signipotens	alv	SYG 227	C	2	5	4	2	4	2	0	5	
4	Martyr Dei egregie	hy	ST 373	F	2	0	-3	-5	-3	-1	2	4	E
8	Martyr Dei egregie	hy	ST 425	G	2	4	5	4	5	4	2	4	G
4	Martyr Dei qui unicum	hy	ST 196	E	-4	-2	1	3	1	0	-2	0	E
2	Martyr Dei qui unicum	hy	ST 313	G	-2	-5	-2	2	0	-2	0	2	G
8	Martyr Dei qui unicum	hy	AM 251	G	-2	-3	-5	-2	2	0	-2	0	G
3	Martyr Dei qui unicum	hy	ST 101	E	-2	3	5	8	7	5	8	7	E
1	Martyr Dei qui unicum	hy	ST 196	D	2	-2	2	5	7	5	2	3	D
8	Martyr Dei qui unicum	hy	ST 101	G	2	0	-2	2	5	4	0	2	G
6	Martyr Dei qui unicum	hy	ST 61 100 AM 642	F	2	4	2	4	2	0	4	7	F
2	Martyr Dei qui unicum	hy	ST 243	C	2	4	5	2	0	5	7	9	D
6	Martyr Dei qui unicum	hy	ST 457	A	3	5	8	7	5	7	5	3	C
8	Martyr Dei qui unicum	hy	ST 404	G	5	2	0	5	7	5	4	2	G
3	Martyr Dei Venantius	hy	AR 711 LU 1469	E	1	3	1	0	-2	0	-2	-4	E
3	Martyr egregie Deo dilecte	hy	ST 388	c	-3	-5	-3	-5	-7	-8	-10	-8	E
3	Martyr fuisti studio	an	WA 313	E	3	-2	5	8	7	5	3	5	E
1	Martyres Christi ad praesidem	an	WA 378	D	-2	0	3	0	-2	0	3	2	D
tp	Martyres Domini Dominum	an	AR [42] LU 1154 AM 648 LA 520	D	-2	0	3	5	7	5	7	5	G
7	Martyres sancti per fidem	re	WA 422	G	2	0	2	0	2	5	7	5	G
8	Martyres sancti quanta passi	an	WA 423	G	-5	-2	0	2	0	2	0	-2	G
4	Martyris Christi colimus triumphum	hy	ST 298	F	-3	-5	-3	0	-1	-3	-1	0	E

8 Martyris Christi colimus triumphum	hy	ST 396	G	2	0	-3	-2	0	2	0	2	G
8 Martyris Christi colimus triumphum	hy	ST 432	G	2	0	-2	2	5	4	2	0	G
7 Martyris ecce dies Agathae	hy	ST 376	G	2	0	-2	2	4	5	4	2	G
7 Martyris ecce dies Agathae	hy	ST 88 427	G	2	0	-2	2	5	4	2	5	G
4 Martyris ecce dies Agathae	hy	ST 426	G	2	5	4	2	5	4	2	0	b
8 Martyrum chorus laudate Dominum	an	AR [42] LU 1154 *AM 648 LA 520	c	-1	0	-3	-5	-3	-5	-7	-5	G
8 Martyrum rector diadema splendor	hy	ST 150	G	-2	2	5	4	2	0	2	4	G
4 Mater Christi gloriosa	an	PM 279	C	2	4	5	4	5	4	2	4	E
1 Maternitas tua Dei genitrix	an	AM 1085	D	-2	3	5	3	7	5	2	3	D
4 Maternitas tua Dei genitrix	an	AR 882[6] LU 1687	D	2	3	5	3	0	2	3	2	E
4 Matthaee sancte	hy	ST 402	F	-3	-5	-3	0	-3	-5	0	2	E
4 Matthaee sancte	hy	ST 241	F	-1	-3	-5	-3	0	-3	-1	0	E
4 Matthia juste	hy	ST 403	F	-3	-5	-3	0	-3	-5	0	2	E
4 Matthia juste	hy	ST 241	F	-1	-3	-5	-3	0	-3	-1	0	E
8 Matris sub almae numine	hy	AR 640 LU 1388	G	-2	-3	-2	0	-2	0	2	5	G
8 Mauri laudes propheticis	an	LR 284	G	5	2	0	-2	2	5	4	0	G
3 Maurus a teneris annis	re	PM 124 LR 275	D	5	7	5	7	5	7	10	9	E
8 Maurus junior cum bonis	an	LR 274	G	5	2	0	2	0	2	0	2	G
7 Maxima pars fratrum	re	LR 285	a	5	2	5	3	5	7	3	2	G
8 Maximilla Christo amabilis	an	AR 580 LU 1308 AM 756 LA 504	G	5	2	0	-2	0	2	0	4	G
Me autem propter innocentiam Domine spes mea	grv	GR 518 LU 1494	c	2	0	2	0	-1	0	2	-1	
Me enim de die	see	Me etenim de die										
2 Me etenim de die	an	AR 361 AM 335 *LA 126 *WA 85	D	-5	-3	-2	0	2	0	2	0	D
2 Me exspectaverunt peccatores	int	GR [55] LU 1220 SYG 41 GB 44[v] GS 226	F	-3	0	2	0	2	0	-3	0	D
3 Me oportet minui	re	LA 18 *WA 11	G	5	2	5	2	0	2	4	5	E
7 Me suscepit dextera tua	an	AR 397 [178] LU 1802 *AM 1163 *WA 438 *LA 559	d	-3	0	2	3	0	-3	-2	-3	G
8 Mea doctrina non est mea	an	LA 164	G	-2	2	5	7	5	4	2	4	G
Mea nox obscurum Beatus Laurentius clamavit	rev	LA 438 WA 349										
Mecum enim est maxima	see also	Mecum est maxima										
Mecum enim est maxima merces Dum sacrum mysterium	rev	PM 197 WA 386										
7 Mecum enim est maxima merces	an	WA 386	G	7	9	7	5	9	10	12	10	G

7 Mecum enim habeo custodem	an	AM 786 *LU 1340 *AR 603 LA 338	d	-3	0	2	0	-2	0	2	0	G
5 Mecum enim habeo custodem	an	WA 255	c	-3	0	2	4	0	-2	0	-3	F
Mecum est maxima	see also	Mecum enim est maxima										
7 Mecum est maxima merces	re	WA 387	G	4	5	7	9	7	10	9	5	G
Mecum sunt divitiae et gloria Ego diligentes me	trv	GR 61**	G	2	4	5	4	5	7	5	0	
Media autem nocte	see also	Media nocte										
Media autem nocte clamor Haec est virgo prudens	rev	LA 545										
Media autem nocte clamor Prudentes virgines	rev	LR 222										
Media nocte clamor factus Haec est virgo sapiens	rev	LR 225 LA 544										
5 Media nocte clamor factus	re	LR 226	a	-4	0	3	5	3	2	3	5	F
Media nocte clamor factus Audivi vocem	rev	PM 236 *WA 394	a	-2	-4	-2	0	3	-2	-4	-2	
4 Media nocte clamor factus	an	LR 224 *WA 434 LA 546	a	-2	0	3	5	3	5	7	3	a
2 Media nocte dominica	an	WA 402	D	-2	-5	-2	0	2	0	2	3	D
4 Media vita in morte sumus	re	AR 152* PM 45 VP 106	D	2	3	5	3	2	0	7	5	E
4 Mediae noctis tempore	hy	ST 448	C	5	4	5	2	4	5	7	5	E
Medicinam carnalem corpori Qui me dignatus	rev	LA 361 WA 274										
1 Medicinam carnalem corpori	an	AR 625 LU 1371 *AM 807 *WA 276 LA 363	D	2	3	5	7	5	7	5	3	D
1 Medicinam carnalem corpori	re	WA 275	D	3	0	-2	3	5	7	5	3	D
8 Medicinam carnalem corpori	re	LA 362	D	3	5	7	5	7	5	7	5	G
2 Meditabor in mandatis tuis	of	GR 114 301 OTT 109 LU 548 894 SYG 78 *GB 70 *GS 40 48 139 168	E	3	5	8	3	7	5	3	5	a
1 Meditatio cordis mei	int	GR 148 SYG 107 GB 95 GS 69	a	-4	-2	0	-2	3	2	0	3	D
4 Meditatio cordis mei	an	LR 334	F	-3	-1	0	2	-1	0	-3	0	E
Mel et lac ex ejus ore Amo Christum	rev	LA 333 WA 254										
1 Mel et lac ex ejus ore	an	LA 332	F	2	4	0	2	0	2	0	-1	D
6 Mel et lac ex ejus ore	re	LA 337 WA 254	c	2	4	2	4	2	0	2	-3	c
7 Mel et lac ex ejus ore	an	WA 254	G	4	5	7	9	7	5	7	9	G
Melior est enim fructus Ego diligentes me	trv	GR 61**	G	2	4	5	4	5	4	0	2	

	Chant		Sources										
	Melius illi erat si natus Judas mercator	rev	OHS 389 LU 644										
4	Mella cor obdulcantia	hy	AM 833	F	-1	-3	-1	2	4	0	-1	2	E
	Memento Domine animae Rogamus te Domine	rev	LA 557	c	-1	-5	-3	-1	-3	-1	0	-3	
	Memento Domine David Mihi autem absit	intv	GR 426 LU 1354										
	Memento Domine David Sacerdotes ejus	intv	GB 212 SYG 209 GS 224										
	Memento Domine David Sacerdotes Sion	intv	GR 88** GS 224										
	Memento Domine David Sacerdotes tui	intv	GR [35] LU 1186 1495 GS 220 GB 28 SYG 27										
	Memento Domine David Statuit ei	intv	GR [3] [32] LU 1182										
	Memento Domine David Suscitabo mihi	intv	GR [117]										
	Memento Domine David	alv	SYG 181	b	3	0	1	-2	-4	-2	0	-2	
	Memento Domine et ostende Recordare mei Domine	ofv	SYG 259	D	2	0	-2	0	2	3	2	3	
	Memento Domine filiorum Edom Super flumina	ofv	OTT 119 *GB 102^V *SYG 115	d	-2	0	3	2	3	2	0	-2	
2	Memento mei Deus in bono	re	WA 179	D	-2	0	-2	-5	-2	-3	-2	0	D
	Memento mei Deus meus Memento mei Deus	rev	WA 179										
2	Memento mei Deus quia ventus	re	AR [164] LU 1791 LA 284 WA 172	D	-2	0	-2	-5	-2	-3	-2	0	D
8	Memento mei Domine Deus	an	AR 439 OHS 515 LU 718 AM 442 443 WA 124 LA 201	G	2	-2	0	2	5	4	5	2	G
7	Memento mei dum bene	re	LA 149 *WA 96	G	2	7	9	7	9	5	4	5	G
	Memento nostri Domine Non discedimus	rev	LA 19										
	Memento nostri Domine Patres nostri in Aegypto	ofv	GB 75^V	D	2	3	5	7	5	7	5	7	
	Memento nostri Domine Confitemini Domine	trv	GR 113 LU 547 GB 75 SYG 86	F	2	4	2	4	2	4	5	2	
1	Memento nostri Domine	int	GB 11 *GS 11	D	3	0	2	3	5	3	5	10	D
2	Memento rerum conditor	hy	AR [133]	a	-2	-5	-7	-2	0	3	2	0	a
4	Memento verbi tui serva·tuo	co	GR 379 LU 1065 SYG 116 GB 103^V GS 76 165	F	2	4	2	4	2	4	0	2	E
	Mementote mirabilium ejus Impetum inimicorum	rev	LA 296 WA 181										
5	Mementote mirabilium ejus	gr	GR 85**	F	2	4	0	2	-3	0	-1	2	F

7	Memor Christus Dominus	an	LR 126	G	5	4	5	7	5	7	9	7	G
	Memor esto congregationis ... adquisisti O Pastor apostolice	rev	WA 290	a	-2	0	-2	-4	-2	-4	-5	-9	
5	Memor esto congregationis ... possedisti	an	AR 156 LU 279[N]	c	-3	-1	0	-1	0	2	0	2	F
	Memor esto fili Omni tempore benedic	rev	WA 176										
7	Memor esto fili	re	LA 289 *WA 176	a	-2	0	3	5	3	5	8	5	G
8	Memor esto fili	an	WA 175	D	3	2	3	5	7	5	7	9	G
4	Memor fui judiciorum	gr	GR 564 LU 1580	C	2	5	4	5	4	5	2	5	E
1	Memor humanae conditionis	an	SYG 69	D	7	9	7	5	7	10	9	10	D
	Memor multitudinis misericordiae Patres nostri in Aegypto	ofv	GB 75[V]	D	3	5	2	3	2	5	3	5	
4	Memor sit Dominus sacrificii	an	LR 121 LU 928	F	-1	-3	0	2	4	2	0	-1	E
4	Memor sit Dominus sacrificii	gr	SYG 232	F	2	-3	-5	-3	0	2	0	2	E
4	Memor sit Dominus omni	of	SYG 233	D	3	2	5	3	5	2	3	5	E
4	Memorare o piissima virgo Maria		AR 124*	F	-1	-3	-1	2	4	2	4	7	E
	Memores erunt nominis tui Exsultabit cor meum	grv	GR 587[1] LU 1612[1]	a	3	5	7	5	3	2	3	0	
	Memoria memor ero Accepit Jesus	rev	LR 128 LU 932	F	2	0	2	4	5	4	2	0	
	Memoriam abundantiae suavitatis Magnificentiam	trv	GR 99**	F	2	4	2	0	2	0	-3	-1	
	Memoriam fecit mirabilium	sr	AR 538[12] LU 976										
	Mens mea solidata Agatha laetissime	rev	LA 357										
7	Mens mea solidata	an	WA 273 *LA 360	d	-3	0	2	3	0	-5	-2	-3	G
8	Mense septimo festa	co	GR 372 LU 1055 *SYG 253 *GB 259 *GS 173	c	-3	0	-3	-1	0	-1	-3	-5	G
2	Mensuram bonam	an	WA 187	D	-2	0	2	3	5	3	0	-2	D
4	Mentem sanctam spontaneum	an	WA 275 *LA 361	F	-1	0	-1	0	2	0	-1	-3	E
3	Mercenarius est cujus non sunt	an	AR 470 AM 484 *LA 235	G	5	2	0	4	5	7	9	7	E
8	Merito haec patimur	re	LA 151 *WA 97	F	2	4	2	4	6	4	2	4	G
	Merito haec patimur Dixit Ruben fratribus	rev	LA 150 *WA 97	G	5	4	0	4	5	7	5	7	
5	Merito sanctitatis et gradu	re	WA 294	a	-2	-4	0	3	5	3	5	7	F
7	Meruit esse hostia	re	WA 350	G	2	0	2	5	7	5	4	5	G
2	Meruit esse hostia	re	LA 439	C	2	4	2	5	4	5	2	4	D
4	Metuebat Herodes Joannem	re	LA 451 *WA 362	F	-1	-3	0	-1	0	2	4	2	E
8	Meum est consilium et aequitas	tr	GR 26**	G	2	4	2	0	2	0	-2	0	G

2	Meus cibus est	an	WA 100	F	-1	0	-1	-3	-1	-5	-3	-5	D
2	Michael archangele veni	an	WA 380 *LA 465	D	5	3	2	-2	0	3	2	0	D
8	Michael archangelus venit	re	LA 470	F	2	4	2	4	2	4	6	2	G
7	Michael et angeli ejus	re	PM 191	G	2	0	2	-2	2	5	4	5	G
8	Michael Gabriel cherubim et seraphim	an	PM 154 *WA 381 *LA 468	F	2	4	0	2	4	7	6	4	G
7	Michael praepositus paradisi	an	WA 380 *LA 465	G	7	4	5	7	2	4	0	5	G
5	Mihi absit gloriari	int	GR 65**	c	-3	0	-3	-1	0	-5	-3	-5	F
	Mihi autem absit gloriari Qui gloriatur	trv	GR 546	G	-5	0	2	2	5	4	5		
4	Mihi autem absit gloriari	gr	GR 481	C	2	5	4	5	4	5	2	5	E
2	Mihi autem absit gloriari	int	GR 426 602 LU 1354 1643	C	2	5	7	5	7	5	7	2	D
7	Mihi autem adhaerere	int	GR(34)	c	2	-3	0	4	2	0	2	5	G
3	Mihi autem adhaerere	of	GR 498 LU 1467	G	2	5	4	5	4	5	7	5	E
4	Mihi autem adhaerere	re	WA 68	D	3	2	0	2	3	5	3	2	E
3	Mihi autem nimis honorati	of	GR 394 OTT 128 LU 1306 SYG 201 GB 203 GS z 203	E	1	3	5	6	3	5	1	0	E
2	Mihi autem nimis honorati	int	GR 392 LU 1304 SYG 54 GB 235 GS w	C	2	5	7	5	7	5	7	2	D
3	Mihi osculum non dedisti	an	WA 338	G	2	5	4	2	4	2	0	2	E
	Mihi vivere Christus Qui gloriatur	trv	GR 546	c	2	0	-5	0	2	4	-1	0	
1	Mihi vivere Christus	an	WA 330 *LA 422	F	2	4	0	2	4	2	4	0	D
7	Mihi vivere Christus	re	LA 425 ×WA 331	G	2	4	5	4	2	4	0	2	G
3	Miles Christi gloriose	re	WA 391	E	-2	3	5	7	5	3	5	8	E
	Militia est vita Quare detraxistis	rev	WA 172										
	Millia millium ministrabant Angelis suis	rev	PM 193										
	Millia millium ministrabant Factum est silentium	rev	LA 465 WA 380										
4	Minor sum cunctis	re	WA 92	F	2	5	4	2	5	7	4	5	a
	Minuisti eum Domine paulo minus	alv	GR 451	G	5	4	2	4	0	2	0	-2	
3	Minuisti eum paulo minus	int	GR 517 LU 1493	E	1	-2	3	8	5	3	5	7	E
2	Mira nocturnis modulante lingua	hy	LR 455	A	5	3	5	8	7	5	7	8	D
	Mira res hanc speculationem Intempesta noctis hora	ofv	GB 55	C	4	2	4	-1	0	2	0	-1	
7	Mirabantur omnes de his	co	GR 73 LU 491 SYG 43 *GS 24	G	2	0	2	4	5	4	2	5	G
1	Mirabantur omnes de his	co	GB 40	D	2	3	2	0	-2	3	5	7	D

	Mirabantur omnes de his	alv	SYC 42	C	2	4	5	7	5	4	2	5	
8	Mirabantur omnes in verbis	an	LR 310	G	2	0	4	2	5	4	2	0	G
1	Mirabantur omnes qui audiebant	an	LA 343	D	-2	3	5	3	5	7	5	7	D
7	Mirabantur omnes qui audiebant	co	SYG 45	G	2	-2	2	0	2	0	2	5	G
8	Mirabile mysterium declaratur	an	AR 296 *AM 274 717 *WA 51 *LA 65	G	-2	-3	-5	-2	-5	-3	-2	0	G
4	Mirabilem Deum in sanctis	inv	WA 429	C	2	5	4	5	4	2	5	4	E
6	Mirabilia opera tua	an	AR 180 LU 301	F	2	4	2	0	-1	0	2	-3	F
8	Mirabilis Deus in sanctis	of	GR [24] OTT 141 LU 1165 SYG 175 GB 171 *GS 217	D	2	3	5	7	5	7	5	7	G
	Mirabilis Dominus noster	alv	GR 414 GS 216 SYG 176 *GB 268v	a	-2	-4	-5	-9	-5	-2	-4	-5	
	Mirabilis in excelsis Dominus Deus enim firmavit	ofv	OTT 16 GB 16 SYG 16	G	2	-2	0	2	0	2	0	2	
8	Miraculum laudabile	hy	ST 7	D	3	5	3	7	5	0	3	5	G
7	Mirificavit Dominus sanctos	an	LR 381 *WA 395 *LA 474	G	4	7	5	2	5	4	2	5	G
4	Miris modis repente liber	hy	AR 797 LU 1578	F	-1	-3	-5	-3	0	-1	0	2	E
7	Miroque modo inermi	an	WA 386	G	4	5	7	5	9	7	4	7	G
5	Mirum dictu hinc	an	WA 292	a	-2	0	-2	0	-2	-4	0	3	F
4	Miseratio hominis circa proximum	int	GR 631 LU 1693	D	3	2	3	2	3	5	7	5	E
2	Miserator Dominus escam	an	AR 525 LU 956 AM 544	A	3	5	3	5	7	8	5	3	D
7	Misereor super turbam	an	AR 558 LU 1009 *AM 596 *WA 188 *LA 312	b	3	0	3	5	3	5	3	1	G
1	Miserere Domine plebi tuae	an	WA 229	C	2	9	11	9	12	9	11	12	D
7	Miserere Domine plebi tuae	an	GB 161	G	5	4	5	7	5	4	2	5	G
2	Miserere Domine populo tuo	re	WA 179	E	3	5	8	7	8	7	5	7	a
1	Miserere et parce clementissime		AR 159*	G	2	0	5	4	5	4	2	0	D
6	Miserere mei Deus	an	AM 38 LA 89 *WA 64	F	2	4	0	2	4	2	0	[0]	F
1	Miserere mei Deus et a delicto	an	AR 341 AM 312 *WA 74 *LA 113	a	-5	-2	2	0	3	2	3	0	D
	Miserere mei Deus miserere	sr	LA 92 WA 65										
	Miserere mei Deus miserere Misereris omnium	intv	GR 87 LU 525 GS 30 GB 62 SYG 65										
	Miserere mei Deus miserere Ne perdideris	rev	WA 62										
1	Miserere mei Deus miserere	gr	GR 88 LU 526 SYG 65 GB 62 *GS 31	D	-2	2	0	3	0	-2	0	3	D
	Miserere mei Deus miserere	alv	SYG 234	G	2	0	-2	2	5	0	2	0	

	Incipit	Type	Sources										
	Miserere mei Deus quoniam conculcavit In Deo laudabo	intv	GR 127 GS 56 GB 83^V SYG 94										
	Miserere mei Deus secundum Asperges me	anv	GR 1* 4* LU 11 13 PM 9										
	Miserere mei Deus secundum In diebus illis	anv	GS 96										
8	Miserere mei Deus secundum	an	AR 75	G	-2	-3	-5	-3	-2	0	2	0	G
	Miserere mei Deus secundum		AR 154*	F	-1	-3	-1	0	-3	-5	-3	-1	D
2	Miserere mei Domine quoniam	tr	GR [145]	D	-2	0	-2	-5	-2	0	-2	0	D
8	Miserere mei fili David	an	AR 358 LU 518 AM 332 *WA 83 *LA 125	G	2	0	2	5	4	0	2	0	G
	Miserere mei secundum eloquium Meditabor in mandatis	ofv	OTT 109 GB 70 SYG 78	C	2	5	7	5	7	5	4	5	
8	Miserere mihi Domine et exaudi	an	AR 58 OHS 168 LU 266	G	2	0	-2	0	2	0	-2	0	G
8	Miserere mihi Domine quoniam ad te	int	GR 363 LU 1044 SYG 249 GB 256 *GS 159	G	5	2	0	2	-2	0	2	5	G
	Miserere mihi Domine quoniam conculcavit In Deo laudabo	intv	GB 83^V										
3	Miserere mihi Domine quoniam conculcavit	int	GR 156 SYG 111 GB 99 GS 73	E	1	-2	3	5	3	7	5	7	E
	Miserere mihi Domine quoniam conculcavit Deus vitam meam	grv	GR 128 *GS 56 GB 83^V *SYG 94	G	5	7	5	4	5	7	9	7	
7	Miserere mihi Domine quoniam infirmus	gr	GR 133 *SYG 96 *GB 85^V GS 58	G	-5	0	-2	0	-3	-2	0	-5	G
	Miserere mihi Domine quoniam infirmus Domine convertere	ofv	OTT 84 GB 99^V SYG 111	C	2	5	7	5	4	7	9	5	
5	Miserere mihi Domine quoniam tribulor	int	GR 163 SYG 116 *GB 103^V *GS 76	a	3	0	-2	0	-4	-2	0	3	F
8	Miserere mihi Domine secundum magnam	of	GR 118 OTT 35 SYG 88 GB 77^V *GS 50	G	2	4	5	4	5	2	0	2	G
	Miserere miserere miserere O vera ... unitas	anv	WA 162	F	-1	-3	-1	2	4	2	0	-1	
	Miserere miserere miserere O beata benedicta	anv	WA 161	C	2	4	2	5	4	5	7	5	
	Miserere nobis Domine Ad te levavi	trv	GR 124 LU 554 *GS 55 *GB 82^V *SYG 93	G	2	4	5	4	2	5	4	2	
8	Miserere nostri Domine	an	LA 96	F	2	4	2	0	4	6	7	4	G
1	Misereris omnium, Domine	int	GR 87 LU 525 *SYG 65 GB 62 GS 30	F	2	4	2	4	2	0	2	4	D
4	Misericordia Domini plena	int	GR 263 LU 816 *SYG 164 *GB 146 *GS 127	D	3	2	3	2	3	2	3	5	E

#	Incipit	Genre	Source	Mode									Final
	Misericordia et veritas obviaverunt Deus tu convertens	ofv	OTT 6 *SYG 4 *GB 3	c	-1	0	2	4	0	-1	-3	0	
7	Misericordia et veritas obviaverunt	an	LR 265	G	4	5	7	5	4	5	7	9	G
1	Misericordia et veritas praecedent	an	AR 179 LU 279^R	a	-2	-4	-2	0	-2	-4	-5	-7	D
	Misericordia et veritas praeibunt Tui sunt caeli	ofv	OTT 18 *GB 19^V	F	4	2	0	-1	0	-5	-1	2	
	Misericordia mea	see Misericordiam meam											
1	Misericordia tua Domine ante oculos	an	AR 133 LU 279^J	D	-2	0	3	2	3	5	3	2	D
1	Misericordia tua Domine magna	re	LA 100 *WA 69	D	-2	3	5	3	7	3	5	7	D
3	Misericordiam et justitiam	re	LA 103	G	2	5	4	2	0	4	5	2	E
	Misericordiam meam non dispergam Veritas mea	ofv	OTT 148 GB 41^V *SYG 38	E	-4	-2	5	6	5	3	8	5	
	Misericordias Domini in aeternum	sr	WA 164										
	Misericordias Domini in aeternum Semel juravi	cov	SYG 209										
	Misericordias Domini in aeternum Gaudens gaudebo	intv	GR 77**										
	Misericordias Domini in aeternum Humiliavit semetipsum	intv	GR [106]										
	Misericordias Domini in aeternum Redemisti nos	intv	GR 536 LU 1532										
	Misericordias Domini in aeternum Statuit ei	intv	GS 220										
	Misericordias Domini in aeternum	alv	SYG 245	C	2	4	0	2	4	7	5	4	
	Misericordias tuas Domine in aeternum	sr	LA 100										
	Misericordias tuas Domine in aeternum Statuit ei Dominus	intv	GB 41										
	Misericordias tuas Domine in aeternum Confitebuntur caeli	grv	GR 512	F	-3	0	-1	0	2	4	2	0	
	Misericordias tuas Domine in aeternum Confitebuntur caeli	ofv	OTT 138 *GB 153 *SYG 170	F	2	6	9	6	7	4	2	4	
	Misericordias tuas Domine in aeternum Confitebuntur caeli	grv	SYG 190	G	5	7	5	4	5	7	9	7	
2	Misericors et miserator Dominus escam	an	AR 538^1 LU 965 AM 561	C	2	4	5	2	0	2	9	7	D
2	Misericors et miserator Dominus longanimis	tr	GR [113] LU 972	D	-2	0	-2	-5	-2	0	-2	0	D
	Misericors et miserator et juste Rogamus te Domine	rev	VP 241	a	-2	-4	-2	1	0	1	3	1	
7	Misertus Dominus destitutae	re	WA 313	G	7	5	7	5	2	5	9	7	G
	Misertus enim est Deus Igitur Joseph	rev	WA 95	F	-1	0	-1	-3	2	0	-1	-3	
8	Misi digitum meum in fixuras	an	AR 466 AM 480	F	2	4	7	6	7	4	2	4	G
	Misit de caelo Miserere mei Deus	grv	GR 88 LU 526 *GS 31 GB 62 SYG 65	D	7	5	7	3	7	8	7	5	

	Incipit		Sources											
8	Misit denique aquam	an	SYG 133	F	2	4	2	4	2	4	2	0	G
	Misit Deus misericordiam Dominus qui eripuit	rev	LA 268 WA 165										
	Misit Deus misericordiam Misit Dominus angelum ... conclusit	rev	LA 303 WA 184										
5	Misit Dominus angelum ... conclusit	re	LA 303 *WA 184	F	4	7	4	7	9	7	9	7	F
7	Misit Dominus angelum ... de manu	an	AR 751 800 PM 173 LU 1515 1577 AM 935 990 WA 328 LA 416	b	1	3	5	3	5	1	-2	1	G
7	Misit Dominus angelum ... de medio	an	AR 814 LU 1597 AM 1006 WA 350 LA 336 441	b	1	3	5	3	5	1	-2	1	G
7	Misit Dominus manum suam	an	LR 347 WA 320 LA 400	d	-3	0	2	0	2	0	-2	-5	G
	Misit Dominus manum suam Priusquam te formarem	grv	GR 524 LU 1500 *GS 1 *GB 198^v *SYG 196	a	2	-1	0	-3	-5	-3	-1	0	
	Misit Dominus manum suam In medio ecclesiae	rev	PM 227	a	3	0	-2	0	1	-2	-4	-2	
5	Misit Dominus verbum suum	gr	GR 68 LU 485v SYG 35 GB 37^v GS 21	F	2	4	0	2	0	-1	-3	2	F
8	Misit Herodes rex manus	re	PM 183 *LA 450 *WA 362	D	5	3	5	7	5	7	5	7	G
	Misit in eos Dominus Operarii	rev	LR 282	C	2	5	4	5	7	4	2	5	
8	Misit me vivens pater	re	AR 116* LR 131 LU 938	D	5	3	5	7	5	7	9	7	G
	Misit rex incredulus Misso Herodes	rev	LA 452										
2	Misit rex incredulus	re	LA 453	C	2	4	2	5	4	5	2	4	D
8	Misit rex incredulus	an	AR 830 LU 1621 *AM 1029 WA 363	G	5	2	0	-2	0	2	0	4	G
7	Misit rex spiculatorem	of	OTT 176	F	2	4	7	4	2	0	2	4	G
	Misso Herodes spiculatore Herodes enim tenuit	rev	WA 362										
	Misso Herodes spiculatore Joannes baptista	rev	LA 451 WA 362										
	Misso Herodes spiculatore Misit rex incredulus	rev	LA 453										
1	Misso Herodes spiculatore	an	AR 828 LU 1618 *AM 1025 *WA 363 *LA 454	F	-5	-3	4	2	0	2	4	0	D
4	Misso Herodes spiculatore	re	WA 363	F	-3	0	-1	0	2	0	-1	0	E
	Misso Herodes spiculatore	alv	GS 196	a	-2	-5	-4	-2	-4	-2	-7	-9	
8	Misso Herodes spiculatore	re	LA 452	D	5	3	5	7	5	7	5	7	G

	Incipit		Sources										
	Missus est angelus Domini	alv	GR 637	E	1	0	-2	3	5	3	1	3	
2	Missus est angelus Gabriel ... ad virginem	an	AR 648 LU 1400 AM 837	D	-5	-2	0	-2	0	3	2	0	D
8	Missus est angelus Gabriel ... in civitatem	an	PM 246	G	2	0	-2	0	2	5	4	2	G
8	Missus est angelus Gabriel ... in civitatem	an	AM 886	F	2	0	4	7	9	7	4	2	G
1	Missus est angelus Gabriel ... in civitatem	an	AR 688	C	2	5	2	4	2	0	2		D
8	Missus est angelus Raphael	an	AR 890 LU 1701	F	2	0	2	4	5	4	2	0	G
8	Missus est Gabriel a Deo	an	WA 200	G	2	0	-2	0	-2	2	5	4	G
3	Missus est Gabriel angelus	int	SYG 57	E	1	-2	0	1	3	5	3	8	E
7	Missus est Gabriel angelus	re	PM 23 *LA 3 377	G	2	0	2	0	2	5	7	5	G
8	Missus est Gabriel angelus	an	AR 247 668 [139] LU 1416 AM 222 861 *WA 18 *LA 24 376	F	2	0	2	4	5	4	2	0	G
8	Missus sum ad oves	an	WA 94 *LA 143	c	-1	-5	-1	0	-3	-5	-3	-5	G
8	Mittat tibi auxilium / Memor sit Dominus	grv	SYG 232	c	2	0	-3	0	-3	-7	-3	-5	
	Mittat tibi auxilium / Memor sit Dominus	ofv	SYG 232	D	2	3	5	10	7	5	3	2	
	Mittat tibi Dominus	alv	SYG 232	c	-1	2	0	-1	0	2	0	-3	
	Mittat vobis Dominus	alv	GR [123] LU 1289	c	-1	2	0	-1	0	2	0	-3	
	Mitte illam a sede / Da mihi Domine	rev	LA 277 WA 169										
6	Mitte manum tuam	co	GR 263 407 LU 811 1328 SYG 164 GB 146 GS h 125	F	2	0	2	4	2	0	2	4	F
8	Mitte manum tuam	an	AR 465 AM 478 WA 137 LA 230 233	F	2	4	2	4	2	0	4	7	G
2	Mittens Dominus et alios	an	WA 371	C	2	4	2	0	2	4	2	0	D
1	Mittens haec mulier	an	WA 110 *LA 185	D	7	9	7	5	7	5	3	2	D
7	Mittite in dexteram navigii	an	AR 450 OHS 795 AM 462 *WA 135 LA 219	d	-3	0	2	0	2	0	-2	-5	G
	Mixto rore		see Mixtum rorem										
	Mixtum rorem balsami / Felix Maria	rev	PM 169 *WA 337	a	-2	-4	-2	-7	-5	-9	-5	-7	
8	Modicum et non videbitis me alleluia	co	GR 268 LU 24 *SYG 167 GB 149^v GS 129	F	2	4	2	0	2	4	2	4	G
6	Modicum et non videbitis me dicit	an	AR 473 LU 820 AM 487 WA 143 LA *231 236	F	-1	0	-3	-1	-5	-3	0	2	F
	Modicum et non videbitis me dicit	alv	SYG 166 *GB 273^v *GS 128	G	-2	-3	-2	0	2	0	2	4	

6	Modo veniet dominator	re	LA 20 WA 19	e	-4	-2	-4	-5	-4	-2	0	-2	c
	Mole peccatorum gravati 　　O mulier sancta	rev	WA 337	a	3	2	0	3	5	3	0	-2	
1	Monstra te esse matrem	hy	LU 1863	D	7	8	7	5	7	5	7	5	D
1	Montes et colles cantabunt	an	AR 225 LU 332 AM 196 *WA 12 LA 11	D	-2	3	5	3	7	5	7	5	D
5	Montes et omnes colles	an	AR 232 LU 338 AM 205 *WA 16 *LA 16	a	-4	0	3	2	0	3	5	3	F
8	Montes Gelboë nec ros	re	LA 269 *WA 165	G	-2	0	-2	-5	-3	-2	-3	-5	G
1	Montes Gelboë nec ros	an	AR 540 LU 986 *AM 576 WA 164 *LA 274	D	-2	0	3	0	-2	3	0	3	D
	Montes in circuitu ejus 　　Qui confidunt	trv	GR 139 (40) LU 561 *GS 63 GB 90 *SYG 101	D	5	10	7	5	0	5	7	10	
1	Montes Israel ramos vestros	re	LA 5 *WA 23	C	2	5	7	9	7	4	5	2	D
7	Moram faciente sponso	re	PM 139 LR 297	G	5	4	5	7	5	4	7	5	G
	Mortem enim quam salvator 　　Patefactae sunt	rev	LA 46										
	Mortem enim quam salvator 　　Lapides torrentes	rev	WA 36	d	-2	-5	-2	0	-2	0	2	3	
	Mortuus est propter delicta 　　Expurgate vetus	rev	OHS 814 LR 93 LA 212										
	Mortuus est semel 　　Christus resurgens	rev	OHS 822										
1	Mortuus sum et vita mea	an	AR 848 LU 1644	C	2	5	2	0	2	0	5	7	D
	Mox ad primam 　　Deprecatus enim	rev	WA 345										
	Mox illis clamantibus 　　Quadam die tempestate	rev	WA 240	c	-1	2	-1	0	-3	-5	0	-1	
6	Mox pater suos	an	WA 295	E	1	-2	-4	1	3	1	3	1	F
3	Mox ut vocem Domini	re	LA 498 WA 233	F	-3	-1	0	2	4	2	4	0	E
	Moyses et Aaron 　　Decantabat populus	rev	LA 226										
8	Moyses famulus Domini	re	LA 158 WA 101	D	3	5	7	10	9	10	7	3	G
1	Mulier amicta sole	an	AR 630 LU 1380	D	-2	0	3	0	3	7	5	7	D
7	Mulier cum parit tristitiam	an	LA 236	G	4	5	7	9	7	5	9	10	G
	Mulier ecce filius 　　Stabant juxta crucem	intv	GR 595 LU 1633										
	Mulier ecce filius 　　Valde honorandus	rev	LA 49										
8	Mulier quae erat ... attulit	an	AR 793 LU 1568 AM 978 *SYG 132	F	2	4	2	0	4	2	0	4	G
3	Mulier quae erat ... stans	an	AM 585	G	2	4	5	2	0	2	0	2	E

1 Mulier quae erat ... stans	an	AR 548	D	7	10	7	5	7	5	3	5	D
1 Mulier quid ploras	an	LA 221	F	2	4	2	4	0	2	0	-1	D
1 Mulieres sedentes ad monumentum	an	AR 441 OHS 410 625 LU 776^B AM 449 WA 127 LA 206	C	2	9	10	9	7	9	10	9	D
Multa bona opera operatus Quid me quaeritis	rev	LR 413										
4 Multa bona opera operatus	an	AR 418 LU 1099 AM 395 WA 109 *LA 174	G	2	5	7	9	7	5	7	9	a
Multa fecisti tu Domine Exspectans exspectavi	ofv	OTT 104 GB 92 SYG 104	d	-2	0	-2	-3	-5	-7	-5	-2	
3 Multa quidem et alia	an	LA 230 234	G	2	0	2	4	5	4	2	4	E
2 Multa sunt Domine peccata	an	GB 156^V *WA 229	D	-2	0	2	3	2	0	-2	0	D
3 Multa turba Judaeorum	an	SYG 120	E	3	0	-2	3	5	3	7	10	E
2 Multae tribulationes justorum	int	GR 515 (20) LU 1507 SYG 199 GB 201 GS m 212	a	-2	0	-2	-5	-2	0	3	5	a
Multae tribulationes justorum	alv	SYG 200	F	2	4	7	4	6	7	9	7	
Multas denique martyrum Sebastianus Dei cultor	rev	LA 324										
1 Multi ab oriente	an	WA 71	D	-2	0	3	2	0	2	0	-2	D
8 Multi enim sunt vocati	an	WA 76 *LA 116	F	4	2	4	2	4	2	4	2	G
Multifarie olim Deus loquens	alv	GR 49 LU 441 GS H SYG 19 GB 31^V	G	2	0	-2	2	5	0	2	0	
Multiplicabitur ejus imperium Nascetur nobis	rev	LA 21 382 WA 24										
1 Multiplicabitur ejus imperium	an	AR 244	D	-2	0	2	3	5	3	2	0	D
7 Multiplicasti Deus misericordiam	an	AR 150	G	4	5	7	9	7	5	4	0	G
8 Multiplicati sunt qui tribulant	re	LR 415 LA 166 WA 105	D	3	5	7	5	7	3	0	3	G
4 Multitudo angelorum	an	WA 398	E	-2	1	0	1	3	1	0	-2	E
Multitudo Christianorum Febus et Cornelius	rev	WA 409										
2 Multitudo languentium et qui ... ad eum	co	GR 416 LU 1337 *SYG 41 *GB 44^V *GS 218	D	-2	0	2	3	2	0	2	3	C
2 Multitudo languentium et qui ... ad Jesum	co	GR 69**	D	-2	0	2	3	2	0	2	3	D
8 Multitudo languentium veniebant	an	LA 328	G	5	2	0	-2	0	2	0	-2	G
8 Multos hic sanavit	an	WA 293	G	-2	-3	-2	0	2	0	2	0	G
Multum enim valet Orante beatissimo	rev	WA 289										
Mundus autem gaudebit Tristitia vestra	rev	LR 165 LA 386 WA 305										

1 Muneribus datis	an	WA 240	D	3	0	-2	3	5	7	9	7	D
Munimine regio Iste sanctus	rev	LA 522 WA 416										
8 Muro tuo inexpugnabili	re	LA 303 *WA 184	F	2	4	2	4	2	4	6	4	G
1 Muro tuo inexpugnabili	an	AM 591 *AR 553 *LU 996 LA 308 *WA 183 317	C	2	9	11	9	7	9	11	9	D
Myrrha et gutta et casia Diffusa est	rev	LR 254										
2 Mysterium ecclesiae	hy	ST 7	E	-2	0	-2	-4	-2	0	1	3	D
7 Mysterium ecclesiae	hy	ST 40	G	7	5	7	9	5	10	9	7	G
7 Mysterium mirabile	hy	ST 35	G	2	0	-2	0	2	0	5	7	G
2 Mysteriorum signifer	hy	ST 13	D	-2	-5	-7	-2	0	2	3	2	D
2 Mysterium signifer	hy	ST 42	a	-2	-5	-7	-2	0	3	2	0	a

1 N.praeesse dignus	re	PM 231	D	3	0	-2	3	5	7	5	2	D
Nam et ego apostolus Quis es tu	rev	LA 359 WA 273										
Nam sponsum quem quasi leonem Domine Jesu ... pastor	rev	LA 492 WA 407										
Nam ubi pauperum O acceptabilem	rev	WA 285	a	-2	0	-2	-4	-5	-2	0	3	
Nam virtus in infirmitate Ne magnitudo	anv	WA 331 LA 425										
Nam virtus in infirmitate Ne magnitudo	rev	LA 428										
2 Nardi Maria pistici	hy	ST 443	F	4	0	4	2	5	4	2	0	G
2 Narrabo nomen tuum	re	LA 238 *WA 143	A	3	5	7	5	7	5	7	5	D
2 Narrabo omnia mirabilia	co	GR 118 SYG 88 *GB 77^{v} GS 50 142	A	3	7	5	7	3	2	0	3	D
2 Narraverunt mihi iniqui	int	GR 473 LU 1427	F	-1	-3	0	2	0	2	0	-3	D
8 Nascetur nobis parvulus	re	LA 21 382 *WA 24	G	-2	0	-7	-5	-2	0	-2	0	G
Nativitas est hodie Nativitas gloriosae	rev	LA 459 *WA 365	a	7	5	7	5	3	5	7	8	
7 Nativitas est hodie ... pulchritudinem	an	WA 365	G	5	4	5	7	9	7	5	4	G
7 Nativitas est hodie ... vita	an	AR 834 LU 1625 AM 1032 WA 368 LA 461	d	-3	0	2	0	-2	0	-3	-2	G

8 Nativitas gloriosae virginis	an	AR 834 LU 1625 AM 1032 *WA 368 *LA 460	G	-5	-2	0	2	0	2	4	0	G
1 Nativitas gloriosae virginis	re	LA 459 *WA 365	a	3	0	-2	3	5	3	5	7	a
Nativitas gloriosae virginis	alv	GS u	a	3	2	0	3	-2	0	-2	-4	
1 Nativitas tua Dei genitrix	an	AR 837 LU 1627 AM 1035 *WA 364 *LA 455	D	-2	3	5	3	7	5	2	3	D
1 Nativitas tua Dei genitrix	re	WA 366	D	3	5	3	5	7	5	3	5	D
Nativitas tua Dei genitrix	alv	GB 232	A	3	5	3	5	8	5	7	5	
Nativitatem hodiernam perpetuae Regali ex progenie	rev	WA 367										
8 Nativitatem hodiernam perpetuae	an	AR 836 *AM 1034 *WA 368 LA 461	G	2	0	-2	0	2	0	5	2	G
1 Nativitatem hodiernam perpetuae	re	LA 460 WA 366	C	2	5	7	9	7	4	5	2	D
2 Nativitatem virginis Mariae	inv	LR 446	C	2	4	5	2	0	2	5	4	D
8 Nato Domino angelorum	an	LR 61 WA 47 LA 37	F	2	4	0	2	4	2	4	2	G
6 Natura creans omnia	hy	ST 310	G	5	4	7	9	7	5	4	5	c
Natus est nobis hodie salvator O regem caeli	rev	PM 36 LR 397 *LA 35										
8 Natus est nobis hodie salvator	an	WA 48 LA 31	G	-2	2	5	4	0	4	5	2	G
3 Naufragantis carnis pudor	re	WA 249	G	-3	-5	-3	0	2	0	2	5	E
5 Nazaraeus vocabitur puer	an	AR 733 LU 1497 LR 352 *WA 322	F	4	7	5	4	5	7	9	7	F
7 Nazaraeus vocabitur puer	an	LA 403	G	4	7	5	4	5	9	7	0	G
1 Ne abscondas me Domine	re	LA 284 WA 173	C	2	4	2	9	11	9	7	5	D
Ne avertas faciem tuam a me Domine exaudi	intv	GB 104^v										
Ne avertas faciem tuam a me Domine exaudi	trv	GR 191 OHS 324 LU 619 GS 92 GB 114 SYG 127	C	2	5	7	5	2	4	5	4	
2 Ne avertas faciem tuam a puero	gr	GR 190 OHS 322 LU 617 SYG 127 *GB 113^v *GS 91	E	3	5	7	5	8	5	7	8	a
2 Ne avertas faciem tuam a puero	re	WA 107	A	3	5	7	5	8	7	8	10	D
Ne avertas faciem tuam ne avertas Domine exaudi	ofv	OTT 53 GB 114^v SYG 128	D	5	7	10	7	5	7	9	10	
Ne avertas faciem tuam ne avertas Exaudi Deus orationem	ofv	SYG 129	D	5	7	10	7	5	7	9	10	
7 Ne derelinquas me ... Deus	int	GR 118 *SYG 88 GB 78 GS 50	G	5	4	5	7	10	9	10	7	G
Ne derelinquas me ... ne Domine pater	rev	LA 276										
4 Ne derelinquas me ... pater	re	LA 279 *WA 169	a	-2	0	-4	-5	-9	-7	-4	-7	E
4 Ne derelinquas me ... virtus	an	AR 181 LU 302	F	-3	-1	0	2	-1	0	-1	-3	E

	Incipit	Type	Source										
2	Ne discedas a me	an	AR 174 LU 279°	D	-2	0	3	2	0	-2	3	5	D
	Ne discesseris a me Exaudi me	trv	GR 9**	D	3	2	3	5	2	5	3	2	
	Ne forte satiatus Verbum iniquum	rev	WA 169										
	Ne forte veniant Sepulto Domino	rev	WA 125										
6	Ne in ira tua arguas	an	WA 63	C	2	5	4	2	5	7	5	7	F
5	Ne in ira tua arguas	an	LA 87	F	4	7	6	4	6	7	9	4	F
	Ne in ira tua corripias	an	OHS 238 (nm)										
	Ne intres in judicium Ne perdideris	rev	LA 94										
	Ne irascaris Domine Aspice Domine de sede	rev	WA 183										
1	Ne magnitudo revelationum	an	WA 331 LA 425	D	-2	0	3	5	3	5	7	5	D
6	Ne magnitudo revelationum	re	LA 428	c	2	0	-1	-5	-3	0	-1	0	c
	Ne perdas cum impiis	sr	AR 43 LU 248										
2	Ne perdas cum impiis	re	LA 168 *WA 109	A	3	5	7	5	8	7	8	5	D
	Ne perdideris me Domine Peccavi super numerum	rev	WA 166										
6	Ne perdideris me Domine	re	LA 94 *WA 62	c	2	0	2	5	4	2	5	2	c
	Ne permittas Domine Jesu Beatus Andreas	rev	WA 235										
	Ne quaeso Domine irascaris Ait autem Abraham	rev	WA 81	a	3	2	3	5	3	2	3	2	
6	Ne recorderis peccata	re	AR [166] LU 1792 LA 555 *WA 437	D	-2	3	5	7	5	3	5	3	F
4	Ne reminiscaris Domine delicta mea	an	AR 547 LU 992 1840 *AM 584 *WA 176	C	2	0	2	4	2	4	2	0	E
4	Ne reminiscaris Domine delicta nostra	an	PM 328 LA 293	C	2	0	2	4	5	4	2	4	E
1	Ne tacueris Deus	an	AR 202 LU 279[v]	D	2	3	5	2	3	0	-2	3	D
8	Ne timeas a facie	an	LR 347 *LA 400	G	5	2	0	2	0	-2	0	2	G
1	Ne timeas a facie ... ut eruam	an	WA 320	D	7	5	7	10	9	7	5	3	D
8	Ne timeas Maria invenisti	an	AR 218 668 [139] LU 1417 AM 190 862 *WA 8 *LA 6 379	G	5	2	0	2	-2	0	2	0	G
	Ne timeas Zacharia ... deprecatio	alv	SYG 198	E	-2	0	1	3	1	0	1	0	
	Ne timeas Zacharia ... oratio Descendit angelus	rev	LA 402 WA 321										
	Ne timeas Zacharia ... oratio	alv	SYG 196 *GB 196[v]	G	2	5	7	9	10	12	9	5	
7	Ne timeas Zacharia ... oratio	int	GR 521 *SYG 195 *GB 196 GS 188	G	5	7	9	7	5	4	5	7	G
	Ne timeas Zacharias		see Ne timeas Zacharia										

Ne timueris cum divite	an	OHS 299 (nm)									
Ne tradas Domine sceptrum tuum Recordare mei	rev	PM 114									
Ne tradas me a desiderio Eripe me	trv	GR 208 OHS 534 LU 725 GS 99 GB 116^V *SYG 137	F	2	4	2	4	2	4	5	2
7 Ne tradideris me Domine in animas	co	GR 165 *SYG 117 GB 104 GS 77	G	2	5	4	5	2	0	5	7	G
Ne tradideris me in animas Ne perdas	rev	WA 109									
Nec fecit proximo Propter intolerabiles	rev	WA 288									
8 Nec illud silendum est	an	WA 388	G	5	2	0	-2	0	2	0	5	G
8 Nec observavimus neque fecimus	an	GB 154^V	G	-5	-2	0	2	0	-5	-2	0	G
8 Nefarium tamen apud Christianorum	an	WA 258	a	3	2	0	-2	-4	-2	0	-2	G
1 Nemini dixeritis visionem	an	WA 90	D	3	0	-2	5	3	2	-2	0	D
1 Nemo in eum misit manum	an	AR 402 LU 1094 AM 377 WA 104	D	-2	0	2	3	5	3	2	0	D
2 Nemo te condemnavit mulier nemo	co	GS 63	D	-2	0	-2	-3	-2	0	-2	0	D
8 Nemo te condemnavit mulier nemo	co	SYG 100	D	2	3	2	3	5	3	5	7	G
3 Nemo te condemnavit mulier nemo	an	AR 396 LU 558 *AM 371 *WA 100	G	2	5	4	2	0	2	4	5	E
7 Nemo te condemnavit mulier nemo	an	LA 156	G	5	4	5	7	5	4	2	0	G
8 Nemo te condemnavit mulier nemo	co	GR 138 *GB 89^V	G	5	4	5	7	5	4	2	4	G
2 Nemo te condemnavit mulier quae	co	SYG 100	C	2	4	2	4	5	4	5	4	D
8 Nemo tollet a me	an	WA 115 *LA 175	G	2	5	4	2	5	7	5	7	G
Nequando dicant gentes Adjuva nos	trv	GR [131]	F	2	0	2	0	-3	0	2	-1
Nequando dicat inimicus Multiplicati sunt	rev	LR 415 LA 166 WA 105									
8 Nequando rapiat ut leo	an	AR [157] LU 1784 WA 436 *LA 553	a	-4	-2	0	-2	0	-2	0	-2	G
Neque irrideant me Ad te Domine	rev	LA 84 WA 61									
1 Nesciat sinistra tua	an	WA 84 (inc illeg)									D
6 Nesciens mater virgo virum	an	PM 39 *WA 32 *LA 39	F	2	0	2	0	2	4	0	4	F
7 Nesciens mater virgo virum	re	PM 250 *LA 35 *WA 48	G	4	5	7	9	10	9	5	7	G
3 Nigra sum sed formosa	an	AR [115] LR 219 LU 1784 AM 707 *WA 353 LA 543	G	4	5	2	5	4	0	2	4	E
2 Nihil inquinatum in eam	gr	GR 48**	a	-5	0	2	0	-2	0	-2	0	a
8 Nihil inquinatum in eam	re	LR 267	G	2	0	2	-2	0	2	0	2	G
Nihil inquinatum in eam	alv	GR 51**	G	2	0	5	4	5	7	9	5

Incipit		Type	Source	Mode									Final
8	Nihil inquinatum in eam	re	AM 1191	F	2	4	2	4	6	4	2	4	G
	Nihil proficiet et inimicus / Inveni David	rev	LR 198 LA 532										
	Nihil proficiet inimicus in eo / Inveni David	grv	GR [3] LU 1130 *GS 221 *GB 41 *SYG 37	D	7	5	7	10	7	9	5	3	
6	Nimis exaltatus est alleluia	an	LR 100 *WA 148 *LA 247	F	-1	2	4	-1	0	-3	-5	0	F
	Nimis honorati sunt amici tui	sr	AR [10] LU 1114 1522 WA 415										
	Nimis honorati sunt amici tui / Constitues eos	rev	LR 143 LA 510 WA 413										
	Nimis honorati sunt amici tui / Non sunt loquelae	rev	LR 147										
	Nimis honorati sunt amici tui	alv	SYG 207 *GS y	G	-2	-3	-2	0	2	0	4	2	
	Nimis honorati sunt amici tui	alv	GR 644 LU 1720 GB 267V	c	-1	2	0	-1	0	2	0	-3	
2	Nimis honorati sunt amici tui	gr	GR 391 LU 1326 *SYG 54 *GB 235 *GS w	G	4	2	5	2	4	5	2	0	a
4	Nisi diligenter perfeceris	an	WA 274 *LA 359	D	7	5	7	9	7	5	7	5	E
	Nisi Dominus aedificaverit / Sapientia reddidit	intv	LU 1440										
	Nisi ego abiero / Non conturbetur	rev	WA 149										
	Nisi ego abiero / Non relinquam vos	rev	LA 249										
	Nisi ego abiero / Tempus est	rev	LR 101										
1	Nisi ego abiero	an	WA 150 LA 247	D	-2	3	5	3	5	7	10	7	D
5	Nisi granum frumenti	an	WA 419 LA 439	F	4	7	5	4	2	7	9	7	F
	Nisi quia Dominus erat / Anima nostra	cov	SYG 206										
	Nisi quod Dominus erat / Anima nostra	ofv	OTT 145 *GB 27V SYG 26	a	-2	0	3	5	3	5	3	2	
1	Nisi tu Domine conserves	an	LA 96	F	2	4	6	4	2	-1	2	4	D
	Nobilissimis orta natalibus / Agatha laetissima	rev	WA 273										
1	Nobilissimus siquidem natalibus	an	WA 238	D	3	0	-2	3	5	7	10	5	D
	Nobis ergo petimus piis / O constantia martyrum	rev	PM 195	D	7	5	7	5	3	5	7	8	
	Nocte ae die in profundum / Ter virgis	alv	WA 265 331 LA 426										
4	Nocte os meum perforatur	re	LA 285 WA 173	F	-1	0	2	4	2	-1	0	2	E
8	Nocte surgentes vigilemus omnes	hy	ST 250	a	-2	-4	-2	0	-2	-4	0	3	G
4	Nocte surgentes vigilemus omnes	hy	ST 85	E	1	0	-2	0	-2	-4	-2	0	E

8 Nocte surgentes vigilemus omnes	hy	ST 212	G	2	-2	-3	-2	0	2	0	-2	G
8 Nocte surgentes vigilemus omnes	hy	ST 359	G	2	0	-2	0	2	0	-2	2	G
4 Nocte surgentes vigilemus omnes	hy	ST 155	C	2	5	4	2	5	4	5	2	E
2 Nocte surgentes vigilemus omnes	hy	ST 165	G	2	5	4	5	7	5	7	10	d
4 Nocte surgentes vigilemus omnes	hy	ST 263	D	3	5	7	5	3	2	0	3	E
6 Nocte surgentes vigilemus omnes	hy	ST 263	C	4	2	5	2	0	5	7	5	F
7 Noctem illam tenebrosus	an	LA 287	b	1	3	5	3	5	3	1	0	G
Noe vero et filii Quadraginta dies	rev	LA 117 WA 76										
Noe vero et uxor		see Noe vero et filii										
8 Noe vir justus	re	LA 116	C	2	7	5	7	9	11	9	7	G
Noli aemulari in eo	an	OHS 236 (nm)										
Noli aemulari in malignantibus Justus non conturbabitur	intv	GB 229 GS 205										
Noli aemulari in malignantibus Os justi	intv	GR [42] [48] LU 1200 GS 204 GB 40 SYG 33										
Noli aemulari in malignantibus Salus autem justorum	intv	GR [28] LU 1169 GS 211 GB 196 SYG 193										
Noli aemulari inter malignantibus		see Noli aemulari in malignantibus										
8 Noli esse mihi Domine	re	LA 177 *WA 111	G	2	0	2	0	2	0	5	4	G
Noli flere Maria	sr	WA 142										
6 Noli flere Maria	an	WA 136	F	2	0	-1	2	4	0	-1	-3	F
8 Noli me derelinquere pater	an	LA 433	G	2	4	5	2	0	-2	0	2	G
8 Noli me derelinquere pater	re	LA 435 WA 348	D	5	3	5	7	5	7	5	7	G
8 Nolite diligere mundum	tr	GR 22**	G	2	4	2	0	2	0	-2	0	G
8 Nolite expavescere	an	LR 90 *WA 133 LA 216	G	5	2	0	-2	0	2	0	4	G
8 Nolite judicare ut non judicemini	an	AR 523 LU 916 AM 542 WA 187 LA 311	G	5	2	0	-2	0	2	0	4	G
1 Nolite me considerare	an	AM 1046	C	2	5	2	4	2	0	5	7	D
1 Nolite me considerare	an	AR 842 LU 1631	C	2	5	4	5	7	9	7	5	D
8 Nolite soliciti esse dicentes	an	AR 565 810 AM 605 1003 *WA 189 *LA 316	G	5	2	0	2	4	2	0	2	G
Nolite timere eos qui corpus Sancti et justi	rev	LA 389										
8 Nolite timere eos qui corpus	an	LA 520	G	5	2	0	-2	0	2	0	4	G
Nolite timere et opprobria In conspectu gentium	rev	LA 467										

	Incipit		Source										
7	Nolite timere non separabuntur	re	LA 327	G	2	0	2	0	2	5	4	5	G
8	Nolite timere non separabuntur	an	LA 326	G	5	2	0	-2	0	2	0	4	G
8	Nolite timere quinta enim die	an	AR 245 AM 219 WA 20 LA 24	G	5	2	0	-2	0	2	0	7	G
	Nolo multa fortitudine / Antequam comedam	rev	LA 282 WA 172										
	Nolo multa fortitudine / Desiderium meum	rev	WA 175										
8	Nomen eorum permanet	an	AR 642	G	-2	-5	-2	-3	-2	0	-2	0	G
7	Nomen sempiternum dabo	an	AM 980	G	4	5	7	9	7	5	2	5	G
2	Nomine aeterno haereditavit	an	WA 251	D	-2	-5	-2	0	5	3	5	7	D
1	Non abscondas me Domine	re	PM 112	C	2	4	2	9	10	9	7	5	D
	Non abscondi misericordiam tuam / Annuntiavi	trv	GR [2^2] LU 1122^4	G	-5	0	2	4	2	5	7	5	
	Non adorabitis Deum alienum / In die sollemnitatis	ofv	OTT 61 GB 139^v *SYG 159	F	-1	-3	-1	-3	0	-3	0	-3	
2	Non auferetur sceptrum	re	LA 18 *WA 23	D	2	0	3	0	2	0	-2	3	D
1	Non auferetur sceptrum	an	WA 13	C	2	5	4	2	0	2	5	4	D
	Non calor hunc coxit / Sanctas primitias	rev	PM 267	C	2	5	7	5	4	5	7	4	
	Non comparavi illi omnem lapidem / Super salutem	rev	PM 111										
2	Non confundetur dum loquetur	an	LA 99	F	-3	0	-1	-3	-1	-3	-5	0	D
	Non conturbetur cor		see also Non turbetur cor										
4	Non conturbetur cor	re	WA 149	E	1	-2	-4	3	5	3	5	3	E
	Non derelinquet Dominus sanctos / Multae tribulationes	intv	GR(20)										
	Non derelinquet Dominus sanctos	alv	GR 446	C	2	5	4	5	7	5	4	2	
3	Non dico tibi septies	an	WA 100	G	2	5	2	5	4	2	0	2	E
	Non diebus neque noctibus / Cilicio Caecilia	rev	LA 491 WA 406										
	Non dilexerunt animas suas	alv	GR 109**	D	-2	0	3	0	-2	2	3	5	
8	Non discedimus a te	re	LR 19 WA 24	D	3	5	7	5	7	5	7	9	G
7	Non duplices sermonem	of	GR 32**	G	4	7	5	7	9	7	10	12	G
8	Non ego te desero	an	WA 347 *LA 433	G	5	2	0	2	0	-2	0	2	G
	Non enim habet amaritudinem / Alleluia: delectatio	rev	WA 144										
	Non enim in justificationibus / Qui caelorum contines	rev	LA 306										
8	Non enim judicavi me scire	of	GR 477 LU 1429	a	-2	2	0	-2	0	3	2	3	G
	Non enim loquetur a semetipso / Si enim non abiero	rev	LR 106 LA 246										

2 Non enim loquetur a semetipso	an	LA 242	D	-2	0	3	2	3	5	3	2	D
8 Non enim loquetur a semetipso	an	AR 482 AM 498	G	5	2	0	2	0	-2	0	2	G
1 Non enim misit Deus	an	LA 265	D	-2	0	-2	0	3	0	-2	0	D
7 Non enim misit Deus	an	WA 155	G	5	4	5	7	9	7	4	5	G
Non enim vos estis 　　Dum steteritis	rev	LR 138 LA 506 WA 412										
Non erat ille lux 　　Fuit homo missus	rev	LA 401										
8 Non eris inter virgines	re	WA 432	D	3	5	7	5	7	5	7	5	G
Non est alia natio 　　Qui manducat	rev	LR 131	c	-1	-3	-5	0	2	4	2	0	
4 Non est ei species	an	AR 843 LU 1639 *AM 1047	G	2	5	7	5	7	9	7	5	a
7 Non est hic aliud	an	LR 237 WA 318 LA 547	d	-3	0	2	0	-2	0	-3	-2	G
7 Non est inventus similis	an	AR [56] LU 1176 AM 657 *LA 536 WA 427	d	-3	0	2	0	-3	-2	-3	-7	G
Non est inventus similis 　　Ecce sacerdos	grv	GR [32] LU 1183 1495^{A} GS 220 GB 28^{V} *SYG 27	F	4	2	7	9	7	2	7	9	
3 Non est privatus	an	WA 315	E	-2	3	5	8	7	8	10	8	E
Non esurient neque sitient 　　Absterget Deus	rev	LR 178 LA 514 WA 420										
6 Non habemus hic manentem	of	GR 23**	F	2	0	2	4	2	0	2	0	F
4 Non haberes in me potestatem	an	AR 428 OHS 226 AM 407 WA 114 *LA 185	G	2	5	7	5	7	9	7	5	a
7 Non illam crucians ungula	hy	AR 617	G	4	5	7	9	7	5	7	0	G
Non in fermento malitiae 　　Expurgate vetus	rev	WA 134										
1 Non in justificationibus	an	GB 160	F	2	0	2	4	2	4	2	0	D
Non in perpetuum irascetur 　　Misericors	trv	GR [113] LU 972	C	2	5	7	5	7	9	7	5	
5 Non in solo pane	an	AR 371 LU 538 AM 344 *WA 87	c	-3	0	2	4	0	-1	0	2	F
1 Non in solo pane	an	LA 130	D	-2	0	3	0	2	3	2	0	D
8 Non intres in judicium	an	WA 439	G	5	4	2	0	-2	0	2	0	G
3 Non invenientes Jesum regressi	an	AR 653 LU 1406 *AM 842	E	1	0	-2	3	5	3	5	8	E
2 Non judicavi me scire	tr	GR 476	D	-2	0	-2	-5	-2	0	-2	0	D
Non judicavi me scire 　　Mihi autem absit	grv	GR 481	E	1	-2	3	5	8	7	8	7	
8 Non licet mihi facere	an	AR 347 AM 318 WA 75	G	5	2	0	2	0	-2	0	2	G

7	Non lotis manibus	an	AR 393 LU 1091 AM 368	G	4	5	7	9	7	5	4	2	G
7	Non lotis manibus	an	WA 100 *LA 155	G	5	4	5	7	4	7	9	5	G
8	Non me permittas	an	WA 237 *LA 500	G	-2	-3	-2	0	2	0	2	0	G
7	Non meis meritis ad vos	an	AR 927 LU 1760 AM 1145 WA 410 LA 496	d	-3	0	2	0	-2	0	-3	-2	G
	Non Moyses dedit vobis panem Comedetis carnes	rev	LR 123 LU 927	D	-2	0	3	5	3	5	7	5	
	Non nobis Domine non nobis	alv	GB 261^v	G	5	4	5	7	2	5	4	2	
2	Non nos demergat Domine	an	GB 159^v	A	3	5	7	5	7	8	7	8	D
8	Non omnis qui dicit mihi	an	WA 188 *LA 313	G	5	2	0	2	0	-2	0	3	G
4	Non participentur sancta	of	GR [120]	F	4	2	4	0	-3	2	0	-1	E
6	Non pepercisti animae tuae	an	AR 3 (sup 1)	F	2	0	4	7	4	7	9	4	F
1	Non potest arbor bona	an	AR 559 LU 1013 *AM 597	C	2	5	2	0	2	5	7	4	D
8	Non potest filius a se	an	LA 165	G	5	2	0	2	0	2	0	-2	G
	Non privabit bonis eos Beatus vir	trv	GR 450 LU 1394	G	-5	0	2	0	2	5	4	5	
1	Non pro his rogo tantum	co	GB 177^v	C	2	5	4	2	4	0	-2	3	D
4	Non profanorum sinitur vagari	hy	LR 456	a	-2	0	-2	-4	-5	-4	-2	-5	E
1	Non recedet laus tua	an	AR 638 LU 1384 *AM 821	C	2	4	5	2	0	4	2	0	D
7	Non recedet memoria	an	WA 373	G	5	2	5	7	5	4	0	2	G
	Non relinquam vos	see also Non vos relinquam											
2	Non relinquam vos orphanos	re	LR 98 LA 249	D	-5	-2	0	2	0	-2	0	2	D
	Non satis Deo carus est Si tibi gratum	rev	WA 244										
	Non secundum peccata nostra Misericors	trv	GR [113] LU 972	D	-5	-2	0	3	0	-2	0	-2	
	Non sicut ego volo Pater si non potest	cov	SYG 124										
7	Non sit vobis vanum	inv	LA 127 *WA 85	G	5	4	5	7	5	9	7	9	G
7	Non sum missus nisi ad oves	an	LA 135	G	4	5	7	9	7	5	7	9	G
	Non sunt loquelae Caeli enarrant	rev	WA 410										
	Non sunt loquelae Ibant gaudentes	rev	LR 166 LA 393										
	Non sunt loquelae In omnem terram	rev	LA 510										
3	Non sunt loquelae	re	LR 147	G	2	4	5	4	2	4	5	4	E
	Non sunt loquelae In omnem terram	ofv	SYG 54	D	2	9	11	9	7	9	12	11	

Non tantum sollicitus Aperi nobis	rev	WA 345										
Non tradas me		<u>see</u> Ne tradas me										
Non turbetur cor		<u>see also</u> Non conturbetur cor										
6 Non turbetur cor ... alleluia	an	WA 148 *LA 253	F	2	0	-1	2	4	0	-1	-3	F
3 Non turbetur cor ... ego	re	LR 102 LA 248 *WA 147	F	-1	-3	2	4	2	4	7	6	E
6 Non turbetur cor ... neque	an	AR 694 LU 1465[A] AM 892 *LA 392 WA 308	F	-1	0	-3	-1	-3	-5	-3	0	F
8 Non veritus incredulae	an	WA 385	G	5	2	0	2	0	2	0	2	G
Non vos inquit Paschasius dixit	rev	WA 245										
8 Non vos me elegistis	re	LR 118	G	2	0	2	0	2	5	7	5	G
Non vos me elegistis	alv	SYG 172 GS y	C	2	5	2	4	5	2	4	2	
5 Non vos me elegistis	an	WA 307	F	2	5	2	5	4	0	4	7	F
Non vos me elegistis Vitone laudabilis	rev	PM 204	D	7	10	7	5	7	3	2	0	
Non vos relinquam		<u>see also</u> Non relinquam vos										
Non vos relinquam ... dicit	alv	GB 182[V]	F	2	9	7	4	7	9	2	0	
1 Non vos relinquam ... vado	alv	GR 289 LU 856 GS K SYG 187	D	2	3	2	0	-2	0	-2	3	
Non vos relinquam ... vado	an	AM 519 *AR 502 *LU 862 WA 151 *LA 255	C	2	4	2	0	5	4	2	0	D
2 Non vos relinquam ... veniam	re	WA 148	D	-2	0	-2	-5	-2	0	2	0	D
6 Non vos relinquam ... veniam	an	WA 151	F	2	0	-1	2	4	0	-1	-3	F
5 Non vos relinquam ... veniam	co	GR 303 LU 899 *SYG 188 *GB 194 GS b	a	3	2	3	0	-2	0	3	-2	F
2 Non vos relinquam ... venio	an	LA 255	C	2	4	2	0	2	4	5	4	D
Non vult mortem peccatoris Derelinquat impius	rev	LA 131										
4 Nonne cognoscit Deus	re	WA 174	G	-3	-2	-3	-2	0	2	-2	-3	E
Nonne cor nostrum ... dum loqueretur	alv	GB 131	D	2	0	3	0	2	0	-2	0	
1 Nonne cor nostrum ... dum loqueretur	an	AR 480 AM 495 WA *63 133 LA 218	C	2	0	5	2	5	7	9	10	D
Nonne cor nostrum ... dum loqueretur	alv	SYG 155 GS 118	D	2	3	2	0	-2	0	-2	3	
Nonne cor nostrum ... dum nobiscum	alv	SYG 164	E	3	0	-2	3	5	7	5	3	
8 Nonne decem mundati	an	WA 189	F	2	4	2	4	2	4	2	0	G
Nonne ecce omnes isti Facta autem hac	rev	WA 155										

	Incipit	Genre	Sources	Mode									Final
	Nonne iste est David / Percussit Saul	rev	LA 268										
8	Nonne iste est David	an	WA 164 *LA 273	G	5	2	0	-2	0	2	0	2	G
1	Nonne Moyses dedit	an	LA 164	D	7	9	10	7	5	3	5	7	D
8	Nonne sic oportuit pati	an	AR 472 *AM 486 *WA 138 *LA 218 232	F	2	4	7	6	7	4	7	2	G
8	Nonne vides quanta sit	an	WA 343	G	-5	-2	-3	-2	0	2	0	-2	G
2	Norma tu vitae speculumque sanctae	hy	LR 273	A	5	3	5	8	7	5	7	8	D
4	Norunt infantes laudare	an	WA 43	F	-1	-3	-1	0	2	0	-1	2	E
2	Nos alium Deum nescimus	re	LA 291 *WA 177	A	3	5	7	5	8	7	8	5	D
7	Nos autem gloriari	an	AR 701 LU 1460 AM 900 1041 WA 371 LA 463	d	-3	0	2	0	2	0	-3	-2	G
6	Nos autem gloriari	co	GB 234^V	F	2	0	-1	0	2	5	0	2	F
	Nos autem gloriari	alv	GB 165 *GS v	D	7	5	7	5	2	3	2	0	
3	Nos autem gloriari ... in quo	co	GB 167^V	a	-2	-5	-2	0	2	0	-2	0	E
8	Nos autem gloriari ... in quo	an	SYG 142	a	-2	-4	-2	0	-2	-4	-2	0	G
1	Nos autem gloriari ... in quo	re	WA 309	C	2	4	5	4	2	4	2	4	D
4	Nos autem gloriari ... in quo	int	GR 195 490 OHS 257 439 LU 667 1454 *SYG 125 GB 112^V GS 90 235	D	3	2	3	5	3	0	3	2	E
	Nos ejus norma / Gloria Christe	rev	WA 300	G	2	0	-2	-3	0	2	5	7	
	Nos enim quasi senes / Noli me derelinquere	rev	LA 435 WA 348										
	Nos quasi senes	see	Nos enim quasi senes										
tp	Nos qui vivimus benedicimus	an	AM 132 133	C	2	5	7	9	10	9	7	5	G
4	Nos scientes sanctum nomen	an	WA 407 *LA 490	G	-3	0	2	0	-2	0	-3	-7	E
2	Nostrae matris praeconia	hy	ST 136	D	2	3	5	3	2	0	-2	3	D
	Nostras deprecationes ne despicias	sr	AR 7 (sup 1)										
	Notam facite in populis / Exsulta et lauda	grv	GR 54**	F	4	2	7	9	7	4	7	9	
	Notam fecisti in gentibus	see	Notam fecisti in populis										
	Notam fecisti in populis / Quis Deus ... tu es	rev	LR 342 WA 159	b	1	3	1	-2	-4	1	0	1	
	Notas fecisti mihi vias / Benedicam Dominum	ofv	OTT 88 *GB 76^V SYG 87	F	2	4	2	4	2	0	2	0	
8	Notas mihi fecisti Domine	re	LA 82 *WA 60	F	2	4	2	4	2	4	6	4	G
7	Notas mihi fecisti vias	co	GR 134 *SYG 97 *GB 86 *GS 59	e	-2	0	-2	0	-2	-4	-2	0	G

Notum fecit Dominus alleluia	sr	AR 269 LU 411 AM 273 WA 48										
6 Notum fecit Dominus alleluia	an	LU 388 *LR 61 LA 33 *WA 49	F	-1	2	4	0	-3	-5	0	-1	F
4 Notum fecit Dominus opus	an	LR 266	F	-3	-1	0	2	4	2	4	2	E
Notum fecit Dominus salutare Cantate Domino canticum	alv	SYG 248	D	2	0	-2	0	2	0	-2	0	
Notum fecit Dominus salutare Cantate Domino canticum	alv	SYG 247	D	3	0	3	0	2	3	7	10	
Notum fecit Dominus salutare Viderunt omnes	grv	GR 33 LU 409 GS G GB 17ᵛ SYG 19	F	4	2	7	9	7	4	7	9	
Notus in Judaea Deus Vovete et reddite	cov	SYG 251										
8 Notus in Judaea Deus	tr	GR [136] LU 1286	G	2	4	2	0	2	0	-2	0	G
Notus in Judaea Deus Terra tremuit	ofv	OTT 55 *GB 128 SYG 153	D	3	7	10	7	5	7	5	8	
5 Nova bella elegit Dominus	gr	GR 40**	F	2	0	2	4	5	4	7	4	F
5 Nova regis praeconia	hy	ST 139	F	-1	-3	-1	0	2	0	-1	2	F
7 Novissime veniunt	an	WA 431	G	5	4	5	7	9	7	9	7	G
8 Novit Dominus viam justorum	an	LR 381 *WA 395 *LA 474	G	2	5	4	5	4	2	5	4	G
1 Novo decurrens lumine	hy	ST 306	D	7	8	7	5	7	8	10	7	D
1 Novus athleta Domini	hy	VP 195	D	7	8	7	5	7	5	3	2	D
4 Nox atra rerum contegit	hy	ST 363	G	-3	0	-2	-3	-2	-5	-3	-2	E
3 Nox atra rerum contegit	hy	ST 214	D	2	3	5	3	5	3	2	3	E
4 Nox et tenebrae et nubila	hy	AR 128 AM 57	E	-4	-2	1	0	1	3	1	0	E
1 Nox et tenebrae et nubila	hy	AM 57	a	2	0	-2	-4	-2	0	-2	-4	D
3 Nox et tenebrae et nubila	hy	ST 214	D	2	3	5	3	5	3	2	3	E
8 Nox et tenebrae et nubila	hy	ST 363	D	2	3	5	7	3	5	0	2	G
8 Nubes lucida	an	WA 90	F	2	4	2	4	2	4	2	4	G
Nudus egressus sum de utero Si bona	rev	LR 422										
6 Nullis te genitor blanditiis trahit	hy	AR 682	F	-5	-3	0	2	0	2	4	2	F
6 Numquam inquinatum corpus	re	WA 245	c	2	0	2	4	0	2	0	-3	c
4 Numquid Dominus supplantat	re	LA 285 *WA 173	a	3	0	3	5	3	2	3	2	b
1 Numquid est in idolis	an	WA 231	F	4	2	0	4	2	4	5	4	D
Numquid fortitudo lapidum Vir erat	ofv	OTT 122 *GB 262 SYG 256	b	1	-2	1	0	1	3	1	0	
4 Numquid redditur pro bono	an	AR 98 409 AM 107 122 389 *LA 171 WA 108	G	2	5	7	5	7	9	7	5	a
8 Numquid scis quare	re	WA 185	D	3	5	7	5	7	9	7	3	G

Mode	Incipit	Type	Source										
	Numquid sicut dies 　　Quis mihi tribuat	rev	WA 173										
2	Nunc ad Sicelidem mittitur insulam	hy	LR 450	G	2	5	4	0	2	4	5	2	a
2	Nunc autem ad te venio	an	LA 254	D	-2	0	2	3	2	0	-2	0	D
	Nunc autem manent 　　Maneant in vobis	anv	OHS 450 SYG 131										
7	Nunc autem manent	an	WA 214	d	3	0	2	0	2	0	2	0	G
	Nunc Christe te deprecor 　　Libera me Domine de morte	rev	LA 557	D	-2	0	2	3	5	3	0	2	
	Nunc cum eo regnas	alv	LU 1476^D	F	2	4	2	0	2	0	-3	-1	
2	Nunc dimittis Domine	re	WA 270	D	-2	-5	-2	0	-2	0	3	5	D
7	Nunc dimittis Domine	an	WA 272 *LA 350	G	4	5	7	9	7	5	7	9	G
	Nunc dimittis servum tuum 　　Lumen ad revelationem	anv	GS 180 SYG 47										
8	Nunc dimittis servum tuum	tr	GB 49	G	2	4	2	0	2	0	5	7	G
8	Nunc dimittis servum tuum	tr	GR 434 LU 1363 *SYG 50 *GS k	D	3	5	3	5	3	0	2	-2	G
	Nunc ergo egressus 　　Numquid scis	rev	WA 185										
8	Nunc ergo filii audite me	tr	GR 587^3 LU 1612^3	G	2	4	2	0	2	0	5	7	G
6	Nunc ergo nomen Domini	an	WA 287	c	2	4	2	0	2	0	2	4	c
	Nunc ergo ora pro nobis	alv	GR 39**	a	-2	-4	0	3	0	3	-2	-5	
8	Nunc facies fortiter	an	WA 386	G	5	2	0	-2	0	2	0	7	G
3	Nunc facta est salus	re	LA 469	G	2	4	5	4	2	-2	0	2	E
8	Nunc sancte nobis spiritus	hy	ST 360 AM 84 94 109	G	-5	-2	0	2	0	-2	0	5	G
8	Nunc sancte nobis spiritus	hy	ST 173	G	-5	0	2	0	-2	0	2	5	G
4	Nunc sancte nobis spiritus	hy	ST 137	E	-4	0	3	5	3	1	3	1	E
1	Nunc sancte nobis spiritus	hy	AR 217 LU 318	E	-4	0	3	5	7	5	3	5	a
8	Nunc sancte nobis spiritus	hy	ST 155	G	-3	-2	0	-3	-5	0	2	4	G
8	Nunc sancte nobis spiritus	hy	ST 204	c	-3	-2	0	-2	-3	-5	0	2	c
2	Nunc sancte nobis spiritus	hy	AR [124] AM 710	a	-2	-5	-7	-2	0	3	2	0	a
1	Nunc sancte nobis spiritus	hy	AR 461 LU 808	a	-2	-4	-2	0	-7	-2	-4	-7	D
8	Nunc sancte nobis spiritus	hy	AR 268 LU 407	G	-2	-3	-5	-2	2	0	-2	0	G
6	Nunc sancte nobis spiritus	hy	ST 328	G	-2	-3	-2	0	-2	[0	0	0]	F
8	Nunc sancte nobis spiritus	hy	ST 173	a	-2	0	-2	0	-4	0	-2	-4	G
8	Nunc sancte nobis spiritus	hy	AR 84 AM 93 108	a	-2	0	-2	0	-2	-4	-2	-4	G
8	Nunc sancte nobis spiritus	hy	ST 321	a	-2	0	-2	[0	0	0	0	0]	G
2	Nunc sancte nobis spiritus	hy	ST 27	E	-2	0	-2	0	1	0	-2	-4	D

2 Nunc sancte nobis spiritus	hy	ST 4	D	-2	0	3	0	-2	0	-2	0	D
2 Nunc sancte nobis spiritus	hy	ST 77 266 AM 84	D	-2	0	3	2	0	-2	0	-2	D
2 Nunc sancte nobis spiritus	hy	AR 25 LU 235	D	-2	0	3	2	0	2	0	-2	D
2 Nunc sancte nobis spiritus	hy	AM 244 554	D	-2	0	3	2	0	3	5	3	D
2 Nunc sancte nobis spiritus	hy	ST 174	a	-2	0	3	2	0	3	5	3	a
8 Nunc sancte nobis spiritus	hy	ST 77	G	-2	2	0	2	0	2	0	-2	G
3 Nunc sancte nobis spiritus	hy	AR 538[10] LU 969	E	-2	3	5	8	7	5	3	5	E
6 Nunc sancte nobis spiritus	hy	ST 173	F	-1	0	-1	-3	-5	0	2	0	F
4 Nunc sancte nobis spiritus	hy	AR 493 LU 846	F	-1	0	2	4	2	0	-3	0	E
4 Nunc sancte nobis spiritus	hy	ST 267	b	1	-2	0	-2	-4	-2	0	-2	b
2 Nunc sancte nobis spiritus	hy	ST 441	D	2	-2	-3	-2	0	2	3	2	D
1 Nunc sancte nobis spiritus	hy	ST 179	G	2	0	-3	-2	0	2	0	2	D
8 Nunc sancte nobis spiritus	hy	AM 93 108	G	2	0	-2	0	2	0	2	5	G
7 Nunc sancte nobis spiritus	hy	ST 27	G	2	0	-2	0	2	0	5	7	G
8 Nunc sancte nobis spiritus	hy	AM 472 LU 808	G	2	0	2	4	5	2	4	5	G
2 Nunc sancte nobis spiritus	hy	ST 346	F	2	4	0	2	0	-1	-3	-5	D
2 Nunc sancte nobis spiritus	hy	AM 185	C	2	4	0	2	4	5	4	2	D
8 Nunc sancte nobis spiritus	hy	AR 26 LU 235	G	2	4	0	2	5	4	2	4	G
1 Nunc sancte nobis spiritus	hy	AM 339	F	2	4	2	0	2	4	2	-1	D
8 Nunc sancte nobis spiritus	hy	AM 85 94 109	G	2	4	2	0	2	4	5	4	G
2 Nunc sancte nobis spiritus	hy	AR 413 OHS 85 203 LU 569 AM 387	C	2	4	5	4	2	0	2	4	D
6 Nunc sancte nobis spiritus	hy	ST 319	F	2	4	5	4	2	4	0	2	F
8 Nunc sancte nobis spiritus	hy	AR 316 LU 458 AM 294	F	2	4	7	2	4	0	2	7	G
6 Nunc sancte nobis spiritus	hy	ST 136	G	2	5	4	2	0	2	4	2	F
5 Nunc sancte nobis spiritus	hy	ST 246	C	2	5	4	2	0	7	9	7	C
5 Nunc sancte nobis spiritus	hy	ST 207	C	2	5	9	11	12	9	5	7	C
2 Nunc sancte nobis spiritus	hy	ST 115	D	3	0	-2	3	5	3	5	7	D
1 Nunc sancte nobis spiritus	hy	AR 894[10] LU 1708	D	3	0	-2	3	5	7	5	10	D
4 Nunc sancte nobis spiritus	hy	AM 568 1095	D	3	2	0	2	5	2	3	2	E
1 Nunc sancte nobis spiritus	hy	AR 370 LU 531	E	3	5	3	1	3	5	3	0	D
3 Nunc sancte nobis spiritus	hy	ST 154	E	3	5	7	5	3	5	3	7	E
5 Nunc sancte nobis spiritus	hy	ST 320	F	4	7	9	7	4	7	5	4	F
8 Nunc scimus quia scis	an	WA 146	a	-2	-4	-2	0	3	2	3	2	G
3 Nunc scio vere quia misit	int	GR 532 LU 1518 *SYG 202 *GB 204 GS o 189	F	-3	2	0	-1	2	4	7	6	E

8 Nunc tempus acceptabile	hy	ST 381	G	-2	0	2	5	4	5	7	5	G
8 Nunc tibi virgo virginum	hy	ST 433	G	2	0	-2	2	5	4	2	0	G
8 Nunc tibi virgo virginum	hy	ST 399	G	2	0	2	0	-2	0	2	5	G
7 Nuntiaverunt Jacob	re	LR 410 *LA 152 WA 98	G	2	0	2	0	2	0	2	5	G
4 Nuntium vobis fero de supernis	hy	ST 83	F	-3	-1	2	4	2	4	5	4	E
1 Nuntium vobis fero de supernis	hy	ST 372	D	3	0	3	0	2	-2	2	5	D
1 Nuptiae factae sunt	an	WA 62 *LA 106	D	-2	3	5	3	5	7	8	7	D
Nuptiae factae sunt	alv	SYG 35	C	2	4	0	2	4	5	7	4	
8 Nuptiae factae sunt	an	AR 336 AM 306	F	2	4	2	0	4	7	4	2	G
1 Nuptiae quidem paratae sunt	an	WA 190 LA 318	D	3	0	-2	3	5	3	5	7	D
1 0 acceptabilem Deo	re	WA 285	D	-2	0	3	5	0	3	2	-2	D
6 0 admirabile beati Gregorii	an	WA 291	b	1	-2	-4	1	3	5	3	1	c
6 0 admirabile commercium	an	AR 294 LU 442 AM 271 *WA 50 LA 64	F	-3	-5	0	2	0	2	4	2	F
0 admirabile mysterium Beata et venerabilis	rev	WA 48										
1 0 admirabile nomen Jesu	an	VP 98	C	2	5	4	2	0	5	7	9	D
1 0 admirabile pretium	an	WA 215 *SYG 140	a	-7	-9	0	-2	3	2	5	3	D
0 admirabile pretium Dum fabricator	anv	GS 103	D	7	0	7	5	10	9	12	10	
2 0 Adonai et dux	an	AR 235 LU 340 AM 209 *WA 21 LA 27	C	5	4	5	2	4	2	0	2	D
0 adoranda trinitas	alv	SYG 261	G	2	-2	2	5	0	2	0	-2	
4 0 beata anima quae meruit	an	AM 1131	E	-2	0	1	-2	0	-2	-4	0	E
1 0 beata beatissimae	an	WA 334	D	2	0	-2	0	3	2	3	5	D
2 0 beata benedicta	an	WA 161	D	-2	-5	-2	0	-2	0	2	3	D
3 0 beata Caecilia quae duos fratres	re	PM 212 *LA 489 WA 408	G	2	5	4	5	4	2	5	4	E
1 0 beata et benedicta	an	WA 161	C	2	5	7	5	4	2	0	5	D
2 0 beata infantia	an	PM 37 VP 88 WA *31 200 *SYG 18	D	3	0	-2	0	3	2	3	5	D

8	O beata lactentium	an	WA 44	G	2	0	-2	0	2	5	4	2	G
1	O beata Radegundis	an	PM 176	C	5	4	5	2	4	2	0	2	D
1	O beata trinitas te laudamus	re	PM 91	D	-5	-2	0	3	2	0	-2	0	D
1	O beata virgo Maria	an	AR 826² LU 1612	D	3	2	3	5	2	0	3	2	D
7	O beate Joannes corona	re	VP 210	a	-2	-5	-2	0	3	2	0	3	G
1	O beate Oswalde	an	WA 392	D	-2	0	3	2	0	2	0	-2	D
1	O beati martyres	re	WA 377	D	-2	0	3	0	2	0	-2	0	D
1	O beati viri Benedicti	an	WA 301	D	-2	0	3	2	0	2	0	-2	D
4	O beati viri N.	re	LR 210 *WA 297	F	-3	0	-1	0	-1	2	0	-1	E
1	O beatum pontificem	an	AR 919 LU 1750 AM 1118 LA 487	C	2	5	4	2	4	2	0	2	D
1	O beatum praesulem	re	WA 295	D	2	0	-2	0	3	5	3	2	D
2	O beatum virum cujus anima	an	AR 916 LU 1746 AM 1114 *WA 403 LA 480	C	5	4	5	2	4	2	0	2	D
3	O beatum virum in cujus transitu	int	SYG 224	E	1	3	0	3	5	10	8	7	E
8	O beatum virum in cujus transitu	re	VP 243 *LA 485 *WA 401	D	5	3	5	7	5	7	9	7	G
8	O beatum virum Martinum	re	LA 482 *WA 400	D	5	3	5	7	5	7	5	7	G
	O beatum virum Martinum / O virum ineffabilem	ofv	GB 243ᵛ	A	3	7	5	7	5	3	5	3	
1	O beatum virum qui spreto	an	AM 777	D	-2	0	3	2	0	2	0	-2	D
6	O beatum virum qui spreto	an	VP 101	C	5	7	5	7	9	5	9	12	F
	O bona crux diu desiderata / Cum vidisset beatus Andreas	rev	LA 498										
	O bona crux diu desiderata / O bona crux quae	rev	WA 235										
	O bona crux quae decorem / Videns crucem	rev	LA 502										
8	O bona crux quae decorem	re	LA 501 *WA 235	G	-2	-5	-3	-2	-3	-5	-7	-5	G
1	O caelestis norma vitae	an	AM 968 *PM 145 *VP 129	D	3	0	-2	3	5	7	5	3	D
5	O Christi mater caelica	hy	ST 320	c	-3	-7	-5	-3	-2	-3	-5	-7	F
5	O Christi mater caelica	hya	ST 49	c	-3	-5	-3	-2	-3	-5	-7	-5	F
8	O Christi mater caelica	hy	ST 355	a	-2	0	3	0	-7	-2	-4	-2	G
2	O Christi mater caelica	hy	ST 352	D	-2	0	3	5	3	2	0	5	D
6	O Christi pietas omni prosequenda	an	PM 119 WA 242	F	2	4	0	2	0	-3	-5	0	F
1	O claviger regni caelorum	re	VP 182 WA 280 (inc. illeg.)	D	-2	0	3	0	2	0	-2	0	D
2	O clavis David	an	AR 236 LU 341 AM 210 *WA 21 LA 28 LA 28	C	5	4	5	2	4	2	0	2	D

1 O constantia martyrum laudabilis	re	PM 195	D	3	0	-2	0	3	5	3	2	D
4 O crucifer bone lucis sator	hy	ST 479	G	2	0	2	5	4	0	2	0	E
1 O crux admirabile ... adorandus	an	SYG 142	C	2	4	5	4	2	4	2	9	D
1 O crux admirabile ... effusus	an	SYG 141	D	7	5	7	5	3	5	7	3	D
O crux admirabilis evacuatio 　　O crux benedicta	rev	WA 308										
O crux admirabilis evacuatio 　　O crux gloriosa	rev	LA 397										
1 O crux admirabilis evacuatio	an	WA 370	C	2	9	7	9	7	5	4	7	D
1 O crux ave spes unica	hy	LU 1461	F	2	4	5	4	2	0	2	4	D
O crux benedicta quae sola 　　Adoramus te	trv	GR [104]	F	2	-3	0	-5	-3	-1	0	2	
1 O crux benedicta quae sola	an	AR 839 LU 1631 *AM 1046 *WA 370 *LA 395 *SYG 141	C	2	5	7	9	7	4	5	2	D
2 O crux benedicta quae sola	re	LA 396 *WA 308	A	5	3	5	7	5	3	8	5	D
8 O crux benedicta quia in te	an	WA 308 *LA 395 *SYG 142	G	-2	0	-5	-2	0	2	0	2	G
O crux gloriosa	an	WA 370 (inc illeg)										
O crux gloriosa 　　Nos autem gloriari	rev	WA 309										
O crux gloriosa 　　O crux benedicta	rev	LA 396										
7 O crux gloriosa	re	LA 397 *WA 369	G	2	0	2	0	2	4	5	4	G
3 O crux gloriosa	re	VP 151	E	3	0	-2	3	5	8	7	5	E
1 O crux mirabile signum	an	SYG 141	C	2	0	2	4	5	4	2	0	D
1 O crux splendidior cunctis	an	AR 699 LU 1453 AM 898 1039 *WA 309 *LA 399 *SYG 140	C	2	5	2	0	5	7	9	7	D
2 O crux viride lignum	an	VP 152	D	-2	-5	-2	0	-2	0	3	2	D
O custos hominum 　　Nocte os meum	rev	LA 285 WA 173										
8 O Cuthberte	an	WA 296	G	2	0	2	0	5	4	5	7	G
1 O decus virginitatis	re	WA 356	D	3	0	3	2	0	-2	0	-2	D
5 O Dei sapientia	hy	ST 343	F	2	4	2	0	2	4	7	9	F
3 O dignissima Christi sponsa	an	AM 1133 *PM 210	E	-2	1	-2	0	1	0	1	3	E
6 O diligens Christum	re	WA 337	G	5	7	5	7	9	7	9	10	c
2 O doctor optime ecclesiae	an	AR 577[17] [66] LU 262[5] 1188 *AM 665 741	C	5	4	5	2	4	2	0	2	D
8 O Domine quia ego servus	of	GR 453 74** LU 1395	F	4	2	-3	0	-1	0	-3	-1	G

2	O Domine salvum me fac	an	AR 365 AM 341 WA 88 LA 132	F	-1	-3	-1	0	-3	-5	-3	-1	D
2	O Emmanuel rex	an	AR 237 LU 342 AM 211 *WA 22 LA 28	C	5	4	5	2	4	2	0	2	D
	O ... et magnum Gloriosus es Oswaldus	rev	WA 390 (inc illeg)										
1	O felicem virum beatum Joseph	an	AR 183* PM 143 VP 126	D	-2	0	3	2	0	2	0	-2	D
1	O felix Anna peperisti prolem	re	PM 171	a	-2	0	-2	-4	-2	1	0	-2	D
1	O felix Joachim genuisti prolem	re	PM 182	a	-2	0	-2	-4	-2	-4	-2	1	D
6	O felix obedientia	an	PM 125	F	-3	0	-1	0	2	0	-1	-3	F
2	O genitrix aeterni	hy	ST 462	G	2	-2	0	2	4	5	7	9	a
2	O gente felix hospita	hy	AR 325	C	2	5	4	2	0	5	7	9	D
4	O gloriosa Dei genitrix	an	PM 272	E	-2	1	-2	0	-2	-4	0	-2	E
2	O gloriosa domina	hy	ST 87 AM 709 864 1016	d	-2	-5	-7	-2	0	3	2	0	d
2	O gloriosa domina	hy	ST 223	d	-2	-3	-2	-5	-7	-2	0	3	d
3	O gloriosa domina	hy	ST 356	E	1	0	-2	3	1	0	3	5	E
2	O gloriosa virginum	hy	AR [122] LU 1314	a	-2	-5	-7	-2	0	3	2	0	a
6	O gloriosum praesulem	re	PM 131	F	-1	-3	-1	-3	-5	-3	-5	-3	F
1	O grande cunctis gaudium	hy	ST 37	D	7	8	7	5	7	10	9	7	D
2	O Gregori dulcissimum	an	PM 141	C	5	4	5	4	0	2	4	2	D
7	O Hippolyte si credideris	an	WA 349	d	-3	0	2	0	-2	0	-3	-2	G
8	O Hippolyte si credideris	re	WA 351	D	3	5	7	5	7	5	7	9	G
	O inclyte atque sublimis Immaculatas hostiarum preces	ofv	SYG 220	C	2	4	5	7	4	2	5	2	
8	O ineffabilem virum	an	WA 400 *LA 481	c	-1	-3	0	-1	-3	-5	-1	-3	G
5	O insignissime pater	an	WA 284	a	-2	-4	0	3	5	3	0	3	F
	O Joachim sancte conjux	alv	GR 585 LU 1609	D	2	3	2	-2	2	3	0	-2	
	O Juda et Jerusalem		see also Judaea et Jerusalem										
	O Juda et Jerusalem Sanctificamini filii	rev	WA 25										
7	O Juda qui dereliquisti	re	WA 120	G	2	5	4	2	4	0	2	0	G
1	O laudanda sancti Benedicti	re	LR 326	D	-2	0	3	2	0	2	0	-2	D
2	O lux beata caelitum	hy	AR 321 LU 475	C	2	5	4	2	0	5	7	9	D
8	O lux beata trinitas	hy	ST 85	a	-2	-4	-7	-4	-5	-4	-2	0	G
8	O lux beata trinitas	hy	ST 252	a	-2	-4	-7	-4	0	-4	-2	0	G
1	O lux beata trinitas	hy	AM 163	a	-2	0	-2	-4	-5	-7	-9	-5	D
8	O lux beata trinitas	hy	AM 163 533	G	2	0	-2	-5	-3	-2	0	2	G

8 0 lux beata trinitas	hy	ST 211 364	G	2	0	-2	-5	-2	0	2	0	G
8 0 lux beata trinitas	hy	ST 180	G	2	0	-2	-3	-2	-5	-2	-3	G
2 0 lux beata trinitas	hy	ST 271	C	5	4	2	0	2	5	2	4	D
2 0 magni meriti Maria	re	WA 335	D	-2	0	-2	0	2	3	2	0	D
3 0 magnum mysterium et admirabile	re	LU 382 *LR 61 *LA 35 *WA 28	G	2	4	5	4	5	4	2	4	E
7 0 magnum pietatis opus	an	AR 700 LU 1459 AM 899 1040 WA 369 LA 462	d	-3	0	2	0	2	0	-3	-2	G
8 0 Maria Jesse virga	an	PM 253 SYG 17	G	5	4	2	0	-2	0	2	5	G
6 0 Maria mater pia	an	WA 339	c	-1	0	-3	-1	-3	-5	0	2	c
1 0 Martine o pie	an	WA 402	D	3	2	0	-2	0	2	0	3	D
1 0 martyr egregie Victor	re	PM 345	C	2	5	7	5	4	2	4	2	D
1 0 mi pastor egregie	hy	ST 329	D	7	8	7	5	7	3	2	0	D
0 mira Christi regis Rex noster in cruce	anv	WA 131 223	D	5	7	5	7	10	12	10	9	
8 0 mira res filia	an	PM 252	G	-2	-5	-3	-2	-3	-5	-7	-5	G
8 0 mirae pietatis homo	re	WA 250	G	2	0	-3	-2	-5	0	2	0	G
1 0 mirum et magnum miraculum	re	VP 190	D	-2	0	-2	0	3	5	3	5	D
4 0 mors ero mors tua	an	AR 440 OHS 618 LU 773 AM 445 *WA 127 LA 206	c	2	0	2	4	0	2	-3	2	a
4 0 mulier magna est fides	an	AR 377 LU 1084 AM 350 *WA 92 *LA 135 140	G	2	5	7	5	7	9	5	7	a
8 0 mulier sancta lacrimarum	re	WA 337	G	2	0	-2	2	0	-2	0	2	G
2 0 mundi domina regis	an	PM 252	C	5	4	5	2	4	2	0	2	D
4 0 mundi lampas et margarita	an	PM 170	E	-2	1	-2	0	-2	-4	-2	0	E
1 0 nata lux de lumine	hy	ST 161	a	-7	0	-2	-4	-5	-2	0	1	D
8 0 nata lux de lumine	hy	ST 422	G	2	0	-2	0	2	4	0	-2	G
1 0 Nazarene dux Bethleem	hy	ST 117	D	-2	2	3	2	0	3	7	5	D
4 0 nimis felix meritique celsi	hy	AM 926	E	-2	0	1	3	5	3	5	3	E
1 0 nimis felix meritique celsi	hy	AR 738	D	-2	0	3	0	3	5	3	5	D
2 0 nimis felix meritique celsi	hy	ST 95	D	-2	0	3	2	0	2	0	-2	D
4 0 nimis felix meritique celsi	hy	ST 233	E	-2	0	3	5	3	5	3	1	E
2 0 nimis felix meritique celsi	hy	AR 737	C	2	5	2	4	2	0	2	4	D
2 0 oriens splendor lucis	an	AR 236 LU 342 *AM 210 *WA 21 LA 28	C	5	4	5	2	4	2	0	2	D
1 0 pastor aeterne	an	WA 238	D	3	0	-2	3	5	7	9	7	D
4 0 pastor apostolice	re	WA 290	D	5	3	7	5	3	5	3	2	E

2	0	O pater sancte mitis atque pie	hy	ST 456	a	-2	0	-2	0	2	0	-2	0	D
2	0	O pater sancte mitis atque pie	hy	ST 391	D	-2	0	2	3	0	3	0	-2	D
2	0	O pater sancte mitis atque pie	hy	ST 423	F	2	0	2	4	2	0	2	4	D
8	0	O per omnia laudabilem	an	WA 242	G	-2	-5	-2	0	2	0	-2	0	G
1	0	O Petre pastor summe	an	WA 325	D	3	0	-2	3	5	3	5	7	D
2	0	O pie Deus qui primum hominem	of	OTT 178 *SYG 237	D	2	3	2	0	-2	0	2	0	D
6	0	O pietatis Deus qui mundum	an	GB 158^v	D	-2	-5	-2	0	-2	0	3	2	F
5	0	O praeclara Constantia	hy	ST 321	F	2	4	5	4	2	0	2	0	F
1	0	O praeclara stella maris	re	VP 187	D	-2	0	3	5	3	2	0	2	D
2	0	O praeferenda gloria	hy	ST 39	a	-2	3	2	0	7	5	3	2	a
2	0	O prima virgo prodita	hy	AR 1 (sup 3) LU 1600	a	-2	-5	-7	-2	0	3	2	0	a
1	0	O princeps apostolorum	re	WA 278	a	-2	0	-2	-4	-2	0	-4	0	D
2	0	O qualem gloriam meruerunt	an	PM 43	C	5	4	5	2	4	2	0	2	D
6	0	O quam admirabile est nomen	an	WA 33	F	2	0	2	4	2	0	2	0	F
6	0	O quam admirabile nomen	an	LR 289	F	2	5	4	2	0	2	5	2	F
2	0	O quam admirabilis vir	re	WA 390	a	-2	0	3	7	5	3	2	0	a
	0	O quam beata es virgo	alv	GB 223	G	2	0	2	5	7	5	4	5	
4	0	O quam beata femina	hy	ST 152	D	3	2	0	2	5	2	3	2	E
2	0	O quam beatus es pie	re	WA 392	D	2	-2	0	2	5	3	2	0	D
	0	O quam beatus est Dei	alv	GB 227	G	2	0	2	5	7	5	4	5	
6	0	O quam bonus et suavis	an	AR 4 (sup 2)	F	-3	-5	0	2	0	2	4	0	F
	0	O quam bonus et suavis	alv	GR 303 LU 898	a	-2	-5	-4	-2	-4	-2	-7	-9	
	0	O quam bonus et suavis Emitte spiritum	trv	GR [93] LU 1279	D	-2	0	3	5	7	3	2	5	
7	0	O quam casta mater	an	SYG 17	G	2	-2	2	5	2	4	2	0	G
	0	O quam dulcem vocem Dixit Dominus Mariae	rev	WA 336	D	7	5	7	5	3	2	0	3	
3	0	O quam glorifica luce coruscas	hy	ST 398	E	-2	0	3	1	0	3	5	3	E
2	0	O quam glorifica luce coruscas	hy	AR 134* PM 180 LU 1864 VP 43 ST 41 96 193	D	-2	0	3	2	0	2	0	-2	D
3	0	O quam glorifica luce coruscas	hy	ST 132	E	1	-2	3	5	8	7	5	3	E
8	0	O quam glorifica luce coruscas	hy	ST 207	G	2	4	0	5	2	0	-2	0	G
1	0	O quam glorifica luce coruscas	hy	ST 192	C	2	5	7	5	2	0	2	0	D
6	0	O quam gloriosum ... gaudent innocentes	an	WA 45	E	1	-2	-4	1	3	1	3	5	F
6	0	O quam gloriosum ... gaudent omnes	an	AR 903 LU 1732 AM 1107 1123 *LA 479	F	-3	-5	0	2	0	2	4	0	F

	Text		Source										
1	O quam gloriosum ... gaudent omnes	re	WA 396	F	-3	-1	-3	-1	-3	-5	-3	4	D
1	O quam gloriosum ... regnant innocentes	re	VP 84	D	-2	0	3	5	3	2	0	2	D
	O quam gloriosum ... regnant omnes	alv	SYG 222	G	2	5	7	9	7	5	7	9	
2	O quam gloriosus est beatus Stephanus	an	LA 48	C	5	4	5	4	2	4	2	0	D
6	O quam metuendus est locus	an	AR [113] LU 1249 AM 702 *WA 317 *LA 553	F	-3	-5	0	2	0	2	4	0	F
1	O quam metuendus est locus	re	LR 239 *LA 550	D	2	3	5	3	0	3	5	3	D
	O quam mirifica		see also O quam glorifica										
3	O quam mirifica luce coruscas	hy	ST 129	c	-3	-1	0	2	-1	0	-1	-3	E
4	O quam praeclara sunt	an	AM 817	E	1	3	1	-2	-4	-2	0	3	E
6	O quam praeclara sunt	an	VP 106	D	3	5	7	3	5	8	7	5	F
	O quam pretiosum est regnum	alv	GB 239^V	G	5	7	9	7	5	7	9	7	
7	O quam pulchra est casta generatio	an	LR 213 WA 432 LA 541	d	-3	0	2	0	-2	0	-3	-2	G
	O quam pulchra est casta generatio	alv	GR 104**	D	2	3	2	-2	2	3	0	-2	
	O quam pulchra est casta generatio	alv	GR [58] LU 1223 GB 223^V	C	2	4	2	0	5	7	9	10	
1	O quam pulchri super montes	re	VP 252	D	-2	0	3	2	0	2	-2	3	D
1	O quam speciosa est Maria	an	PM 180	D	3	2	0	-2	0	3	2	0	D
6	O quam speciosi pedes	an	AR 778 LU 1550	F	-3	-5	0	2	0	2	4	0	F
6	O quam suavis est Domine	an	AR 529 97* LU 917 *AM 548 VP 8 4*	F	2	4	0	2	0	-1	-3	-5	F
1	O quam veneranda es egregie	an	LA 537	C	2	0	5	7	5	4	2	5	D
1	O quanta qualia sunt illa sabbata	hy	ST 324	D	3	5	7	9	7	5	7	0	D
1	O quantum in cruce spirant amorem	an	PM 157 VP 169	D	3	2	3	7	5	7	3	5	D
4	O quantus erat luctus hominum	re	LA 486 *WA 401	F	-3	2	-1	0	2	4	2	4	E
1	O quantus luctus hominum	an	LA 487 *WA 402	C	2	5	2	4	2	0	2	0	D
2	O radix Jesse	an	AR 235 LU 341 AM 209 *WA 21 LA 28	C	5	4	5	2	4	2	0	2	D
3	O redemptor sume carmen	hy	ST 496	G	2	0	-2	-3	-2	-3	-2	0	E
2	O redemptor sume carmen	hy	OHS 425	D	3	0	-2	0	3	5	3	2	D
2	O redemptor sume carmen	hy	ST 495	D	3	0	-2	3	5	7	5	7	D
2	O redemptor sume carmen	hy	WA 212	D	3	2	-2	0	3	5	3	2	D
1	O redundans flos caelestis	an	VP 192	D	3	0	2	0	-2	0	-2	3	D
1	O regem caeli cui talia	re	PM 36 LR 397 *LA 35 *WA 30	a	-2	0	-2	-4	-2	1	0	-2	D
1	O rex benigne Domine	hy	ST 245	D	3	2	0	-2	3	5	7	5	D

2	0	rex gentium	an	AR 236 LU 342 AM 211 *WA 22 LA 28	c	5	4	5	2	4	2	0	2	D
2	0	rex gloriae Domine	an	AR 496 LU 853 AM 512 *WA 150 LA 252	C	5	4	5	2	4	2	0	2	D
2	0	rex gloriae et tuorum	an	PM 346	C	5	4	5	2	4	2	0	2	D
2	0	rex justitiae	an	WA 248	C	5	4	5	4	2	4	2	0	D
	0	robur apostolice Pretiosus vir	rev	WA 312	D	7	5	7	5	3	2	0	2	
4	0	Roma felix quae tantorum principum	hy	ST 96	F	-1	-3	-5	-3	0	-1	0	2	E
4	0	sacerdotum nobilissime	re	WA 392 (inc illeg)										
5	0	sacrum convivium	an	AR 535 98* LU 959 AM 555 VP 9 4*	a	-2	-4	0	3	5	3	5	7	F
5	0	salutaris hostia fulget dies	hy	ST 314	a	-1	0	2	0	2	0	2	4	F
4	0	salutaris hostia quae caeli	hy	AR 93*	F	-1	0	2	4	2	0	-3	0	E
7	0	salutaris hostia quae caeli	hy	AR 94* LU 1854	G	2	0	-2	0	2	0	2	4	G
6	0	salutaris hostia quae caeli	hy	ST 459	F	2	4	2	4	5	0	2	0	F
8	0	salutaris hostia quae caeli	hy	AR 93*	G	2	5	4	2	0	-2	2	0	G
1	0	salutaris hostia quae caeli	hy	AR 94*	C	2	9	10	9	7	9	7	5	D
2	0	sancta mundi domina	hy	ST 236	D	-2	0	3	0	-5	0	-2	0	D
2	0	sancta mundi domina	hy	ST 300	D	-2	0	3	2	0	2	3	0	D
8	0	sancta mundi domina	hy	ST 399	G	2	0	2	0	-2	0	2	5	G
	0	sancte Dei pretiose Sancte Christi	rev	VP 258	D	3	0	-2	0	3	2	3	5	
8	0	sancte N. concivis	re	WA 418	G	2	0	2	0	-2	2	5	2	G
	0	sancte N. sidus Sancte N. confessor	rev	WA 428	D	2	0	-2	0	3	2	3	2	
2	0	sapientia quae ex ore	an	AR 234 LU 340 AM 208 WA 21 *LA 27	C	5	4	5	4	2	4	2	0	D
4	0	sator rerum reparator aevi	hy	ST 422	G	4	5	7	9	7	5	4	2	b
7	0	singularis femina	hy	ST 398	G	2	4	5	4	2	0	5	7	G
8	0	sol salutis intimis	hy	AR 366	G	-2	-3	-2	2	0	-2	0	2	G
2	0	sol salutis intimis	hy	AR 367	A	3	5	8	5	3	5	3	7	D
3	0	sola magnarum urbium	hy	AM 292	D	2	3	5	7	0	2	3	5	E
3	0	sola magnarum urbium	hy	AR 313 LU 456	D	2	3	5	7	0	2	5	3	E
4	0	Thoma Christi	hy	ST 240	F	-1	-3	-5	-3	0	-3	-1	0	E
2	0	Thoma Didyme	an	WA 247 *LA 28	C	5	4	5	4	2	4	2	0	D
7	0	venerabiliter pia	re	WA 338	G	-2	0	3	2	0	2	0	3	G

	Incipit		Source										
6	O veneranda martyrum gloriosa	re	VP 255 *WA 423	F	2	0	2	4	2	4	7	2	F
2	O veneranda trinitas laudanda	hy	ST 392	D	-2	0	2	3	0	3	0	-2	D
2	O veneranda trinitas laudanda	hy	ST 422	F	2	0	2	4	2	0	2	4	D
3	O vera summa sempiterna trinitas	an	WA 162	G	2	5	4	2	4	2	0	2	E
4	O vera summa sempiterna unitas	an	WA 162	E	1	3	5	3	1	0	-2	0	E
4	O verbum fidelissimum	hy	ST 236	E	-2	0	3	1	0	-2	0	3	E
4	O vere beatum in cujus ore	re	LA 482	F	-1	-3	-1	-3	-1	0	2	4	E
3	O vere beatum o ineffabilem pietate	an	PM 206 *WA 405	G	2	5	2	0	2	5	0	4	E
1	O Verena sponsa Christi	hy	ST 323	a	1	0	-2	0	-2	-4	-5	-7	D
	O virgo ineffabiliter Quae est ista quae penetravit	rev	VP 204										
4	O virgo Maria quae genuisti	an	PM 273	D	3	2	0	5	3	5	7	5	E
5	O virgo sole purior	hy	ST 21	G	2	0	-3	-7	-2	-3	-5	-7	C
7	O virgo super virgines benedicta	an	PM 255	G	2	5	7	5	7	0	2	0	G
2	O virgo virginum quomodo fiet	an	PM 246 *WA 22 LA 28	C	5	4	5	2	4	2	0	2	D
	O viri ad vos clamito Adversio parvulorum	rev	WA 171	c	2	5	4	5	4	2	4	2	
1	O viri misericordiae	an	AM 973	C	2	9	11	9	7	5	7	9	D
	O virum ineffabilem O vere beatum	rev	LA 482										
	O virum ineffabilem Oculis ac manibus	rev	WA 400										
8	O virum ineffabilem	an	AR 917 LU 1749 AM 1115 *WA 402 LA 486	G	2	0	-2	2	4	2	0	-2	G
2	O virum ineffabilem	of	GB 243[V]	A	3	5	7	5	3	5	7	5	D
	O vos omnes ... sicut	sr	AR 846 LU 1632										
	O vos omnes ... [sicut] Caligaverunt	rev	OHS 508 LU 712 LA 203 WA 123										
8	O vos omnes ... sicut	an	AR 441 PM 189 OHS 623 LU 776[B] AM 448 449 WA 127 LA 206	c	-3	-1	-3	-5	-3	-5	-7	-3	G
	O vos omnes ... sicut Stabat sancta Maria	trv	GR 471 LU 1634	F	2	4	2	0	2	4	2	4	
	O vos omnes ... sicut	alv	GR 597 LU 1634[V]	F	4	2	4	0	-1	-3	0	2	
8	O vos omnes ... similis	re	OHS 610 LU 767 LA 204 WA 125	c	-3	-1	-3	-5	-3	-5	-7	-3	G
2	O vos unanimes Christiadum chori	hy	AM 908 *LR 452	G	2	4	2	0	2	5	2	0	a
7	Obaudite me divini fructus	an	PM 193	G	5	4	2	0	2	5	7	5	G
8	Obduxere polum nubila caeli	hy	ST 493	G	2	4	2	0	2	5	4	2	G

	Title	Type	Sources		1	2	3	4	5	6	7	8	
7	Obedientiae pennis elatus	an	AM 778	G	4	5	7	5	4	5	7	9	G
7	Obedientiae speculum Maurus	an	LR 279	G	4	5	7	5	4	5	7	9	G
2	Oblatus est quia ipse voluit	an	AR 433 OHS 404 LU 657 AM 418 419 LA 194 WA 120	F	-1	-3	-5	-3	0	2	0	4	D
1	Obsecro Domine aufer	an	AR 541 LU 987 AM 577 *LA 275	D	-2	2	3	5	3	0	-2	3	D
5	Obsecro Domine memento	an	AR 543 LU 989 *AM 579	F	4	7	9	7	9	12	11	9	F
5	Obsecro Domine mitte	re	LA 5 *WA 5	a	-4	0	3	2	3	2	0	3	F
6	Observa fili praecepta	an	AR 545 LU 991 *AM 582 *LA 281	E	1	-2	-4	1	3	1	3	5	F
	Observa igitur et audi Audi Israel	rev	LA 160 WA 102										
	Obtulerunt discipuli Domino	alv	SYG 156	G	2	4	2	0	2	4	5	4	
1	Obtulerunt discipuli Domino	an	AR 482 AM 497 WA 134 LA 219	C	2	9	10	9	7	5	7	9	D
	Obtulerunt discipuli Domino	alv	GB 133^v	D	3	5	7	5	3	5	3	0	
4	Obtulerunt pro eo Domino	re	WA 269	F	-3	0	-1	0	-1	0	-1	0	E
2	Obtulerunt pro eo Domino	re	GR 431 PM 136 LU 1360 LA 351	A	3	5	7	5	8	7	8	5	D
8	Obtulerunt pro eo Domino	an	AR 621 LU 1366 AM 803 WA 270 LA 355	F	4	7	6	2	6	7	4	2	G
	Obtulerunt sacrificium In dedicatione	rev	LA 548										
8	Obviam procedunt Cherubim	an	WA 359	G	-2	-5	-2	-3	-2	0	-7	-5	G
8	Obviam sacratissimis	re	LR 370	F	2	4	2	4	2	4	6	4	G
3	Occasum tanti pontificis	re	WA 285	E	-2	3	5	8	7	5	7	8	E
6	Occurrit beato Joanni	an	WA 39 LA 49	c	2	0	2	0	2	4	0	2	c
7	Occurrit piissimae genetrici	an	WA 359	G	2	4	5	7	9	7	5	7	G
8	Occurrunt turbae cum floribus	an	GR 174 OHS 97 LU 584 *WA 114 209 *LA 183 *GB 107 *SYG 118	a	-4	-2	0	-2	-4	0	3	5	G
8	Occurrunt turbae cum floribus ... in excelsis	an	PM 58	a	-4	-2	0	-2	-4	0	3	5	G
7	Octava decima die	re	WA 22	G	5	4	5	7	5	2	5	4	G
4	Oculi Domini respexerunt	an	LR 176	a	-2	0	3	5	3	5	7	5	a
1	Oculi mei ad fideles	of	GR (36)	D	7	8	7	10	7	5	7	5	D
4	Oculi mei semper ad Dominum	an	WA 60 *LA 80	b	-4	-2	1	3	1	-1	1	-1	a
7	Oculi mei semper ad Dominum quia	int	GR 123 LU 552 SYG 92 GB 82 *GS 54	G	7	9	7	9	5	7	4	2	G

	Incipit		Sources										
7	Oculi omnium in te sperant	gr	GR 314 [96] LU 944 SYG 97 GB 86^v *GS 59 164	G	2	4	5	7	5	4	2	0	G
7	Oculi tui Deus respexerunt	an	WA 283	G	4	5	7	9	7	5	4	2	G
7	Oculi tui sancta Dei genitrix	an	WA 353	G	4	5	7	5	9	7	4	7	G
	Oculi tui sicut columbae Pulchra es o virgo	rev	PM 263	a	-2	0	1	0	-2	0	-2	-4	
	Oculis ac manibus in caelum Dum sacramenta	rev	LA 483										
	Oculis ac manibus in caelum	alv	GB 242^v	D	-2	0	2	3	5	7	5	3	
4	Oculis ac manibus in caelum	re	LA 483 WA 400	C	2	5	2	4	5	4	5	7	E
	Oculis ac manibus in caelum	alv	SYG 225	G	4	5	4	2	0	2	4	2	
7	Oculis ac manibus in caelum	an	AR 918 LU 1749 AM 1116 *WA 402 LA 487	G	4	5	7	9	7	5	9	10	G
	Oculus Dei respexit illum	alv	GR 604 LU 1646	D	-2	-5	-2	0	-2	2	5	2	
7	Oculus Dei respexit illum	int	GR 448 LU 1392	G	7	10	9	10	9	10	7	9	G
7	Odo princeps altissime	hy	ST 64	a	2	3	5	2	3	0	2	3	G
4	Odor nominis tui o Maria	an	PM 188	C	2	5	4	5	2	4	2	0	E
	Offenditur ultro condonat O mirae pietatis	rev	WA 250	a	3	2	-2	2	0	2	3	0	
	Offerens autem urceum		see Afferens autem urceum										
	Offerentur regi		see Afferentur regi										
4	Oleo caput meum	an	WA 338	E	-2	0	3	5	3	1	3	1	E
	Oleum effusum nomen tuum Domine Deus virtutum	trv	GR 53	G	-5	0	2	5	2	5	7	5	
	Oleum effusum nomen tuum Inveni quem diligit	trv	GR (11)	G	2	4	5	4	5	7	5	0	
8	Oleum effusum nomen tuum	an	AR 301 LU 445 *AM 279	G	5	2	0	2	0	-2	0	2	G
7	Omne quod dat mihi Pater	an	AR [146] LU 1776 AM 1154 WA 438 LA 560	d	-3	0	2	0	2	0	-2	0	G
7	Omne quod dat mihi Pater	co	GB 266^v	D	-3	0	2	0	3	2	0	-2	G
	Omne quod est in mundo Nolite diligere	trv	GR 22**	G	-5	0	2	5	2	5	7	5	
3	Omnes amici mei derelinquerunt	re	OHS 485 LU 693 *LA 195 *WA 122	G	4	5	2	4	5	4	2	0	E
5	Omnes angeli ejus	an	AR 354 WA 79 *LA 92 124	F	2	0	4	7	9	7	9	7	F
4	Omnes autem vos fratres	an	AR 383 LA 144	C	2	4	5	4	5	7	4	5	E
8	Omnes collaudant nomen	an	OHS 101 LU 588	G	-3	-2	-3	-5	-3	-5	-2	0	G
8	Omnes collaudant nomen	an	WA 113	F	2	4	2	4	2	0	4	7	G

	Omnes de Saba venient	sr	LA 75											
	Omnes de Saba venient Reges Tharsis	rev	LR 72 WA 55											
8	Omnes de Saba venient	an	AR 333 LU 482 AM 300	c	-1	-5	-1	0	-3	-5	-3	-5	G
7	Omnes de Saba venient ... laudem	re	LR 76 *LA 70 *WA 53	d	-5	-3	-2	0	-2	0	2	0	G
8	Omnes de Saba venient ... laudem	an	WA 57	F	2	4	2	0	4	7	6	4	G
5	Omnes de Saba venient ... laudem	gr	GR 57 LU 459 *SYG 30 *GB 33 GS J 19	F	2	4	2	4	7	9	6	7	F
8	Omnes gentes per gyrum	an	AR 928 LU 1761 *AM 1146 *WA 410 LA 496	c	2	0	-1	0	-3	0	-1	-5	G
	Omnes gentes plaudite manibus Viri Galilaei	intv	GR 285 LU 846 GB 178ᵛ										
6	Omnes gentes plaudite manibus	int	GR 336 LU 1009 SYG 178 *GB 177 *GS 133 148	F	-3	-5	-3	0	4	2	4	0	F
	Omnes gentes plaudite manibus	alv	GR 337 LU 1011 *SYG 241 *GS 133 *GB 177	F	2	5	7	2	0	7	5	7	
	Omnes gentes plaudite manibus Ascendit Deus	ofv	OTT 75 SYG 179 *GB 177	D	7	9	7	10	9	7	5	9	
4	Omnes gentes quascumque fecisti	an	LR 73 *WA 54 LA 69 *GB 119	F	-3	0	-3	-1	0	2	0	-1	E
8	Omnes gentes quascumque fecisti	co	GR 55 LU 449	F	2	4	2	4	2	0	2	0	G
1	Omnes gentes quascumque fecisti	gr	GR 78**	D	3	0	3	0	3	7	5	3	D
	Omnes in unum congregati Corde et animo	rev	WA 367										
	Omnes inimici mei adversum Contumelias et terrores	rev	LA 178										
	Omnes inimici mei adversum Eram quasi agnus	rev	OHS 396 LU 649 LA 192 WA 119										
	Omnes inimici mei adversum Qui custodiebant	rev	LA 170 WA 107										
7	Omnes inimici mei audierunt	an	AR 431 OHS 308 AM 410 *WA 117 LA 187	G	4	5	7	9	7	5	9	10	G
	Omnes montes qui in circuitu Montes Gelboe	rev	LA 269 *WA 165	G	5	4	0	2	4	2	5	7	
7	Omnes nationes venient	an	AR 333 AM 299 WA 57	G	4	5	7	5	9	7	9	5	G
	Omnes pariter congregati Corde et animo	rev	LA 459										
1	Omnes qui habebant infirmos	an	AR 394 LU 1091 AM 369 *WA 157	D	2	3	5	2	3	2	0	-2	D

	Incipit	type	Sources										
2	Omnes qui in Christo baptizati	co	GR 261 OHS 829 LU 807 SYG 162 GB 144^v GS 124	D	-5	-2	0	-2	0	2	3	0	D
	Omnes qui videbant me Deus Deus meus	trv	GR 180 OHS 109 LU 594 GS 86 *GB 109 *SYG 122	F	-3	0	-3	0	2	0	2	4	
8	Omnes sancti quanta passi	an	AR [41] LU 1153 AM 647	G	-5	-2	0	2	0	2	-2	0	G
6	Omnes sancti qui estis	re	WA 397	c	2	0	2	4	2	0	-3	-2	c
	Omnes scribentur in libro Ambulabunt mecum	rev	WA 45										
8	Omnes sitientes venite	an	AR 214 LU 324 *AM 188 WA 7 *LA 6	d	-3	0	2	0	-3	0	2	0	G
8	Omnes sunt administratorii	an	AM 1066 *AR 865	F	2	4	2	0	2	4	0	2	G
4	Omnes superni ordines	hy	ST 237	E	1	-2	1	-2	-4	-2	0	-2	E
8	Omnes terrarum incolae	hy	ST 166	F	2	4	2	4	2	0	4	2	G
2	Omnes terrarum incolae	hy	ST 94	C	2	9	10	9	7	9	7	5	D
	Omnes virtutes et omnis Agmina sacra	rev	WA 391										
8	Omni tempore benedic Deum	re	LA 288 *WA 176	D	3	5	7	5	7	9	7	5	G
	Omnia enim corda Quae sunt in corde	rev	LA 280 WA 170										
	Omnia enim judicia tua Peto Domine	rev	LR 423 LA 288 WA 176										
	Omnia judicia tua	see Omnia enim judicia											
	Omnia per ipsum facta In principio erat	rev	LR 66										
	Omnia per ipsum facta Verbum caro	rev	LU 390										
3	Omnia quae fecisti nobis	int	GR 377 LU 1063 *SYG 114 *GB 102 *GB 76 164	G	5	2	5	0	5	2	7	5	E
3	Omnia quaecumque voluit	an	AM 143 WA 67 *LA 96	G	2	5	4	2	0	2	0	-2	E
	Omnia quaecumque voluit ... in caelo Laudabile miraculum	rev	WA 289	d	-2	0	3	0	3	2	3	5	
	Omnibus omnia factus sum	alv	GR 68**	G	2	5	2	4	2	0	5	7	
2	Omnipotens adorande colende	re	PM 128 *LA 337 *WA 255	E	3	5	8	5	8	7	5	7	a
7	Omnipotens Deus maestorum	an	GB 159	F	2	4	7	4	2	4	2	4	G
8	Omnipotens Deus supplices	an	WA 230	F	2	4	7	4	2	4	2	4	G
2	Omnipotens sermo tuus	an	AR 252 LU 357 *AM 228 *WA 19 25 *LA 22	F	-1	0	-3	-5	-3	0	-1	-5	D
	Omnipotentem semper adorant	see Omnipotentem semper adorent											

	Incipit	Type	Sources										
4	Omnipotentem semper adorent	hy	ST 489 GS 172	C	2	0	2	5	4	5	4	5	E
4	Omnipotentem semper adorent	hy	SYG 252	C	2	4	5	4	5	7	5	4	E
2	Omnipotentem semper adorent	hy	ST 489	C	2	5	2	4	2	0	5	7	D
	Omnis enim natura Si quis putat	trv	GR 31**	C	2	5	4	5	7	5	7	2	
4	Omnis expertem maculae Mariam	hy	AR 635 LU 1382	E	-2	1	-2	-4	0	1	3	5	E
2	Omnis gloria ejus filiae	tr	GR 104**	D	-2	0	-2	-5	-2	0	-2	0	D
3	Omnis gloria ejus filiae	int	GR 47**	E	1	0	-2	3	5	3	5	8	E
3	Omnis interea populus	an	WA 234	c	-1	-3	-1	-3	-5	-3	-1	-3	E
8	Omnis plebs ut vidit	an	WA 83	c	2	0	-1	0	-3	-5	-1	-5	G
1 2	Omnis pulchritudo Domini	re	PM 85 LR 97 LA 245 *WA 147	F	-1	0	-3	-5	-3	-1	0	2	D
8	Omnis qui invocaverit nomen	an	AR 298 LU 451 AM 276	G	-5	-2	0	2	0	2	0	-2	G
1	Omnis qui petit accipit	an	LA 243	D	2	3	5	2	3	5	2	3	D
1	Omnis qui se exaltat	an	WA 189	D	-2	0	2	3	5	2	5	7	D
2	Omnis sanctorum concio	hy	AM 984	a	-2	-5	-7	-2	0	3	2	0	a
8	Omnis sapientia a Domino	an	AR 544 LU 990 AM 581 WA 168 *LA 280	F	2	4	2	4	2	-1	0	2	G
7	Omnis spiritus laudet Dominum	an	AR 189 [180] LU 1803 AM 1165 1166 WA 438 *LA 559	G	4	5	7	9	7	5	2	4	G
	Omnis terra adoret te	sr	AR 704 LU 1459										
4	Omnis terra adoret te	an	LR 70 *WA 53 LA 67	F	-3	0	-3	-1	0	2	0	-1	E
4	Omnis terra adoret te	int	GR 67 LU 484 SYG 35 GB 37 GS 21	F	-3	0	-1	2	4	2	4	7	E
	Omnis terra adoret te	alv	SYG 35 GB 37^v	C	2	4	2	4	5	4	5	4	
5	Omnis vallis implebitur	an	WA 20 *LA 27	F	4	7	6	4	2	4	2	0	F
4	Omnium Christe pariter tuorum	hy	ST 64	E	-2	-4	0	-2	0	3	0	-2	E
2	Omnium Christe pariter tuorum	hy	ST 98	G	7	9	7	5	7	10	9	7	d
	Omnium est enim artifex Spiritus Domini	rev	LR 118 LA 256 WA 155										
1	Omnium sanctorum chori	an	LA 478	D	-2	0	3	0	2	3	2	0	D
2	Opera manuum tuarum	an	AR [145] LU 1775 *AM 1153 1154 *WA 435 *LA 560	F	-1	-3	-5	-3	-5	0	2	0	D
8	Opera quae ego facio	an	WA 95	G	5	2	0	-2	0	2	0	-2	G
8	Operamini non cibum	an	WA 100 *LA 155	G	-2	-5	-2	0	2	0	2	0	G
2	Operarii qui de illius fama	re	LR 282	D	-2	0	3	2	0	-2	0	2	D

	Incipit		Source										
2	Operibus sanctis Nicholaus	re	WA 239	D	-2	-5	-2	0	3	2	0	-2	D
	Operuisti omnia peccata Benedixisti Domine	ofv	OTT 8 *GB 6 *SYG 7	G	-3	2	5	2	4	5	4	5	
	Operuit caelos majestas Domine audivi	trv	GR 206 OHS 529 LU 721 GS 98 GB 116 SYG 136	F	2	4	2	0	2	0	-3	-1	
1	Opes decusque regium reliqueras	hy	AR 782	D	-2	0	2	3	7	5	2	3	D
	Opes et divitiae		see also Gloria et divitiae										
	Opes et divitiae in domo Beatus vir qui timet	trv	LU 1442	G	2	4	5	4	5	7	5	0	
	Oportebat pati Christum	alv	GR 267 LU 822 GS 126 SYG 155 GB 133^v	E	-2	0	-2	-4	-2	-4	-2	-4	
8	Oportebat pati Christum	an	AR 486 *AM 503 WA 139 *LA 219 232	F	2	4	2	0	4	7	6	2	G
8	Oportet nos mundum	an	GB 158	G	5	2	0	2	0	2	0	-2	G
3	Oportet te fili gaudere	co	SYG 92	G	2	4	2	4	5	4	2	4	E
3	Oportet te fili gaudere	co	GB 81^v	G	4	2	4	5	4	5	4	2	E
8	Oportet te fili gaudere	co	GR 122 *GS 54	G	5	2	0	2	-2	2	0	2	G
2	Oppressit me dolor	an	AR 847 LU 1642 AM 1051	D	-2	0	3	0	3	0	-2	0	D
2	Opprobrium factus sum nimis	re	OHS 185 (nm) LA 180	A	3	5	7	5	8	7	8	10	D
	Optans suorum Maria Maria Magdalene ut cognovit	rev	WA 336	c	4	7	5	7	5	4	7	9	
2	Optatus votis omnium	hy	ST 10	E	-2	0	-2	-4	-2	0	1	3	D
8	Optatus votis omnium	hy	ST 419	G	2	0	-2	0	2	4	0	-2	G
1	Optatus votis omnium	hy	ST 36	D	7	8	7	5	7	10	9	7	D
1	Optatus votis omnium	hy	PM 84 VP 155	D	7	9	7	5	7	10	9	7	D
8	Optimam partem elegit	co	GR (33)	G	2	0	-2	0	2	4	5	0	G
	Optimam partem elegit	alv	GS p 191	a	3	2	0	3	-2	0	-2	-4	
	Optimam partem quae non valet Relinquens Maria	rev	WA 336	c	-1	-3	-5	0	2	5	4	2	
	Ora pro hiis ovibus Simon Barjona	rev	WA 341	a	-2	0	3	2	-2	3	0	-2	
8	Ora pro nobis beata Anna	an	WA 340	G	5	2	0	-2	0	2	0	4	G
	Ora pro nobis beate Clemens	alv	GB 245	D	-2	0	2	3	5	7	5	3	
2	Ora pro nobis beate Martine	gr	SYG 225	D	2	3	2	3	2	0	3	5	D
8	Ora pro nobis beate Martine	an	WA 402	G	5	2	0	-2	0	2	0	4	G
4	Ora pro nobis beate Martine	re	WA 401	D	5	2	3	0	2	0	5	7	E
	Ora pro populo interveni pro clero Felix namque	rev	AR 127* PM 242 LR 255 LA 447 WA 357										

	Incipit		Sources										
8	Orabat Judas Deus	an	WA 309 *LA 398	G	5	4	2	4	2	0	4	5	G
1	Orabat sanctus Benedictus	an	WA 298	D	3	0	-2	3	5	3	5	7	D
7	Orabat sanctus Joannes	an	WA 40	G	5	4	5	7	9	7	5	4	G
1	Oramus te beatissime	an	WA 334	D	2	0	-2	0	3	2	3	5	D
1	Oramus te virgo virginum	an	PM 279	D	-2	0	3	2	3	0	-2	0	D
	Orans jacentem suscitat / Servus Dei Benedictus	rev	WA 299	a	-2	-4	0	3	1	0	-2	3	
5	Orante beatissimo ad Dominum	re	WA 289	F	4	7	9		4	7	2	4	F
7	Orante sancta Lucia apparuit	an	AM 769 *AR 592 *LU 1324 LA 322 WA 243	G	7	4	7	9	7	9	7	5	G
8	Orante sancto Clemente apparuit	re	PM 213 LA 495 *WA 409	D	3	5	7	5	7	5	7	5	G
7	Orante sancto Clemente apparuit	an	AM 1145 *AR 927 *LU 1760 LA 496 WA 410	G	7	4	7	9	7	9	7	5	G
8	Orantibus in loco isto	re	LR 238	D	3	5	7	5	7	9	7	5	G
8	Oratio mea munda est	of	GR 577 OTT 164 SYG 212 GB 216^V *GS 193	D	2	3	5	7	10	7	5	10	G
4	Oravi Deum meum ego Daniel	of	GR 367 OTT 107 LU 1050 *SYG 250 *GB 256^V *GS 161	D	3	0	2	3	0	5	3	0	E
8	Oravit Jacob et dixit	re	LA 140 *WA 92	G	-2	-3	-2	0	-2	0	2	0	G
	Oravit Jesus ad patrem / Pater si non potest	cov	SYG 124										
	Oravit Moyses Dominum / Sanctificavit Moyses	ofv	OTT 114 GB 259^V SYG 254	E	3	5	3	5	8	7	3	5	
8	Oravit sanctus Andreas	re	LA 501 *WA 235	D	3	7	5	7	5	7	5	7	G
8	Oravit sanctus Hyppolitus	an	WA 352	G	-5	-2	0	2	0	-3	-2	0	G
8	Orbata pontifice	re	WA 284	G	-2	0	-7	-5	-7	-5	-2	0	G
1	Orbis exsultans celebret hoc festum	hy	ST 120	D	2	-2	0	7	10	9	5	3	D
1	Orbis exsultans celebret hoc festum	hy	ST 108	D	2	0	-2	0	3	2	0	2	D
5	Orbis patrator optime	hy	AM 1069	F	4	7	9	6	7	9	11	7	F
8	Ordines angelorum videntes	an	WA 57	G	-3	-2	0	2	0	-2	2	0	G
5	Ordo sanctorum militum	hy	ST 128	c	-7	-3	0	2	0	2	4	5	F
3	Oremus dilectissimi nobis	an	GB 158^V *WA 230	D	5	7	5	7	5	3	2	3	E
7	Oremus omnes ad Dominum dixit	re	WA 409	G	2	0	2	0	2	0	2	5	G
8	Oremus omnes ad Dominum Jesum	an	AR 926 LU 1758 AM 1144 WA 408	G	2	0	-2	0	2	0	2	5	G
6	Oremus omnes ad Dominum Jesum ... dixit	re	LA 494	F	2	0	-1	-3	-5	-3	0	2	F
8	Oremus omnes ad Dominum ut ostendat	an	WA 409	G	2	0	-2	0	2	0	2	5	G

4 Oriens sol justitiae	an	WA 292	E	1	3	5	3	1	0	-2	-4	E
Orietur diebus	<u>see</u> Orietur in diebus											
3 Orietur in diebus Domini	an	LU 379 *LR 56 *WA 27 LA 33	G	4	5	0	4	5	2	0	4	E
Orietur in diebus ejus Laetentur caeli	rev	LA 5 WA 5										
Orietur in diebus ejus Modo veniet dominator	rev	WA 19										
Orietur in diebus ejus Reges Tharsis	ofv	OTT 21 *GB 34 *SYG 31	F	4	7	9	7	9	7	9	7	
8 Orietur sicut sol	an	AR 257 AM 234 *WA 26 LA 30	G	-5	-2	0	2	0	-2	0	2	G
8 Orietur stella ex Jacob	re	LA 23 WA 5	D	3	5	7	5	7	5	7	5	G
8 Oris divini	an	WA 312	G	-2	-5	-3	-2	0	2	0	-2	G
Ornatam monilibus Ostendit mihi	rev	LR 272										
8 Ornatam monilibus	re	PM 259 LR 253 VP 220 *LA 445 WA 356	D	3	5	7	5	7	5	7	10	G
Ornaverunt faciem templi In hymnis	rev	PM 115 LA 296 WA 181										
7 Ornaverunt faciem templi	re	LA 296 *WA 181	c	-1	0	2	0	2	4	2	0	G
1 Ornaverunt faciem templi	an	LA 301	C	2	4	2	0	2	5	2	4	D
8 Ortu Phoebi jam proximo	hy	ST 402	G	-5	-2	0	2	0	-2	0	5	G
8 Ortu Phoebi jam proximo	hy	ST 439	a	-2	0	2	3	0	2	0	-2	G
3 Ortu Phoebi jam proximo	hy	ST 241	E	-2	3	5	8	7	5	8	7	E
Ortus est sicut sol Dies sanctificatus	alv	SYG 19	D	7	5	7	9	5	3	7	5	
Os justi meditabitur	sr	AR [84] LU 1194 AM 667 668 1176 1177										
1 Os justi meditabitur	gr	GR [38] LU 1191 SYG 206 GB 53 GS 204	D	-2	0	3	0	-2	0	3	0	D
6 Os justi meditabitur	int	GR [42] [48] LU 1200 SYG 33 GB 40 GS 204	F	2	0	-5	-3	-5	-3	0	-3	F
Os justi meditabitur	alv	GB 40^v	G	2	4	5	7	4	5	2	0	
Os justi meditabitur Apud Dominum	trv	GR 528	C	2	5	7	2	0	2	5	7	
Os justi meditabitur	alv	SYG 199	C	2	9	11	9	7	9	5	4	
Os meum loquetur sapientiam	an	OHS 298 (nm)										
7 Os suum aperuit sapientiae	re	LR 226	G	2	0	2	0	2	-2	0	2	G
1 Osculetur me osculo	an	WA 162	C	2	5	2	4	0	2	4	5	D

	Incipit		Sources										
	Ostende mihi faciem tuam	alv	GR 440 LU 1377	G	2	5	2	4	5	4	5	7	
1	Ostende mihi faciem tuam	an	WA 356	D	3	-2	3	5	7	5	3	2	D
3	Ostende nobis Domine lucem	an	AM 78 79 *AR 189	G	2	4	5	2	0	2	4	2	E
	Ostende nobis Domine misericordiam	sr	AR 36 LU 243 AM 182 LA 16 WA 12										
	Ostende nobis Domine misericordiam Emitte agnum	rev	LR 395 LA 26 382										
	Ostende nobis Domine misericordiam	alv	GR 2 LU 320 SYG 2 GB 1 *GS 1	c	-1	2	0	-1	0	2	0	-3	
2	Ostende nobis Domine misericordiam	gr	GR 11 SYG 9 GB 8 *GS 7	F	2	4	0	2	4	0	-3	0	a
	Ostende nobis Domine misericordiam Benedixisti Domine	ofv	OTT 8 *GB 6 *SYG 7	G	4	5	2	4	2	4	2	0	
	Ostendens quia hic est Saulus qui et Paulus	anv	WA 331 LA 425										
7	Ostendit mihi angelus fontem	re	LA 227 *WA 141	G	2	0	2	0	2	4	5	7	G
8	Ostendit mihi Dominus civitatem	re	LR 272	D	3	5	7	5	7	5	7	10	G
1	Ostendit mihi Dominus fluvium	an	AR 849	F	-5	-3	4	5	4	2	4	5	D
	Ostendit mihi thesauros Mel et lac	rev	LA 337	c	2	5	4	5	4	2	4	2	
4	[Ostendit sanctus Gamaliel]	an	WA 341 (inc illeg)										E
	Oswalde sydus aureum O sacerdotum	rev	WA 392										
7	Oswaldus bajulus crucis	re	WA 284	G	4	5	7	5	2	4	5	7	G
4	Oves meae vocem meam	an	AR 418 LU 1099 AM 395 WA 109 *LA 174	G	2	5	7	5	7	9	7	5	a
	Pacem meam do vobis Tempus est ut ... dicit	rev	LA 249 WA 148										
5	Pacem meam do vobis	co	GR 301 LU 895 SYG 186 GB 192 GS 139	c	-1	-3	0	-1	-3	-5	-3	-2	F
6	Pacem meam do vobis	an	WA 148 *LA 253	F	2	0	-1	2	4	0	-1	-3	F
5	Pacem relinquo vobis ... dicit	co	GR [138] LU 1287	c	-1	-3	0	-1	-3	-5	-7	-5	F
6	Pacem relinquo vobis ... non	an	AR 511 AM 527 *LA 266	F	-3	-1	0	-5	-3	0	2	0	F
4	Pacem tuam da nobis Domine	an	AR 144* VP 30	F	-1	-3	-1	-3	-5	-3	0	-1	E

5 Pacifice loquebantur mihi	gr	GR 164 SYG 116 GB 103ᵛ GS 77	D	3	5	3	5	7	3	5	3	F
8 Pacifice loquebantur mihi	re	LA 170 WA 107	D	3	5	7	5	7	5	7	9	G
8 Pacificus vocabitur et thronus	an	AR 894¹ LU 1715 *AM 1088	G	-2	-5	-2	0	2	0	2	0	G
5 Paganorum multitudo fugiens	an	AR 626 AM 809 WA 276 *LA 364	F	4	7	6	7	6	4	7	0	F
5 Pande tuis caelis	an	WA 277	a	-2	-4	3	5	8	7	3	7	F
Panem caeli dedit eis	sr	AR 534 LU 942 AM 551										
8 Panem caeli dedit eis	co	GR 520 LU 1495	G	2	5	2	5	4	0	4	5	G
5 Panem de caelo dedisti nobis	co	GR 356 LU 1035 *SYG 248 *GB 254ᵛ GS 156	F	2	0	4	2	0	2	0	2	F
4 Pange lingua gloriosae lanceae	hy	ST 334	F	-1	-3	0	-1	-3	-5	-3	-1	E
1 Pange lingua gloriosi corporis	hy	AR 104* GR 153* VP 7* LU 950 AM 547	D	-2	3	5	7	8	10	8	7	D
3 Pange lingua gloriosi corporis	hy	AR 527 103* GR 198 152* PM 93 OHS 469 VP 9 5* LU 957	E	1	0	-2	3	5	8	10	8	E
1 Pange lingua gloriosi lauream	hy	GR 218 222 OHS 56 (nm) 578 LU 742	D	2	5	7	5	7	10	9	7	D
2 Pange lingua gloriosi proelium	hy	ST 417	c	-3	-1	0	-3	-5	-3	-1	0	a
3 Pange lingua gloriosi proelium	hy	ST 52	F	-3	-1	0	2	4	2	0	2	E
2 Pange lingua gloriosi proelium	hy	ST 227	a	-2	-4	-2	0	-7	-4	-2	-5	D
1 Pange lingua gloriosi proelium	hy	ST 385	D	-2	3	5	7	9	10	9	5	D
3 Pange lingua gloriosi proelium	hy	ST 188	a	-2	3	5	8	10	8	5	8	a
3 Pange lingua gloriosi proelium	hy	ST 90	E	-2	3	5	8	10	8	5	8	E
6 Pange lingua gloriosi proelium	hy	ST 452	F	-1	-3	-1	0	-1	0	-1	-3	C
3 Pange lingua gloriosi proelium	hy	ST 286	E	1	0	-2	3	8	10	8	5	E
6 Pange lingua gloriosi proelium	hy	ST 342	F	2	4	5	4	2	0	4	2	F
1 Pange lingua gloriosi proelium	hy	ST 52	C	2	5	7	5	4	2	0	5	D
1 Pange lingua gloriosi proelium	hy	LR 437	D	2	5	7	5	7	10	9	7	D
3 Pange lingua praeconium	hy	ST 336	E	1	0	-2	3	5	3	1	0	E
8 Pange sanctae Katherinae	hy	ST 15	G	2	0	-3	-5	0	2	4	5	G
7 Panis angelicus fit panis hominum		AR 96*	G	4	5	7	9	7	5	7	0	G
4 Panis angelicus fit panis hominum		AR 95* *VP 6	D	7	9	7	5	7	9	10	9	E
3 Panis enim Dei est	an	WA 100	d	-3	0	2	0	-2	0	-3	-2	E
4 Panis quem ego dabo	re	LR 124	F	2	0	-3	0	-1	2	4	0	E

1 Panis quem ego dedero	co	GR 362 LU 1043 *SYG 80 GB 71^v *GS 41 158	D	5	7	8	7	5	7	5	3	D
4 Pantata enyosa	an	GB 119	F	-1	-3	0	-3	-1	0	2	0	E
8 Paraclitus autem spiritus	an	AR 514 LU 900 AM 531	G	-5	-2	0	2	0	2	0	-2	G
Paraclitus spiritus sanctus	alv	GS 138	D	3	2	5	3	2	3	0	-2	
4 Paradisi januae per te	an	WA 353	G	2	5	7	9	7	5	7	9	a
1 Paradisi porta per Evam	an	WA 135 LA 442	D	-2	3	5	3	5	7	5	3	D
Paradisi porta per Evam Assumpta est	ofv	OTT 167 *GB 226	F	2	5	2	0	-3	-5	-3	0	
4 Paradisi portae per te	an	LR 374 VP 201 LA 442	G	2	5	9	7	5	7	9	7	a
8 Paradisi portas aperuit nobis	re	PM 51 LA 129 WA 86	G	2	0	2	5	4	5	7	5	G
Paras mihi mensam	alv	LU 1623^C	c	-1	2	0	-1	0	2	0	-3	
Parasti in conspectu meo mensam Ego autem cum mihi	trv	GR 566	G	2	4	5	4	5	7	5	0	
Parasti in dulcedine tua pauperi Unus panis	rev	AR 113* LR 129 VP 16										
Paratum cor meum Deus Da nobis Deus	intv	GR 106**										
5 Paratum cor meum Deus	re	LA 94 *WA 66	a	-4	0	3	2	0	3	5	8	F
Paratum cor meum Deus	alv	GR 378 LU 1064 *GB 259^v *SYG 253 *GS 158	C	2	4	5	7	5	7	9	10	
5 Paratur nobis mensa	an	LR 122	F	4	7	4	7	9	7	9	12	F
3 Paratus esto Israel	re	PM 25 *LA 18 *WA 14	G	4	2	4	2	0	5	4	5	E
2 Paratus esto Israel	an	AR 244 *WA 8 *LA 26	D	5	3	2	-2	0	3	0	3	D
7 Parcat tibi soror	an	AM 815	c	-1	-3	0	2	4	2	-5	-3	G
1 Parce Domine parce ... ne in aeternum		AR 93* LU 1868	a	-2	-4	0	-2	-4	-2	-4	-5	D
5 Parce Domine parce ... quem redemisti	an	AR 208* *WA 228	c	-3	-1	0	-3	0	-3	0	2	F
4 Parce Domine parce ... quem redemisti	an	GB 154	C	2	4	5	4	2	4	2	0	E
Paries quidem filium Suscipe verbum	rev	PM 245 LA 14 379 WA 4										
Pariet autem filium Angelus Domini	rev	LR 310										
Pars mea Domine dixi custodire Meditabor in mandatis	ofv	OTT 109 *GB 70 SYG 78	C	2	5	7	5	7	5	2	7	
4 Partem beatae resurrectionis	co	SYG 238	C	2	4	5	7	5	4	5	7	E
8 Participem me fac	re	LA 132 *WA 88	D	3	5	3	5	0	3	5	7	G

	Title	Type	Sources										
8	Parvulus filius hodie	an	AR 265 LR 64 LU 399 *AM 242 *WA 32 *LA 35	F	2	4	0	2	4	2	-1	0	G
	Pascha nostrum immolatus	alv	GR 242 OHS 710 LU 779 GS 117 *SYG 153 GB 125^V	c	-1	2	4	2	4	2	4	2	
	Pascha nostrum immolatus Epulemur in azymis	alv	GS 117	d	3	0	-2	-5	-7	-2	-7	-2	
6	Pascha nostrum immolatus	co	GR 243 OHS 716 LU 781 SYG 154 *GB 128^V *GS 117	F	4	2	4	0	-1	-3	-1	0	F
	Pascha nostrum immolatus Immolabit haedum	rev	AR 114* LR 122 LU 926	D	7	5	7	5	3	2	0	5	
3	Paschale mundo gaudium	hy	AR [30]	E	1	3	1	0	-2	0	-2	-4	E
2	Paschalis festi gaudium	hy	ST 463	C	2	5	4	2	0	5	7	5	D
5	Paschasius dixit cessabunt	re	WA 245	a	-4	0	3	5	3	2	3	5	F
6	Paschasius proconsularis	an	WA 244	c	2	0	-1	0	2	5	4	2	c
1	Passer invenit sibi domum	co	SYG 94	D	-2	0	2	3	0	-2	3	5	D
1	Passer invenit sibi domum	co	GR 126 LU 556 *GS 55 *GB 83	c	5	2	4	7	4	5	4	5	a
4	Pastis visceribus ciboque sumpto	hy	ST 480	G	-3	0	-2	-3	-5	-2	-5	-3	E
4	Pastis visceribus ciboque sumpto	hy	ST 480	F	-3	0	2	4	2	0	2	4	E
3	Pastor bonus animam suam	an	AR 470 AM 483 *LA 235	G	2	4	5	4	5	7	9	7	E
3	Pastor eximius pastoralis	an	AM 832	c	-1	-5	-1	0	-3	-5	-3	-5	E
8	Pastores dicite quidnam	an	WA 48 LA 40	G	-2	-3	-2	0	2	0	2	0	G
7	Pastores venerunt festinantes	an	AR 320 LU 468	G	7	5	7	10	9	7	9	10	G
	Pastorum princeps O claviger	rev	WA 280										
2	Pastorum summo jubilemus	inv	WA 277	C	2	5	2	4	2	0	4	2	D
2	Patefactae sunt januae	an	LA 47	D	-2	0	2	3	5	3	2	0	D
4	Patefactae sunt januae	re	LA 46 *WA 36	D	3	0	2	3	2	3	2	3	E
8	Pater Abraham miserere	an	WA 187 *LA 145	F	2	4	2	0	2	4	2	0	G
	Pater cum essem cum eis	alv	SYG 178	E	1	3	1	5	7	5	3	5	
4	Pater cum essem cum eis	co	GR 289 LU 856 *SYG 179 *GB 183 *GS L 134	F	2	0	-1	0	-3	2	4	6	E
7	Pater de caelis	an	WA 59 LA 77	G	7	5	4	7	9	5	7	5	G
8	Pater diligit filium	an	WA 105	c	-1	0	2	0	-1	-3	0	-1	G
6	Pater fidei nostrae	an	AR 353 LU 510 AM 326	F	-3	-5	0	2	4	2	4	2	F
2	Pater insignis confessor Benedicte	re	VP 128	D	-2	-5	-2	0	-2	0	3	2	D

4 Pater juste mundus te	an	AR 421 OHS 46 LU 578 *AM 399	F	-1	-3	0	-1	-3	-1	0	2	E
6 Pater manifestavi nomen	an	AR 490 LU 844 AM 507 LA 244	F	-3	-1	0	-3	0	2	4	5	F
1 Pater manifestavi nomen	an	WA 146	F	-3	0	-1	-3	-5	-3	-5	-3	D
Pater peccavi in caelum	an	WA 95 (inc illeg)										
7 Pater peccavi in caelum	re	LR 407 LA 145 *WA 87	G	5	2	4	2	0	4	5	7	G
4 Pater sancte serva eos	an	LA 249 252	F	-3	0	-3	-1	0	2	0	-1	E
4 Pater sanctus dum intentam	an	LR 324 *WA 300 *LA 375	F	-1	-3	0	-1	-3	-1	0	2	E
4 Pater sanctus dum intentam	re	LA 371 *WA 298	D	3	2	5	3	0	2	0	2	E
8 Pater si non potest	co	GR 184 OHS 146 LU 603 *SYG 124 GB 111 GS 89	c	-1	-3	-5	-1	-3	0	-3	-5	G
3 Pater superni luminis	hy	AR 789 LU 1565	G	2	4	2	5	4	2	0	2	E
8 Pater superni luminis	hy	AM 975	G	2	4	5	4	2	0	2	-2	G
1 Pater venit hora	an	AR 487 *AM 503	D	-2	3	5	3	7	5	8	7	D
Paternarum traditionum Saulus adhuc	anv	LA 340										
4 Patres nostri in Ægypto	of	GB 75[V]	A	2	3	5	7	8	10	7	12	E
3 Patriarchae nostri Abrahae	re	WA 293	E	-2	3	5	8	5	7	5	3	E
Patruum imitans Excellenti prosapia	rev	WA 282	D	-2	0	3	5	3	2	0	-2	
6 Paucitas dierum meorum	re	LA 284 *WA 173	c	2	0	2	0	-1	0	-1	-3	c
4 Paule pie sanctorum mitissime	hy	ST 402	F	-3	-5	-3	0	-3	-5	0	2	E
8 Paulus et Joannes dixerunt ad Terentianum	an	AR 743 LU 1509 WA 324	G	-5	-2	0	2	0	2	0	2	G
1 Paulus et Joannes dixerunt ad Terentianum	an	LA 410	D	-2	3	5	3	5	7	5	2	D
8 Paulus et Joannes dixerunt Juliano	an	AR 742 LU 1509 WA 324 LA 410	G	5	2	0	-2	0	2	0	4	G
Pauper et inops laudabunt	alv	GR 424 LU 1352[V]	a	-2	1	0	-2	0	-4	-5	-4	
Pauper sum ego et in laboribus	sr	AR 329 LU 473										
1 Pax aeterna ab aeterno patre	an	PM 240	D	7	5	3	5	7	8	7	5	D
6 Pax vobis ego sum alleluia	an	AM 478 496 *AR 464 481 LA 230	F	-1	2	4	-1	0	-3	-5	0	F
8 Pax vobis nolite timere	an	AR 891 LU 1702	c	-1	-3	0	-1	-5	-7	-5	-3	G
1 Peccantem me quotidie	re	AR [171] LU 1797 LA 556 *WA 437	F	4	2	4	0	2	4	5	4	D
1 Peccata mea Domine sicut sagittae	re	LA 84 WA 62	a	-2	3	5	7	5	7	5	3	a
1 Peccata mea Domine sicut sagittae	an	PM 50 *WA 60	D	3	0	-2	2	3	5	3	0	D

	Incipit	Type	Sources										
7	Peccati aculeus conteritu	an	VP 96 WA 59 LA 77	G	7	5	4	7	9	7	5	7	G
	Peccatorum indulgentia Per beatum Dionysium	rev	WA 388										
3	Peccavi super numerum	re	LA 270 *WA 166	c	-5	-3	-1	0	-1	-3	-1	-3	E
	Peccavimus cum patribus Memento nostri Domine	intv	CS 11										
	Peccavimus cum patribus Emendemus in melius	rev	LA 128										
	Peccavimus cum patribus Sustinuimus pacem	rev	WA 184										
	Peccavimus cum patribus Tribulationes civitatum	rev	LA 291 WA 177										
2	Peccavimus Domine et tu iratus	an	WA 229 *GB 157	A	3	5	7	5	8	7	8	10	D
4	Peccavimus Domine peccavimus tibi	an	GB 154^v	G	-2	0	-3	0	-2	0	-2	-3	E
	Peccavimus impie egimus Sustinuimus pacem	rev	LA 303										
7	Pectore sincero Maria	re	WA 337	G	2	0	5	4	5	7	5	4	G
	Pedes eorum pedes Facies et pennas	rev	WA 373										
1	Per arma justitiae	an	AR 97 PM 51 *AM 107 122 WA 89	D	-2	3	5	3	5	7	10	7	D
8	Per beatum Dionysium	re	WA 388	G	2	0	-2	0	2	5	4	5	G
2	Per ipsam te deprecor	re	WA 243	A	3	5	7	5	3	5	8	5	D
	Per ipsum nobis Per signum crucis	trv	SYG 129	C	2	4	5	7	5	2	4	5	
	Per lignum crucis		see also Per signum crucis										
4	Per lignum crucis de inimicis	co	GB 246^v	D	3	7	5	3	0	2	0	-2	E
8	Per lignum servi facti sumus	an	OHS 584 LU 746	G	-5	-2	0	2	0	2	0	-2	G
8	Per lignum servi facti sumus	an	PM 53	G	-5	-2	0	2	0	2	0	-2	G
8	Per lignum servi facti sumus	co	SYG 175 *GS 186 236	G	2	0	2	0	-2	0	2	5	G
	Per manus autem apostolorum	alv	GS y	F	-1	0	-3	-1	-3	-5	-3	-1	
8	Per manus reverendi pontificis	an	PM 132	G	-5	-2	0	2	0	2	0	-2	G
6	Per memetipsum juravi	re	LA 118 *WA 78	GG	2	4	5	4	5	7	5	9	C
	Per quatuor partes Statura erat	rev	WA 374										
	Per quem mihi mundus Mihi vivere	anv	LA 422 WA 330										
	Per quem mihi mundus Mihi vivere	rev	LA 425 WA 331										
	Per quem omnes gentes Tu es vas	anv	WA 264 330 LA 423										

	Per signum crucis		<u>see also</u> Per lignum crucis										
2	Per signum crucis de inimicis	tr	SYG 129	D	-2	0	-2	-5	-2	0	-2	0	D
2	Per signum crucis de inimicis	an	AM 1041 *SYG 142 *WA 371	D	-2	3	2	0	2	0	-2	0	D
8	Per signum crucis de inimicis	an	AR 701 LU 1460 AM 900	c	2	0	-1	0	-3	0	-1	-3	G
4	Per signum crucis de inimicis	co	GR 492 LU 1457	G	4	7	5	4	0	2	0	2	b
4	Per signum sanctae ac venerandae crucis	an	SYG 142	F	-1	-3	-1	0	-1	0	2	0	E
	Per signum sanctae crucis	alv	SYG 174	D	3	5	3	2	0	3	0	7	
8	Per singulos dies	an	AM 156 157 *LA 102	c	-1	-3	-5	-3	-5	-7	-5	-3	G
	Per te Dei genitrix	alv	GR 552 LU 1557 *GS u	D	7	5	7	5	0	3	2	5	
8	Per te Lucia virgo	an	AR 592 LU 1324 AM 770 WA 243 LA 322	G	5	2	0	-2	0	2	0	4	G
	Per te omnes gentes Tu es vas	trv	GR 420 LU 1346 *GS 178 *SYG 44	D	-2	0	3	2	3	0	2	0	
	Per totam Judaeam Ibat igitur Saulus	anv	WA 262 (inc illeg)										
	Per totam Judaeam Ibat igitur Saulus	rev	LA 344 WA 263										
1	Per unum hominem peccatum	re	LR 262	D	-2	0	3	0	2	0	-2	0	D
8	Per viscera misericordiae	an	AR 170 AM 73 LA 102	G	5	2	0	2	0	-2	0	2	G
5	Peractis centum	re	WA 77	c	2	0	-3	-2	-5	-3	0	2	F
	Peracto passionis suae Sacram praesentis	rev	WA 257										
	Perambulabam in innocentia Misericordiam et judicium	rev	LA 103										
7	Perambulabant in innocentia	an	LR 141	G	4	5	7	4	7	9	7	5	G
	Percipietis immarcescibilem Venite benedicti	trv	SYG 75	c	2	0	-3	0	2	4	-1	0	
8	Percussit Saul mille	re	LA 268	D	3	5	7	5	7	9	7	5	G
	Percussus sum sicut foenum Domine exaudi	trv	GR 191 OHS 324 LU 619 GS 92 GB 114 SYG 127	F	2	4	2	0	2	0	-3	-1	
	Perdam sapientiam sapientium Sapientia hujus mundi	grv	GR 475	a	-4	0	-2	-5	-4	-7	-5	-7	
	Pereant peccatores a facie Mirabilis Deus	ofv	OTT 141 GB 171 SYG 175	a	3	5	7	5	7	5	7	3	
	Pereunt pericula cessat Si quaeris	rev	VP 176	c	-1	-3	-1	-5	-3	-5	-8	-5	
	Perfecisti eis qui sperant Quam magna multitudo	rev	LA 88 WA 63										

	Incipit		Sources										
	Perfecisti eis qui sperant Quam magna multitudo	grv	GR 449 LU 1393	F	4	2	7	9	7	4	7	9	
3	Perfecto corde Maria	re	WA 336	E	-2	3	5	7	3	5	8	5	E
4	Perfice gressus meos	of	GR 79 LU 508 OTT 90 SYG 61 GB 58^v GS 27 147	C	2	5	4	5	2	0	2	5	E
	Periit fuga a me Educ de carcere	rev	LA 163 WA 103										
1	Perpetuis nos Domine	an	WA 363	D	3	0	3	2	0	-2	0	-2	D
	Perpetuum nobis Domine Archangeli Michaelis	rev	LA 470 WA 383										
1	Perpetuum nobis Domine	an	WA 384	D	-2	3	5	3	5	7	10	7	D
2	Persequar inimicos meos	tr	GR 463 LU 1420	D	-2	0	-2	-5	-2	0	-2	0	D
	Persequar inimicos meos Factus est Dominus	ofv	OTT 42 GB 96^v SYG 108	D	3	5	7	3	5	7	10	7	
	Perseverans usque in finem Erectus in culmine	rev	WA 285										
4	Perseverans ulcus illud	an	WA 250	F	-1	-3	-5	-3	-1	-3	-5	-3	E
	Persistens gemma monachorum Sancte Benedicte	rev	WA 301										
4	Personet aula Dei	inv	WA 281	C	2	5	4	2	4	2	0	2	E
6	Pes enim meus stetit	co	SYG 86	D	3	0	3	5	7	10	7	9	F
	Petiit puella caput Joannis Da mihi in disco	rev	LA 453										
4	Petiit puella caput Joannis	an	LA 453	D	2	5	7	9	7	5	7	9	E
	Petite et accipietis quaerite Domus mea	rev	LR 241										
1	Petite et accipietis quaerite	co	GR 284 [142] LU 843 SYG 178 GB 162^v *GS 133	F	2	4	2	-1	0	2	0	-1	D
8	Petite et accipietis quaerite	an	AR 485 AM 501 *WA 146 *LA 242	F	2	4	2	0	2	4	7	6	G
8	Petite et accipietis ut gaudium	an	AR 485 AM 501	F	2	4	2	7	6	4	6	2	G
8	Petite et dabitur vobis	an	LA 243	a	-4	-2	-4	0	3	0	3	5	G
8	Peto Domine ut de vinculo	an	LA 293	G	-2	-3	-2	0	2	0	-2	2	G
1	Peto Domine ut de vinculo	re	LR 423 LA 288 WA 176	a	-2	0	-4	0	-2	-4	-2	-4	D
	Petrae scissae sunt Velum templi	rev	OHS 488 LU 695 LA 199										
4	Petre amas me	re	LR 361 LA 417 WA 279	F	-1	0	2	4	2	-1	0	2	E
4	Petre amas me	an	WA 281 *LA 420	G	2	5	7	5	7	9	7	5	a
3	Petre pontifex inclite	hy	ST 234	E	-2	3	5	8	7	5	8	7	E
8	Petrus ad se reversus	an	WA 340	F	2	4	7	6	4	2	0	2	G

	Chant	Type	Source										
3	Petrus apostolus dixit paralitico	an	WA 326	G	2	5	4	2	5	4	5	7	E
8	Petrus apostolus et Paulus doctor	an	AR 775 LU 1547 *AM 959 WA 332 *LA 426	G	5	2	0	-2	0	2	0	4	G
1	Petrus autem servabatur	an	WA 340	C	2	9	11	9	7	5	4	5	D
4	Petrus beatus catenarum laqueos	hy	ST 96	F	-1	-3	-5	-3	0	-1	0	2	E
	Petrus ergo et Paulus In visione	rev	WA 312	D	7	5	7	5	3	2	0	3	
8	Petrus et Joannes ascendebant	an	AR 751 LU 1515 *AM 934 WA 328 *LA 412	G	5	2	0	-2	0	2	0	4	G
8	Petrus et Paulus duo sunt	an	WA 332	F	2	4	2	0	2	4	2	4	G
1	Petrus quidem servabatur	an	LA 415	F	2	0	2	4	2	-1	0	2	D
3	Petrus quidem servabatur	an	AR 799 LU 1577 AM 989	G	2	0	2	4	5	4	0	2	E
	Philippe qui me videt	see Philippe qui videt me											
8	Philippe qui videt me	an	WA 307	G	-5	-2	0	2	5	4	2	0	G
7	Philippe qui videt me	an	AR 694 LU 1465^E AM 893 *LA 394	G	4	5	7	4	7	9	7	5	G
5	Pie colamus annua	hy	ST 114	C	2	4	0	2	5	4	2	4	C
3	Pinguis est panis Christi	an	AR 530 LU 940 *AM 550	G	2	4	5	4	5	7	5	4	E
3	Pius adolescens Dunstanus	re	WA 312	E	-2	3	5	3	5	7	8	5	E
8	Placare Christe servulis	hy	AR 895 LU 1730	G	2	0	-2	2	5	4	0	2	G
2	Placare Christe servulis	hy	AR 663 892	D	3	0	-2	0	3	2	3	5	D
2	Placebo Domino in regione	an	LA 560	E	-2	-4	-2	0	-2	-4	-2	0	D
3	Placebo Domino in regione	an	AR [142] LU 1772 *AM 1150 *WA 435	G	4	5	2	4	2	0	2	0	E
5	Placentes Deo facti	an	WA 373	G	2	0	2	-2	2	5	7	5	F
	Placita enim erat Deo Consummatus in brevi	grv	GR 70**	D	7	5	7	10	7	10	5	3	
5	Plange quasi virgo	re	OHS 603 LU 761 *LA 202 *WA 125	b	3	1	-2	0	-2	1	0	1	F
4	Plangent eum quasi unigenitum	an	AR 440 OHS 620 LU 775 AM 445 446 WA 127 *LA 206	G	2	5	7	5	7	9	7	5	a
	Plangent se super se Libera me Domine de morte	rev	LA 557 *WA 438	D	-2	0	2	3	5	3	0	2	
	Plantatus in domo Domini Justus germinabit	rev	LR 151 LA 522 WA 416										
	Plantatus in domo Domini	alv	SYG 189	D	3	2	5	3	2	3	0	7	
	Plantatus in domo Domini Justus ut palma	ofv	OTT 150 *SYG 24 *GB 25^V	D	5	7	10	9	12	10	9	10	
	Plantaverat autem ... lignum Plantaverat autem	rev	WA 72										

	Incipit		References										
	Plantaverat autem ... paradisum Tulit ergo Dominus	rev	LA 109 WA 72										
4	Plantaverat autem ... paradisum	re	LA 109 *WA 72	F	-3	0	-1	0	2	0	-1	0	E
4	Plantaverat autem ... paradisum	an	WA 75	F	-1	-3	-1	2	4	2	0	2	E
1	Plasmator hominis Deus	hy	AM 158 ST 363	F	2	4	0	2	0	-1	2	0	D
8	Plasmator hominis Deus	hy	AM 157	D	3	5	3	7	5	0	3	5	G
2	Plasmator hominis Deus	hy	ST 214	D	3	5	7	3	5	3	5	2	D
1	Plateae tuae Jerusalem	re	LA 228 *WA 141	G	-2	0	-2	-3	0	2	0	2	D
1	Plaudat chorus fidelium	hy	ST 130	D	3	5	7	5	2	0	3	7	D
3	Plaudat laetitia lux hodierna	hy	ST 239	b	1	-2	-4	-2	-4	-6	-7	-9	E
	Plenus gratia et fortitudine Videbant omnes Stephanum	rev	LA 42										
	Plorans ploravit in nocte Aspice Domine quia facta	rev	LA 302 WA 183										
7	Ploremus coram Domino	inv	LA 136	G	2	-2	0	2	0	2	0	2	G
7	Poenas cuccurrit fortiter	hy	ST 44	G	4	5	7	9	7	5	4	5	G
8	Polycarpus presbyter dixit	an	LA 326	G	5	4	2	0	-2	2	0	2	G
	Ponam arcum meum in nubibus Per memetipsum	rev	LA 118 WA 78										
1	Ponam arcum meum in nubibus	re	LA 118 *WA 78	F	2	4	2	4	2	0	2	4	D
8	Ponam in Sion salutem	an	AR 254 *AM 230 *LA 17	F	2	4	2	0	2	0	4	2	G
6	Ponens Petrus genua	an	WA 326	c	-1	-3	-1	-3	-5	0	2	4	c
5	Ponent Domino gloriam	an	WA 18 *LA 20	c	-1	-3	-5	-7	-3	-7	-3	0	F
2	Ponis nubem ascensum tuum	re	PM 84 LR 105 AM 1186 LA 249 WA 149	D	-5	-2	0	2	0	2	0	-2	D
	Ponit nubem	see	Ponis nubem										
5	Pontifex sacerdos magnus inter fratres	gr	GR [118]	F	2	0	2	4	0	2	0	-1	F
1	Pontificalis apex	an	WA 277	C	2	0	2	5	2	0	5	7	D
7	Pontifices almi divina	an	WA 240	G	5	4	5	7	4	5	2	0	G
4	Popule meus quid feci	an	AR 93 409 AM 102 117 389 *WA 108 *LA 171	a	-2	0	3	5	3	5	7	5	a
	Popule meus quid feci		SYG 139	D	2	-1	0	2	3	5	3	2	D
	Popule meus quid feci		GR 211 *WA 214 GB 118 *GS 101	C	2	4	5	4	2	0	2	4	D
7	Popule meus quid feci	re	WA 103	G	2	5	4	5	4	5	7	5	G
6	Populi autem non credentibus	an	WA 404	F	2	4	0	-5	-3	0	2	0	F
	Populo qui nascetur Deus Deus meus	trv	GR 180 OHS 109 LU 594 *GS 86 GB 109 SYG 122	C	2	0	2	5	2	0	2	0	

	Incipit		Sources										
5	Populum humilem salvum	of	GR 341 LU 1015 OTT 93 *SYG 107 GB 95^v *GS 69 149	F	2	0	2	0	2	4	7	4	F
7	Populus acquisitionis annuntiate	co	GR 255 OHS 810 LU 799 *SYG 159 *GB 139^v *GS 122	G	2	4	5	4	5	4	5	2	G
7	Populus Domini et oves	inv	LA 146 *WA 100	G	2	5	4	5	4	2	5	7	G
4	Populus meus ait Dominus	an	AR 147 AM 63 64	F	-3	-1	0	2	-1	0	-1	-3	E
8	Populus Sion convertimini	an	GB 154 *WA 227	G	2	5	4	5	4	5	2	7	G
7	Populus Sion ecce Dominus	int	GR 4 LU 327 *SYG 3 *GB 2^v *GS 2	G	5	7	5	7	5	4	5	7	G
4	Porta Sion clausi portam	re	PM 268	F	-3	-1	-5	-3	-1	-3	0	-1	E
	Portae ejus non claudentur Haec est Jerusalem	rev	LA 228 WA 142										
	Portae Jerusalem ex sapphiro Lapides pretiosi	rev	PM 239 LR 242										
8	Portas caeli aperuit Dominus	of	GR 251 OHS 798 OTT 60 LU 795 SYG 158 GB 136^v GS 121 139	F	2	4	7	4	2	6	4	2	G
8	Portio mea Domine	an	AM 154 155 WA 70 LA 102	c	-1	0	-3	-5	-1	-3	-1	0	G
	Positis autem genibus		see also Positis genibus										
	Positis autem genibus beatus Video caelos	cov	SYG 23										
	Positis autem genibus beatus Lapidabant Stephanum	rev	LA 44 WA 35										
	Positis autem genibus beatus	alv	SYG 22	D	-2	0	3	5	3	5	7	5	
1	Positis autem genibus beatus	an	WA 35	F	-1	-3	-5	-1	-3	0	-1	-3	D
	Positis autem genibus clamabat Patefactae sunt	rev	WA 36										
	Positis autem genibus Stephanus Elegerunt apostoli	ofv	OTT 161 GB 22	C	2	5	7	9	7	5	9	12	
	Positis genibus		see also Positis autem genibus										
1	Positis genibus beatus Stephanus	an	LA 41	D	-2	0	3	2	3	5	3	2	D
	Positis genibus beatus Stephanus	alv	SYG 22	C	2	4	5	2	0	7	5	4	
	Positis namque genibus Vir Domini Cuthbertus	rev	WA 293										
8	Post dies octo ... ingressus	an	AR 463 LU 815 AM 477 WA 136 *LA 230	c	2	0	-1	0	-1	-3	0	-1	G
	Post dies octo ... stetit	alv	GR 262 LU 810 GS 124 GB 144^v	G	2	5	4	5	7	9	10	9	
	Post dies octo ... stetit	alv	SYG 163	D	3	2	5	3	2	3	0	2	
	Post excessum beatissimi Martini	alv	SYG 227	D	2	3	5	3	2	0	2	3	

No.	Incipit	Genre	Sources										
1	Post excessum beatissimi Martini	an	WA 403	C	2	9	11	9	7	9	11	9	D
1	Post matutinis laudibus	hy	ST 381	D	3	0	-2	3	5	7	5	10	D
	Post partum virgo inviolata	sr	AR 879 LU 1678 AM 1073 WA 358										
4	Post partum virgo inviolata	an	LR 251 *LA 350 383 477	a	-2	0	3	5	3	5	7	5	a
	Post partum virgo inviolata	alv	GR [77] LU 1265 *GS r *SYG 48 *GB 220^V	F	-1	0	-3	-1	-3	-5	-3	0	
8	Post partum virgo inviolata	of	GR 76**	F	2	4	7	4	2	0	2	4	G
1	Post passionem Domini	re	WA 385	D	3	5	3	0	3	5	3	5	D
3	Post passionem suam	re	LR 96 LA 245 *WA 147	F	-3	-1	0	2	4	2	4	5	E
8	Post Petrum primum principem	hy	ST 7	G	-2	-3	-2	0	-2	-5	-7	-8	G
6	Post Petrum primum principem	hy	ST 424	E	-2	0	-4	-2	0	3	5	3	C
7	Post Petrum primum principem	hy	ST 44	G	-2	2	0	2	4	5	4	2	G
8	Post Petrum primum principem	hy	ST 401	G	2	0	-2	0	2	5	7	5	G
8	Post triduum invenerunt Jesum	an	AR 324 LU 474	a	-4	-2	0	-2	-4	0	2	3	G
8	Post triduum jussus tamen	hy	ST 42	G	-2	0	2	5	4	5	7	5	G
	Postquam audissem et vidissem Ostendit mihi angelus	rev	LA 227 WA 141										
	Postquam autem impleti		see also Postquam impleti										
	Postquam autem impleti sunt dies Obtulerunt pro eo	rev	GR 431 PM 136 LU 1360 LA 351 WA 269										
2	Postquam domi puerilem	an	WA 238	D	-2	-5	-2	0	2	0	-2	3	D
8	Postquam ergo lavit	an	SYG 133	a	-2	-4	-2	0	-2	0	-2	0	G
	Postquam impleti		see also Postquam autem impleti										
3	Postquam impleti sunt	re	LA 351	F	2	0	-3	-1	-3	0	-1	0	E
8	Postquam sexaginta annos	re	LR 286	D	5	3	5	7	5	7	5	7	G
7	Postquam resurrexit a mortis	an	SYG 149	G	2	0	-2	2	5	4	2	5	G
4	Postquam surrexit Dominus a coena	an	WA 213 *GS 97	d	-7	-5	-2	0	-2	0	3	5	b
4	Postquam surrexit Dominus a coena	an	GR 200 OHS 447 LU 672 *SYG 130	E	-2	0	3	5	3	5	3	5	E
4	Postula a me et dabo tibi	of	GR 642 LU 1713	C	2	5	4	5	4	5	7	5	E
1	Postulavi patrem meum alleluia	an	OHS 754 WA 128 *LA 210 224	C	2	5	7	9	7	5	7	9	D
	Fosuerunt me in lacu inferiori Aestimatus sum	rev	OHS 617 LU 772 LA 205 WA 126										
1	Posuerunt mortalia servorum	co	GR 644 LU 1492^B *SYG 191 *GB 195^V *GS 219	F	2	4	2	4	2	0	2	4	D

Posuerunt mortalia servorum Vindica Domine	grv	GR 643 GS 214 *GB 195 SYG 190	F	4	7	9	7	9	11	7	9	
1 Posuerunt super caput ejus	an	AR 439 OHS 409 516 LU 718 AM 443 WA 124 LA 201	C	2	9	10	9	7	9	10	9	D
Posui adjutorium meum super potentem Veritas mea	ofv	OTT 148 GB 41^v SYG 38	F	2	0	4	2	0	-1	0	-3	
Posui adjutorium super potentem	alv	GB 272	D	-2	0	2	3	5	7	5	3	
1 Posui adjutorium super potentem	re	PM 314 LR 199 LA 531 WA 425	D	-2	3	5	7	5	3	5	7	D
Posui adjutorium super potentam	alv	GS 224	G	2	0	5	7	5	7	2	0	
Posui super eum spiritum Ecce puer meus	rev	LA 54										
Posui vos ut eatis	alv	GR 568	D	-2	0	2	3	5	2	3	0	
8 Posuisti Domine in capite ejus	of	GR 48 [14] OTT 136 LU 438 1140 GS 204 GB 233^v	F	2	4	7	4	2	0	2	4	G
6 Posuisti Domine in capite ejus	co	GR [10] LU 1135 SYG 34 GB 41 GS 209	C	2	5	4	7	9	5	7	5	F
1 Posuisti Domine in capite ejus	gr	GR (6) *SYG 43 GS 206	C	2	9	10	9	10	9	7	9	D
Posuisti Domine super caput	sr	AR [20] LU 1124 AM 638 1172 WA 419										
2 Posuisti Domine super caput	re	LR 156 *LA 526	D	2	-2	0	3	0	2	0	-2	D
8 Posuisti Domine super caput	tr	GB 46	G	2	4	2	0	2	0	5	7	G
Posuisti Domine super caput	alv	GR [17] LU 1148 GS 206 *GB 270	C	2	5	7	4	2	5	4	5	
4 Posuisti Domine super caput	an	LR 153 WA 416 *LA 523	G	2	5	7	9	7	5	7	9	a
1 Posuisti Domine super caput	gr	GR (6) GB 45^v GS 206 SYG 43	C	2	9	10	9	10	9	7	9	D
Posuisti Domine super caput	alv	SYG 217	D	3	0	-2	3	5	3	5	7	
Posuisti in capite Desiderium animae	rev	WA 416										
Posuisti super caput ejus Desiderium animae	trv	GR [5] LU 1131 GS 208 *GB 51^v *SYG 52	G	2	5	4	2	5	2	0	2	
2 Posuit coronam capiti meo	re	LR 152 LA 525 *WA 418	C	2	4	2	5	4	5	7	2	D
Posuit in ea verba signorum Mementote mirabilium	grv	GR 85**	F	4	7	9	7	9	7	9	4	
Posuit me desolatam	sr	AR 678										
7 Posuit os meum Dominus	an	LR 351 *LA 403	d	-3	0	2	0	-2	0	-3	-2	G
Posuit os meum quasi gladium Inflammatum	gr	GR 622[1] LU 1681[2]	D	7	5	7	10	7	10	5	3	

	Incipit		Sources										
	Posuit signum in faciem Dexteram meam et collum	rev	LA 333 WA 253										
7	Posuit signum in faciem	an	WA 253 *LA 332	d	-2	-3	0	-2	-3	0	2	-2	G
8	Potens es Domine eripere	an	AR 397 AM 372 *WA 103 LA 162	F	2	4	0	2	4	7	6	7	G
	Potens es Domine et veritas Inveni David	ofv	OTT 147 GB 28^v SYG 27	G	2	0	-2	0	2	5	4	5	
	Potens in terra erit semen Beatus vir qui metuit	rev	LA 384 WA 304										
	Potens in terra erit semen	alv	GR 585	a	-2	0	2	3	5	7	5	3	
8	Potens in terra erit semen	an	WA 415 LA 421	G	-2	2	5	4	0	4	5	2	G
	Potens in terra erit semen Beatus vir qui timet	trv	GR [8] LU 1442 *GS 203 *GB 52^v *SYG 55	G	2	4	5	4	5	7	5	0	
	Potens in terra erit semen Dispersit dedit pauperibus	grv	GR 576 LU 1608 GS 193 GB 216^v SYG 212	a	3	5	7	5	3	2	3	0	
	Potens in terra erit semen Beatus vir qui timet	grv	GR [11] LU 1136 GS 206 GB 51 SYG 51	F	4	7	9	7	4	7	4	2	
	Potestas ejus potestas aeterna Aspiciebam in visu	rev	LA 3										
	Potestas ejus potestas aeterna	alv	GR 639 LU 1711	C	2	0	2	5	7	5	4	2	
4	Potestatem habeo ponendi animam	an	AR 430 OHS 226 AM 409 WA 115 *LA 187	G	2	5	7	9	7	5	7	9	a
	Potuit enim transgredi Beatus vir	rev	PM 229 LR 209										
2	Potum meum cum fletu	co	GR 194 OHS 346 LU 624 SYG 128 GB 115 GS 93	D	-2	0	2	3	2	0	2	0	D
7	Prae timore autem ejus	an	AR 444 OHS 727 768 LU 782 *AM 454 LA 214 233 *WA 129 137	G	4	5	7	4	5	7	9	7	G
1	Praebe fili cor tuum	re	LA 280 *WA 170	a	-2	0	-4	-2	0	-7	-4	-2	D
7 8	Praecedam vos in Galilaeam	an	AR 465 AM 478 LA 222 *WA 131 136	d	-2	-3	-2	0	2	0	2	-2	G
	Praecepitque ei Dominus Dixit Dominus ad Adam	rev	WA 73										
1	Praeceptor per totam noctem	an	AR 555 AM 593 LU 1001 WA 187 LA 311	C	2	9	10	9	7	9	10	9	D
	Praeceptum Domini lucidum Justitiae Domini	ofv	OTT 94 GB 82^v SYG 93	F	4	2	0	4	2	0	4	7	
	Praecinxisti me virtute Factus est Dominus	ofv	OTT 42 GB 96^v *SYG 108	E	1	3	5	3	5	3	1	3	
3	Praecipita Domine omnes	re	WA 185	E	-2	3	5	8	7	5	8	7	E

2 Praeclara custos virginum	hy	LR 259	a	-2	-5	-7	-2	0	3	2	0	a
1 Praeclara festivitas	an	WA 248	D	3	0	-2	3	5	7	5	7	D
8 Praeclara salutis aurora	an	AR 633	G	5	2	0	2	0	-2	0	2	G
2 Praeclara dies ortus est	an	PM 344	D	3	2	-2	0	3	2	3	5	D
7 Praeco praeclarus sacer et propheta	hy	ST 393	c	-1	-3	-1	0	-5	-3	-5	-7	G
2 Praecursor Christi magne baptista	an	PM 159	D	2	3	2	0	2	0	-2	0	D
8 Praecursor Domini venit	re	LR 356 384 AM 1197 *LA 405 *WA 322	D	3	5	7	5	3	7	9	10	G
7 Praecursor Joannes exsultat	an	WA 59 LA 79 *VP 97	G	7	5	2	5	9	7	9	5	G
Praecursor pro nobis ingreditur Intuemini quantus	rev	LA 20 381 WA 24										
7 Praecursor pro nobis ingreditur	re	LA 25 WA 22	c	2	0	-1	2	4	2	0	2	G
1 Praedicabant apostoli	co	OHS 437 LU 664	F	-1	0	2	4	0	-1	-3	-5	D
1 Praedicans praeceptum Domini	an	LR 149 LA 522 *WA 416	D	7	9	7	5	7	5	3	5	D
Praedicator veritatis et doctor Tu es vas	trv	GR 420 GS 178	F	-1	0	2	4	2	-1	0	2	
6 Praeditus hinc juvenis	re	WA 284	c	2	0	2	4	2	0	2	5	c
7 Praeoccupemus faciem Domini	inv	WA 420	G	5	4	5	7	5	7	9	7	G
Praeoccupemus faciem ejus Venite exsultemus	alv	SYG 245 GS 154	G	5	4	5	7	5	7	9	7	
1 Praeparate corda vestra Domino	re	PM 110 LR 420 LA 268 *WA 166	C	2	4	2	9	11	9	7	9	D
Praeparavit cor suum Biennio ante mortem	rev	LR 284										
3 Praepositus paradisi januae	an	WA 379	G	2	5	4	2	5	4	5	7	E
Praesentibus indicens Eodem vero anno	rev	LA 372										
Praesentibus indicens Ipso anno	rev	LR 331										
Praestet nobis gratiam Summae trinitati	rev	WA 161	d	-2	0	-2	0	3	0	3	2	
1 Praesul Christi Dunstanus	re	WA 312	C	2	0	2	4	5	2	0	2	D
5 Praesul Christi Wulstanus	re	WA 250	F	4	2	7	9	7	12	11	9	F
4 Praesul insignis Oswalde	an	WA 286	E	-2	1	-2	-4	-2	0	-2	0	E
2 Praevaluit David in Philisthaeum	re	LA 269 WA 165	A	3	5	7	5	8	5	3	5	D
8 Praevaluit David in Philisthaeum	an	AR 539 LU 986 AM 575 WA 164 LA 273	G	5	2	0	2	0	2	0	-2	G
6 Praevenisti eam Domine	co	GR 37**	C	2	5	2	0	5	7	9	7	F

	Incipit		Source										
7 8	Precatus est Moyses in conspectu	of	GR 352 OTT 97 LU 1030 *SYG 89 *GB 79 *GS 52 155	G	2	5	0	-2	0	2	0	2	G
	Precibus tuis sanctis O venerabiliter	rev	WA 238	d	-2	-3	-2	0	-2	0	2	0	
	Pretiosa in conspectu Domini	sr	WA 310										
	Pretiosa in conspectu Domini	alv	GB 164	G	-2	2	5	4	2	0	-2	0	
7	Pretiosa in conspectu Domini	an	LA 473 512	c	-1	0	2	0	2	4	2	0	G
	Pretiosa in conspectu Domini	alv	GR [19] LU 1151 *SYG 218	E	1	-4	-2	3	8	5	3	5	
7	Pretiosa in conspectu Domini	an	WA 394	G	5	4	5	7	5	7	9	7	G
7	Pretiosa in conspectu Domini	re	LR 166 *LA 386 WA 307	G	5	4	5	7	5	7	9	7	G
3	Pretiosa sunt Thebaeorum corpora	an	WA 377	E	-2	3	5	8	7	8	10	8	E
3	Pretiosi Dei sancti	an	PM 200	G	2	0	2	5	4	2	0	2	E
4	Pretiosus martyr Christi	an	WA 36	C	2	0	2	5	4	2	4	2	E
1	Pretiosus martyr Vincentius	re	WA 260	D	-2	0	3	0	2	0	-2	0	D
4	Pretiosus vir Domini	re	WA 312	C	2	5	4	2	5	4	2	0	E
8	Prima autem azymorum	an	GS 78	F	2	4	2	7	6	7	4	2	G
8	Prima autem die azymcrum	an	SYG 120 *WA 208	G	2	0	5	4	5	2	0	2	G
4	Primo dierum omnium	hy	ST 358	G	-3	0	-2	-3	-2	-5	-3	-2	E
4	Primo dierum omnium	hy	ST 84	D	2	3	5	2	5	3	2	3	E
3	Primo dierum omnium	hy	ST 210 250 262	D	2	3	5	3	5	3	2	3	E
4	Primo dierum omnium	hy	ST 181	D	2	3	5	7	5	3	2	0	E
1	Primo proscriptos patria	hy	ST 307	D	7	9	10	7	5	3	5	7	D
	Primorum princeps et athleta O claviger regni	rev	VP 182										
8	Primum quaerite regnum Dei	co	GR 359 LU 1039 SYG 245 *GB 252^v GS 151	G	2	0	-2	-3	-2	-5	-2	-3	G
	Primus ad Sion dicet	alv	SYG 170 *GS v 204	F	4	6	7	9	7	2	6	4	
1	Primus vocatione maximus	an	WA 278	D	7	5	3	5	3	5	7	0	D
3	Princeps ecclesiae pastor		SYG 265	G	2	5	4	2	0	2	4	2	E
1	Princeps gloriosissime Michael	an	AR 862 LU 1662 AM 1063 LA 473	C	2	5	7	5	4	2	5	4	D
1	Princeps gloriosissime Raphael	an	AR 894 LU 1703	C	2	5	7	5	4	2	5	4	D
	Princeps hujus mundi Magnificate Dominum	rev	LR 269										
1	Princeps sancte caelestis	re	WA 383	D	-2	0	3	5	3	2	0	2	D
6	Principes persecuti sunt me	re	LA 182 *WA 113	c	2	0	2	4	0	-3	0	2	c

	Incipit		Sources										
1	Principes persecuti sunt me	co	GR [68] LU 1238 *GB 229^V *GS t 230	F	2	4	5	4	7	4	2	0	D
8	Principes populorum congregati	an	LR 135 *WA 411 LA 505	G	2	0	-2	2	5	4	2	5	G
1	Principes sacerdotum consilium	an	AM 397 *AR 420 *LU 1101 *WA 110 LA 174	D	-2	0	3	2	0	3	0	-2	D
1	Principes sacerdotum et pharisaei	an	OHS 631 LU 776^G	D	-2	0	3	2	0	3	0	-2	D
	Priusquam fierent montes / Repleti sumus	ofv	OTT 175 GB 163 SYG 171	D	7	8	7	10	9	7	5	9	
	Priusquam montes fierent / Domine refugium	intv	GR 101 GS 38 165 GB 68 SYG 76										
	Priusquam montes fierent / Domine refugium	grv	GR 381 LU 1067 GB 262 SYG 256 GS 34 165	a	3	5	7	5	3	2	3	0	
5	Priusquam te formarem	gr	GR 524 LU 1500 SYG 196 GB 198^V *GS 1	F	2	0	2	-3	0	2	4	2	F
8	Priusquam te formarem	an	LR 346 *WA 320 *LA 400	G	5	2	0	-2	0	2	4	5	G
7	Priusquam te formarem	re	LR 349 *LA 402 *WA 322	G	5	2	0	2	4	7	5	7	G
	Pro eo quod audisti / In sudore vultus	rev	LA 111 WA 74										
6	Pro eo quod non credidisti	an	LA 409	c	-3	-5	0	2	0	2	4	2	c
	Pro eo quod obedisti	see	Pro eo quod audisti										
	Pro eo ut diligerent me / Domine fac mecum	ofv	OTT 37 *GB 85^v *SYG 96	b	1	0	1	0	-4	-2	0	-2	
	Pro eo ut me diligerent / Vir iste in populo	rev	LA 503 WA 236										
1	Pro fidei meritis vocitatur	an	PM 109	C	2	4	5	2	4	2	0	5	D
	Pro hac orabit ad te / Laetamini in Domino	ofv	OTT 140 *GB 44 SYG 41	F	2	4	2	0	4	2	0	2	
	Pro omnibus mortuus est Christus	alv	GR 480 LU 1434	E	-2	1	0	-2	0	1	0	-2	
8	Pro pace regum et principum	an	GB 155	F	4	7	4	6	4	2	4	2	G
	Pro patribus tuis nati sunt / Constitues eos	grv	GR 393 533 LU 1519 GS x GB 204 SYG 202	F	4	7	6	4	7	6	2	4	
7	Pro quorum memoria	co	GS 233	G	5	4	5	7	9	7	9	10	G
	Pro salute et augmento gregis / Fidelis namque	rev	PM 309	a	-2	1	0	-2	0	-2	-4	-5	
6	Pro te Jesu Christe morte	re	WA 249	c	2	4	2	0	2	0	-3	-2	c
	Proba me Domine / Lavabo inter innocentes	ofv	SYG 86	d	-2	-3	-2	-3	-5	-3	-5	-2	
4	Proba me Domine	gr	SYG 85	D	-2	5	3	0	-2	5	3	5	E
	Probasti Domine cor meum / Igne me examinasti	anv	WA 348 LA 436										

#	Incipit	Type	Sources		1	2	3	4	5	6	7	8	
	Probasti Domine cor meum In craticula	rev	LA 439 WA 349										
7	Probasti Domine cor meum	int	GR 586 *GB 217^v *SYG 217 *GS 195	G	2	-2	2	0	2	0	2	5	G
5	Probasti Domine cor meum	gr	GR 579 LU 1594 SYG 213 GB 217^v GS 194	D	3	7	8	7	5	7	5	3	F
8	Probasti nos Deus igne	tr	GR 108**	G	2	4	2	0	2	0	5	7	G
	Probavit me Dominus sicut aurum Oratio mea	ofv	OTT 164 *GB 216^v *SYG 212	G	4	7	5	4	7	9	7	9	
8	Procedat e thalamo suo	hy	ST 30	G	-2	-3	-5	-2	2	0	-2	0	G
	Produxitque Dominus Deus Plantaverat autem	rev	LA 109										
1	Profana dum succenderet	hy	ST 43	C	2	4	7	5	4	2	5	4	D
7	Proficiat nobis Domine	co	SYG 230	G	2	-2	2	0	2	5	4	5	G
	Proficiebat sapientia Descendit Jesus	rev	LR 316	G	5	4	0	2	4	2	5	7	
1	Profitemur enim Christianae	an	WA 258	C	2	9	11	9	12	9	7	9	D
8	Prolapso in lacum Placido	re	LR 276	G	-2	-5	-3	-2	-3	-5	-7	-5	G
3	Proles de caelo prodiit	hy	ST 442	E	3	5	3	5	8	7	5	8	E
5	Proles de caelo prodiit	hy	ST 443	F	4	7	9	6	7	9	11	7	F
	Prolongaverunt iniquitatem sibi Saepe expugnaverunt	trv	GR 153 LU 571 *GS 72 *GB 97^v *SYG 110	G	-5	0	2	4	2	5	7	5	
	Promittentes tecum in carcerem Vadis propitiator	rev	PM 188	G	4	7	9	7	5	4	7	9	
4	Proni rogamus	hy	ST 241	F	-1	-3	-5	-3	0	-3	-1	0	E
4	Prope es tu Domine	int	GR 11 *SYG 9 *GB 8 GS 6	D	3	2	3	2	3	5	7	5	E
5	Prope est Dominus	gr	GR 21 LU 354 *SYG 8 *GB 7 *GS 6	F	-3	0	2	0	-3	0	2	-1	F
6	Prope est jam Dominus	inv	LA 22 WA 17	c	2	0	2	4	0	2	4	2	c
4	Prope est jam Dominus	inv	LA 18	C	2	4	5	4	5	7	4	5	E
3	Prope est ut veniat tempus	re	LA 14 *WA 15	G	2	4	5	4	2	5	2	0	E
	Prope esto Domine	see	Prope es tu Domine										
4	Propheta magnus surrexit	an	AR 403 567 LU 1044 1096 AM 380 607	a	-2	0	3	5	3	5	7	5	a
1	Prophetae praedicaverunt nasci	an	AR 240 AM 215 LA 24 377 WA 18	D	-2	0	3	2	0	-2	3	5	D
	Prophetae praedixerunt	see	Prophetae praedicaverunt										
	Propitius esto Domine peccatis	alv	GR [148] LU 841 SYG 234	C	2	4	5	2	0	4	5	7	

N	Incipit	Type	Sources	Mode									Fin
5	Propitius esto Domine peccatis	gr	GR 107 LU 999 *SYG 81 GB 78^v GS 42 51 145 170	D	3	5	3	5	7	5	7	5	F
8	Propitius esto peccatis	an	WA 67 *LA 97	c	-1	-3	-5	-3	-1	-3	-5	-3	G
5 7	Proprio filio suo non pepercit	an	AR 438 OHS 509 LU 712 AM 438 *LA 200 WA 124	d	-3	0	2	3	2	0	-2	-3	G
	Propter David servum tuum Surge Domine	trv	GR [119] 90**	G	-5	0	2	5	7	4	5	2	
7	Propter fidem castitatis	an	WA 274 LA 360	d	-3	0	2	0	2	0	-3	-2	G
5	Propter fratres meos	gr	GR 527 LU 1512	F	2	0	2	4	0	2	0	-1	F
5	Propter insuperabilem	an	WA 38 *LA 49^v	a	-4	0	3	2	0	3	5	3	F
2	Propter intolerabiles rerum	re	WA 288	D	-2	0	-2	-5	-2	0	-2	0	D
8	Propter lignum servi	an	LA 215	G	-5	-2	0	2	0	2	0	-2	G
	Propter nimiam caritatem Ecce jam venit	rev	WA 23										
8	Propter nimiam caritatem	an	AR 293 LU 440 AM 270 *LA 40	G	-2	-5	-2	0	2	0	-2	0	G
8	Propter nomen tuum	an	AR 170	G	-5	-2	0	-2	0	2	-2	0	G
	Propter nos egenus	sr	AR 328 LU 470										
	Propter quod et Deus Christus factus est	grv	GR 196 AR 434 LU 669 OHS 444 GS v 94 235 GB 115 *SYG 129	F	4	2	7	9	7	2	7	9	
4	Propter Sion non tacebo	an	AR 240 AM 215 *WA 18 *LA 24	G	2	5	7	5	7	9	5	7	a
1	Propter testamentum Domini	re	PM 207 LR 186 *LA 517 WA 422	D	3	5	3	0	3	5	3	5	D
	Propter veritatem Diffusa est gratia	rev	LA 542										
	Propter veritatem Dilexisti	rev	LR 221 LA 543 WA 431										
	Propter veritatem Vidisti Domine	rev	LA 358 WA 275										
	Propter veritatem ... et deducet Diffusa est gratia	trv	SYG 49	E	-2	0	1	3	1	3	1	0	
5	Propter veritatem ... et deducet	gr	GR 583 620 (31) LU 1676 SYG 215 GB 222^v GS s	F	2	0	2	4	2	4	0	2	F
1	Propter veritatem ... et deducet	re	LR 221 LA 545 *WA 431	D	2	3	5	3	0	3	5	3	D
	Propter veritatem ... et deducet Diffusa est gratia	trv	GS 228	F	2	4	2	4	2	0	2	0	
	Propter veritatem ... et deducet Diffusa est gratia	grv	GR [69] LU 1240 GS 227 GB 29^v SYG 28	F	4	7	9	7	4	7	0	4	
	Propter veritatem ... et deducet Specie tua	grv	GR [60] LU 1226 GS 226 SYG 39	F	4	7	9	7	4	7	0	4	

	Propter veritatem ... et deducet	alv	GR [67] LU 1237	D	5	7	5	3	0	5	3	5	
	Propter veritatem ... exaltabit	alv	SYG 232	D	2	0	-2	0	3	2	0	2	
	Propterea benedixit te Deus / Constitues eos	ofv	OTT 131 *GB 206^v / *SYG 203	F	-5	-3	-1	0	-1	0	2	-1	
	Propterea confitebor tibi / Persequar inimicos	trv	GR 463	C	2	5	4	5	2	5	2	4	
	Propterea dimissa sunt ei / In diebus illis mulier	anv	SYG 130										
	Propterea laetamini caeli / Nunc facta est salus	rev	LA 469										
	Propterea unxit te Deus / Dilexisti	grv	GR [52] LU 1216 / GS 226 GB 4 SYG 5	G	-2	0	-2	2	5	2	0	2	
	Prostratus est saevissimus / A Christo	anv	WA 264 LA 345										
7	Prostratus est saevissimus	an	LA 343	G	5	2	0	4	5	7	9	7	G
	Protector meus et cornu / Firmamentum meum	rev	LA 82										
4	Protector noster aspice Deus	int	GR 357 LU 1036 / *SYG 248 *GB 255 / GS 157	F	-3	-1	0	2	4	2	7	4	E
5	Protector noster aspice Deus	gr	GR 108 LU 1003 / *SYG 75 *GB 67^v / GS 37 43 144 171	D	3	5	3	0	3	5	2	3	F
2	Protege Domine plebem tuam	of	GR 594 LU 1630 / OTT 168 SYG 174 / GB 167 GS 185 236	D	-2	-5	-2	0	2	0	-2	0	D
	Protege Domine templum / Praecipita Domine	rev	WA 185										
7	Protexisti me Deus a conventu	int	GR [15] LU 1146 / SYG 169 GB 153 / GS 205	G	2	0	2	5	7	5	7	9	C
	Prudentes autem virgines / Offerentur regi	rev	LA 544										
	Prudentes autem virgines / Simile est regnum ... decem	rev	WA 432										
5	Prudentes virgines acceperunt oleum	co	GR 101**	F	2	4	6	7	2	0	2	0	F
4	Prudentes virgines aptate lampades	an	AR 577^21 [87] / LU 2629 1215 / AM 683 746	a	-2	0	3	5	3	5	7	5	a
	Prudentes virgines aptate vestras / Media nocte	rev	LR 226										
7	Prudentes virgines aptate vestras	re	LR 222	G	5	4	5	7	9	7	5	7	G
8	Psallat chorus caelestium	hy	ST 110	G	2	0	-2	-3	-5	-3	-2	0	G
6	Psallentes Christo Christum	inv	WA 248	c	2	0	2	4	0	2	0	4	c
1	Psallite Deo nostro	an	LR 70 WA 53 LA 66	D	-2	0	3	2	0	2	0	-2	D
8	Psallite Deo qui ascendit	re	WA 150	G	2	0	2	0	-2	0	2	0	G
2	Psallite Domino omnes	re	WA 396	D	-2	0	-2	0	3	2	0	2	D

Psallite Domino qui ascendit	alv	GB 182	D	-2	0	2	3	2	0	-2	0	
1 Psallite Domino qui ascendit	co	GR 287 LU 849 SYG 180 GB 182 GS 136	D	-2	0	3	2	3	5	3	2	D
Psallite Domino qui ascendit	alv	SYG 180	d	3	0	-2	-5	-7	-2	-7	-2	
Psalmum dicite nomini ejus In ecclesiis	rev	LA 238										
3 Pudore bono repletus	an	WA 239	E	-2	3	5	8	7	8	10	8	E
Puellae saltanti imperavit Accedentes discipuli	rev	WA 363										
1 Puellae saltanti imperavit	an	AR 829 LU 1620 AM 1026 *WA 363 *LA 454	D	-2	3	5	3	7	3	5	7	D
Puellae saltanti imperavit Misit rex	ofv	OTT 176	F	2	9	11	9	11	7	6	7	
2 Puellae saltanti imperavit	re	LA 452 *WA 362	A	3	5	7	5	8	7	8	10	D
1 Puer fletum subsecute	re	WA 299	A	3	5	3	5	8	5	0	3	D
1 Puer Jesus crescebat	an	LA 62	D	7	9	7	9	10	7	5	7	D
6 Puer Jesus proficiebat	an	AR 289 LU 437 AM 267	F	-5	-3	0	2	0	2	4	7	F
1 Puer Jesus proficiebat	an	WA 58	E	-4	-2	1	3	1	3	5	8	D
Puer meus dicit Dominus	alv	SYG 213	G	2	5	7	4	2	5	4	5	
7 Puer meus noli timere	re	LA 434 *WA 349	c	-1	0	2	0	2	4	2	4	G
7 Puer natus est nobis	int	GR 33 LU 408 SYG 18 GS G	G	7	9	7	5	7	5	9	7	G
1 Puer natus in Bethlehem alleluia		AR 149*	D	3	2	3	5	3	2	0	3	D
7 Puer qui natus est nobis	an	AR 741 LU 1505 AM 928 *LA 405	G	7	9	7	5	2	5	9	7	G
8 Puer quidam parvulus	an	WA 298 *LA 375	G	-2	-3	-2	0	2	0	2	0	G
7 Puer Samuel ministrabat	an	AR 536 LU 960 AM 556	G	2	5	7	5	7	9	10	12	G
1 Puer trimus amne	re	WA 250	D	3	2	0	-2	0	3	5	7	D
1 Pueri Hebraeorum portantes	an	GR 170 AR 423 OHS 77 93 LU 581 AM 402 *PM 53	D	3	0	-2	3	5	3	7	10	D
1 Pueri Hebraeorum tollentes	an	WA 113 207 LA 182 GS 78	D	3	0	-2	3	5	3	5	7	D
1 Pueri Hebraeorum vestimenta	an	AR 424 GR 170 OHS 85 94 LU 582 AM 402 *PM 53 *WA 113 207 *LA 182 *GS 78	D	3	0	-2	3	5	3	7	10	D
Pulcher virtutibus Immaculatas hostiarum	ofv	SYG 220	A	3	5	3	7	8	7	5	7	
1 Pulchra es et decora	an	AR 821 LU 1606 AM 1015 *LR 220 *LA 448 *WA 358	F	4	5	2	4	0	4	2	4	D

1 Pulchra es o virgo Maria	re	PM 263	C	2	5	2	0	2	4	2	4	D
1 Pulchra et decora filia	an	WA 358	F	4	5	2	0	4	2	4	2	D
8 Pulchra facie sed pulchrior	re	WA 433	G	-3	-2	0	2	0	-2	0	2	G
Pulchra facie sed pulchrior	alv	SYG 42	E	1	0	-2	3	5	7	8	5	
5 Pulchra facie sed pulchrior	re	LR 218 *LA 336 *WA 255	F	4	7	9	7	9	11	7	4	F
Pulchra facie sed pulchrior In sanctitate fulgida	rev	WA 431	G	5	4	0	-2	0	2	4	2	
Pulchra Sion filia pro mortali Surge virgo	rev	PM 209	E	-2	3	5	8	5	3	5	8	
2 Pulchrae sunt genae tuae	an	WA 162	D	-2	0	3	2	0	-2	0	3	D
Pulchriores sunt oculi ejus Non auferetur	rev	LA 18 WA 23										
Puri cordis munditiae Pius adolescens	rev	WA 312	c	-1	-3	-5	-3	0	-1	2	0	
4 Qua Christus hora sitiit	hy	ST 319	a	-2	0	-2	0	-2	0	-2	-4	E
8 Qua Christus hora sitiit	hy	ST 382	c	2	0	-1	-3	0	-3	0	-1	G
3 Quadam die cum ex more	re	LR 295	G	2	5	4	2	0	-2	0	2	E
3 Quadam die tempestate	re	WA 240	G	2	0	2	5	2	4	5	4	E
7 Quadraginta annis proximus	inv	LA 166	G	2	0	-2	0	2	5	7	5	G
5 Quadraginta dies et noctes	re	LA 117 WA 76	F	4	7	4	7	9	7	6	7	F
Quae apparuit intercessori Oswaldus bajulus	rev	WA 284	d	2	3	2	0	-2	0	-2	-3	
Quae cum exisset Puellae saltanti	rev	WA 362										
Quae cum non inveniret Anima Scholasticae	rev	LR 300										
Quae datura eras Per ipsam te	rev	WA 243										
Quae est enim fortitudo mea Inclinans faciem	rev	WA 175										
Quae est enim ... fortitudo mea Vir erat	ofv	OTT 122 GB 262 SYG 256	c	2	0	-1	0	2	0	5	0	
Quae est ista quae ascendit de	sr	AR 634 LU 1375										
4 Quae est ista quae ascendit de	an	WA 356	F	-1	-3	0	-1	0	2	0	2	E

	Quae est ista quae ascendit per Quae est ista quae processit	rev	LA 443										
	Quae est ista quae ascendit per Vidi speciosam	rev	AM 1200 PM 178 LR 376 WA 355										
1	Quae est ista quae ascendit sicut	an	AR 821 LU 1600[4] AM 1017 WA 358 LA 449	C	2	9	10	9	7	9	7	9	D
1	Quae est ista quae penetravit	re	VP 204	F	-3	-1	-3	-5	-3	-5	0	2	D
4	Quae est ista quae processit	re	PM 261 LR 253 *LA 443 WA 355	F	-1	-5	-3	0	-1	2	0	-1	E
8	Quae est ista quae progreditur	co	GR 399	G	-2	0	-5	-3	-2	0	2	0	G
	Quae est ista quae progreditur	alv	GR 75**	D	-2	0	3	0	-2	2	3	5	
8	Quae est ista speciosa	an	AR 871 LU 1679 *AM 1072	a	-4	-2	0	-2	0	-2	-4	0	G
	Quae Gabrielis archangeli dictis Gaude Maria	trv	GR [78] LU 1266	D	-2	0	3	5	3	0	2	3	
1	Quae in sinu beati patris	re	LR 282	D	7	5	7	10	9	7	5	7	D
	Quae meruit Dominum progenerare Candida virginitas	rev	PM 264 VP 40	D	3	5	7	5	3	5	3	2	
1	Quae mihi fuerunt lucra	co	GR 622[5] LU 1681[6]	D	2	3	2	3	5	3	2	5	D
6	Quae mulier habens drachmas	an	AR 538[16] LU 985 AM 573 *LA 311	F	-3	-5	0	2	0	2	4	0	F
	Quae nec oculus vidit Venite benedicti	trv	SYG 75	G	2	4	5	4	2	4	5	4	
8	Quae sunt haec maleficia	re	WA 246	G	-5	0	-2	-5	0	-2	0	-2	G
2	Quae sunt in corde hominum	re	LA 280 *WA 170	D	-2	0	2	3	2	0	-2	0	D
3	Quaerentes eum tenere	an	WA 95	G	-3	-2	0	-2	-3	-5	0	4	E
3	Quaerentes eum tenere	an	AR 385 LU 1088 *AM 360 LA 145	G	2	5	2	5	4	0	2	4	E
	Quaerite autem primum	see	Quaerite primum										
4	Quaerite Dominum dum inveniri	an	AR 221 AM 192 *WA 9 *LA 7	a	-2	0	3	5	3	5	7	5	a
3	Quaerite Dominum et confirmamini	of	GR 110**	c	-3	-1	0	2	0	-3	-5	-1	b
8	Quaerite Dominum et inveniet	an	WA 66	G	-2	2	5	4	0	4	5	2	G
8	Quaerite Dominum et vivet	an	LA 95	G	-2	2	5	4	2	4	5	2	G
1	Quaerite primum regnum Dei	an	AR 566 810 LU 1040 1591 *AM 605 1004 *LA 316 *WA 189	F	-5	-3	4	5	4	2	4	5	D
1	Qualem caritatem corde	an	AM 875	C	2	4	5	4	5	4	2	4	D
	Qualis pater talis filius	alv	SYG 261										
	Quam admirabile est nomen	an	OHS 58 (nm)										
	Quam amabilia sunt tabernacula Protector noster aspice	intv	GB 255										

#	Text	Type	Source	Start									End
8	Quam bonus Deus	an	LA 95	c	2	0	-5	-3	-7	-3	-1	-3	G
	Quam bonus Israel Deus Factum est cor meum	intv	GR 505 LU 1477										
	Quam bonus Israel Deus Mihi autem adhaerere	intv	GR (34)										
	Quam bonus Israel Deus Oculus Dei respexit	intv	GR 448 LU 1392										
	Quam bonus Israel Deus Tenuisti manum	intv	GR 462 LU 1418 GS 86										
	Quam bonus Israel Deus Tenuisti manum	grv	GR 179 OHS 108 LU 593 GS 86 *GB 109 *SYG 122	F	-3	2	5	2	4	5	4	5	
1	Quam bonus Israel Deus	an	WA 67	a	-2	0	-2	-4	-2	3	0	-2	D
8	Quam bonus Israel Deus	an	AR 155 LU 279^{N}	c	2	0	-5	-3	-5	-7	-5	-3	G
	Quam dilecta tabernacula Passer invenit	cov	SYG 94										
	Quam dilecta tabernacula Dilectio Dei	intv	GR 603 LU 1645										
	Quam dilecta tabernacula Exsultet gaudio	intv	GR 59 LU 470										
	Quam dilecta tabernacula Illuxerunt coruscationes	intv	GR 571 LU 1585										
	Quam dilecta tabernacula Protector noster	intv	GR 357 LU 1036 GS 157 SYG 248										
	Quam dilecta tabernacula tua Sub umbra illius	intv	GR 625 LU 1689										
	Quam dilecta tabernacula tua Terribilis est locus	intv	GR [71] LU 1250										
	Quam dilecta tabernacula Domine dilexi	rev	LA 548										
7	Quam dilecta tabernacula	re	LR 240	G	5	7	9	10	7	5	7	5	G
	Quam dulcia faucibus De ore prudentis	rev	LA 384										
	Quam dulcia faucibus Deus docuisti	trv	GR 72**	F	2	7	9	11	7	2	7	9	
	Quam elevata est Domine Dominus noster	cov	SYG 87										
8	Quam felix es Gallia	re	PM 347	G	-2	-5	-2	0	5	2	0	4	G
6	Quam jocunda et suavis	an	WA 252	c	-3	-5	0	2	4	2	4	5	c
	Quam magna multitudo	alv	GR 628	a	-2	0	-4	-7	-9	-7	-5	-4	
	Quam magna multitudo In te speravi	ofv	OTT 101 *GB 68^{V} *SYG 76	G	2	3	2	0	-2	0	-2	0	
1	Quam magna multitudo	re	LA 88 *WA 63	D	2	3	5	3	0	3	5	3	D
3	Quam magna multitudo	co	GR 507 LU 1480	c	4	2	4	0	-1	-3	-5	-3	E
5	Quam magna multitudo	gr	GR 449 LU 1393	F	4	7	4	7	6	7	9	7	F

#	Title		Sources										
1	Quam magna multitudo	of	GR 57**	D	7	8	7	5	3	5	3	5	D
	Quam magnificata sunt	sr	AM 128 LA 87 WA 63										
	Quam magnificata sunt / Bonum est confiteri	ofv	OTT 26 *GB 57 *SYG 59	G	2	0	-5	0	2	5	7	5	
7	Quam magnificata sunt	an	AR 187	G	4	7	5	2	5	4	2	0	G
	Quam nemo principum / Non judicavi	trv	GR 476	C	2	5	7	5	2	5	7	9	
4	Quam pulchra es amica mea	re	LR 224	F	-3	0	-1	2	0	-1	0	-1	E
8	Quam pulchra es et quam	an	WA 361	G	2	4	5	2	5	4	2	0	G
3	Quam pulchra es Gertrudis	an	AM 1128	E	-2	3	5	7	8	7	8	10	E
1	Quam pulchra es Maria	an	PM 272	D	7	8	7	5	7	5	3	2	D
4	Quam pulchri super montes	co	GR 60**	F	-1	2	4	7	4	2	4	2	E
7	Quam salubre invocatum	an	WA 249	G	2	5	4	5	7	9	7	5	G
	Quam supra nonaginta / Dico vobis gaudium	cov	SYG 260										
7	Quandam vexatam demone	an	WA 293	G	7	5	7	10	7	9	7	5	G
	Quando certa lege / Gyrum caeli	rev	WA 168	a	2	0	2	0	2	5	4	5	
	Quando enim infirmor / Libenter gloriabor	anv	LA 430 WA 266										
	Quando enim infirmor / Libenter gloriabor	rev	WA 265										
3	Quando nata est virgo	an	WA 364	E	-2	3	5	8	10	8	7	5	E
3	Quando natus es ineffabiliter	an	AR 294 LU 443 *AM 271 WA 50 *LA 64	E	-2	3	5	8	7	3	7	8	E
2	Quando orabas cum lacrimis	of of	GR 556 LU 1563	D	-5	-2	0	2	-2	0	2	3	D
	Quando praeparabat caelos / In principio Deus	rev	LR 421 LA 276										
3	Quantam denique messem	re	WA 239	G	2	0	2	4	5	4	2	4	E
7	Quantas habeo iniquitates	an	WA 171	G	7	5	7	10	9	7	5	7	G
1	Quantas sancti corpore poenas	hy	ST 499	F	-3	-1	0	-1	-5	-1	-3	0	D
	Quanti mercenarii / Pater peccavi	rev	LR 407 LA 145 WA 87										
8	Quanto eis praecibiebat	an	WA 189	G	5	2	0	-2	0	2	0	2	G
3	Quare detraxistis sermonibus	an	LA 287	E	-2	3	5	3	5	7	8	10	E
1	Quare detraxistis sermonibus	re	LA 283 *WA 172	D	2	3	5	3	2	0	2	3	D
8	Quare ergo rubrum est	an	AR 760 LU 1537 AM 946	c	-1	-3	-1	0	-5	-7	-3	0	G
	Quare fremuerunt gentes / Servite Domino in timore	cov	SYG 68										

	Quare fremuerunt gentes Dominus dixit	intv	GR 27 LU 392 GS 13 GB 13ᵛ SYG 14									
	Quare fremuerunt gentes Astiterunt reges	rev	OHS 616 LU 771 LA 205									
8	Quare jejunavimus	an	LA 126	c	-1	0	2	0	-1	-3	-5	-3	G
	Quare me repulisti Judica me Deus	intv	GB 97									
	Quasi apis argumentosa O beata Caecilia	rev	PM 212									
	Quasi arena maris Utinam appenderentur	rev	LA 283 WA 172									
	Quasi cedrus exaltate es	alv	GB 224	c	2	4	2	4	5	4	2	0	
6	Quasi modo geniti alleluia	int	GS 124	C	2	5	7	5	7	9	7	5	F
6	Quasi modo geniti infantes	int	GR 261 LU 809 *SYG 162 GB 144ᵛ	C	2	5	7	5	0	5	7	4	F
	Quasi modo geniti infantes	alv	GB 144ᵛ	C	2	7	5	4	2	0	2	0	
	Quasi palma exaltata	alv	GR 34**	G	2	0	7	9	7	9	7	9	
	Quasi qui invenit Principes persecuti	rev	LA 182 WA 113									
	Quasi rosa plantata	alv	GR 614 LU 1669	G	-2	0	7	9	7	9	7	9	
	Quasi sponsum decoratum Induit me	rev	LR 228									
	Quasi trames aquae Quae in sinu	rev	LR 282	a	-2	0	-2	-4	-5	-2	0	-2	
3	Quasi unum ex paradisi	an	PM 34 WA 38 *LA 48	G	2	0	2	5	4	5	7	5	E
	Quasi unus de paradisi	scc	Quasi unum ex paradisi									
6	Quatuor animalia ibant	re	WA 373	c	2	-2	0	2	-3	-5	-7	0	c
2	Quatuor facies uni	re	WA 372	C	2	5	4	2	5	4	5	7	D
3	Quem crescentem virtutibus	an	WA 311	E	1	0	-2	3	5	8	7	5	E
8	Quem dicunt homines	an	WA 281	G	-2	-3	-2	-3	-2	0	2	0	G
1	Quem dicunt homines	re	LR 366 *LA 419 *WA 279	D	3	0	3	0	3	5	7	5	D
	Quem dilexerat viventem Valde mane	rev	WA 338	a	-2	-4	-5	-2	0	2	0	-7	
	Quem Dominus post apostolos Adest namque beati	rev	WA 387									
	Quem ex Indorum Exsultemus cuncti in Deo	grv	GB 227	D	7	5	7	3	7	9	7	5	
8	Quem in superna patria	hy	ST 377	G	-2	0	2	5	4	5	7	5	G
	Quem Michael assumpsit O beatum virum	intv	SYG 224									
3	Quem parentes	an	WA 248	E	-2	3	5	8	7	5	3	5	E

	Quem perfuderat Deus Sebastianus vir	rev	LA 325									
	Quem proposuit Deus Gratificavit nos	trv	GR 538	C	2	5	7	2	5	4	5	4	
	Quem quaeris mulier	sr	WA 145										
	Quem te petimus Pectore sincero	rev	WA 337	G	5	4	5	7	9	7	5	7	
1	Quem terra pontus aethera	hy	ST 131	a	-7	0	2	-2	0	2	3	2	D
4	Quem terra pontus aethera	hy	ST 29	a	-2	-5	-7	-2	0	3	0	-2	E
2	Quem terra pontus aethera	hy	ST 87 184 LR 245 273	d	-2	-5	-7	-2	0	3	2	0	d
8	Quem terra pontus aethera	hy	ST 298	G	-2	-3	-5	-7	-2	0	3	2	G
2	Quem terra pontus aethera	hy	ST 223	d	-2	-3	-2	-5	-7	-2	0	3	d
4	Quem terra pontus aethera	hy	ST 132	G	2	0	-2	-5	-2	-3	0	-2	E
8	Quem terra pontus aethera	hy	ST 398	G	2	0	-2	0	2	4	0	-2	G
1	Quem terra pontus aethera	hy	ST 122	D	7	9	7	5	3	2	5	7	D
	Quem unum caelestis Elegit Deus	rev	PM 342	G	5	4	0	2	4	2	5	7	
2	Quem vidistis pastores	an	AR 264 LU 395 AM 240 WA 31 *LA 40	F	-1	0	-3	0	-1	-5	-3	0	D
4	Quem vidistis pastores	re	LU 377 *LR 58 *LA 36 *WA 30	D	3	0	2	5	3	2	3	2	E
	Quem visurus sum ego ipse Credo quod redemptor	rev	AR [158] PM 320 LU 1785 LA 554 WA 436										
	Quemadmodum desiderat cervus Reliqui domum meam	intv	GR 18**										
5	Quemadmodum desiderat cervus	gr	GR 506 LU 1478	D	3	5	3	5	7	5	7	5	F
	Qui a Judaeis Lucianus presbyter	rev	WA 343										
	Qui ad justitiam erudiunt	alv	GR 497 LU 1467	G	7	9	7	5	7	5	2	4	
2	Qui ambulat fraudulenter	gr	GR 30**	E	3	5	8	5	7	8	5	3	a
1	Qui autem diligit me	an	WA 151	D	2	0	-2	3	5	3	5	7	D
1	Qui biberit aquam	co	SYG 99 *GS 61	F	-1	-3	0	2	0	2	0	-1	D
3	Qui biberit aquam	co	GR 136 *GB 88	E	3	1	0	3	5	1	3	1	E
1	Qui caelorum contines	an	AR 553 LU 997 AM 592 WA 183 *LA 309	C	2	5	4	2	0	2	5	4	D
2	Qui caelorum contines	re	LA 306 WA 185	A	3	5	7	5	8	7	8	10	D
8	Qui Christe natus virgini	hy	ST 179	G	2	4	2	4	5	4	2	0	G
4	Qui Christiano nomini	hy	ST 291	C	2	4	5	4	2	0	2	5	E

#	Text	Type	Sources	Mode									End
	Qui cogitaverunt malitias Eripe me	trv	GR 208 OHS 534 LU 725 GS 99 *SYG 137 *GB 116^v	D	-2	0	3	5	3	0	2	3	
	Qui cogitaverunt supplantare Custodi me	ofv	OTT 52 *SYG 126	a	-2	0	-2	0	3	2	3	5	
	Qui cogitaverunt supplantare Eripe me	trv	GR 208 OHS 534 LU 725 GS 99 *GB 116^v *SYG 137	D	-2	0	3	5	7	3	2	5	
	Qui cogitaverunt supplantare Custodi me Domine	ofv	GB 113	C	5	7	5	2	5	7	5	7	
8	Qui cognoscis Domine	int	SYG 234	G	2	0	-2	0	2	5	4	5	G
8	Qui confidunt in Domino	gr	GB 75	G	-3	0	-2	0	-3	-2	0	-5	G
	Qui confidunt in Domino	alv	GB 266^v	D	-2	0	2	3	5	3	2	0	
	Qui confidunt in Domino	alv	SYG 255 GS 163	a	2	0	-2	0	-2	-4	-2	0	
8	Qui confidunt in Domino	tr	GR 139(40) LU 561 SYG 101 GB 90 GS 63	G	2	4	2	0	2	0	-2	0	G
	Qui confidunt in illum Tamquam aurum	rev	LR 184 LA 519										
1	Qui consolabatur me	re	WA 175	D	3	5	3	0	3	5	3	5	D
5	Qui cum audissent	re	WA 240	F	4	2	7	9	7	4	2	7	F
	Qui cum imminere Post passionem	rev	WA 385										
1	Qui custodiebant animam	re	LA 170 *WA 107	D	2	3	5	3	0	3	5	7	D
	Qui custodit veritatem Lauda anima	ofv	OTT 67 GB 149 *SYG 166	C	2	5	7	9	4	7	5	4	
	Qui custos est Domini Fidelis servus	rev	AM 1193 *LR 316	a	-2	0	-2	-4	-2	0	-2	0	
	Qui dat salutem Deus canticum	rcv	WA 145										
3	Qui de rupe promisit	an	WA 295	G	2	5	4	2	5	4	5	4	E
	Qui de terra est Ecce agnus	rev	LR 64										
3	Qui de terra est	an	WA 49 *LA 63	E	-2	3	5	8	7	8	10	7	E
1	Qui diligitis Dominum	an	LR 387	C	2	9	10	9	7	9	7	5	D
	Qui docet manus meas Deus qui praecinxit	grv	GR 463 LU 1419	G	5	7	5	7	5	7	4	5	
	Qui docti fuerint fulgebunt	alv	GR 496 LU 1466	C	2	9	10	9	7	9	5	4	
1	Qui dum eremum	an	WA 300	D	3	0	-2	3	5	3	5	7	D
	Qui facis angelos tuos Ponis nubem	rev	LA 249 WA 149										
	Qui facit angelos suos	alv	GR 461 GB 168^v	C	2	4	2	9	10	9	7	4	
8	Qui gloriatur in Domino	tr	GR 546	G	2	4	2	0	2	0	-2	0	G

	Qui habitant in domo Quam dilecta	rev	LR 240										
8	Qui habitas in caelis	an	AR 119 OHS 287 LU 285 AM 116 *WA 66 LA 93	a	-4	-2	0	2	3	0	2	3	G
	Qui habitat in adjutorio Invocabit me	intv	GR 93 LU 532 GS 34 GB 64v SYG 72										
8	Qui habitat in adjutorio	an	LR 237 *WA 318 *LA 549	a	-4	-2	0	-4	-5	-7	-4	-2	G
2	Qui habitat in adjutorio	tr	GR 95 LU 533 SYG 73 GB 65 GS 35	D	-2	0	-2	-5	-2	0	-2	0	D
1	Qui in sancta ecclesia	an	WA 315	D	-5	-2	0	-2	0	2	0	2	D
	Qui insurgunt in me confundantur Confitebor Domino	ofv	OTT 74 *GB 162 SYG 178	F	4	7	9	7	6	7	6	4	
	Qui intingit mecum manum Unus ex discipulis	rev	OHS 391 LU 645 LA 191 WA 118										
4	Qui Lazarum resuscitasti	re	PM 320	F	-3	0	2	0	-3	-1	-3	0	E
4	Qui Lazarum resuscitasti	re	AR [159] LU 1786 *LA 554 *WA 436	D	3	2	0	2	3	2	5	3	E
	Qui liberas Israel Tu Domine universorum	rev	LA 299										
	Qui ligandi et solvendi O princeps	rev	WA 278	D	7	9	7	5	7	5	3	5	
8	Qui major est	an	WA 94	G	-2	-5	-2	0	2	0	3	2	G
	Qui maledixerit tibi Ecce odor filii	rev	LA 137 WA 91										
6	Qui manducat carnem meam	co	GR 344 LU 1019 SYG 90 *GB 80 GS 52 159	C	2	5	7	5	9	7	5	7	F
7	Qui manducat meam carnem	re	LU 938 LR 131	G	7	5	4	5	7	9	7	5	G
1	Qui me confessus fuerit	an	AR [15] LU 1125 AM 640 WA 419 LA 527	D	-2	3	5	3	5	7	8	7	D
1	Qui me dignatus est	re	WA 274	D	3	5	3	5	7	5	3	5	D
6	Qui me dignatus est	co	GR 437 LU 1370 *SYG 51 GB 50v GS 181	D	3	5	7	5	7	5	3	5	F
7	Qui me dignatus est	an	AR 626 LU 1371 AM 808 WA 276 *LA 363	G	4	5	7	9	7	9	7	5	G
6	Qui me dignatus est	re	LA 361	G	5	7	9	7	9	7	5	7	c
	Qui me invenerit inveniet	sr	AR 635 LU 1380										
	Qui me invenerit inveniet	alv	GR 26**	D	-2	0	3	5	0	3	2	0	
	Qui me invenerit inveniet Nunc ergo filii	trv	GR 587³	G	2	4	5	4	5	7	5	0	

1 Qui me misit mecum est	an	AR 382 LU 1085 AM 356 WA 94 *LA 144	D	2	3	5	2	3	2	0	-2	D
1 Qui me sanum fecit	an	AR 377 LU 1084 AM 350 *WA 90	D	-2	3	5	3	7	3	5	7	D
Qui me segregavit Qui operatur	anv	WA 329 LA 422										
1 Qui me segregavit	an	WA 330	D	-2	0	3	5	7	5	3	5	D
3 Qui meditabitur in lege	co	GR 90 LU 529 *SYG 67 *GB 63 GS 32	E	-2	3	5	3	5	8	7	5	E
1 Qui mihi ministrat	an	AR [16] LU 1125 AM 640 *WA 419 *LA 528	D	-2	3	5	3	7	8	7	5	D
5 Qui mihi ministrat	co	GR [15] LU 1141 SYG 213 GB 219 GS q 210	F	4	5	7	4	5	7	5	4	F
1 Qui non colligit mecum	an	AR 389 LU 556 AM 364 *WA 97 LA 153	D	2	3	5	2	3	2	0	3	D
3 Qui odit animam suam	an	AR 577[13] [19] LU 262 1129 *AM 642 737 WA 419 *LA 525	G	2	5	4	2	4	2	0	2	E
Qui operatur justitiam	an	OHS 177 (nm)										
Qui operatus est Petro Gratia Dei sum	rev	LA 429										
5 Qui operatus est Petro	re	LA 424 *WA 330	a	-4	0	3	0	3	5	3	2	F
1 Qui operatus est Petro	an	WA 329 LA 422	D	-2	0	3	5	2	3	0	3	D
5 Qui operatus est Petro	gr	GR 418 LU 1345 SYG 204 GB 208 GS 178 h (inc)	F	2	0	2	4	5	4	2	0	F
Qui oravit Dominum Dormivit Abraham	rev	WA 82	D	3	0	-2	5	3	2	0	7	
5 Qui pacem ponit fines	an	AR 526 LU 957 AM 545	F	4	7	4	7	9	7	9	12	F
Qui pascit me ab adolescentia Jam laetus	rev	PM 142	F	2	5	4	5	4	2	4	2	
Qui percussit in deserto Oremus omnes	rev	LA 494 WA 409										
7 Qui persequebantur justum	an	AR 580 LU 1308 *AM 756 *LA 504	G	4	5	7	4	7	9	7	9	G
7 Qui persequebantur populum	re	LA 158 WA 101	G	5	4	5	7	5	7	9	7	G
4 Qui post me venit	an	AR 229 LU 1083 AM 202 *WA 13 LA 12 15	G	2	5	9	7	5	7	9	5	a
Qui posuit fines tuos	alv	GR [137] LU 1286 GS f	a	-2	1	0	-2	0	-4	-5	-4	

Qui posuit fines tuos Lauda Jerusalem Dominum	alv	SYG 259	a	-2	2	0	-2	0	-4	-5	-4
Qui primum adversum Sanctus Joannes	rev	WA 345									
Qui pro mundi salute Protege Domine	ofv	OTT 168	C	2	4	5	4	5	4	5	7
Qui propitiatur omnibus Benedic anima mea	ofv	OTT 110 GB 72 SYG 80	a	-2	0	3	5	7	5	3	5
2 Qui Raphaelem archangelum	an	WA 292	D	-2	-5	-2	0	2	0	-2	0	D
Qui regis Israel intende Adjutor et protector	intv	GR 485 LU 1277[A]									
Qui regis Israel intende Domine Deus virtutum	intv	GR 111**									
Qui regis Israel intende Populus Sion	intv	GR 4 LU 327 GS 2 GB 2[V] SYG 3									
Qui regis Israel intende Recordare Domine	intv	GR [139]									
Qui regis Israel intende Veni et ostende	intv	GR 13 LU 343 GS 7 GB 8[V] SYG 10									
Qui regis Israel intende Aspice Domine de sede	rev	LA 301									
Qui regis Israel intende Aspiciens a longe	rev	PM 18 LA 2									
Qui regis Israel intende Orantibus in loco	rev	LR 238									
8 Qui regis Israel intende	tr	GR 19 LU 351 SYG 11 GB 10 GS 10	G	2	4	2	0	2	0	2	0	G
Qui regis Israel intende Excita Domine	grv	GR 15 LU 347 GS 9 GB 9 SYG 10	a	3	5	7	5	3	2	3	0
Qui regis Israel intende Hodie scietis	grv	GR 24 LU 360 SYG 13 GB 12[V] GS 12	a	3	5	7	5	3	2	3	0
Qui regis Israel intende Qui sedes	grv	GR 7 LU 335 GB 5[V] *SYG 6 GS 4	G	7	5	7	9	5	2	7	5
7 Qui regni claves	re	LR 367 LA 418 *WA 328	F	2	9	11	9	11	7	6	7	G
7 Qui regni claves	an	WA 278	G	5	4	5	7	9	7	9	7	G
Qui reminiscimini Domini Super muros tuos	rev	LA 302 WA 184									
Qui sanat contritos corde	alv	SYG 258 *GS d	E	1	-2	3	5	7	10	8	5

	Incipit		Sources										
7	Qui sedes Domine super Cherubim	gr	GR 7 LU 335 SYG 6 GB 5^v GS 4	a	3	5	3	5	0	3	2	0	G
	Qui sedes super Cherubim / Qui regis Israel	trv	GR 19 LU 351 *GS 10 *GB 10 *SYG 11	G	2	4	5	4	5	7	5	0	
8	Qui seminant in lacrimis	tr	GR [24] LU 1164 *SYG 51 *GB 50 GS 217	D	3	5	2	3	5	0	-2	0	G
	Qui sequitur me non ambulat	alv	GR [13] LU 1139	D	2	0	-2	2	3	5	3	2	
3	Qui sequitur me non ambulat ... dicit	an	AR 405 [16] LU 1097 1125 *AM 381 640 WA 419 LA 527	G	5	2	0	2	5	2	5	4	E
2	Qui sine peccato templi est oblatus	hy	ST 486	F	2	0	2	4	5	2	0	2	D
	Qui statis in domo Domini / Laudate Dominum	ofv	OTT 40 *GB 90 *SYG 102	G	2	5	7	5	2	5	7	5	
8	Qui sunt hi sermones	an	AR 448 OHS 778 LU 788 AM 461 *LA 217 231	F	2	0	2	4	2	4	6	2	G
8	Qui sunt hi sermones ... respondens	an	LA 218	G	2	0	-2	0	2	0	2	4	G
7	Qui sunt isti qui ut nubes	re	LA 510	G	2	0	2	5	4	5	7	5	G
1	Qui sunt isti qui ut nubes	re	LR 146 WA 414	D	7	5	7	3	5	7	5	3	D
	Qui tantae ejus gloriae / Cum sanctus Benedictus	rev	LR 327 LA 370 WA 299										
	Qui tantae ejus gloriae / Sanctus Benedictus post	rev	LR 298										
3	Qui te posthabitis	hy	AM 776	D	2	3	5	7	5	7	10	12	E
	Qui timent Dominum sperent	alv	GR 385 LU 1072 GS 160 *SYG 249	C	2	9	7	10	9	10	7	5	
	Qui timent te videbunt me	alv	GR 73**	E	1	0	-2	3	5	8	5	8	
4	Qui timet Dominum in mandatis	an	AR 46 OHS 158 LU 254	G	-3	-2	0	2	0	2	0	-3	E
	Qui timetis Dominum benedicite / Laudate Dominum	ofv	OTT 40 *GB 90 SYG 102	a	-5	-2	0	2	3	2	0	2	
	Qui timetis Dominum laudate / Narrabo nomen	rev	LA 238 WA 143										
	Qui timetis Dominum laudate / Deus Deus meus	trv	GR 180 OHS 109 LU 594 GS 86 GB 109 SYG 122	C	2	5	7	2	5	7	5	4	
1	Qui timetis Dominum laudate	gr	GR 467	C	2	9	10	9	10	9	7	9	D
	Qui tres pueros / Summe Dei confessor	rev	WA 241	G	7	5	4	2	5	7	5	2	
	Qui tribulant me / Usqueque exaltabitur	rev	LA 167 WA 114										
	Qui venturus es judicare vivos / Qui Lazarum	rev	AR [159] PM 320 LU 1786 LA 554										
6	Qui venturus est veniet	re	LA 13 *WA 14	C	2	4	5	2	5	2	0	2	C

No	Incipit	Type	Sources										
1	Qui verbum Dei retinent	an	AR 350 LU 504 AM 322 325 *WA 79 *LA 119	D	-2	3	5	3	5	7	5	7	D
1	Qui verbum meum audit	an	LA 165	D	-2	3	5	3	7	9	7	5	D
7	Qui vicerit dabo ei	co	GR 512 LU 1485	d	-2	-3	0	2	-2	-5	-7	-5	G
2	Qui vicerit faciem illum	re	LA 51 WA 39	A	3	5	7	5	8	7	8	10	D
1	Qui vult venire	an	AR 577[13] [21] LR 157 LU 262 1128 *AM 644 737	D	-2	3	5	3	5	7	8	7	D
1	Qui vult venire ... sequatur	co	GR [12] LU 1138 *SYG 44 GB 46 217 GS 209	D	3	2	5	7	8	7	3	5	D
1	Qui vult venire ... sequatur ...dicit	an	LA 527	D	-2	3	5	3	5	7	5	3	D
	Quia accusatus non negavi Beatus Laurentius dixit Domine	anv	LA 433 WA 347										
	Quia apud te propitiatio est De profundis clamavi ad te	trv	GR 75 LU 499 *GS 25 GB 56^v *SYG 59	G	-5	0	2	4	5	0	-2	0	
	Quia cogitaverunt supplantare		see Qui cogitaverunt										
	Quia defecerunt sicut fumus Domine exaudi	trv	GR 191 OHS 324 LU 619 GS 92 GB 114 SYG 127	D	-5	-2	0	2	0	3	5	7	
	Quia delectasti me Domine Bonum est confiteri	trv	GR 497	D	2	-2	0	3	5	0	3	5	
	Quia ecce captaverunt Eripe une	ofv	OTT 46 *GB 101^v SYG 113	a	3	5	3	5	3	5	3	5	
	Quia ecce venio Exsulta satis	ofv	OTT 11 *GB 10 *SYG 12	G	2	5	4	7	5	4	5	4	
8	Quia ego tecum sum	an	WA 115	G	2	-2	0	2	0	-2	0	2	G
	Quia eripuit animam Convertere animam	grv	GB 265^v	D	3	5	7	5	3	2	3	0	
	Quia factus es adjutor Eripe me	ofv	OTT 46 GB 101^v SYG 113	G	2	5	2	0	2	4	2	0	
	Quia factus es susceptor	alv	GR 470	D	3	2	3	5	7	8	5	3	
6	Quia fecisti viriliter	of	GR 52**	C	2	5	7	5	2	4	5	7	F
	Quia humilis fuit in oculis Christianissimus	rev	LR 283										
	Quia illic sederunt Laetatus sum in his	trv	SYG 101	C	2	5	7	5	2	5	7	9	
	Quia in eo laetabitur Anima nostra sustinet	grv	GR 111**	F	4	2	7	9	7	4	7	4	
	Quia ipse Dominus novit Beatus Laurentius dixit mea	anv	LA 434 WA 347										
	Quia januas tuas Gratias ago	anv	WA 349										
1	Quia mirabilia fecit	an	LA 101	a	-2	0	-2	-5	-4	-2	-4	-7	D
4	Quia mirabilia fecit	an	WA 69	E	-2	0	-2	-4	-2	1	-2	0	E

	Incipit		Sources										
	Quia misericordiam et veritatem Dum oraret in	rev	WA 288										
	Quia non derelinquet Qui confidunt	grv	GB 75	G	7	10	7	5	2	0	2	-2	
	Quia oblitus sum manducare Domine exaudi	ofv	OTT 53 SYG 128	G	-2	-3	-2	-3	-5	-3	-5	-2	
5	Quia respexit Deus	an	LA 96	a	-4	0	3	2	0	3	5	3	F
	Quia respexit humilitatem Magnificat anima	trv	GR 50**	G	-5	0	2	0	2	5	4	5	
	Quia satiavit animam inanem Confiteantur Domino	grv	GR 631 LU 1694	E	1	-2	3	5	3	5	7	8	
	Quia viderunt oculi mei Cum inducerent ... dicens	rev	LA 352										
	Quia viderunt oculi mei Nunc dimittis	trv	GR 434 LU 1363 *GS k *GB 49 *SYG 50	G	2	4	5	4	5	7	5	0	
8	Quia vidisti me Thoma	an	AR 466 595 LU 1326 AM 479 774 WA 138 *LA 230	G	-2	2	5	4	0	4	5	2	G
	Quibus ipse ait haec Via recto	rev	LR 332 LA 374										
4	Quicumque Christum quaeritis	hy	AM 995	a	-2	-5	-7	-2	0	2	0	-2	E
4	Quicumque Christum quaeritis	hy	AR 803 LU 1590	F	-1	0	2	4	2	0	-3	0	E
4	Quicumque Christum quaeritis	hy	LR 445	F	-1	2	4	2	0	-3	0	-1	E
1	Quicumque Christum quaeritis	hy	ST 445	D	7	5	3	5	7	0	2	3	D
1	Quicumque fecerit voluntatem	co	GR 456 SYG 206 GB 211^V GS p	D	3	2	3	5	2	3	2	0	D
	Quid bonum ejus est	alv	GR 55**	E	-2	3	5	7	8	5	3	5	
5	Quid bonum ejus est	of	GR 628 LU 1691	F	2	0	2	4	5	4	5	4	F
8	Quid cruciaris quid	re	WA 246	G	-5	0	2	5	2	4	2	0	G
	Quid dormitis surgite Una hora	rev	OHS 397 LU 650 LA 192 WA 119										
	Quid enim prodest Dixit Judas fratribus	rev	LA 147										
	Quid ergo		see also Quod ego										
	Quid ergo miserrimus Libera me Domine de morte	rev	WA 438	F	-1	-3	-1	-3	-5	-3	-5	-3	
8	Quid est homo quia magnificas	an	LR 334	c	-1	-3	0	-1	-3	-5	-3	-1	G
	Quid est homo quod memor Gloria et honore	ofv	OTT 133 GB 23^V SYG 34	D	7	8	7	10	7	5	9	7	
4	Quid faciam quia dominus	an	AR 560 LU 1016 AM 598 *LA 313	F	-1	-3	-1	0	2	0	-1	-3	E
	Quid gloriaris in malitia Ego autem sicut oliva	intv	GR [1] GS 202 GB 22^V SYG 170										
1	Quid hic statis tota die	an	AR 344 LU 502 AM 314 *WA 75 *LA 114	C	2	9	10	9	7	9	7	9	D

	Quid in me ergo displicuit Noli me derelinquere	anv	LA 433										
	Quid in me ergo displicuit Quo progrederis	rev	WA 348 *LA 435	c	-1	-5	-3	0	2	0	-1	-3	
8	Quid me quaeritis interficere	re	LR 413	G	-2	0	-7	-5	-2	2	0	-2	G
7	Quid me quaeritis interficere	an	AR 401 LU 1094 *AM 377 *WA 104	b	1	3	5	3	1	-2	1	3	G
1	Quid molesti estis	an	WA 110 LA 183	D	-2	3	5	3	5	7	10	7	D
8	Quid retribuam Domino	an	AR 538[2] LU 965	c	2	0	-1	0	2	0	-3	0	G
4	Quid vobis videtur	an	WA 190	E	-4	-2	1	0	1	3	1	0	E
4	Quid vobis videtur	an	AR 568 LU 1051 *AM 609 *LA 317	E	1	0	-4	-2	1	0	1	3	E
1	Quidam autem Judaei	an	WA 109	C	2	5	4	2	5	7	4	5	D
4	Quidquid antiqui cecinere vates	hy	LR 317	a	-2	0	-2	-4	-5	-4	-2	-5	E
	Quidquid fiebat sub ipso Fuit Dominus	rev	LR 305										
	Quiescat Domine ira Recordare Domine testamenti	rev	LA 271 WA 166										
	Quinimmo perpetuum Gratias tibi Domine	rev	WA 385										
1	Quinquaginta annos	an	WA 108 *LA 172	C	2	9	7	5	7	9	5	4	D
	Quinque autem ex eis Simile est	rev	LR 229 LA 543										
2	Quinque autem ex eis	an	WA 430	D	-2	0	3	2	3	5	3	2	D
3	Quinque fatuae virgines	an	WA 430	E	-2	3	5	8	7	5	7	5	E
1	Quinque mihi Domine	an	WA 426	D	-2	3	5	3	5	7	9	7	D
	Quinque prudentes virgines	alv	GS 231	G	2	-2	2	5	4	2	5	7	
	Quinque prudentes virgines	alv	GR 416 LU 1339 *GS 231 *SYG 45 *GB 273[v]	G	2	0	-2	2	5	4	2	5	
5	Quinque prudentes virgines	co	GR [64] LU 1228 SYG 42 GB 45 *GS 230	F	2	0	2	4	6	7	2	0	F
7	Quinque prudentes virgines	an	WA 434	G	2	5	4	5	7	5	4	7	G
2	Quique cupitis ardire	hy	ST 65	G	2	0	-3	-2	0	-2	-5	0	D
	Quique terrigenae et filii hominum Aspiciens a longe	rev	PM 18 LA 2										
	Quis ascendet in montem Tollite portas	grv	GR 9 LU 1269 *GS 5 *GB 6[v] *SYG 8	a	3	5	3	5	7	8	7	3	
3	Quis ascendet in montem	of	GR 520 LU 1495 GS 57	G	5	2	4	5	4	7	9	7	E
5	Quis dabit ex Sion salutare	co	GR 129 *SYG 95 GB 84[v] GS 57	c	-3	0	-3	0	4	2	0	2	F

	Quis dabit mihi pennas Surge propera	intv	GR (9)										
	Quis det ut veniat Nonne cognoscit	rev	WA 174										
3	Quis Deus magnus ... praeelegit	re	LR 271	G	2	-3	-2	0	2	0	2	4	E
3	Quis Deus magnus ... tu es	re	LR 342 WA 159	G	2	5	2	4	0	2	5	2	E
1	Quis enim in omnibus	an	WA 164 LA 273	C	2	9	11	9	7	9	11	9	D
7	Quis es tu qui venisti	an	AM 807 *AR 624 *LU 1370 LA 363 *WA 276	d	-3	0	2	0	2	0	-3	-2	G
8	Quis es tu qui venisti	re	LA 359 WA 273	F	2	4	2	4	2	4	6	2	G
7	Quis est iste qui venit	an	AR 759 LU 1536 AM 945	G	4	7	5	4	2	0	2	5	G
4	Quis ex vobis arguet	an	WA 108	C	2	0	2	4	5	4	2	4	E
3	Quis ex vobis homo	an	AR 538[15] LU 1102 *AM 571 *LA 310	E	-2	3	5	3	5	8	10	8	E
1	Quis igitur ille est	re	LA 138	D	3	0	-2	3	5	7	5	7	D
6	Quis infelici fletus aquam capiti	hy	ST 465	F	2	-3	-1	-5	-3	0	2	4	F
	Quis loquetur potentias Confitemini Domino	trv	GR 113 LU 547 GB 75 *SYG 86	C	2	5	7	5	2	4	5	4	
8	Quis mihi tribuat	re	WA 173	c	2	0	2	0	-1	0	2	-3	G
8	Quis possit amplo famine praepotens	hy	ST 432	G	5	2	4	2	0	2	4	2	G
4	Quis scit si convertatur	an	WA 84	F	-1	-3	0	-1	0	2	0	-1	E
	Quis sicut Dominus Deus	alv	GR 19**	E	1	0	-2	3	5	8	7	5	
5	Quis sicut Dominus Deus	gr	GR 369 GS 168 SYG 251 GB 257[V]	D	3	5	7	3	5	3	2	0	F
7	Quis tibi videtur	an	WA 189	G	4	5	7	5	7	5	4	5	G
	Quis vestrum habebit	alv	SYG 177	E	-2	3	5	7	8	10	7	8	
3	Quo abiit dilectus tuus	an	AR 675 LU 1423	E	-2	3	5	8	7	5	7	10	E
6	Quo abiit dilectus tuus	an	AR 843 LU 1639	C	2	5	7	5	7	9	10	9	F
8	Quo amplius gentilitatis	an	WA 384	G	5	2	0	2	0	-2	0	2	G
	Quo mereamur tuo fulti O martyr egregie	rev	PM 346	a	3	0	-2	0	-2	-4	-5	-2	
7	Quo progrederis sine filio	an	WA 347 LA 433	b	1	3	5	3	1	-2	1	0	G
8	Quo progrederis sine filio	re	LA 435 *WA 348	D	5	3	5	3	2	3	5	2	G
	Quo virtute precum Festa dies mundo	rev	WA 350	c	2	5	4	5	4	2	4	2	
1	Quod autem cecidit	an	WA 79	D	-2	0	3	2	0	2	0	-2	D
1	Quod autem cecidit	an	AR 352 AM 324	C	2	9	10	9	7	9	10	9	D
1	Quod autem cecidit	an	LA 120	D	3	0	-2	3	5	7	10	7	D

	Incipit		Source										
1	Quod chorus vatum venerandus olim	hy	VP 103	a	-2	0	-2	-4	-5	-7	-2	-4	D
1	Quod chorus vatum venerandus olim	hy	ST 87	a	-2	0	-2	-4	-5	-2	-4	-5	D
2	Quod chorus vatum venerandus olim	hy	ST 222	D	-2	0	3	2	0	-2	0	3	D
2	Quod chorus vatum venerandus olim	hy	ST 257 276	D	-2	0	3	2	0	2	0	-2	D
8	Quod chorus vatum venerandus olim	hy	ST 276	G	2	0	-3	-2	0	2	-2	2	G
8	Quod chorus vatum venerandus olim	hy	ST 426	G	2	0	-2	-3	-2	0	-2	0	G
1	Quod chorus vatum venerandus olim	hy	ST 374	C	5	2	5	2	0	5	7	9	D
1	Quod chorus vatum venerandus olim	hy	ST 184	D	7	5	7	5	3	2	3	5	D
	Quod confractum fuerat Ego pascam	trv	GR 66**	c	-1	0	-1	-5	-3	0	-1	0	
	Quod dico vobis in tenebris Ego vos elegi	cov	SYG 190										
4	Quod dico vobis in tenebris ... dicit	co	GR [31] LU 1173 *GB 231 *GS t 220	D	2	3	5	3	0	3	2	-2	E
	Quod ego facio tu nescis Domine tu mihi	anv	GR 201 OHS 448 LU 673 SYG 130										
	Quod ego		see also Quid ergo										
	Quod ego miserrimus Libera me Domine de morte	rcv	LA 557	D	-2	0	3	0	2	0	-2	0	
	Quod enim verbis docebat Merito sanctitatis	rev	WA 294										
	Quod factum est In principio ... omnia	rev	WA 30										
	Quod justum est judicate Quare detraxistis	rev	LA 283										
	Quod parasti ante faciem Nunc dimittis	rev	WA 270										
	Quod parasti ante faciem Nunc dimittis	trv	GR 434 LU 1363 GS k *GB 49 *SYG 50	G	2	5	2	5	7	5	4	0	
	Quod perierat requiram Ego pascam	trv	GR 66**	G	-5	0	2	5	4	2	0	-2	
8	Quod seminavit lacrimans	hy	ST 377	G	-2	0	2	5	4	5	7	5	G
1	Quod uni ex minimis	an	AR 373 AM 346 *WA 89 *LA 134	D	2	3	5	7	5	2	3	2	D
4	Quodcumque in orbe nexibus revinxeris	hy	AR 597 LU 1334	F	-1	-3	-5	-3	0	-1	0	2	E
5	Quodcumque in orbe nexibus revinxeris	hy	ST 19	C	4	5	7	9	7	9	11	12	C
1	Quodcumque ligaveris	re	WA 280 (inc illeg)										D
	Quodcumque ligaveris Simon Petre	rev	LR 359 VP 181 LA 413 WA 277										
	Quodcumque ligaveris Solve jubente Deo	rev	LR 364										
	Quodcumque ligaveris Tu es pastor	rev	PM 160 LR 363 AM 1198										

	Incipit	Type	References										
	Quodcumque ligaveris / Tu es Petrus	rev	LR 360 WA 278										
8	Quodcumque ligaveris	an	AR 600 753 / LU 1517 AM 825 937 / 991 WA 277 LA 420	a	-4	-2	0	-2	-4	-5	-4	-2	G
	Quodcumque ligaveris / Tu es Petrus	trv	GR 409 LU 1332 / GS 182 *SYG 53	C	2	5	7	5	2	5	7	9	
4	Quodcumque vinclis	hy	ST 394	F	-3	-5	-3	0	-1	0	2	0	E
4	Quodcumque vinclis	hy	LR 432 AM 822	F	-1	-3	-5	-3	-1	0	2	0	E
7	Quomodo fiet istud angele	an	AR 249 669 / LU 1415 AM 225 864 / *LA 22 377	G	4	5	7	5	2	5	0	4	G
7	Quomodo fiet istud quia virum	an	WA 238	G	5	4	5	7	5	2	5	2	G
	Quomodo fiet istud quoniam virum / Ave Maria	rev	PM 244 LA 3 378										
	Quomodo fiet istud quoniam virum / Maria ut audivit	rev	WA 302										
1	Quomodo fiet istud respondens	re	WA 302	D	-2	-5	-2	0	2	0	2	3	D
	Quomodo in me fiet hoc / Ave Maria	ofv	OTT 13 GB 12	F	2	4	2	4	0	2	0	-3	
	Quomodo inquit fiet istud / Ave Maria	trv	GR 459 LU 1412	D	3	2	3	5	7	5	7	5	
4	Quomodo multiplicasti tuam	an	WA 288	F	-1	-3	-1	0	2	0	2	4	E
	Quoniam ad te orabo Domine / Verba mea	intv	GR 136 GB 88^v / SYG 99										
	Quoniam ad te orabo Domine / Gloriabuntur in te	ofv	OTT 135 GB 201^v / SYG 200	a	3	5	3	0	3	5	3	2	
	Quoniam aedificavit Dominus / Timebunt gentes nomen	grv	GR 71 LU 489 / GS 23 159 / GB 39 SYG 42	F	4	2	7	9	7	4	7	4	
	Quoniam alieni insurrexerunt / Deus in nomine	intv	GR 141 GS 64 / SYG 103										
	Quoniam angelis suis mandavit / Qui habitat	trv	GR 95 LU 533 / GS 35 GB 65 / SYG 73	D	-2	0	3	5	3	5	3	0	
	Quoniam angelis suis mandavit / Scapulis suis	ofv	OTT 32 *GB 66^v / *SYG 74	G	5	7	4	5	2	0	5	2	
	Quoniam apud te est fons / Filii hominum	trv	GR 55**	G	-5	0	2	4	2	5	4	5	
	Quoniam confirmata est super nos / Laudate Dominum	trv	GR 110 237 / LU 776^{II} OHS 683 / *GS 46 115 173 / *GB 74 *SYG 83	G	-5	0	2	0	2	5	4	5	
	Quoniam confirmata est super nos	alv	SYG 250	E	-2	3	5	7	8	5	3	5	
	Quoniam confortavit seras / Filiae Jerusalem	rev	LR 169 LA 389 / WA 304										
	Quoniam confortavit seras / Plateae tuae	rev	LA 228										

	Quoniam declinaverunt in me Contristatus	trv	GR 6223	D	-2	0	3	2	3	5	2	5	
	Quoniam defecit in dolore Miserere mei	trv	GR [145]	D	-2	0	3	5	7	3	2	5	
	Quoniam Deus magnus Dominus	alv	GR 361 LU 1042 GS 156 SYG 246 GB 255v	G	2	0	5	7	9	7	10	7	
7	Quoniam Deus magnus Dominus	inv	LA 80 WA 72	G	5	4	5	7	5	7	9	7	G
	Quoniam Domini est regnum Videns ergo vir	rev	WA 288										
	Quoniam Dominus excelsus terribilis Omnes gentes	intv	GR 336 LU 1009										
	Quoniam Dominus summus terribilis Ascendit Deus	ofv	OTT 75 GB 177 SYG 179	D	3	0	3	0	5	7	5	3	
	Quoniam elevata est magnificentia Ex ore infantium	intv	GB 26										
	Quoniam elevata est magnificentia Gloria et honore	rev	WA 418										
	Quoniam elevata est magnificentia Domine Dominus	grv	GR 342 LU 1017 GS 150 GB 252 SYG 244	F	4	2	7	9	7	9	7	11	
	Quoniam elevata est magnificentia Gloria et honore	grv	SYG 217	F	4	7	9	11	7	9	7	9	
3	Quoniam in aeternum	an	AM 144 145 *LR 338 *WA 67 *LA 96	G	2	5	4	2	0	2	0	-3	E
	Quoniam in me speravit Qui habitat	trv	GR 95 LU 533 GS 35 GB 65 SYG 73	D	-2	0	3	5	0	3	5	7	
8	Quoniam in te confidit	an	WA 65 *LA 92	G	-2	2	5	4	0	4	5	2	G
8	Quoniam in te confidit	an	AM 46	F	2	4	7	6	7	4	2	4	G
	Quoniam iniquitatem meam Abscondi tamquam	rev	WA 61										
	Quoniam iniquitatem meam Domine non secundum	rev	WA 437										
	Quoniam iniquitatem meam Peccata mea Domine	rev	LA 84										
	Quoniam iniquitatem meam Peccavi super numerum	rev	LA 270										
	Quoniam iniquitatem meam Miserere mihi	ofv	OTT 35 *GB 77v SYG 88	G	5	7	5	2	-2	2	5	2	
	Quoniam ipse liberavit Qui habitat	trv	GR 95 LU 533 GS 35 *GB 65 SYG 73	D	-2	0	3	5	3	0	3	5	
	Quoniam magnus Dominus Annuntiate inter gentes	trv	GR [128] LU 1295	G	-5	0	2	4	5	2	5	9	
	Quoniam magnus es tu Te Deum patrem	rev	WA 161										

Quoniam magnus es tu 　Te Deum	trv	GR [84] LU 1273	G	-5	0	2	5	4	5	0	-2	
Quoniam magnus es tu 　Omnes gentes	grv	GR 78**	D	7	5	7	10	7	10	5	3	
8 Quoniam non fuit dolus	an	WA 288	E	1	-2	1	0	1	3	5	3	G
Quoniam non in finem 　Adjutor in opportunitatibus	grv	GR 74 LU 498 *GS 24 GB 56 *SYG 58	E	-2	3	5	7	8	10	7	8	
Quoniam ... non revertetur oculus 　Vir erat	ofv	OTT 122 *SYG 256 *GB 262	a	5	3	5	3	0	2	0	5	
Quoniam omnes dii gentium 　Annuntiate inter gentes	trv	GR [128] LU 1295	G	2	5	4	5	2	5	2	0	
Quoniam peccatorum mole 　Christi mater	rev	VP 268 WA 303	D	7	5	7	8	7	5	7	5	
Quoniam percussit petram 　Sancti tui	rev	LR 182 LA 515										
Quoniam praevenisti eum in 　benedictione 　　Desiderium animae	trv	GR [5] LU 1131 GS 208 *GB 51^{V} *SYG 52	G	-5	0	2	4	2	5	4	0	
Quoniam praevenisti eum in 　benedictionibus 　　In virtute tua	intv	GR [10] LU 1135 GS 205										
Quoniam praevenisti eum in 　benedictionibus 　　Corona aurea	rev	LR 158 LA 524 WA 417										
Quoniam praevenisti eum in 　benedictionibus 　　Desiderium animae	rev	LR 155										
Quoniam praevenisti eum in 　benedictionibus 　　Gloria et honore	rev	LR 160 LA 526										
Quoniam praevenisti eum in 　benedictionibus 　　Corona aurea	grv	GR 12**	G	2	0	2	5	4	5	7	5	
Quoniam praevenisti eum in 　benedictionibus 　　Desiderium animae	rev	LA 525	b	5	3	5	6	5	3	5	3	
Quoniam praevenisti eum in 　benedictionibus 　　Desiderium cordis	grv	GR 82**	D	7	10	7	5	7	5	2	3	
Quoniam quis in nubibus 　Confitebuntur caeli	ofv	OTT 138 *GB 153 *SYG 170	G	5	9	7	9	7	5	9	7	
5 Quoniam respexisti humilitatem	gr	GR (35)	F	2	0	2	4	2	4	2	0	F
Quoniam tecum est Dominus 　Sicut fui	rev	LA 160 WA 102										
Quoniam tribulatio proxima 　Circumdederunt me	rev	PM 52 OHS 63(nm) 303(nm) LA 183 WA 113	D	7	5	7	8	7	5	7	5	
Quoniam tu Deus exaudisti 　Factus es spes	trv	GR 424 LU 1353	G	-5	0	2	4	2	5	7	5	

	Title	Type	Source									
	Quoniam tu es protector Beatus Andreas de cruce	rev	LA 502									
	Quorum meritis gaudet O beati martyres	rev	WA 377									
	Quorum remiseritis peccata Jam non dicam	rev	LA 257 WA 154									
	Quos redemit de manu Dicant nunc qui	rev	LR 418 LA 241									
7	Quotiescumque manducabitis	co	GR 320 [99] LU 950	G	7	0	7	5	10	9	10	7	G
8	Rabbi quid peccavit homo	an	AR 402 LU 1095 AM 378	F	2	0	4	7	9	7	6	4	G
8	Rabbi quis peccavit hic	an	WA 104 LA 164	F	2	0	4	7	9	7	6	4	G
8	Radix Jesse floruit	hy	ST 367	G	2	0	2	0	-2	0	2	5	G
8	Radix Jesse quae exsurget	re	LA 20 378 *WA 15	G	-2	-5	-3	-2	-3	-5	-7	-5	G
7	Ramos virentes sumpserat	hy	ST 35	G	4	5	7	9	7	5	4	5	G
	Recedentibus discipulis Congratulamini ... quem	rev	OHS 803 LR 91 WA 132									
1	Recedite a me amare	an	AR 843 LU 1639 *AM 1047	C	2	9	10	9	12	9	7	9	D
	Recessit igitur scienter Vir Dei Benedictus	intv	SYG 56 GB 54									
	Recessit igitur scienter Fuit vir	rev	LR 320 LA 367 WA 297									
7	Recessit igitur scienter	an	LR 320	d	-3	0	2	0	-2	0	-3	-2	G
4	Recessit igitur scienter	an	WA 297 *LA 367	F	-1	-5	-3	-1	0	2	0	2	E
7 8	Recessit pastor noster ... nam	re	OHS 608 LU 766 *LA 203 *WA 125	F	2	9	11	9	6	9	7	9	G
7	Recessit pastor noster ... portas	re	LR 341	F	2	9	11	9	6	9	7	9	G
6	Recordare Domine quid acciderit	an	GB 160	D	-5	-2	0	2	0	2	3	2	F
4	Recordare Domine testamenti	re	LA 271 WA 166	C	2	5	4	5	4	5	7	5	E
4	Recordare Domine testamenti	int	GR [139]	D	3	0	2	3	2	0	3	2	E
8	Recordare mei Domine et tuere	an	WA 114 LA 185	c	-1	0	2	0	2	0	-1	-3	G
1	Recordare mei Domine omni	of	GR 385 OTT 125 LU 1072 *GS e	D	-2	3	7	5	7	5	8	7	D
1	Recordare mei Domine omni	re	PM 114	G	3	0	3	0	2	0	2	3	D

2	Recordare mei Domine omni	of	GB 263^v *SYG 259	G	4	2	0	4	2	0	2	4	a
	Recordare quod steterim / Attende Domine	rev	OHS 63(nm) LA 176 WA 110										
	Recordare quod steterim / Recordare mei	ofv	OTT 125 *SYG 259	C	2	5	2	5	2	5	7	9	
1	Recordare quod steterim	of	GS 78	D	3	5	3	5	7	3	2	5	D
3	Recordare virgo mater Dei	an	AR 3 (sup 1)	E	-2	3	5	7	8	10	8	7	E
1	Recordare virgo mater in conspectu	of	GR 600 47** LU 1557 1637	D	3	5	3	5	7	3	2	5	D
	Recordatus Dominus Noe / Peractis centum	rev	WA 77	c	-2	-3	-5	0	-2	0	-2	-3	
	Recordatus est Deus / Ascendens ergo Deus	rev	WA 81	a	-2	0	-2	-4	-5	-2	0	-7	
8	Rector potens verax Deus	hy	AM 88 99 114	G	-5	-2	0	2	0	-2	0	5	G
4	Rector potens verax Deus	hy	ST 267	F	-3	0	-3	0	-1	0	2	4	E
1	Rector potens verax Deus	hy	ST 164	a	-2	-5	-2	0	-2	-4	-2	0	D
1	Rector potens verax Deus	hy	ST 162	G	-2	-5	-2	2	0	-2	0	-2	D
6	Rector potens verax Deus	hy	ST 317	a	-2	0	-4	-2	0	1	3	1	F
8	Rector potens verax Deus	hy	ST 174	a	-2	0	-2	0	-4	0	-2	-4	G
8	Rector potens verax Deus	hy	AR 89 AM 98 113	a	-2	0	-2	0	-2	-4	-2	-4	G
2	Rector potens verax Deus	hy	ST 28	E	-2	0	-2	0	1	0	-2	-4	D
2	Rector potens verax Deus	hy	ST 5	D	-2	0	3	0	-2	0	-2	0	D
2	Rector potens verax Deus	hy	ST 78 267 361 AM 87	D	-2	0	3	2	0	-2	0	-2	D
8	Rector potens verax Deus	hy	ST 78	G	-2	2	0	2	0	2	0	-2	G
8	Rector potens verax Deus	ly	AR 32 LU 240	G	2	-2	0	2	-2	0	2	4	G
1	Rector potens verax Deus	hy	ST 174	D	2	-2	2	5	7	5	2	3	D
8	Rector potens verax Deus	hy	AM 98 113	G	2	0	-2	0	2	0	2	5	G
2	Rector potens verax Deus	hy	ST 148	a	2	3	0	3	0	3	0	3	a
8	Rector potens verax Deus	hy	AR 32 LU 241	G	2	4	0	2	5	4	2	4	G
8	Rector potens verax Deus	hy	AM 88 99 114	G	2	4	2	0	2	4	5	4	G
2	Rector potens verax Deus	hy	OHS 147 215 (nm)	C	2	4	5	4	2	0	2	4	D
1	Rector potens verax Deus	hy	ST 246	G	2	5	0	2	0	2	0	5	D
5	Rector potens verax Deus	hy	ST 137	C	4	7	9	7	5	4	2	4	C
2	Rectos decet collaudatio	an	WA 63 LA 87	a	-2	0	-2	-5	-4	-2	-4	-7	D
2	Rectus Dominus Deus	an	AR 192	D	5	3	2	-2	0	3	2	-2	D
	Reddam tibi vota mea / Jubilate Deo	ofv	OTT 69 GB 38 SYG 36	D	7	8	7	5	7	5	3	5	
	Reddet Deus mercedem	alv	SYG 191	D	-2	0	3	2	0	3	2	0	
	Reddet Deus mercedem	alv	GS 216	D	-2	0	3	5	0	3	2	0	

	Incipit		Sources										
1	Reddit muto consonantis	an	WA 249	D	3	2	0	-2	0	3	5	3	D
1	Reddite ergo quae sunt Caesaris	an	AR 573 LU 1073 *AM 614 *LA 319	F	-5	-3	4	5	4	2	4	2	D
	Redemisti nos Domine	sr	AR 767 LU 1532 AM 946 947										
8	Redemisti nos Domine Deus	an	AR 899 LU 1729 *AM 1103 WA 397	G	-5	-2	0	2	0	2	0	2	G
3	Redemisti nos Domine	int	GR 536 LU 1532	E	1	-2	3	0	3	5	10	8	E
3	Redemit Dominus populum	re	LA 305 WA 184	F	-1	0	2	4	2	4	2	4	E
	Redemptionem misit ... in populo	alv	GR 266 LU 822 *SYG 248	D	-2	0	3	5	3	2	3	5	
7	Redemptionem misit ... populo	an	AR 271 LU 412 AM 246 WA 32 LA 38	G	4	7	5	2	5	4	2	0	G
1	Redemptor meus vivit	re	LA 560	D	-2	0	2	3	2	0	-2	0	D
2	Redemptor mundi signo crucis	co	SYG 130	F	-1	-3	-1	-3	-5	-3	-1	-3	D
1	Redime Domine de interitu	an	GB 157	F	-1	-3	-1	0	-1	-3	0	-1	D
7	Redime me Deus Israel	co	GR 159 SYG 113 GB 100^v *GS 74	c	-1	0	-3	-1	-3	-5	-3	-1	G
	Redime me Domine et miserere	sr	AR 96 LU 521										
2	Redime me Domine et miserere	int	GR 115 SYG 87 GB 76 GS 48	D	3	2	3	5	3	5	3	2	D
1	Redimet Dominus animas	co	GB 76	F	-1	0	-3	-5	0	2	4	2	D
8	Refulsit sol in clypeos	an	AR 550 LU 994 AM 588	G	-5	-2	0	2	0	2	0	-5	G
8	Refulsit sol in clypeos	an	LA 300	G	2	0	-2	0	2	-2	2	0	G
2	Refulsit sol in clypeos	re	LA 295 WA 182	A	3	5	7	5	8	7	8	5	D
	Regali ex progenie Nativitatem hodiernam	rev	LA 460 WA 366										
6	Regali ex progenie	an	AR 834 LU 1626 AM 1032 *WA 368 *LA 461	F	2	0	2	0	2	4	0	4	F
7	Regali ex progenie	re	LA 458 *WA 367	G	2	4	5	4	2	4	0	2	G
4	Regali ex progenie	of	LU 1476^F	E	3	0	3	5	3	1	-2	1	E
6	Regali solio fortis Iberiae	hy	AR 680	F	-5	-3	0	2	0	2	4	2	F
3	Regali solio fortis Iberiae	hy	ST 335	G	-3	-2	0	2	0	5	7	5	E
3	Regem angelorum Dominum	inv	LR 449	G	2	0	2	5	4	2	5	2	E
3	Regem apostolorum Dominum	inv	LR 134 *WA 411	G	2	0	2	5	4	2	5	2	E
4	Regem apostolorum Dominum	inv	LA 505	C	2	4	5	4	5	7	4	5	E
6	Regem apostolorum Dominum	inv	LR 162	D	3	5	3	5	7	5	3	5	F
3	Regem archangelorum Dominum	inv	LR 447 *LA 464	G	2	0	2	5	4	2	5	2	E
3	Regem baptizatum Dominum	inv	WA 58	G	2	0	5	4	2	5	2	5	E

4	Regem confessorum Dominum	inv	LR 190	C	2	5	4	5	7	4	5	2	E
6	Regem confessorum Dominum	inv	LR 190	D	3	5	3	5	7	5	3	5	F
6	Regem cui omnia vivunt	inv	AR[152] LU 1779	F	2	0	2	4	0	2	4	2	F
4	Regem martyrum Dominum	inv	LR 148 175 *LA 513	C	2	5	4	5	7	4	5	2	E
3	Regem praecursoris Dominum	inv	LR 345 *LA 400 *WA 320	G	2	0	2	5	4	2	5	2	E
2	Regem regum Dominum	inv	LR 380 *LA 474 WA 395	C	2	4	5	2	0	2	5	4	D
6	Regem venturum Dominum	inv	WA 8	F	2	0	2	4	0	2	4	2	F
5	Regem virginum Dominum	inv	LR 211	a	-4	0	3	0	3	5	3	5	F
6	Regem virginum Dominum	inv	LR 211	D	3	5	3	5	7	5	3	5	F
	Reges terrae afferent Fundata est	rev	LA 549										
1	Reges terrae et omnes populi	an	AR 397 AM 373 WA 103 LA 162	F	-1	-3	-1	0	2	4	2	-1	D
	Reges Tharsis et insulae	sr	AR 316 LU 458 AM 292 LA 74 WA 58										
	Reges Tharsis et insulae Omnes de Saba	rev	LR 76 WA 53 LA 70										
5	Reges Tharsis et insulae	of	GR 59 OTT 21 LU 461 *SYG 31 GB 34 GS 19	c	-3	0	-3	0	4	2	0	-1	F
2	Reges Tharsis et insulae	re	LR 72 LA 71 WA 55	D	-2	0	-2	-5	-2	0	3	2	D
1	Reges Tharsis et insulae	an	LR 70 WA 53 LA 67	F	-1	-3	-1	0	2	4	2	4	D
	Reges videbunt et consurgent	sr	LA 408										
8	Reges videbunt et consurgent	an	LR 351 *WA 321 LA 403	c	2	0	-1	0	-1	-3	-1	0	G
	Regi autem saeculorum	alv	SYG 262	D	2	0	-2	0	3	2	0	2	
4	Regi ... jubilemus	inv	WA 329	C	2	5	4	0	2	4	2	7	E
2	Regi polorum debitas	hy	ST 11	D	-2	0	3	5	0	-2	0	-2	D
1	Regi saeculorum immortali	an	WA 71	D	3	0	3	2	0	-2	3	5	D
	Regina adstat ad dexteram Ipse habet	grv	LU 1476D	C	2	9	10	9	7	9	7	9	
1	Regina caeli laetare alleluia	an	PM 257 335	F	-3	-5	0	2	0	-3	-5	0	D
1	Regina caeli laetare alleluia	an	AR [131] AM 718 LA 215	D	-2	3	5	3	0	-2	3	2	D
6	Regina caeli laetare alleluia	an	AR 67 OHS 743 LU 275 AM 176	F	2	0	2	4	5	4	2	5	F
6	Regina caeli laetare alleluia	an	AR 69[1] OHS 744 LR 48 LU 278 AM 179	F	2	0	2	4	5	4	2	5	F
1	Regina mundi dignissima	co	GR 552 LU 1558	D	-2	0	3	2	3	5	3	0	D
8	Regis immensi militis triumphis	hy	ST 450	G	5	4	2	4	0	2	0	-2	G

7	Regis iram non formidans	re	WA 251	G	4	5	7	9	7	5	7	9	G
8	Regis superni nuntia	hy	AR 883 LU 1688 AM 1086	G	2	4	5	4	2	0	2	-2	G
	Regna terrae cantate Deo Confirma hoc	ofv	OTT 79 *GB 189[v] *SYG 183	D	3	0	3	5	3	2	0	3	
	Regnabit Deus super gentes	alv	SYG 180	C	2	0	-3	0	2	-5	-7	-3	
	Regnavit Dominus super omnes	alv	GR 288 LU 855 GS K *GB 179[v]	D	-2	2	0	3	5	2	0	3	
3	Regni caelestis per fructum	re	PM 268	E	-2	3	5	8	5	3	5	8	E
8	Regnum ejus regnum sempiternum	an	AR 894[1] OHS 831 LU 1715 AM 1088	c	2	0	-1	0	-1	-3	-1	0	G
5	Regnum mundi et omnem	re	LR 227 PM 234 VP 260 *WA 432	F	4	7	4	2	7	9	7	9	F
7 8	Regnum tuum Domine	an	AM 160 *WA 60 *LA 105	c	2	0	2	0	-1	-3	0	-1	G
4	Regrediente anima	an	AM 965	D	2	3	5	2	3	2	0	2	E
2	Regressus Lucianus presbyter	an	WA 345	C	2	5	2	4	0	2	5	4	D
7	Relicta domo rebusque patris	an	LR 319	d	-3	0	2	0	2	0	-3	-2	G
8	Relicta domo rebusque patris	an	WA 297 *LA 367	G	-2	-5	-2	-3	-2	0	2	0	G
2	Relictis retibus suis	an	LA 497	D	-2	0	2	3	5	3	2	0	D
	Religio munda et immaculata Indicabo tibi	rev	LA 306										
3	Religio munda et immaculata	co	GR 557 LU 1564	G	4	2	5	4	2	0	5	2	E
5	Relinquens Maria activam	re	WA 336	F	4	2	7	4	2	7	9	7	F
5	Relinquens Wulstanus	an	WA 248	F	4	2	7	5	4	2	7	9	F
1	Reliqui domum meam	int	GR 18**	D	3	0	2	-2	3	5	7	5	D
8	Reliquit eum temptator	an	WA 88	G	2	5	2	5	4	2	0	4	G
2	Remansit puer Jesus	an	AR 323 LU 469 AM 301	C	4	2	5	4	0	2	5	4	D
4	Reminiscere miserationum tuarum	int	GR 111 LU 545 *SYG 77 *GB 69 GS 39 47	D	3	0	2	3	0	3	2	3	E
	Remissionem peccatorum Gratificavit nos	trv	GR 538	D	-2	0	3	5	3	0	2	3	
	Repentino namque sonitu Disciplinam	rev	LR 114 LA 257 WA 154										
3	Repleatur os meum laude tua	int	GR 302 LU 897 *SYG 186 *GB 192[v] *GS 140	E	1	-2	3	8	5	8	5	3	E
8	Repleatur os meum laude ut hymnum	re	LA 97 *WA 67	D	3	5	7	5	7	9	7	5	G
	Replebimur in bonis domus Te decet hymnus Deus	alv	SYG 242	F	2	9	11	9	11	12	14	12	
	Replebitur majestate ejus Benedictus Dominus	rev	AM 1188 LR 337 WA 159										

2 Repleta est malis	gr	GR 9**	A	3	5	7	5	0	3	5	7	D
1 Repleta est spiritu sancto	re	PM 164	D	-2	0	3	2	5	3	2	3	D
Repleti fructu justitiae	alv	GR 545 LU 1545	D	7	3	5	7	5	3	2	3	
Repleti quidem spiritu Virtute magna	rev	PM 217 OHS 779 LR 87 LA 210 WA 133 305										
1 Repleti sumus mane	of	GR(19) OTT 175 *SYG 171 *GS 209 *GB 163	D	-2	0	2	3	5	8	5	3	D
Repleti sunt apostoli	alv	GB 192	F	2	4	2	-1	0	2	0	2	
Repleti sunt omnes spiritu	sr	AR 508 LU 883 LA 263 WA 155 157										
Repleti sunt omnes spiritu Facta autem hac	rev	LA 260										
Repleti sunt omnes spiritu Loquebantur	rev	LR 113 LA 259 WA 156										
Repleti sunt omnes spiritu Spiritu sancto	rev	WA 156										
Repleti sunt omnes spiritu	alv	SYG 186	D	2	0	-2	0	2	0	2	3	
6 Repleti sunt omnes spiritu	inv	LA 264 *WA 154	D	3	5	3	5	3	5	3	5	F
2 Repleti sunt omnes spiritu	re	AM 1187 LU 875 *PM 90 *LR 110 LA 256 WA 152	A	3	5	7	5	8	10	8	7	D
8 Repleti sunt omnes spiritu	an	AR 504 LU 884 *AM 521 WA 63 153 LA *254 261	G	5	2	0	-2	0	2	0	2	G
6 Repletus sancto spiritu	gr	GB 54	a	3	5	3	0	3	7	8	5	c
6 Repletus sancto spiritu	gr	SYG 56	D	3	5	3	7	5	7	5	3	F
Repletus sum consolatione	alv	GR 547	D	3	5	3	5	0	-2	3	5	
8 Replevit et inebriavit me	an	LA 187	G	5	4	0	4	5	2	0	2	G
Reposita est mihi corona Scio cui credidi	rev	LA 424 WA 330										
1 Reposita est mihi corona	co	GR 477 LU 1430	F	-1	0	-3	-5	-3	-1	-3	-1	D
2 Reposita est mihi corona	re	LA 427 WA 331	A	3	5	7	5	8	7	8	10	D
8 Reposita est mihi corona	an	LA 426 WA 331	G	5	2	0	-2	0	2	0	4	G
Requiem aeternam dona ei Domine Subvenite sancti Dei	rev	GR 107* AR [183]										
Requiem aeternam dona ei Domine Rogamus te Domine	rev	LA 557	c	-1	0	2	0	-1	0	-1	-3	
Requiem aeternam dona eis Domine Lux aeterna	cov	GR 102* LU 1815 GS 233 *SYG 236										
Requiem aeternam dona eis Domine Domine quando veneris	rev	AR [160] PM 319										
Requiem aeternam dona eis Domine Qui Lazarum	re	LU 1823 WA 436										

	Text		Source	Mode									
	Requiem aeternam dona eis Domine Congregati sunt	rev	AR 197*	a	-2	-4	-2	0	2	0	-7	-5	
	Requiem aeternam dona eis Domine Libera me Domine de viis	rev	AR [173] PM 318 LU 1798	a	-2	0	-2	-4	-5	-2	0	1	
	Requiem aeternam dona eis Domine Redemptor meus vivit	rev	LA 560	a	-2	0	2	0	-2	0	-2	-4	
	Requiem aeternam dona eis Domine Domine Jesu Christe	ofv	OTT 189 *SYG 235	D	-2	0	3	2	0	-2	0	2	
	Requiem aeternam dona eis Domine Libera me Domine de morte	rev	AR [174] PM 321 GR 102* LU 1767 *LA 557	F	-1	0	-3	-1	-3	-1	0	2	
	Requiem aeternam dona eis Domine In loco viridi	rev	VP 242	f	-1	0	2	0	-1	-3	-1	0	
6	Requiem aeternam dona eis Domine	int	GR 94* LU 1807 SYG 235 *GB 265^v GS 232	F	2	0	2	4	2	0	2	0	F
	Requiem aeternam dona eis Domine Ne recorderis	rev	AR [166] LU 1792	F	2	5	4	5	4	2	4	2	
2	Requiem aeternam dona eis Domine	gr	GR 95* LU 1808 *SYG 235 *GB 265^v *GS 232	G	4	2	5	2	4	5	2	0	a
	Requiem aeternam dona eis Domine Absolve Domine	rev	LA 558	G	5	4	5	7	5	7	10	9	
6	Requievit arca mense septimo	re	WA 77	c	2	4	2	5	4	2	0	-2	c
4	Rerum creator optime	hy	ST 363	G	-3	0	-2	-3	-2	-5	-3	-2	E
3	Rerum creator optime	hy	ST 213	D	2	3	5	3	5	3	2	3	E
8	Rerum Deus tenax vigor	hy	AM 90 104 119	G	-5	-2	0	2	0	-2	0	5	G
8	Rerum Deus tenax vigor	hy	ST 175	a	-2	0	-2	0	-4	0	-2	-4	G
8	Rerum Deus tenax vigor	hy	AR 93 LU 519 AM 103 118	a	-2	0	-2	0	-2	-4	-2	-4	G
2	Rerum Deus tenax vigor	hy	ST 28	E	-2	0	-2	0	1	0	-2	-4	D
2	Rerum Deus tenax vigor	hy	ST 5	D	-2	0	3	0	-2	0	-2	0	D
2	Rerum Deus tenax vigor	hy	ST 175	D	-2	0	3	0	2	0	-2	0	D
2	Rerum Deus tenax vigor	hy	ST 78 AM 90	D	-2	0	3	2	0	-2	0	-2	D
2	Rerum Deus tenax vigor	hy	ST 138	D	-2	0	3	2	0	2	0	-2	D
8	Rerum Deus tenax vigor	hy	ST 78 268	G	-2	2	0	2	0	2	0	-2	G
8	Rerum Deus tenax vigor	hy	AR 38 LU 245 AM 103 118	G	2	0	-2	0	2	0	2	5	G
8	Rerum Deus tenax vigor	hy	AR 38 LU 245	G	2	4	0	2	5	4	2	4	G
8	Rerum Deus tenax vigor	hy	AM 91 104 119	G	2	4	2	0	2	4	5	4	G
2	Rerum Deus tenax vigor	hy	OHS 151 218 (nm)	C	2	4	5	4	2	0	2	4	D
1	Rerum Deus tenax vigor	hy	ST 246	G	2	5	0	2	0	2	0	5	D
4	Rerum salus intermina	hy	ST 281	F	-1	-3	2	0	-1	-3	0	-1	E

8	Respexit Dominus humilitatem	an	AR 143 AM 149	F	2	4	2	0	2	4	7	6	G
	Respexit Dominus populum Misertus Dominus	rev	WA 313										
3	Respexit Elias ad caput	re	LR 124 LU 927	G	2	-3	-2	0	2	0	2	4	E
8	Respexit me et exaudivit	an	AR 115 LU 279^F	G	5	2	0	2	0	2	0	-2	G
7	Respice cuncta quia tua sunt	an	GB 160^v	d	-2	-3	-2	0	2	0	2	0	G
	Respice Domine de sanctuario ... et de Audi Domine hymnum	rev	LA 272 WA 167										
6	Respice Domine de sanctuario ... super	an	LA 549	c	-1	-3	-5	-3	-1	0	2	0	c
5	Respice Domine in testamentum	gr	GR 354 LU 1033 *SYG 106 *GB 94^v GS 68 156	F	2	4	0	2	-3	0	-1	2	F
7	Respice Domine in testamentum	int	GR 354 LU 1032 SYG 247 GB 254 *GS 155	G	7	10	9	10	9	10	7	9	G
	Respice in me et exaudi me Illumina oculos	ofv	OTT 87 GB 81 SYG 92	b	1	-2	0	-4	-2	1	3	1	
6	Respice in me et miserere mei	int	GR 327 LU 981 SYG 240 GB 248 GS 143	F	2	0	2	0	-3	0	2	5	F
	Respice in me et miserere mei Ad te Domine	ofv	OTT 5 SYG 2 *GB 1^v	D	7	10	7	5	7	5	3	5	
2	Resplenduit facies ejus	an	AM 998	D	-5	-2	0	2	0	-2	0	3	D
8	Resplenduit facies ejus	an	AR 805 LU 1589	G	5	2	0	2	0	2	0	-2	G
8	Respondens autem angelus ... nolite	an	AR 444 OHS 728 770 LU 783 AM 454 WA 129 137 LA 216	G	5	2	0	-2	0	2	0	-2	G
	Respondens autem angelus ... quem Angelus Domini descendit	alv	GS 125	C	2	4	5	7	5	9	7	5	
8	Respondens autem Dominus	an	WA 432	G	5	2	0	-2	0	2	0	-2	G
8	Respondens autem infans	an	WA 404	c	-1	-3	0	-1	-5	-1	2	0	G
1	Respondens autem Petrus	an	AM 999	D	-2	0	3	2	0	-2	3	5	D
6	Respondens autem Petrus	an	AR 806 LU 1589	F	2	4	5	2	0	2	4	0	F
5	Responderunt prudentes virgines	an	WA 431	F	4	7	6	4	2	7	9	7	F
	Respondit Hippolytus quare Coepit Hippolytus	rev	WA 352										
6	Responsum acceperat Simeon	re	LA 349 *WA 269	a	3	5	3	7	8	10	5	3	c
	Responsum accepit Simeon ... Christum	sr	WA 272										
	Responsum accepit Simeon ... Christum Simeon justus	rev	LA 349 WA 269										
2	Responsum accepit Simeon ... Christum	an	GR 430 PM 135 LU 1359 SYG 47 *GS i	F	-1	-3	-1	0	-1	-3	-8	-5	D

8	Responsum accepit Simeon ... Christum	co	GR 435 LU 1365 *SYG 50 *GB 49^v GS 181	D	3	7	5	7	5	7	5	3	G
3	Responsum accepit Simeon ... Dominum	an	WA 272	c	2	5	2	5	4	2	0	2	a
7	Responsum accepit Simeon ... Dominum	an	AR 620 LU 1366 *AM 802 *LA 355	G	4	7	5	2	5	4	5	2	G
	Restitue animam meam	an	OHS 234 (nm)										
	Restitui numerum gaudet Regni caelestis	rev	PM 268	c	-1	2	0	-1	-3	-5	-3	-5	
4	Resurrexi et adhuc tecum sum	int	GR 240 OHS 708 LU 777 *SYG 152 *GB 123 GS K	D	3	0	3	0	2	0	3	2	E
	Resurrexit Dominus alleluia	sr	WA 142 LA 241										
8	Resurrexit leo fortis	hy	ST 459	F	-3	-1	0	-3	-1	0	-1	-3	G
	Resurrexit tamquam dormiens	alv	GB 126	D	3	2	3	5	3	5	7	5	
	Retribuet mihi Dominus	an	OHS 179 (nm)										
	Revela Domino viam Delectare in Domino	rev	LA 88										
	Revelabit Dominus condensa Tollite hostias	grv	GR 162 *GS 76 GB 102 SYG 114	F	4	2	7	9	7	4	7	9	
1	Revelabitur gloria Domini	co	GR 26 LU 362 *SYG 14 *GB 13^v *GS 13	D	3	2	3	7	5	3	2	3	D
1	Revelabunt caeli iniquitatem	re	WA 120	C	2	5	4	0	2	5	4	2	D
	Revelavit Dominus		*see* Revelabit Dominus										
1	Reversus est angelus	an	AR 868 *AM 1069	C	2	9	10	9	7	5	7	5	D
8	Revertenti Abraham	re	WA 80	G	2	0	-2	2	5	4	2	0	G
7	Revertere in terram Juda	an	WA 52 *LA 355	G	4	7	4	7	9	5	4	5	G
7	Revertere revertere Sunamitis	an	LR 214	G	4	7	9	10	9	5	2	5	G
	Revertere virgo Israel Prope est ut veniat	rev	LA 14 WA 15										
	Revertimini unusquisque Scindite corda	rev	WA 86										
8	Rex aeterne Domine	hy	ST 386	a	-2	0	2	3	0	2	0	-2	G
8	Rex aeterne Domine	hy	ST 92	a	-2	0	3	2	0	-2	3	-2	G
6	Rex angelorum praepotens	hy	ST 386	c	2	4	2	0	2	4	5	4	c
8	Rex autem David	an	WA 165 *LA 275	G	-2	-3	-2	-3	-2	0	-2	0	G
8	Rex Christe clementissime	hy	ST 126	G	2	4	2	0	-3	-2	0	2	G
8	Rex Christe factor omnium	hy	ST 228 287	G	-2	-3	-2	0	-2	-3	-2	-5	G
8	Rex Christe factor omnium	hy	ST 386	G	-2	0	2	5	4	5	7	5	G
4	Rex Christe Martini decus	hy	LR 454	F	-1	-3	-1	2	4	0	-1	2	E
7	Rex Christe Martini decus	hy	ST 461	G	2	4	0	2	4	0	5	4	G

6	Rex Christe Martini decus	hy	ST 400	c	2	4	5	4	2	0	2	4	c
8	Rex Christe Martini decus	hy	ST 99 435	G	2	5	4	2	0	2	4	5	G
2	Rex Christe tu mirificas	hy	ST 99	D	-2	0	3	0	2	0	-2	3	D
8	Rex confessorum gloria	hy	ST 402	G	2	4	2	0	-2	2	0	2	G
2	Rex gloriose martyrum	hy	ST 404	D	-2	-5	-2	0	3	0	2	0	D
4	Rex gloriose martyrum	hy	AR [27] LU 1145	E	-2	-4	0	3	1	-2	-4	-2	E
3	Rex gloriose martyrum	hy	ST 307	E	-2	3	5	8	7	8	10	8	E
3	Rex gloriose martyrum	hy	AR [26] LU 1144 AM 631 881	E	1	3	1	0	-2	0	-2	-4	E
4	Rex gloriose martyrum	hy	ST 242	E	1	3	1	0	-2	3	5	3	E
2	Rex gloriose martyrum	hy	ST 60	D	2	0	-2	0	2	3	2	0	D
8	Rex gloriose martyrum	hy	ST 101 103	G	2	0	-2	2	5	4	0	2	G
4	Rex gloriose martyrum	hy	AR [42] ST 101 103	F	2	0	-1	2	4	2	0	-1	E
4	Rex gloriose martyrum	hy	ST 103	D	2	3	5	7	0	2	5	3	E
4	Rex gloriose martyrum	hy	AM 649	E	3	0	3	5	3	1	0	-2	E
8	Rex gloriose martyrum	hy	AR [43]	C	5	4	5	7	9	7	5	7	G
7	Rex magnus natus est	re	WA 56	G	5	7	9	7	10	7	9	10	G
	Rex meus et Deus meus Verba mea	intv	GS 61										
4	Rex noster adveniet	re	LA 10 *WA 12	F	-3	-1	0	-1	-5	-3	-1	0	E
4	Rex noster adveniet	inv	LA 13	C	2	5	2	4	5	7	2	4	E
3 4	Rex noster in cruce	an	WA 130 223	G	2	0	-2	-5	0	2	0	-2	D
8	Rex pacificus magnificatus	an	AR 259 LU 364 AM 236 *WA 26 LA 30	G	-2	-5	-2	0	2	0	2	0	G
6	Rex saeculorum quem laudat	an	WA 301	F	-3	-5	-3	0	2	4	2	0	F
4	Rex sanctorum angelorum	hy	ST 491 GS 114	G	2	5	4	2	4	0	4	7	b
4	Rex sempiterne Domine	hy	LR 82	E	1	3	1	0	-2	0	1	-2	E
3	Rex sempiterne lucis auctor unice	hy	ST 141	E	1	3	1	-2	1	0	1	3	E
4	Rex sine fine manens	an	PM 110	F	-1	-3	-1	-3	-5	-3	-1	2	E
5	Rex virtutum assis nobis	an	WA 252	F	4	7	9	7	5	7	4	5	F
	Roga quae ad pacem Laetatus sum in his	trv	SYG 101	F	2	4	2	0	2	4	2	4	
2	Rogabo patrem meum	an	LA 246 WA 148	D	-2	0	3	2	0	-2	3	5	D
1	Rogamus te Domine Deus noster ut	re	VP 241	C	2	9	10	9	7	5	7	5	D
1	Rogamus te Domine Deus quia	an	GB 156	C	2	4	2	0	2	4	5	4	D
8	Rogamus te Domine Deus	re	LA 557	G	-5	0	2	4	5	2	4	5	G
1	Rogamus te virgo	an	WA 354	D	-2	0	3	2	0	-2	0	-2	D
7	Rogate quae ad pacem	gr	GR [135] LU 1285	c	2	0	2	0	-3	2	0	2	G

#	Title	Type	Sources										
3	Rogavi Dominum meum	re	LA 321 *WA 246	c	-5	-3	-1	0	-1	0	2	0	E
	Rogavi pro te Petre	alv	GR 543 LU 1543	D	7	5	7	8	7	5	7	3	
8	Rogo te pater ut mittas	an	WA 187 *LA 310	a	3	0	-2	-4	0	2	-2	5	G
	Rorate caeli desuper	sr	WA 16										
	Rorate caeli desuper Emitte agnum Domine	rev	WA 18										
	Rorate caeli desuper Montes Israel	rev	LA 5 WA 23										
4	Rorate caeli desuper	an	AR 238 AM 213 *WA 17 *LA 23	a	-2	0	3	5	7	5	3	5	a
1	Rorate caeli desuper	int	GR 21 [81] LU 353 1269 SYG 8 GB 6^v GS 5	C	2	9	10	9	12	9	7	9	D
2	Rorate caeli desuper	re	LA 26 *WA 19	A	3	5	7	5	8	7	8	5	D
1	Rorate caeli desuper ... ne irascaris		AR 145* VP 59 LU 1868	F	2	4	9	7	5	4	2	4	D
	Rosa vernans castitatis	alv	VP 52	G	2	0	5	0	2	0	-3	-5	
	Rubum quem viderat Assumpta est virgo	rev	LA 446										
4	Rubum quem viderat	an	AR 295 LU 443 AM 272 WA 50 *LA 65	D	2	3	5	3	0	2	3	2	E
6	Sacerdos Dei Lucianus	re	WA 344	F	4	7	9	7	9	11	9	11	c
7	Sacerdos Dei Martine aperti	an	WA 400 LA 483	G	4	7	5	2	5	4	2	5	G
8	Sacerdos Dei Martine pastor	an	WA 400 *LA 483	G	-2	0	2	0	-2	2	5	4	G
	Sacerdos Dei Martine pastor	alv	SYG 226	G	2	0	-2	2	5	4	2	0	
6	Sacerdos Dei Martine pastor	co	GB 243^v	D	3	5	3	2	5	7	3	5	F
2	Sacerdos Domini Oswaldus	an	WA 283	D	-2	0	3	2	0	3	0	-2	D
1	Sacerdos et pontifex ... ora pro nobis	an	AR 577^15 [55] LU 262^4 1173 AM 656 739 *PM 336	D	-2	0	3	5	0	3	0	-2	D
1	Sacerdos et pontifex ... sic placuisti	an	AR 81* LU 1840 *PM 308 *LA 537	D	-2	0	3	5	0	3	0	-2	D
1	Sacerdos in aeternum Christus	an	AR 525 LU 956 AM 543	D	3	0	-2	3	5	3	7	10	D

	Incipit		Source		1	2	3	4	5	6	7	8	
1	Sacerdos magnus qui in vita	co	GR 570 LU 1583	D	3	2	3	5	0	-2	2	5	D
	Sacerdos sit sanctus	alv	GR [119]	D	3	2	3	5	7	8	5	3	
5	Sacerdotes Dei benedicite ... aeternum	an	WA 393	F	4	7	6	4	7	9	7	6	F
6	Sacerdotes Dei benedicite ... sancti	int	GR [7] LU 1132 *SYG 55 GS 220 GB 52	D	-4	-2	0	-2	3	5	3	5	F
8	Sacerdotes Dei benedicite ... sancti	re	WA 429	G	2	0	-2	0	2	4	2	0	G
7	Sacerdotes Dei benedicite ... servi	an	AR [56] LU 1176 AM 658 *LA 536	d	-3	0	2	0	-3	-2	-5	-3	G
4	Sacerdotes Domini incensum	of	GR 319 [98] LU 949	F	-3	-1	0	-1	0	2	4	0	E
	Sacerdotes ejus		see also Sacerdotes Sion										
2	Sacerdotes ejus induam salutari	int	GB 212 *SYG 209 GS 224	D	-3	-2	0	-2	3	2	0	2	D
8	Sacerdotes ejus induam salutari	tr	LU 1623^C	G	2	4	2	0	2	0	5	7	G
1	Sacerdotes ejus induam salutari	gr	GR [36] LU 1187 SYG 209 GB 212 GS 225	C	2	9	10	9	10	9	7	9	D
	Sacerdotes ejus induant		see Sacerdotes ejus induam										
	Sacerdotes procedentes Tu Domine universorum	rev	WA 182										
4	Sacerdotes sancti incensum	an	AR 531 LU 940	F	-1	-3	-1	-3	0	-1	0	2	E
4	Sacerdotes sancti incensum	an	AM 551	D	3	2	3	5	3	0	-2	0	E
	Sacerdotes Sion		see also Sacerdotes ejus										
2	Sacerdotes Sion induam salutari	int	GR 88**	a	-4	-2	0	-2	3	2	0	2	a
	Sacerdotes tui Domine Deus	alv	GR 89**	G	2	4	2	0	2	4	5	4	
3	Sacerdotes tui Domine induant	int	GR [35] LU 1186 1495 SYG 27 GB 28 GS 220	F	-3	0	-1	0	2	4	0	-3	E
	Sacerdotes tui induantur Surge Domine	trv	GR [119] 90**	G	-5	0	2	5	4	5	2	5	
	Sacerdotes tui Domine induantur	alv	SYG 211 GB 272	G	2	4	2	0	2	4	5	4	
5	Sacrae parentes virginis	hy	ST 344	F	2	4	0	6	4	6	4	6	F
8	Sacram hujus diei	an	WA 256	G	-5	-2	0	2	0	2	0	2	G
7	Sacram praesentis diei	re	WA 257	d	-2	-3	-2	0	2	0	2	0	G
	Sacramentorum codicem mystico Gregorius praesul	rev	PM 140 VP 123										
	Sacramentum regni uno ore Isti sunt triumphatores	rev	WA 412										
3	Sacrata nobis gaudia	hy	AM 879	E	1	3	1	0	-2	0	-2	-4	E
6	Sacratum hoc templum Dei	hy	ST 423	E	-2	0	-4	-2	0	3	5	3	C
6	Sacri Christe pontificis	hy	ST 395	c	2	4	2	0	2	4	5	4	c

4	Sacri pontificis annuis emicat	hy	ST 469	C	2	4	5	7	5	4	2	4	E
8	Sacri triumphale tui	hy	ST 12	G	2	0	-2	-5	-2	0	2	0	G
8	Sacrificabo hostiam laudis	an	AR 299 LU 452	c	-1	-5	-1	0	-3	-5	-3	-5	G
2	Sacrificent Domino sacrificium laudis	gr	GR 89**	E	3	5	8	5	7	8	5	3	a
1	Sacrificium Deo spiritus	an	WA 70	D	2	3	5	3	5	3	2	0	D
6	Sacris reliquiarum muneribus	an	LR 280	F	-3	-1	-5	-3	-5	0	-1	2	F
1	Sacris solemniis juncta sint gaudia	hy	AR 109* GR 154* LU 952 ST 346	D	-2	0	3	2	0	-2	0	3	D
8	Sacris solemniis juncta sint gaudia	hy	ST 46	G	2	0	-2	2	5	4	2	0	G
6 8	Sacris solemniis juncta sint gaudia	hy	ST 348	c	2	4	5	4	2	-1	0	-3	c
1	Sacris solemniis juncta sint gaudia	hy	ST 304	D	3	5	3	2	3	5	7	5	D
1	Sacris solemniis juncta sint gaudia	hy	PM 94 LR 120 VP 10	D	7	8	7	10	9	7	5	7	D
4	Sacris solemniis juncta sint gaudia	hy	AR 106* GR 153* VP 9* LU 920	D	7	9	7	5	7	9	10	9	E
8	Saepe expugnaverunt me	tr	GR 153 LU 571 SYG 110 GB 97^{v} *GS 72	G	-2	-5	-3	-7	-5	-2	0	2	G
2	Saepe expugnaverunt me	an	AM 135	F	-1	-3	-1	0	2	4	2	-1	D
1	Salus autem justorum a Domino	int	GR [28] LU 1169 SYG 193 GB 196 GS 211	a	-4	-2	-7	-9	-7	-4	-7	-4	D
7	Salus nostra in manu ... respice	an	AR 8 (sup 1)	G	5	4	5	7	9	7	5	7	G
2	Salus nostra in manu ... respiciat	re	WA 98	C	2	5	4	5	7	5	4	2	D
4	Salus populi ego sum	int	GR 375 LU 1059 SYG 97 GB 86 *GS 59 163	F	-3	-1	0	2	5	4	2	4	E
5	Salus populi ego sum	of	GR 79**	F	2	4	5	4	5	4	2	4	F
6	Salutare vultus mei	an	AR 107 AM 46 *WA 65 *LA 92	F	2	4	0	2	4	2	0	-1	F
7	Salutem ex inimicis	an	LA 95	G	4	5	7	9	7	4	5	7	G
8	Salutis aeternae dator	hy	AR 900 LU 1722	G	2	0	-2	2	5	4	0	2	G
4	Salutis humanae sator	hy	AR 488 GR 155* LU 852	F	-1	0	2	4	2	0	-3	0	E
	Salutis nostrae auctorem Tria sunt munera	rev	LA 72 WA 55										
	Salva me ex ore leonis In te jactatus	rev	LA 169 WA 106										
	Salva nos Christe	alv	SYG 173	C	2	5	2	4	2	0	5	7	
3	Salva nos Christe	an	AR 700 LU 1460 *AM 899 1040 *WA 371 LA 462	G	2	5	2	5	4	0	2	4	E
3	Salva nos Domine vigilantes	an	AR 64 OHS 172 LU 271	G	2	5	7	5	4	2	4	2	E

	Incipit	Type	Source	Mode	1	2	3	4	5	6	7	8	End
	Salvabit sibi dextera	see Salvavit sibi											
	Salvabo populum meum Israel	alv	GR [140]	D	-2	0	3	2	3	5	2	0	
7	Salvasti enim nos Deus	gr	GR 98**	a	3	5	3	5	7	3	2	3	G
2	Salvasti nos Domine	an	AR 119 LU 279^H	D	-2	0	3	2	-2	2	0	2	D
7	Salvator mundi Domine	hy	ST 83	G	2	0	-2	0	2	0	5	7	G
	Salvator mundi salva ... et cuncta Protege Domine	ofv	OTT 168 *GB 167 *SYG 174	A	3	5	3	5	3	5	3	2	
1	Salvator mundi salva ... sancta	an	LA 474	D	-2	0	2	3	2	3	0	2	D
7	Salvator mundi salva ... qui per crucem	an	OHS 584 LU 747 *LA 463 *SYG 141	G	4	5	7	9	7	4	5	7	G
3	Salvatorem exspectamus Dominum	re	LA 4 *WA 4	G	2	4	5	4	2	4	5	4	E
	Salvavit eum dextera	see Salvavit sibi											
	Salvavit sibi dextera ejus Cantate Domino	intv	GR 268 LU 826 GS 129 GB 149^V SYG 167										
7	Salve crux pretiosa suscipe	an	AR 579 LU 1307 AM 755 WA 236 LA 504	d	-3	0	2	0	2	0	-3	-2	G
	Salve crux quae in corpore Doctor bonus	rev	LA 499 WA 234										
8	Salve crux quae in corpore	an	LA 500	c	-1	0	-3	-5	0	2	4	2	G
7	Salve crux quae in corpore	re	WA 235	G	2	-2	2	5	7	2	5	4	G
4	Salve crux sancta salve mundi gloria	hy	ST 389	F	-3	-5	-3	0	-3	-5	0	2	E
4	Salve crux sancta salve mundi gloria	hy	ST 230	F	-1	-3	-5	-3	0	-3	-1	0	E
1	Salve crux sancta salve mundi gloria	hy	ST 454	F	2	4	2	6	4	2	4	6	D
1	Salve crux sancta salve mundi gloria	hy	AR 163* ST 120	D	3	2	3	5	7	5	3	2	D
4	Salve festa dies	hy	ST 482 *WA 223 *GS 116 134 173	F	2	-1	2	4	0	-1	-3	-1	E
4	Salve festa dies	hy	AR 166* PM 62	E	3	0	3	5	1	0	-2	0	E
5	Salve mater misericordiae mater Dei		AR 139*	G	5	4	2	0	2	0	-3	0	C
	Salve mater misericordiae mater spei	alv	GR 44**	C	2	5	4	5	7	5	4	2	
1	Salve regina mater	an	AR 68 LU 276 *AM 176	a	-2	0	-7	0	-2	-4	-5	-4	D
5	Salve regina mater	an	AR 69^1 LR 48 LU 279 AM 180	C	4	7	9	7	9	12	11	9	C
1	Salve regina misericordiae	an	WA 352	a	-2	-7	0	-2	-4	-5	-7	-5	D
	Salve regina misericordiae	alv	LU 1476^E	c	-1	2	0	-1	0	2	0	-3	
2	Salve sancta parens	int	GR [75] LU 1263 CS q *GB 220	A	3	5	7	5	3	5	7	8	D
	Salve stella maris O decus	rev	WA 356	a	-4	-2	0	3	5	3	2	0	
	Salve virga florens	alv	VP 53	G	2	0	5	4	2	-5	-2	-3	

4	Salve virginale Christi	re	PM 265 VP 41	C	2	4	2	4	5	7	9	12	E
8	Salvete cedri Libani	hy	AM 1123	G	2	0	-2	2	5	4	0	2	G
3	Salvete Christi vulnera	hy	AM 950	E	-2	3	5	8	7	5	3	5	E
2	Salvete Christi vulnera	hy	AR 765 LU 1529	C	2	4	5	7	5	4	2	0	D
8	Salvete flores martyrum	hy	AM 261	G	-2	-3	-5	-2	2	0	-2	0	G
3	Salvete flores martyrum	hy	ST 221	E	-2	3	5	8	7	5	8	7	E
2	Salvete flores martyrum	hy	ST 447	F	-1	-3	-5	-3	0	2	-3	0	D
8	Salvete flores martyrum	hy	ST 413	G	2	0	-2	0	2	4	0	-2	G
3	Salvete flores martyrum	hy	ST 277	D	2	3	5	7	0	2	3	5	E
1	Salvete flores martyrum	hy	ST 369	C	2	4	7	5	4	2	0	4	D
1	Salvete flores martyrum	hy	AR 285 LU 431	C	2	4	7	5	4	2	4	5	D
3	Salvos fac nos Domine	gr	GR 51 LU 447	F	-5	-3	-1	0	-1	2	-1	2	E
2	Salvos nos fac Domine	int	GR [133]	A	3	5	8	5	3	5	8	10	D
7	Salvum fac populum tuum	gr	GR 119 SYG 88 GB 78 GS 43 50 171	G	2	-2	2	5	2	5	7	5	G
1	Salvum fac servum tuum	gr	GR 105 GS 41 SYG 80 GB 72	C	2	4	7	4	2	0	2	4	D
	Salvum me fac Deus Exaudi nos Domine quoniam	anv	GR 84 GB 61^v SYG 64 GS 29										
	Salvum me fac Deus Vidi aquam	anv	SYG 145										
	Salvum me fac Deus Adversum me exercebantur	cov	SYG 126										
	Salvum me fac Deus Cor meum conturbatum	intv	GR 8**										
8	Salvum me fac Deus	re	LA 177 *WA 111	G	-2	-5	-3	-2	-3	-5	-7	-5	G
	Salvum me fac Deus	alv	GR [139]	F	-1	-3	-1	0	2	7	6	4	
	Salvum me fac Deus Ne avertas faciem	grv	GR 190 OHS 322 LU 617 GS 91 GB 113^v SYG 127	a	3	5	7	5	3	2	3	0	
	Salvum me fac Deus Improperium exspectavit	ofv	OTT 49 *GB 110^v *SYG 123	D	3	5	7	5	10	7	5	3	
3	Salvum me fac Deus	of	GR 10**	G	5	2	0	2	0	-2	2	5	E
	Salvum me fac Domine Tu Domine servabis nos	cov	SYG 91										
8	Salvum me fac Domine	an	AR 105 OHS 229 LU 285	a	-4	-2	0	-4	-2	-4	-7	-5	G
	Sana animam meam	sr	AM 43 50 57 64 71 80										
	Sana contritiones ejus Commovisti Domine terram	trv	GR 78 LU 507 GS 27 GB 58 SYG 60	G	5	7	9	5	0	5	7	9	
2	Sana Domine animam meam	an	AR [168] LU 1794 *WA 64 437 *LA 88 556	F	-1	0	-1	-3	0	-1	0	-1	D

	Sana me Domine et sanabor Peccata mea	rev	WA 62											
2	Sancta Dei genitrix moesta comitata	hy	ST 347	D	-2	0	3	0	3	0	-2	0	D
	Sancta Dei genitrix semper virgo	sr	AR 878 LU 1675 WA 7 310											
1	Sancta Dei genitrix virgo	an	WA 353 LA 449	D	-2	3	5	3	5	7	8	7	D
2	Sancta et immaculata virginitas	re	LR 62 247 PM 38 AR 130* LU 384 AM 1184 VP 39 *LA 34 *WA 29	D	3	0	-2	0	2	-2	0	3	D
1	Sancta legio Agaunensium	re	PM 190	D	3	0	-2	3	5	7	5	3	D
3	Sancta legio Agaunensium	an	WA 377	G	5	4	0	2	4	5	7	5	E
1	Sancta Maria clemens et pia	re	WA 357	D	-2	0	2	0	-2	0	2	3	D
7	Sancta Maria Dei genitrix	inv	LR 245	G	5	4	5	7	5	7	9	7	G
1	Sancta Maria succurre ... assumptionem	re	WA 353	C	2	5	2	4	2	0	2	0	D
4	Sancta Maria succurre ... festivitatem	an	AR [121] LU 1254	E	1	3	-2	-4	-2	0	3	5	E
1	Sancta Maria succurre ... festivitatem	an	AM 705	C	2	5	2	4	2	0	2	0	D
4	Sancta Maria succurre ... maternitatem	an	AR 882[5] AM 1083 *WA 354	E	1	3	-2	-4	-2	0	3	5	E
1	Sancta Maria virginum piissima	an	PM 278	D	3	7	5	3	2	0	-2	0	D
1	Sancta mater Anna	an	WA 339	D	-2	0	3	5	3	2	0	3	D
6	Sancta mater istud agas	hy	AR 676	F	2	4	2	4	7	5	4	2	F
3	Sancta virgo Scholastica	re	LR 292	G	2	0	5	4	2	0	2	4	E
	Sanctae trinitatis fidem Martinus Hic est Martinus	rev	PM 343 LA 481 WA 399											
7	Sanctae trinitatis fidem Martinus	an	WA 398 *LA 480	G	4	5	7	4	7	9	7	4	G
2	Sanctas primitias offert genitus	re	PM 267	D	-2	0	-5	-2	0	3	2	0	D
1	Sancte Benedicte confessor	re	WA 301	D	3	0	-2	3	5	7	5	3	D
	Sancte Benedicte qui in caelis	alv	SYG 207	C	2	5	2	4	5	2	4	2	
2	Sancte Christi confessor audi	re	VP 258	D	-2	-5	-2	0	2	-2	0	2	D
4	Sancte Cuthberte confessor	an	WA 294	C	2	5	4	2	4	2	0	2	E
2	Sancte Dei pretiose protomartyr	hy	ST 82	a	-2	-4	-2	0	-7	-4	-2	-5	D
4	Sancte Dei pretiose protomartyr	hy	ST 219	E	-2	1	-2	-4	-2	0	-2	0	E
1	Sancte Dei pretiose protomartyr	hy	VP 80	D	7	8	7	5	3	5	0	3	D
4	Sancte Luca	hy	ST 403	F	-3	-5	-3	0	-3	-5	0	2	E
2	Sancte Martine Christi	re	LA 485	D	-2	-5	-2	0	2	3	5	3	D
	Sancte Michael archangele	sr	LA 473											
6	Sancte Michael archangele	an	LA 468	c	-3	-5	0	2	0	2	4	2	c

8	Sancte Michael archangele	an	WA 381	G	5	2	0	-2	0	2	0	-2	G
	Sancte Michael archangele	alv	GR 609 LU 1655	D	5	7	5	3	0	2	0	2	
2	Sancte Michael archangelorum	re	LA 470	F	-1	0	-3	-5	-3	0	-3	-5	D
	Sancte N. confessor	sr	WA 424										
2	Sancte N. confessor	re	WA 428	D	-2	-5	-2	0	3	2	3	5	D
3	Sancte pater Aredi	int	SYG 219	E	1	0	-2	3	10	8	7	8	E
	Sancte pater Benedicte	sr	AM 847 848 960 961										
1	Sancte pater Cuthberte	an	WA 294	D	-2	0	3	5	3	2	0	3	D
	Sancte Paule apostole intercede	alv	GB 208^v	F	2	4	6	7	2	4	2	0	
	Sancte Paule apostole praedicator	alv	GR 534 LU 1526	D	5	7	5	3	0	2	0	2	
1	Sancte Paule apostole praedicator ... ad Deum	re	LA 428 WA 266 (inc illeg)	D	-2	-5	-2	0	-2	0	2	3	D
8	Sancte Paule apostole praedicator ... ad Deum	an	AR 598 612 755 LU 1350 AM 796 824 940 *LA 430 WA 266	G	-2	-5	-2	2	-2	0	2	0	G
5	Sancte Paule apostole praedicator ... ad Deum	re	VP 185	F	4	7	9	7	6	7	4	7	F
4	Sancte sacerdos Domini	an	WA 251	C	2	5	2	4	7	9	7	9	E
	Sancte Vincenti levita	alv	GB 46	G	4	5	4	2	0	2	4	2	
8	Sancti angeli custodes	an	AR 869 LU 1667 *AM 1071	G	5	4	2	0	2	0	-2	0	G
8	Sancti Dei dedit vobis	re	WA 393	G	-2	0	2	5	4	2	5	4	G
7	Sancti Dei omnes intercedere	an	AR [132] *WA 398	G	4	5	7	9	7	10	9	10	G
3	Sancti Dei omnes qui estis	an	WA 398	E	-2	3	5	8	7	8	7	8	E
7 8	Sancti Dei vobis apertus est	an	PM 205	c	-1	-3	0	-1	-3	-1	-5	-3	G
tp	Sancti Domini Dominum	an	AM 1122	C	2	5	7	9	7	9	7	5	G
8	Sancti estis dicit Dominus	an	AM 878	c	-1	-3	-5	-3	-5	-7	-8	-7	G
	Sancti et justi in Domino	sr	AR [34] LU 1119 AM 634										
8	Sancti et justi in Domino	an	AR 577^{12}_1 $[36]_1$ LU 262_1 1122_1 AM 637^A 736 910 *LA 391	G	-2	0	-2	-5	-3	-2	0	2	G
	Sancti et justi in Domino	alv	GS 215	G	2	0	-2	2	5	0	2	0	
	Sancti et justi in Domino	alv	SYG 222	G	2	0	2	0	-2	2	5	7	
8	Sancti et justi in Domino	re	LA 389	F	2	4	2	4	2	4	6	4	G
	Sancti immensitas amoris Gloriosa es	rev	WA 335	a	-2	0	-2	-4	-5	-7	-2	0	
6	Sancti infantes martyres	hy	ST 370	c	2	4	2	5	4	2	0	2	c
8	Sancti mei qui in carne	re	LR 187 LA 517 *WA 429	G	2	4	5	4	2	4	5	4	G

	Sancti mei qui in isto saeculo		see also	Sancti mei qui in carne										
7	Sancti mei qui in isto saeculo	an	AM 878		G	4	5	7	5	9	7	5	7	G
7	Sancti omnes intercedant	an	AR 53 [129]		d	-3	-2	0	2	0	3	2	3	G
8	Sancti omnes intercedant	an	AM 166 713 1011		c	-1	0	-3	-5	-3	-5	-7	-5	G
	Sancti per fidem vicerunt 　　Isti sunt viri	rev	LR 145 LA 509											
	Sancti per fidem vicerunt 　　Verbera carnificum	rev	LA 516											
2	Sancti per fidem vicerunt	an	AR [47] LU 1156 AM 652 WA 420		D	-2	0	3	2	0	-2	0	3	D
	Sancti per fidem vicerunt 　　Isti viventes	rev	WA 413		c	-1	0	2	0	-1	0	-1	-3	
3	Sancti per fidem vicerunt	re	LR 180		G	2	4	5	4	2	4	5	4	E
1	Sancti qui sperant in Domino	an	PM 223 LR 177 *LA 514		D	7	10	7	5	7	3	2	0	D
	Sancti sanctum genuere 　　Praesul Christi Dunstanus	rev	WA 312											
4	Sancti spiritus dono	an	WA 290		D	3	2	3	5	3	2	0	2	E
1	Sancti spiritus et animae	an	AR 743 LU 1510 AM 878 981 *WA 324 423 *LA 411 477		D	7	10	7	5	7	3	5	3	D
	Sancti spiritus psallebant 　　Dunstanus archiepiscopus	rev	WA 314		a	3	2	-2	0	2	0	3	5	
	Sancti tui Domine benedicent	sr	LA 512 WA 420											
3	Sancti tui Domine benedicent	int	GR [18] LU 1149 *SYG 169 *GB 152ᵛ GS 211		F	-3	-1	-3	2	4	9	7	6	E
	Sancti tui Domine benedicent	alv	GR 415 LU 1336 *GS 215 GB 269ᵛ SYG 40		D	-2	0	2	3	5	7	5	3	
	Sancti tui Domine florebunt	sr	WA 306											
	Sancti tui Domine florebunt	alv	SYG 222		d	-2	-3	-7	-5	-3	-2	0	-2	
	Sancti tui Domine florebunt	alv	GR [19] LU 1150 GS 215 GB 239		F	2	4	2	4	2	0	4	2	
8	Sancti tui Domine florebunt	an	AR [29] LU 1120 *AM 632 *WA 132		G	5	2	5	4	0	7	5	2	G
7	Sancti tui Domine florebunt	an	LA 391		G	5	4	5	7	5	4	2	4	G
7	Sancti tui Domine mirabile	re	LR 182 LA 515 *WA 421		G	5	4	5	7	4	5	7	5	G
4	Sanctifica nos Domine	an	SYG 142		E	-2	-4	-2	0	1	3	5	3	E
8	Sanctificamini filii Israel	re	LA 29 WA 26		D	3	5	5	7	5	5	7	5	G
7	Sanctificamini hodie	re	LA 29 WA 25		G	5	4	5	7	5	2	5	4	G
	Sanctificati sunt ergo 　　Decantabat populus	rev	WA 141											

	Text	Type	Sources										
6	Sanctificavit Dominus tabernaculum	an	LA 547	F	2	4	2	0	2	4	2	0	F
1	Sanctificavit Dominus tabernaculum ... quia haec	an	AR [106] LU 1242 *AM 696	F	-5	-3	4	5	4	2	4	5	D
5	Sanctificavit Moyses altare	of	GR 374 OTT 114 LU 1057 *SYG 254 *GB 259^v GS 162	F	2	0	2	4	2	4	5	4	F
7	Sanctificavit tabernaculum ... altissimus	an	LR 335	G	4	5	7	9	7	5	4	2	G
6	Sanctificavit tabernaculum ... venite	inv	WA 319	D	3	5	3	5	3	2	3	5	F
3	Sanctimonia et magnificentia	an	LR 265	E	-2	3	5	8	7	8	10	8	E
6	Sanctimonialis autem femina	an	LA 372	c	-3	-5	0	2	0	2	4	2	c
4	Sanctis qui in terra sunt	an	LR 177 LA 514 WA 421	F	-3	-1	0	2	0	-3	0	-1	E
2	Sanctissima Christi sponsa	an	AM 1128	D	-5	-2	0	3	2	0	2	0	D
8	Sanctissima membra	an	LR 369	G	5	2	0	2	5	0	2	0	G
1	Sanctissime confessor Christi Benedicte	re	PM 145 LR 330 AM 1194 LA 372 WA 299	C	2	5	7	9	7	4	5	2	D
4	Sanctissime confessor Domini	an	PM 332 341 AM 855 967 WA 298	F	-1	-3	-1	2	4	2	0	2	E
2	Sanctissimi martyris Stephani	re	WA 36	D	-2	0	-2	-5	0	-2	0	-2	D
1	Sanctissimus monachorum pater	re	PM 168 LR 371	D	-2	0	3	5	3	0	2	0	D
	Sanctitate quoque insignis — Sanctus Vincentius Christi	rev	WA 257										
2	Sanctitate quoque insignis	an	WA 256	D	-2	0	3	2	3	5	3	2	D
	Sanctorum corporum sacer sanguis — Sancta legio	rev	PM 190										
7	Sanctorum corpora sacer	an	WA 377	G	4	2	5	7	5	4	0	4	G
3	Sanctorum meritis inclyta gaudia	hy	AR [38] LU 1159 ST 102	D	2	3	5	7	5	7	10	12	E
3	Sanctorum meritis inclyta gaudia	hy	ST 403	D	2	3	5	7	10	12	10	9	E
2	Sanctorum meritis inclyta gaudia	hy	ST 61	G	2	4	0	2	5	4	2	0	a
2	Sanctorum meritis inclyta gaudia	hy	AM 646	G	2	4	2	0	2	5	2	0	a
2	Sanctorum meritis inclyta gaudia	hy	ST 198	C	2	5	4	0	2	4	5	0	D
2	Sanctorum meritis inclyta gaudia	hy	AR [36] LU 1157	G	2	5	4	0	2	5	0	2	a
2	Sanctorum meritis inclyta gaudia	hy	ST 102	G	2	5	4	0	2	5	4	0	a
1	Sanctorum meritis inclyta gaudia	hy	ST 199	a	3	5	3	2	0	-2	0	-4	D
3	Sanctorum meritis inclyta gaudia	hy	ST 242	D	3	5	7	5	7	5	10	12	E
1	Sanctorum meritis inclyta gaudia	hy	ST 135	F	4	2	0	-1	-3	2	0	-5	D
5	Sanctorum meritis inclyta gaudia	hy	ST 197	C	4	5	7	9	7	5	7	0	C
8	Sanctorum meritis inclyta gaudia	hy	ST 198	C	4	5	7	9	7	9	12	14	G

	Incipit		Source										
1	Sanctorum meritis inclyta gaudia	hy	ST 43	D	7	8	7	5	7	10	9	7	D
4	Sanctorum meritis inclyta gaudia	hy	ST 199	D	7	9	7	5	7	9	7	3	E
8	Sanctorum precibus istorum	an	AM 829	G	4	5	2	5	4	2	0	4	G
	Sanctorum sicut aquilae	alv	SYG 210	G	2	5	7	5	7	9	10	12	
8	Sanctorum velut aquilae	an	AR [47] LU 1156 AM 652 *LA 520	G	2	-2	0	2	5	4	0	4	G
4	Sanctum est verum lumen	an	WA 398 *LA 478	E	-2	1	0	-2	-4	-2	0	-2	E
5	Sanctum et terribile nomen	an	AR 298 LU 451 AM 276	a	-2	0	-4	0	3	5	3	5	F
1	Sanctus antistes Cuthbertus	an	WA 293	D	-2	0	3	2	3	5	3	2	D
7	Sanctus Benedictus dilectum	re	LR 277	G	2	0	2	5	4	2	5	7	G
2	Sanctus Benedictus per viam	an	AM 858	C	5	4	5	2	4	2	0	2	D
1	Sanctus Benedictus plus appetiit	re	PM 144 LR 321 LA 368 WA 297	D	-2	0	3	5	3	5	0	2	D
7	Sanctus Benedictus post triduum	re	LR 298	G	2	0	5	4	5	7	5	7	G
8	Sanctus Bricius satisfaciens	an	WA 404	G	-5	-2	0	2	0	2	0	-2	G
1	Sanctus Dionysius qui tradente	an	WA 384	D	-2	3	5	3	5	7	5	3	D
7	Sanctus Gamaliel per visum	re	WA 344	a	5	7	5	7	3	2	3	5	G
1	Sanctus Joannes episcopus	re	WA 345	C	2	5	7	5	4	2	5	2	D
8	Sanctus Martinus obitum suum	an	WA 402 (inc illeg)	G									G
8	Sanctus Mauritius legionem	an	WA 376	G	-5	-2	0	2	0	-2	0	2	G
8	Sanctus quidem	an	WA 240	G	-2	0	2	0	2	0	-2	2	G
2	Sanctus sanctus sanctus XI		GR 40* LU 47	D	-5	-2	0	-2	2	0	2	3	D
2	Sanctus		THAN #201	D	-5	-2	0	2	0	-2	0	2	D
2	Sanctus		THAN #200	D	-5	-2	0	2	0	-2	0	3	D
1	Sanctus		THAN #199	D	-5	-2	0	3	7	5	3	2	D
2	Sanctus		THAN #198	D	-5	0	2	-2	-3	-5	-2	0	D
3	Sanctus		THAN #38	b	-4	0	1	0	-2	-4	-6	-4	E
8	Sanctus		THAN #37	b	-4	0	1	3	5	3	1	0	G
6	Sanctus		THAN #35	c	-3	-7	-12	-7	-3	-5	-7	-3	F
6	Sanctus		THAN #34	c	-3	-7	-5	-7	-3	0	2	0	F
5	Sanctus IX		GR 34* LU 42 OHS 459 THAN #33	c	-3	-7	-5	-3	-5	-7	-3	-5	F
5	Sanctus		THAN #1	g	-3	-7	-2	-3	-5	-3	-5	-8	b
5	Sanctus		THAN #31	c	-3	-5	-7	-5	-3	-5	-7	-5	F
5	Sanctus		THAN #30	c	-3	-5	-7	-5	-3	-5	-7	-3	F
5	Sanctus		THAN #29	c	-3	-5	-7	-5	-3	-5	-7	-2	F
8	Sanctus		THAN #94	G	-3	-5	-7	-5	-3	-2	-3	-5	G

6 Sanctus	THAN #93	G	-3	-5	-7	-3	-5	-3	-2	-5	C
5 Sanctus XVII	GR 56* LU 61 OHS 145 THAN #32	c	-3	-5	-7	-3	0	2	0	-3	F
8 Sanctus	THAN #28	c	-3	-5	-7	-3	0	2	0	2	c
5 Sanctus	THAN #27	c	-3	-5	-7	-2	-3	-5	-7	-3	F
4 Sanctus	THAN #26	c	-3	-5	-3	-5	-7	-3	0	2	a
2 Sanctus XVI	GR 54* LU 59 THAN #131	F	-3	-5	-3	0	-1	-3	-5	-3	D
8 Sanctus	THAN #25	c	-3	-5	0	-5	-3	-5	-7	0	c
8 Sanctus	THAN #92	G	-3	-5	0	2	0	2	4	5	G
2 Sanctus	THAN #24	c	-3	-5	0	2	4	-1	[0	0]	a
8 Sanctus	THAN #91	G	-3	-2	-3	-5	0	2	4	5	G
5 Sanctus	THAN #23	c	-3	-2	0	-3	-5	-7	-5	-3	F
8 Sanctus	THAN #22	c	-3	-2	0	-2	-3	-5	0	2	c
8 Sanctus	THAN #21	c	-3	-2	0	2	0	2	4	5	c
5 Sanctus	THAN #20	c	-3	-1	0	2	4	2	0	-1	F
5 Sanctus	THAN #19	c	-3	0	-5	-3	-7	-8	-10	-8	F
1 Sanctus	THAN #90	G	-3	0	-5	-2	-3	-5	0	7	D
1 Sanctus	THAN #6	d	-2	-5	-9	-7	-12	-9	-12	-14	D
5 Sanctus	THAN #18	c	-2	-5	-3	-2	0	2	5	4	F
2 Sanctus	THAN #196	D	-2	-5	-2	0	2	3	5	3	D
2 Sanctus	THAN #197	D	-2	-5	-2	0	2	3	5	3	D
2 Sanctus	THAN #195	D	-2	-5	-2	0	5	7	3	2	D
8 Sanctus	THAN #89	G	-2	-5	-2	2	-2	0	-2	2	G
4 Sanctus	THAN #43	a	-2	-4	0	-2	0	-2	0	-2	E
2 Sanctus	THAN #155	E	-2	-4	0	1	3	1	0	-2	D
7 Sanctus	THAN #5	d	-2	-3	-5	-3	-7	-3	-7	-9	F
8 Sanctus	THAN #88	G	-2	-3	-5	-2	0	2	0	2	G
8 Sanctus	THAN #87	G	-2	-3	-2	0	2	0	2	4	G
8 Sanctus	THAN #86	G	-2	-3	-2	0	2	4	0	2	G
1 Sanctus	THAN #42	a	-2	0	-7	-4	-5	-4	-2	0	D
2 Sanctus	THAN #4	d	-2	0	-2	-5	-3	-5	-7	-2	C
Sanctus	GR 169 58* 101* LU 1814 THAN #41	b	-2	0	-2	-4	-2	0	-2	0	a
4 Sanctus I	GR 6* OHS 686 LU 18 THAN #154	b	-2	0	-2	-4	-2	0	-2	0	b
4 Sanctus	THAN #153	E	-2	0	-2	-4	0	-2	-4	-2	E
Sanctus	THAN #10	a	-2	0	-2	0	-2	0	-2	3	a

4 Sanctus	THAN #152	E	-2	0	1	-2	-4	0	1	3	E
1 Sanctus	THAN #39	a	-2	0	2	3	-2	0	2	3	D
Sanctus	THAN #194	D	-2	0	2	3	-2	0	2	3	
4 Sanctus	THAN #193	D	-2	0	2	3	0	2	0	-2	E
2 Sanctus	THAN #192	D	-2	0	2	3	2	0	-2	0	D
1 Sanctus	THAN #191	D	-2	0	3	2	0	-2	2	3	D
1 Sanctus	THAN #190	D	-2	0	3	2	0	3	7	5	D
1 Sanctus	THAN #189	D	-2	0	3	2	3	5	2	0	D
1 Sanctus	THAN #188	D	-2	0	3	7	5	2	0	3	D
1 Sanctus	THAN #130	F	-1	-3	-5	-3	-1	-3	-1	2	D
5 Sanctus	THAN #129	F	-1	-3	-1	-3	-5	2	4	2	C
8 Sanctus	THAN #128	F	-1	-3	-1	0	-5	0	-1	-3	G
3 Sanctus VI	GR 24* LU 33 THAN #17	c	-1	-3	-1	0	2	-1	0	-3	E
5 Sanctus	THAN #127	F	-1	-3	4	2	-1	0	-3	4	F
5 Sanctus	THAN #126	F	-1	0	-3	-5	0	2	0	7	F
6 Sanctus	THAN #16	c	-1	0	-3	-1	-3	-5	2	-1	C
5 Sanctus	THAN #2	f	-1	0	-1	-3	-5	-12	-10	-8	F
Sanctus	THAN #15	c	-1	0	-1	0	-3	0	-1	-3	b
2 Sanctus	THAN #125	F	-1	0	2	4	2	0	-1	0	D
6 Sanctus	THAN #124	F	-1	0	2	4	2	0	4	6	F
3 Sanctus	THAN #151	E	1	-2	0	-4	0	3	5	3	E
3 Sanctus	THAN #3	e	1	0	-2	0	-7	-4	-2	0	a
4 Sanctus	THAN #36	b	1	0	-2	0	-4	-6	-7	-4	E
3 Sanctus	THAN #150	E	1	0	-2	0	3	0	-4	-2	E
4 Sanctus	THAN #149	E	1	0	-2	0	3	1	0	-2	E
3 Sanctus	THAN #148	E	1	0	-2	0	3	5	0	3	E
3 Sanctus	THAN #147	E	1	0	-2	0	3	5	7	8	E
3 Sanctus	THAN #146	E	1	0	-2	0	7	8	7	5	E
3 Sanctus	THAN #145	E	1	0	-2	3	0	1	0	-2	E
3 Sanctus	THAN #144	E	1	0	-2	3	5	7	8	7	E
3 Sanctus	THAN #143	E	1	0	-2	5	3	0	1	-2	E
3 Sanctus	THAN #142	E	1	0	-2	5	3	5	0	1	E
3 Sanctus	THAN #141	E	1	0	-2	5	3	5	3	1	E
3 Sanctus	THAN #140	E	1	0	-2	5	7	3	0	-4	E
3 Sanctus	THAN #139	E	1	3	0	1	0	-2	3	5	E
8 Sanctus	THAN #85	G	2	-3	-2	-3	-5	0	2	0	G

8 Sanctus	THAN #84	G	2	-2	0	-2	2	5	4	2	G
7 Sanctus	THAN #83	G	2	-2	0	2	5	4	5	2	G
5 Sanctus	THAN #123	F	2	-1	-5	-3	-1	0	4	6	F
8 Sanctus XIII	GR 46* LU 52 THAN #82	G	2	0	-3	-2	-5	-3	0	2	G
5 Sanctus	THAN #14	c	2	0	-3	-2	-3	-7	-5	-7	F
3 Sanctus	THAN #81	G	2	0	-2	-3	-2	0	2	0	F
8 Sanctus	THAN #80	G	2	0	-2	0	2	-2	0	2	G
1 Sanctus	THAN #187	D	2	0	-2	0	3	5	3	2	D
6 Sanctus	THAN #122	F	2	0	-1	-3	0	2	4	5	F
Sanctus	THAN #13	c	2	0	2	0	-1	-3	-1	0	c
8 Sanctus	THAN #79	G	2	0	2	0	4	5	2	5	G
8 Sanctus	THAN #12	c	2	0	2	4	0	2	0	2	c
8 Sanctus	THAN #78	G	2	0	2	4	5	4	2	0	G
5 Sanctus	THAN #11	c	2	0	2	4	5	4	2	0	F
6 Sanctus	THAN #121	F	2	0	2	4	6	4	2	0	F
1 Sanctus	THAN #186	D	2	0	3	5	3	2	0	7	D
3 Sanctus	THAN #77	G	2	0	4	5	4	0	2	-2	E
6 Sanctus	THAN #120	F	2	0	4	6	2	0	-3	-1	F
7 Sanctus	THAN #76	G	2	0	5	2	0	4	0	2	G
8 Sanctus ad lib. III	GR 91* LU 87 THAN #230	G	2	0	5	4	2	4	0	2	G
7 Sanctus	THAN #75	G	2	0	5	4	2	4	0	7	G
8 Sanctus	THAN #74	G	2	0	5	4	2	4	2	0	G
5 Sanctus	THAN #118	F	2	0	5	4	5	2	0	4	F
5 Sanctus	THAN #119	F	2	0	6	4	0	2	0	4	F
1 Sanctus	THAN #185	D	2	3	0	5	3	2	0	-2	D
1 Sanctus XIV	GR 49* LU 55 THAN #184	D	2	3	2	-2	3	2	0	3	D
1 Sanctus	THAN #183	D	2	3	2	0	-2	0	3	2	D
1 Sanctus	THAN #182	D	2	3	2	3	0	7	3	0	D
1 Sanctus	THAN #179	D	2	3	5	2	3	2	0	5	D
1 Sanctus	THAN #180	D	2	3	5	2	3	2	0	5	D
1 Sanctus	THAN #181	D	2	3	5	2	3	2	0	5	D
2 Sanctus	THAN #178	D	2	3	5	7	5	3	2	3	D
6 Sanctus	THAN #117	F	2	4	0	-5	-3	-5	0	-5	G
7 Sanctus	THAN #73	G	2	4	0	-3	2	0	7	4	G

6 Sanctus VIII	GR 30* LU 38 THAN #116	F	2	4	0	2	0	-1	-3	-5	F
5 Sanctus	THAN #10	c	2	4	0	2	0	4	7	5	c
8 Sanctus	THAN #63	G	2	4	0	2	4	5	4	2	G
8 Sanctus	THAN #66	G	2	4	0	2	4	5	4	2	G
8 Sanctus	THAN #9	c	2	4	0	2	4	5	4	5	c
1 Sanctus ad lib. I	GR 90* LU 86 THAN #229	C	2	4	0	2	5	7	2	4	D
5 Sanctus	THAN #113	F	2	4	0	5	4	2	4	0	F
5 Sanctus	THAN #114	F	2	4	0	5	4	2	4	0	F
6 Sanctus	THAN #115	F	2	4	0	6	4	2	0	-1	F
8 Sanctus	THAN #72	G	2	4	0	7	5	4	0	2	G
1 Sanctus	THAN #71	G	2	4	2	0	-3	0	-3	-2	D
4 Sanctus	THAN #70	C	2	4	2	0	-2	0	-3	0	E
8 Sanctus	THAN #69	G	2	4	2	0	-2	2	0	4	G
8 Sanctus	THAN #68	G	2	4	2	0	2	0	2	4	G
5 Sanctus	THAN #112	F	2	4	2	0	2	0	4	7	F
8 Sanctus	THAN #111	F	2	4	2	0	2	4	2	0	G
2 Sanctus	THAN #227	C	2	4	2	0	2	4	2	4	D
2 Sanctus	THAN #228	C	2	4	2	0	2	4	2	4	D
8 Sanctus	THAN #67	G	2	4	2	0	2	4	5	4	G
6 Sanctus	THAN #110	F	2	4	2	0	6	4	2	0	F
8 Sanctus	THAN #109	F	2	4	2	4	0	2	4	2	G
8 Sanctus	THAN #65	G	2	4	2	4	2	0	-2	0	G
8 Sanctus	THAN #64	G	2	4	2	4	5	4	2	4	G
6 Sanctus	THAN #108	F	2	4	2	4	6	4	6	4	F
4 Sanctus	THAN #226	C	2	4	2	5	7	9	7	5	E
1 Sanctus	THAN #225	C	2	4	5	2	0	2	7	5	D
8 Sanctus	THAN #62	G	2	4	5	2	4	2	0	2	G
1 Sanctus	THAN #224	C	2	4	5	2	4	5	4	2	D
2 Sanctus XV	GR 53* LU 58 THAN #223	C	2	4	5	2	4	7	4	5	D
7 Sanctus	THAN #61	G	2	4	5	2	5	4	5	2	G
8 Sanctus	THAN #60	G	2	4	5	4	0	2	4	5	G
8 Sanctus	THAN #59	G	2	4	5	4	2	0	-3	-2	G
8 Sanctus	THAN #58	G	2	4	5	4	2	0	-2	0	G
6 Sanctus	THAN #107	F	2	4	5	4	2	0	-1	0	F
6 Sanctus	THAN #222	C	2	4	5	4	2	0	2	0	C

8 Sanctus	THAN #57	G	2	4	5	4	2	0	2	4	G
4 Sanctus	THAN #221	C	2	4	5	4	2	0	2	5	E
1 Sanctus	THAN #220	C	2	4	5	4	2	0	2	9	D
4 Sanctus	THAN #219	C	2	4	5	4	2	0	4	5	E
5 Sanctus	THAN #106	F	2	4	5	4	2	0	4	7	F
5 Sanctus	THAN #105	F	2	4	5	4	2	0	7	9	F
4 Sanctus	THAN #218	C	2	4	5	4	2	4	0	4	E
4 Sanctus	THAN #217	C	2	4	5	4	2	4	2	4	E
2 Sanctus	THAN #216	C	2	4	5	4	2	4	5	7	D
4 Sanctus	THAN #215	C	2	4	5	4	2	7	5	7	E
4 Sanctus	THAN #214	C	2	4	5	4	2	9	7	5	E
1 Sanctus	THAN #213	C	2	4	5	7	5	7	9	7	D
5 Sanctus	THAN #212	C	2	4	7	9	7	9	11	12	C
5 Sanctus	THAN #104	F	2	4	7	9	7	9	12	11	F
4 Sanctus III	GR 14* LU 24 THAN #56	G	2	5	2	0	-2	0	-3	0	E
2 Sanctus	THAN #211	C	2	5	2	4	5	7	5	4	D
8 Sanctus	THAN #55	G	2	5	4	2	0	2	5	4	G
1 Sanctus	THAN #210	C	2	5	4	2	4	0	4	7	D
2 Sanctus	THAN #209	C	2	5	4	2	4	2	4	5	D
4 Sanctus ad lib. II	GR 91* LU 86 THAN #208	C	2	5	4	2	7	5	7	4	E
8 Sanctus VII	GR 27* LU 36 THAN #54	G	2	5	4	5	2	0	7	9	G
7 Sanctus	THAN #53	G	2	5	4	5	2	0	7	9	G
1 Sanctus	THAN #207	C	2	5	4	5	4	2	0	2	D
8 Sanctus	THAN #52	G	2	5	4	5	7	5	4	2	G
2 Sanctus	THAN #206	C	2	5	7	5	4	2	4	2	D
1 Sanctus	THAN #205	C	2	5	7	9	7	4	2	5	D
5 Sanctus	THAN #103	F	2	6	0	2	0	-1	0	-1	F
4 Sanctus	THAN #138	E	3	-2	3	1	0	3	5	7	E
4 Sanctus	THAN #138	E	3	-2	3	1	0	8	5	3	E
4 Sanctus X	GR 37* LU 45	E	3	0	1	-2	-4	-2	1	-2	E
3 Sanctus	THAN #136	E	3	0	1	0	-4	-2	0	3	E
3 Sanctus	THAN #135	E	3	0	1	0	-2	0	3	5	E
3 Sanctus	THAN #134	E	3	1	0	1	0	-2	1	0	E
2 Sanctus XII	GR 43* LU 50 THAN #177	D	3	2	0	-2	0	3	7	8	D

1 Sanctus	THAN #176	D	3	2	0	2	-2	-3	-2	0	D
1 Sanctus	THAN #175	D	3	2	0	3	0	-2	3	5	D
1 Sanctus	THAN #174	D	3	2	5	2	-2	0	2	5	D
1 Sanctus	THAN #173	D	3	5	3	2	0	3	2	0	D
8 Sanctus	THAN #172	D	3	5	7	5	0	3	5	7	G
1 Sanctus	THAN #171	D	3	5	7	5	3	5	3	2	D
2 Sanctus	THAN #133	E	3	5	8	7	8	7	5	3	a
1 Sanctus	THAN #170	D	3	7	5	3	0	2	0	2	D
4 Sanctus	THAN #51	G	4	2	0	-2	0	-2	-3	-2	E
4 Sanctus	THAN #204	C	4	2	0	2	4	5	7	5	E
1 Sanctus II	GR 10* LU 21 OHS 850 THAN #203	C	4	2	7	5	4	5	2	9	D
6 Sanctus	THAN #102	F	4	5	4	2	4	2	-1	0	F
7 Sanctus	THAN #8	c	4	5	7	4	2	4	7	5	c
7 Sanctus	THAN #50	G	4	5	7	5	9	7	5	4	G
5 Sanctus	THAN #100	F	4	5	7	9	12	11	9	7	F
5 Sanctus	THAN #101	F	4	6	7	4	2	7	9	7	F
5 Sanctus	THAN #99	F	4	7	4	2	7	9	7	9	F
5 Sanctus	THAN #98	F	4	7	4	12	11	7	4	0	F
5 Sanctus	THAN #97	F	4	7	6	4	2	7	9	7	F
5 Sanctus	THAN #96	F	4	7	9	7	4	5	4	2	F
5 Sanctus	THAN #95	F	4	7	9	7	4	7	6	4	F
8 Sanctus IV	GR 17* LU 27 OHS 421 THAN #49	G	5	2	0	-3	-2	0	4	5	G
8 Sanctus	THAN #48	G	5	4	2	0	-3	-2	0	2	G
8 Sanctus	THAN #47	G	5	4	2	4	2	0	2	4	G
8 Sanctus	THAN #46	G	5	4	2	4	2	0	4	5	G
8 Sanctus	THAN #45	G	5	4	7	5	4	2	0	4	G
3 Sanctus	THAN #7	c	5	4	7	9	11	4	5	4	b
8 Sanctus	THAN #169	D	5	7	5	7	10	9	5	7	G
1 Sanctus	THAN #168	D	7	0	3	5	7	5	2	3	D
4 Sanctus V	GR 20* LU 30 THAN #167	D	7	5	0	5	3	2	0	2	E
1 Sanctus	THAN #166	D	7	5	3	2	0	3	2	5	D
1 Sanctus	THAN #165	D	7	5	3	2	0	7	5	3	D
1 Sanctus	THAN #164	D	7	5	3	2	3	2	0	-2	D
1 Sanctus	THAN #163	D	7	5	3	2	3	2	0	12	D

1 Sanctus		THAN #162	D	7	5	3	5	2	0	5	7	D
1 Sanctus		THAN #161	D	7	5	3	5	7	5	12	10	D
7 Sanctus		THAN #44	G	7	5	4	5	7	5	4	5	G
3 Sanctus		THAN #132	E	7	5	7	3	1	0	1	0	E
1 Sanctus		THAN #160	D	7	5	7	5	3	2	0	-2	D
1 Sanctus		THAN #159	D	7	5	7	8	7	5	7	5	D
1 Sanctus		THAN #157	D	7	8	7	5	3	2	0	3	D
1 Sanctus		THAN #158	D	7	9	7	5	3	2	0	-2	D
1 Sanctus		THAN #156	D	7	9	7	5	3	2	3	0	D
5 Sanctus sanctus sanctus ... omnipotens	an	WA 159	b^b	2	-1	-5	-1	2	4	2	0	F
5 Sanctus sanctus sanctus ... omnipotens	an	PM 92	F	4	7	9	7	9	12	11	7	F
1 Sanctus Sebastianus dixit	re	LA 329	D	-2	0	3	5	3	5	0	2	D
4 Sanctus terrarum illustret petimus	hy	ST 488	D	3	0	-2	0	2	0	2	0	E
1 Sanctus Vincentius a pueritia	an	WA 256	E	-4	-2	5	7	5	3	1	3	D
1 Sanctus Vincentius Christi	re	WA 257	D	3	0	2	0	-2	3	5	7	D
5 Sanguinis et aquae fluenta	re	PM 156 LR 344	c	2	0	-3	0	-7	-3	0	2	F
Sanguis Jesu Christi filii Dei	sr	AR 768 LU 1536										
5 Sanguis sanctorum martyrum	an	LR 182 WA 421 LA 516	a	-4	0	3	1	0	1	3	5	F
1 Sapientia aedificavit ... excidit	gr	GR 398	C	2	9	10	9	7	5	9	7	D
7 Sapientia aedificavit ... excidit ... subdidit	an	AR 543 LU 989 AM 580 *LA 280 *WA 168 317	G	2	5	7	5	7	9	10	7	G
1 Sapientia aedificavit ... miscuit	an	AM 550 *AR 530 *LU 939	C	2	9	11	9	7	9	7	5	D
8 Sapientia clamitat in plateis	an	AR 545 LU 990 AM 581 *WA 168 LA 281	C	2	5	7	9	7	9	12	7	G
4 Sapientia Domini evangelii	an	WA 372	C	2	5	4	2	5	4	2	0	E
Sapientia hujus mundi	alv	GR 473 LU 1428	C	2	4	2	4	2	0	4	5	
1 Sapientia hujus mundi	gr	GR 475	C	2	9	10	9	12	9	7	5	D
3 Sapientia reddidit justis	int	LU 1440	E	-2	3	5	8	5	7	8	10	E
Sapientia requiescit in corde De ore prudentis	rev	OHS 780 PM 230 LR 88 WA 306										
3 Sapientiam antiquorum	an	WA 374	G	2	5	4	2	5	4	2	5	E
Sapientiam eorum ... pronuntiet		see Sapientiam sanctorum ... pronuntiet										
8 Sapientiam eorum narrabunt	an	WA 373	G	2	0	-2	-3	-2	0	2	5	G
Sapientiam ipsorum narrent	alv	GR 445 LU 1386	C	2	9	12	9	7	9	7	4	
1 Sapientiam sanctorum ... nuntiet	int	GR [25] LU 1166 SYG 189 GB 194^v GS 211	a	-2	-4	-2	-4	-2	0	-2	1	D

	Incipit		Ref										
4	Sapientiam sanctorum ... pronuntiat	an	AM 981	E	1	3	1	0	3	5	3	1	E
	Sapientiam sanctorum ... pronuntiet 　　Corpora sanctorum	rev	PM 200 LR 188 LA 519										
4	Satiavit Dominus quinque millia	an	AR 399 LU 563 AM 374 WA 104 *LA 159	G	2	5	7	9	7	5	7	9	a
	Saturninus pontifex magnus	alv	SYG 230	D	-2	0	2	3	5	7	5	3	
8	Saul et Jonathas amabiles	an	LA 274	G	-2	0	-2	-5	-3	-2	2	0	G
4	Saule frater Dominus misit	an	LA 342	F	-1	-3	-5	-3	-1	0	-5	0	E
1	Saule Saule quid me persequeris	an	WA 262 LA 341	C	2	9	11	9	7	9	7	5	D
1	Saulus adhuc spirans	re	LA 341 *WA 263	C	2	4	5	4	2	4	0	2	D
1	Saulus adhuc spirans	an	WA 262 LA 340	D	3	0	-2	3	5	3	5	7	D
	Saulus autem cadens 　　Viri autem qui	anv	LA 341										
	Saulus autem consentiens 　　Sepelierunt Stephanum	rev	LA 45										
4	Saulus autem multo magis	an	WA 264 (inc illeg)										E
4	Saulus autem tremens	an	WA 262 (inc illeg) LA 339	F	-3	-5	-3	0	-1	0	-1	0	E
8	Saulus qui et Paulus	an	WA 331 *LA 425	G	5	2	0	-2	0	2	0	4	G
5	Scande thronum prolis	re	WA 355	a	-4	-2	0	1	0	-4	0	3	F
	Scapulis suis obumbrabit	sr	AR 36 LU 244 AM 336										
	Scapulis suis obumbrabit 　　Qui habitat	trv	GR 95 LU 533 GS 35 *GB 65 *SYG 73	G	-2	0	-2	-5	-3	-2	0	-2	
8	Scapulis suis obumbrabit ... 　　Dominus et	of	GR 98 OTT 32 LU 537 *SYG 74 GB 66^v GS 36	a	-2	2	0	-2	0	3	2	0	G
3	Scapulis suis obumbrabit ... et	co	GR 99 LU 537 SYG 75 GB 67 *GS 37	G	2	5	4	5	4	2	4	2	E
	Scholasticae mox nuntiat 　　In columbae specie	trv	GB 54^v	F	2	7	2	7	4	6	7	4	
1	Sciant gentes quoniam nomen	gr	GR 78 LU 506 SYG 60 GB 58 GS 26	D	3	0	3	0	3	7	5	3	D
4	Sciens Jesus quia venit	int	GR 53**	F	-3	-1	0	2	4	0	-3	0	E
4	Sciens Jesus quia venit	an	AR 6 (sup 2)	F	-1	-3	0	-1	-3	-1	0	2	E
	Scimus quidem desiderare 　　Dixerunt discipuli	rev	LA 484 WA 399										
1	Scimus quidem te pater	an	WA 403	D	3	2	0	2	0	-2	0	2	D
4	Scindite corda vestra	re	LA 129	F	-3	0	-1	0	2	0	-1	0	E
6	Scindite corda vestra	re	WA 86	F	2	0	2	4	2	0	2	-3	F
	Scio cui credidi 　　Bonum certamen	rev	LA 427 WA 330										

	Text	Type	Sources	Mode									
	Scio cui credidi 　Reposita est mihi	rev	WA 331										
1	Scio cui credidi	an	WA 330 LA 422	a	-4	-2	0	-2	0	-4	-5	-7	D
1	Scio cui credidi	int	GR 417 LU 1344 *SYG 204 *GB 207^v *GS 189	a	-2	0	-2	0	-2	0	1	0	D
1	Scio cui credidi	re	LA 424 WA 330 (inc illeg)	C	2	4	5	2	0	2	4	5	D
6	Scio Domine quia morti	re	WA 174	c	4	2	5	4	2	4	0	2	c
6	Scio quem quaeritis	an	WA 135	F	2	4	2	5	4	2	0	2	F
3	Scitote quia Dominus	an	AR 301 LU 445 *AM 279	G	2	5	2	5	4	2	0	2	E
8	Scitote quia prope est	an	AR 260 LU 365 AM 237 *WA 26 LA 30	a	-4	-2	0	-2	-4	-2	0	-4	G
	Scitote quod Dominus 　Jubilate Domino omnis terra	trv	GR 82 LU 513 GS 28 GB 59^v SYG 62	F	4	7	6	2	4	2	0	2	
	Scitote quoniam Dominus	alv	GR [129] LU 1296	G	2	4	5	4	5	4	2	0	
8	Scriptum est enim in lege	an	WA 269	G	-5	-2	0	2	0	2	0	-2	G
8	Scriptum est enim percutiam	an	AR 425 OHS 163 LU 605 AM 404 *LA 185	F	2	4	2	4	2	0	2	4	G
8	Scriptum est enim quia domus	an	AR 374 561 LU 1019 AM 347 600 *WA 188 LA 314	F	2	4	2	0	-1	0	-3	-1	G
2	Scuto bonae voluntatis	an	LR 149 *WA 416 *LA 522	F	-1	-3	-1	0	-1	-5	-3	0	D
	Scuto circumdabit te	sr	AR 42 LU 248										
	Scuto circumdabit te 　Qui habitat	trv	GR 95 LU 533 GS 35 GB 65 *SYG 73	F	-3	0	-3	0	2	0	2	4	
2	Sebastiani martyris	hy	ST 20	D	-2	3	5	3	5	7	5	7	D
1	Sebastianus Dei cultor	an	LA 330	F	2	4	2	4	0	2	4	0	D
8	Sebastianus Dei cultor	re	LA 324	D	3	5	7	5	7	5	7	9	G
7	Sebastianus dixit ad Nicostratum	an	LA 331	G	4	5	7	5	9	7	5	7	G
8	Sebastianus dixit Marcelliano	an	LA 326	G	5	4	0	4	5	7	5	2	G
7	Sebastianus Mediolanensium	re	LA 325	G	2	0	2	5	7	5	4	5	G
7	Sebastianus Mediolanensium	an	LA 323	G	4	5	7	5	9	7	9	7	G
4	Sebastianus vir Christianissimus	re	LA 325	F	-3	0	-1	0	2	0	-1	0	E
7	Sebastianus vir Christianissimus	an	LA 324	G	4	5	7	5	9	7	5	7	G
1	Secundum magnam misericordiam	an	AR 348 AM 319 *WA 65 LA 92	F	2	4	2	0	2	4	2	0	D

	Secundum multitudinem dolorum Tribularer si nescirem	rev	LR 404										
1	Secundum multitudinem miserationum	an	AR 353 AM 326 WA 78 LA 123	D	-2	3	5	3	5	7	10	7	D
	Secundum nomen tuum Deus Vir Dei Benedictus	intv	GR(27)										
	Secundum nomen tuum Deus Suscepimus Deus	trv	GR 113**	G	-5	0	2	4	2	5	4	0	
	Secundum quod dictum est Quem vidistis	rev	WA 30	a	-2	-4	-2	-4	-5	-9	-7	-5	
	Securus et gaudens venio O bona crux	rev	LA 501										
	Securus et gaudens venio Salve crux quae in corpore	rev	WA 235										
4	Secus decursus aquarum	an	LR 176 *WA 420 LA 513	D	2	3	5	0	3	2	0	2	E
	Sed et lingua mea Gaudebunt labia mea	rev	LA 98 WA 68										
	Sed sic eum volo manere Exiit sermo	grv	GR 39 LU 422 GS 16 GB 24^v *SYG 24	F	4	2	7	9	7	2	7	9	
	Sed surge et ingredere Saule Saule	anv	LA 341										
2	Sede a dextris meis	an	WA 63	D	-2	0	3	2	0	-2	3	5	D
6	Sedebit Dominus rex	co	GR 642 LU 1714	C	2	5	2	0	5	7	9	7	F
7	Sedere autem mecum	an	LA 144	G	4	5	7	9	5	7	4	5	G
5	Sederunt principes	gr	GR 36 LU 416 *SYG 22 *GB 21 *GS 15	D	3	7	5	7	3	5	3	5	F
	Sedes super thronum Sperent in te	ofv	OTT 85 *GB 100 *SYG 112	G	2	5	4	7	5	2	-2	2	
8	Sedibus caeli nitidis receptos	hy	AR 776 LU 1551	G	2	0	-3	-2	0	2	-2	2	G
	Sedisti super thronum	an	OHS 58 (nm)										
8	Sedit angelus ad sepulchrum	an	WA 222	G	2	0	-2	0	2	0	-2	0	G
4	Semel juravi in sancto meo	co	GR [6] LU 1132 *SYG 209 *GB 211^v GS 191	G	-2	-3	0	-2	-3	0	2	0	E
8	Semen cecidit ... aliud	an	AR 350 LU 509 *AM 322 325 *WA 79 LA 119	c	-1	0	-1	-5	-1	2	0	2	G
1	Semen cecidit ... centuplum	an	WA 79	D	-2	3	5	7	10	12	9	10	D
7	Semen cecidit ... centuplum	an	LA 119	G	4	5	7	9	7	2	5	4	G
8	Semen cecidit ... in patientia	an	AR 350 LU 504 *AM 321 LA 118	c	-1	0	-1	-5	-1	2	0	2	G
3	Semen est verbum Dei	an	AR 352 *AM 324 **WA 79 *LA 120	G	2	5	4	2	0	2	4	5	E

Seminavit in benedictionibus 　　Ecce virum	rev	WA 249										
Semper mortificationem 　　Christo igitur	trv	GR 482	D	-5	-2	0	-2	0	3	2	3	
8 Senex puerum portabat	re	LA 348 WA 270	c	2	0	2	0	-1	-3	-1	-5	G
1 Senex puerum portabat	an	AR 619 LU 1355 AM 801 LA 356 *WA 272	C	2	3	0	-2	0	3	0	2	D
Senex puerum portabat	alv	GR 434 LU 1363 *GB 47^v	F	4	2	-1	0	2	0	2	-3	
1 Seniores populi consilium	re	OHS 398 LU 651 LA 193 *WA 119	D	2	3	5	3	0	3	5	3	D
Separemur a sinistris 　　Princeps sancte	rev	WA 383	D	7	5	7	10	9	7	5	3	
8 Sepelierunt Stephanum	an	AR 278 LU 420 1583^B AM 254 LA 43	G	-2	2	5	4	0	4	5	2	G
7 Sepelierunt Stephanum	re	LA 45	G	2	0	2	0	2	4	5	7	G
Sepivi te et lapides elegi 　　Vinea mea	rev	OHS 490 LU 697 LA 196										
2 Septies in die laudem	re	LA 154 WA 99	D	-5	-2	0	-2	0	3	2	3	D
2 Sepulto Domino signatum est	re	OHS 618 LU 773 *LA 202 *WA 125	C	2	5	2	5	4	5	2	4	D
Seraphim stabant super illud 　　Vidi Dominum	rev	PM 201 LR 383 AM 1204 LA 301 WA 183										
3 Sermo meus et praedicatio	int	GR 544 LU 1543	E	1	-2	3	8	5	8	5	3	E
7 Serve bone et fidelis intra	an	AR [75] LU 1196 AM 671 LA 536	b	1	3	1	3	1	-2	1	0	G
3 Serve bone et fidelis intra	an	AR [56] LU 1177 *AM 658 *WA 427	G	2	0	2	5	4	2	0	2	E
4 Serve bone et fidelis quia	an	AM 673 743	E	1	3	0	3	5	3	1	0	E
8 Serve nequam omne debitum	an	WA 191	G	-3	-2	0	2	0	2	5	2	G
6 Serve nequam omne debitum	an	AR 572 LU 1070 AM 613 *LA 319	c	-3	-1	-5	-3	0	2	4	0	c
4 Servi Dei benedicite	an	WA 286	F	2	0	-1	-3	-1	2	4	2	E
7 Servi Domini benedicite	an	AM 832	G	4	0	2	4	5	7	5	4	G
8 Servite Domino in timore	an	WA 64 *LA 89	G	5	2	4	2	0	-2	0	2	G
8 Servite Domino in timore et exsultate	an	OHS 57 (nm) AM 5	a	-4	-2	0	-2	-4	-2	0	-4	G
8 Servite Domino in timore et exsultate	re	LA 83	F	2	4	2	4	2	4	6	4	G
5 Servite Domino in timore et exsultate	co	GR 93 (43) *SYG 68 *GB 64^v *GS 34	a	3	2	3	0	-4	0	-2	-4	F
2 Servivit Domino beatus Oswaldus	an	WA 282	D	-2	0	3	2	0	2	0	-2	D
Servus autem Domini 　　Cumque ad mensam	rev	LR 292										

6	Servus Dei Benedictus	re	WA 299	c	-3	-7	-3	0	2	0	2	4	F
8	Servus Dei Nicholaus	re	WA 241	D	3	2	3	5	7	3	8	7	G
8	Servus tuus ego sum	re	LA 143 WA 94	G	2	0	-2	0	2	4	5	7	G
6	Sexaginta sunt reginae	an	WA 163	F	-3	0	2	4	5	2	0	-3	F
8	Sexto die portari se	re	LR 331 *LA 373	F	2	4	2	4	2	4	7	2	G
	Sexto namque die	<u>see</u> Sexto die											
	Si alia decem milia Quae sunt haec	rev	WA 246										
8	Si ambulavero in medio tribulationis	of	GR 376 OTT 118 LU 1061 *SYG 97 GB 86^v *GS 59 163	G	2	0	-2	0	5	2	4	2	G
4	Si ambulavero in medio umbrae	co	GR 42**	a	-2	-4	-2	0	-2	-5	-2	-5	E
1	Si ambulem in medio umbrae	gr	GR 137 SYG 99 GB 88^v GS 61	D	3	5	3	2	3	2	0	2	D
2	Si bona suscepimus	re	LR 422 LA 282 *WA 171	A	3	5	7	5	8	7	8	5	D
7	Si cognovissetis me	an	AR 695 PM 152 LU 1465^E AM 893 *WA 307 *LA 394	G	5	4	5	7	9	7	5	9	G
	Si consistant adversum me castra Dominus illuminatio	intv	GR 330 LU 998 GS 144 GB 248^v SYG 241										
7	Si consurrexistis cum Christo	co	GR 249 OHS 787 LU 791 SYG 157 GB 135 GS 120	G	5	2	0	5	4	5	7	5	G
7	Si coram hominibus tormenta	an	WA 420 LA 513	d	-3	0	2	0	-2	0	-3	-2	G
7	Si culmen veri honoris	an	AR 352 AM 324 *WA 79 LA 120	d	-3	0	2	0	2	0	-3	-2	G
	Si dederit homo omnem Aquae multae	grv	GR (10)	F	4	7	9	7	4	7	0	4	
	Si dictis inquit O Hippolyte	anv	WA 349										
	Si dictis inquit O Hippolyte	rev	WA 351										
7	Si diligeretis me gauderetis	an	LA 394	G	4	5	7	9	7	9	10	12	G
3	Si diligis me Simon Petre	int	GR [2^1] LU 1122^1	E	-2	3	5	8	7	8	5	10	E
6	Si diligis me Simon Petre	re	LR 360 LA 413 WA 277	F	5	2	0	4	0	2	5	7	F
3	Si diligitis me mandata	an	AR 695 LU 1465^F AM 894 *WA 151	G	5	2	0	4	5	7	5	4	E
	Si Dominus Deus meus fuerit Erit mihi Dominus	rev	LA 139										
1	Si Dominus Deus meus fuerit	re	LA 139 WA 92	D	3	0	-2	3	5	7	5	7	D
1	Si duo ex vobis consenserint	an	AR 392 LU 1090 AM 366 LA 154	C	2	9	10	9	12	9	7	9	D

#	Incipit		Sources										
4	Si ego Dominus et magister	an	GR 202 OHS 449 LU 674 *SYG 130	E	-2	0	3	5	3	5	7	8	E
6	Si ego verus Christi	an	LA 330	a	3	0	2	3	2	-2	5	3	c
	Si enim credimus	gr	SYG 236										
4	Si enim credimus	int	SYG 236	E	3	0	1	3	5	3	5	3	E
	Si enim hoc egero / Angustiae mihi	rev	LA 304 WA 185										
	Si enim non abiero / Ego rogabo	rev	LR 104 LA 248										
	Si enim non abiero	alv	SYG 168	E	-2	3	5	7	8	5	3	5	
3	Si enim non abiero	re	LR 106 LA 246	G	2	4	5	2	4	5	4	2	E
	Si exprobramini in nomine / Communicantes	grv	GR 508 LU 1482	F	4	2	7	9	7	4	7	9	A
	Si filii et heredes	alv	GR 480 LU 1434	G	-2	3	5	8	7	5	7	10	
7	Si gloriam dignitatis	an	WA 79	d	-3	0	2	0	2	0	-2	-3	G
8	Si ignem adhibeas	an	WA 274 *LA 357	G	5	2	0	-2	0	2	0	4	G
4	Si ignoras te	an	WA 162	E	3	5	3	1	0	-2	0	3	E
3	Si in digito Dei ejicio	an	AR 389 LU 552 *AM 363 *WA 99 LA 150	G	5	2	0	2	5	2	4	5	E
	Si iniquitatem observaveris		see Si iniquitates observaveris										
	Si iniquitates observaveris / De profundis	trv	GR 75 LU 499 GS 25 *GB 56^V *SYG 59	G	-5	0	2	5	4	5	2	5	
7	Si iniquitates observaveris	an	LA 560	d	-2	-3	-2	0	2	0	-2	-3	G
8	Si iniquitates observaveris	an	AR [144] LU 1779 AM 1152 WA 435	G	-2	-3	-2	0	2	0	-2	0	G
	Si iniquitates observaveris / De profundis	ofv	OTT 126 GB 265 SYG 258	D	-2	0	-5	-7	-5	-7	-5	-2	
3	Si iniquitates observaveris	int	GR 383 LU 1070 *SYG 259 *GB 263^V GS d	E	-2	3	5	8	7	8	7	5	E
1	Si male locutus sum	an	LA 187	D	-2	3	5	3	5	7	9	7	D
7	Si manseritis in me	co	GR (15)	G	2	5	4	5	2	0	5	7	G
7	Si manseritis in me	an	AR 696 LU 1465^F AM 895 LA 394	G	4	5	7	9	7	5	9	12	G
	Si mei non fuerint / Ab occultis meis	grv	GR 130 GS 57 SYG 81 *GB 84^V	a	3	5	7	5	3	2	3	0	
1	Si mihi Dominus salvator	an	AR 348 AM 320	F	-1	-3	0	2	4	2	0	2	D
	Si oblitus fuero tui / Super flumina	ofv	OTT 119 GB 102^V SYG 115	a	3	5	3	5	8	10	8	7	
8	Si oblitus fuero tui	re	LR 417 LA 237 WA 143	D	3	5	7	5	7	5	3	7	G
1	Si offers munus tuum	an	AR 556 LU 1005 AM 594 *WA 188 LA 312	D	2	3	0	2	0	3	2	0	D

	Incipit		References										
	Si oportuerit me mori	rev	LR 360 LA 413										
	Si diligis		WA 277										
	Si peccaverit in te	rev	LA 271 WA 167										
	Domine si conversus												
	Si praecepta mea	rev	AM 1189										
	Sicut dilexit												
	Si quae illi sunt	rev	WA 438	G	5	4	5	7	5	7	5	7	
	Absolve Domine												
8	Si quaeris miracula mors	re	VP 176	G	2	-2	0	-2	-3	-5	0	2	G
3	Si quis diligit me sermonem	an	AR 510 LU 889	G	5	2	0	4	5	7	5	4	E
			AM 526 *WA 153										
			*LA 262										
1	Si quis fecerit voluntatem	an	WA 89	C	2	5	4	5	2	5	7	5	D
	Si quis in verbo non offendit	trv	GR 31**	D	3	2	3	5	7	5	3	5	
	Si quis putat												
1	Si quis introierit	an	WA 156 *LA 265	D	-2	3	5	3	5	7	10	9	D
	Si quis manducaverit	rev	LR 124 LU 927	c	2	0	-1	-3	-5	-3	0	-5	
	Respexit Elias												
1	Si quis mihi ministraverit	an	AR [16] LU 1126	D	3	0	-2	3	5	3	5	7	D
			AM 641 WA 419										
			LA 437 527										
8	Si quis per me intraverit	an	LA 527	c	-1	-3	-5	-3	-1	-3	-5	-3	G
2	Si quis putat se religiosum esse	tr	GR 31**	A	3	5	2	3	5	0	-2	0	D
6	Si quis sitit veniat ad me	co	GR [116] LU 975	F	-3	0	2	0	2	4	2	0	F
4	Si quis sitit veniat et bibat	an	AR 416 LU 1098	C	2	5	7	5	7	9	7	5	a
			AM 394 WA 109										
			*LA 173										
	Si reversus fuero	rev	WA 92										
	Erit mihi Dominus												
	Si tacuero non quiescit	rev	WA 172										
	Memento mei Deus												
	Si testimonium hominum	alv	GR 538 LU 1534	E	1	0	-2	3	5	3	5	8	
3	Si tibi gratum vis	re	WA 244	F	-1	2	-1	0	-3	-1	-3	0	E
7	Si vere fratres divites	an	AR 351 LU 509	d	-3	0	2	0	-3	-2	0	-5	G
			*AM 323 *WA 79										
			*LA 119										
7	Si vos manseritis in sermone	an	WA 90	G	5	4	5	7	5	7	9	7	G
7	Sic benedicam te in vita	an	AR 365 AM 341	G	5	4	5	7	5	4	2	4	G
			*WA 88 LA 132										
8	Sic Deus dilexit mundum	an	AR 510 AM 525	G	-2	-5	-3	-2	0	2	0	2	G
			WA 155 *LA 264										
8	Sic erunt novissimi primi	an	AM 318 WA 76 LA 111	a	-4	-2	0	-2	-4	-2	0	3	G
3	Sic eum volo manere	an	WA 42 *LA 56	c	-1	-3	0	-3	-5	-3	-7	-5	E
8	Sic eum volo manere	re	LA 53 WA 41	D	3	5	7	5	7	5	7	5	G

2 Sic patres vitam peragunt	hy	AR 638	D	-2	0	3	2	0	2	0	-2	D
Sic secum matrem Ecclesiae sponsum	rev	PM 269	G	5	4	0	2	4	2	0	4	
8 Sic ter quaternis trahitur	hy	ST 188	G	-2	-3	-5	-2	2	0	-2	0	G
4 Sic veniet quemadmodum	an	WA 151 *LA 244 245	F	-1	0	-3	0	2	0	-1	0	E
Sicque illi sunt Domine Absolve Domine	rev	LA 558	G	5	4	5	7	5	7	10	9	
4 Sicut ablactatus est	an	LR 338	a	-2	0	3	5	7	5	3	5	a
Sicut audivimus ita et vidimus Suscepimus Deus	grv	GR 433 LU 1362 SYG 48 GB 47ᵛ GS j	F	4	2	7	9	7	9	7	11	
4 Sicut cedrus exaltata sum	re	PM 260 LR 252 *LA 443 *WA 355	D	3	2	5	3	0	2	0	3	E
8 Sicut cervus desiderat	tr	GR 232 OHS 673 LU 776ᴮᴮ SYG 151 GB 120 GS 112	G	2	4	2	0	2	0	-2	0	G
Sicut cinnamomum et balsamum	alv	GR 34**	D	-2	-5	-2	0	-2	2	5	2	
7 Sicut civitas Catinensium	an	WA 247	c	2	0	-1	0	2	4	2	0	G
Sicut dies verni		see also Et sicut dies verni										
2 Sicut dies verni	an	WA 359	D	-2	0	3	0	-2	0	-2	0	D
Sicut dilexit me pater Ego sum vitis	rev	OHS 790 LR 89										
4 Sicut dilexit me pater	re	AM 1189	E	3	1	-2	0	-2	1	3	1	E
Sicut enim amor Dei Beata Caecilia dixit	rev	LA 492										
Sicut enim mihi Deus Beata Caecilia dixit	rev	WA 407										
Sicut enim per me		see Et sicut per me										
Sicut fons aquarum Sancta virgo	rev	LR 292										
2 Sicut fui cum Moyse	re	LA 160 WA 102	A	3	5	7	5	8	5	7	5	D
4 Sicut fuit Jonas in ventre	an	AR 375 AM 348 *LA 135 *WA 89	G	2	5	7	9	7	5	7	9	a
5 Sicut in holocausto arietum	of	GR 338 (42) LU 1012 OTT 92 *SYG 243 GB 250ᵛ GS 148	F	2	4	5	4	5	4	2	0	F
4 Sicut laetantium omnium habitatio	an	LR 335	F	-3	-1	0	2	0	-1	0	2	E
7 Sicut laetantium omnium habitatio ... Scholastica	an	LR 293	G	4	5	7	5	4	5	7	9	G
7 Sicut laetantium omnium nostrum	an	LR 250 LA 350 WA 269	d	-3	0	2	0	-2	0	-3	-2	G
2 Sicut lilium inter spinas	an	WA 354 *LA 456	C	2	5	4	2	0	-3	0	2	D
5 Sicut lilium inter spinas	gr	GR 75**	F	4	5	4	2	4	2	0	2	F

1	Sicut malum inter ligna	an	WA 353	C	2	5	2	0	2	5	4	2	D
8	Sicut mater consolatur	re	LA 8 *WA 10	D	3	5	7	5	7	5	7	5	G
	Sicut misit me pater / Non vos me elegistis	rev	LR 118										
4	Sicut myrrha electa	an	LR 246 *WA 268 / LA 347 383	G	2	5	9	7	5	7	9	5	a
4	Sicut novellae olivarum	an	AR 526 LU 956 / AM 545	F	-1	-3	0	2	4	2	0	2	E
5	Sicut novit me pater	an	AR 471 AM 485 / WA 142 LA 235	F	4	7	6	4	2	7	9	7	F
4	Sicut oculi servorum in manibus	int	GR 99 *SYG 75 / *GB 67 *GS 37	E	3	1	0	1	3	5	3	5	E
	Sicut oliva fructifera	alv	GR 622^4	G	5	7	5	9	7	5	2	5	
4	Sicut ovis ad occisionem	re	OHS 596 LU 755 / *LR 339 *LA 205 / *WA 126	F	-3	-1	0	-1	0	-3	-5	-3	E
2	Sicut pastor portat ovem	an	GB 159^v	D	-5	0	-2	0	3	0	3	2	D
4	Sicut pater suscitat	an	WA 105	G	2	5	7	5	7	9	7	5	a
7	Sicut portavimus imaginem	int	SYG 237	G	5	4	5	9	7	10	9	10	G
	Sicut unguentum in capite / Ecce quam bonum	grv	GR 384 455 / LU 1071 GS *d *n 214 / GB 201 *SYG 199	D	7	10	7	5	3	2	5	7	
6	Sidera scansurus terrisque	an	WA 277	F	-3	-1	-3	-5	-3	0	2	0	F
8	Sidus Mariae inclitum	hy	ST 399	G	2	0	-2	0	2	5	7	5	G
3	Sidus solare revehit	hy	ST 160	E	-2	3	5	3	1	3	1	0	E
	Signa autem eos / Ite in orbem	rev	LA 258										
7	Signa eos qui in me credunt	co	GR 575 SYG 192 / *GB 216 GS 193	d	-3	0	2	0	2	0	-2	2	G
4	Signatus est beatus Oswaldus	an	WA 282	C	2	4	5	4	2	4	7	9	E
8	Signifer invictissime	hy	LR 443	G	-2	-3	-5	-2	2	0	-2	0	G
8	Signifer invictissime	hy	ST 468	G	2	4	2	4	5	7	5	4	G
1	Significavit Dominus Petro	an	WA 332	D	-2	0	2	3	5	2	5	7	D
8	Signum crucis mirabile	hy	ST 389	G	-7	0	2	0	2	4	5	4	G
7	Signum magnum apparuit	re	PM 120 LR 268	d	-2	0	2	-2	-3	-7	-5	-2	G
7	Signum magnum apparuit	int	GR 582 LU 1601	G	2	-2	2	0	2	5	9	7	G
8	Signum salutis pone Domine	an	PM 108	D	2	3	5	7	5	3	5	7	G
2	Signum salutis pone Domine	an	GB 157^v	A	3	5	7	5	3	5	7	8	D
6	Silvester pastor inclite	hy	ST 371	c	2	4	2	0	2	4	5	4	c
8	Silvestri almi praesulis	hy	ST 370	G	2	4	2	0	-2	2	0	2	G
8	Silvestri almi praesulis	hy	ST 445	G	2	4	2	4	5	4	2	0	G

	Title		References										
	Simeon in manibus / Suscipiens Jesum	rev	WA 270										
7	Simeon justus et timoratus	re	LA 349 *WA 269	G	2	4	5	4	2	4	2	0	G
3	Simeon justus et timoratus	an	AR 620 LU 1366 / AM 802 *LA 355	G	4	5	2	5	4	2	0	2	E
1	Simeon justus et timoratus	an	WA 272	F	4	5	2	5	4	2	0	2	D
1	Similabo eum viro sapienti	an	AR 577^18 [73] / LU 262^7 1193 / AM 669 743 / *WA 427 *LA 536	C	2	5	2	4	5	4	0	5	D
4	Simile est regnum caelorum decem	re	LR 229 *LA 543	F	-3	0	-1	0	-1	2	0	-1	E
2	Simile est regnum caelorum decem	re	WA 432	C	2	4	2	5	4	5	7	5	D
1	Simile est regnum caelorum decem	an	WA 430	C	2	9	11	9	12	9	7	9	D
1	Simile est regnum caelorum decem ... quinque	an	WA 435	C	2	0	2	5	2	4	2	0	D
1	Simile est regnum caelorum fermento	an	AR 340 LU 495 / AM 310	D	7	8	7	5	7	10	9	7	D
7	Simile est regnum caelorum grano	an	AR 340 LU 1109 / *AM 310	G	7	5	4	2	5	7	9	7	G
8	Simile est regnum caelorum homini negotiatori	co	GR [66] 115** / LU 1231 SYG 29 / GB 30^V GS 230	G	2	0	-5	0	4	2	0	5	G
1	Simile est regnum caelorum homini negotiatori	an	AM 685 746	C	2	0	2	5	2	4	2	0	D
7 8	Simile est regnum caelorum homini negotiatori	an	AR [92][97] *577^21 / LU 262 1231 / *AM 680 745 / *WA 339 434 *LA 546	G	2	5	2	4	2	0	7	5	G
1	Simile est regnum caelorum homini patrifamilias	an	AM 313 *AR 343 / *WA 75 *LA 114	D	7	9	7	5	7	9	7	5	D
1	Simile est regnum caelorum sagenae	an	WA 430	D	2	0	2	0	-2	3	5	7	D
4	Simile est regnum caelorum thesauro	co	GR 110**	D	2	3	5	7	5	7	5	3	E
	Similitudo aspectus animalium	re	WA 373	F	2	4	2	4	0	2	4	2	F
3	Similitudo vultus animalium	re	WA 372	C	2	0	2	4	2	5	4	5	E
1	Simon Barjona tu vocaberis	re	WA 341	D	-2	0	3	0	2	-2	0	3	D
4	Simon Barjona tu vocaberis	an	WA 341 *LA 365	E	1	3	-2	0	-2	5	3	1	E
8	Simon dormis non potuisti	an	AR 431 OHS 193 / *AM 411 *WA 117 / *LA 188	G	5	2	-2	0	2	0	4	5	G
	Simon ecce Sathanas / Ego pro te rogavi	rev	LA 417 WA 278										
	Simon Joannis diligis me / Petre amas me	rev	LR 361 LA 417 / *WA 279										
6	Simon Joannis diligis me	co	GR 531 SYG 204 / GS o *GB 203^V	F	2	0	4	2	0	2	0	4	F
8	Simon Joannis diligis me	an	WA 281 *LA 420	G	5	2	0	-2	0	2	0	4	G

7	Simon Petre antequam de navi	re	LR 359 VP 181 LA 413 WA 277	G	7	9	7	9	5	4	5	7	G
8	Simon Petrus cum audisset	an	LA 220	G	2	0	2	4	5	4	5	7	G
8	Sine macula sanctus Stephanus	an	WA 34	G	5	2	0	2	0	-2	0	2	G
4	Sinite me inquit	an	WA 404	F	-3	-5	-3	0	-1	0	2	0	E
8	Sinite parvulos venire	co	GR 590 LU 1616	F	2	4	2	4	2	4	2	0	G
3	Sint lumbi vestri	an	LR 201 *LA 534	G	2	5	4	2	5	4	0	2	E
1	Sint lumbi vestri ... et vos	re	PM 228 LR 202 LA 535 WA 430	D	-2	-5	-2	0	3	2	0	2	D
3	Sint lumbi vestri ... et vos	co	GB 234	C	2	4	0	2	5	4	5	7	E
1	Sint lumbi vestri ... et vos	an	WA 393 430	C	2	5	4	2	4	2	0	5	D
4	Sion noli timere	an	AR 223 LU 1081 AM 194 WA 9 20 *LA 22	c	2	0	2	4	2	0	2	-3	a
4	Sion renovaberis	an	AR 229 LU 1083 AM 201 *WA 13 *LA 12	c	2	0	2	4	0	2	-3	2	a
8	Sisti jubet martyram	hy	ST 41	G	-2	0	2	5	4	5	7	5	G
4	Sit laus sit honor Christo	an	WA 337	F	-1	-3	-1	2	4	2	0	2	E
	Sit nomen Domini ... ex hoc	sr	AR 304 LU 446 AM 280										
	Sit nomen Domini ... ex hoc Laudate pueri	intv	GR 550 GS 190 GB 211 SYG 206										
2	Sit nomen Domini ... ex hoc	an	LU 1825	D	-2	0	3	2	0	2	3	0	D
	Sit nomen Domini ... ex hoc Laudate pueri Dominum	alv	SYG 206 *GS p 123	D	7	9	7	9	7	5	7	10	
7	Sit nomen Domini ... in saecula	an	AR 47 OHS 159 LU 254 AM 127 LA 87	d	-3	-2	0	2	0	-2	-3	-5	G
2	Sitientes venite ad aquas	int	GR 149 LU 565 SYG 108 GS 70 GB 96	G	2	5	2	0	2	5	7	5	a
	Sitivit anima mea ad Deum fortem Quemadmodum desiderat	grv	GR 506 LU 1478	c	2	0	-1	-3	2	-1	0	2	
8	Sitivit anima mea ad Deum vivum	an	LA 556	a	-4	-2	0	-2	0	-2	-4	-2	G
2	Sitivit anima mea ad Deum vivum	an	AR [169] LU 1795 *WA 437	E	-4	-2	1	0	-2	0	-2	-4	D
	Sitivit anima mea ad Deum vivum Sicut cervus	trv	GR 232 OHS 673 LU 776^{BB} *GS 112 *GB 120 *SYG 151	G	2	4	5	7	5	0	2	0	
4	Sitivit anima mea ad nomen	an	AR 302 LU 450 AM 279	E	1	3	1	0	-2	-4	-2	1	E
	Sitivit in te anima mea Deus Deus meus	ofv	OTT 66 GB 147^{V} SYG 165	D	-2	0	3	0	-2	0	3	5	
	Sobrie et juste et pie Salvatorem exspectamus	rev	LA 4 WA 4										

	Socius enim factus es Egregie Christe	rev	PM 127										
1	Sol et luna laudate Deum	an	AR 388 AM 362 WA 99 LA 153	F	2	4	2	4	2	-1	0	2	D
8	Sol ille verus qui Deus omnia	hy	ST 324	G	2	5	2	0	2	0	7	5	G
	Sola namque sine exemplo Super salutem	rev	PM 263 LR 377										
1	Solem justitiae regem	re	AR 128* PM 185 VP 211 WA 366	D	2	0	-2	3	2	0	2	0	D
2	Solemne tempus vertitur	hy	ST 450	C	5	7	9	7	5	4	2	4	D
2	Solemnis dies advenit	hy	ST 369	G	-3	-2	0	2	0	-2	-3	-5	D
2	Solemnis dies advenit	hy	ST 412	G	-2	0	2	0	-2	0	3	2	G
3	Solemnis dies advenit	hy	ST 256	D	2	3	5	7	0	2	3	5	E
3	Solemnis dies advenit	hy	ST 220	D	2	3	5	7	0	2	5	3	E
4	Solemnis redit temporis	hy	ST 373	a	-2	-5	-7	-2	0	3	0	-2	E
	Solemnitas gloriosae virginis	alv	GR 620 LU 1676[A]	G	5	4	2	4	0	2	0	-2	
8	Solemnitatem hodiernam sanctissimi	hy	AM 1078	G	2	0	-2	0	2	0	4	5	G
8	Solemnitatem hodiernam sanctissimi	an	AR 877	G	2	0	-2	0	2	0	5	2	G
8	Solemnitatem Magdalenae	an	WA 336	F	2	4	2	0	2	4	2	4	G
2	Solemnitatem rosarii virginis	inv	LR 448	C	2	4	5	2	0	2	4	2	D
3	Solemnizet laete festa	hy	ST 317	E	1	3	-2	3	1	0	-2	0	E
4	Solis o virgo radiis amicta	hy	AR 3 (sup 3) LU 1600[2]	F	-3	-1	2	4	2	4	6	4	E
	Sollemnis, sollemnitas etc.	see	Solemnis, solemnitas										
	Solve jubente Deo terrarum	sr	LA 420										
8	Solve jubente Deo terrarum	an	AM 993 *WA 328 LA 420	d	-3	0	2	0	2	0	-3	-2	G
	Solve jubente Deo terrarum	alv	GR 563 LU 1576 GS 192 *SYG 203	D	2	3	5	3	0	2	3	2	
4	Solve jubente Deo terrarum	an	AR 801 LU 1579 WA 278	C	2	5	4	2	4	2	0	2	E
7	Solve jubente Deo terrarum	re	LR 364 *LA 418 WA 280	G	7	9	7	9	5	7	5	7	G
5	Solvite templum hoc	an	AR 401 LU 1094 AM 376 *WA 104 *LA 164	a	-4	0	3	5	3	5	7	5	F
4	Somno refectis artubus	hy	ST 362	G	-3	0	-2	-3	-2	-5	-3	-2	E
2	Somno refectis artubus	hy	ST 163	c	-3	[0	0	0	0	0	0	0]	a
3	Somno refectis artubus	hy	ST 86 182 213	D	2	3	5	2	5	3	2	3	E
4	Somno refectis artubus	hy	ST 279	D	2	3	5	3	5	3	0	2	E
4	Somno refectis artubus	hy	ST 252	D	2	3	5	3	5	3	2	3	E
1	Sonant ibi jugiter	an	LA 326	D	-2	3	5	3	5	7	5	3	D

2 Sonet vox tua	an	WA 356	D	-5	-2	0	2	0	-2	0	3	D
8 Soror mea Lucia virgo	an	AR 593 LU 1325 AM 770 WA 246 *LA 322	G	-2	-5	-3	-2	0	2	0	2	G
8 Soror nostra parvula	an	WA 163	G	-2	0	2	5	4	2	0	-3	G
Specie tua et pulchritudine	sr	AR [93][94] LU 1256 AM 680 WA 430										
Specie tua et pulchritudine Afferentur regi	rev	LR 223										
Specie tua et pulchritudine Diffusa est	rev	LR 216										
Specie tua et pulchritudine Propter veritatem	rev	LR 221 LA 545										
Specie tua et pulchritudine Pulchra facie	rev	LR 218 LA 336 WA 255										
Specie tua et pulchritudine Veni electa	rev	PM 237 LR 216 WA 355										
7 Specie tua et pulchritudine	an	LR 214 246 375 WA 432 *LA 541	d	-3	0	2	0	-3	-2	0	-2	G
8 Specie tua et pulchritudine	re	LR 217 LA 542	G	-2	-5	-3	-2	-3	-5	-7	-5	G
Specie tua et pulchritudine	alv	SYG 41	D	-2	0	2	3	5	3	2	0	
Specie tua et pulchritudine Diffusa est gratia	trv	GS 228	D	-2	0	3	5	7	3	2	5	
Specie tua et pulchritudine	alv	GR [70] LU 1218 GS 227 SYG 29 GB 273	c	-1	2	0	-1	0	2	0	-3	
5 Specie tua et pulchritudine	gr	GR [60] LU 1226 SYG 39 GB 42[v] GS 226	F	-1	2	4	2	0	-3	0	2	F
Specie tua et pulchritudine Veni sponsa	trv	GR [52] LU 1217	c	2	0	-5	0	2	4	-1	0	
Specie tua et pulchritudine Diffusa est	ofv	OTT 156 *GB 49 *SYG 46	D	2	3	7	5	8	7	5	3	
Specie tua et pulchritudine Diffusa est	trv	SYG 49	C	2	5	7	5	2	4	5	4	
Specie tua et pulchritudine Audi filia ... quia concupivit	grv	GR 655 LU 1755 GS t *GB 243[v] *SYG 228	G	5	7	9	7	10	7	9	7	
8 Species firmamenti super caput	re	WA 375	F	2	4	2	0	2	4	7	4	G
Speciosa facta es et suavis	sr	AR 879 LU 1678 AM 1077 WA 8 310 352										
Speciosa facta es et suavis Veniens a Libano	rev	LA 229										
8 Speciosa facta es et suavis	re	WA 139	G	-2	2	5	7	5	4	5	7	G
4 Speciosa facta es et suavis	an	AR [116] LU 1259 AM 708 WA 268 *LA 347	G	2	5	7	9	7	5	7	9	a

6 Speciosa facta es et suavis ... viderunt	an	PM 276	F	2	0	2	4	0	4	7	4	F
Speciosum fecit rex angelorum	alv	SYG 219	D	7	9	7	5	7	5	3	5	
2 Speciosus forma prae filiis	an	OHS 296 (nm) WA 27 *LA 63	F	2	-1	-3	0	-3	-1	-5	0	D
3 Speciosus forma prae filiis	gr	GR 45 103** LU 434 SYG 30 GB 31	G	2	5	4	5	2	4	5	7	E
2 Spem in alio numquam habui	re	WA 179	A	3	5	7	5	8	7	8	7	D
Spera in Domino Delectare	rev	WA 64										
Spera in Domino Indicabo tibi	rev	WA 186										
6 Spera in Domino	an	WA 63 *LA 87	F	-1	2	4	2	4	2	0	[0]	F
1 Spera in Domino	gr	GR 423 LU 1352^v	D	7	8	7	5	7	5	3	7	D
Speravit in Domino Deus Deus meus	trv	GR 180 OHS 109 LU 594 *GS 86 *GB 109 *SYG 122	F	2	0	2	0	-3	2	-1	0	
3 Sperent in te omnes qui noverunt	of	GR 329 OTT 85 LU 983 *SYG 112 GB 100 *GS 74 144	G	2	5	4	5	4	5	4	7	E
Sperent in te qui noverunt	alv	GR 94**	E	1	-2	3	5	8	7	10	8	
1 Speret Israel in Domino	an	LA 93	a	-2	-5	-4	-2	-4	-5	-7	-9	D
ir Speret Israel in Domino	an	AM 139	a	-2	-4	-2	0	1	-2	1	0	a
4 Speret Israel in Domino	an	WA 66	G	-2	-3	-2	2	-2	-5	-2	-3	E
4 Spes mea Domine	re	LA 115 WA 75	G	2	5	2	0	2	4	0	2	E
5 Spes nostra salus	an	WA 158	E	1	5	8	10	12	10	8	10	F
1 Spiritu intelligentiae replevit	an	WA 373	D	5	3	2	0	2	0	-2	0	D
1 Spiritu principali confirma	an	AM 66 *WA 69 *LA 101	F	-1	-3	-5	0	2	0	3	2	D
5 Spiritu sancto replevit	re	WA 156	F	2	0	2	4	2	4	2	0	F
8 Spiritus carnem et ossa	an	AR 481 AM 497 *LA 219	F	2	4	7	2	4	0	2	4	G
Spiritus Dei ornavit	see also Spiritus ejus ornavit											
Spiritus Dei ornavit caelos	alv	SYG 185	G	-2	2	4	2	0	-2	0	2	
Spiritus Domini replevit orbem	sr	AR 507 LU 878 AM 522 LA 262										
Spiritus Domini replevit orbem	alv	GS a 140	E	1	-2	3	5	8	7	10	8	
8 Spiritus Domini replevit orbem	of	SYG 185	F	2	0	-1	-5	-3	0	2	4	G
8 Spiritus Domini replevit orbem	re	LR 118 *LA 256 *WA 155	G	2	0	2	0	-2	-5	-3	-2	G
Spiritus Domini replevit orbem	alv	SYG 183	E	3	5	7	10	8	5	8	5	

#	Incipit	Type	Sources										
8	Spiritus Domini replevit orbem	an	AR 504 875 LU 884 1677 AM 520 1076 *WA 153 *LA 261	D	3	7	5	7	5	3	2	0	G
8	Spiritus Domini replevit orbem	int	GR [91] LU 1279 GS M 234 SYG 183	D	3	7	5	7	5	7	5	3	G
8	Spiritus Domini replevit orbem ... alleluia	int	GR 292 LU 878 GB 185 SYG 183 GS M 234	D	3	7	5	7	5	7	5	3	G
2	Spiritus Domini super me evangelizare	an	AR 240 *AM 215 *WA 18 LA 24	D	2	3	0	-2	0	3	2	-2	D
2	Spiritus Domini super me propter	int	GR 58**	D	-2	0	3	5	3	2	-2	0	D
5	Spiritus Domini super me propter	gr	GR [100] LU 1283^A	F	2	0	2	4	2	4	2	0	F
	Spiritus Domini super me propter	alv	GR [102] LU 1283^C	C	2	9	7	9	10	9	7	9	
3	Spiritus Domini super me propter	int	GR 564 LU 1579	G	5	4	2	7	5	7	5	0	E
	Spiritus ejus ornavit	see also Spiritus Dei ornavit											
	Spiritus ejus ornavit caelos	alv	GR 305 LU 902	F	2	4	7	2	4	2	0	2	
	Spiritus est Deus	alv	SYG 187	c	-1	2	0	-1	0	2	0	-3	
	Spiritus est qui vivificat	alv	GR 304 LU 901	G	4	5	4	0	2	4	2	0	
8	Spiritus et animae justorum	an	AR [29] LU 1121 AM 633 *WA 307	F	2	0	2	4	0	-1	-3	2	G
	Spiritus omnia scrutatur	alv	SYG 186	G	-2	0	2	0	2	0	5	4	
	Spiritus paraclitus alleluia	sr	AR 508 LU 883 AM 518										
6	Spiritus paraclitus alleluia	an	LA 263	F	-1	2	4	0	-3	-5	0	-1	F
	Spiritus paraclitus docebit	alv	GB 192	a	-4	0	-4	0	-2	-4	-5	-7	
2	Spiritus qui a Patre procedit	co	SYG 186	E	-2	0	-4	0	3	1	0	-2	D
	Spiritus qui a Patre procedit	alv	GB 191^V	D	-2	0	2	0	-2	0	-2	0	
8	Spiritus qui a Patre procedit	an	AR 513 LU 896 AM 529	F	2	0	4	2	7	6	7	9	G
8	Spiritus qui a Patre procedit	co	GR 299 LU 892 *GB 191^V *GS 139	F	2	0	4	2	7	6	7	9	G
	Spiritus qui a Patre procedit	alv	SYG 185	C	2	4	5	4	2	4	5	7	
	Spiritus sancti gratia Virgo est electa	rev	LA 53										
	Spiritus sancti gratia	alv	SYG 24	G	5	4	5	7	5	2	0	2	
8	Spiritus sanctus docebit vos	co	GR 298 LU 889 GB 191 *GS 138	G	-5	-2	0	2	0	2	5	4	G
6	Spiritus sanctus docebit vos	an	LA 263	F	-1	2	4	0	-3	-5	0	-1	F
8	Spiritus sanctus docebit vos	co	SYG 185	F	2	4	2	4	2	4	2	0	G
	Spiritus sanctus docebit vos	alv	GR 299 LU 891 GB 191	F	2	4	7	9	7	6	2	4	

	Title		Sources										
	Spiritus sanctus in te descendet ... Dei genitrix	alv	SYG 2	a	2	0	-2	-4	-2	0	2	0	
8	Spiritus sanctus in te descendet ... et virtus	an	AR 667 LU 1414 AM 861	G	-5	-2	0	2	0	2	0	-2	G
8	Spiritus sanctus in te descendet ... ne timeas	an	AR 216 [137] AM 189 WA 7 LA 6 376	G	-5	-2	0	2	0	2	0	-2	G
	Spiritus sanctus procedens	alv	GS M 137	D	-2	-5	-2	0	-2	2	5	3	
3	Spiritus sanctus procedens	re	PM 87 LR 111 LA 261 *WA 154	E	-2	3	5	8	5	8	3	5	E
7	Spiritus sanctus replevit totam	re	LR 116 *LA 258 WA 156	G	2	0	2	0	2	5	4	5	G
	Spiritus sanctus superveniet Dixit Maria	rev	WA 302										
	Spiritus sanctus superveniet Ave Maria	trv	GR 459 LU 1412 GS 183 SYG 57	F	2	4	2	0	2	4	2	4	
8	Spiritus ubi vult spirat	co	GR 307 LU 906 *SYG 187 GB 193 GS a 140	F	2	4	2	4	2	0	2	4	G
	Spiritus ubi vult spirat	alv	SYG 186	E	3	5	7	10	8	5	8	5	
8	Splendent Bethlehemitici campi	an	PM 36	G	-5	-2	0	2	0	2	-2	2	G
3	Splendet Bethlehemiticus campus	an	WA 43	G	2	0	-2	0	2	0	-2	2	E
8	Splendida facta est facies	re	LA 159 WA 101	D	5	3	5	7	5	7	5	7	G
6	Splendor paternae gloriae	hy	ST 253 270	F	-5	-3	0	2	0	-5	-3	0	F
4	Splendor paternae gloriae	hy	ST 86 AR 73 AM 44	E	-4	-2	1	0	1	3	1	0	E
6	Splendor paternae gloriae	hy	ST 270	F	-3	-5	0	2	0	-3	-5	-1	F
2	Splendor paternae gloriae	hy	ST 163	d	-3	0	2	0	2	0	[0	0]	d
4	Splendor paternae gloriae	hy	ST 2	E	-2	-4	-2	0	1	3	1	0	E
4	Splendor paternae gloriae	hy	ST 183	E	-2	-4	-2	1	3	1	0	-4	E
5	Splendor paternae gloriae	hy	ST 2	D	-2	0	3	2	0	2	3	2	C
2	Splendor paternae gloriae	hy	ST 26	D	-2	0	3	2	0	3	-2	0	D
1	Splendor paternae gloriae	hy	AM 44	a	2	0	-2	-4	-2	0	-2	-4	D
6	Splendor paternae gloriae	hy	ST 441	F	2	0	2	4	2	0	2	0	F
3	Splendor paternae gloriae	hy	ST 213	D	2	3	5	3	5	3	2	3	E
8	Splendor paternae gloriae	hy	ST 362	D	2	3	5	7	3	5	0	2	G
8	Sponsae Christi eximiae	hy	ST 353	G	-2	-3	0	2	4	5	4	2	G
	Sponsus amat sponsam Virgo flagellatur	rev	PM 214 VP 251	F	2	4	5	4	5	4	2	4	
4	Squalent arva soli pulvere multo	hy	ST 494	C	2	4	5	4	2	0	2	5	E
1	Stabant juxta crucem Jesu	int	GR 595 LU 1633	D	7	8	7	5	3	7	5	8	D
2	Stabat mater dolorosa	hy	ST 336	a	-2	0	3	2	0	2	0	-2	a

	Text	Type	Source										
8	Stabat mater dolorosa	hy	ST 47	G	-2	2	0	2	4	5	4	2	G
6	Stabat mater dolorosa	hy	AR 672 162* VP 136 LU 1424	F	2	4	2	4	7	5	4	2	F
7	Stabat mater dolorosa	hy	ST 334	G	2	4	2	5	4	2	0	4	G
6	Stabat mater dolorosa	hy	ST 444	F	2	4	5	2	4	5	7	4	F
2	Stabat sancta Maria	tr	GR 471 LU 1634	D	-2	0	-2	-5	-2	0	-2	0	D
	Stabat sancta Maria	alv	GR 596 LU 1633^V	D	2	3	2	0	-2	3	5	7	
8	Stabunt justi in magna constantia	an	WA 308	G	-2	-5	-3	-2	0	2	0	-2	G
	Stabunt juste in magna constantia	alv	SYG 172	D	2	0	-2	2	3	5	7	5	
	Stabunt justi in magna constantia	alv	GS 185	D	2	3	2	0	-2	3	5	7	
8	Stabunt justi in magna constantia	an	LR 164	D	2	3	5	7	5	7	10	9	G
1	Stans a dextris ejus	an	AR 613 LU 1351^V AM 798 *PM 129	D	-2	3	5	3	7	8	7	5	D
1	Stans a longe publicanus	an	AR 562 LU 1105 AM 601 WA 189 LA 314	C	2	5	4	2	0	2	0	5	D
	Stans autem Jesus jussit Caecus sedebat	rev	LR 401 LA 123 WA 83										
1	Stans autem Jesus jussit	an	AR 357 LU 516 AM 331 *WA 83 LA 125	C	2	5	2	4	2	0	5	7	D
1	Stans beata Agatha	an	AR 624 LU 1372 *AM 806 WA 276 (inc illeg) LA 364	C	2	0	2	5	2	4	2	0	D
1	Stans beata Agnes	an	AR 606 LU 1341 AM 789 *WA 267 *LA 339	D	3	0	-2	3	5	7	3	5	D
5	Stans in aede	re	WA 251	F	4	7	9	7	5	7	4	2	F
7	Stans Jesus clamabat	an	AR 538^7 LU 977 AM 565	d	-3	0	2	0	2	0	-3	-2	G
	Stantes erant pedes Laetatus sum	trv	SYG 101	F	-1	0	2	4	2	4	2	0	
	Stantes erant pedes Laetatus sum	alv	SYG 3 *GB 3	D	7	9	7	9	7	5	7	5	
1	Stat a dextris ejus	an	WA 255 LA 335	D	-2	3	5	3	5	7	9	7	D
	Statimque pauci Cum non posset	rev	WA 283	a	-2	0	-2	-4	-2	-4	-5	-7	
	Statimque solutos a vinculis Audiens Christi	rev	WA 240	D	7	5	3	5	7	5	7	5	
1	Statuit Dominus supra petram	re	LA 91 *WA 65	D	7	8	7	10	7	9	10	7	D
7	Statuit ea in aeternum	an	AR 379 AM 353 *WA 93 LA 142	G	4	5	7	9	5	7	4	5	G
1	Statuit ei Dominus testamentum pacis	int	GR [3] [32] LU 1182 SYG 37 GB 41 GS 220	D	7	8	7	10	7	8	7	8	D

	Incipit	Genre	Sources									
	Statuit ei Dominus testamentum sempiternum / Ecce vere Israelita	rev	LR 195 LA 533 WA 390									
	Statuit supra petram pedes meos / Exspectans exspectavi	ofv	OTT 104 GB 92 SYG 104	c	2	0	2	0	2	0	-1	-3
	Statura erat rotarum / Euntibus animalibus	rev	WA 374									
8	Statura erat rotarum	re	WA 374	G	2	0	2	0	-2	0	2	5	G
7	Stella ista sicut flamma	an	AR 313 LU 464 *AM 291 *WA 52 *LA 71	b	1	3	5	3	5	1	3	1	G
	Stella quam viderant Magi / Videntes stellam	rev	PM 40									
8	Stella quam viderant Magi	re	LR 78 LA 71 *WA 54	F	2	4	2	4	6	4	2	4	G
4	Stella quam viderant Magi	an	WA 57	G	2	5	7	9	7	5	7	9	a
2	Stephano primo martyri	hy	ST 411	G	-3	-2	0	-2	-3	-5	0	-2	D
2	Stephano primo martyri	hy	ST 368	G	-3	-2	0	2	0	-2	-3	-5	D
2	Stephano primo martyri	hy	ST 39	a	-2	3	2	0	7	5	3	2	a
1	Stephano primo martyri	hy	ST 8	D	2	3	-2	0	2	3	-2	0	D
3	Stephano primo martyri	hy	ST 220	D	2	3	5	7	0	2	3	5	E
	Stephanus autem plenus gratia / Videbant omnes	rev	WA 34									
3	Stephanus autem plenus gratia	re	LA 41	F	-3	0	-1	0	2	0	-3	2	E
8	Stephanus autem plenus gratia	an	AR 276 LU 413 AM 252 LA 40	c	-1	-3	-5	-7	-5	-3	-7	-8	G
8	Stephanus autem plenus gratia	re	WA 34	F	2	4	2	4	2	4	6	2	G
	Stephanus Dei gratia plenus / Impetum fecerunt	rev	WA 34	a	-2	-4	-5	-7	-4	-7	-9	-7	
	Stephanus plenus gratia	sr	WA 37									
8	Stephanus servus Dei	re	PM 30 LA 44 *WA 36	F	2	4	2	4	6	4	2	4	G
4	Stephanus servus Dei	an	WA 35 *LA 43	C	2	5	4	2	4	2	0	-1	E
	Stephanus vidit caelos / Hesterna die	rev	WA 36									
8	Stephanus vidit caelos	an	AR 274 AM 251 LU 1583A *WA 37 LA 43	F	2	0	4	7	6	4	6	7	G
	Stetit angelus		see also Sedit angelus									
7	Stetit angelus ad sepulcrum	an	SYG 146	G	2	-2	0	2	0	-2	0	2	G
	Stetit angelus juxta aram	sr	AR 859 860 LU 1652 1653 AM 1068 LA 472 WA 384									

Stetit angelus juxta aram Hic est Michael	rev	LA 468									
Stetit angelus juxta aram In conspectu gentium	rev	WA 380									
Stetit angelus juxta aram Michael archangelus	rev	LA 470									
1 Stetit angelus juxta aram	of	GR 610 OTT 170 LU 1656 *GB 170^v GS 197	F	-3	-5	-3	0	4	2	4	0	D
7 Stetit angelus juxta aram	re	LA 466 *WA 380	G	2	4	5	4	2	4	0	2	G
4 Stetit angelus juxta aram	an	AR 856 LU 1659 AM 1058 WA 379 *LA 465	G	2	5	7	5	7	9	7	5	a
8 Stetit Jesus in medio	an	AR 449 OHS 782 *AM 462 WA 134 *LA 219 232	F	2	0	2	4	7	6	2	6	G
Stetit Jesus in medio	alv	SYG 162	G	2	4	5	4	2	4	5	7	
8 Stetit Moyses coram Pharaone	re	LA 156 WA 101	G	2	0	2	0	2	4	0	-2	G
1 Stetit pontifex inter mortuos	of	GR [140]	F	-3	-5	-3	0	4	2	4	0	D
2 Stirps Jesse virgam produxit	re	AR 129* PM 186 WA 303	D	-2	0	2	3	2	0	2	3	D
Stola		see also Stolam									
Stola jucunditatis induit eum	sr	WA 415									
Stola jucunditatis induit eum Beatus vir qui suffert	rev	WA 418									
7 Stola jucunditatis induit eum	re	LR 156 *LA 524 *WA 417	G	2	4	5	4	2	4	2	0	G
Stolam		see also Stola									
1 Stolam jucunditatis induit eum	an	LA 538	D	-2	3	5	3	5	7	9	7	D
7 Strinxerunt corporis membra	an	WA 348 *LA 436	d	-3	0	2	0	-3	-2	-3	-7	G
2 Strinxerunt corporis membra	re	LA 437 WA 348	A	3	5	7	5	8	7	8	10	D
Stupebant autem omnes Ingressus Paulus	anv	LA 343 WA 264									
Stupebant autem omnes Ingressus Paulus	rev	LA 345 WA 265									
1 Suavi jugo tuo dominare	an	AR 538^1 LU 965 AM 560	C	2	9	10	9	12	9	7	9	D
8 Suavis Dominus universis	an	AR 204 OHS 44 LU 311	G	5	2	0	2	0	-2	0	2	G
Sub altare Dei audivi voces Sub throno Dei	rev	WA 44									
7 Sub altare Dei audivi voces	re	PM 35 LA 57 WA 43	a	-2	-4	-2	0	3	2	3	5	G
3 Sub altare Dei clamabant	an	WA 44	E	-2	3	5	8	7	8	7	8	E
8 Sub manu continuo	an	LA 342 *WA 264	G	5	2	0	2	0	-2	2	0	G

	Sub pennis eorum Quatuor facies	rev	WA 372	F	2	4	2	-1	-3	0	3	2
	Sub tanto pastore lupus Beatus Hugo	rev	PM 149	.								
	Sub throno Dei Cantabant sancti	rev	LA 58 WA 45									
	Sub throno Dei Vidi sub altare	rev	LA 60									
4	Sub throno Dei	re	LA 60 *WA 44	C	2	5	2	5	7	5	4	5	E
8	Sub throno Dei	an	AR 284 LU 431 AM 261 *WA 46 LA 61	G	4	2	4	5	4	0	2	0	G
4	Sub tuam protectionem	an	WA 353	D	7	5	7	9	7	5	7	5	E
7	Sub tuum praesidium confugimus	an	AR [134] 123* PM 287 VP 37 18* LU 1861 AM 1258	G	4	5	7	4	5	7	9	7	G
	Sub tuum praesidium omnes	sr	AR 6 (sup 1)									
5	Sub umbra illius	int	GR 625 LU 1689	F	4	7	4	7	4	6	7	2	F
4	Sub umbra illius	co	GR 53**	G	4	7	5	4	0	2	0	-2	b
	Subiecit populos nobis et gentes Omnes gentes	intv	GB 177 SYG 178 GS 133 148[1]									
	Subiecit populos nobis et gentes Ascendit Deus	ofv	OTT 75 SYG 179 GB 177	D	-2	0	3	0	3	5	0	3	
1	Subiit ergo in montem	an	AR 400 LU 564 *AM 376 *LA 163	F	-5	-3	4	5	4	7	4	2	D
8	Subiit ergo Jesus in montem	an	WA 104	G	-2	0	2	0	-2	2	5	0	G
2	Substrato cilicio in ecclesia	re	LR 287	A	3	5	7	5	8	7	8	5	D
1	Subvenite sancti Dei	an	WA 8	C	2	9	11	9	7	5	7	9	D
4	Subvenite sancti Dei	re	AR [183] GR 107* LU 1765 *AM 1168	D	3	0	2	3	2	5	3	2	E
2	Succedit nocti lucifer	hy	AM 982	a	-2	-5	-7	-2	0	3	2	0	a
4	Succurre nobis genitrix Christi	an	PM 280	D	3	2	0	2	0	-2	0	2	E
4	Sufficiebat nobis paupertas	re	LA 289 *WA 176	F	-3	0	-1	0	-1	0	-1	0	E
	Sumite de optimis terrae Tollite hinc	rev	LR 409 LA 149 WA 97									
7	Sumite psalterium jucundum	re	PM 192	G	2	0	2	0	-2	2	5	4	G
8	Summa ingenuitas ista est	an	LA 357 *WA 273	c	-1	-3	-1	0	-3	-5	-7	-3	G
2	Summa laus dulcis melodia	an	PM 174 *WA 379	C	2	0	2	5	4	2	5	2	D
8	Summae Deus clementiae	hy	LR 441	G	2	-2	-3	-2	-5	-3	-2	0	G
3	Summae Deus clementiae	hy	ST 214	D	2	3	5	3	5	3	2	3	E
2	Summae Deus clementiae	hy	AR 844 AM 1049	C	2	4	5	4	2	0	2	4	D
7	Summae trinitati simplici	re	WA 161	G	7	5	7	5	7	10	9	7	G

4	Summe confessor sacer et sacerdos	hy	ST 404	D	2	3	5	7	5	3	2	0	E
7	Summe Dei confessor	re	WA 241	d	-2	-3	-2	0	-2	3	2	-2	G
7	Summe largitor praemii	hy	ST 383	c	-3	0	-5	0	-3	-1	-3	-5	G
8	Summe largitor praemii	hy	ST 285	a	-2	-4	0	-2	-4	0	3	-2	G
2	Summe largitor praemii	hy	ST 32 89 186	G	2	4	0	2	5	4	2	4	a
2	Summe largitor praemii	hy	ST 284	C	2	4	5	0	2	5	4	2	D
2	Summe largitor praemii	hy	ST 284	C	2	4	5	2	0	2	5	4	D
1	Summe sacerdos rector et custos	hy	ST 157	a	-2	0	-2	-4	-5	-7	-2	0	D
3	Summi parentis unice	hy	AR 791	G	2	4	2	5	4	2	0	2	E
2	Summi vatis praeconium	hy	ST 13	D	-2	0	3	5	0	-2	0	-2	D
7	Summum regem gloriae	inv	LR 445	G	5	4	5	7	9	10	9	7	G
4	Summum venerantes bonum	inv	WA 341	C	2	4	5	2	4	5	7	5	E
1	Sunt de hic stantibus	an	AM 256 *AR 280 WA 42 LA 56	D	-2	3	5	3	5	7	8	7	D
	Super aspidem et basiliscum Angelis suis	rev	LA 130 WA 87										
	Super aspidem et basiliscum Angelis suis	trv	GR [144]	D	3	2	3	5	7	5	3	5	
	Super aspidem et basiliscum Qui habitat	trv	GR 95 LU 533 *GS 35 *GB 65 *SYG 73	D	3	2	3	5	7	5	3	5	
	Super aspidem et basiliscum ... liberabo Scapulis suis	ofv	OTT 32 GB 66^{V} SYG 74	G	5	7	5	7	5	7	2	5	
	Super flumina Babylonis Si oblitus	rev	LR 417 LA 237 WA 143										
1	Super flumina Babylonis	of	GR 379 OTT 119 LU 1065 *SYG 115 *GB 102^{V} GS 76 165	F	2	4	5	4	2	4	0	2	D
	Super ipsum continebunt Rex noster adveniet	rev	LA 10										
2	Super mira potentia	an	WA 340	C	2	4	5	4	2	0	5	7	D
	Super misericordia tua In conspectu angelorum	rev	AM 1202 LR 384 VP 217 WA 381										
	Super montem	see	Supra montem										
6	Super muros tuos Jerusalem	re	LA 302 *WA 184	c	2	4	2	4	2	4	0	2	c
1	Super muros tuos Jerusalem	an	AR 554 LU 997 *AM 592 *LA 308	C	2	5	4	2	5	2	0	2	D
1	Super nivem dealbabuntur	an	AM 877	F	2	4	2	4	2	-1	0	2	D
	Super omnia ligna cedrorum Crux fidelis	rev	PM 152 WA 369										
1	Super omnia ligna cedrorum	an	AR 701 AM 901 1042 *WA 371 LA 463 SYG 144	C	2	5	4	2	4	5	2	4	D

	Title	Type	Sources										
	Super quem continebunt Radix Jesse	rev	WA 15										
3	Super salutem et omnem ... dilecta	re	PM 263 LR 377 *WA 357	E	-2	3	5	8	5	8	3	5	E
3	Super salutem et omnem ... dilexi	re	PM 111 LA 279 *WA 169	E	-2	3	5	8	5	8	3	5	E
	Super solium David Ecce virgo	rev	LA 5 380 WA 5										
8	Super solium David	an	AR 232 AM 206 WA 12 *LA 12 384	G	-5	-2	0	2	0	-2	0	2	G
	Super te Jerusalem orietur	sr	AR 42 LU 248 LA 6 WA 17										
4	Super te Jerusalem orietur	an	AR 228 LU 1082 AM 200 WA 13 *LA 12	G	2	5	7	9	7	5	7	9	a
1	Superna mater inclita	hy	ST 124	D	7	5	3	2	0	-2	3	2	D
5	Supplex sacramus canticum	hy	ST 21	F	-1	0	2	4	5	4	2	0	F
	Supra montem excelsum Clama in fortitudine	rev	LR 394 LA 23 WA 17										
2	Supra pectus Domini	an	WA 38 LA 48	D	-2	0	3	2	0	2	0	-2	D
1	Surgam et ibo ad patrem	re	VP 117	c	2	4	5	4	2	7	5	4	a
	Surge amica mea speciosa mea Flores apparuerunt	grv	GR 439 LU 1376	c	2	0	-3	0	2	0	-1	0	
8	Surge aquilo et veni auster	an	LA 543	c	-3	0	-5	0	-3	0	2	-1	G
	Surge Domine in requiem Alleluia: audivimus	rev	WA 144										
8	Surge Domine in requiem	tr	GR [119] 90**	G	-2	-5	-3	-7	-5	-2	0	2	G
1	Surge ergo et vade	an	WA 343	D	3	0	-2	0	3	5	3	2	D
7	Surge et accipe puerum	re	LR 312	G	7	9	7	9	10	9	7	5	G
	Surge et illuminare Jerusalem Omnes de Saba	grv	GR 57 LU 459 GS 19 J GB 33 SYG 30	c	2	0	-3	0	2	0	-1	0	
	Surge illuminare Jerusalem	sr	WA 57										
7	Surge pater et comede	re	LA 137	c	-1	0	2	0	2	4	2	4	G
7	Surge Petre et indue te	re	PM 172 LR 363 *LA 416 *WA 327	G	7	9	7	9	5	4	5	7	G
7	Surge propera amica mea	an	AM 820 *PM 140	G	7	4	5	7	9	7	9	7	G
7	Surge propera amica mea	int	GR (9)	G	7	9	7	5	7	2	5	4	G
3	Surge virgo et nostras	re	PM 209	D	5	7	5	10	9	7	5	7	E
	Surge virgo regia Veni electa	rev	LA 446	C	2	4	5	7	5	4	2	0	
	Surgens Dominus Jesus et stans	alv	SYG 156	C	2	0	5	4	2	9	7	11	
1	Surgens Dominus Jesus stans	an	SYG 149	C	2	0	4	5	4	2	4	2	D
	Surgens ergo mane Jacob O quam metuendus	rev	LA 550										

	Incipit		Source										
	Surgens ergo mane Jacob Si Dominus Deus meus	rev	LA 139 WA 92										
7	Surgens ergo mane Jacob	re	LA 550	G	2	0	2	0	2	0	2	5	G
	Surgens Jesus Dominus ... stans	alv	SYG 163	D	7	9	7	5	3	5	7	5	
7	Surgens Jesus Dominus ... stans ... gavisi	re	OHS 812 *LR 92 *LA 210 WA 133	G	7	9	5	4	5	7	9	7	G
	Surgens Jesus Dominus ... stetit	alv	GS 119	C	2	5	2	4	5	4	0	2	
8	Surgens Jesus imperavit	an	WA 71 *LA 107	G	-5	-2	-3	-5	0	-2	-7	-5	G
8	Surgens Jesus mane	an	AR 464 *AM 477 *LA 232	G	5	2	0	-2	0	2	0	4	G
8	Surgens Jesu mane	an	WA 130	G	5	2	0	-2	0	2	0	5	G
8	Surgit Jesus a coena	an	SYG 133	G	-2	-3	-5	-2	2	0	-2	0	G
8	Surgite sancti de mansionibus	an	WA 226	G	2	4	2	0	2	0	-2	2	G
2	Surgite vigilemus venite	inv	LA 8 WA 9	C	2	4	5	2	4	2	0	2	D
	Surrexerunt autem quidam ex Judaeis Elegerunt apostoli	ofv	OTT 161 *SYG 23	C	2	5	7	9	10	9	7	9	
	Surrexerunt quidam de Synagoga Stephanus autem	rev	LA 41										
2	Surrexerunt quidam de Synagoga	re	LA 42	A	3	5	7	5	7	5	8	7	D
	Surrexit altissimus de sepulcro	alv	SYG 158 *GS 127	G	2	0	2	4	5	4	5	4	
	Surrexit altissimus de sepulcro	alv	SYG 168	D	7	10	7	5	7	2	3	5	
	Surrexit altissimus Dominus	alv	GB 146	G	2	4	5	4	5	4	2	0	
	Surrexit autem Saulus Ad manus autem	anv	LA 342 WA 262										
6	Surrexit Christus de sepulcro	an	AM 31 474	F	2	4	2	0	2	4	0	2	F
4	Surrexit Christus et illuxit	an	WA 135	F	-1	0	2	0	-1	-3	-1	0	E
	Surrexit Christus et illuxit	alv	GR 271 LU 831 GS 127 SYG 165	C	2	4	5	4	2	0	4	5	
	Surrexit Christus jam non moritur	alv	GS 131	D	3	5	8	7	8	5	3	7	
	Surrexit Christus qui creavit	alv	GR 254 OHS 808 LU 798 *SYG 159 GB 150 GS 129	A	3	5	3	5	8	5	7	5	
	Surrexit Dominus de sepulcro	sr	AR 31 LU 239 AM 455 470 LA 214 WA 136										
	Surrexit Dominus de sepulcro Surrexit pastor	rev	WA 133										
8	Surrexit Dominus de sepulcro	an	WA 134 225	a	-4	-2	0	-2	-4	0	-2	-4	G
1	Surrexit Dominus de sepulcro	an	WA 131	F	2	4	2	0	4	6	2	0	D
	Surrexit Dominus de sepulcro Angelus Domini	ofv	GB 132	F	2	4	7	4	2	0	2	4	
1	Surrexit Dominus de sepulcro	re	LA 213	C	2	5	7	9	7	4	5	2	D
	Surrexit Dominus de sepulcro	alv	GR 248 LU 790 OHS 785 *GB 137^v	D	7	10	7	5	7	5	2	3	

#	Text	Type	Sources										
6	Surrexit Dominus et apparuit	co	GR 246 OHS 777 LU 788 SYG 156 GB 132ᵛ GS 118	a	3	0	3	5	7	10	7	8	c
	Surrexit Dominus et occurrens	alv	SYG 163 *GS 120	D	7	5	3	5	3	2	0	-2	
	Surrexit Dominus vere	sr	AR 37 LU 244 AM 455 458 466 LA 216 WA 136										
6	Surrexit Dominus vere	an	LA 221	F	-1	2	4	0	-1	0	-3	-5	F
	Surrexit Dominus vere	alv	GR 251 OHS 797 LU 794 GS 130 SYG 155 *GB 135ᵛ	F	2	4	7	2	4	2	0	2	
6	Surrexit Dominus vere	inv	OHS 746 LR 82 LU 765 *LA 217 *WA 131	D	3	5	3	5	3	2	3	5	F
4	Surrexit enim sicut dixit	an	WA 138	a	-2	-4	0	-2	-4	0	-2	0	E
7	Surrexit Odo plenus spiritu	an	AM 874	G	7	4	7	9	7	5	7	5	G
	Surrexit pastor bonus ... grege	alv	GS 128	G	-2	-3	-2	-5	-3	-2	0	2	
1	Surrexit pastor bonus ... grege	re	OHS 759 *LR 86 415 *LA 212 WA 133	C	2	9	10	9	7	9	12	14	D
	Surrexit pastor bonus ... ovibus	alv	SYG 164	C	2	4	5	2	4	0	2	0	
	Surrexit quasi ignis	alv	GR 66**	C	2	0	5	4	2	4	0	5	
8	Suscepimus Deus misericordiam	an	LR 56 70 LU 378 WA 27 53 *LA 31	G	2	0	-2	0	2	5	4	2	G
1	Suscepimus Deus misericordiam	int	GR 339 432 LU 1361 SYG 48 GB 47 GS j 149	C	2	9	10	9	**12**	9	7	9	D
8	Suscepimus Deus misericordiam	tr	GR 113**	D	3	5	2	3	5	0	-2	0	G
5	Suscepimus Deus misericordiam	gr	GR 433 LU 1362 *SYG 48 *GB 47ᵛ GS j	D	3	5	3	5	7	5	7	5	F
8	Suscepisti me Domine	an	AR 117 LU 279ᶠ	G	2	0	-2	0	2	-2	-3	-5	G
7	Suscepit Deus Israel	an	AR 206 LU 313 AM 163	G	2	5	4	5	7	9	7	9	G
4	Suscipe verbum virgo Maria	re	PM 245 LA 14 379 *WA 4	F	-3	0	2	0	-3	-1	-3	0	E
8	Suscipe voces pariterque laudes	hy	ST 405	G	2	0	-3	-2	0	2	0	2	G
	Suscipiant montes pacem Reges Tharsis	ofv	OTT 21 GB 34 SYG 31	F	4	7	4	7	9	4	7	9	
	Suscipiant montes pacem Benedictus Dominus	grv	GR 64 LU 478 GS 20 GB 36 *SYG 32	G	5	7	9	7	5	7	5	4	G
	Suscipiat te Christus Subvenite sancti	rev	AR [183] GR 107* LU 1765 AM 1168										
7	Suscipiat vos Christe	an	WA 8	d	-3	0	2	0	-3	-2	0	-5	G
6	Suscipiens Jesum in ulnas	re	VP 102 *LA 350 *WA 270	D	3	5	3	5	3	2	3	5	F

Incipit		Source	Mode									Final
Suscipiens Simeon puerum 　Cum inducerent	rev	WA 270										
2 Suscitabit Deus caeli regnum	an	AR 894^6 LU 1705 AM 1092	D	2	-2	0	5	7	3	2	-2	D
3 Suscitabo mihi sacerdotem	int	GR [117]	F	-3	0	-1	0	2	4	0	-3	E
Suscitans a terra inopem 　Quis sicut Dominus	grv	GR 369 GS 168 GB 257^V SYG 251	c	2	0	-3	0	2	0	-1	0	
Suscitans a terra inopem	alv	GR 20**	D	7	8	7	5	7	5	2	3	
1 Sustinuimus pacem et non venit	an	LA 309	D	-2	0	3	0	2	0	-2	3	D
8 Sustinuimus pacem et non venit	re	LA 303 *WA 184	D	3	5	7	5	7	3	0	2	G
Suxerunt mel de petra	alv	GB 151^V	D	-2	2	3	5	3	2	3	2	
2 Synagoga populorum circumdederunt	re	OHS 242 (nm) WA 111	D	3	5	7	5	7	5	8	7	D
1 Tali namque ad Dominum	an	WA 389	D	-2	3	5	3	5	7	5	3	D
8 Talis est dilectus meus	an	LA 458	G	2	4	2	0	2	4	2	0	G
8 Tamquam ad latronem existis	re	OHS 496 LU 702 *LA 196	D	5	3	5	7	5	7	5	3	G
Tamquam agnus coram tondente 　Ecce quomodo	rev	OHS 611 LU 768 LA 198										
7 Tamquam aurum in fornace	an	LR 176 WA 420 LA 513	d	-3	0	2	0	2	0	-3	-2	G
8 Tamquam aurum in fornace	re	LR 184 LA 519	D	3	5	7	5	7	5	3	5	G
Tamquam filiis dico	alv	GR 547	G	2	4	5	4	2	4	5	4	
8 Tamquam lignum quod plantatum	of	GR (25)	F	2	0	-1	-5	-3	0	2	4	G
Tamquam nugaces aestimati 　Dixerunt impii	rev	OHS 302 (nm) LA 179										
Tamquam nugaces aestimati 　Viri impii	rev	WA 116										
Tamquam prodigium factus	alv	GR 622^2 LU 1681^3	G	2	0	-2	2	5	4	2	7	
Tamquam sponsus Dominus 　Descendit de caelis Deus	rev	LR 59	a	-2	0	-2	-4	-2	0	-2	0	
8 Tamquam sponsus Dominus	an	LU 372 *LR 55 WA 49 *LA 31	G	2	0	-2	0	2	5	4	2	G
Tamquam sponsus Dominus 　Descendit de caelis Deus	rev	LA 32	a	3	0	-2	0	2	-2	-4	-2	
Tamquam sponsus Dominus 　Descendit de caelis missus	rev	PM 27 WA 31	a	3	0	-2	0	2	-2	-4	-2	
5 Tandem ad sponsi	an	WA 244	F	4	7	4	2	7	9	7	9	F
1 Tantam gratiam ei	an	LR 324 *WA 298	D	7	10	7	5	7	5	7	2	D

	Text	Type	Source										
	Tantam gratiam et virtus / Intempestae noctis	ofv	SYG 57	D	2	3	5	7	5	10	7	5	
	Tantaque circa eum / Hodie dilectus	cov	SYG 57										
7	Tantas per illum Dominus	re	WA 387	G	2	0	2	5	7	5	4	5	G
8	Tantas per illum Dominus	an	WA 385	G	5	2	0	-2	0	2	0	-2	G
	Tanto namque feliciores / Valerius igitur	rev	WA 257	a	-2	0	-2	-4	-5	-2	0	3	
4	Tanto namque feliciores	an	WA 256	F	-1	0	-1	-3	-1	0	2	4	E
7	Tanto pondere eam fixit	an	AR 594 LU 1325 *AM 773	d	-3	0	2	0	-3	-2	0	-5	G
4	Tanto tempore vobiscum eram	an	LA 188	C	2	5	4	2	4	5	7	4	E
4	Tanto tempore vobiscum sum ... credis	co	GR 489 LU 1465^D *SYG 172 *GB 165 *GS 185	D	3	0	3	2	3	5	3	2	E
	Tanto tempore vobiscum sum ... credis	alv	GR 489 LU 1465^C	G	5	4	2	0	2	4	2	0	G
4	Tanto tempore vobiscum sum ... creditis	re	PM 151 *WA 307	D	3	0	3	2	3	5	3	0	E
3	Tanto tempore vobiscum sum ... meum	an	AR 695 LU 1465^E *AM 893 *LA 394	G	2	5	4	2	4	5	4	0	E
1	Tantum ergo sacramentum	hy	AR 89* AM 1258	D	-2	3	5	7	8	10	8	7	D
3	Tantum ergo sacramentum	hy	AR 88* GR 158* LU 954	E	1	0	-2	3	5	8	10	8	E
5	Tantum ergo sacramentum	hy	AR 89* LU 1851	C	2	4	2	0	2	4	7	5	C
5	Tantum ergo sacramentum	hy	AR 90* LU 1852 AM 1259	F	2	4	2	6	7	4	2	4	F
2	Te beata sponsa Christi	hy	AM 813	C	2	0	5	4	2	0	5	7	D
1	Te Christe patris verbum / virtus inclita	hy	ST 57	C	2	4	5	7	9	7	5	4	D
1	Te Christe rex piissime	hy	ST 44	C	2	4	7	5	4	2	5	4	D
	Te confiteor labiis / Omnipotens adorande	rev	PM 128 LA 337 WA 255										
8	Te decet hymnus	an	AM 53 54 *AR 126 WA 67 *LA 95	c	-1	-3	-5	-3	-5	-3	-1	[0]	G
	Te decet hymnus ... et tibi / Requiem aeternam	intv	GR 94* LU 1807 GS 232 SYG 235										
	Te decet hymnus ... et tibi	alv	GR 346 LU 1022 GS 148 SYG 242 GB 252	G	7	9	7	9	7	9	7	9	
2	Te decet laus te decet hymnus	hy	AM 1261 *AR 209 *LR 42	A	3	5	7	5	7	5	3	5	D
1	Te decet laus te decet hymnus	hy	AR 209* AM 1260 LR 42 *WA 6	G	7	9	7	5	7	5	2	5	a
8	Te deprecante corporum	hy	AR 887	G	-2	-3	-2	0	-2	0	2	5	G

3 Te Deum laudamus			WA 5	D	3	5	3	5	7	5	0	3	E
3 Te Deum laudamus			AR 66* GR 141* LU 1832 *AM 1250 LR 34 OHS 761 PM 96 VP 22 15*	E	3	5	3	5	7	8	7	5	E
3 Te Deum laudamus			AR 69* GR 144* LR 37 LU 1834 OHS 791 VP 25	E	3	5	3	5	7	8	7	5	E
3 Te Deum laudamus			GR 147*	E	3	5	3	5	7	8	7	5	E
8 Te Deum patrem	tr		GR [84] LU 1273	D	3	5	2	3	5	0	-2	0	G
4 Te Deum patrem ... et ore	an		AR 523 LU 916 AM 541 VP 28 18* WA 158	E	1	3	1	0	-2	0	3	5	E
4 Te Deum patrem ... et ore	re		WA 161	C	2	5	4	2	5	2	4	2	E
8 Te Deus omnipotens	an		WA 382	G	2	0	-2	0	2	4	2	4	G
2 Te gestientem gaudiis	hy		AR 880 LU 1680 AM 1079	a	-2	-5	-7	-2	0	3	2	0	a
6 Te gestientem gaudiis	hy		ST 22	F	4	5	7	9	7	4	0	4	F
Te gloriosus apostolorum	alv		GR 588 LU 1613	C	2	5	4	5	7	5	4	2	
7 Te gloriosus apostolorum ... te	an		AR 901 LU 1724 AM 1105 WA 397 LA 478	G	2	5	4	5	7	9	7	9	C
4 Te invocamus te adoramus	an		WA 158	F	-1	-3	-1	-3	-5	-3	-1	-3	E
1 Te Joseph celebrent agmina	hy		AR 650 LR 436 LU 1447 AM 839 884	D	3	2	3	5	7	0	-2	3	D
5 Te jure laudant	an		WA 162	a	-2	-4	0	3	5	3	5	7	F
7 Te laudamus Domine			AR 210* *VP 170	d	-3	-2	0	2	0	-2	0	-2	G
4 Te laudant angeli	re		WA 28	F	-1	-3	-1	0	-1	0	-1	0	E
8 Te lucis ante terminum	hy		ST 362	G	-5	-2	0	2	0	-2	0	5	G
8 Te lucis ante terminum	hy		ST 6	G	-5	0	2	4	5	2	0	4	G
Te lucis ante terminum	hy		ST 330	d	-3	-2	-3	-5	-3	-2	0	2	c
8 Te lucis ante terminum	hy		ST 28 AR 60 LU 268 AM 171	G	-3	0	2	4	5	2	0	4	G
2 Te lucis ante terminum	hy		AR 61 AM 172	a	-2	-5	-7	-2	0	3	2	0	a
2 Te lucis ante terminum	hy		AM 337	E	-2	-4	-2	0	1	0	-2	1	D
8 Te lucis ante terminum	hy		AR 263 LU 367	G	-2	-3	-5	-2	2	0	-2	0	G
2 Te lucis ante terminum	hy		AM 549	D	-2	0	3	2	0	3	5	3	D
2 Te lucis ante terminum	hy		ST 78 84	D	-2	0	3	5	7	5	3	5	D
3 Te lucis ante terminum	hy		AR 538^6 LU 966	E	-2	3	5	8	7	5	3	5	E
4 Te lucis ante terminum	hy		AR 490 LU 844	F	-1	0	2	4	2	0	-3	0	E
4 Te lucis ante terminum	hy		AR 59 LU 267	F	-1	2	4	2	0	2	4	2	E
2 Te lucis ante terminum	hy		AR 364 LU 540	E	1	-2	-4	-2	0	1	-2	-4	D

8 Te lucis ante terminum	hy	ST 269	G	2	-2	-3	-2	0	2	0	2	G
2 Te lucis ante terminum	hy	ST 254	G	2	0	-2	-3	-2	0	-3	-2	D
6 Te lucis ante terminum	hy	ST 331	a	2	0	-2	0	-2	-4	-2	0	F
8 Te lucis ante terminum	hy	ST 176	c	2	0	-1	-3	-5	-3	0	-3	G
6 Te lucis ante terminum	hy	ST 343	F	2	0	-1	-3	-1	0	-1	-3	C
8 Te lucis ante terminum	hy	AM 469	G	2	0	2	4	5	2	4	5	G
2 Te lucis ante terminum	hy	AR 407 LU 577	C	2	4	5	4	2	0	2	4	D
8 Te lucis ante terminum	hy	ST 440	G	2	4	5	4	2	5	7	4	G
8 Te lucis ante terminum	hy	AR 311 LU 455 AM 290	F	2	4	7	2	4	0	2	7	G
2 Te lucis ante terminum	hy	AR 212 LU 326	C	2	5	0	2	5	4	2	4	D
2 Te lucis ante terminum	hy	ST 247 269	D	3	0	-2	0	3	2	3	5	D
1 Te lucis ante terminum	hy	AR 502 894^5 LU 862 1704 AM 520	D	3	0	-2	3	5	7	5	10	D
4 Te lucis ante terminum	hy	AM 564 1091	D	3	2	0	2	5	2	3	2	E
8 Te lucis ante terminum	hy	ST 79 84	a	3	5	3	2	0	-2	0	2	G
8 Te lucis ante terminum	hy	AR 58 AM 170	a	3	5	3	2	0	2	0	-2	G
8 Te lucis ante terminum	hy	AR 59 LU 266	G	4	2	5	4	2	5	0	2	G
8 Te lucis ante terminum	hy	AM 170	G	4	2	5	4	2	5	4	0	G
5 Te lucis ante terminum	hy	ST 330	F	4	2	7	9	7	12	11	9	F
1 Te lucis auctor personant	hy	ST 289	D	3	0	-2	0	3	2	3	5	D
1 Te lucis auctor personant	hy	ST 288	D	7	5	7	10	9	7	5	7	D
Te martyr inclite O sancte N. concivis	rev	WA 418	a	3	2	-2	0	2	-2	3	5	
Te martyrum candidatus	alv	GR [30] LU 1171 *GS 18 217 *SYG 192 *GB 268^v	C	2	5	4	5	7	5	4	2	
2 Te mater alma numinis	hy	AR 882^4 AM 1083	a	-2	-5	-7	-2	0	3	2	0	a
3 Te poli cives super astra Christe	hy	ST 150	a	-2	0	3	2	0	2	3	0	E
7 Te qui in spiritu	an	WA 58 LA 78 *VP 95	G	7	5	4	7	9	5	7	5	G
1 Te saeculorum principem	hy	AR 894^2 LU 1716	C	2	9	10	9	7	9	7	5	D
1 Te saeculorum principem	hy	AM 1090	D	7	5	7	10	9	7	5	7	D
Te sancta Dei crux Protege Domine	ofv	OTT 168	D	-2	-5	-7	-2	0	2	3	0	
1 Te sanctum Dominum in excelsis	re	AR 196* *PM 109 VP 216 *WA 382	D	-2	0	2	3	0	-2	0	3	D
3 Te semper idem esse	an	WA 158	G	2	5	4	2	0	2	0	4	E
4 Te splendor et virtus patris	hy	AR 707 LU 1463	E	-2	-4	0	3	1	-2	-4	-2	F

2	Te splendor et virtus patris	hy	AR 854 LU 1661	D	3	0	-2	0	3	2	3	5	D
8	Te trina Deus unitas	hy	ST 423	G	2	0	-2	0	2	4	0	-2	G
6	Te unum in substantia	an	WA 158	D	-2	0	2	3	0	-2	0	3	F
1	Tecum principium in die virtutis	an	AR 270 LU 412 *AM 245 *WA 32 *LA 38	F	-5	-3	4	5	4	2	4	0	D
2	Tecum principium in die virtutis	gr	GR 28 LU 393 *SYG 14 GB 13ᵛ GS 13	a	-5	0	2	0	-2	0	-2	0	a
1	Telluris alme conditor	hy	AR 122 LU 518	F	2	4	2	0	-1	2	-1	0	D
	Telluris ingens conditor	hy	ST 363 AM 142	F	2	4	0	2	0	-1	2	0	D
8	Telluris ingens conditor	hy	AM 141	D	3	5	3	7	5	0	3	5	G
2	Telluris ingens conditor	hy	ST 213	D	3	5	7	3	5	3	5	2	D
2	Tellus ac aethra jubilent	hy	ST 326	D	2	3	5	3	2	0	3	2	D
4	Tellus ac aethra jubilent	hy	SYG 135	D	2	3	5	7	0	2	5	3	E
2	Templum Domini sanctum est	an	LR 237 *WA 318 *LA 549	F	-1	-5	-3	0	-1	-3	0	4	D
8	Templum tuum nos effice	hy	ST 179	G	2	4	2	4	5	4	2	0	G
6	Tempore laetitiae juste	an	WA 336	F	2	5	4	2	0	2	4	-3	F
1 2	Temptavit Deus Abraham	re	LA 121 *WA 81	D	3	5	0	2	3	2	0	-2	D
4	Tempus est ut revertar ... dicit	re	LR 101 *LA 249 *WA 148	E	1	-2	1	3	1	0	1	0	E
	Tempus est ut revertar ... vos Benedicite Deum caeli	rev	WA 177										
2	Tempus est ut revertar ... vos	re	LA 290 *WA 177	F	-1	0	-3	0	2	0	-1	-3	D
4	Tempus meum nondum advenit	an	AR 417 LU 1098 AM 394 *LA 173	G	2	5	7	5	7	9	7	5	a
7	Tenebrae factae sunt	re	OHS 497 LU 703	G	2	-2	0	2	0	2	0	2	G
7	Tenebrae factae sunt ... tunc	re	LA 200 WA 123	G	2	-2	0	2	0	2	0	2	G
7	Tenuisti manum dexteram	int	GR 462 LU 1418	G	2	0	2	5	7	5	7	10	G
4	Tenuisti manum dexteram	gr	GR 179 OHS 108 LU 593 *SYG 122 GB 109 *GS 86	C	2	0	7	5	2	0	2	7	E
8	Ter virgis caesus sum	an	AR 610 757 LU 1349 *AM 794 942 WA 265 331 *LA 426	G	5	2	0	-2	0	2	0	4	G
8	Ternis ter horis numerus	hy	ST 382	c	2	0	-1	-3	0	-3	0	-1	G
8	Terra tremuit et quievit	an	OHS 392 LU 647 LR 87 WA 119 LA 192	c	-1	-5	-3	0	2	0	-1	0	G
4	Terra tremuit et quievit	of	GR 243 OHS 712 OTT 55 LU 781 *SYG 153 *GB 128 GS 117	D	3	2	3	0	3	2	3	5	E

7	Terribile est Christe judicium	an	GB 161	G	5	4	7	9	7	5	4	5	G
2	Terribilis est locus iste	int	GR [71] LU 1250 *SYG 263 GB 172^v GS 174	D	-2	-5	-2	0	3	5	3	2	D
1	Terribilis est locus iste	re	LR 235 WA 317	D	-2	0	3	2	3	0	2	3	D
	Terrore subjuncti / Hi sancti viri	rev	WA 388										
	Tertia jejunii nocte / Electus et dilectus	rev	WA 290										
3	Tertio Christum Petrus	an	WA 278	E	-2	3	5	7	3	5	7	5	E
	Testimonium ergo perhibebat / Cogitaverunt autem	rev	WA 112 GS 83	G	5	4	5	7	5	4	5	4	
	Testimonium in Joseph posuit illud / Exsultate Deo adjutori	intv	GR 368 GS 168 GB 257^v SYG 251										
8	Testimonium perhibuit Joannes	re	LA 73	D	5	3	5	7	5	7	9	10	G
7	Testis mihi est Deus	gr	GR 544 LU 1544	G	-2	0	2	0	2	4	5	4	G
7	Tetradius cognita Dei	an	WA 400 *LA 481	G	7	4	7	9	7	4	7	9	G
4	Thesaurizate vobis thesauros	an	AR 359 AM 333 *WA 84 LA 126	a	-2	0	3	7	5	3	5	7	a
1	Thomas qui dicitur Didymus	an	WA 137	D	3	0	-2	3	5	3	5	7	D
2	Tibi Christe splendor patris	hy	ST 399	G	-2	-3	-5	-3	-2	-5	-7	-3	D
	Tibi Christe splendor patris	hy	ST 461	G	-2	-3	-5	-3	-2	-5	-7	-2	
4	Tibi Christe splendor patris	hy	ST 237	E	-2	1	-2	-4	-2	0	-2	0	E
8	Tibi Christe splendor patris	hy	ST 460	G	2	0	-3	-2	0	4	0	2	G
[1]	Tibi Christe splendor patris	hy	ST 194	C	2	0	2	5	4	2	0	5	[D]
2	Tibi Christe splendor patris	hy	ST 97	C	2	0	4	5	4	2	0	5	D
2	Tibi Christe splendor patris	hy	ST 58 429 LR 447 AM 1056	C	2	0	5	4	2	0	5	7	D
	Tibi derelictus est pauper / Exsurge Domine	trv	GR [101] LU 1283^B	G	2	4	5	4	2	5	4	2	
3	Tibi dixit cor meum	int	GR 117 *GB 77 *SYG 88 GS 49	G	5	2	5	4	2	0	2	-2	E
3	Tibi Domine derelictus est	gr	GR 149 LU 566 *SYG 108 *GB 96 *GS 70	C	4	7	5	4	5	7	9	7	E
6	Tibi Domine psallam	an	AR 126	F	-1	0	-3	-5	-3	0	2	0	F
	Tibi enim a Domino / Tu es pastor	rev	LA 416 WA 279										
	Tibi enim Domine derelictus est		see also Tibi enim derelictus est										
	Tibi enim derelictus est / Deus qui sedes	rev	LA 81 WA 60										
	Tibi enim gemina / Levita Vincentius	rev	WA 257										

	Incipit	type	sources										
	Tibi gloria hosanna	alv	GR [109]	G	5	7	9	7	5	7	5	2	
	Tibi junctus igitur / Sanctissimi martyris Stephani	rev	WA 36	D	7	5	7	5	3	5	7	10	
8	Tibi laus perennis auctor	hy	ST 483	a	-2	-4	-7	-4	-5	-4	-2	0	G
	Tibi laus tibi gloria / O beata trinitas	rev	PM 91	a	-2	0	-2	-4	-5	-2	0	-2	
2	Tibi laus tibi gloria	an	WA 161	a	-2	0	-2	0	2	0	-2	0	D
	Tibi laus tibi gloria / O vera ... trinitas	anv	WA 162	G	2	5	4	2	5	4	5	7	
	Tibi laus tibi gloria / Te jure laudant	anv	WA 162	F	4	7	9	11	7	11	12	9	
7	Tibi laus tibi gloria ... / in saecula	re	WA 160	G	2	0	2	5	4	5	7	5	G
4	Tibi revelavi causam meam	an	AR 424 OHS 147 / LU 604 AM 402 / *LA 183	G	2	5	9	7	5	7	9	7	a
8	Tibi soli peccavi Domine	an	AR 150 *AM 58 / *WA 68 *LA 98	F	2	0	4	7	4	6	7	4	G
	Tibi soli peccavi et malum / Abscondi tamquam aurum	rev	LA 85										
	Tibi soli peccavi et malum / Quomodo confitebor	rev	WA 438										
	Tibi soli peccavi et malum / Miserere mihi	ofv	OTT 35 GB 77^v / SYG 88	G	7	9	7	5	7	5	7	5	
	Timeamus et amemus Deum / Ubi caritas	anv	GR 204 OHS 451	F	2	0	2	4	0	2	0	-3	
	Timeat eum omne semen / Qui timetis	grv	GR 467	D	7	5	7	10	7	9	5	3	
	Timebunt gentes nomen tuum	alv	SYG 249	C	2	4	2	4	5	4	5	4	
	Timebunt gentes nomen tuum	alv	GR 373 LU 1056 / GS 167 GB 39^v	D	3	0	-2	3	5	3	5	7	
5	Timebunt gentes nomen tuum	gr	GR 71 LU 489 / *SYG 42 GB 39 / GS 23 159	D	3	5	7	3	5	3	2	0	F
	Timentibus Deum nihil / Deum time	rev	WA 88	a	-2	-4	-2	-4	-5	-7	-5	-9	
1	Timete Dominum omnes sancti	gr	GR 648 LU 1726 / SYG 192 GB 216 / GS 213	D	-2	0	3	2	3	5	3	2	D
	Timete Dominum omnes sancti	alv	SYG 192	D	-2	0	3	5	3	2	0	3	
	Timete Dominum omnes sancti / Gustate et videte	trv	GR 95**	G	2	4	5	4	5	4	5	7	
	Timete Dominum omnes sancti	alv	SYG 212	G	2	4	5	7	2	0	4	7	
1	Timete Dominum omnes sancti	an	LR 385 WA 395 / LA 475	D	3	0	-2	3	5	7	5	7	D
3	Timete Dominum omnes sancti	int	GR 574 *SYG 192 / *GB 215^v *GS 211	G	5	2	0	5	4	2	5	4	E

8 Timor et tremor ... in Nineven	an	GB 155^v WA 230	G	2	0	-2	0	2	0	2	5	G
Timor et tremor ... super me Domine ne in ira	rev	LR 398 LA 81 *WA 60	a	-2	0	-2	-4	-2	0	-2	0	
Tobias et Sara in tribulatione In illo tempore	rev	PM 198	G	5	4	0	2	4	2	5	7	
7 Tolle arma tua	re	LR 405 *LA 136 *WA 91	G	2	5	4	2	5	0	2	0	G
7 Tolle puerum et matrem	co	GR 46 LU 436 SYG 30 GB 31^v GS H	G	2	0	2	5	4	5	7	5	G
Tolle puerum et matrem	alv	SYG 30	G	2	4	5	7	9	7	5	7	
3 Tolle puerum et matrem	an	WA 52 *LA 350	G	2	5	4	2	5	4	0	4	E
8 Tolle quod tuum est	an	AR 346 AM 317 *WA 75 *LA 115	c	-1	-3	-5	-3	-5	-7	-5	-3	G
Tollite de optimis	see Sumite de optimis											
7 Tollite hinc vobiscum	re	LR 409 *LA 149 *WA 97	G	2	0	2	0	2	5	7	5	G
4 Tollite hostias et introite	co	GR 374 LU 1058 *SYG 255 GB 261 GS 162	d	-2	-3	0	2	0	2	-2	0	b
5 Tollite hostias et introite	gr	GR 162 *SYG 114 *GB 102 GS 76	F	2	4	2	0	2	4	2	4	F
Tollite jugum meum	sr	AR 538^{11} LU 970 AM 566										
Tollite jugum meum	alv	GR 325 [112] LU 972	E	1	3	1	0	-2	0	3	5	
7 Tollite jugum meum	re	LR 137 *LA 506 WA 411	G	2	0	2	0	2	5	7	5	G
1 Tollite jugum meum	an	WA 412	F	2	4	2	4	2	0	2	0	D
3 Tollite jugum meum	an	LA 507	G	2	5	2	0	2	0	-3	-2	E
Tollite portas principes Aspiciens a longe	rev	PM 18										
3 Tollite portas principes	an	LR 232 WA 317 *LA 547	G	2	5	4	2	5	4	0	2	E
2 Tollite portas principes	of	GR 26 OTT 14 LU 362 *SYG 14 *GB 13 *GS 13	E	3	5	7	5	7	8	10	7	a
2 Tollite portas principes	gr	GR 9 LU 1269 *SYG 8 *GB 6^v *GS 5	G	4	2	5	2	4	5	2	0	a
2 Torcular calcavi solus	an	AR 760 LU 1537	D	-2	0	3	5	2	3	0	-2	D
2 Torquebatur animo Pascasius	an	WA 247	D	3	-2	0	3	2	3	5	3	D
Torrentem pertransivit anima nostra Anima nostra	ofv	OTT 145 GB 27^v SYG 26	G	2	5	7	5	0	2	5	2	
Tota decora ingreditur filia Audi filia ... concupiscet	grv	GR 583	G	5	7	9	7	10	7	9	7	

4 Tota die contristatus	re	LA 168 *WA 106		D	3	0	3	2	3	5	3	0	E
Tota die miseretur Justus non conturbabitur	grv	GB 162ᵛ *GS 206		F	4	7	9	7	9	7	9	11	
Tota die miseretur Justus cum ceciderit	grv	GR [13] LU 1139		F	4	7	9	7	9	11	7	9	
1 Tota formosa et suavis es	gr	GR 60**		D	7	8	7	5	3	7	5	7	D
4 Tota pulchra es amica	an	AR 124* PM 274 VP 54 *WA 360		F	-1	-3	-1	2	4	2	4	7	E
Tota pulchra es Maria	alv	GR 402 LU 1318		D	2	3	2	0	-2	0	2	0	
1 Tota pulchra es Maria	an	AR 586 LU 1320 AM 763		F	4	5	2	0	4	0	2	0	D
Tota pulchra es Maria Tu gloria	trv	GR 441 LU 1378		G	5	7	9	5	0	5	7	9	
Totus caelesti gaudio In columbae specie Scholastica	rev	LR 299 AM 1192											
1 Tradent enim vos in conciliis	an	AR [8] LU 1112 AM 621 WA 414 LA 508		D	-2	3	5	7	5	3	5	7	D
1 Tradetur enim gentibus	an	AR 384 LU 1087 AM 358 WA 94		D	-2	3	5	3	5	7	8	7	D
1 Tradiderunt corpora sua ad supplicia	an	LA 516		C	2	9	11	9	7	5	7	9	D
1 Tradiderunt corpora sua in mortem	an	LR 181		C	2	9	10	9	12	9	7	9	D
Tradiderunt corpora sua propter Fuerunt sine querela	rev	LR 138 LA 509 WA 413											
Tradiderunt corpora sua propter Isti sunt sancti qui pro testamento	rev	LA 390											
Tradiderunt corpora sua propter Verbera carnificum	rev	LR 183											
1 Tradiderunt corpora sua propter ... et	re	LR 179 LA 515 WA 421		C	2	4	2	9	10	9	7	9	D
8 Tradiderunt corpora sua propter ... ideo	re	LA 388		G	-2	0	2	0	2	5	4	5	G
6 Tradiderunt me in manus	re	LU 710 OHS 505 *LA 197 *WA 123		G	2	5	4	5	4	2	4	2	c
Tradidit auribus meis Induit me Dominus	rev	LA 335 WA 253											
Tradidit in mortem animam Sicut ovis	rev	OHS 596 LR 339 LU 755 LA 205											
1 Traditor autem dedit eis	an	AR 434 OHS 406 LU 658 *AM 420 *WA 120 *LA 194		F	-5	-3	4	5	4	2	-1	0	D
2 Traduntur igni martyres	hy	ST 44		D	-2	-3	-2	0	-2	0	2	5	D
Trahe me post te curremus Inveni quem diligit	trv	GR (11)		G	-5	0	2	5	2	5	7	5	
3 Trahe me post te in odorem	an	LR 219		E	-2	3	5	8	7	8	7	5	E
3 Trahe nos virgo	an	AR 587 LU 1321 *AM 764		E	-2	3	5	8	7	8	10	8	E

1	Transeunte Domino clamabat	an	AR 356 LU 511 AM 329 *WA 83 *LA 122 125	D	-2	3	5	3	5	7	5	8	D
8	Transiens ex hoc mundo	re	WA 314	G	-2	-5	-2	0	-2	0	2	5	G
8	Transite ad me omnes	re	LR 263	D	3	5	7	5	8	5	7	5	G
	Transite ad me omnes In me gratia	grv	GR 43**	F	4	7	9	11	7	9	7	9	
	Transitoriam felicitatem Quantam denique	rev	WA 239	G	2	5	4	2	4	5	4	2	
6	Transiturus de mundo	re	LR 132	D	3	5	3	8	7	5	3	5	F
	Transivimus per ignem Probasti nos	trv	GR 108**	G	2	4	5	4	2	5	2	0	
1	Translate ad caelestia	re	WA 315	C	2	4	5	2	0	2	5	7	D
4	Translato ad caelestia	an	WA 314	E	-2	1	0	-2	0	-2	1	0	E
	Transtulisti illos mare rubrum Magna enim sunt	rev	LA 279										
	Transtulisti illos per mare In mari via	rev	WA 101										
	Tremens factus sum ego Libera me Domine de morte	rev	AR [174] PM 321 LU 1767 GR 102* LA 557	F	-1	0	-1	-3	-1	-3	-5	-3	
	Tres enim adhuc dies Memento mei dum bene	rev	LA 149 WA 96										
8	Tres pueri jussu regis	an	AR 4 AM 30	G	2	0	-2	0	2	0	-2	2	G
	Tres sunt qui testimonium dant Hic est qui venit	grv	GR 537 LU 1533	G	2	4	5	4	5	4	5	4	
	Tres sunt qui testimonium dant Duo seraphim	rev	PM 107 AR 179* LR 419	D	7	5	7	5	3	5	7	3	
7	Tres viri isti	re	WA 389	G	5	4	5	7	5	7	9	7	G
1	Tria sunt munera pretiosa	re	LA 72 WA 55	D	-2	3	5	7	5	7	5	3	D
4	Tria sunt munera quae	an	AR 332 *AM 298 LR 75 *WA 56 *LA 69	F	-3	-1	0	2	0	-1	2	0	E
8	Tribularer si nescirem	re	PM 48 LR 404 VP 119 LA 130 WA 87	D	3	5	7	5	7	5	3	5	G
7	Tribulationes civitatum audivimus	re	LA 291 WA 177	G	5	4	5	7	5	7	5	4	G
5	Tribulationes cordis mei dilatatae	gr	GR 112 LU 546 SYG 77 GB 69^v GS 39 47	F	4	7	6	9	7	9	7	4	F
1	Tribus miraculis ornatum	an	AR 318 LU 466 AM 296 LA 79	D	-2	0	2	3	5	3	2	0	D
8	Tricesimo ordinationis	an	WA 403	G	-5	-2	0	2	0	-2	0	2	G
4	Triduanas a Domino poposci	an	AR 925 LU 1757 AM 1141 WA 408 *LA 490	D	2	3	5	7	5	3	5	3	E

2 Trinitati altissimae	hy	ST 14	C	2	4	5	2	4	2	0	2	D
Trinitati lux Honor virtus	rev	WA 160	c	2	5	4	5	7	9	7	5	
4 Tristes erant apostoli	hy	LR 163	F	-1	2	4	2	0	-3	0	-1	E
3 Tristes erant apostoli	hy	AR [22] LU 1121 AM 630	E	1	3	1	0	-2	0	-2	-4	E
3 Tristes erant apostoli	hy	LR 162	E	1	3	1	0	-2	0	1	-2	E
8 Tristis est anima mea	re	OHS 378 LU 635 *LA 189 *WA 118	F	2	4	0	4	7	6	7	9	G
Tristitia implebit cor	alv	SYG 168	D	3	5	3	2	0	3	0	2	
8 Tristitia implevit cor	an	AR 476 AM 490 *WA 143 304	a	-4	-2	0	3	2	0	-2	0	G
8 Tristitia vestra alleluia convertetur	re	LR 165 *LA 386 *WA 305	G	5	2	0	2	0	2	0	2	G
6 Tristitia vestra alleluia vertetur	an	AR 477 *AM 491	F	-1	2	4	-1	0	-3	-5	0	F
Tristitia vestra vertetur	sr	WA 307										
8 Tristitia vestra vertetur ... et	an	AR 475 *AM 490	G	5	2	0	-2	0	2	0	4	G
8 Trium puerorum cantemus	an	AR 379 AM 352 WA 93 LA 85	G	2	0	2	0	-2	0	2	-2	G
2 Triumphant sancti martyres	an	WA 376	C	2	5	4	2	0	2	5	2	D
Tu autem confessor Ora pro nobis beate Martine	rev	WA 401										
1 Tu autem cum oraveris	an	AR 361 AM 335 WA 85 LA 126	D	-2	3	5	3	5	7	8	7	D
Tu autem Domine in aeternum Dies mei sicut umbra	grv	GB 104ᵛ	a	3	5	7	5	3	2	3	0	
Tu autem Domine miserere Ego dixi Domine	rev	WA 65										
Tu autem Domine ne longe Deus meus es tu ne	rev	LA 167										
1 Tu autem Domine scis omne	an	AR 431 OHS 307 347	D	-2	0	3	2	0	-2	2	3	D
Tu autem Domini susceptor Synagoga	rev	WA 111										
Tu autem in sancto habitas Deus Deus meus	trv	GR 180 OHS 109 LU 592 GS 86 GB 109 SYG 122	C	2	5	7	5	2	5	7	9	
3 Tu Bethlehem terra Juda	an	AR 246 *AM 221 *WA 17 *LA 23	G	2	5	4	0	2	4	5	4	E
8 Tu Christe nostrum gaudium	hy	ST 94	G	2	4	2	0	-2	2	0	2	G
4 Tu decus virgineum virgo Dei	an	PM 271	C	2	5	4	5	7	5	4	2	E
Tu Domine cui humilium Dominator Domine	rev	PM 113 LA 292 WA 178										
Tu Domine pater noster	alv	GB 151ᵛ	G	2	5	4	5	7	5	2	5	
Tu Domine pater noster Salvos fac nos	grv	GR 51 LU 447	E	3	0	3	5	3	2	-2	0	

#	Incipit		Sources										
3	Tu Domine servabis ... a	co	GR 121 SYG 91 GB 80^v *GS 53	G	5	4	5	7	2	4	5	4	E
8	Tu Domine servabis ... in	an	AR 125 OHS 291 LU 289	a	-4	-2	0	-2	-4	-2	-4	-2	G
1	Tu Domine universorum	an	LA 300	C	2	5	4	2	4	2	0	2	D
2	Tu Domine universorum	re	VP 246 LA 299 WA 182	A	3	5	7	5	8	7	8	10	D
	Tu elegisti Domine domum Tu Domine universorum	rev	VP 246										
	Tu es altissimus	alv	GB 178^v	C	2	9	11	9	7	5	4	2	
5	Tu es Deus qui facis	an	LA 97	c	-3	0	2	-3	-5	-3	-1	-5	F
6	Tu es Deus qui facis	an	WA 67	F	-3	0	2	0	2	0	[0	0]	F
3	Tu es Deus qui facis	gr	GR 81 LU 512 *SYG 62 GB 59^v GS 28	C	2	5	7	5	4	5	7	9	E
	Tu es Domine qui restitues		see also Tu es qui restitues										
8	Tu es Domine qui restitues	an	PM 329 VP 274 LU 1845	G	5	2	0	-2	0	2	0	-2	G
	Tu es inquit Petrus Quodcumque	rev	WA 280										
	Tu es magister meus Oravit sanctus Andreas	rev	LA 501 WA 235										
8	Tu es pastor ovium ... tradidit	re	PM 160 *AM 1198 LR 363 LA 416 *WA 279	G	2	0	-3	0	-2	0	2	-2	G
2	Tu es pastor ovium ... tradidit	inv	LR 431 LA 412 WA 325	C	2	4	5	2	0	2	5	4	D
1	Tu es pastor ovium ... traditae	an	AM 792 823 933 943 988 PM 126 *AR 598 750 798 *LU 1330 1516 LA 411 *WA 281 328	D	-2	3	5	3	5	7	10	7	D
1	Tu es Petrus	of	GR 411 OTT 187 LU 1333 SYG 53	F	-3	-5	-3	0	4	2	4	0	D
6	Tu es Petrus	co	GR 412 534 [2^4] LU 1122^6 1521 *SYG 54 GB 207 GS 183 *189	F	-3	0	2	0	-5	-3	-5	-3	F
7	Tu es Petrus	an	AR 752 800 141* LU 1515 1578 AM 935 990 VP 17 13* WA 280 *LA 420	d	-3	0	2	0	-3	-2	-3	-7	G
2	Tu es Petrus	tr	GR 409 LU 1332 SYG 53 GS 182	D	-2	0	-2	-5	-2	0	-2	0	D
	Tu es Petrus	alv	GB 202^v	D	-2	0	2	3	5	7	5	3	
7	Tu es Petrus	int	SYG 53	G	2	-2	2	0	2	5	7	5	G
	Tu es Petrus	alv	GR 409 534 LU 1122^3 1520 SYG 203	F	2	4	2	0	2	0	-3	-1	
7	Tu es Petrus	re	LR 360 LA 414 WA 278	G	7	9	7	9	5	4	5	7	G

	Tu es qui restitues Notas mihi fecisti	rev	LA 82 WA 60										
8	Tu es qui venturus es an alium	an	AR 227 LU 333 AM 199 *WA 16 *LA 11	F	2	4	2	7	6	4	7	6	G
7	Tu es qui venturus es Domine	an	AR 229 LU 1083 *AM 201 *WA 13 *LA 12	d	-3	0	2	0	-2	0	-2	-7	G
	Tu es sacerdos in aeternum	sr	AR [64] LU 1175										
	Tu es sacerdos in aeternum	alv	GR [4][33] LU 1183 1495^B *SYG 38 *GB 272^V	F	2	4	6	7	4	2	6	2	
	Tu es Simon Bar Jona	alv	GS 189 SYG 203	D	2	0	-2	2	3	5	3	2	
	Tu es vas electionis Sancte Paule	rev	VP 185										
8	Tu es vas electionis	an	WA 264 330 *LA 423	a	-4	-2	0	-2	0	-2	0	3	G
1	Tu es vas electionis	re	PM 162 *LA 429 *WA 263	C	2	5	2	0	2	5	4	7	D
	Tu es vas electionis	alv	SYG 205	D	3	0	3	7	10	7	5	9	
2	Tu es vas electionis	tr	GR 420 LU 1346 *SYG 44 *GS 178	A	3	5	2	3	5	0	-2	0	D
	Tu exsurgens Domine misereberis	sr	LA 16 WA 8										
	Tu exsurgens Domine misereberis Domine exaudi	trv	GR 191 OHS 324 LU 619 GS 92 GB 114 *SYG 127	F	2	4	2	4	2	0	2	0	
	Tu exsurgens misereberis Domine exaudi	ofv	OTT 53 *SYG 128	G	2	0	-2	0	-2	0	2	5	
	Tu gloria Jerusalem ... Bethlehem Salve virginale	rev	PM 265 VP 41	D	7	5	7	8	7	5	3	2	
8	Tu gloria Jerusalem ... nostri	an	AR 586 631 LU 1320 1381 AM 764	c	-1	0	-3	-5	-7	-5	-3	-5	G
	Tu gloria Jerusalem ... nostri	alv	GR 403	G	2	4	5	7	9	7	5	7	
8	Tu gloria Jerusalem ... nostri	tr	GR 441 LU 1378	D	3	5	2	3	5	0	-2	0	G
	Tu gloria Jerusalem ... nostri Benedicta es	grv	GR 401 LU 1317	F	4	7	6	4	7	6	2	4	
7	Tu gloria Jerusalem ... tui	an	AR 784	b	1	3	1	0	1	-2	-4	0	G
	Tu humiliasti sicut vulneratum Tui sunt caeli	ofv	OTT 18 GB 19^V *SYG 20	F	4	7	4	6	7	2	4	6	
	Tu locutus es Minor sum	rev	WA 92										
5	Tu mandasti mandata tua	co	GR 377 LU 1062 SYG 98 *GB 87 *GS 60 164	c	-3	0	2	0	-3	-5	-3	-2	F
7	Tu natale solum protege	hy	AR 615	G	4	5	7	9	7	5	7	0	G
1	Tu principatum tenes in choro	an	PM 32 *WA 35 *LA 40	D	-2	0	3	2	3	0	2	0	D
1	Tu principum leges attendis	an	WA 245	D	3	0	-2	3	5	7	9	7	D

	Tu puer propheta	sr	WA 332									
	Tu puer propheta ... praeibis ... Dominum	alv	GR 524 LU 1501 *GS 1, 188 GB 197^v *SYG 196	D	-2	0	2	3	5	7	5	3	
3	Tu puer propheta ... praeibis ... Dominum	an	AR 736 LU 1504 *AM 925 *WA 321 *LA 408	G	5	4	2	4	5	4	0	2	E
2	Tu puer propheta ... praeibis ... faciem	co	GR 525 LU 1502 *SYG 199 *GB 200^v GS m	D	3	5	7	5	7	3	0	3	D
1	Tu puer propheta ... praeibis ... faciem	re	LR 358	D	3	5	7	5	7	3	0	3	D
1	Tu quae in columbina	re	LR 300	D	-2	0	3	0	2	3	5	3	D
	Tu quae in puerili aetate Tu quae in columbina	rev	LR 300									
	Tu quidem gressus Scio Domine quia	rev	WA 174									
	Tu scis quae cogitant Congregatae sunt gentes	rev	LA 298 WA 181									
6	Tu solus altissimus	an	WA 68	G	2	0	-2	0	-2	0	-2	-3	F
1	Tu solus altissimus	an	LA 98	F	2	4	2	0	2	4	2	0	D
1	Tu solus peregrinus es et non	an	AR 471 AM 485 WA 132	C	2	9	10	9	7	9	7	5	D
1	Tu solus peregrinus in Jerusalem	an	LA 217	C	2	9	11	9	7	9	7	5	D
4	Tu trinitatis unitas	hy	ST 363	G	-3	0	-2	-3	-2	-5	-3	-2	E
8	Tu trinitatis unitas	hy	AR 520 LU 907	a	-2	-4	-7	-5	-4	-2	0	-2	G
8	Tu trinitatis unitas	hy	AM 537	G	2	0	-2	-5	-3	-2	0	2	G
3	Tu trinitatis unitas	hy	ST 214	D	2	3	5	3	5	3	2	3	E
3	Tu vincis in martyribus	hy	AM 636	E	1	3	1	0	-2	0	-2	-4	E
1	Tua est potentia	an	AR 551 LU 995 AM 589	D	-2	3	5	3	5	7	5	3	D
2	Tua est potentia	re	AM 1203 *VP 262 LA 295 *WA 180	C	2	4	2	5	4	5	2	4	D
2	Tua est potentia	an	LA 299	C	5	4	5	2	4	2	0	2	D
3	Tua est potentia	an	WA 180	D	5	7	5	3	5	7	10	9	E
1	Tua sunt haec Christe	an	WA 376	C	2	4	2	0	2	4	5	2	D
3	Tuam coronam adoramus	of	GR 15**	G	2	5	4	5	4	7	5	2	E
8	Tuam crucem adoramus ... exaltationem	an	LA 463	G	2	5	4	2	4	2	0	2	G
	Tuam crucem adoramus ... passionem Adoramus te Christe	rev	WA 369									
8	Tuam crucem adoramus ... passionem	co	SYG 130	F	2	0	2	0	2	4	0	-3	F
6	Tuam crucem adoramus ... passionem	re	WA 369	c	2	0	2	0	2	4	0	-3	c
8	Tuam crucem adoramus ... passionem	an	SYG 142	G	2	4	5	4	2	4	2	0	G

	Text		Source										
	Tuam crucem adoramus ... passionem Adoramus te	trv	GR [104]	D	3	2	3	5	7	5	7	5	
	Tuam crucem adoramus ... passionem	alv	SYG 173	F	4	2	-1	0	2	0	2	-3	
2	Tuam Deus deposcimus pietatem	an	WA 398	F	-1	-3	-5	-3	-1	0	2	0	D
	Tuam Deus deposcimus pietatem Erue Domine	ofv	OTT 177 SYG 236	C	2	4	5	7	9	7	9	5	
4	Tuam Domine excita potentiam	an	WA 8	G	2	5	7	5	7	9	7	5	a
6	Tuam ipsius animam	an	AR 673 LU 1422 AM 867	F	2	4	0	-1	-3	-5	0	2	F
4	Tui sunt caeli	of	GR 35 OTT 18 LU 410 *SYG 20 *GB 19^V *GS 15	F	-3	-1	-3	0	-1	0	2	0	E
7	Tulerunt Dominum meum	an	AR 451 OHS 811 LU 800 *AM 464 *WA 135 LA 221	b	3	0	3	5	3	5	6	5	G
8	Tulerunt Dominum meum	re	OHS 802 LR 90 LA 211 WA 131	D	3	5	7	5	7	5	7	5	G
4	Tulerunt Jesum parentes ejus	of	GR 63 LU 472	C	2	5	4	5	7	2	7	5	E
1	Tulerunt lapides Judaei	an	AR 414 LU 574 AM 392 LA 172	D	-2	0	2	3	5	3	2	0	D
7	Tulerunt lapides ut jacerent	an	WA 107	G	4	5	7	9	7	9	5	2	G
8	Tulit ergo Dominus hominem	re	LA 109 *WA 72	F	2	0	-1	0	2	4	2	-1	G
4	Tulit ergo paralyticus	an	AR 569 LU 1059 AM 610 *LA 318	C	2	4	5	4	2	4	2	4	E
	Tum rex tum proceres Orbata pontifice	rev	WA 284	c	-1	-5	-1	-3	0	2	0	-3	
	Tunc acceptabis sacrificium Elegit Dominus	rev	LA 534										
7	Tunc acceptabis sacrificium	an	AR 396 AM 371 WA 103 *LA 161	G	4	5	7	5	9	7	4	7	G
7	Tunc ad locum dilectae	an	LR 325 *LA 370	b	1	3	1	5	3	5	3	1	G
	Tunc aperientur oculi Confortamini et jam	ofv	OTT 9 *GB 7 *SYG 8	F	-3	0	-1	0	2	4	2	-1	
2	Tunc assumpsit eum diabolus	an	AR 370 LU 531 *AM 343 WA 89 LA 133	F	-1	0	-3	-1	-3	-5	-3	0	D
6	Tunc in viscera ejus	an	WA 247	F	-3	-1	-3	-5	-3	0	2	0	F
7	Tunc invocabis et Dominus	an	AR 363 LU 530 AM 340 *WA 84	G	4	5	7	5	9	7	4	7	G
1	Tunc praecepit eos	an	WA 309 *LA 397	D	7	8	7	5	7	5	3	2	D
	Tunc praecinxit se	an	SYG 132										
8	Tunc sanctus Andreas	an	WA 234	c	-1	-3	0	-1	-5	-3	-5	-7	G
	Tunc surrexerunt omnes virgines Venite et accendite	anv	SYG 47										
1	Tunc surrexerunt omnes virgines	an	PM 237 WA 434 LA 546	D	-2	0	3	2	0	-2	3	5	D

1 Tunc Valerianus in conspectu	an	WA 352	D	-2	0	2	3	5	7	10	9	D
8 Tunc Valerianus perrexit	an	LA 490 *WA 407	G	2	4	5	2	0	-2	0	2	G
4 Turba multa quae convenerat	an	AR 423 GR 175 LU 585 *AM 401 PM 58 OHS 73 98 *WA 113 *LA 182	G	-2	0	-2	-3	-2	0	-2	0	E
6 Ubi caritas et amor	an	GR 204 OHS 451 LU 675	F	2	4	2	4	5	4	2	4	F
Ubi collisi sunt currus / Nova bella elegit	grv	GR 40**	F	4	7	9	7	6	4	7	6	
4 Ubi duo vel tres congregati	an	AR 392 LU 1090 AM 367 *WA 99 *LA 155	G	2	5	9	7	5	7	9	7	a
7 Ubi est Abel frater tuus	re	LA 112 WA 74	G	2	0	2	0	2	5	4	5	G
7 Ubi est caritas et dilectio	an	WA 214 SYG 131	G	4	5	7	9	7	9	10	9	G
1 Ubi est thesaurus tuus	an	WA 84	C	2	5	7	9	7	9	7	4	D
7 Ubi fratres in unum	an	SYG 131	G	2	5	9	7	5	7	9	7	G
1 Ubi sunt misericordiae tuae	an	GB 160	F	-1	0	-1	0	4	2	4	6	D
5 Ultimo festivitatis die	co	GR 291 LU 861 *SYG 182 GB 184^v *GS L	a	-2	0	-2	-5	-7	-2	0	3	F
Ululate pastores et clamate / Plange quasi	rev	WA 125										
Umbra futurorum praesens / Magne Deus	rev	WA 318	c	2	4	5	4	2	0	2	4	
Una ergo sabbatorum / Surgens Jesus	rev	OHS 812 LR 92 LA 210 WA 133										
Una fides unum baptisma / Beati martyres	rev	LA 410 WA 324										
7 Una hora non potuistis	re	OHS 397 LU 650 LA 192 *WA 119	d	-3	0	-2	0	2	-2	-3	-7	G
8 Una igitur pater	an	WA 159	G	2	0	-2	-3	-2	0	2	5	G
7 Unam petii a Domino ... omnibus	co	GR 334 LU 1005 *SYG 242 GB 249^v GS 146	d	-3	0	2	0	2	0	-2	-5	G
5 Unam petii a Domino ... omnibus	gr	GR 60 1** LU 471	F	2	0	2	4	2	4	2	0	F

#	Text		Sources										
5	Unam petii a Domino ... ut videam	gr	GR 92 *SYG 68 GB 64 GS 33	F	2	0	2	4	2	4	2	0	F
5	Unam quam petiit virgo	re	PM 266	a	-2	-4	0	3	5	7	5	3	F
6	Unde huic sapientia	co	LU 1444	F	-1	0	-3	-1	-3	-5	0	2	F
1	Unde veniet auxilium	an	LA 96	a	-2	0	-2	-5	-4	-2	-4	-5	D
7	Undecim discipuli in Galilaea	an	AR 451 AM 464 OHS 815 WA 135 LA 222	d	-2	-3	-2	0	2	0	-2	-3	G
1	Unguentum effusum nomen	an	WA 435 *LA 541	D	-2	3	5	3	5	7	9	7	D
4	Unguentum in capite	co	SYG 233	D	-2	3	5	3	7	5	7	5	E
	Universae angelorum virtutes	alv	GB 169	G	-2	2	5	4	2	0	-2	0	
1	Universi qui te exspectant	gr	GR 2 LU 320 SYG 1 GB 1 GS B 1	C	2	5	7	5	2	4	0	-3	D
8	Unum in tribus colimus	hy	ST 391	G	2	0	2	0	-2	0	2	5	G
	Unum locutus sum / Auditu auris	rev	WA 175										
4	Unum opus feci	an	WA 104	G	2	5	7	5	7	9	7	5	a
	Unumquodque duabus alis / Species firmamenti	rev	WA 375										
	Unus autem ex illis Caiphas / Collegerunt pontifices	rev	GR 166 GS 84	C	2	0	2	4	5	7	4	2	
1	Unus autem ex illis ut vidit	an	AR 565 LU 1036 AM 604 *WA 189 *LA 316	C	2	5	4	0	4	2	0	5	D
	Unus autem ex ipsis Caiphas / Collegerunt pontifices	anv	WA 210 *SYG 117 *GB 105^v	F	2	0	2	5	7	4	2	0	
8	Unus est Dominus	re	WA 161	G	2	0	-2	2	5	2	0	4	G
2	Unus est enim magister	an	AR 382 LU 1086 AM 356 *WA 94 *LA 144	F	-1	-5	-1	-3	-5	0	2	0	D
8	Unus ex discipulis meis	re	OHS 391 LU 645 *LA 191 *WA 118	G	2	0	2	0	2	4	5	4	G
1	Unus ex duobus qui secuti	an	AR 579 LU 1304 AM 754 *WA 232 *LA 502	D	-2	3	5	3	7	5	3	5	D
	Unus ex tribus / Sanctus Gamaliel	rev	WA 344										
7	Unus militum lancea	co	GR 326 [116] LU 975	d	-3	0	2	0	-3	-2	-5	-7	G
1	Unus militum lancea	an	AR 538^6 LU 977 AM 565	D	2	3	5	7	5	2	5	7	D
7	Unus panis et unum corpus	co	GR [134]	d	-3	0	2	0	2	0	-2	-5	G
1	Unus panis et unum corpus	re	AR 113* LR 129 VP 16	D	-2	0	3	0	2	0	-2	0	D
	Unus spiritus et una fides / Viri sancti gloriosum	rev	PM 221 LR 178 LA 514 WA 420										

	Incipit		Sources										
	Unusquisque propriam mercedem Ego plantavi	anv	LA 430 WA 266										
8	Unxerunt Salomonem Sadoc	an	AR 541 LU 987 AM 577	G	2	0	-2	0	2	5	4	2	G
2	Urbis cives Andegavae	hy	ST 149	G	2	4	0	2	5	7	5	4	a
2	Urbs beata Jerusalem	hy	ST 423	c	-3	-1	0	-3	-5	-3	-1	0	a
4	Urbs beata Jerusalem	hy	ST 106	F	-3	0	-3	-5	-3	-1	0	-1	E
4	Urbs beata Jerusalem	hy	ST 240	E	-2	1	-2	-4	-2	0	-2	0	E
1	Urbs beata Jerusalem	hy	ST 59	D	2	-2	2	5	2	5	7	9	D
1	Urbs beata Jerusalem	hy	ST 106	D	7	5	3	5	7	0	3	7	D
7	Urbs fortitudinis nostrae	an	AR 224 LU 332 AM 195 WA 12 LA 11	G	7	10	7	5	7	3	7	5	G
4	Urbs Jerusalem beata	hy	LR 231 AM 694	E	-2	1	-2	-4	-2	1	-2	0	E
2	Usque modo non petistis	an	AR 483 LU 830 *AM 499 *WA 146 *LA 231 242	C	2	4	5	7	9	7	4	5	D
	Usque modo non petistis	alv	SYG 168 *GS 130	C	4	5	4	2	0	2	4	0	
	Usquequo Domine oblivisceris Cantabo Domino	cov	SYC 240										
	Usquequo Domine oblivisceris Domine in tua misericordia	intv	GR 310 GS 141 GB 247 SYG 238										
	Usquequo Domine oblivisceris Illumina oculos	intv	GR [147]										
	Usquequo Domine oblivisceris Illumina oculos	ofv	OTT 87 *GB 81 SYG 92	E	-2	3	5	8	7	8	5	3	
4	Usquequo exaltabitur inimicus	re	LA 167 *WA 114	F	-3	0	-1	0	2	0	-1	0	E
	Ut a peccatis cunctis O magni meriti	rev	WA 335										
	Ut ad videndam faciem Perfecto corde	rev	WA 336	b	-2	-4	-2	0	3	5	3	1	
	Ut adimpleretur quod dictum Surge et accipe	rev	LR 312										
	Ut annuntiem omnes Mihi autem adhaerere	rev	WA 68										
	Ut apud Christum Beatus Nicholaus	rev	WA 241	c	2	5	4	5	4	2	4	2	
3	Ut audivit salutationem	an	AR 771 LU 1541 *AM 954	E	-2	3	5	8	7	8	10	8	E
3	Ut autem sciatis	an	WA 157	G	5	4	2	0	2	5	4	5	E
	Ut caelestis regni Miles Christi	rev	WA 391	b	-2	-4	-2	0	1	3	1	0	
4	Ut cognoscamus Domine	an	AR 239 AM 214 *WA 17 *LA 23	a	-2	0	3	5	7	5	3	5	
	Ut confisus fiducia Sacerdos Dei Lucianus	rev	WA 344										

Ut credentibus timorem Rogavi Dominum	rev	LA 321 WA 246										
Ut digni efficiamur Sancte Paule apostole	anv	LA 430 WA 266										
Ut digni efficiamur Sancte Paule apostole	rev	LA 428 WA 266										
Ut discam mandata Servus tuus	rev	LA 143 WA 94	G	2	0	2	0	-2	0	2	5	
Ut ditem diligentes Meum est consilium	trv	GR 26**	G	-5	0	2	5	4	5	7	0	
Ut fugiant a facie arcus Commovisti	trv	GR 78 LU 507 GS 27 GB 58 SYG 60	F	2	7	9	11	7	2	7	9	
Ut in nomine Jesu omne Christus pro nobis	intv	SYG 128										
Ut misericors fieret Pontifex sacerdos	grv	GR [118]	F	4	2	7	9	7	9	7	11	
1 Ut non delinquam	an	WA 64 LA 88	a	-2	0	-2	-5	-4	-2	-4	-5	D
8 Ut nox tenebris obsita	hy	ST 384	G	-2	-3	-2	0	2	0	-2	0	G
Ut probetis potiora ut sitis Testis mihi	grv	GR 544 LU 1544	G	5	7	5	7	4	5	7	2	
Ut profiteretur cum Maria Ascendit Joseph	rev	LR 311										
1 Ut queant laxis resonare fibris	hy	ST 295	a	-2	0	-2	-4	-7	-2	-4	-2	D
2 Ut queant laxis resonare fibris	hy	ST 393	D	-2	0	2	3	0	3	0	-2	D
2 Ut queant laxis resonare fibris	hy	ST 94	D	-2	0	3	2	0	2	0	-2	D
4 Ut queant laxis resonare fibris	hy	ST 233, 259, 295	E	-2	0	3	5	3	5	3	1	E
4 Ut queant laxis resonare fibris	hy	ST 158	D	2	-2	0	2	3	5	3	5	E
4 Ut queant laxis resonare fibris	hy	ST 352	C	2	4	7	9	7	2	7	5	E
2 Ut queant laxis resonare fibris	hy	AR 733 LU 1504 AM 922	C	2	5	2	4	2	0	2	4	D
2 Ut queant laxis resonare fibris	hy	ST 474	C	2	5	2	5	2	0	2	4	D
4 Ut queant laxis resonare fibris	hy	ST 475	C	4	2	0	2	0	2	4	7	E
4 Ut queant laxis resonare fibris	hy	ST 429	G	4	5	7	9	7	5	4	2	b
Ut qui Deus repulisti in finem Respice Domine	intv	GR 354 LU 1032 GS 155 GB 254 SYG 247										
Ut quid Domine recessisti	an	OHS 59 (nm)										
Ut quid Domine recessisti Tibi Domine derelictus	grv	GR 149 LU 566 *GS 70 *GB 96 SYG 108	G	2	5	4	5	7	4	5	4	
Ut quid repulisti	see	Ut quid Deus repulisti										
Ut sciat omnis terra Praevaluit David	rev	LA 269 WA 165										

	Ut testimonium perhiberet	grv	GR 522 GS 1 188 GB 196ᵛ SYG 195	F	4	2	7	9	7	9	7	11	
2	Ut tibi clarum resonemus hymnum	hy	ST 56	a	-2	0	-2	-4	0	-4	0	3	a
	Ut tuo nos interventu Sancta Maria clemens	rev	WA 357	a	3	5	0	-4	-2	0	-2	0	
	Ut valeant famuli Adjuva sancte tuos	grv	SYG 230	F	4	2	7	9	7	9	7	4	
7	Ut videam voluntatem Domini	an	WA 318	G	4	5	7	9	10	9	5	9	G
	Ut videam voluptatem Domini et visitem Unam petii	grv	GR 1** GB 64 SYG 68 GS 33	F	4	7	9	7	9	7	9	4	
	Ut videam voluptatem Domini et protegar Unam petii	grv	GR 92 GS 33	F	4	7	9	7	9	7	9	4	
	Ut vidit beatus Sebastianus Clarissimis viris	rev	LA 327										
8	Ut vidit beatus Sebastianus	an	LA 323	G	-5	-2	0	2	0	2	0	-2	G
	Ut vitium virtus operiret Ad nutum Domini	rev	AR 130* PM 187 *WA 365	E	1	3	1	-2	3	1	0	3	
4	Utinam appenderentur peccata	re	LA 283 WA 172	F	-3	0	-1	0	2	0	-1	0	E
	Utinam appenderentur peccata Vir erat	ofv	OTT 122 SYG 256 GB 262	c	2	0	-1	0	2	0	2	0	
	Utinam hodie vocem Domini	inv	OHS 55 (nm)										
	Utriusque gloria Regis iram	rev	WA 251										
2	Uxor tua sicut vitis	gr	GR [122] LU 1289	G	4	2	5	2	4	5	2	0	a

---

1	Vadam ad montem myrrhae	an	AR 674 LU 1422	D	7	10	12	10	9	7	5	7	D
1	Vadam ad patrem meum	an	AR 386 LU 1088 AM 360 *WA 95 LA 146	D	7	10	7	5	7	5	2	3	D
1	Vade Anania et quaere	re	LA 344 *WA 264	C	2	5	2	0	5	7	9	7	D
7	Vade Anania et quaere	an	AR 608 LU 1343 AM 791 WA 263	G	4	5	7	5	9	7	9	7	G
4	Vade jam et noli peccare	an	WA 90	c	2	0	2	4	2	0	2	-3	a
3	Vade Luciane et dic	re	WA 342	G	2	5	4	2	4	0	2	5	E
1	Vade Satana non temptabis	an	WA 88 LA 133	F	2	4	2	0	2	0	2	4	D
7	Vadis propitiator ad immolandum	re	PM 188 *WA 122	G	2	0	4	5	7	5	4	7	G

	Text		Sources										
1	Vado ad eum ... et nemo	an	AR 478 LU 825 AM 493 LA 241	D	7	10	7	5	3	5	7	3	D
1 2	Vado ad eum ... sed quia	an	AR 480 LU 829 AM 495 *WA 145 *LA 241	F	-1	-3	-1	-3	-5	-3	0	-1	D
	Vado ad eum ... sed quia	alv	GS 130 *SYG 167	C	2	4	5	2	0	7	5	4	
3	Vado parare vobis locum	an	PM 86 WA 150 307	G	2	5	4	0	2	0	2	0	E
1	Vado parare vobis locum	an	LA 254	D	7	10	7	5	7	5	3	5	D
2	Vae nobis quia peccavimus	an	SYG 139	D	2	0	-5	-2	-3	-5	-7	0	D
	Valde eam nos oportet Super salutem	rev	WA 357										
	Valde honorandus est	sr	WA 42										
	Valde honorandus est Iste est Joannes	rev	LA 53 WA 41										
8	Valde honorandus est	an	AR 279 LU 421 *AM 255	G	-5	-3	-2	0	2	0	2	5	G
	Valde honorandus est	alv	SYG 24	C	2	4	2	4	2	0	4	7	
4	Valde honorandus est	an	LA 52	D	2	5	9	7	5	7	9	5	E
2	Valde honorandus est	re	LA 49 WA 39	A	5	3	5	7	5	7	5	7	D
1	Valde mane die	re	WA 338	D	-2	0	2	3	0	2	0	-2	D
8	Valde mirabilis es o Maria	co	GR 47**	G	2	0	-2	0	2	4	5	0	G
7	Valerianus in cubiculo	an	AR 924 LU 1756 AM 1140 WA 408 LA 493	G	4	5	7	5	9	7	9	5	G
1	Valerius igitur episcopus	re	WA 257	D	-2	0	3	0	2	0	-2	0	D
3	Valerius igitur episcopus	an	WA 256	E	-2	3	5	3	5	8	7	8	E
	Vectus amne spatio Puer trimus	rev	WA 250										
	Vehementer mundaverunt Facto diluvio	rev	WA 76										
	Velociter exaudi me Eripe me	ofv	OTT 51	a	-2	0	3	0	-2	0	-2	0	
8	Velociter exaudi me ... quia	re	LA 104	F	2	4	7	9	7	6	7	9	G
2	Velum templi scissum est	re	OHS 488 LU 695 LA 199 WA 123	D	-2	0	-2	-5	-2	0	3	2	D
4	Venerandae virginis	hy	ST 309	E	1	3	1	0	-2	3	1	0	E
1	Venerunt ad monumentum	an	AR 467 AM 480	D	-2	3	5	3	7	9	10	9	D
	Venerunt de tribulatione	alv	GR 108**	C	2	4	5	7	9	7	12	11	
7	Venerunt pastores festinantes	an	LR 303	G	7	9	5	9	10	9	7	9	G
	Venerunt quoque Aegypti Salus quoque	rev	WA 98										
	Veni ad liberandum nos	sr	AR 30 LU 238 AM 184 LA 6 WA 7										

8 Veni creator spiritus	hy	AR 500 73* GR 150* PM 89 ST 38 94 LU 885 AM 518 1254	G	2	0	-2	0	2	0	5	7	G
8 Veni creator spiritus	hy	ST 232 260 294 390 420	G	2	0	-2	0	2	5	7	5	G
1 Veni creator spiritus	hy	ST 349	D	3	2	0	-2	0	-2	0	3	D
Veni de Libano sponsa mea Electa mea	rev	LR 263										
3 Veni de Libano sponsa mea	int	GR 613 LU 1668	G	5	2	5	4	2	0	5	2	E
7 Veni de Libano sponsa mea	an	PM 234	G	5	4	2	4	2	0	4	5	G
1 Veni desiderator bone	an	PM 175 *WA 351	C	2	5	7	5	4	2	0	2	D
5 Veni dilecte mi	an	WA 163	F	4	5	7	5	7	4	2	7	F
Veni Domine et noli Festina ne tardaveris	rev	LA 10 WA 15										
Veni Domine et noli	alv	GR 22 LU 354 *SYG 7 *GB 11 *GS 12	C	2	4	5	7	5	7	9	10	
7 Veni Domine et noli ... et revoca	re	LA 14 *WA 15	c	-3	0	2	0	-2	0	-2	0	G
4 Veni Domine et noli ... Israel	an	AR 243 AM 218 WA 20 *LA 26	G	2	5	7	5	7	9	7	5	a
7 Veni Domine visitare	an	AR 223 LU 327 AM 195 WA 9 LA 7	G	2	5	7	5	7	9	10	12	G
Veni Domine visitare	alv	SYG 13	D	7	5	7	9	7	5	3	2	
1 Veni electa mea	an	AR [88] [98] LU 1211 1233 AM 679 687	D	-2	3	5	3	7	5	7	5	D
Veni electa mea ... quia Veni sponsa	rev	PM 233 LR 215 LA 542										
Veni electa mea ... quia	alv	GS 227	D	3	2	5	3	2	3	0	3	
2 Veni electa mea ... quia	re	PM 237 LR 216 *LA 446 *WA 355	A	3	5	8	5	3	5	8	3	D
8 Veni et libera nos	an	WA 8	F	2	4	7	6	7	4	2	0	G
2 Veni et ostende nobis	int	GR 13 LU 343 *SYG 10 *GB 8v *GS 7	A	3	5	7	5	3	5	7	8	D
1 Veni hodie ad fontem	re	LA 122 *WA 83	a	-2	0	2	3	5	3	2	0	D
7 8 Veni in hortum meum soror mea	an	PM 275 WA 355 *LA 458	G	7	5	4	5	7	5	2	0	G
8 Veni redemptor gentium	hy	ST 81	G	-2	-3	-5	-2	2	0	-2	0	G
2 Veni redemptor gentium	hy	ST 273	D	-2	0	3	2	0	2	3	5	D
2 Veni redemptor gentium	hy	ST 217	D	-2	0	3	2	0	3	5	3	D
3 Veni redemptor gentium	hy	ST 177	E	1	0	-2	3	5	8	7	8	E
7 Veni redemptor gentium	hy	ST 365	G	2	0	-2	0	-2	2	5	7	G

	Incipit		Source										
7	Veni redemptor gentium	hy	ST 409	F	2	4	7	4	2	6	4	2	G
8	Veni redemptor gentium	hy	ST 80	G	2	5	2	0	-2	-3	-5	-2	G
2	Veni redemptor gentium	hy	ST 328	C	2	5	2	5	4	5	7	4	D
8	Veni sancte spiritus reple	an	AR 72* LU 1837 *PM 332 VP 158 *WA 157 LA 262	G	-3	-2	-5	-2	2	0	-2	0	G
	Veni sancte spiritus reple Emitte spiritum	trv	GR [93] LU 1279	F	2	4	2	4	5	2	0	4	
	Veni sancte spiritus reple	alv	GR 293 [92] LU 880 GB 187 *GS 138 234	C	2	4	5	4	2	0	2	4	
1	Veni spiritus alme	an	WA 153	D	-2	3	2	0	5	3	2	0	D
7	Veni sponsa Christi accipe coronam	an	AR 577[20] [96] *LR 219 LU 262[8] 1214 AM 682 745 WA 434	d	-3	0	2	0	-3	-2	-3	-7	G
8	Veni sponsa Christi accipe coronam	tr	GR [52] LU 1217	G	-2	-5	-3	-7	-5	-2	0	2	G
	Veni sponsa Christi accipe coronam	alv	GB 273[V]	c	-1	2	0	-1	2	0	-3	0	
	Veni sponsa Christi accipe coronam	alv	SYG 208	D	2	5	7	3	2	5	2	3	
8	Veni sponsa Christi accipe coronam	an	AR 577[20] [86] LU 262[8] 1209 *AM 678 744 LA 545	G	5	2	0	-2	0	2	0	4	G
	Veni sponsa Christi accipe coronam	alv	GB 272[V]	G	5	2	0	2	4	2	0	5	
3	Veni sponsa Christi accipe coronam	re	PM 233 LR 215 *LA 542	G	5	2	4	5	4	2	0	2	E
	Veni sponsa Christi accipe coronam	alv	SYG 208	D	7	10	7	5	7	5	3	2	
	Veniant super me miserationes Levabo oculos	ofv	OTT 34 GB 67[V] SYG 76	G	-2	0	-7	-5	-2	0	2	0	
6	Veniat dilectus meus	an	WA 354 *LA 456	c	2	0	2	5	2	4	2	0	c
1	Veniens a Libano	re	PM 235 LA 229 *WA 140	E	-2	0	3	5	3	5	8	5	D
	Veniens veniet Dominus Ecce veniet Dominus princeps	rev	LA 15										
8	Veniens vir splendidissimus	of	GB 166[V] *SYG 174	G	-2	2	0	2	0	-2	2	0	G
8	Venient ad te	an	AR 334 AM 300 LR 78 *LA 76 *WA 57	G	-2	-5	-3	-2	0	2	4	0	G
2	Veniente Domino Jesu	an	SYG 119	A	3	5	8	5	3	5	3	5	D
	Venientes autem venient Fundata est domus	rev	PM 239 LR 234										
	Venientes autem venient Non eris inter virgines	rev	WA 432										
	Venientes autem venient Qui seminant	trv	GR [24] LU 1164 GS 217 *GB 50 *SYG 51	G	2	5	4	2	5	2	0	2	
1	Veniet dies Domini	an	WA 9	c	2	4	2	4	2	0	-1	0	a

	Incipit		Sources										
4	Veniet Dominus cum potestate	an	WA 20	b	-4	-2	1	3	1	3	5	3	a
1	Veniet Dominus et non tardabit	an	AR 231 LU 338 AM 204 WA 16 LA 16	a	-2	0	-2	-5	-4	-2	0	-4	D
8	Veniet fortior me	an	AR 221 AM 192 WA 9 LA 7	c	-1	0	2	0	-1	0	2	0	G
8	Veniet nobis salus a Domino	re	LA 27	F	2	4	2	4	6	4	2	4	G
3	Venit ad Petrum	an	SYG 134 *GS 97	E	3	5	8	3	5	3	1	3	E
	Venit autem ad Simonem / Coena facta sciens	anv	SYG 133	C	2	4	2	4	5	4	5	4	
1	Venit enim princeps mundi	an	LA 266	D	-2	0	2	0	3	0	-2	0	D
	Venit ergo ad Simonem Petrum / Domine tu mihi	anv	GR 201 OHS 448										
1	Venit lumen tuum	an	AR 312 LU 463 *AM 290 WA 56 *LA 73	F	2	4	2	4	2	0	2	0	D
8	Venit lumen tuum	re	LR 80	F	2	4	2	4	2	4	2	4	G
7	Venit Maria Magdalene	an	SYG 146	c	-1	0	2	-3	-5	-7	-3	-5	G
7	Venit Maria nuntians	an	WA 135 *LA 221 233	G	4	5	7	9	5	7	5	4	G
8	Venit Michael archangelus	re	LA 468 *WA 381	F	2	4	2	4	2	4	2	4	G
5	Venit sponsus et virgines	co	GR 106**	c	-3	0	2	4	2	0	-1	2	F
	Venite ad me et ego dabo / Fecit me Dominus	rev	LR 306										
4	Venite ad me omnes	an	AR 538[7] LU 977 *AM 566	F	-1	-3	-1	0	2	-1	2	4	E
	Venite ad me omnes	alv	GR 648 [114] LU 973 1726 *SYG 218	G	2	0	5	7	5	2	4	2	
	Venite ad me sancti mei	alv	SYG 207	G	-2	0	2	0	2	0	2	0	
2	Venite adoremus Deum et procidamus	int	GR 371 LU 1052 *SYG 252 GS 170 GB 258	c	2	-5	-3	-7	-5	-3	0	2	a
4	Venite adoremus et procidamus	inv	WA 90	F	-3	0	-1	0	2	0	-1	0	E
	Venite adoremus eum / Dies sanctificatus	rev	LR 73 LA 70 WA 55										
8	Venite adoremus eum	an	VP 92	G	5	4	0	4	5	2	0	2	G
4	Venite adoremus regem confessorum	inv	WA 424	C	2	5	2	4	5	4	2	0	E
4	Venite adoremus regem regum	inv	LR 373 LA 442 *WA 354	C	2	4	5	4	2	4	5	7	E
	Venite ascendamus ... et ad domum / Docebit nos	rev	LA 15 WA 10										
8	Venite ascendamus ... et videte	an	AM 1049 *AR 845	a	-4	-2	-4	0	3	2	0	3	G
6	Venite audite et narrabo	int	GR 398	D	3	0	5	8	7	5	3		F
	Venite benedicti patris / Sancti mei ... carne	rev	LR 187										

	Incipit	Type	Sources										
	Venite benedicti patris Sancti mei ... isto	rev	LA 517 WA 429										
	Venite benedicti Patris ... cum gaudio	alv	GB 267^V	G	2	0	-2	0	2	4	2	4	
8	Venite benedicti patris ... quod	tr	SYG 75	G	2	0	2	4	2	0	2	0	G
7	Venite benedicti patris ... quod	an	AR 373 *AM 346 *WA 89 *LA 134	G	5	2	4	5	7	5	7	9	G
7	Venite benedicti Patris ... quod	int	GR 250 OHS 795 LU 792 *SYG 157 *GB 135 GS 120	G	5	7	9	7	5	4	5	7	G
8	Venite comedite panem meum	an	AR 3 (sup2)	G	2	-2	0	2	5	4	0	4	G
	Venite comedite panem meum Homo quidam	rev	AR 112* PM 105 LR 419 VP 15 AM 1189	F	2	4	5	2	0	2	4	5	
	Venite comedite panem meum Ab ortu solis	trv	GR [97] LU 1282	D	3	0	3	7	3	5	3	5	
	Venite comedite panem meum	alv	GR 627	D	7	10	7	5	7	5	3	2	
1	Venite et accendite	an	SYG 47	a	-2	0	3	5	3	2	0	-2	D
	Venite et videte Deum Vadis propitiator	rev	WA 122										
8	Venite et videte locum	an	WA 138 LA 223	G	5	4	0	4	5	2	0	2	G
	Venite et videte opera Benedicite gentes	ofv	OTT 71 GB 93^V *SYG 105	C	2	9	10	9	12	9	7	5	
4	Venite exsultemus Domino	inv	LA 87	E	-2	0	1	0	1	-2	0	-2	E
6	Venite exsultemus Domino	inv	WA 63	F	2	0	2	4	2	0	2	4	F
	Venite exsultemus Domino jubilemus Venite adoremus	intv	GR 371 LU 1052 GS 170 GB 258										
7	Venite exsultemus Domino jubilemus	inv	LA 79	G	5	4	5	7	5	9	7	9	G
	Venite exsultemus Domino jubilemus	alv	GR 358 LU 1038 GS 154 GB 255 SYG 245	G	5	4	7	9	7	5	7	10	
1	Venite filii audite me	int	GR 589 LU 1615	a	-4	-2	0	-2	3	2	0	3	D
4	Venite filii audite me	of	GR 425 LU 1353^V 1623^E	C	2	5	4	5	7	2	7	5	E
5	Venite filii audite me	gr	GR 336 (39) LU 1010 *SYG 105 GB 93 GS 67 *148 168	D	3	5	7	5	7	3	5	3	F
	Venite filii audite me	alv	GB 250^V	G	5	4	5	7	9	7	9	7	
	Venite justi ad prandium	alv	SYG 44	d	-2	0	2	0	2	3	5	3	
7	Venite omnes exsultemus	an	WA 200	G	4	5	7	5	7	9	7	5	G
2	Venite populi ad collaudandum	inv	WA 262	D	-2	-5	-2	0	2	3	2	0	D
1	Venite populi ad sacrum	an	AR 99* *PM 105 *VP 14 *SYG 154	F	2	0	-1	0	2	4	2	-1	D
8	Venite post me dicit Dominus	an	LA 497	G	5	2	0	-2	0	2	0	4	G

#	Text		Refs										
1	Venite post me faciam vos fieri	re	WA 233	C	2	5	0	4	2	5	2	4	D
8	Venite post me faciam vos piscatores	co	GR 395 LU 1306 *SYG 231 GB 246^v *GS h	G	-5	0	-3	0	5	4	5	2	G
6	Venite venite venite filii	an	GS 94	F	-3	-5	0	-3	-5	0	2	4	F
2	Vera fides geniti	co	GS u	D	-2	0	3	2	0	-2	0	3	
8	Verax est pater	an	WA 159	c	-1	-3	-5	-3	-1	-3	-5	-3	G
	Verba mea auribus percipe Gloriabuntur in te	ofv	OTT 135	c	2	0	2	0	2	0	2	0	
	Verba mea auribus percipe Intende voci	ofv	OTT 83 GB 87^v *SYG 98	c	2	0	2	0	2	0	2	0	
	Verba mea auribus percipe	alv	GR 312 *SYG 239 *GS 141 *GB 247^v	C	2	5	4	5	7	5	2	5	
5	Verba mea auribus percipe	int	GR 136 SYG 99 GB 88^v GS 61	F	4	7	4	7	4	6	7	2	F
6	Verba quae locutus sum	an	LA 263	F	-1	2	4	0	-1	0	-3	-5	F
7	Verbera carnificum	re	LR 183 LA 516 *WA 421	G	5	4	5	7	4	5	7	5	G
	Verbo Domini caeli firmati	sr	AR 522 LU 913										
	Verbo Domini caeli firmati	alv	SYG 240	C	2	4	5	2	4	0	2	4	
	Verbo Domini caeli firmati	alv	GR 300 LU 893	C	2	4	5	7	5	4	5	7	
	Verbo Domini caeli firmati Beata gens	grv	GR 366 [91] LU 1048 GS 67 160 234 GB 93 SYG 105	D	7	10	7	5	7	5	3	7	
	Verbum caro factum est	sr	AR 269 LU 407										
6	Verbum caro factum est alleluia	an	WA 29 *LA 31	F	-1	2	4	0	-1	-3	-5	0	F
8	Verbum caro factum est ... cujus	re	WA 30	D	5	3	5	7	5	7	9	7	G
	Verbum caro factum est ... et habitavit	sr	AM 242 248 WA 32										
	Verbum caro factum est ... et vidimus	sr	LA 39										
8	Verbum caro factum est ... et vidimus	an	WA 37 *LA 39	G	-2	-5	-3	-2	0	2	0	2	G
8	Verbum caro factum est ... et vidimus	re	LR 67 LU 390 LA 34	D	5	3	5	7	5	7	9	7	G
8	Verbum caro factum est ... plenum	an	AR 323 LU 469	G	-2	-5	-3	-2	0	2	0	2	G
	Verbum frequens in ore Beatus Wulstanus	rev	WA 250										
	Verbum iniquum et dolosum Domine pater	rev	WA 169										
1	Verbum iniquum et dolosum	re	LA 278 WA 169	C	2	4	2	0	2	0	2	0	D
2	Verbum patris principium	hy	ST 370	D	2	0	-2	3	5	7	2	0	D
8	Verbum salutis omnium	hy	ST 365	D	-2	0	3	5	7	5	7	5	G
8	Verbum salutis omnium	hy	ST 409	G	2	5	4	2	0	4	2	0	G

2	Verbum supernum prodiens a patre	hy	ST 408	d	-7	-5	-2	0	2	0	2	-2	d
2	Verbum supernum prodiens a patre	hy	ST 70	E	-4	0	3	5	7	5	3	5	a
2	Verbum supernum prodiens a patre	hy	ST 170	G	-2	-5	-2	0	-2	3	5	3	G
2	Verbum supernum prodiens a patre	hy	ST 171	E	-2	0	3	5	7	5	3	5	a
8	Verbum supernum prodiens a patre	hy	ST 272	D	-2	0	3	5	7	5	7	3	G
8	Verbum supernum prodiens a patre	hy	ST 365	D	-2	0	3	5	7	5	7	5	G
2	Verbum supernum prodiens a patre	hy	ST 216	D	-2	0	3	5	8	5	8	3	G
2	Verbum supernum prodiens nec patris	hy	ST 10	E	-2	0	-2	-4	-2	0	1	3	D
3	Verbum supernum prodiens nec patris	hy	ST 344	E	1	0	-2	0	3	5	3	1	E
6	Verbum supernum prodiens nec patris	hy	ST 350	G	2	0	2	4	5	4	2	0	F
8	Verbum supernum prodiens nec patris	hy	AM 552	G	2	4	2	0	-2	2	0	2	G
8	Verbum supernum prodiens nec patris	hy	AR 531 111* PM 95 VP 12 11* LU 940 AM 552	G	2	5	4	2	0	-2	2	0	G
	Vere Dominus est in loco Dum exiret Jacob	rev	LA 138 WA 91										
7	Vere Dominus est in loco	re	WA 91	G	2	5	4	2	4	0	2	0	G
6	Vere felicem praesulem	re	WA 289	c	2	0	2	4	2	0	2	0	c
7	Vere gratia plena es	hy	ST 40	G	7	5	7	9	5	10	9	7	G
	Vere languores nostros Ecce vidimus	rev	OHS 381 LR 336 LU 637 LA 190 WA 118										
2	Vere languores nostros	tr	GR [108]	D	-2	0	-2	-5	-2	0	-2	0	D
	Vere mirabilis Deus [Laudemus Dominum]	rev	WA 391										
	Vere tu es rex	alv	GR 61 LU 472	G	2	-2	-3	-5	-3	-2	0	-2	
8	Veri adoratores adorabunt	an	LA 155 WA 100 (inc illeg)	G	2	0	4	2	5	4	0	4	G
7	Veriloquus vates	re	WA 294	G	2	0	-2	2	5	4	5	7	G
8	Veritas de terra	an	LU 380 *LR 60 *WA 29 *LA 33	c	-1	-3	-5	-1	-3	-5	-7	-3	G
2	Veritas mea et misericordia	of	GR [6] [44] OTT 148 LU 1203 SYG 38 GB 41^v GS 223	D	2	0	-2	0	3	0	3	0	D
6	Veritas mea et misericordia	co	GR 64** GS 223	F	2	0	4	2	0	2	0	2	F
	Versa est in luctum Adesto dolori	rev	WA 174										
2	Versa est in luctum	re	LA 286 *WA 174	C	2	4	2	5	4	5	7	2	D
2	Verso crucis vestigio	hy	ST 42	a	-2	3	2	0	7	5	3	2	a
	Verumtamen existimo omnia	alv	GR 474 LU 1428	C	2	4	2	5	7	5	4	2	

Title	Type	Sources										
Verumtamen justi confitebuntur Eripe me	trv	GR 208 OHS 534 LU 725 GS 99 GB 116^v SYG 137	C	2	5	7	2	5	7	5	4	
Verumtamen non sicut ego Pater si non potest	cov	GB 111										
8 Vespere autem sabbati	an	AR 442 GR 239 *AM 450 *WA 127 *LA 207 234	G	5	2	0	-2	0	2	0	4	G
7 Vespere sabbati quae lucescit	an	SYG 146	E	5	3	5	1	-2	0	1	0	G
8 Veste sancta utetur pontifex	co	GR [121]	F	2	4	2	0	2	4	2	4	G
8 Vestimentum tuum candidum	an	AR 586 LU 1320 AM 764	G	-2	2	5	4	0	2	0	-2	G
4 Vestitus erat veste	an	AR 759 LU 1537 AM 946	a	-2	0	3	5	3	5	7	5	a
5 Vestri capilli capitis	an	AR 577^{14} [44] LU 262^3 1161 AM 650 738 *WA 423	a	-4	0	3	1	0	1	3	5	F
7 Veterem hominem renovans	an	VP 95 *LA 78 *WA 58	G	7	5	4	7	9	7	5	7	G
1 Vexilla Christus inclyta	hy	AR 894^8 LU 1706	D	3	0	-2	3	5	7	5	10	D
1 Vexilla Christus inclyta	hy	AM 1094	D	7	5	7	10	9	7	5	7	D
1 Vexilla regis prodeunt fulget	hy	ST 227 257 286	F	2	4	2	0	2	4	2	0	D
2 Vexilla regis prodeunt fulget	hy	ST 417	F	2	4	5	4	0	2	4	2	D
1 Vexilla regis prodeunt fulget	hy	AR 405 697 GR 225 227 OHS 161 ST 34 90 188 384 LU 575 AM 383 897 1038	F	2	4	5	4	2	0	2	4	D
1 Vexilla regis prodeunt fulget	hy	ST 18	c	2	5	4	2	-3	2	0	-3	a
2 Via justorum recta	an	WA 420	D	3	0	-2	0	3	2	-2	0	D
Via recta	see	Via recto										
2 Via recto Oriente	re	LR 332 *LA 374	C	2	4	2	4	2	0	2	5	D
Viam iniquitatis Domine Benedictus ... in labiis	ofv	OTT 28 *GB 60 *SYG 62	C	7	9	7	5	4	5	4	5	
8 Viam mandatorum tuorum	of	GR 502 LU 1474	G	2	0	-2	0	5	4	5	7	G
Viam mandatorum tuorum Benedictus es ... in labiis	ofv	GB 60	a	7	2	3	2	3	2	3	2	
Viam veritatis elegi Confitebor tibi	ofv	OTT 44 GB 98 SYG 110	D	7	3	5	7	10	7	10	9	
Vias tuas Domine demonstra Ad te levavi	intv	GR 1 LU 318 GS A GB 1 SYG 1										
Vias tuas Domine notas Universi qui te	grv	GR 2 LU 320 GS B 1 GB 1 SYG 1	D	7	5	7	5	3	5	7	3	
Vicerunt draconem propter sanguinem	alv	GR 99**	G	2	0	-2	2	5	4	2	5	

	Victo senatu Vox tonitrui	rev	WA 41	b	-4	-2	-6	-7	-9	-4	-2	-6	
4	Victor Nabor Felix pii	hy	ST 10	F	-3	-1	-3	-5	-3	-1	2	4	E
	Victoriarum vivens sumpsit Virtutum pennis	cov	SYG 220										
	Victricem manum tuam Sancti tui Domine	rev	WA 421										
8	Victricem manum tuam	int	GR 252 OHS 805 LU 796 SYG 158 GB 137 *GS 121	G	4	7	5	2	5	0	4	2	G
8	Vide Domine afflictionem	an	AR 408 AM 388 WA 108 LA 171	a	-4	-2	0	-2	0	-2	-4	-2	G
7	Vide Domine et considera	an	AR 428 OHS 243 249 AM 407 WA 115 LA 186	b	1	3	5	3	5	3	1	0	G
	Vide humilitatem meam Alleluia: judica	rev	WA 144										
	Vide humilitatem meam In toto corde	rev	WA 144										
4	Vide humilitatem meam	an	WA 64	F	-1	-3	-1	0	2	4	2	0	E
	Vide humilitatem meam Tribulationes cordis	grv	GR 112 LU 546 GS 39 47 GB 69ᵛ SYG 77	c	2	0	-3	0	-7	-3	0	2	
2	Vide quia tribulor	re	WA 107	c	2	-1	0	2	-3	-7	-3	0	a
	Vide quoniam tu laborem Exsurge Domine	trv	GR [101] LU 1283ᴮ	G	5	7	9	5	0	5	7	9	
	Vide si tunica Videns Jacob	rev	LA 148 WA 96										
5	Videbam coram me vitem	of	GR 37**	F	4	7	4	2	4	5	2	0	F
	Videbant faciem ejus Elegerunt apostoli	ofv	OTT 161	G	2	-2	0	2	0	2	5	4	
4	Videbant omnes Stephanum	re	LA 42 *WA 34	F	-3	0	-1	0	2	0	-1	0	E
	Videbitis et gaudebit cor vestrum	alv	GR 510 LU 1483	F	2	4	7	4	6	7	9	7	
4	Videbunt gentes justum tuum	re	LA 25 *382 *WA 23	F	-3	0	-1	0	-1	0	2	0	E
1	Videbunt in quem transfixerunt	co	GR 17**	F	2	0	-3	-1	-5	-3	0	2	D
8	Videns Andreas crucem	an	PM 118 *WA 234 *LA 499	G	-2	-5	-3	-2	0	2	0	2	G
1	Videns crucem Andreas	re	LA 502	a	-2	0	-2	-4	-2	0	3	0	D
1	Videns Dominus flentes sorores	co	SYG 108	a	-2	0	-4	-2	0	-2	-4	-5	D
1	Videns Dominus flentes sorores	an	PM 348	F	-1	-3	-1	0	2	-1	0	-3	D
1	Videns Dominus flentes sorores	co	GR 148 GS 69	F	-1	-3	-1	0	2	-1	0	-1	D
4	Videns Dominus flentes sorores	co	GB 96	E	1	3	5	7	5	3	5	1	
3	Videns ergo vir beatus	re	WA 288	G	2	0	2	5	2	4	5	4	E

6 Videns Jacob vestimenta	re	LA 148 WA 96	F	2	0	2	0	2	4	2	4	F
7 Videns praeses beatorum	an	WA 378	G	4	5	7	9	7	9	10	12	G
Videns vidi afflictionem Locutus est Dominus ad Moysen	rev	LA 156 WA 100										
8 Videntes autem turbae	an	WA 190	G	5	4	2	0	2	0	-2	0	G
8 Videntes Joseph a longe	re	LR 408 *LA 146 WA 96	G	2	0	2	0	2	0	2	5	G
4 3 Videntes stellam Magi	re	PM 40 LA 72 WA 55	F	-3	-1	-3	-1	0	2	4	2	E
7 Videntes stellam Magi	an	AR 331 LU 481 *AM 298 WA 55 *LA 74	G	4	5	7	9	7	5	10	9	G
Vidents enim creatorem Intempestae noctis	rev	LR 328 LA 371										
5 Videntibus cunctis splendor	an	WA 234	F	4	7	6	4	2	7	9	7	F
8 Videntibus illis elevatus est	an	AR 492 LU 851 AM 509 *WA 149 LA 250	G	5	4	0	4	5	2	0	2	G
Video caelos apertos	alv	GR 37 LU 416 *GS 15 GB 21^v SYG 22	D	-2	0	2	3	5	7	5	3	
8 Video caelos apertos	co	GR 38 LU 418 *SYG 23 *GB 22^v GS 16	F	2	4	2	4	2	4	2	0	G
7 Viderunt eam ... et beatam	an	AR 882^3 LU 1687 AM 1082	G	4	5	7	5	4	5	7	9	G
Viderunt eam ... et beatissimam Vidi speciosam	rev	LA 443										
3 Viderunt eam ... vernantem	an	AM 1073	E	-2	3	5	7	8	7	10	8	E
3 Viderunt eam ... vernantem	an	AR 872 LU 1680	G	5	2	0	2	5	2	4	5	E
7 Viderunt oculi mei	an	WA 272	G	7	4	7	9	7	9	10	9	G
Viderunt omnes fines terrae	sr	AR 270 LU 411										
1 Viderunt omnes fines terrae	co	GR 35 LU 410 SYG 21 *GB 20^v *GS 15	F	2	0	-3	-1	-5	-3	0	2	D
5 Viderunt omnes fines terrae	gr	GR 33 LU 409 SYG 19 GB 17^v GS G	F	4	7	9	7	4	7	11	9	F
7 Viderunt omnes termini terrae	an	LR 338	G	4	5	7	9	7	5	7	4	G
Viderunt te aquae Deus In mari via tua	intv	GR (3)										
2 Viderunt te aquae Deus	re	LA 237 *WA 144	C	2	4	2	5	4	5	7	2	D
8 Vides o frater Luciane	re	WA 344	D	5	3	5	7	5	7	5	7	G
8 Videte manus meas	an	AR 449 OHS 787 LU 792 *AM 462 WA 139 *LA 219	F	2	0	2	4	7	6	2	6	G

	Text	Genre	Sources		Interval profile	
3	Videte miraculum matris	re	PM 251 *LA 353 WA 271	G	2 -3 -2 0 2 0 2 4	E
8	Videte quoniam non soli mihi	co	GR 530 LU 1514	D	3 7 5 7 5 7 5 7	G
8	Vidi angelum ascendentem	re	LR 390	F	2 4 2 4 2 4 6 4	G
	Vidi angelum Dei fortem / Vidi conjunctos	rev	PM 216 LR 141 LA 507 WA 412			
	Vidi angelum Dei volantem / Audivi voces in caelo	rev	LA 226			
8	Vidi aquam egredientem	an	GR 2* OHS 706 LU 12 PM 10 WA 130 222 GS 116 SYG 145	G	2 -2 2 0 2 0 2 5	G
5	Vidi civitatem ... novam ... et	re	LR 244	c	2 0 -3 -1 -3 0 -1 0	F
1	Vidi civitatem ... novam ... et	re	LA 551	D	3 0 -2 3 5 7 5 3	D
8	Vidi civitatem ... novam ... sicut	int	GR 439 LU 1376	D	3 5 7 3 7 10 9 7	G
8	Vidi civitatem ... ornatam	an	WA 135	F	2 0 4 7 6 4 7 6	G
8	Vidi civitatem ... ornatam	re	LA 388	F	2 4 2 4 6 4 2 4	G
	Vidi civitatem ... tamquam / Vidi civitatem ... novam	rev	LA 551			
	Vidi civitatem ... tamquam / Vidi portam	rev	LR 170 LA 227 WA 140 306			
4	Vidi conjunctos viros	re	PM 216 LR 141 *LA 507 *WA 412	F	-1 2 0 -3 -1 -3 0 -3	E
8	Vidi Domine afflictionem	an	AR 408	a	-4 -2 0 -2 0 -2 -4 -2	G
6	Vidi Dominum facie ad faciem	re	LA 141 *WA 93	e	-4 -2 -4 -5 -4 -2 0 -2	c
1	Vidi Dominum sedentem ... elevatum	re	PM 201 AM 1204 LR 383 LA 301 WA 183	a	-4 -2 -4 -5 -7 -9 -7 -5	D
1	Vidi Dominum sedentem ... plena	an	AR 552 LU 995 AM 590 *WA 183 *LA 308	a	-2 0 -2 -4 0 3 0 2	D
1	Vidi Jerusalem descendentem	re	LA 228 *WA 141	G	2 4 2 5 2 0 4 5	D
	Vidi non servantes pactum / Benedictus ... non tradas	ofv	OTT 48 *GB 104 *SYG 116	b	1 0 1 -2 1 -4 -2 0	
7 8	Vidi portam civitatis	re	LR 170 LA 227 *WA 140 306	G	2 5 2 4 2 0 2 0	G
	Vidi speciosam sicut columbam	alv	SYG 177	C	2 4 5 4 2 0 2 4	
3	Vidi speciosam sicut columbam	re	AM 1200 *PM 178 *LR 376 *LA 443 *WA 355	E	3 1 -2 0 -2 0 1 3	E
	Vidi sub altare Dei / Sub altare	rev	PM 35 LA 57 WA 43			
8	Vidi sub altare Dei	re	LA 60	D	5 3 5 7 5 7 5 7	G
	Vidi supra montem agnum / Orante sancto Clemente	rev	PM 213 WA 409			
7	Vidi supra montem agnum	an	AR 927 LU 1760 AM 1145 *LA 496	d	-3 0 2 0 -3 -2 -3 -7	G

1 Vidi turbam magnam	an	AR 898 LU 1728 AM 1102 *WA 397	D	-2	3	5	3	7	10	7	5	D
Vidimus stellam ejus Magi veniunt	rev	LR 76										
Vidimus stellam ejus ... et venimus	alv	GR 58 LU 460 *GS 19 GB 33ᵛ SYG 31	D	-2	0	2	3	5	7	5	3	
4 Vidimus stellam ejus ... et venimus	an	AR 332 *AM 299 LA 67	F	-1	-3	-1	0	2	4	2	4	E
4 Vidimus stellam ejus ... et venimus	co	GR 59 LU 462 SYG 32 GB 35 GS 19	E	1	3	5	3	5	3	1	3	E
Vidisti Domine agonem Ipse me coronavit	rev	LA 360 WA 274										
7 Vidisti Domine agonem	an	WA 274 LA 359	d	-3	0	2	0	2	0	-3	-2	G
Vidisti Domine Deus meus ne sileas	see Vidisti Domine ne sileas											
5 Vidisti Domine et exspectasti	re	LA 358 *WA 275	a	-4	0	3	2	3	2	0	3	F
Vidisti Domine iniquitatem Dominus mecum est	rev	LA 178										
Vidisti Domine ne sileas Pacifice loquebantur	grv	GR 164 GS 77 GB 103ᵛ SYG 116	F	4	2	7	9	7	9	7	11	
7 Vidit Dominus Petrum et Andream	an	LA 497	d	-3	0	2	0	-3	-2	0	-2	G
3 Vidit igitur assistere	an	WA 342	E	-2	3	5	8	7	8	10	8	E
Vidit Jacob in somnis Terribilis est	rev	LR 235										
7 Vidit Jacob scalam summitas	an	PM 240 LR 241 WA 318 LA 547	G	4	2	5	4	0	5	4	5	G
Vidit Maria Dominum O mirum et magnum	rev	VP 190										
Vidit nocte illa oculis Veniens vir	ofv	GB 166ᵛ	a	2	0	-2	-4	0	-2	-4	0	
2 Vidit populus claudum	an	WA 340 LA 413	D	2	3	5	2	3	2	0	3	D
Vidit supra montem	see also Vidi supra montem											
1 Vidit supra montem	an	WA 410	D	-2	3	5	3	5	7	9	7	D
Viditque Deus cuncta Igitur perfecti	rev	LA 112										
4 Vigilate animo in proximo	an	AR 248 AM 223 WA 20 LA 25	E	1	3	1	3	1	0	1	3	E
Vigilate ergo quia nescitis Sint lumbi vestri	rev	PM 228 LR 202 *LA 535 *WA 430	D	7	5	7	5	3	2	5	7	
Vigilate et orate In monte Oliveti	rev	GR 168 LU 633 OHS 375 LA 189 WA 118										
3 Vigilate et orate	co	GR 11**	G	2	5	2	5	0	2	0	-2	E
8 Vim faciebant qui quaerebant	an	OHS 491 LU 698 WA 122 LA 196	G	2	0	-2	0	2	5	4	2	G

1 Vim virtutis suae oblitus	an	AR 388 AM 362 WA 99 *LA 152	D	7	10	7	5	7	8	7	5	D
Vim virtutis tuae		see Vim virtutis suae										
Vincenti dabo edere Qui vicerit faciem	rev	LA 51 WA 39										
5 Vincenti dabo manna	an	AR 531 LU 940 AM 551	a	-2	-4	0	3	5	3	5	8	F
Vinculis carnis absolutus Iste sanctus digne	rev	LR 203 WA 391										
Vindica Domine sanguinem Effuderunt sanguinem	rev	LA 58 *WA 44										
Vindica Domine sanguinem Isti sunt sancti qui passi	rev	LA 60										
Vindica Domine sanguinem Sub throno Dei	rev	LA 60										
5 Vindica Domine sanguinem	gr	GR 643 *SYG 190 *GB 195 GS 214	F	-3	0	2	0	-3	0	2	-1	F
4 Vindica Domine sanguinem	an	WA 421	F	-1	-3	-5	-3	-1	0	2	0	E
Vindica Domine sanguinem ... super terram Effuderunt sanguinem	trv	GR 42 LU 429 *GB 26^v *SYG 26	G	-5	0	2	5	4	2	5	2	
Vindica Domine sanguinem ... super terram	alv	SYG 175 191 *GB 269	a	-2	2	0	-2	0	-4	-5	-4	
8 Vindica Domine sanguinem ... super terram	an	LR 182 LA 516	c	-1	-3	-5	-3	-1	-3	-5	-3	G
Vindica Domine sanguinem ... super terram	alv	SYG 210	D	2	0	-2	0	3	0	2	0	
Vindica sanguinem servorum Adjuva nos	trv	GR [131]	F	2	4	5	4	2	4	0	-3	
Vinea enim Domini Vinea facta est	trv	SYG 150	F	4	7	6	2	4	2	0	2	
8 Vinea facta est dilecto	tr	GR 230$_s$ OHS 654 LU 776^s SYG 150 GB 120 GS 111	G	2	4	2	0	2	0	5	7	G
4 Vinea mea electa	an	SYG 139	D	-2	2	3	5	3	5	3	2	E
8 Vinea mea electa	re	OHS 490 LU 697 *LA 196 *WA 122	F	2	4	2	0	4	6	7	6	G
4 Vir angelice puntatis	an	WA 315	F	-3	-5	-3	0	-1	-3	-1	-3	E
Vir autem Domini Erat vultu	rev	LA 373 WA 333										
6 Vir Dei Benedictus mundi gloriam	int	SYG 56	F	2	0	-5	-3	-5	-3	0	2	F
8 Vir Dei Benedictus mundi gloriam	int	GR (27) GB 54	G	2	0	-2	0	2	0	2	0	G
Vir Dei Benedictus omnium justorum	alv	GR (25)	F	2	0	5	4	2	4	0	2	
2 Vir Dei Benedictus signum crucis	an	AM 964	C	5	4	5	2	0	2	4	2	D
4 Vir Dei Gamaliel	an	WA 342	F	-1	-3	-1	-5	-3	0	-1	0	E

No.	Title	Type	Reference										
	Vir dilectus a Deo / Priusquam te formarem	rev	LR 349										
	Vir Domini Benedictus	alv	SYG 207	a	-4	0	-2	-5	-4	-7	-9	-7	
1	Vir Domini Benedictus	an	AM 853 WA 300 *LA 375	D	2	0	-2	0	3	5	3	2	D
4	Vir Domini Cuthbertus	re	WA 293	C	2	5	4	5	4	5	7	5	E
2	Vir erat in terra nomine Job	of	GR 382 OTT 122 LU 1069 SYG 256 GB 262 GS 166	E	3	5	7	5	3	5	8	5	a
1	Vir inclitus Dionysius	re	WA 387	D	-2	0	3	0	2	0	-2	0	D
	Vir iste in populo / Dilexit Andream	rev	WA 236										
	Vir iste in populo / Hic est fratrum	rev	LA 298										
4	Vir iste in populo	re	LA 503 *WA 236	D	2	3	2	-2	0	2	3	2	E
	Vir obediens loquetur	alv	GR (5)	G	2	0	-2	2	5	4	7	5	
3	Virga de Jesse generata stirpe	hy	ST 240	E	-2	3	5	7	8	5	3	1	E
	Virga Jesse floruit	alv	GR [79] LU 1267	G	2	0	5	4	2	0	7	9	
	Virga recta est virga regni / Filiae regum	ofv	OTT 157 GB 43 *SYG 39	G	7	9	7	5	10	7	9	5	
	Virga tua et baculus tuus / Si ambulem	grv	GR 137 GS 61 GB 88^V SYG 99	a	-4	0	-2	-5	-4	-7	-9	-7	
1	Virgam virtutis tuae	an	WA 415 LA 512	D	7	8	7	10	7	5	7	8	D
5	Virgines laudent nomen	int	GR 102**	F	4	7	9	7	9	7	6	2	F
2	Virginis alme Deus soboles	hy	ST 126	C	2	4	5	4	2	4	7	5	D
8	Virginis proles opifexque matris	hy	ST 202	a	-2	-4	-2	0	3	2	0	-2	G
1	Virginis proles opifexque matris	hy	ST 162	a	-2	0	3	2	0	3	2	-2	D
4	Virginis proles opifexque matris	hy	LR 212 213	F	-1	0	2	4	2	0	-3	-1	E
8	Virginis proles opifexque matris	hy	ST 245	G	2	0	-3	-2	-5	-3	0	2	G
4	Virginis proles opifexque matris	hy	ST 105 405	D	2	3	5	7	5	3	2	0	E
8	Virginis proles opifexque matris	hy	ST 105	D	2	3	5	7	5	7	5	9	G
8	Virginis proles opifexque matris	hy	ST 202	C	2	5	4	5	7	9	12	11	G
1	Virginitas caelum post lapsum	re	AR 132* VP 203	D	-2	2	3	0	2	-2	2	3	D
	Virgo concepit et virgo peperit / Videte miraculum	rev	PM 251 LA 353 WA 271										
4	Virgo concepit et virgo peperit	an	WA 269	C	2	5	2	5	2	5	4	5	E
1	Virgo Dei genitrix ex qua	an	WA 303	D	-2	0	3	2	0	-2	0	3	D
	Virgo Dei genitrix quem totus / Continet in gremio	rev	WA 50										
2	Virgo Dei genitrix quem totus	hy	ST 79	F	-1	-3	-1	-3	-5	-3	0	-1	D

2 Virgo Dei genitrix quem totus	hy	AR 133* VP 42 LU 1865	F	-1	-3	-1	-3	-5	-3	0	2	D
1 Virgo Dei genitrix quem totus	an	PM 272 *WA 47 *LA 39	C	2	5	4	0	4	2	0	5	D
Virgo Dei genitrix quem totus Benedicta es virgo	grv	GS q	a	3	0	-2	0	-5	-4	-2	-5	
Virgo Dei genitrix quem totus Benedicta et venerabilis	grv	GR [76] LU 1264 *GB 220	a	3	0	-2	0	-5	-4	-2	-5	
Virgo Dei genitrix quem totus Dolorosa	grv	GR 595 LU 1633[V]	a	3	0	-2	0	-5	-4	-2	-5	
Virgo Dei genitrix quem totus	alv	GR 623 LU 1684	D	3	2	5	3	2	3	0	2	
Virgo Dei genitrix virga est Stirps Jesse	rev	AR 129* *PM 186 *WA 303	C	2	4	5	7	5	7	9	7	
Virgo Dei N. rutilans Pulchra facie	rev	WA 433	G	5	4	0	-2	0	2	4	2	
Virgo est electus Valde honorandus	rev	WA 39										
7 Virgo est electus	an	LA 52	d	-3	0	2	0	2	0	-2	0	G
7 Virgo est electus	re	LA 53	d	-2	0	-2	-3	-2	0	2	0	G
6 Virgo flagellatur crucianda	re	PM 214 VP 251	F	2	0	2	4	0	2	0	5	F
2 Virgo gloriosa semper evangelium	an	AR 926 LU 1757 AM 1143 *LA 488 WA 405	F	-1	0	-3	-5	-3	0	-3	-1	D
8 Virgo gloriosa semper evangelium	re	LA 490 *WA 406	F	2	4	2	4	2	4	6	2	G
6 Virgo hodie fidelis	an	VP 73 WA 30 *LA 38	F	2	0	2	4	0	4	5	4	F
8 Virgo Israel revertere	re	LA 19 381 WA 23	G	-2	0	-2	-5	-2	-3	-2	0	G
7 Virgo Maria non est tibi similis	an	PM 186	G	4	5	7	9	10	9	7	9	G
6 Virgo parens Christi benedicta	re	AR 131* VP 39 LU 1862	F	2	0	2	4	0	2	0	5	F
6 Virgo potens sicut turris	an	AR 871 LU 1679 AM 1072	F	2	0	2	4	0	2	5	4	F
1 Virgo prudentissima	an	AR 819 LU 1600 AM 1012[B]	D	3	0	-2	3	5	7	5	2	D
2 Virgo verbo concepit	an	PM 148 *WA 47 *LA 39	C	2	5	4	0	4	2	0	2	D
6 Virgo virginum praeclara	hy	AR 675 LU 1424	F	2	4	2	4	7	5	4	2	F
Viri autem qui comitabantur Saulus autem	anv	WA 262 LA 341(339)										
1 Viri autem qui comitabantur	an	LA 341	D	-2	0	2	0	-2	0	3	2	D
1 Viri Galilaei quid admiramini	of	OTT 172 *SYG 180 *GS 133 *GB 180[V]	F	-3	-5	-3	0	4	2	4	0	D
7 Viri Galilaei quid admiramini	re	LR 105 LA 250 WA 149	G	2	0	2	0	2	5	4	5	G
7 Viri Galilaei quid admiramini	int	GR 285 LU 846 SYG 179 GB 178[V] GS 135	G	5	4	5	7	5	9	7	9	G

	Text	Type	Sources										
7	Viri Galilaei quid aspicitis	an	AR 491 LU 850 AM 508 *LA 250 WA 149	G	4	5	7	5	9	7	4	7	G
1	Viri impii dixerunt opprimamus	re	OHS 184 (nm) WA 116	a	-2	-4	-2	0	-2	-4	-2	-4	D
8	Viri sancti gloriosum sanguinem	re	PM 221 LR 178 *LA 514 *WA 420	G	2	5	2	0	2	4	2	-2	G
	Viri usque gloria / Regis iram non	rev	WA 251	d	2	3	2	0	-2	-3	-2	0	
	Viribus corporis cepit / Beatus Martinus obitum	rev	LA 484										
	Viribus corporis cepit / Martinus igitur obitum	ofv	SYG 225	D	-2	0	3	0	3	2	0	2	
	Viriliter agite et confortetur	alv	GR (36)	G	-2	0	2	0	-2	0	-2	2	
	Viriliter agite et confortetur / Diligite Dominum	grv	GR 93**	D	7	10	7	5	3	2	5	7	
3	Virtute magna reddebant	re	OHS 779 *PM 217 *LR 87 *LA 210 WA 133 305	E	-2	3	5	7	5	8	3	5	E
	Virtutes caeli movebuntur	alv	SYG 4 GS 3	G	-2	2	5	4	2	0	2	4	
1	Virtutum pennis ad astra	co	SYG 220	F	2	0	-1	-3	-1	0	2	0	D
	Visi sunt oculis / Justorum animae	intv	SYG 224										
	Visi sunt oculis / Justorum animae	grv	GR 413 LU 1547 GS 213 GB 171 SYG 194	F	4	7	9	7	9	7	9	4	
	Visi sunt oculis / Justorum animae ... malitiae	rev	WA 422	G	5	4	0	-2	0	2	4	2	
1	Visionem quam vidistis	an	AR 378 LU 550 AM 351	D	2	3	5	2	5	7	3	2	D
1	Visionem quam vidistis	co	GR 573 LU 1587	D	2	3	5	2	5	7	3	2	D
8	Visita nos Domine	an	WA 70 LA 104	c	-1	0	-3	-5	-1	-3	-1	0	G
1	Visitasti terram et inebriasti	co	GR 443 LU 1379	D	2	3	5	3	2	0	-2	3	D
2	Visitationem virginis Mariae	inv	LR 442	C	2	4	5	2	0	2	5	4	D
2	Visitavit nos oriens	an	WA 68	D	-2	0	3	0	2	0	3	5	D
8	Visus est Gregorius	re	PM 155	G	5	3	5	7	5	7	9	7	G
	Vita nostra est abscondita	alv	GR 63	D	3	0	-2	2	5	7	5	10	
1	Vita sanctorum Deus angelorum	hy	ST 387	D	3	0	3	0	2	-2	2	5	D
2	Vita sanctorum Deus angelorum	hy	ST 291 (var)	D	3	0	3	0	3	-2	3	5	D
2	Vita sanctorum Deus angelorum	hy	ST 291	D	3	0	3	0	3	0	-2	3	D
1	Vita sanctorum Deus angelorum	hy	ST 228 258	D	3	0	3	2	0	3	-2	2	D
7	Vita verbo est Wulstanus	an	WA 248	c	2	0	2	4	0	2	0	5	c
	Vitam petiit a te / Desiderium animae	rev	LR 207										

#	Incipit		Sources										
	Vitam petiit a te Domine praevenisti	rev	PM 219 LR 159 205 LA 523 WA 416										
8	Vitam petiit a te	an	LR 196 *WA 425 LA 531	F	2	4	2	7	6	4	7	6	G
	Vitam petiit et tribuisti Desiderium animae	ofv	OTT 153 *SYG 215	F	2	0	2	0	-5	-3	-5	0	
	Vitam petiit et tribuisti Domine praevenisti	grv	GR [48] LU 1207 GS 222 GB 53 *SYG 224	a	3	0	-2	0	-5	-4	-2	-5	
	Vitam petiit et tribuisti In virtute	ofv	OTT 152 GB 51^v SYG 52	c	4	0	2	4	2	0	-3	0	
4	Vitone laudabilis Hydulphe mirabilis	re	PM 204	D	3	0	2	3	0	-2	0	3	E
7	Vivit Dominus et benedictus Deus	an	AM 24 OHS 181 (nm) *LA 105	b	1	3	5	3	1	-2	1	0	G
	Vivit Dominus quoniam adimplevit Transite ad me	rev	LR 263										
8	Vivo autem ego	an	AM 1128	G	2	5	2	0	-2	0	2	0	G
3	Vivo ego dicit Dominus	an	AR 81 AM 5 *WA 89	c	-3	-5	-3	0	-1	-5	-3	0	E
	Vix justus salvabitur Libera me Domine de morte	rev	LA 557	E	5	7	5	3	1	3	5	7	
6	Vobis datum est nosse	an	AR 351 LU 510 AM 323 WA 77 *LA 119	F	2	4	0	-1	-3	-1	-3	-5	F
	Voca me et respondebo Ne abscondas	rev	LA 284 WA 173										
8	Voca operarios et redde	an	AR 344 LU 502 *AM 315 WA 73 *LA 114	G	5	2	0	-2	0	2	0	4	G
1	Vocabis nomen ejus	an	AR 306 LU 453 AM 283	C	2	9	10	9	7	4	7	9	D
	Vocatus quoque a Domino Temptavit Deus	rev	WA 81										
8	Vocavit angelus Domini	re	LA 122	D	3	5	7	5	7	5	7	5	G
	Voce mea ad Dominum Mihi autem absit	intv	GR 602 LU 1643										
7	Voce mea ad Dominum	an	AR 186	d	-3	0	2	3	0	-3	-2	0	G
6	Voce mea ad Dominum	co	SYG 76 *GS 38	F	4	2	0	2	0	2	5	4	F
	Voce quippe de caelo Operibus sanctis	rev	WA 239	C	2	5	7	5	7	9	7	5	
3	Vocem jucunditatis annuntiate	int	GR 270 LU 830 SYG 168 GB 151 GS 130	E	1	-2	3	0	3	5	8	7	E
	Vocem tuam audivi Dum deambularet	rev	LA 111 WA 73										
1	Volavit ad me	co	GR 32**	D	3	2	3	7	5	3	2	3	D
8	Volens Noe scire	re	WA 77	G	-2	-5	-2	2	0	-2	0	5	G

	Text		Sources										
1	Volo pater ut ubi ego sum	an	AR [16] LU 1126 AM 641 *WA 419 *LA 441 527	F	-1	-3	0	-1	2	4	2	0	D
	Vos amici mei estis Jam non dicam	rev	PM 330 LR 110 VP 276 LU 1847										
1	Vos amici mei estis	an	AR [3] 511 LU 1111 AM 622 *WA 414 *LA 477	D	7	10	7	5	7	5	3	5	D
1	Vos amici mei qui secuti	an	WA 331	D	-2	0	2	3	5	3	0	2	D
1	Vos ascendite ad diem	an	AR 417 LU 1099 AM 394 WA 109 *LA 174	C	2	5	4	5	7	4	7	9	D
	Vos autem dixi amicos Hoc est praeceptum	rev	LA 510										
8	Vos estis cives sanctorum	an	PM 310	G	5	2	0	-2	0	2	0	4	G
	Vos estis lux mundi	alv	SYG 218 GB 235^v	G	2	0	2	0	2	0	2	4	
	Vos estis qui permansistis	alv	GR 548 LU 1548	G	2	-2	0	-2	2	5	4	2	
5	Vos qui aliquando eratis	re	VP 186	G	2	0	2	0	-2	2	5	4	F
	Vos qui in pulvere Constantes estote	rev	LA 29 WA 25										
2	Vos qui in turribus	re	WA 178	D	3	2	3	2	-2	0	3	2	D
1	Vos qui reliquistis omnia	co	SYG 219	D	2	0	-2	0	3	2	0	3	D
1 2	Vos qui reliquistis omnia	an	AR [8] *AM 624 882 1124 *WA 332 *LA 428	D	2	3	5	7	3	2	0	-2	D
4	Vos qui secuti ... dicit Dominus	co	GB 236^v	D	2	3	0	5	3	2	3	0	E
1	Vos qui secuti ... regeneratione	co	SYG 55	D	-2	3	5	3	5	7	9	7	D
	Vos qui secuti ... sedebitis	alv	GB 267^v	G	2	0	-5	-3	-5	-3	-7	0	
1	Vos qui secuti ... sedebitis	co	GR 448 LU 1392	D	3	5	7	5	2	3	5	2	D
1 2	Vos qui secuti ... sedebitis ... dicit	an	AR 611 757 PM 217 AM 794 942	D	-2	0	2	3	5	3	0	2	D
2	Vos qui secuti ... sedebitis ... dicit	co	GR 588 LU 1614 GS z 203	D	-2	0	2	3	5	3	0	2	D
8	Vos qui secuti ... sedebitis ... dicit	re	WA 413	G	2	0	5	4	5	7	9	5	G
8	Vos qui transituri estis	re	LA 161 *WA 102	G	2	0	2	0	-2	0	-2	-5	G
5	Vos qui transituri estis	re	LR 412	G	2	0	2	0	-2	2	5	4	F
2	Vos vocatis me magister	an	GS 97	D	-5	-2	0	2	0	2	3	2	D
8	Vos vocatis me magister	an	WA 214 *SYG 133	G	-2	-5	-2	0	2	0	2	4	G
3	Vota mea Domino ... coram	an	AR 99 OHS 222 LU 281	G	2	4	5	4	5	4	2	4	E
	Vota mea Domino ... in conspectu	alv	GR 36**	G	2	5	7	9	7	9	10	12	
4	Votiva cunctis orbita	hy	ST 395	D	2	3	5	7	0	2	3	5	E

2	Vovete et reddite Domino	co	GR 368 LU 1050 SYG 251 GB 257 GS 161	C	2	4	2	0	2	5	7	5	D
5	Vox clamantis in deserto	an	AR 228 LU 1082 AM 200 *WA 13 *LA 12	F	2	0	4	7	9	7	9	7	F
8	Vox clara ecce intonat	hy	ST 171	G	-5	0	2	0	-2	0	2	5	G
2	Vox clara ecce intonat	hy	ST 71	E	-4	0	3	5	7	5	3	5	a
8	Vox clara ecce intonat	hy	ST 408	G	-2	-3	-5	-3	-2	-3	-5	-7	G
2	Vox clara ecce intonat	hy	ST 216	G	-2	-3	-2	-5	-7	-2	0	3	G
2	Vox clara ecce intonat	hy	ST 272	D	-2	0	3	2	0	3	2	3	D
2	Vox clara ecce intonat	hy	ST 171 AM 184	E	-2	0	3	5	7	5	3	5	a
8	Vox clara ecce intonat	hy	ST 365	D	-2	0	3	5	7	5	7	5	G
	Vox de caelo	see Vox de caelis											
	Vox de caelis o vos / Libera me de morte	rev	WA 438	D	7	5	0	3	7	5	2	3	
4	Vox de caelis sonuit	an	WA 57 *LA 75	F	-1	-3	0	-1	0	2	0	-1	E
	Vox enim tua dulcis / Domine Deus virtutum	trv	GR 53	G	2	4	5	4	5	7	5	0	
8	Vox exsultationis et salutis	re	LA 390	G	-2	0	2	4	5	7	5	4	G
	Vox exsultationis et salutis	alv	GB 269 *SYG 176 *GS 215	C	2	4	5	4	2	0	4	5	
2	Vox in Rama audita ... plorans	an	AR 284 AM 261 *WA 46 LA 61	D	-2	0	2	3	5	3	2	0	D
4	Vox in Rama audita ... ploratus	re	LA 59	F	-3	0	-1	0	2	0	-1	0	E
7	Vox in Rama audita ... ploratus	co	GR 44 LU 430 SYG 27 *GB 28 GS 18	d	-2	0	-2	0	2	0	-2	-3	G
1	Vox in Rama audita ... ploratus	re	WA 46	C	2	5	7	9	7	4	5	4	D
	Vox laetitiae et exsultationis / Lux perpetua	rev	LA 387 WA 306										
8	Vox laetitiae in tabernaculis	an	WA 132	G	-2	-5	-2	0	2	0	-2	2	G
8	Vox laetitiae in tabernaculis	an	PM 221	a	-2	-4	-2	0	-2	0	-4	0	G
8	Vox tonitrui tui	re	WA 41	G	2	5	0	2	-2	0	-2	-3	G
6	Vox tua o bone Jesu	an	WA 40	F	-3	-1	-5	0	2	0	2	4	F
	Vox turturis audita est	alv	GR 442 LU 1379[1]	G	-3	-5	0	2	0	2	4	5	
2	Vultum tuum deprecabuntur	int	GR [64] LU 1229 SYG 28 GB 29 221 GS 231	D	-2	0	-2	-5	-2	0	-2	0	D
	Vultum tuum deprecabuntur / Audi filia	trv	GR [62] LU 1227	C	2	5	2	5	4	5	2	5	
8	Wulstane praesul inclite fulget dies	hy	ST 178	G	2	4	2	4	5	4	2	0	G

8 Zachaee festinans descende	an	AR [110] LU 1244 AM 700 *WA 319 *LA 546	F	4	2	4	7	6	4	2	4	G
8 Zelo Christi succensa	an	WA 256	G	-3	-2	-3	-5	0	2	0	2	G
8 Zelus domus tuae comedit me	an	OHS 367 LU 626 *WA 117 *LA 189	c	2	0	-1	0	2	0	-3	0	G
8 Zeno pontifex inclite	hy	ST 387	G	-2	0	2	5	4	5	7	5	G
7 Zoe uxor Nicostrati	re	LA 327	G	2	0	2	0	2	5	4	5	G
8 Zoe uxor Nicostrati	an	LA 331	G	5	2	0	2	0	-2	2	0	G

1	Agnus Dei	SCH #54	a	-7	-9	-4	-2	0	2	0	-4	D
2	Agnus Dei	SCH #240	D	-5	-3	-2	0	2	0	2	-2	[D]
2	Agnus Dei	SCH #107	G	-5	-2	-3	-2	0	-2	0	-5	G
2	Agnus Dei	SCH #246	D	-5	0	-2	-3	-5	-2	0	2	D
7	Agnus Dei	SCH #44	B	-4	-2	0	-4	-2	-4	-6	1	[G]
5	Agnus Dei	SCH #31	c	-3	-7	-12	-7	-5	-3	-5	-7	F
5	Agnus Dei	SCH #41	c	-3	-7	-12	-7	-3	-5	-7	-3	F
5	Agnus Dei	SCH #34	c	-3	-7	-5	-7	-3	0	2	0	F
5	Agnus Dei	SCH #110	G	-3	-7	-5	-3	-2	2	4	5	[F]
5	Agnus Dei	SCH #30	c	-3	-7	-5	-1	-3	-5	-7	-5	F
4	Agnus Dei	SCH #106	G	-3	-5	-7	-2	-3	-2	0	-5	C
5	Agnus Dei	SCH #33	c	-3	-5	-7	0	2	0	5	4	[F]
5	Agnus Dei	SCH #29	c	-3	-5	-3	-5	-7	-3	0	2	[F]
5	Agnus Dei	SCH #32	c	-3	-5	-3	-5	-7	-3	0	2	F
6	Agnus Dei	SCH #154	F	-3	-5	-3	0	4	2	4	2	F
8	Agnus Dei	SCH #105	G	-3	-5	0	2	0	4	5	7	G
1	Agnus Dei	SCH #13	d	-3	-2	-5	-2	-5	-9	-10	-9	D
5	Agnus Dei	SCH #27	c	-3	-2	-3	-5	-7	-3	0	2	F
5	Agnus Dei	SCH #28	c	-3	-1	-3	-5	-7	-3	0	2	F
8	Agnus Dei	SCH #40	c	-3	-1	-3	-5	0	2	4	5	c
8	Agnus Dei	SCH #39	c	-3	-1	0	-1	-3	-5	-3	-1	c
7	Agnus Dei	SCH #38	c	-3	-1	0	2	0	4	5	7	
5	Agnus Dei	SCH #37	c	-3	0	-5	-3	-7	-8	-10	-5	F
1	Agnus Dei	SCH #109	G	-3	0	-5	-2	-3	-5	0	7	D
7	Agnus Dei	SCH #36	c	-3	0	2	0	2	4	2	0	[G]
1	Agnus Dei	SCH #12	d	-2	-5	-9	-7	-12	-9	-12	-14	D
1	Agnus Dei	SCH #8	d	-2	-5	-7	-5	-9	-7	-5	-9	D
2	Agnus Dei	SCH #239	D	-2	-5	-2	0	3	7	3	2	D
1	Agnus Dei	SCH #65	a	-2	-4	-5	-7	-5	-4	-2	0	E
1	Agnus Dei	SCH #64	a	-2	-4	-5	-7	-4	-2	-4	-5	[D]
1	Agnus Dei	SCH #63	a	-2	-4	-5	-4	-5	0	2	3	[D]
1	Agnus Dei	SCH #53	a	-2	-4	-5	-4	-2	-4	-5	-7	D
	Agnus Dei	SCH #62	a	-2	-4	-2	0	-2	0	-2	-4	
5	Agnus Dei	SCH #61	a	-2	-4	-2	0	3	5	3	1	a
4	Agnus Dei	SCH #186	E	-2	-4	-2	0	3	5	3	1	E
5	Agnus Dei	SCH #51	a	-2	-4	0	3	5	3	0	-2	F

5 Agnus Dei	SCH #52	a	-2	-4	0	3	5	3	5	7	F
5 Agnus Dei	SCH #60	a	-2	-4	0	3	5	3	5	7	F
7 Agnus Dei	SCH #11	d	-2	-3	-5	-7	-2	0	2	5	[G]
4 Agnus Dei	SCH #104	G	-2	-3	-5	-3	-2	-3	-7	-5	G
2 Agnus Dei	SCH #245	D	-2	-3	-5	-3	-2	0	2	0	[D]
8 Agnus Dei	SCH #103	G	-2	-3	-5	-2	0	2	0	2	G
7 Agnus Dei	SCH #10	d	-2	-3	-2	0	-3	-2	-5	0	d
1 Agnus Dei	SCH #108	G	-2	-3	-2	0	-2	-3	-5	-3	G
2 Agnus Dei	SCH #9	d	-2	0	-2	-5	-3	-5	-7	-2	d
Agnus Dei	SCH #59	a	-2	0	-2	-4	-2	0	-2	0	
2 Agnus Dei	SCH #185	E	-2	0	-2	-4	-2	1	0	-4	D
8 Agnus Dei	SCH #102	G	-2	0	-2	-3	-5	0	2	0	[G]
7 Agnus Dei	SCH #58	a	-2	0	-2	0	-2	0	-2	-4	[G]
7 Agnus Dei	SCH #43	B	-2	0	1	0	-2	0	-2	-4	[G]
2 Agnus Dei	SCH #244	D	-2	0	2	-2	0	3	5	3	[D]
1 Agnus Dei	SCH #57	a	-2	0	2	0	-2	-4	-2	0	D
1 Agnus Dei	SCH #56	a	-2	0	2	3	-2	0	2	3	D
3 Agnus Dei	SCH #243	D	-2	0	2	3	-2	0	2	3	GG
1 Agnus Dei	SCH #238	D	-2	0	2	3	5	7	5	10	[D]
3 Agnus Dei	SCH #184	E	-2	0	3	5	3	0	1	0	E
1 Agnus Dei	SCH #242	D	-2	0	3	5	7	3	7	10	D
8 Agnus Dei	SCH #55	a	-2	3	5	3	5	0	-4	0	G
4 Agnus Dei	SCH #241	D	-2	5	3	2	0	2	5	7	[E]
5 Agnus Dei	SCH #3	f	-1	-5	-3	-5	-8	-5	-10	-8	F
5 Agnus Dei	SCH #26	c	-1	-3	-5	-3	-7	-8	-3	-5	F
5 Agnus Dei	SCH #2	f	-1	-3	-5	-3	-1	0	-1	-3	F
4 Agnus Dei	SCH #162	F	-1	-3	-5	-1	2	4	2	0	E
8 Agnus Dei	SCH #25	c	-1	-3	-5	0	2	4	5	7	c
4 Agnus Dei	SCH #153	F	-1	-3	-1	-3	-5	2	4	2	[E]
5 Agnus Dei	SCH #24	c	-1	-3	-1	0	-1	-3	-5	-7	F
4 Agnus Dei	SCH #161	F	-1	-3	-1	0	-1	-3	-5	-3	E
7 Agnus Dei	SCH #35	c	-1	-3	0	2	4	5	7	5	[G]
1 Agnus Dei	SCH #152	F	-1	-3	2	0	-1	-3	-1	0	E
5 Agnus Dei	SCH #160	F	-1	-3	4	2	-1	0	-3	4	F
6 Agnus Dei	SCH #23	c	-1	0	-3	-1	-3	-5	2	-1	c
1 Agnus Dei	SCH #159	F	-1	0	-3	0	2	4	7	6	D

5 Agnus Dei	SCH #1	f	-1	0	-1	-3	-5	-12	-10	-8	F
4 Agnus Dei	SCH #158	F	-1	0	2	0	2	0	-1	0	E
6 Agnus Dei	SCH #157	F	-1	0	2	4	2	0	4	6	F
3 Agnus Dei	SCH #156	F	-1	0	2	4	6	4	2	4	G
6 Agnus Dei	SCH #155	F	-1	2	0	2	4	2	-1	-3	F
3 Agnus Dei	SCH #183	E	1	0	-4	-2	0	3	5	3	E
4 Agnus Dei	SCH #42	B	1	0	-2	0	-4	-6	-7	-4	E
4 Agnus Dei	SCH #180	E	1	0	-2	0	1	-2	-4	-2	E
3 Agnus Dei	SCH #178	E	1	0	-2	0	3	0	-4	-2	E
3 Agnus Dei	SCH #179	E	1	0	-2	0	3	0	-4	-2	E
3 Agnus Dei	SCH #177	E	1	0	-2	0	3	5	0	3	E
3 Agnus Dei	SCH #176	E	1	0	-2	0	3	5	7	8	E
3 Agnus Dei	SCH #175	E	1	0	-2	0	7	8	7	5	E
4 Agnus Dei	SCH #174	E	1	0	-2	1	3	5	3	1	[E]
3 Agnus Dei	SCH #173	E	1	0	-2	3	5	8	7	8	E
5 Agnus Dei	SCH #5	e	1	0	-2	5	3	1	0	-2	[F]
3 Agnus Dei	SCH #172	E	1	0	-2	5	3	5	0	1	E
3 Agnus Dei	SCH #171	E	1	0	-2	5	3	5	3	1	E
1 Agnus Dei	SCH #170	E	1	0	1	5	3	1	0	1	D
5 Agnus Dei	SCH #4	e	1	3	0	-2	0	-4	-5	-7	F
4 Agnus Dei	SCH #169	E	1	3	0	1	0	-2	3	5	E
2 Agnus Dei	SCH #168	E	1	3	1	-2	0	-2	0	3	[D]
4 Agnus Dei	SCH #167	E	1	3	1	0	-2	0	-2	3	E
4 Agnus Dei	SCH #166	E	1	3	1	0	-2	0	1	0	[E]
1 Agnus Dei	SCH #7	d	2	-5	3	2	0	-2	0	2	[D]
4 Agnus Dei	SCH #227	D	2	-2	0	2	-2	0	2	5	E
8 Agnus Dei	SCH #93	G	2	-2	2	-2	0	2	0	5	[G]
1 Agnus Dei	SCH #226	D	2	-2	2	3	2	0	2	0	D
2 Agnus Dei	SCH #225	D	2	-2	3	2	5	7	2	0	D
2 Agnus Dei	SCH #92	G	2	0	-5	-2	-3	-5	-3	-2	G
5 Agnus Dei	SCH #21	c	2	0	-3	-5	-7	-8	-7	-5	F
4 Agnus Dei	SCH #91	G	2	0	-2	-3	-5	-3	-2	0	[E]
8 Agnus Dei	SCH #100	G	2	0	-2	-3	-5	-2	0	2	G
1 Agnus Dei	SCH #235	D	2	0	-2	0	-2	0	3	5	D
8 Agnus Dei	SCH #89	G	2	0	-2	0	2	0	2	5	G
8 Agnus Dei	SCH #99	G	2	0	-2	0	2	4	2	4	G

4 Agnus Dei	SCH #236	D	2	0	-2	0	2	5	7	5	[E]
1 Agnus Dei	SCH #224	D	2	0	-2	0	3	5	3	2	D
5 Agnus Dei	SCH #50	a	2	0	-2	2	0	-2	0	-4	F
2 Agnus Dei	SCH #223	D	2	0	-2	2	3	5	3	2	[D]
8 Agnus Dei	SCH #90	G	2	0	-2	2	4	5	4	2	[G]
1 Agnus Dei	SCH #49	a	2	0	-2	5	3	2	0	-2	F
7 Agnus Dei	SCH #20	c	2	0	-1	-5	-3	-1	0	-1	[G]
6 Agnus Dei	SCH #140	F	2	0	-1	-3	-1	0	5	4	F
2 Agnus Dei	SCH #149	F	2	0	-1	-3	0	2	4	5	F
Agnus Dei	SCH #101	G	2	0	2	-2	0	[0	0	0]	G
2 Agnus Dei	SCH #222	D	2	0	2	0	-2	0	2	0	[D]
2 Agnus Dei	SCH #221	D	2	0	2	0	2	3	2	0	D
Agnus Dei	SCH #19	c	2	0	2	0	2	4	2	0	
Agnus Dei	SCH #86	G	2	0	2	0	2	4	2	0	G
6 Agnus Dei	SCH #139	F	2	0	2	4	0	-3	-1	0	d
6 Agnus Dei	SCH #138	F	2	0	2	4	0	2	0	-3	F
8 Agnus Dei	SCH #18	c	2	0	2	4	0	2	0	2	c
6 Agnus Dei	SCH #148	F	2	0	2	4	0	2	0	5	F
8 Agnus Dei	SCH #88	G	2	0	2	4	2	0	-2	2	[G]
6 Agnus Dei	SCH #142	F	2	0	2	4	5	4	2	0	F
8 Agnus Dei	SCH #87	G	2	0	2	4	5	4	2	5	G
6 Agnus Dei	SCH #151	F	2	0	4	2	0	-1	2	4	F
5 Agnus Dei	SCH #141	F	2	0	5	4	0	2	0	2	F
5 Agnus Dei	SCH #22	c	2	0	5	4	2	0	-1	-3	c
1 Agnus Dei	SCH #147	F	2	0	5	4	2	4	-3	0	F
1 Agnus Dei	SCH #220	D	2	3	0	-2	0	2	5	7	D
5 Agnus Dei	SCH #219	D	2	3	0	7	0	2	3	7	F
7 Agnus Dei	SCH #48	a	2	3	2	-2	0	2	3	2	[G]
2 Agnus Dei	SCH #218	D	2	3	2	0	-2	0	2	3	D
1 Agnus Dei	SCH #217	D	2	3	2	0	-2	0	2	5	D
2 Agnus Dei	SCH #84	G	2	3	2	0	2	3	5	7	[G]
1 Agnus Dei	SCH #216	D	2	3	2	3	0	7	3	0	D
1 Agnus Dei	SCH #215	D	2	3	5	2	3	2	0	5	D
2 Agnus Dei	SCH #213	D	2	3	5	3	2	0	-2	0	[D]
2 Agnus Dei	SCH #214	D	2	3	5	3	2	0	3	2	[D]
1 Agnus Dei	SCH #234	D	2	3	5	7	3	0	2	0	D

1 Agnus Dei	SCH #212	D	2	3	7	5	2	3	0	7	[D]
6 Agnus Dei	SCH #135	F	2	4	-3	-1	0	2	4	6	F
6 Agnus Dei	SCH #134	F	2	4	0	-5	-3	-5	0	-5	[F]
6 Agnus Dei	SCH #150	F	2	4	0	2	-1	0	2	0	[F]
2 Agnus Dei	SCH #133	F	2	4	0	2	0	2	0	2	[D]
5 Agnus Dei	SCH #132	F	2	4	0	5	4	2	4	0	F
6 Agnus Dei	SCH #131	F	2	4	0	5	4	2	4	2	F
8 Agnus Dei	SCH #85	G	2	4	0	7	5	4	0	2	G
3 Agnus Dei	SCH #79	G	2	4	2	0	-2	0	4	7	E
6 Agnus Dei	SCH #136	F	2	4	2	0	-1	0	2	4	F
8 Agnus Dei	SCH #98	G	2	4	2	0	2	-2	0	[0]	G
6 Agnus Dei	SCH #130	F	2	4	2	0	7	4	9	7	[F]
6 Agnus Dei	SCH #129	F	2	4	2	4	0	2	0	2	F
4 Agnus Dei	SCH #264	C	2	4	2	4	2	0	5	7	C
8 Agnus Dei	SCH #81	G	2	4	2	4	5	4	0	2	G
Agnus Dei	SCH #83	G	2	4	2	4	5	4	0	2	
8 Agnus Dei	SCH #80	G	2	4	2	4	5	4	2	0	G
6 Agnus Dei	SCH #128	F	2	4	2	4	5	4	2	0	F
Agnus Dei	SCH #82	G	2	4	2	4	5	4	2	4	
8 Agnus Dei	SCH #97	G	2	4	2	4	5	4	2	4	G
6 Agnus Dei	SCH #126	F	2	4	2	4	5	4	5	4	F
6 Agnus Dei	SCH #127	F	2	4	2	4	6	4	2	0	F
2 Agnus Dei	SCH #263	C	2	4	2	5	4	2	5	4	D
8 Agnus Dei	SCH #77	G	2	4	5	2	0	2	4	2	[G]
8 Agnus Dei	SCH #76	G	2	4	5	2	0	2	4	5	[G]
6 Agnus Dei	SCH #123	F	2	4	5	4	2	0	-1	0	F
4 Agnus Dei	SCH #262	C	2	4	5	4	2	0	2	0	C
5 Agnus Dei	SCH #124	F	2	4	5	4	2	0	4	7	F
3 Agnus Dei	SCH #261	C	2	4	5	4	2	0	4	7	[E]
4 Agnus Dei	SCH #260	C	2	4	5	4	2	4	0	4	E
8 Agnus Dei	SCH #78	G	2	4	5	4	2	4	2	0	[G]
8 Agnus Dei	SCH #17	c	2	4	5	4	2	4	5	4	c
8 Agnus Dei	SCH #75	G	2	4	5	4	2	5	4	5	[G]
4 Agnus Dei	SCH #258	C	2	4	5	4	2	7	5	7	E
4 Agnus Dei	SCH #259	C	2	4	5	4	2	7	5	7	E
5 Agnus Dei	SCH #257	C	2	4	5	4	7	5	4	0	C
6 Agnus Dei	SCH #125	F	2	4	6	4	2	0	-3	-5	F

5 Agnus Dei	SCH #146	F	2	4	6	7	4	0	2	0	F
3 Agnus Dei	SCH #122	F	2	4	6	7	4	6	2	-1	[E]
5 Agnus Dei	SCH #121	F	2	4	7	5	4	2	0	2	F
5 Agnus Dei	SCH #256	C	2	4	7	9	7	9	11	12	C
5 Agnus Dei	SCH #120	F	2	5	0	2	0	-3	-1	-3	F
8 Agnus Dei	SCH #96	G	2	5	2	4	2	0	2	0	[G]
2 Agnus Dei	SCH #255	C	2	5	2	4	2	0	2	5	[D]
7 Agnus Dei	SCH #74	G	2	5	4	2	0	2	4	5	[G]
4 Agnus Dei	SCH #265	C	2	5	4	2	0	4	9	7	G
2 Agnus Dei	SCH #253	C	2	5	4	2	4	2	0	2	[D]
7 Agnus Dei	SCH #16	c	2	5	4	2	4	5	4	2	[G]
8 Agnus Dei	SCH #73	G	2	5	4	2	5	7	9	7	G
8 Agnus Dei	SCH #119	F	2	5	4	5	2	4	2	0	G
1 Agnus Dei	SCH #254	C	2	5	4	5	4	2	0	2	D
8 Agnus Dei	SCH #72	G	2	5	7	5	2	4	2	0	G
2 Agnus Dei	SCH #252	C	2	5	7	5	4	2	0	2	D
2 Agnus Dei	SCH #251	C	2	5	7	9	7	5	9	2	[D]
1 Agnus Dei	SCH #211	D	2	5	7	10	7	5	7	10	[D]
6 Agnus Dei	SCH #137	F	2	6	2	4	2	0	4	7	F
Agnus Dei	SCH #266	C	2	9	[0	0	0	0	0	0]	
4 Agnus Dei	SCH #182	E	3	-2	3	1	0	8	5	3	E
6 Agnus Dei	SCH #47	a	3	0	-4	-2	-4	-9	-7	-4	F
4 Agnus Dei	SCH #207	D	3	0	-2	0	2	5	7	5	E
2 Agnus Dei	SCH #210	D	3	0	-2	0	3	5	7	9	D
1 Agnus Dei	SCH #209	D	3	0	-2	2	0	5	7	5	D
1 Agnus Dei	SCH #208	D	3	0	-2	2	5	7	9	5	[D]
1 Agnus Dei	SCH #206	D	3	0	3	5	7	9	7	5	D
1 Agnus Dei	SCH #164	E	3	1	0	-4	-2	0	-2	0	D
2 Agnus Dei	SCH #165	E	3	1	0	1	0	-2	-4	-2	D
1 Agnus Dei	SCH #237	D	3	2	-2	0	-2	0	3	5	D
4 Agnus Dei	SCH #201	D	3	2	0	-2	0	2	3	5	E
2 Agnus Dei	SCH #46	a	3	2	0	-2	0	3	5	7	a
1 Agnus Dei	SCH #233	D	3	2	0	-2	0	3	5	7	D
2 Agnus Dei	SCH #205	D	3	2	0	-2	0	3	7	8	D
1 Agnus Dei	SCH #204	D	3	2	0	2	-2	-3	-2	0	D
1 Agnus Dei	SCH #203	D	3	2	0	3	0	-2	3	5	[D]

1 Agnus Dei	SCH #202	D	3	2	5	2	-2	0	2	5	D
1 Agnus Dei	SCH #200	D	3	5	3	2	0	2	-2	-3	D
4 Agnus Dei	SCH #181	E	3	5	3	7	5	7	5	[0]	[E]
2 Agnus Dei	SCH #232	D	3	5	7	5	3	2	3	5	G
1 Agnus Dei	SCH #199	D	3	5	7	9	7	5	7	5	D
1 Agnus Dei	SCH #45	a	3	5	8	7	5	3	0	-2	[D]
2 Agnus Dei	SCH #267	A	3	5	8	7	8	7	5	7	D
7 Agnus Dei	SCH #6	d	3	5	9	7	5	3	0	-2	[G]
1 Agnus Dei	SCH #231	D	3	7	5	3	0	2	0	2	D
1 Agnus Dei	SCH #230	D	3	7	5	3	0	2	0	7	D
2 Agnus Dei	SCH #15	c	4	2	0	2	0	-1	-3	-1	[a]
8 Agnus Dei	SCH #71	G	4	2	0	4	5	7	4	5	G
5 Agnus Dei	SCH #117	F	4	2	0	4	7	6	4	7	F
6 Agnus Dei	SCH #118	F	4	2	0	4	7	9	7	4	F
1 Agnus Dei	SCH #250	C	4	2	5	7	5	4	2	5	D
1 Agnus Dei	SCH #249	C	4	2	7	5	4	5	2	0	[D]
8 Agnus Dei	SCH #95	G	4	5	2	0	4	2	0	-3	G
8 Agnus Dei	SCH #70	G	4	5	2	4	2	4	2	0	G
5 Agnus Dei	SCH #116	F	4	5	4	2	4	2	-1	0	[F]
8 Agnus Dei	SCH #69	G	4	5	7	5	9	7	5	7	[G]
7 Agnus Dei	SCH #14	c.	4	5	7	9	7	5	4	5	c
5 Agnus Dei	SCH #115	F	4	5	7	9	12	11	9	7	F
5 Agnus Dei	SCH #144	F	4	6	7	9	7	4	0	2	F
5 Agnus Dei	SCH #114	F	4	7	4	2	7	9	7	9	F
3 Agnus Dei	SCH #248	C	4	7	4	12	11	7	4	0	C
5 Agnus Dei	SCH #113	F	4	7	6	9	7	6	7	12	F
5 Agnus Dei	SCH #112	F	4	7	9	7	4	5	4	2	F
5 Agnus Dei	SCH #145	F	4	7	9	7	6	7	4	0	[F]
4 Agnus Dei	SCH #247	C	4	7	9	7	9	11	9	7	[E]
5 Agnus Dei	SCH #111	F	4	7	9	11	9	7	9	7	F
8 Agnus Dei	SCH #68	G	5	2	0	-3	-2	0	4	5	G
5 Agnus Dei	SCH #143	F	5	4	2	0	7	9	12	11	F
8 Agnus Dei	SCH #94	G	5	4	2	4	7	2	4	2	[G]
1 Agnus Dei	SCH #192	D	7	0	3	5	7	5	2	3	D
1 Agnus Dei	SCH #198	D	7	5	3	2	0	3	5	7	E
1 Agnus Dei	SCH #197	D	7	5	3	2	3	0	3	5	D

1 Agnus Dei	SCH #229	D	7	5	3	2	3	2	0	-2	D
1 Agnus Dei	SCH #228	D	7	5	3	2	3	2	0	12	D
1 Agnus Dei	SCH #196	D	7	5	3	5	3	2	0	2	[D]
1 Agnus Dei	SCH #195	D	7	5	3	5	7	5	12	10	D
1 Agnus Dei	SCH #191	D	7	5	3	5	7	10	9	7	D
7 Agnus Dei	SCH #67	G	7	5	4	5	7	5	12	10	G
1 Agnus Dei	SCH #194	D	7	5	7	0	3	2	0	-2	D
4 Agnus Dei	SCH #163	E	7	5	7	3	1	0	1	0	E
1 Agnus Dei	SCH #193	D	7	5	7	5	3	2	0	9	D
1 Agnus Dei	SCH #190	D	7	8	7	5	3	2	0	-2	D
1 Agnus Dei	SCH #189	D	7	9	7	5	7	0	3	2	D
1 Agnus Dei	SCH #188	D	7	9	7	5	7	5	3	2	D
1 Agnus Dei	SCH #187	D	7	9	7	12	10	7	9	7	[D]
7 Agnus Dei	SCH #66	G	7	9	10	12	7	4	9	10	[G]